Aristotle
and
Modern Politics

ARISTOTLE

AND

MODERN

POLITICS

The Persistence
of Political Philosophy

edited by

ARISTIDE TESSITORE

UNIVERSITY OF NOTRE DAME PRESS

Notre Dame, Indiana

Manufactured in the United States of America

Library of Congress Cataloging-in-Publication Data
Aristotle and modern politics : the persistence of political philosophy /
Aristide Tessitore, editor.
p. cm.
Includes bibliographical references and index.
ISBN 0-268-02013-2 (alk. paper)
ISBN 0-268-02014-0 (pbk. : alk. paper)
1. Aristotle—Contributions in political science. 2. Political
science—Philosophy. I. Tessitore, Aristide.
JC71.A7 A75   2002
320'.01—dc21
2002008812

∞ *This book is printed on acid-free paper.*

Contents

Part Two
VIRTUE

Part Three
LAW, ECONOMICS, AND POLITICS

Part Four
THE FOUNDATIONS OF MODERN POLITICS

Acknowledgments

During the heaviest editorial phase of this project, I received much needed help from Dr. A. V. Huff, Academic Dean of Furman University, and my colleagues in the department of political science for making possible a research leave in Fall 2000, as well as generous financial support from the Earhart Foundation during the summer of 2000. I gratefully acknowledge these sources of assistance without which this project would not have found its way into print. I also wish to thank the Duke Endowment and Knight Foundation for their generosity in the form of Furman University Research and Professional Growth grants (2000–2001), which have helped to defray a number of costs associated with the final assembly of this collection of essays.

Earlier versions of two essays have been published elsewhere. Chapter One of the present volume is a revised version of the first chapter of *The Problems of a Political Animal: Community, Justice, and Conflict in Aristotelian Political Thought* (Berkeley: University of California Press, 1993). Chapter Two was originally published in *Liberalism and the Good,* edited by R. Bruce Douglass, Gerald M. Mara, and Henry S. Richardson (New York and London: Routledge Press, 1990). Permission to reprint these essays is gratefully acknowledged.

Introduction

The Renaissance
in Aristotelian Studies and
the Persistence of Political Philosophy

ARISTIDE TESSITORE

If the study of modern politics is increasingly a study of liberal orders, the collapse of Soviet communism and the fall of the Berlin Wall have all but ensured that this will be the case for the foreseeable future. A remarkable and in some sense global consensus concerning the legitimacy of liberal regimes has emerged in the wake of the now defeated ideologies of fascism and communism. Indeed, the rout is of such an order of magnitude that Francis Fukuyama has famously hazarded the thesis that liberalism may in fact signal the "end of history." While acknowledging the persistence of injustice and social problems in stable democracies, and even allowing that some countries might lapse into theocracy or military dictatorship, Fukuyama contends that liberal democracy may still constitute the "final form of human government" at least as an *ideal* form of government, one that will not be surpassed.[1]

In light of the unprecedented political and theoretical triumph of liberal democracy in the aftermath of the Cold War, it may come as something of a surprise that one of the defining debates of the last two decades concerns the nature and future of modern liberalism. This debate crosses traditional disciplinary boundaries and spans the conventional divide between purely academic and informed popular writing. Vigorous discussion about modern liberalism is as likely to arise in journalistic forums as it is in traditional courses in political science, philosophy, religion, or sociology. For citizens living in modern societies, the problems involved are of urgent

1

concern and, given the number of unresolved issues, the ferment of intellectual and political activity surrounding liberalism is not likely to dissipate any time soon.

The many-sided debate about the nature and future of modern politics is delimited by those who celebrate the triumph of liberalism and those who question whether it possesses resources sufficient to sustain itself. Between these two extremes are a growing number who might best be characterized as anti-utopian partisans of liberalism—those who recognize and appreciate the merits of liberalism over possible alternatives while, at the same time, seeking to articulate characteristic defects or blindnesses inherent in liberal (as in all) political arrangements. One of the most surprising features of this debate, however, is the frequency with which another figure, one unacquainted with modern politics, has entered the fray. If it is true that Aristotle has always cast a long shadow over the moral-political discourse of the West, contemporary debate about liberalism has all but resuscitated him. Despite the profound divide separating classical and modern theories of government, contemporary thinkers have, with surprising frequency, turned to the political teaching of Aristotle in order to assess both the possibilities and limitations for politics in liberal societies.

THE RENAISSANCE IN ARISTOTELIAN STUDIES

The renewal of interest in Aristotle arises from a multiplicity of sources. Notwithstanding this fact, it is possible to trace this renaissance in its broadest terms to two related developments in modern political thought. The first emerges from liberalism's ongoing and congenital effort to justify its own moral foundations and especially to stave off charges of moral relativism. The second development arises from attempts to sort out the vexed relationship between theory and practice or, more generally, science and politics—a problem that emerged with especial poignancy after the first World War and has yet to receive definitive resolution.[2]

With respect to the first development, the defense of liberalism was for many years shaped by the debate between John Stuart Mill's utilitarian principle (maximizing general welfare) and Kant's subordination of any form of instrumentalism to the intrinsic dignity of individuals understood as ends in themselves.[3] In recent years this debate has been largely settled in favor a neo-Kantian rights-based ethic, due in large measure to the influence of John Rawls's *A Theory of Justice*. In Rawls's view the rights of individuals necessarily trump concerns for the general welfare because rights are fundamental and, as a consequence, must be regarded as prior to any utilitarian calculus regarding a common or, more likely, majoritarian interest.

As Rawls puts it, "rights secured by justice are not subject to political bargaining or to the calculus of social interests."[4] What is needed to sustain this position and what Rawls seeks to provide is an account of rights that does not depend on any particular conception of the good; that is, one that does not presuppose the superiority of one way of life over any other. As a result, Rawls attempts to justify liberalism as a neutral framework of rights, one that is deliberately agnostic toward competing understandings of the good.[5] It is in this sense that liberal societies are based on a notion of fairness rather than an idea of the good. In the language of Kantian liberals, the right is prior to the good both in the sense that individual rights cannot be sacrificed for the sake of a general good and in the sense that these rights do not derive from any particular version of the good. Rather, rights provide the framework within which individuals are able to pursue the good as they understand it, subject only to the condition that this same liberty be extended to others pursuing different or rival goods.

As this rights-based ethic has come to prevail over its utilitarian rival, a new and growing challenge to its hegemony has come increasingly into view during the last fifteen years. Communitarian critics of liberalism question the priority of the right over the good and typically ground their critique in Aristotle.[6] Notwithstanding the deep differences and genuine diversity characteristic of those who at one time or another have been associated with the communitarian movement, it is possible to identify a set of recurring concerns. Among many issues, communitarians question whether it is possible to abstract from the particular and always contingent narrative history that contributes to the shape of individual identity, deny the possibility of regime neutrality that modern liberalism claims for itself (or at least aspires to), and question the adequacy of understanding persons as "unencumbered selves."[7] Underlying this challenge to liberal ascendancy is a critical assessment of the implicit conception of a self as independent of and distinct from the particular aims, choices, and attachments that make up a human life, an assessment that bears directly on the concern about liberal culture's capacity to sustain itself.

The communitarian turn to Aristotle is perhaps not surprising insofar as Aristotle's "philosophy of human affairs" (*NE* 10.9.1181b15) (an investigation that includes the study of both ethics and politics) is imbued with an awareness of the indispensable and formative power of associations.[8] Individuals do not spring fully grown from the head of Zeus. Rather, as both the *Ethics* and *Politics* make clear, human beings develop as participants in different communities, most notably the family and the political association. Even at the sharpest point of individuation, Aristotle insists on the inescapable and formative contribution of a particular *ethos* in the development of character.[9]

Although several authors in this volume are critical of communitarian appropriations of Aristotle,[10] the fact remains that part of the pervasive presence of Aristotle in contemporary debate is attributable to this source. Even if communitarian theorists are sometimes characterized by un-Aristotelian hopes for communal harmony, they rightly point to the implausibility of liberal theories that abstract from the institutions and practices that shape character and choice. To this extent at least, communitarians are indebted to the persistence of a genuinely Aristotelian insight into the formative context of political life, an insight typically obscured by contemporary and characteristically liberal elevations of the individual self.

The second and deeper source of renewed interest in Aristotle can be traced to a pervasive sense of crisis that gripped the intellectual world of Weimar Germany after World War One. The powerful and often forgotten influence of the Weimar conversation for subsequent debates about liberalism and the changing relationship between theory and practice has been ably excavated in John Gunnell's *The Descent of Political Theory* (Chicago: University of Chicago Press, 1993). Although Gunnell's theme is the alienation of political theory in the increasingly empirical discipline of political science, he traces this estrangement to an older but persistent quarrel between the authority of knowledge and political authority. Max Weber's addresses on the bifurcation of science and politics as vocations (1918; 1919), the culmination of a dialogue about academic and public discourse in which he had participated for twenty-five years, mark a problematic touchstone for the controversies that have followed.[11] Weber claimed that in an increasingly pluralistic world, the idea that the academy could speak with a single voice, one that also possessed political authority, had become obsolete. Paradoxically, he maintained that the restoration of any relationship between academic and political discourse presupposed their rigorous separation. This line of thought culminated in Weber's celebrated and maligned distinction between facts and values. However permeable the membrane separating facts and values, Weber's articulation of this distinction laid bare an underlying crisis in practical judgment. Since value judgments could not be justified or determined by logic or science, there could be no rational basis for discriminating between different and competing judgments in personal or political life. Rather, value judgments represent expressions of preference, decision, or faith—a position prepared by the valorization of the will in Kantian and especially Nietzchean philosophy. For Weber there was and could be no philosophic or scientific solution to the problem of practical judgment.

In the years leading up to the rise of the Third Reich, Heidegger was the most influential philosopher on the continent. His attack on modernity and neo-Kantian philosophy, fusing of philosophy and history, return to Greek philosophy, and emphasis on the political as exemplified in the polis (among many themes), profoundly influenced those coming of age during this period. Even those who resisted his doctrines and politics were nevertheless influenced by his thought. In this way, Heidegger directly and indirectly facilitated the turn to Aristotelian practical philosophy—both in his own use of Aristotle and, perhaps most deeply, in the subsequent reaction provoked by Heidegger's radical historicism.[12] Against the contemporary bifurcation of politics and science, Heidegger found in Aristotle a basis for his own intensification of the practical dimension of Greek political thought. As Carnes Lord—writing from a very different perspective—puts it, for Aristotle the "human sciences are preeminently 'practical' (*praktikai*) sciences whose express purpose is not simply to increase knowledge but rather to benefit human life or human action (*praxis*)."[13] Against the reigning historicist orthodoxies in philosophy and social science that devolve from Heidegger's thought, several of Heidegger's most influential students (and the traditions of scholarship to which they gave rise) found in Aristotle a complex and nuanced understanding of *human nature,* one that is inescapably embedded in a particular and variable political context.

The resurgence of interest in Aristotle derives from philosophic positions that, while quite distinct from one another, were later brought together under the designation of "neo-Aristotelianism." Franco Volpi locates the beginning of this renaissance with the advent of two books written by students of Heidegger.[14] Hannah Arendt's *The Human Condition* appeared in the United States in 1958 (translated into German in 1960) and Georg Gadamer's *Truth and Method* was published two years later. Whereas Arendt drew attention to the Aristotelian account of *praxis* for understanding the nature of "the political" (as distinguished from politics), Gadamer maintained the continuing relevance of Aristotle's notion of *phronēsis* (prudence) as a kind of knowledge guiding human action and life. Volpi notes that these were but two of the "most famous examples of a widespread recovery of the Aristotelian notion of praxis and the ethical and political knowledge with which it is concerned."[15] Whatever the merits of Aristotle's writing on physics, metaphysics, and biology, the practical character of his treatises in the human sciences put down deep roots in modern German thought.[16] In the broadest sense, the renaissance in Aristotelian studies centers on the problem of practical judgment, the recognition of and need for a credible notion of practical philosophy.

The influence of the Weimar conversation and its aftermath found its way into the Anglo-American world especially through a tide of German émigrés during the Nazi period. Among the most influential were Hannah Arendt, Leo Strauss, and Eric Voegelin, all of whom found an initial outlet for their ideas in the recently founded *Review of Politics.* The express purpose of the *Review* was "to revive the Aristotelian conception of politics," albeit from a Christian vantage point, by applying the Aristotelian and Christian tradition to modern problems in social and political philosophy.[17] Faced with the increasingly positivist and historicist discipline of political science, these authors, despite the very real differences between them, criticized the naivetés of modern political *science* by holding up the relevance of classical political *philosophy*.[18] Arendt emphasized the pervasive eclipse of the political dimension of life; Voegelin called for a return to the search for transcendent principles characteristic of classical medieval Christian thought; and Strauss sought a recovery of the truth of classical political philosophy exemplified in the work of Plato and Aristotle.[19] Despite pointed differences barely suggested here, all three émigrés found in classical philosophy a standard by which to assess the problem articulated by Weber. If Weber's distinction between science and politics as vocations was part of an attempt to save both science and politics, it also brought with it an insufficiently critical acceptance of relativism and historicism in the social sciences. From significantly different vantage points, Arendt, Voegelin, and Strauss uncovered Aristotelian conceptions of practical rationality as responses to the crisis in modern rationality, particularly as it applies to the study of politics. The continuing influence of these émigrés on succeeding generations of scholars has pushed Aristotle increasingly into the forefront in debates about the nature and limitations of modern politics.

The Persistence of Political Philosophy

Contemporary debate has centered on a number of crucial issues that are at the heart of modern politics, none of which is likely to disappear soon. To what extent is political community possible in the highly individualistic culture of liberal societies and what constitutes a realistic expectation for community in civic life? To what extent does liberalism presuppose virtue on the part of its citizens and how is virtue to be understood? How does one foster the kind of deliberation necessary to sustain democratic practice? To what degree can a polity rely on law and economics to ensure continued political vitality? What is the relationship between law and prudence and what are or ought to be the uses and limits of private property? In what is the theory and practice of liberalism grounded? Can conceptions of political culture or autonomy furnish a basis for a theoretically consistent understanding of liberalism?

Although Aristotle antedates liberalism by over 2,000 years, his political teaching is characterized by sustained reflection on the fundamental issues embedded in current debates. Each question raised in the preceding paragraph can be subsumed into one of four general themes that Aristotle considered at depth: (1) the problem of political community; (2) the possibilities and limitations of virtue in politics; (3) the relationship between law, economics, and politics; and (4) the foundations of political theory and practice. Explorations of these four themes furnish the organizational principle for the present volume. By assessing present-day issues from an Aristotelian perspective, the following essays bring to light the often surprising ways in which Aristotle engages and advances recent discussion. In doing so, they reveal not only the continued vitality of Aristotelian political thought, but, by bringing Aristotle into dialogue with some of the most vexed problems and acute analyses of modern political discourse, the persistence of political philosophy itself.

Part One of the book is comprised of three essays that address modern concerns about the possibility of community in modern politics. In the first of these, Bernard Yack takes issue with the appropriation of Aristotle by communitarian critics of modern life and thought. Much of modern social theory is predicated on useful but misleading dichotomies resulting from individualist-communitarian polemics that date back to the eighteenth century. By disentangling Aristotle's own consideration of community from subsequent distortions, Yack uncovers an understanding of community that avoids the twin abstractions of modern social theory—liberal fantasies about self-constituting individuals and exaggerated communitarian dreams for moral and social harmony. Aristotle's concrete analysis of the character, possibilities, and limitations of community gives full weight to the formative power of social contexts for individual character and action without, however, suggesting the necessity of any specific form of communal life. For Aristotle, Yack writes, "political community appears as the *scene* of conflict rather than its *remedy.*" Aristotle's broad and realistic understanding of community encourages readers to explore all forms of communal behavior, including instrumental associations and everyday social phenomena. In so doing, Aristotle provides the critical distance necessary to analyze the advantages and disadvantages of the dichotomous language of modern social theory.

Chapter Two offers Martha Nussbaum's classic "Aristotelian Social Democracy." This essay brings together much of her thought on the relevance of Aristotelian essentialism for contemporary understandings of politics, and sets the agenda for her normative and empirical work on comparative qualities of life. Taking her inspiration from Aristotle, Nussbaum sketches a political conception that is intended to provide a basis for evaluative judgments in politics. Following Aristotle, Nussbaum reverses the liberal framework by arguing for the priority of the good in evaluating political arrangements, something she calls the "thick vague theory of the good."

Nussbaum is careful to point out that this idea of the good does not rely on any extra-historical conception of truth or import controversial metaphysical assumptions incapable of eliciting consensus—views that are often but wrongly attributed to Aristotle. It is "thick" in that it takes its bearings from a finite list of functional capabilities that characterize a human life, a set of capabilities that is recognizable across cultures. It is at the same time "vague" in the sense that it allows a great deal of latitude in concrete specification and is sensitive to variations in local traditions. This latter quality allows some rapprochement with the sensibilities of liberalism. Nussbaum finds in Aristotle a useful paradigm that gives to politics the task of ensuring that all citizens receive the institutional, material, and especially educational, support necessary to develop those capabilities proper to human functioning, something that governments ought to undertake in a proactive rather than residual way.

Part One concludes with Susan Collins's careful examination of the virtue most requisite for political community—namely, justice. Collins notes that many contemporary students in politics and philosophy are drawn to Aristotle's consideration of virtue because of the "dual roots" that characterize his analysis: Aristotle's teaching on virtue comes to sight both as a necessary support for any given political order and as the core ingredient of human flourishing. However, most neo-Aristotelians depart from Aristotle by emphasizing one or the other of these dimensions in contrast to Aristotle's more comprehensive analysis of the crucial relationship between them. It is especially in Aristotle's consideration of justice in the *Nicomachean Ethics* that he examines the clearest point of intersection between the civic concern for virtue as constitutive of the common good and the more individual preoccupation with virtue as a constituent of human flourishing. Collins contends that Aristotle lays out the dilemma of moral virtue with greatest clarity in his analysis of justice. Although Aristotle was as eager as present-day neo-Aristotelians to bring virtue and the human good to the attention of politicians and political thinkers, his unflinching clarity about the relationship between virtue's dual roots caused him to be more sober about the possibilities for politics than many of the modern scholars who invoke his teachings. Collins denies that this moderation is adequately understood as skepticism. Rather, it is the fruit of long reflection on virtue, politics, and the human good—a reflection that poses at one and the same time Aristotle's greatest challenge and most generous gift to students of modern politics.

Part Two of the volume turns to the question of virtue in a thematic way. This section begins with Aristide Tessitore's sympathetic critique of the work of Alasdair MacIntyre, who, since the publication of *After Virtue*, has become the most prominent neo-Aristotelian in America. Tessitore's overview of MacIntyre's project as a whole focuses on the most original dimension of MacIntyre's contribution—his effort to transpose Aristotle into a contemporary key by developing the three core notions of practice, tradition, and narrative unity. Taken together, these three themes constitute MacIntyre's critical response to those aspects of Aristotle's work that, he believes, relegate it to an antiquarian status—a jejune belief in the unity of virtue, reliance on a now defunct polis, and dependence on a properly discredited metaphysical biology. MacIntyre's novel solution attempts to relocate the essential structure of Aristotle's thought within a dynamic historical tradition. While appreciative of his contribution, Tessitore turns the tables by offering a critical evaluation of MacIntyre's neo-Aristotelianism as it might appear from an Aristotelian perspective. The distinctive elements of MacIntyre's thesis are juxtaposed to the particular Aristotelian difficulties that MacIntyre attempts to surmount: authoritative practice and the unity of virtue; tradition and the Greek polis; narrative unity and metaphysical biology. In each case, Tessitore brings to light the possibility and fruitfulness of a dialogue that illuminates the often hidden pretenses of a historical consciousness that has not confronted at full depth Aristotle's claims on behalf of nature. While acknowledging that MacIntyre's corpus brilliantly reflects the contemporary predicament in a way that ensures its continued relevance, Tessitore contends that engagement with the thought of Aristotle furnishes the basis for a critical examination of the predicament itself.

In the second essay in this section David O'Connor uncovers a dispute between Martin Heidegger and Leo Strauss about the character of Aristotelian virtue. O'Connor maintains that Strauss's interpretation of Aristotle needs to be understood, at least in part, as the vehicle of his response to Heidegger. Based on a close reading of Heidegger's infamous address upon assuming the rectorship of the University of Freiburg in 1933 ("The Self-Assertion of the German University") and Strauss's debate with Alexandre Kojève (whom Strauss treats as a sort of surrogate for Heidegger), O'Connor brings to light two features of Heidegger's appropriation of Aristotle opposed by Strauss. Strauss resists both the practical and the patriotic features of Heidegger's Aristotle, while preserving what he takes to be Aristotle's emphasis on both the *continuity* between the values and commitments of those engaged in political life and the concepts and emphases of those engaged in political science, and the *discontinuity* between the philosophic life and the political life as objects of human aspiration. O'Connor contends that one effect of the debate between Heidegger and Strauss is that each is forced to intensify or systematize aspects of Aristotle's teaching in a way that resolves tensions that Aristotle's texts leave open. His analysis demonstrates the crucial and typically overlooked influence of this debate on Strauss's interpretation of Aristotle. O'Connor maintains that Strauss offers an account of Aristotelian virtue, philosophy, and politics that would keep philosophy from being colored by practice and patriotism even for those inclined to accept the Heideggerian view of man as the shepherd of Being.

The final essay in Part Two addresses the thorny matrix constituted by the intersection of virtue, contemporary liberalism, and Christian theology. Charles Pinches argues that Peter Berkowitz's recent attempt (*The Making of Modern Liberalism*) to reconnect contemporary liberalism to Aristotle and virtue fails because it imports key liberal assumptions about the instrumentality of virtue, assumptions that effectively deprive liberalism of the very "virtue capital" it needs to sustain itself. Berkowitz's wish to appropriate virtue for political purposes fails because particular virtues are not detachable from the way of life, history, tradition, and truth claims about the best and most complete human life within which they arise. Pinches finds in Richard Rorty's *Achieving Our Country* a more revealing window onto the problematic relationship between liberalism, virtue, and Christian theology. Unlike Berkowitz, Rorty follows Aristotle in rooting virtue in a particular cultural tradition—not, to be sure, in the fourth-century polis of ancient Greece, but in the story of the American liberal past, particularly as it is envisioned in Rorty's accounts of Dewey and Whitman. Moreover, his return to the language of American pride and forthright disavowal of the penumbra of sin makes good Aristotelian sense. But this raises a problem about Rorty's (and liberalism's) long-term commitment to equality given the historical roots of equality in Christianity's vision of sinners equally in need of God's grace. Freed from this biblical story, by means of which Aristotle was so thoroughly transformed by Aquinas, why should Aristotle's account of natural inequality not also accompany Rorty's return to the moral centrality of pride? Pinches concludes that, despite itself, Rorty's liberalism may continue to trade on the Christian view of sin it most especially eschews.

Part Three of the volume puts Aristotelian political philosophy into dialogue with contemporary issues in law and economics. Miriam Galston takes up the work of contemporary liberal legal theorists who reject legal formalism and natural law theory, on the one hand, and relativism and subjectivism, on the other—a group she dubs "theorists of the middle way." These theorists believe that legal reasoning and legal precepts can be correct even if they cannot be demonstrated syllogistically or with certainty. Galston analyzes two distinct approaches within this group: one that is reluctant to have recourse to substantive moral and political principles that exist independent of a particular legal order (the process-oriented approach), and one that recognizes and is willing to incorporate such substantive standards at specific junctures in legal reasoning. Galston argues that Aristotle's writings are useful for both of these approaches but contends that there is deeper agreement between Aristotle's thought and that of Ronald Dworkin (the main representative of theorists willing to turn to moral standards external to a legal system for guidance) than there is between Aristotle and the process-oriented theorists. She maintains that proponents of the process-oriented approach could learn (from a comparative study of Aristotle and Dworkin) that some of the constraints they stipulate to ensure fair and accurate deliberation amount to a recognition that people are more capable of rational thought if they possess a certain kind of character. Galston concludes that, in the interests of truth, contemporary liberal theorists of the middle way would profit by viewing Aristotle as a participant in their deliberations and, thus, entitled to the same open and fair consideration they accord one another.

In the second essay in this section, Jill Frank considers the many meanings of private property in contemporary legal and political theory. Private property understood as an individual right to the possession, use, and disposition of material things; key to individual liberty, independence, and security; guarantor against arbitrary exercises of governmental power; and inducement to efficient economic activity is said to be central to a *liberal*-democratic regime. But property's protection of a private sphere of individual autonomy, independence, and exclusion, makes the claim of centrality to the democratic side of the liberal-*democratic* equation suspect. Liberal-*democratic* politics depends not only on privacy but also on reserves of public goods; it requires not only autonomy and independence but some form of collective action and interdependence; it relies not only on protection against arbitrary redistribution but on equality. Against the dominant liberal conception, which understands property in terms of exchange value, Frank develops an Aristotelian understanding of property as an activity of use bound to the practices of citizenship. She finds traces of this perspective in both contemporary legal practice and political theory as well as in the writings of Thomas Jefferson and James Madison. But it is especially in Aristotle's more ancient understanding of "the democratic virtue of property" that Frank finds a perspective that better fulfills both the *liberal* and *democratic* commitments of liberal democracy.

In the final essay in this section, Douglas Den Uyl and Douglas Rasmussen offer a libertarian account of the usefulness of Aristotle for understanding moral issues that arise from the economic theory and practices of liberalism. They begin by grounding the natural right to liberty within a neo-Aristotelian understanding of human flourishing. Self-direction pertains to the very core of human flourishing and as such constitutes the condition for the possibility of self-perfection however that might be understood.

They maintain that the place of self-direction in the self-perfecting life is crucial for a proper understanding of the natural right to liberty. Den Uyl and Rasmussen also address the right to private property, arguably the most controversial aspect of the modern natural rights tradition and, given Aristotle's apparent antipathy toward commerce, the most problematic dimension of Aristotle's analysis for the libertarian position they wish to uphold. They argue that an examination of the issue of property according to Aristotelian principles supports a social theory that gives an important role to private property and, as a consequence, provides at least an openness to commercial life. With respect to Aristotle's apparent antipathy toward commerce, Den Uyl and Rasmussen turn to Aristotle's analysis of "advantage-friendships," where they find that commercial transactions furnish the paradigm for this kind of friendship. Moreover, they maintain that civic friendship is best understood as a type of advantage-friendship. By developing Aristotle's teaching on friendship, Den Uyl and Rasmussen offer a new way of conceiving the liberal commercial order, one that is based on an Aristotelian mean between the prevailing Hobbesian notion of self-interest (characteristic of social contract theory and taken over by rational choice) and a romanticized and ultimately untenable invocation of character friendship with its dependence on a virtuous citizenry.

The concluding section of this volume is comprised of three essays that address the theoretical foundations of modern liberalism. One of the most significant developments in liberal political philosophy is its recognition of the importance of political culture, the most influential recent statement of which is John Rawls's *Political Liberalism*. This perspective argues that support for liberal institutions should not be based on any supposed metaphysics of the person, but on a recognition of the priorities of liberal culture. Political liberalism responds to incompatible comprehensive doctrines about the good by decoupling public justification of liberal institutions from comprehensive doctrines of any sort.

Gerald Mara begins with a sympathetic critique of this development in contemporary theory but goes on to argue that Aristotle offers a different and preferable perspective on the uses of political culture within political philosophy. Mara makes this case by presenting a groundbreaking reading of Aristotle's *Constitution of Athens* (*Athēnaiōn Politeia*) as a critical and reconstructive assessment of the political culture of democracy. He interprets this work not simply as a historical or descriptive account (one of the many constitutions "collected" by Aristotle's students), but as an examination of how one particular democratic society could be improved so as to strengthen its potentials and diminish its pathologies. Read as a work of practical political education, the *Constitution of Athens* encourages constructive criticism of the Athenian regime and, by extension, democratic political culture, generally. Taken together with the *Politics,* the *Constitution of Athens* reveals an understanding of political theory that is neither dismissive of nor bound by the cultural priorities and political processes of decent, yet flawed, regimes. Mara concludes that we may be better positioned to appreciate both the decencies and flaws of modern politics by supplementing contemporary liberalism's cultural turn with Aristotelian insights.

Stephen Salkever maintains that the major theorists of deliberative democracy, John Rawls and Jürgen Habermas, treat the ideal model of democratic politics as complete in itself, independent of any fundamental ground. This strategy is part of a deliberate effort to avoid metaphysics and, in so doing, to appeal to a broader political base; Rawls and Habermas write as if they were legislators as well as philosophers. Salkever contends that political theorists who create normative models should consider metaphysical questions—indeed, the failure to do so is likely to result in metaphysical dogmatism. It leads Rawls and Habermas to endorse uncritically a number of questionable Kantian assumptions that lessen the appeal of the deliberative model wedded to it. Salkever argues that deliberative democrats would do well to consider an Aristotelian alternative—specifically, the doctrine of "species teleology" and the "ethics of natural questions" that follows from it. Once loosened from its Kantian moorings, the deliberative model can better inform practical reason by supplying the alternative to instrumental cost-benefit calculation that both Habermas and Rawls desire. With respect to the grounding of deliberative democracy, Salkever maintains that, paradoxically, political models are less dogmatic and more fruitful if they refuse to abstract from metaphysical controversy. Moreover, he contends that a consideration of Aristotle's theory of nature and being, along with the options offered by Hobbes and Kant, can strengthen the model of deliberative democracy as a guide to present-day practice.

Like Salkever, Fred Miller finds the pervasive liberal reliance on the doctrines of Kant—particularly the core doctrine of personal autonomy—to be problematic. Whereas Miller embraces the underlying liberal commitment to personal autonomy, the philosophical analysis and justification of this ideal has proven to be a daunting task. The controversial nature of Kant's doctrines about human rationality have led several liberal theorists to seek new foundations for autonomy in the philosophic psychology of David Hume. But Hume's location of human motivation in the passions and consequent demotion of reason to an instrumental status is also rife with difficulties. Given the persistent problems that plague modern theories of autonomy, Miller sets himself the task of reconstructing the cherished liberal concept of autonomy within an Aristotelian framework. He grounds his argument in Aristotle's emphasis on the rule of reason, a notion that recognizes the essential role of both reason and natural inclinations in an individual's soul. Moreover, political autonomy, understood as the self-government of citizens under law, both presupposes and contributes to the development of some measure of individual autonomy—that is, citizens with virtuous, self-governing souls. Miller concludes that Aristotle provides the basis for a theory of autonomy that is detached from both the Humean danger of ethical noncognitivism (the view that ethical principles are subjective and cannot be justified on rational grounds) and the Kantian need to abstract entirely from human nature (with an appeal to the self-legislation of pure practical reason alone). In so doing, Aristotle offers a philosophic analysis and justification of autonomy that is able to encompass both reason and desire, one that also points to the challenging task of providing for an educated citizenry.

As is clear from even this cursory consideration, the authors in this volume differ on the nature of Aristotle's contribution to current understandings of modern politics. In fact, a deliberate effort has been made to include essays from a variety of different points of view and disciplines, something that is intended to reveal both the range and depth of Aristotle's influence in contemporary discussion. Aristotle's appeal for thinkers on both the left and the right is one indication of his capacity to lift present-day readers beyond the more partisan divisions that often obstruct deeper and even fundamental considerations of politics. Notwithstanding the diversity of perspectives canvassed in these essays, all of the contributors are united by the conviction that citizens of modern political societies stand to benefit from serious engagement with the thought of Aristotle.

In addition to gleaning something of the magnitude of Aristotle's presence in ongoing debates and demonstrating some of the ways in which Aristotle sheds new light on current problems, the book as a whole exhibits the persistence of political philosophy at a time when the pervasive influence of "ideology" and "historicism" lead many to deny this possibility. It is characteristic of modern politics that it draws its fundamental principles from the critical reflections of reason over against the imposition of authority under its various guises. Modern politics can best sustain itself by nurturing the critical attitude that initially brought it into being. Paradoxically, serious engagement with the "pre-liberal" thought of Aristotle can render contemporary debate less narrow and less dogmatic by bringing to light otherwise hidden limitations that necessarily impinge upon the political discourse of any era, including our own. If the modern understanding of freedom is primarily freedom to speak and think for oneself, the essays in this volume exhibit the persistence of political philosophy by thinking beyond the hidden limits often constricting contemporary paradigms.

Notes

1. Francis Fukuyama, *The End of History and the Last Man* (New York: Avon Books, 1992), xi.

2. For a recent statement on the persistence of the problematic relationship between political science and political philosophy, see the published version of a symposium on this subject in *PS: Political Science and Politics* 33, no. 2 (June 2000): 189–97.

3. Consider especially John Stuart Mill, *On Liberty* and Immanuel Kant, *Groundwork for a Metaphysics of Morals.*

4. Rawls, *A Theory of Justice* (Cambridge, Mass.: Harvard University Press, 1971), 4.

5. Rawls's theory of the good has now become extremely complex, especially with the publication of *Political Liberalism,* where he qualifies, but does not disavow, the core thesis of *A Theory of Justice.* Rawls writes, "Even though political liberalism seeks common ground and is *neutral in its aim,* it is important to emphasize that it may still affirm the superiority of certain forms of moral character and encourage certain moral virtues while remaining neutral in its aim" (*Political Liberalism* [New York: Columbia University Press, 1993], 194, emphasis added). The theme of *Political Liberalism* is explicitly addressed by Gerald Mara in part four of this volume.

6. *Liberalism and Its Critics,* ed. Michael Sandel (New York: New York University Press, 1984), represents an early collection of authors associated with the communitarian movement. Sandel's introduction traces the origin of the communitarian critiques to Aristotle, Hegel, and the civic republican tradition (pp. 5, 7).

7. On the narrative unity of human life see Alasdair MacIntyre's *After Virtue* (Notre Dame, Ind.: University of Notre Dame Press, 1981), especially chapter 15. William Galston argues against the possibility of regime neutrality in *Liberal Purposes: Goods, Virtues, and Diversity in the Liberal State* (Cambridge: Cambridge University Press, 1991), especially chapter 4. The notion of the "unencumbered self," a self understood as prior to and independent of purposes and ends, was first put forward in Michael Sandel's seminal article, "The Procedural Republic and the Unencumbered Self," *Political Theory* 12, no. 1 (February 1984): 81–95.

8. Thomas Smith aptly observes that "a guiding assumption in Aristotelian social and political theory is the formative power of contexts" ("Aristotle and the Conditions for and Limits of the Common Good," *American Political Science Review* 93, no. 3 [September 1999]: 625–36, at 631).

9. Ronald Beiner lucidly brings into focus the importance of *ethos* for understanding and defending Gadamer's version of neo-Aristotelianism in "Do We Need a Philosophic Ethics?" in *Action and Contemplation: Studies in the Moral and Political Thought of Aristotle,* ed. Robert Bartlett and Susan Collins (Albany: State University of New York Press, 1999), 37–52. Beiner writes, "What Gadamer ultimately draws from Aristotle's practical philosophy is the notion that one is always already participating in shared norms by which one is antecedently shaped, and that 'the ideal of the nonparticipating observer' who stands above it all is therefore a bogus one" (ibid., 41).

10. See especially essays by Bernard Yack and Susan Collins in this volume.

11. For Gunnell's more detailed account of Weber's role in the Weimar conversation and its consequences for the development of American social science, see *Descent of Political Theory*, especially 147–55.

12. In part two of this volume, David O'Connor examines the relationship between Heidegger and one of his most influential students, Leo Strauss, particularly as it bears on the crucial differences in their understanding and appropriation of Aristotle.

13. Carnes Lord's "Introduction" to *Essays on the Foundations of Aristotelian Political Science*, ed. Carnes Lord and David O'Connor (Berkeley: University of California Press, 1991), 2. This volume seeks to recover a genuinely Aristotelian approach to the social sciences by avoiding both the overly historical and insufficiently historical approaches to Aristotle's thought that often impair genuine understanding of Aristotle's enduring historical and philosophical interest.

14. Franco Volpi, "The Rehabilitation of Practical Philosophy and Neo-Aristotelianism" in *Action and Contemplation*, 3–25, at 4–5.

15. Ibid., 5.

16. Consider Volpi, "Rehabilitation of Practical Philosophy," and Lord and O'Connor, *Foundations of Aristotelian Political Science*, esp. 2–3 and nn. 2–3.

17. Gunnell, *Descent of Political Theory*, 141.

18. Volpi, "Rehabilitation of Practical Philosophy," 5.

19. Arendt, *The Origins of Totalitarianism* (New York: Harcourt, Brace, 1951); Voegelin, *The New Science of Politics* (Chicago: Chicago University Press, 1952); Strauss, *Natural Right and History* (Chicago: Chicago University Press, 1953).

PART ONE

THE PROBLEM
OF COMMUNITY

CHAPTER ONE

Community

An Aristotelian Social Theory

BERNARD YACK

Aristotle's name figures prominently in most contemporary critiques of liberal individualism. Aristotle, it is said, can help us see that our political life is nothing but "civil war carried on by other means," "a war of all against all . . . we make for ourselves, not out of whole cloth but out of an intentional distortion of our social natures."[1] He teaches us that a healthy political life "presupposes a wide range of agreement [on] a community of goods and virtues," and that "it is this agreement which makes possible the kind of bond between citizens which constitutes" the political community.[2]

Given his insistence on the priority of the community to the individual, it is not surprising that Aristotle has been so frequently enlisted as an ally by communitarian critics of modern life and thought. But when we turn to the text of Aristotle's *Politics*, this characterization of his arguments becomes rather difficult to sustain. For the central books of the *Politics* (3–6) are a study of conflict, competition, and compromise. Political community appears here as the *scene* of conflict rather than its *remedy*, a disordered reality rather than a vision of lost or future harmony. All the cruel, mindless, and selfish actions that we, sadly, associate with ordinary political life are included prominently among "the political things (*ta politika*)" that Aristotle sets out to study, not just the occasional moments of warmth and heroism. For just as there are peaks of virtue and cooperation that can be found only among citizens, so there are forms of distrust, conflict, and competition that only citizens experience.

Modern scholars exaggerate Aristotle's hostility to social conflict and competition because they tend to associate his understanding of community with their own. But unlike most modern social and political theorists, Aristotle does not develop his conception of community as an answer to the celebrations of social differentiation and competition found in the writings of modern liberal individualists. If anything, he writes to counter the extreme communitarianism of Plato's *Republic,* a book that, he complains, makes social unity the measure of political health (*Pol.* 1261–62). Aristotle argues against Plato that the elimination of social heterogeneity threatens to eliminate political community itself. For, as we shall see, community signifies for him a combination of sharing and differentiation, rather than social unity (*Pol.* 1261a14–1261b15). Aristotle's conception of community seeks to explain rather than eliminate social differentiation and the conflicts that arise therefrom. As long as we identify his communitarianism with our contemporary assaults on individualism and social differentiation, we will seriously misunderstand his account of social and political life.

I am not, however, insisting on removing the layers of communitarian interpretation that have settled on Aristotelian ideas solely in the name of textual fidelity. After all, one may prefer creative distortions to more faithful readings of texts, especially when one challenges, as do so many current readers, the very notion of more or less authentic interpretations. I suggest that we should dig beneath overly communitarian readings of Aristotle's texts primarily because I believe that what we find there can help us analyze and resolve conceptual and theoretical difficulties that are, in large part, a legacy of the polemics between individualists and their communitarian critics. Aristotle built his understanding of ordinary political life upon the soundest of communitarian premises: the social construction of individual identities and aspirations. But, unlike present-day communitarians, he had no need to enlist this premise in a polemical war against advocates of liberal individualism. As a result, his communitarian conception of politics has none of the exaggerated hopes for moral harmony and elevated behavior associated with today's communitarianism. If one is seeking to construct an adequate communitarian understanding of ordinary political life, or even if one is only interested in seeing what might be learned from such an understanding, then one could do no better than to start with Aristotle. But in order to do so, we need first to get a handle on what he means by community, a subject that has received surprisingly little attention from scholars.

THE COMMUNAL ANIMAL

Aristotle uses *koinonia* as a generic term for all social groups.[3] Aristotelian *koinoniai* emerge out of almost every kind of social interaction. They can be as fleeting as a business deal or as enduring as religious customs, as small as a nuclear family or as large as a nation. Wherever individuals hold something in common (*koinon*), be it a household, a contract, a destination, or a political regime, they participate in a *koinonia* according to Aristotle (*NE* 1132b31–1133b, 1159b25–1160a).[4]

I translate *koinonia* as "community," even though Aristotle often uses it—for example, in describing parties to an exchange of goods—when we would be much more comfortable with terms like "partnership" or "association."[5] I do so, first of all, in order to preserve the etymological relation between *koinon* (common) and *koinonia* (community), a relation that is central to Aristotle's understanding of community.[6] Second, while I believe that we should try to distance Aristotle's understanding of community from the images of personal warmth and intimacy that we tend to associate with the word "community," other familiar connotations of the word are very much worth preserving. One of the most striking features of Aristotle's understanding of community is that he associates with *all* social groups many social phenomena, such as friendship ties, that we tend to associate only with smaller and highly integrated communities. By preserving this association in our translation of *koinonia,* we draw attention to the distinctiveness of Aristotle's understanding of human sociability.

Although he focuses most of his attention on the political community, Aristotle insists that the human being is a "communal animal (*zoon koinonikon*)," as well as a political animal (*EE* 1242a25).[7] He notes that human beings are naturally disposed to share a wide variety of communal goods and activities, not just those associated with political community. "Men strive to live together even when they have no need of assistance from one another, though it is also the case that the common advantage brings them together" (*Pol.* 1278b19). Human beings, he suggests, generally shun a solitary existence and find pleasure in regular interaction with each other. Moreover, they are equipped with the reasoning ability to see the mutual advantage to be gained from participating in groups. As a result, they are naturally disposed to establish and maintain a wide range of communities.

Apparently, Aristotle deems the communal nature of human beings to be so self-evident that he sees no need to offer proof of its existence.[8] In the opening pages of the *Politics* he simply assumes our communal nature and rushes on to demonstrate that nature makes us political animals as well. Nevertheless, Aristotle's assumptions about our communal nature have important implications for his account of political life, as becomes clear when we examine his discussion of community in other texts. Some social theorists argue that Aristotle's persistent focus on politics rules out the use of Aristotle's "generic concept *koinonia* as the subject of social predication."[9] But if we are willing to use some imagination in exploring Aristotle's scattered remarks about *koinonia,* then we should be able to distinguish it from his understanding of political community.

Four key features characterize community as Aristotle uses the term. 1) A community consists of individuals that differ from each other in some significant way (*Pol.* 1261a–b). 2) These individuals share something, some good, activity, feature of their identity or any combination thereof (*Pol.* 1252a1; *NE* 1156a–1157b). 3) They engage in some interaction related to what they share. 4) Perhaps most important, they are bound to each other, to a greater or lesser extent, by some sense of friendship (*philia*) and some sense of justice (*NE* 1159b27).[10]

The first of these features, the heterogeneity of community members, may seem like a commonplace, but it plays an important role in Aristotle's understanding of community. As he makes clear in his critique of Plato's *Republic,* it leads Aristotle to conceive of community in terms of the kinds of things that different individuals share, rather than in terms of collective identities.[11] Aristotle ridicules Plato for treating collective identity as the measure of communal health. If we took Plato's standards seriously, he complains, we would have to conclude that the ideal community would be a single individual, since only then could we be sure that we have rid ourselves of the social tensions created by heterogeneity (*Pol.* 1261a). Once we recognize the absurdity of Plato's ideal of collective identity, we must, Aristotle argues, acknowledge that heterogeneity is a necessary element of community, rather than the obstacle to social harmony that community seeks to overcome. Men and women, farmers and shoemakers, sailors and passengers, aristocratic and peasant families—such are the members of Aristotelian communities. The creative—and sometimes destructive—tension that emerges from combinations of sharing and difference is one of the most important features of community, as Aristotle conceives of it. Eliminate differences in social identity in the name of easing this tension, you destroy community itself (*Pol.* 1261b5).[12]

Aristotle does, of course, insist on the priority of the political community, among other communities, to the individual (*Pol.* 1253a19). But in doing so, he is illustrating the necessary role that communities play in the full development of the natural capacities of human beings, not the subordination of individual to collective identities. Nowhere will you find in Aristotle's writings the lyric celebration of such subordination that Rousseau, among others, has taught us to associate with community. Nor will you find a discussion of Rousseau's favorite passion, love of country, in Aristotle's account of the passions in the *Rhetoric.* One can hardly imagine a Rousseauian—or any "civic republican"—account of rhetoric that omitted love of country from the list of popular passions![13] Yet Aristotle finds no place for it in the *Rhetoric,* despite the fact that the *Rhetoric* is devoted to identifying the ways in which orators exploit the passions in order to sway their audience in the court or the assembly. He omits it, I suspect, because a passion for collective identity plays little role in his understanding of community.

Because Aristotle describes business and traveling groups, indeed, all instrumental associations based on shared interest, as communities (*NE* 1132b31, 1159b25), he clearly does not identify community with collective identity.

Instead, he identifies it with the kind of sharing—whether of goods, like property, pleasure, or virtue, or of activities, such as politics, profit-making, or religious worship—that bring individuals together. Of course, shared identities may also bring individuals together, according to Aristotle. The members of families, *poleis,* and many other communities (even members of the human race as a whole [*NE* 1155a29]),[14] often see in each other a certain reflection of themselves, a reflection that leads them to devote special attention to each other (*Pol.* 1262b23). But unless we clearly distinguish such sharing of social identity from collective identity, we are bound to misunderstand Aristotle's account of communal life.

Shared identity refers to common elements in the way in which a group of individuals identify themselves. Collective identity, in contrast, refers to the association of one's own identity with a collective will or actor, such as Rousseau's general will. While Aristotle has a great deal to say about the social identities people share and the common goods that are often associated with such sharing, he does not speak of communities as collective actors expressing a "general will."[15] It is always individual actors—for example, fathers, ship-captains, oligarchs, demagogues, or tyrants—who speak in the name of Aristotelian communities. Such individuals may seek to persuade us that the policies that they choose are for our own or the common good. They may possess the kind of power or superior knowledge that make such persuasion unnecessary. But their choices, even when their decisions genuinely promote the common good of a community, remain the choices of particular individuals, choices that we may or may not be disposed to accept. Sharing some identity—as, for example, members of a family, tribe, or class—with these individuals may make us more likely to accept the choices they make. But it does not presume the existence of a collective identity and will, nor does Aristotle ever suggest that it does. "Who rules?" and "which individuals and groups would rule best?" are the questions that Aristotle asks in his analysis of communities, not "who best represents the general will with which we would all identify if we could only abstract from particular interests."

Aristotle never confuses the intense sense of belonging to a group, what Herman Schmalenbach calls "communion (*bund*),"[16] with community itself. As Schmalenbach points out, those who actually live in communities, as opposed to those who yearn for them, rarely have an intense awareness of collective identity. For them, communities "is nothing but a fact" of life, "an existential circumstance or is simply evident. Life in a family or on the farm makes no explicit claims for community."[17] There is little sense of collective identity among community members precisely because their individual identities are shaped by the communities in which they live. "In the fact that the unconscious is the basis of community, we can consciously apprehend the strongest differentiating quality from communion."[18]

Those who experience "communion," in contrast, consciously experience the loss of separate identity that often comes with an intense sense of belonging to a group. This experience can arise in many different kinds of groups and situations—for example, among soldiers sharing adversity in the trenches, among travelers on a ship who share the pleasures of a cruise, even among people who, like the characters in Thomas Mann's *Magic Mountain*, share nothing but their boredom.[19] But it tends to be a fragile and transitory experience, an experience that comes and goes unexpectedly. (As with a sense of spontaneity, if you seek it, you will probably never experience it.)[20] Communions arise out of the ordinary experiences of social interaction that shape individual character and identity. Given their relatively settled personal identities, "those who grow up in a community easily come to mistrust such communions," when, as is often the case, they are "proposed to a community by someone who is not part of the community."[21]

The failure to distinguish clearly between community and communion (or collective identity) helps explain the romanticization of community life that appears in the works of so many modern social and political theorists since Rousseau, a romanticization that these theorists often read into Aristotle's works as well. Those who participate in communion lose their sense of distinction from one another and are, if only for a brief period of time, disposed toward high levels of mutual trust and relatively rare forms of cooperation. Those who participate in community, in contrast, do not lose this sense of distinction from one another, even if they share important elements of their identities.

As a result, community does not necessarily provide us with the source of increased trust and cooperation that we find in communion. The members of a traditional peasant village may share a relatively familiar and stable sense of who and what they are. But such sharing, as Oscar Lewis has noted, hardly eliminates "distrust, suspicion, envy, violence, reserve, and withdrawal" in "small peasant societies"; it merely channels social conflicts in directions that are relatively unfamiliar to participants in more diffuse, urban cultures.[22] Few conflicts are more intense than those between brothers over an inheritance or between peasant neighbors over a piece of land. But, as Schmalenbach points out, such conflicts take place within the community that brothers and peasants share. Despite their conflicts, "neighbors and brothers remain neighbors and brothers. Neighborliness and brotherhood also persist [among them] psychically. . . . Those who oppose one another are not merely enemies. There is probably no better example anywhere to demonstrate how minor a role feelings play as a basis of community."[23]

Once we distinguish community from communion and collective identity, it becomes clear that for Aristotle community is a structural feature of everyday social interactions, rather than an ideal of solidarity and harmonious living. Sentiments of love, sympathy, and solidarity will often develop in Aristotelian communities. But they will grow out of the same sources as much of the conflict and competition in communal life: the sharing of goods, activities, and identities by different kinds of individuals.

THE FORMS OF FRIENDSHIP AND JUSTICE

Perhaps the most striking feature of Aristotle's understanding of community is his claim that some form of both friendship and justice binds the members of every kind of community.

> In every community there is thought to be some form of justice, and friendship too; at least men address as friends their fellow-voyagers and fellow-soldiers, and so too those sharing with them in any other kind of community. And the extent of their community is the extent of their friendship, as it is the extent to which justice exists between them. (*NE* 1159b27–31)

Because community is Aristotle's generic term for *all* social groups, it follows from this claim that participants in every kind of social group, even in the relatively fleeting and impersonal communities formed by exchangers and travelers, develop some form of both friendship and justice. Clearly, such a claim cuts right across the modern dichotomies—such as the distinctions between community and society or between altruism and self-interest—that tend to shape our social imagination. Contrary to the way in which we ordinarily describe social relations, Aristotle can speak of social phenomena such as the form of friendship that develops among those who exchange goods or the form of justice that develops among family members. We will seriously misunderstand his account of social and political life unless we make an effort to counter our reliance on these familiar dichotomies.

By friendship Aristotle means a disposition to give individuals what is good for them. "We may describe friendly feeling (*to philein*) towards anyone as wishing for him what you believe to be good things, not for your own sake but for his, and being inclined, as far as you can, to bring these things about" (*Rhet.* 1380b36). In every form of friendship "one wishes what is good for the friend," whether that good is profit, pleasure, or virtue. "For friendship asks us to do what we can, not what is due" (*EE* 1244a21; *NE* 1163b15).

Justice, in contrast, asks us to give precisely "what is due" to others (*NE* 1163b15). If friendship asks us to do all that we *can* to help another, justice asks us to do all that some standard of merit *obliges* us to do. For Aristotle, a sense of mutual concern among individuals is thus the mark of friendship, a sense of mutual obligation, the mark of justice. Friendship maintains community by disposing individuals to seek each other's good in some way and to expect such solicitude from each other. Justice brings individuals together by disposing them to hold each other accountable to standards of mutual obligation.

Friendship and justice inspire the emotional bonds that maintain Aristotelian communities. The pursuit of pleasure and advantage naturally leads individuals to associate with each other, according to Aristotle. But pleasure and advantage are not sufficient motivations to maintain the communities established in this way. They offer little incentive to maintain communal actions and goals when alternative, conflicting sources of pleasure and advantage appear, as they inevitably do. Aristotle would probably agree with Jon Elster that a combination of rational pursuit of individual self-interest and emotional attachment to social norms provide "the cement of society."[24] But he would note, in addition, that we would better understand the bewildering variety of social norms that emerges among any collection of human beings if we focused more of our attention on the different forms of friendship and justice promoted by different kinds of sharing.[25]

Clearly, Aristotle uses the Greek word *philia*—which I have been translating as friendship—to describe a much broader range of relationships than we are accustomed to using the word "friendship" to describe. Aristotle's concept of friendship possesses a sociological breadth that is quite foreign to both our theoretical and everyday vocabulary.[26] Indeed, Aristotle seems to use *philia* as a generic term for all expressions of human sympathy and mutual concern.

To a certain extent, Aristotle's concept of friendship reflects ordinary Greek usage, in which *philia* refers to a very broad range of personal relationships, not just to those based on personal intimacy between non-kin.[27] It is therefore tempting to translate *philia* by some term other than friendship when Aristotle applies it to non-intimate relationships such as that between buyers and sellers of goods.[28] But it would be unfortunate if we gave in to this temptation. For we would then lose Aristotle's clear sense that all expressions of mutual concern, from those expressed by contractors to those expressed by kin and by intimate friends, have something important in common.

Aristotle does not merely follow Greek usage when he applies the concept of *philia* to such a broad range of relationships. He also provides the basis for an explanation of our social interactions that might justify that usage. Aristotle's discussion of friendship and community suggests that the emotional attachments formed by intimate friends, family members, travelers, and exchangers of goods are all properly described by one term, *philia*, because they all flow from a similar source: the disposition of human beings to develop a sense of concern for the good of individuals with whom they share goods, identities, and activities. The wide range in depth, breadth, and intensity of these attachments reflect the wide range of goods, identities, and activities that human beings share. Accordingly, Aristotle classifies forms of friendship with reference to the ends shared by individuals: pleasure, advantage, and virtuous activity (*NE* 1156a–57b).

Aristotle's concept of friendship thus reflects a fundamental premise of his approach to social theory, as well as common Greek usage. Friendship is for Aristotle a "state of soul"—that is a settled disposition or character trait rather than a passion like love (*NE* 1157b28)[29]—that develops wherever individuals share ends and actions. "The proverb 'what friends have is common property' expresses the truth," Aristotle notes, "For friendship depends on community" and "the extent of their community is the extent of their friendship" (*NE* 1159b30–32). Sharing ends and actions disposes individuals to express a sense of selective concern for each other, a sense of concern that varies in its degree of depth and intensity in proportion to the kinds of ends and actions they share. One reason we maintain our communities is because we are, in ways and to an extent that varies in different communities, naturally disposed to aid those with whom we share ends, activities, and identities.

That this kind of mutual concern develops in the more tightly knit communities, such as families and other intimate associations, seems undeniable. But do we have any evidence to confirm the plausibility of Aristotle's claim that we will find something like this sense of mutual concern even in more impersonal and transitory social groups? I think that we have. Consider, to begin with, a relatively easy case: our behavior when traveling together with strangers. We are usually far more inclined to put ourselves out to help someone with whom we are sharing a plane or bus ride than we are willing to do after we have reached our destination. When we share a journey, the sense of being 'all in the same boat'—the sense that we are all unavoidably stuck, whatever our differences, with the difficulties and inconveniences created by our shared means of transport—disposes us to make much more of an effort than we ordinarily make to help strangers.

Moving to the more difficult case of contractual and exchange relations, it is not as implausible as it might at first seem to assert that participants in exchanges and other economic dealings develop a limited sense of mutual concern. Exchangers, unlike thieves, engage in activities that they see as mutually advantageous—though, hopefully, as more advantageous to themselves than to the other parties. Consequently, they tend to associate their own gain with the—preferably smaller—gains achieved by their partners. Exchangers hardly seek to maximize the good of their exchange partners, and self-interest, of course, often colors individuals' perceptions of what is good for others. But their participation in what they see as mutually advantageous activity may dispose them, however weakly, to prefer the well-being of their exchange partners, as long as it does not directly harm their own interests. Even the relatively impersonal exchange of goods over the supermarket counter could dispose us to this kind of mutual concern. To the extent that we think of ourselves as acting to promote each other's advantage in such exchanges, we come to be more disposed, however minimally and momentarily, to help each other in ways we would not be disposed to do were we not exchanging with each other.[30]

Exchange relations manifest, at the very least, the expectation that those with whom we exchange things will display some concern for our good, as long as it does not make it impossible for them to benefit from our interactions as well. For confirmation of this expectation, consider how we react to being cheated in an exchange as opposed to how we react to being robbed by a stranger. We certainly get angry with thieves and seek to have them punished. But we do not normally experience when robbed the disappointed expectations we experience when we are cheated unless we share something with the thief, such as a family, a workplace, or a country, that leads us to expect that the thief would show some concern for our welfare.

We share with our exchange partners an activity that is supposed to be mutually advantageous. When someone cheats us by taking more than we agreed to exchange, we are hurt not only by the injustice of the action, but also by the fact that an individual has chosen to harm us despite our agreement to engage in mutually advantageous behavior. That individual has treated us as if we shared nothing at all. The more we share with the individual who cheats us, the greater our displeasure will be. The family member, colleague, or compatriot who cheats us adds greater insult to the injury we suffer. It "is reasonable," Aristotle notes, to react in this way since "in addition to the injury," we also consider ourselves robbed of the expected pleasures and benefits of our friendship with such individuals (*Pol.* 1328a10). But even if all that we share with others is the act of exchanging goods for mutual profit, we still seem to develop the expectation our exchange partners will display at least a minimal concern for our good as long as it does not rule out their own.

Aristotle is not, of course, suggesting that we are normally disposed to sacrifice ourselves for the sake of someone who sells us a stick of gum. Exchange friendship, especially when it is based on a single and relatively unimportant action, will be rather superficial and transitory.[31] It will persist only as long as both participants continue to believe that they gain some advantage from their interaction. Aristotle's major point seems to be that our natural sympathy for others grows out of and is shaped by the kinds of ends and activities we share with them.[32] Even such minimal sharing as an exchange of goods leads us to distinguish, to a certain extent, the individuals with whom we exchange things as objects of our concern. Our selective concern for such individuals may not lead us to sacrifice our lives for them, but it might help explain why most of us, to the consternation of rational choice theorists, avoid cheating on them in our exchanges when we can easily get away with it.[33]

Aristotle also argues that some form of justice develops in every human community, even in communities, such as families, that are bound by an intense and intimate form of friendship.[34] Accordingly, he suggests that there are a variety of different forms of justice, such as domestic, despotic, and political justice (NE 1134b), corresponding to the different forms of communal life.

But justice, as Aristotle conceives of it, functions as a communal bond in a considerably more complex way than friendship. Friendship maintains communities by disposing their members to concern themselves, to some extent, in each other's well-being. This disposition to mutual concern, Aristotle argues, develops naturally among individuals who share goods and activities. But no parallel disposition to act justly emerges naturally out of ordinary social interactions. Like the other Aristotelian moral virtues, justice is a socially acquired "characteristic" rather than a natural disposition. Dispositions toward friendly behavior, like other natural capacities, develop prior to and then express themselves in acts of friendship. The disposition to act justly, in contrast, only emerges, as with all the other moral virtues, after we have repeatedly performed just actions. It requires extensive training and moral education (NE 1103a).

But if the disposition to act justly does not develop naturally, then what does Aristotle have in mind when he insists that some form of justice develops naturally among members of every community? He seems to be saying that even if our natural capacities do not dispose us to act justly, they do dispose us to seek to establish standards in our communities. Aristotle argues that logos, the distinctively human capacity for reason and speech, "is designed to indicate the advantageous and the harmful and, therefore also, the just and unjust ... and it is community in these things that makes a household or a polis" (Pol. 1253a, emphasis added). Acting justly may not be natural for human beings, but talking about acting justly apparently is.

Justice, Aristotle suggests here, develops out of our ability to communicate with each other about the mutual and shared advantages or disadvantages of a particular course of action. Discussion of the advantages and disadvantages of alternative actions naturally leads to assertions of standards of mutual obligation. We do not simply say to others "give us this, we want it." We say, instead, "give us this, you owe it to us (given the shared or mutual advantages that brings us together)." "Community in these things [i.e., the just and unjust] makes a household or a polis" (*Pol.* 1253a), or any other form of human community, because a demand for just behavior emerges naturally in the communities formed by social animals who can speak and reason with each other.[35] It is this concern about justice that most distinguishes human *communities—all* human communities, not just the polis—from the communities formed by other animals. For, while many animals surpass human beings in social friendship and mutual concern, only human beings hold each other accountable to standards of justice.

Moreover, human beings hold each other accountable to such standards in very different ways in different kinds of communities according to Aristotle. Political justice, a form of justice characterized by public legislation, courts, adjudication, and physical compulsion, is the most familiar form of justice, at least to members of political communities. But, as Aristotle makes clear in his discussion of political justice in the *Nicomachean Ethics* (1134a), it is far from the only form of justice. Very different forms of justice develop in the family and other communities.

Unfortunately, Aristotle passes over the non-political forms of justice too quickly in the *Nicomachean Ethics* to provide us with any systematic comparisons of the various forms of justice. It is not entirely clear even what he means by speaking of different forms of justice in different communities. I suggest that he is speaking about different ways in which human beings hold each other accountable to shared standards of obligation, or, in more modern terms, of different forms of the practice of social justice.[36] The way in which Aristotle distinguishes political from non-political forms of justice implies that we hold each other accountable to standards of justice in a variety of different ways in different communities. The most important of these variations concern the ways in which standards of mutual obligation are determined and imposed in different communities.

Because the practice of justice grows out of our efforts to hold others accountable to standards of mutual obligation that they are not naturally disposed to follow, it is bound to involve the compulsion of some individuals by others. Unlike friendship, which involves other-regarding actions we are ourselves disposed to perform, justice primarily concerns other-regarding actions that we are disposed to demand from others. As a result, standards of justice, as Aristotle conceives of them, inevitably reflect a choice that some individuals make and impose on others. The ways in which different kinds of community construct and distribute the power to impose such standards will largely constitute the specific forms of justice that develop within them. What most distinguishes political from domestic justice, for example, is the public legislation and alternation in positions of authority that domestic justice lacks (*NE* 1134a).

Given this understanding of justice, however, it is not immediately clear why Aristotle thinks of justice as a bond rather than a solvent of community. Friendship binds us together by disposing us to help those with whom we share goods and activities. But the only natural disposition that Aristotle associates with justice is a disposition to demand that others conform to what we believe are appropriate standards of behavior. If the practice of social justice consists primarily of angry complaints about each other's behavior, then justice could easily appear to be more of a threat to community than a way of maintaining it.[37]

Why then does justice function as a bond rather than a solvent of community for Aristotle? Again, we have to reconstruct his answer to this question, since he never explicitly addresses it. First of all, to the extent that community members accept the authority of standards of social justice and/or of those who establish them, they share important ends, activities, and sources of identity. But even if, as is most often the case, such acceptance does not fully exist among community members, sharing the various forms of the practice of social justice can still reinforce communal ties. Aristotle believes that nature disposes us to develop different ways of holding each other accountable in the different kinds of community that we form, even if it does not dispose us to behave justly or agree on shared standards of justice.

Practicing justice in these different ways establishes links among individuals that would otherwise be missing. We react very differently to those whom we hold accountable to behave according to shared standards and to those who simply fail to treat us well. We get angry at the former group of individuals. We charge them with injustice and seek to enlist the aid of other community members to correct their behavior. Their behavior brings to mind and reinforces the notion that there is some special link between us, that we share with other community members a practice of holding each other accountable to standards of obligation. Even if that link only structures the way we engage in conflict with each other, it still reinforces the sense that we participate with others in a community. Our disposition to raise and enforce standards of mutual obligation among community members need not promote social order and peace, but it does give rise to the kinds of shared activity and identity that reinforce our sense of living in a community.

Friendship and justice thus support communal life in very different ways according to Aristotle. Our natural disposition to act in a friendly way toward people with whom we share ends and actions leads us to single out community members as objects of special sympathy and concern. Our natural disposition to hold individuals to standards of mutual obligation also leads us to single out community members as objects of special, though not as benevolent, attention. Both dispositions lead us to distinguish and devote special attention to the individuals with whom we share ends and activities.

Aristotelian Community and Modern Social Theory

The Aristotelian social theory reconstructed in this essay differs from the most influential modern social theories in that it begins with a single concept, community (*koinonia*), rather than a conceptual dichotomy. Aristotle assumes that what all social groups have in common is significant enough to provide the basis for a generic concept covering all social groups. He explains the great variety of social groups by referring to the variety of goods and activities that individuals share in their communities. In contrast, the classic modern social theorists, such as Tönnies, Durkheim, and Weber, build their social theories on dichotomies between fundamentally different forms of social order, dichotomies such as "community vs. society," "mechanical vs. organic solidarity," or "communal vs. associative groups."[38] They begin their explanations of the variety of social behavior by determining to which of the two categories a given social group belongs.

Aristotle's understanding of community cuts right across these familiar modern dichotomies. When we look at his famous claim about our political nature with these dichotomies in mind, it appears as if Aristotle is suggesting that human beings are, by nature, altruistic sharers in something like the small highly integrated social group that Tönnies describes as community (*Gemeinschaft*). But Aristotle also repeatedly insists that the bond between members of political communities belongs to the same general category, instrumental or advantage friendship, as the bond between partners to any exchange or contract (*NE* 1160a11; *EE* 1242a6).[39] These claims, when read through the lens provided by modern social theory, seem to suggest that, on the contrary, political communities belong to the category of voluntary, self-interested social interactions that Tönnies calls society or association (*Gesellschaft*).[40]

As long as we continue to apply the basic dichotomies of modern social theory to Aristotle's work, his understanding of community cannot help but seem confused and contradictory.[41] But once we recognize that his concept of community rests upon a very different understanding of social interaction than that manifested in the basic dichotomies of modern social theory, this appearance of confusion and contradiction disappears.

One reason that modern social theorists favor conceptual dichotomies is their interest in identifying and explaining the novelty of characteristically modern forms of social order. Modern social theorists are heirs to the polemical debates between liberal individualists and their communitarian critics of the left (Rousseau and the socialists) and the right (Burke, de Maistre, Bonald, etc.). These critics, like their present-day followers, argue that the increasing acceptance of individualistic political theories and practices threatens the very possibility of social order. The classic modern social theorists agree with these critics that individualistic theories provide inadequate explanations of social order. But they also notice that new forms of social order seemed to be developing in the modern societies, the nations of Western Europe and North America, that were most closely associated with these theories. The problem that they set for themselves is to identify and explain these new forms and sources of social order. Tönnies' concept of *Gesellschaft,* Durkheim's concept of "organic solidarity," Weber's concept of rationalization,[42] even Marx's concept of the capitalist mode of production—they are all inspired by the need to identify and explain the unprecedented forms of social order that develop in a modern, increasingly individualistic world. The great conceptual dichotomies upon which they build their social theories thus represent, more than anything else, an attempt to distinguish a novel modern form of social order from its predecessors.

Aristotle, needless to say, does not share these concerns and challenges. Accordingly, he has far less reason to begin his analysis of community, like modern social theorists, with a dichotomy between two basic forms of social interaction. As a result, his analysis of community can help us gain some critical distance on the advantages and disadvantages of the dichotomous vocabulary of modern social theory.

Viewed from the perspective of Aristotle's understanding of community, the great value of modern approaches to social theory lies in the special insights into the peculiar structures of modern society that they make possible. But these approaches have accompanying disadvantages, such as the tendency to construct overly simplistic conceptions of pre-modern forms of social order. Such over-simplification is probably inevitable when pre-modern forms of social order are constructed as negative images of peculiarly modern forms. (In the context of my reconstruction of Aristotelian social and political thought, the most important example of such oversimplification is the portrayal of the ancient polis as an "undifferentiated," "face-to-face society" bound by the overwhelming moral consensus characteristic of Durkheim's "mechanical solidarity." I challenge this portrayal of the polis in *The Problems of a Political Animal.* See especially the final section of Chapter 2.) Modern social theorists also pay for their insights into peculiarly modern forms of social order with a certain degree of abstractness in their analyses. When examined closely, the actual forms of social order they study fall more readily along a continuum than into the dichotomous categories that they erect. As a result, modern social theorists must abstract from a large part of social reality in order to sustain the "ideal types" that support their conceptual dichotomies.

Weber, among others, concedes that the great majority of relationships he describes as "associative" or instrumental have some of the features of the "communal" relationships from which he distinguishes them. "No matter how calculating and hard-headed the ruling considerations in such a social relationship—as that of a merchant to his customers—may be, it is quite possible for it to involve emotional values which transcend its utilitarian significance."[43] But once we recognize the degree of abstraction from social reality required by the dichotomy between community and society, then we must acknowledge that, valuable as such dichotomies may be for highlighting the contrasts between particular forms of community, we need to correct the distortions that they create by employing alternative approaches to social theory as well.[44] The Aristotelian approach to social theory helps us correct this abstraction by treating all social groups as variations on the theme of community. The greater concreteness of its classification of different kinds of communal life greatly compensates for the relative imprecision of its conceptual categories.

The lack of a widely accepted generic concept, such as Aristotle's concept of *koinonia,* also introduces considerable confusion into the recurring debate about the value of community that has been raging among social and political theorists since the end of the eighteenth century. Aristotle is often drawn into this controversy as a partisan of communitarian political theories and practices. But, as we have seen, Aristotle's understanding of community strongly diverges from most modern understandings of the concept. Once we recognize this divergence, we can use his understanding of community to help us gain some critical distance on the recurrent modern debates between communitarians and liberal individualists.

Modern communitarianism is in large measure a reaction against the limitations of contractarianism and the other liberal political theories that gained popularity in the seventeenth and eighteenth centuries. As a result, it is not surprising that a revival of communitarianism has followed hard on the heels of the recent revival of social contract theory associated with the work of John Rawls.[45] Modern communitarianism also grows out of dissatisfaction with the new kinds of selfishness, dislocation, and injustice that have emerged in the relatively impersonal social and political institutions that have put liberal theories into practice in the modern world.

As a result, most modern communitarians, from Rousseau to Alasdair MacIntyre, raise both theoretical and practical objections against liberal individualism. They tend to argue, first of all, that liberal theories are inadequate because they ignore the ways in which communities constitute the identity and character of individuals. They then usually go on to argue that liberal practices and institutions are inadequate because they undermine the communal attachments that are essential to individual and social health.[46]

The first of these two arguments is considerably sounder than the second. Communitarian critiques of contractarianism and other individualistic social theories rest upon relatively uncontroversial assumptions about the influence of communal life on individuals. Like Aristotle, I accept these assumptions and acknowledge the weakness of theories that abstract from the social sources of individual character and identity. Many liberal theories, especially those associated with contractarianism, are built upon myths about the possibility of self-constituting individuals, individuals who can somehow abstract from social influences on their character in order to determine which institutions a purely rational individual can choose.

But most modern communitarians usually go much further. They tend to argue that the devaluation of community in individualist social and political practices turns modern individuals into alienated and "unencumbered selves,"[47] thereby dissociating them in a way that threatens both individual integrity and a healthy social order. In doing so, they attempt to ground their critiques of the injustice and dislocation created by liberal practices and institutions in their understanding of the failings of individualistic explanations of social and political life. Since this critique of liberal practices sounds like it rests upon the same uncontroversial assumption that supports communitarian critiques of liberal theories, many find it equally plausible. After all, if individualistic theories dissociate individuals, should not the practices that realize these theories do the same?

On closer examination, however, a tension emerges between these two claims. If individualistic theories fail because they abstract from the social constitution of individual character and identity, then whatever their corresponding practices may do to us, these practices cannot dissociate us in the way imagined by individualistic theories. For it is the central premise of the communitarian critique of these theories that self-constituting or dissociated individuals exist only in the fevered imaginations of liberal theorists. It follows from this premise that even if modern individuals *feel* less associated with each other, they still must, like all other individuals, draw a large part of their character and identity from their shared life. Modern individuals may experience a relatively large degree of alienation from each other, but such alienation is no less a social phenomenon, a shared culture, than patriotism or the celebration of tradition.

In fact, the communitarian critique of liberal practices and institutions rests upon a highly controversial assumption about the *value* of community, rather than a relatively uncontroversial assumption about its existence. Communitarians generally assume that social and political health requires the strong sense of belonging to a community that they believe is characteristic of the specific form of social life that Tönnies and others call "community."[48] This assumption is controversial for a number of reasons. First of all, it is very hard to prove. Communitarians have been making vain predictions about the upcoming dissolution of liberal and individualistic societies since the end of the French Revolution. Their favorite examples of such dissolution, such as the collapse of the Weimar Republic,[49] are not very convincing since they occur in societies in which the individualistic practices that are supposed to bring about social collapse were generally quite weak and bitterly opposed by a large and powerful segment of the population. According to communitarian arguments, it should be precisely the communities in which liberal individualism is most firmly entrenched, such as the United States and Great Britain, that experience the dissolution of social order. Thus the relative success of the most liberal and individualistic communities in the twentieth century poses a very powerful objection to assumptions that political communities will self-destruct without a strong shared sense of community.[50]

These assumptions are also controversial because it is not at all clear that communities, as conceptualized by Tönnies and those who follow him, actually do generate a strong sense of belonging to a community among their members. We can assume that they do generate this sense only if, like many modern social theorists, we conflate community with communion. But, as we have seen, there are good reasons for doubting that communion always arises out of community and that the sense of belonging that communitarians seek can be anything more than a temporary social phenomenon. And once we question the connection between community and communion, the reasons for preferring forms of social life that resemble Tönnies' community also come into question. For without communion, there is little reason to believe that pre-modern "communities" are any more harmonious or less conflictual than modern "societies" are.

These problems in communitarian arguments are difficult to discern because contemporary communitarians and their liberal opponents both tend to blur the distinction between generic and specific uses of the term "community." The blurring of this distinction allows communitarians to base their critique of liberal practices and institutions on the relatively uncontroversial premise that grounds their critique of individualistic theories. In effect, they argue that because we are largely constituted by our social experience as a whole, we should live in a very *specific* form of society, usually designated as community. In other words, they argue that because we cannot live without some form of social interaction, we require a particular form of society, unlike our present one, in which individuals express a very strong sense of mutual association.

But, as Michael Oakeshott notes, no particular species of society or community corresponds to the adjective "social" in claims about the social constitution of human character and identity.[51] The defense of community in its specific sense requires, as we have seen, additional and much more controversial arguments. The validity of communitarian critiques of modern practices and institutions rests primarily on the validity of such arguments. An insistence on the generic social constitution of individuals does nothing to justify them.

Nevertheless, it is very difficult to detect the frequent blurring of the distinction between generic and specific uses of terms like "community," "society," and "association" in these arguments as long as we lack a generally recognized term for the genus of all social interactions. Without such a term, we make terms like "community," "society," and "association" do double duty as generic and specific categories and suffer the consequences in conceptual confusion and repetitious intellectual controversies.[52]

Aristotle's concept of community, or something like it, could help us eliminate some of this confusion. Aristotle's understanding of community captures the most sensible and uncontroversial part of communitarian arguments, the insistence upon the way in which all forms of social interactions help shape individual character and identity. But, at the same time, it leaves open questions about the nature and value of any particular form of communal life that one might advocate. It allows us to give full weight to the social constitution of individual character and actions without suggesting the necessity of any specific form of communal life.

Because Aristotle is so often drawn into contemporary debates between individualists and communitarians as a partisan of communitarianism, it might seem rather strange that I suggest using his concepts to referee their disputes. But one of my aims here has been to disentangle Aristotelian insights from these debates. Aristotle undoubtedly rejects explanations of human behavior that rely solely upon examination of individual choice and calculation. But his embrace of communal explanations of human behavior does not blind him to the communal aspects of instrumental associations and other everyday social phenomena. His account of community encourages us instead to identify and explore all the forms of communal behavior created by human beings sharing pleasure, profit, and goodness.

NOTES

This essay is a partially revised version of Chapter 1 ("Community") of Bernard Yack, *The Problems of a Political Animal* (Berkeley: University of California Press, 1993).

1. A. MacIntyre, *After Virtue*, 263; B. Barber, *Strong Democracy*, 75.

2. A. MacIntyre, *After Virtue*, 109.

3. As Niklas Luhmann notes, we could translate *koinonia* as "social system," if that modern generic term did not connote a degree of abstraction wholly absent from Aristotelian social theory (*Soziologische Aufklärung*, 138).

4. The former passage cited here (*NE* 1132b31–33b) describes parties to ordinary exchanges of goods as members of a *koinonia*. (See also *NE* 1164a1.) For an especially insightful commentary on this passage, see M. Finley, "Aristotle and Economic Analysis," 140–58, 144ff. See also E. M. and N. Wood, *Class Ideology and Ancient Political Theory*, 227.

5. Even Carnes Lord, who strives in his translation of the *Politics* for a literal rendition of Aristotle's words, finds it necessary to use more than one term for *koinonia*. Lord translates *koinonia* as "partnership" in the opening sentence of the *Politics*, and shifts between community and partnership throughout. See Aristotle, *Politics*, trans. C. Lord, 35.

6. As does R. Mulgan, *Aristotle's Political Theory*, 16. See also M. Finley, *The Ancient Economy*, 152.

7. See the insightful commentary on this passage by M. Defourny, *Aristote: Études sur la 'Politique*,' 385ff.

8. Unlike many modern social theorists, Aristotle was not spurred on by competing social and political theories that deny the naturalness of human sociality to provide such proof. He did, however, feel the challenge of theories that denied the naturalness of *political* community and responded with his famous argument about our political nature.

9. M. Riedel, "Gesellschaft, Gemeinschaft," in *Geschichtliche Grundbegriffe*, ed. R. Koselleck et al., 2:804; idem, *Metaphysik und Metapolitik*, 39; N. Luhmann, "Moderne Systemtheorien als Form gesamtgesellschaftlicher Anylse," in *Theorie der Gesellschaft oder Sozialtechnologie*, ed. J. Habermas and N. Luhmann, 7.

10. This sketch of Aristotle's conception of *koinonia* combines features of similar sketches by Moses Finley and W. L. Newmann. See M. Finley, "Aristotle and Economic Analysis," 144, and W. L. Newman, *The Politics of Aristotle*, I: 41–42.

11. As R. F. Stalley points out ("Aristotle's Critique of Plato's *Republic*," 182–99, 184–85), Aristotle seems far more interested in exploring the nature of community in this passage than in presenting a careful analysis of Plato's arguments.

12. On this point, see M. Nussbaum, "Shame, Separateness and Political Unity: Aristotle's Criticism of Plato," 395–435, A. Saxonhouse, "Family, Polity, and Unity," and M. Nichols, *Socrates and the Political Community*, 153–80.

13. I discuss how and why Rousseau imposed the idea of such a passion on the ancient political philosophers in *The Longing for Total Revolution*, 62–72.

14. The further one stretches a sense of shared identity, the weaker it is likely to be, as Aristotle makes clear in his critique of Plato's proposal to turn the city into one family (*Pol.* 1262a). Thus the sense of friendship and community shared by the human race as a whole is bound to be very weak. Nevertheless, it is not negligible. In some circumstances it may inspire a very strong, if temporary, bond with other individuals.

15. The passage that comes closest to an account of collective identity, Aristotle's discussion at the beginning of *Politics*, Book 3, about whether a political community derives its identities from its form—its constitution or regime—or its matter—its individual citizens—is in fact a discussion about how we identify communities, not how individuals identify themselves.

16. H. Schmalenbach, "Communion—A Social Category." See also A. Black, *State, Community and Human Desires*, 50–51.

17. H. Schmalenbach, "Communion," 78.

18. Ibid.

19. One of Schmalenbach's major points is that communion is just as likely to arise out of the voluntary and instrumental associations that Tönnies and other social theorists characterize as "societies" as from the more closely knit and constitutive social groups that they describe as "communities."

20. A. Black, *State, Community and Human Desires*, 50–51.

21. H. Schmalenbach, "Communion," 91. To confirm Schmalenbach's point, imagine the suspicion that Rousseau would inspire were he living in a peasant village or in ancient Sparta. Many of the modern intellectuals, like Rousseau, who yearn for community would probably undermine it where it already exists, since it is an identity-dissolving communion, rather than community, that they really seek.

22. O. Lewis, "The Folk-Urban Ideal Types," 498. Lewis goes on to suggest that "in some villages peasants can live out their lives without any deep knowledge or understanding of the people whom they 'know' in face-to-face relationships. By contrast, in modern Western cities, there may be more give and take about one's private, intimate life at a single sophisticated cocktail party than would occur in years in a peasant village."

23. H. Schmalenbach, "Communion," 82.

24. J. Elster, *The Cement of Society*, 15, 97ff.

25. Aristotle's discussion of friendship and justice bears some similarity to a number of later theories about the social passions that temper the individual's pursuit of pleasure and self-interest. Adam Smith, for example, speaks of "beneficence and justice" as the two dispositions that maintain society. He too distinguishes the obligations that we are disposed to impose on other individuals from the friendly, but unenforceable concern for others that we also come to expect from them (*The Theory of Moral Sentiments*, 155–60). Similarly, Amartya Sen speaks of "sympathy" and "commitment" as the two social passions that maintain our communities by restricting self-interest ("Rational Fools: A Critique of the Behavioral Foundations of Economic Theory," 31). What distinguishes Aristotle's account of friendship and justice from theirs is his claim that some sense of *both* friendship and justice, however limited in depth and breadth, develops in *every* social group, from families and religious societies to cities and business partnerships.

26. Modern sociological studies of friendship generally focus on a far narrower range of relationships—voluntary relationships expressing personal intimacy of some sort—than Aristotle's. They usually explore the social influences upon the way in which individuals form such relationships. For an overview, see, for example, G. Allen, *A Sociology of Friendship and Kinship*, idem, *Friendship: Developing a Sociological Perspective*, and G. Suttles, "Friendship as a Social Institution." For a very insightful account of the social context shaping friendship ideals in different historical periods, see A. Silver, "Friendship and Trust as Moral Ideals: A Historical Approach." In "Friendships and Friendly Relations," Suzanne Kurth notes that we have "friendly relations" with a much larger and broader range of individuals than those with whom we have the intimate and non-instrumental ties that we ordinarily associate with friendship. Kurth's concept of "friendly relations" comes closer to Aristotle's understanding of the majority of non-intimate friendships, though it remains considerably more selective. Contemporary studies of patron-client

relations cover some of the sociological ground covered by Aristotle's account of instrumental friendship.

27. On problems in translating *philia* and *philos,* see D. Whitehead, *The Demes of Attica,* 231–32, and W. R. Connor, *The New Politicians of Fifth-Century Athens,* 30–31. For the Greek understanding of friendship in general, see J. C. Fraisse, *Philia: la notion de l'amitié dans la philosophie de l'antique.*

28. I suspect that the only reason commentators have not offered such alternative translations of *philia* is that they devote most of their attention to Aristotle's best form of friendship—the friendship between virtuous individuals—the form of Aristotelian friendship that most closely conforms to modern notions of friendship. For exceptions see J. Cooper, "Aristotle on the Forms of Friendship," idem, "Aristotle on Friendship," K. Alpern, "Aristotle on the Friendships of Utility and Pleasure," and R. Paine, "Anthropological Approaches to Friendship." Contemporary philosophical study of friendship—an increasingly popular topic—also tends to focus on the moral value of such intimate relationships. See, for example, L. Bluhm, *Friendship, Altruism and Morality,* and A. W. Price, *Love and Friendship in Plato and Aristotle.*

29. In this respect, friendship resembles virtue for Aristotle, which helps explain why he discusses it, following his discussion of the virtues, in his ethical writings.

30. Exchange friendship would probably not develop where there is no social interaction between individuals, as, say, in an electronic transfer of stocks or funds generated by a computer program. But when you transfer stocks through a broker Aristotelian exchange friendship would develop between you and the broker and the broker and the buyer, if not between you and the buyer of your stock.

31. That does not mean, as John Cooper argues, that Aristotle limits exchange friendship to relationships between individuals who regularly and repeatedly interact. Cooper insists, contrary to the interpretation I have presented, that "Aristotle does not make the mistake, which a superficial reading would seem to convict him of, of counting as *philia*" the bonds between all participants in exchange communities. Cooper is certainly correct when he suggests "that it would be a mistake to call in English all such relationships friendships; . . . a businessman is no friend to all of his regular customers" (J. Cooper, "Aristotle on Friendship," 316). But that hardly settles any questions about the way in which Aristotle uses Greek.

32. It is thus the different forms of social interaction rather than, as in Adam Smith's *Theory of the Moral Sentiments,* sympathetic observation that inspires concern for the welfare of others, according to Aristotle.

33. See Robert Frank's discussion of the failure of the self-interest model of behavior to explain our general avoidance of cheating in *Passions within Reason: The Strategic Role of the Emotions.*

34. This point about the existence of a sense of justice among family members is made quite strongly in Susan Okin's critique of contemporary communitarianism in Okin, *Justice, Gender and the Family.*

35. It would be a mistake, however, to think of our disposition to demand justice from others as a purely rational or calculating state of mind. This disposition is manifested, as well, in the passion Aristotle calls anger (*orge*). Anger, Aristotle sug-

gests, manifests our desire for revenge against individuals who dishonor us when, according to our own judgment, we do not deserve to be dishonored. He cites, as an illustration, Achilles' complaint that Agamemnon has treated him "'Like an alien honoured by none'" (*Rhet.* 1378b31–34). (Aristotle is quoting Homer, *Iliad,* Book IX, line 648.) We express anger, Aristotle implies, when community members treat us as aliens, as individuals with whom they share no mutual obligations because they share no actions and ends with us. Anger is the passion that arises in us when individuals fail to meet the obligations we believe are entailed by their sharing with us communal ends and activities.

36. "Practice," admittedly, is not a concept that Aristotle ever employs. But we need some concept to explain what Aristotle means by the different forms of justice that develop in different forms of community, as opposed to either the virtue of justice or the just acts and states of affairs that such a virtue disposes us to choose. I try to integrate these different ways of talking about justice in Chapter 5 ("Political Justice") of *The Problems of a Political Animal.*

37. Aristotle, moreover, avoids one obvious solution to this problem, a solution dear to the hearts of many modern social and political philosophers: the notion that this disposition serves to integrate communities by inspiring a fear of punishment that can help coordinate our behavior and reinforce social order. Even Adam Smith, whose notion of social sympathy has attracted numerous critics of individualism, argues that our disposition to resent perceived insults serves to integrate our communities by means of the fear that it inspires. The "terrors of merited punishment" are, he suggests, "the great safeguards of the association of mankind." Without this fear of punishment by the resentful to "overawe" them, human beings "would, like wild beasts, be at all times ready to fly upon him [the innocent man]; and a man would enter an assembly of men as he enters a den of lions." See A. Smith, *The Theory of Moral Sentiments,* 166–68. Aristotle, in contrast, has little to say at all about fear of punishment. He briefly mentions fear of punishment in the *Nicomachean Ethics* (1179b11) and has a more extended discussion of fear as a passion in the *Rhetoric* (1382a–83b). But in neither place does he treat fear of punishment as the cement of social order.

38. As formulated, respectively, by Ferdinand Tönnies in *Community and Society,* Emile Durkheim in *The Division of Labor in Modern Society,* and Max Weber in *Economy and Society* 41–42.

39. Few commentators notice Aristotle's explicit description of political friendship as an instrumental or shared advantage friendship. Moreover, most of those who do try to find some way of explaining it away so it will not contradict their association of Aristotelian political community with altruism and collective identity. See *The Problems of a Political Animal,* Chapter 4.

40. Indeed, Enrico Berti recommends translating *koinonia politike* as political society (*societé politique*) precisely in order to bring the concept into line with Tönnies' distinction between community and society. See E. Berti, "La notion de societé politique chez Aristote," 80.

41. As Pawel Rybicki (*Aristote et la penseé sociale moderne,* 40–41) has suggested, modern social theorists, whether they lean to communitarian or individualist explanations of social behavior, usually fail to appreciate Aristotle's understanding of our

social nature because they reduce it to "a question of knowing whether human beings come into the world with selfish dispositions or are, on the contrary, born with a strong drive to sociability and altruistic dispositions."

42. As noted earlier, Weber also follows Tönnies by distinguishing between "associative (*gesellschaftliche*)" and "communal (*gemeinschaftliche*) groups" in *Economy and Society,* 41–42.

43. M. Weber, *Economy and Society,* 41, 346.

44. One certainly cannot continue to assert, as some do, that this dichotomy "has undergone the rigors of scientific investigation and been found valid" (G. Simpson, *Conflict and Community,* 31).

45. For example, see R. Bellah et al., *Habits of the Heart;* A. MacIntyre, *After Virtue;* M. Sandel, *Liberalism and the Limits of Justice,* and W. Sullivan, *Reconstructing Public Philosophy.*

46. I develop the following argument more fully in "Does Liberal Practice 'Live Down' to Liberal Theory?" See especially 156–59.

47. The "unencumbered self" is Michael Sandel's metaphor for the dissociated condition of modern individuals. See "The Procedural Republic and the Unencumbered Self."

48. For a clear and extended example of such an argument, see S. de Grazia, *The Political Community.*

49. The dissociation of individuals into an inarticulate mass is an important precondition of totalitarianism according to Hannah Arendt (among others) in her influential work *The Origins of Totalitarianism.*

50. Some communitarians, such as Robert Bellah and his associates in *Habits of the Heart,* explain the surprising political health of individualistic societies, such as the American republic, by suggesting that they are living off the moral capital of older, more communal traditions associated with religion and civic republicanism. Once this moral capital is exhausted, the breakdown of political and psychic health that they predict for individualistic societies will proceed apace.

51. M. Oakeshott, *On Human Conduct,* 88, 98.

52. Georg Simmel used the term *Vergesellschaftung,* usually translated by the coinage "sociation," for this purpose. See *The Sociology of Georg Simmel,* ed. K. Wolf, lxiii.

BIBLIOGRAPHY

Aristotle: Editions and Translations Cited

Barnes, Johnathan, ed. *The Complete Works of Aristotle.* Numerous translators. Princeton, N.J.: Princeton University Press, 1984.
Fritz, Kurt von, and Ernest Kapp, trans. *Aristotle's Constitution of Athens and Related Texts.* With an introduction and notes. New York: Hafner, 1950.
Lord, Carnes, trans. *Politics.* Chicago: University of Chicago Press, 1984.

Newman, W. L., ed. *The Politics of Aristotle.* 4 vols. Oxford: Clarendon, 1887.

Ostwald, Martin, trans. *Nicomachean Ethics.* With an introduction and notes. Indianapolis: Bobbs-Merrill, 1962.

Rackham, Horace, trans. *Nicomachean Ethics.* Cambridge, Mass.: Loeb Classical Library, 1956.

———. *Politics.* Cambridge, Mass.: Loeb Classical Library, 1956.

Sinclair, R. K., and Trevor Saunders, trans. *Politics.* London: Penguin, 1989.

Other Works Cited

Allen, Graham. *Friendship: Developing a Sociological Perspective.* London: Harvester Press, 1989.

———. *A Sociology of Friendship and Kinship.* London: Allen & Unwin, 1979.

Alpern, K. L. "Aristotle on the Friendships of Utility and Pleasure." *Journal of the History of Philosophy* 21 (1983): 303–15.

Aquinas, Thomas. *Commentary on the Nicomachean Ethics.* Chicago: Regnery, 1964.

———. *Selected Political Writings.* Edited by P. d'Entrèves. Oxford: Blackwell, 1959.

Arendt, Hannah. *The Human Condition.* Garden City, N.Y.: Doubleday, 1958.

———. *The Origins of Totalitarianism.* New York: Harcourt Brace Jovanovich, 1973.

Barber, Benjamin. *Strong Democracy.* Berkeley: University of California Press, 1984.

Barker, Ernest. *The Political Thought of Plato and Aristotle.* New York: Dover, 1959.

Bellah, Robert et al. *Habits of the Heart.* Berkeley: University of California Press, 1985.

Berti, Enrico. "La notion de societé politique chez Aristote." In *Antike Rechts- und Sozialphilosophie,* edited by M. Fischer and O. Gigon. Frankfurt: Peter Lange, 1988.

Bien, Gunther. *Die Grundlagen der Politische Philosophie bei Aristoteles.* Munich: Alber, 1973.

Black, Anthony. *State, Community and Human Desires.* New York: St. Martin's Press, 1988.

Bluhm, Lawrence. *Friendship, Altruism and Morality.* London: Routledge & Kegan Paul, 1980.

Bodéüs, Richard. "Deux notions aristotéliciennes sur le droit naturel chez les contintenaux d'Amerique." *Revue de Metaphysique et Morale* (1989): 369–89.

———. "Law and the Regime in Aristotle." In *Essays on the Foundations of Aristotelian Political Science,* edited by C. Lord and D. O'Connor, 234–48. Berkeley: University of California Press.

———. *Le philosophe et la cité.* Paris: "Les Belles Lettres," 1982.

Bradfield, Richard. *The Natural History of Associations: A Study in the Meaning of Community.* 2 vols. London: Duckworth, 1973.

Connor, W. R. *The New Politicians of Fifth-Century Athens.* Princeton, N.J.: Princeton University Press, 1971.

Cooley, Charles. *Human Nature and the Social Order.* New York: Macmillan, 1922.

———. *Social Organization.* New York: Macmillan, 1929.

Cooper, John. "Aristotle on the Forms of Friendship." *Review of Metaphysics* 30 (1976–77): 619–48.

———. "Aristotle on Friendship." In *Essays on Aristotle's Ethics*, edited by A. Rorty, 301–40.

Defourny, Maurice. *Aristote: Études sur la Politique*. Paris: Gabriel Buschesne, 1932.

De Grazia, Sebastian. *The Political Community*. Chicago: University of Chicago Press, 1945.

Durkheim, Emile. *The Division of Labor in Modern Society*. New York: Free Press, 1964.

Elster, Jon. *The Cement of Society*. Cambridge: Cambridge University Press, 1989.

Finley, Moses. *The Ancestral Constitution*. Inaugural Lecture. Cambridge: Cambridge University Press, 1971.

———. *The Ancient Economy*. Berkeley: University of California Press, 1973.

———. "Aristotle and Economic Analysis." In *Articles on Aristotle: 2. Ethics and Politics*, edited by J. Barnes et al. London: Duckworth, 1977.

———. *Politics in the Ancient World*. Cambridge: Cambridge University Press, 1983.

Fraisse, J. C. *Philia: la notion de l'amitié dans la philosophie de l'antique*. Paris: PUF, 1974.

Frank, Robert. *Passions within Reason: The Strategic Role of the Emotions*. New York: Norton, 1988.

Jencks, Christopher. "Varieties of Altruism." In *Beyond Self-Interest*, edited by J. Mansbridge, 53–67. Chicago: University of Chicago Press, 1990.

Kullmann, Wolfgang. "Der Mensch als Politische Lebeswesen bei Aristoteles." *Hermes* 108 (1982): 414–43.

———. "Die Politische Philosophie des Aristoteles." In *Antike Rechts- und Sozialphilosophie*, edited by M. Fischer and O. Gigon.

Kurth, Suzanne. "Friendships and Friendly Relations." In *Social Relationships*, edited by G. McCall, 136–70. Chicago: Aldine, 1970.

Labarière, Jean-Louis. "The Political Animal's Knowledge according to Aristotle." In *Knowledge and Politics*, edited by M. Dascaly. Boulder: Westview, 1988.

Lewis, Oscar. "The Folk-Urban Ideal Types." In *The Study of Urbanization*, edited by P. Hauser and L. Schnore, 491–517. New York: John Wiley and Sons, 1965.

Luhmann, Niklas. *The Differentiation of Society*. Edited and translated by S. Holmes and C. Larmore. New York: Columbia University Press, 1982.

———. "Moderne Systemtheorien als Form gesamtgesellschaftlicher Anylse." In *Theorie der Gesellschaft oder Sozialtechnologie*, edited by J. Habermas and N. Luhmann. Frankfurt: Suhrkamp, 1971.

———. *Soziologische Aufklärung*. Opladen: Westdeutsche Verlag, 1970.

MacIntyre, Alasdair. *After Virtue*. 2nd ed. Notre Dame, Ind.: University of Notre Dame Press, 1984.

———. *Whose Justice? Which Rationality?* Notre Dame, Ind.: University of Notre Dame Press, 1988.

Meikle, S. "Aristotle and Exchange Value." In *A Companion to Aristotle's Politics*, edited by D. Keyt and F. Miller, 156–81. Oxford: Blackwell, 1991.

Mulgan, Richard. *Aristotle's Political Theory*. Oxford: Oxford University Press, 1977.

Nichols, Mary. *Socrates and the Political Community*. Albany: SUNY Press, 1987.

Nisbet, Robert. *The Quest for Community*. Oxford: Oxford University Press, 1953.

Nussbaum, Martha. *The Fragility of Goodness*. Cambridge: Cambridge University Press, 1986.

———. "Shame, Separateness and Political Unity: Aristotle's Criticism of Plato." In *Essays on Aristotle's Ethics*, edited by A. Rorty, 395–435.

Oakeshott, Michael. *On Human Conduct*. Oxford: Clarendon, 1975.

O'Connor, David. "Aristotelian Justice as a Personal Virtue." *Midwest Studies in Philosophy* 13 (1988): 417–27.

Okin, Susan. *Justice, Gender and the Family*. New York: Basic Books, 1989.

Oldfield, Adrian. *Citizenship and Community: Civic Republicanism and the Modern World*. London: Routledge, 1990.

Paine, Robert. "Anthropological Approaches to Friendship." *Humanitas* 6 (1970): 139–59.

Plato. *Republic*. Translated by A. Bloom. New York: Basic Books, 1969.

Pocock, J. G. A. *The Machiavellian Moment*. Princeton, N.J.: Princeton University Press, 1975.

Price, A. W. *Love and Friendship in Plato and Aristotle*. Oxford: Clarendon, 1989.

Rawls, John. "Justice as Fairness: Political, Not Metaphysical." *Philosophy and Public Affairs* (1985).

———. *A Theory of Justice*. Cambridge, Mass.: Harvard University Press, 1971.

Redfield, Robert. *The Little Community: Viewpoints for the Study of a Human Whole*. Chicago: University of Chicago Press, 1955.

Riedel, Manfred. "Gesellschaft, Gemeinschaft." In *Geschichtliche Grundbegriffe*, edited by R. Koselleck et al. 5 vols. Stuttgart: Klett-Cotta, 1972–84.

——— . *Metaphysik und Metapolitik, Studien zu Aristoteles und zur politishcen Sprache der neuzeitlichen Philosophie*. Frankfurt: Surhkamp, 1975.

Ritter, Joachim. *Metaphysik und Politik*. Frankfurt: Suhrkamp, 1969.

Rorty, Amelie, ed. *Essays on Aristotle's Ethics*. Berkeley: University of California Press, 1980.

Rousseau, Jean-Jacques. *Confessions*. New York: Modern Library, n. d.

———. *On the Social Contract: with the Geneva Manuscript and Discourse on Political Economy*. Edited by R. Masters. New York: St. Martin's Press, 1978.

Rowe, Christopher J. "Aims and Methods in Aristotle's Politics." In *A Companion to Aristotle's Politics*, edited by D. Keyt and F. Miller, 57–74. Chicago: University of Chicago Press, 1990.

Rybicki, Pawel. *Aristote et la pensée sociale moderne*. Wroclaw: Ossolineum, 1984.

Salkever, Stephen. *Finding the Mean: Theory and Practice in Aristotelian Political Philosophy*. Princeton, N.J.: Princeton University Press, 1990.

Sandel, Michael. *Liberalism and the Limits of Justice*. Cambridge: Cambridge University Press, 1982.

———. "The Procedural Republic and the Unencumbered Self." *Political Theory* 12 (1984): 81–96.

Saxonhouse, Arlene. "Family, Polity, and Unity." *Polity* 15 (1982): 202–19.

Schmalenbach, Herman. "Communion—A Social Category." In *On Society and Experience*, edited by Schmalenbach, 64–125. Chicago: University of Chicago Press, 1977.

Sen, Amartya. "Rational Fools: A Critique of the Behavioral Foundations of Economic Theory." In *Beyond Self-Interest,* edited by J. Mansbridge, 25–43.

Silver, Allan. "Friendship and Trust as Moral Ideals: A Historical Approach." *Archives Européenes de Sociologie* 30 (1989): 274–97.

Simmel, Georg. *The Sociology of Georg Simmel.* Edited by K. Wolff. New York: Free Press, 1950.

Simpson, George. *Conflict and Community.* New York: T. S. Simpson, 1937.

Sinclair, R. K. *Democracy and Participation in Democratic Athens.* Cambridge: Cambridge University Press, 1988.

Smith, Adam. *An Inquiry into the Nature and Causes of the Wealth of Nations.* New York: Modern Library, 1937.

———. *The Theory of Moral Sentiments.* Indianapolis: Liberty Classics, 1976.

Stalley, R. F. "Aristotle's Critique of Plato's *Republic.*" In *A Companion to Aristotle's Politics,* edited by D. Keyt and F. Miller, 182–99. Oxford: Blackwell, 1990.

Sullivan, William. *Reconstructing Public Philosophy.* Berkeley: University of California Press, 1986.

Suttles, Gerald. "Friendship as a Social Institution." In *Social Relationships,* edited by G. McCall, 95–135. Chicago: Aldine, 1970.

Thomas, Laurence. *Living Morally.* Philadelphia: Temple University Press, 1989.

Tönnies, Ferdinand. *Community and Society.* New York: Harper, 1963.

Unger, Roberto. *Law in Modern Society.* New York: Free Press, 1976.

Weber, Max. *Economy and Society.* Berkeley: University of California Press, 1978.

Whitehead, David. *The Demes of Attica.* Princeton, N.J.: Princeton University Press, 1986.

Wood, E. M. and N. Wood. *Class Ideology and Ancient Political Theory.* Oxford: Blackwell, 1978.

Yack, Bernard. "Does Liberal Practice 'Live Down' to Liberal Theory?" In *Community in America: The Challenges of 'Habits of the Heart,'* edited by C. Reynolds, 149–67. Berkeley: University of California Press, 1988.

———. *The Longing for Total Revolution: Philosophic Sources of Social Discontent from Rousseau to Marx and Nietzsche.* Princeton, N.J.: Princeton University Press, 1986.

CHAPTER TWO

Aristotelian Social Democracy

MARTHA C. NUSSBAUM

"NO CITIZEN SHOULD BE LACKING IN SUSTENANCE"

Aristotle spoke about the human being and good human functioning. He also spoke about the design of political institutions in the many areas of life that should, as he saw it, fall within the province of the lawgiver's concern. He connected these two levels of reflection through a certain conception of the task of political planning. That task, as he saw it, is to make available to each and every citizen the material, institutional, and educational circumstances in which good human functioning may be chosen; to move each and every one of them across a threshold of capability into circumstances in which they may choose to live and function well. The aim of this chapter is to give a philosophical outline of a political conception based upon these elements in Aristotle, to describe the relationship of this conception to some forms of liberalism, and to explain why I find it a valuable and promising political conception. As my title indicates, I believe that this conception provides the philosophical basis for a certain sort of social democracy—one that shares a number of important features with some forms of liberalism that have been defended in the recent debate, but one that also breaks with liberalism at some crucial points.

We can begin investigating this conception by reading three passages from Aristotle's *Politics*:

1. *Politics* 1330b11. The things that we use most of and most frequently where our bodies are concerned, these have the biggest impact on health. Water and air are things of that sort. So good political planning should make some decisions about these things.

2. *Politics* 1329b39 ff. We must speak first about the distribution of land and about farming.... For we do not believe that ownership should all

be common, as some people have urged. We think, instead, that it should be made common by way of a use that is agreed upon in mutuality. At the same time, we believe that no citizen should be lacking in sustenance and support. As for the common meals, everyone agrees that they are a valuable institution in a well ordered city. . . . And all citizens should participate in them, but it is not easy for poor people both to bring in the required contribution and to manage the rest of their household affairs. . . . Then we must divide the land into two portions—the one to be held in common, the other to belong to private owners. And we must divide each of these two portions in half again. Of the commonly held portion, one part will be used to support the cost of religious festivals, the other part to subsidize the common meals. Of the privately held portion, the one part will be on the frontiers, the other part near the city. Each citizen will be given two lots, in such a way that all have a share in both sorts of land. That way is both equal and just.

3. *Politics* 1255b20. Political government is government of free and equal citizens.

Our first passage makes a quick transition. From the fact that water and air are of great importance for health, a central part of good human functioning, it is inferred directly that the adequate provision of these resources (by which is meant, we later see, a clean public water supply and healthy air) is the job of government.

Our second passage makes a similar move, with an even more striking result. The argument seems to go as follows. Participation in the common meals is a valuable part of social functioning. But a system of unqualified private ownership will produce a situation in which the poor are unable to join in, so that they will lose out on a valuable part of citizenship. (We shall examine this premise in a moment.) Nor, for reasons not given in this passage (and we shall discuss these reasons later) is a system with no private ownership altogether acceptable. Aristotle's conclusion: We want a system that includes some private ownership, but that also guarantees that no citizen will be lacking in sustenance—both with respect to common meals and, presumably, with respect to other valued functionings. The solution chosen is an extraordinary one, even from the point of view of the contemporary welfare state. For it is clear, first of all, that fully half the city's land will be held in common. Half of the product of this part will subsidize civic festivals (including, for example, the festivals at which tragedies and other music will be performed—so this looks above all like a subsidy for education). The other half will directly subsidize the participation of all citizens in the common meals.

Aristotle here tells us his own solution to a problem he has discussed before. Common meals, he has argued, are a very important part of the provision of nourishment for all, and also of civic participation and sociability (1272a19–21). In Sparta, each citizen is required to pay a subscription to join, out of his private property. The citizen who is unable to pay is excluded, not only from the common meal, but, as a penalty for failing to join, from all civic participation (1271a26–37, 1272a12–21). Aristotle has criticized this system, praising instead the arrangement in Crete which he calls "more common to all"—for the common meals there are subsidized out of publicly held produce and cattle, as well as by a tariff paid in by dependent noncitizen farmers in the surrounding area. Here, in his own ideal city, he follows the Cretan model, but goes even further. For, since he omits the tariff from noncitizen dependents, he is required to devote an extremely large proportion of the city's land to the common project.

But matters do not end there. For Aristotle has told us, as well, that there will be a "common use" of the land that *is* still privately held. What does he mean by this? The passage refers back to one in Book II, in which Aristotle tells us that the lawgiver must make sure that citizens make their property available to others, not only to personal friends, but also for "the common use of all." He gives some examples: "In Sparta, for example, men use one another's slaves as if they were their own, and one another's horses and dogs. And when they are on a journey, if they need food, they take it from the farms in the area" (1263a30 ff.). Aristotle does not tell us there how the lawgiver will effect this result. What is clear is that things in Aristotle's city will be arranged, through and through, with a view to the full sustenance of every citizen at all times. Even where private property is permitted, it is to be held only provisionally, subject to claims of need. This complex result is defended on grounds of both justice and equality.[1]

Finally, our third passage defines government of a political sort—the sort Aristotle is describing in our first two passages—as a government "of free and equal citizens." It becomes clear elsewhere that this "of" has a double sense: for both ruler and ruled are, in fact, to be free and equal, and they are to be the same people, taking turns in exercise of office.[2]

What we see, then, are three elements. First, we have a conception of good human functioning. (This is incompletely specified here, but we see that it includes both good functioning of body and good social interacting.) Second, we have a conception of political rule, which involves full support for these functionings ("no citizen should be lacking in sustenance") and insists that this support is to be done in such a way as to treat citizens as free and equal. Third, we have a sketch of institutional arrangements that both preserve some private ownership and circumscribe it, both by a scheme of common ownership and by a new understanding of private ownership as provisional, subject to claims of need. There are many difficulties in understanding the concrete details of what will go on. But this much appears evident.

My aim is to articulate the connections among these three elements, showing how a certain view of good human functioning gives rise to a political conception, through an understanding of political rule. We must ask, first of all, how the Aristotelian conception defends the need for a substantial theory of the human good prior to the selection of a political structure. A large part of our task will then be to examine this account of good human functioning and to ask how the Aristotelian conception arrives at it. I shall argue that the account of good human functioning is based upon a conception of the human being. I shall call this conception the "thick vague conception of the human being," and the associated conception of good functioning the "thick vague conception of the good," in order to distinguish it from conceptions of the good used in some liberal theories. By this name I mean to suggest that it provides a (partially) comprehensive conception of good human functioning (in contrast to Rawls's "thin" theory), but at a high level of generality, admitting of multiple specifications. I shall argue that this conception of the human being is not metaphysical in the sense in which it is frequently taken to be by liberal theorists who contrast their own conceptions with Aristotle's. It is, instead, an ethical-political account[3] given at a very basic and general level, and one that can be expected to be broadly shared across cultures, providing focus for an intercultural ethical-political inquiry. We shall then see how choice figures in the Aristotelian conception, and ask how political rule is understood to be a rule of free and equal citizens. We shall ask what room this conception allows for pluralism in the specification of ends. All this will put us in a position to describe its relationship to the liberalisms of John Rawls and Ronald Dworkin, and also to some of the theoretical underpinnings of Scandinavian social democracy.

CONTEXT AND MOTIVATION

Before we continue further, I must make some prefatory remarks. First, about the use of Aristotle. I shall call this conception Aristotelian, and I shall refer for illumination to arguments and examples of Aristotle's. I believe, in fact, that the conception is in most essential respects Aristotle's, and I have defended it as such in three other essays, each dealing with a different aspect of the conception. "Nature, Function, and Capability: Aristotle on Political Distribution" (hereafter NFC) deals with the general idea that political arrangement must be based upon a view of good human functioning, and that its aim is to produce capabilities to function. The two other essays deal with the conception of the human being. "Non-Relative Virtues: An Aristotelian Approach" (NRV) examines the way in which this conception claims to organize a nonrelative debate about human ends across societies. "Aristotle on Human Nature and the Foundations of Ethics" (HN) argues that the conception of the human being is evaluative and ethical/political, rather than metaphysical in the sense that some recent writers have claimed.[4] All of these essays contain detailed textual argument; and all (especially NFC and HN) examine strains and apparent or real inconsistencies in Aristotle's account. Here I shall do little of that. Instead, I aim to give a perspicuous philosophical picture of the conception, showing how its different parts fit together and how it provides us, here and now, with an attractive political alternative. If the reader is not convinced by the textual arguments of the other papers, she can just call it Conception X, and assess it anyway. At times, too, I shall be abbreviating philosophical arguments that are developed at greater length in the other essays, in order to present an overview of the conception. I shall say when I am doing this, and I hope that it will produce clarity rather than the opposite. Notes will provide fuller textual references, and comments on Aristotle's relation to the developing view.

Second, I must say a word about my own context in relation to the current liberalism debate. I wrote the first and the final drafts of this chapter in Finland, at an institute for the study of foundational issues in development economics. Most of my work on the Aristotelian conception during the past three years has been done here, in connection with a project that attempts to investigate conceptions of "the quality of life" for developing countries.[5] This context gives me, I feel, a somewhat peculiar relation to the liberalism debate, for two reasons. First, because much of the debate, as it is being carried on, is American in focus and even in argument. It frequently conceives of liberalism as a tradition deriving from the American founding and from its Enlightenment backing; and it asks about problems that are, in many cases, specific to American political life.[6] I shall not altogether ignore these questions. But the reader should be warned that my statement of the problems is not very much shaped by them. And if I seem to defend alternatives that have no relationship to what is at all plausible or within the range of alternatives currently offered on the American political scene, the cause of this is not so much utopianism, or detachment from political reality, as it is detachment from that particular set of alternatives and immersion in a different set of alternatives.

This brings me to a second difference between my approach and that of many recent writers on liberalism. In most of the contemporary debate, the nation-state is taken as the basic unit, and inquiries about distribution concern the basic structure of this unit. John Rawls, in his most recent writings, explicitly states that his results could not be used either to deal with issues of international justice or to approach questions of justice in societies far removed from liberal democratic traditions deriving from the Enlightenment.[7] My view is that this pessimism is both unjustified and dangerous. Especially in light of the increasing interaction among diverse societies and the frequency of communications, cross-cultural debate about questions of justice is both possible and actual. It seems to me to be an advantage in a philosophical view if it can both explain this debate and provide a framework for its continuation and enhancement (see NRV). And it is urgent that this discussion should develop further. Many of the most urgent problems of justice and distribution that face human beings who live within nation-states are problems that are now, in their very nature, international problems, requiring worldwide communication and common effort for their effective solution. Aristotle may have been able to think of water and air as problems that each city can face on its own; now they are urgent problems for all human beings together, and in common. So are the related problems of hunger and famine, and the urgent question of preserving the ecology of the planet.[8] If we are so much as to survive as a species and a planet, we clearly need to think about well-being and justice internationally, and together. It seems to me that a view of justice that does not take account of this situation, and attempt to provide a framework to address it, is incomplete, and somewhat anachronistic. A great merit of the Aristotelian conception, with its emphasis on human functioning, is, by contrast, that, while it asks about institutions starting from the viewpoint of the single polity, it also insists on using basic conceptions that are shared and shareable by human beings in many times and places, conceptions on the basis of which, it is claimed, a conversation across political boundaries could also be organized (NRV).

And in fact, this would seem to be a merit of the Aristotelian conception from the point of view of Rawlsian liberalism itself. For Rawls insists, as does Aristotle, that the goal of philosophical theorizing in politics is not simply theory, but also, and more urgently, practice. The people engaging in inquiry are imagined by Rawls, as by Aristotle, to be searching for a conception of justice by which they can live, and live together. They are not looking for a detached good "out there," but for something that they can bring about in their lives.[9] It would then seem that if a necessary condition of the viability of a conception of justice in today's world is its ability to provide a basis for international dialogue, Rawls should be just as interested in the fulfillment of that condition as is Aristotle. The antecedent of this conditional may be controversial; but I believe that the evidence for it mounts every year.

The Priority of the Good and
the Task of Political Arrangement

The Aristotelian conception believes that the task of political arrangement cannot be understood or well performed without a rather full theory of the human good and of what it is to function humanly. The task of political arrangement is, in fact, defined in terms of such a theory. Aristotle writes, "It is evident that the best *politeia* is that arrangement according to which anyone whatsoever might do best and live a flourishing life." His criterion for excellence in a political arrangement is that the people involved should be enabled, by that arrangement, to choose to function well and to lead a flourishing life, insofar as the polity's material and natural circumstances permit.[10] But this means, he argues, that we cannot understand what good arrangement is, or which arrangements are good, without having, first, an account of good human functioning in terms of which we can assess the various competitors. He concludes, "A person who is going to make a fitting inquiry into the best political arrangement must first get clear about what the most choiceworthy life is—for if this is unclear, the best political arrangement must remain unclear also" (*Pol.* 1323a14–17).

This priority of the good is the most conspicuous difference between the Aristotelian conception and all major liberal theories. But the difference is actually not easy to grasp; and it is a far more subtle difference than has sometimes been supposed. So we must do more work to understand exactly what the Aristotelian conception requires in this regard. We shall proceed in two stages. In this section we shall develop a general account of Aristotle's idea of the priority of the good, by examining his arguments against two alternative views. We then try to situate these arguments in the contemporary debate, giving some examples to show just what is at stake. In the next section we examine the Aristotelian theory of good itself, asking just how far away it is from "thin" theories of the good that a liberal could accept, and how it is used in assessing political arrangements.

The Aristotelian conception argues that the task of political arrangement is both *broad* and *deep*. *Broad,* in that it is concerned with the good living not of an elite few, but of each and every member of the polity. It aims to bring every member across a threshold into conditions and circumstances in which a good human life may be chosen and lived. It is *deep* in that it is concerned not simply with money, land, opportunities, and offices, the traditional political distributables, but with the totality of the functionings that constitute the good human life.[11] It opposes itself to three other conceptions of the relationship between an idea of the good and a political arrangement—all of which have their analogues in contemporary liberal theory. It needs to be stressed that liberal theories, too, give priority to a certain sort of conception of good: for, as Rawls says, we need to know what we are distributing and to know that these things are good.[12] So the question is, how does each conception conceive of the account of good that is to be used in defining the task of political arrangement itself, prior to the selection of distributive patterns and principles?

Aristotle's first opponent defines the good of an arrangement in terms of the total (or average) opulence it produces. The view does not ask what this opulence does for and in people's lives; it also does not ask how the opulence is distributed. Aristotle mentions an example of this sort: the view that the good city is the wealthy city, no matter what this wealth is doing and who has it. And he frequently alludes to political views that have this tendency, finding them in regimes such as that of Sparta.[13] A contemporary example of this sort of view is the tendency to measure economic development in terms of GNP (total or average) and to rank countries accordingly, where development is concerned, without asking any further questions.

The Aristotelian objection to this view is that it treats as an end in itself something that is only a tool. And it imagines that there is no limit to the goodness of money and possessions whereas in fact (according to the Aristotelian) they have no value, beyond what they do for and in the lives of human beings. Since no major liberal theorist in philosophy defends such a crude measure of the good in connection with the choice of political principles, I shall spend no more time on this opponent—beyond noting that, despite its crudeness, it is widely used by liberal democratic governments, especially when it is not the lives of their own citizens that are in question, but those of distant strangers.

The second group of theories still thinks of money and possessions as good. But it asks about their distribution, as well as their total or average amount. A simple example of this type of theory in the ancient world, and a direct ancestor of contemporary liberalisms, is the theory ascribed by Aristotle to Phaleas, according to which a political arrangement is good just in case it distributes property and money equally among the citizens. (Phaleas apparently said nothing about how to promote growth in the total of goods, or about whether one might tolerate some inequalities in order to achieve this result.)[14]

More sophisticated versions of this type of view can be found in the liberal political theories of Dworkin and Rawls. Dworkin defends equality of resources as a criterion of good distribution, and thus of good arrangement.[15] Rawls's theory of the good has by now become extremely complex, and we will need to return to it later on. But we can begin with the core of the theory, in its initial statement. In *The Theory of Justice*, then, Rawls argued that we need, prior to the selection of principles of justice, a "thin theory" of good, "restricted to the bare essentials." The list of "primary goods" is, as Rawls conceives it, a list of things of which rational individuals, whatever else they want and plan, desire "as prerequisites for carrying out their plans of life." "Other things being equal, they prefer a wider to a narrower liberty and opportunity, and a greater rather than a smaller share of wealth and income."[16] An index of primary goods (above all, at that stage, of wealth and income)—and not, for example, an index of capability or activity—is used in order to judge which people in the society are the "worst off," what counts as an improvement in someone's condition, and so forth. Rawls's second principle of justice permits inequalities only if they improve the condition of the worst off, so defined.

The basic intuitive idea used by the Aristotelian conception to argue against this is the idea that wealth, income, and possessions simply are not good in themselves. However much people may actually be obsessed with heaping them up (and Aristotle devotes much critical attention to this *chrematistic* tendency), what they have really, when they have them, is just a heap of stuff. A useful heap, but a heap nonetheless, a heap that is nothing at all unless it is put to use in the doings and beings of human lives.[17] But this means that to answer any of the interesting questions about their distribution—how much we should give, to whom, under what institutional structures—we need to see them at work in human functioning, seeing which of the important functions of human beings they promote or impede, and how various schemes for their arrangement affect these functionings.[18] They all "have a boundary, like tools: all are useful *for* something" (*Pol.* 1323b7–8). The right amount and the right ordering can be seen only by taking a stand on the question, "What *for*?"

Several more concrete observations can be added to support this general argument. First, the Aristotelian insists that more is not, in fact, always better, where wealth and income are concerned. At any rate, we have no right to assume that this is so, in advance of developing a theory of good living. If something has worth in itself, then more of that thing is probably always better. But once we grant that wealth and income are not like that, but are means, albeit of a very versatile sort, it seems inconsistent to assert confidently that more is always better.[19] This is a heretical and a deeply peculiar thought, to those brought up in liberal capitalism. It seems as if more cannot help being better. To Aristotelianism, by contrast, the thought is not peculiar, but obvious and central. The Aristotelian really does not see any point in heaping these things up more and more, either for herself or for others. Too much wealth may produce excessive competitiveness, or excessive focus on technical and managerial tasks, distracting people from social interaction, from the arts, from learning and reflecting. If this is so, then Aristotle is quite prepared to say, so much the worse for wealth. And he entertains perfectly seriously the possibility that wealth might have these bad results.[20]

Second, the Aristotelian recognizes wide individual variation in the functional role of the instrumental goods. In Aristotle's famous example, the right amount of food for Milo the wrestler, given his activity level, size, and occupation, is an amount that would be too much for most people. On the other hand, Milo would be very badly off, from the point of view of functioning, if he had an amount of food that is just right for a small sedentary philosopher. Again, as Aristotle prominently recognizes, the needs of pregnant women for food and other goods associated with health are very different from the needs of a nonpregnant woman. We might add that the protein needs of a child are altogether different from those of an adult. Again, a person with mobility problems, or a missing limb, will require a much larger subvention in order to be minimally mobile than will a person with no such deficiency.[21] If we look further into social context, still more variety appears. Children from disadvantaged minority groups need more money spent on them, if they are really to have access to education, than do middle-class children: we can see this by looking at what they are able to do and to be. Again, as things currently are, women need more support in terms of child care and so forth, if they are to work as they choose, than do others who do not face similar social obstacles.[22] All this is one more reason why the Aristotelian wishes to make the central question not, "How much do they have?" but rather, "What are they able to do and to be?" And she wishes to say that government has not done its job if it has not made each and every one of them capable of functioning well—even if it has given them many *things*.

Rawls's current reply to this point[23] is, first, to insist that we should leave out of account, for the time being, those who have deficiencies so severe that they are not "normally cooperating members of society." This reply seems obscure: for it appears that "normally cooperating" is specified in terms of the two moral powers,[24] excluding only those with severe mental (or moral?) deficiencies. And yet the objection was made, above all, in connection with differences in physical need. It would surely be odd to define a one-legged person as not a normally cooperating member of society. And, as we have said, even among people who could not be construed as suffering from deficiency, there are many and wide differences, at least some of which the legislator ought to take into account. The idea that there is such a thing as a normal body with normal needs is a myth that the Aristotelian, with that view's emphasis on contextual particularity, avoids.

Rawls's second strategy (one shared by Dworkin) is to regard the allotment of primary goods as like insurance.[25] We give, *ex ante*, equal *expectation* of primary goods, though *ex post* a person who has an accident may in fact get more. We reply that accidents are not the only sources of variation in functional need, and probably not the most important. Some of our examples, and many that could be imagined, rest on uninsurable differences. So it seems, at least to me, that Rawls has not yet met the objections he has received on this point.

Turning now from the subject of individual variation to our third objection, we must insist that in any actual and conceivable contemporary structure of allocation, decisions are in fact made one way or another about which resources are allocated, about how and through what channels they are allocated, and about the areas of human life in connection with which they will be allocated. Governments do not, in fact, completely stay out of the business of choosing to support certain human functions rather than others. No modern state simply puts income and wealth into the citizens' pockets; instead, programs are designed to support certain areas of life—health, education, defense, and so forth. Any other approach would produce confusion. Even to answer the question "Which things that we have to hand are the useful and usable resources?" requires *some* implicit conception of the good and of good human functioning. In particular, decisions about how and whether plants, minerals, and animals are to be taken for use requires a conception of good human functioning in relation to other species and to the world of nature. In short: to answer any of the interesting, actual political questions about resources and their allocation through programs and institutions, we need to take some stand, and do all the time take a stand, on the Aristotelian question, "What human functions are important? What does a good human life require?"[26]

Finally, a list of functionings can show us one very important thing that an account of good based on wealth and resources alone cannot show us. It can show us where tensions and conflicts might be present in the ends that human beings try to promote. I am thinking here not of conflicts between persons, as when A's pursuit of A's good conflicts with B's pursuit of B's good. I am thinking of conflicts among the demands of generally agreed components of the good life, as when certain sorts of industrial or scientific progress may come to be in tension with ecological or health-related values, or where the demands of work may compete with the function of child care. Here, first of all, we want to know about these conflicts and who faces them, since these people—for example women or men who combine a full-time career with family responsibilities—will usually need extra resources and support systems if they are to live as well as people without such conflicts. Simply giving them an equal amount will not do enough; and we will not even find out about their problems if we concern ourselves with resources without having a view of the good. Beyond this, the promotion of the good of all citizens, in cases where pervasive conflicts exist among components of the good, will require deep reflection about the good and about how resources and institutional arrangements might mitigate conflict. It will also require reflection about which conflicts government should attempt to miti-gate and which are signs of a tragic tension within the good itself, not to be mitigated without a loss in richness of life. These reflections must take place prior to decisions about the allocations of amounts of resources, and even prior to decisions about which things are resources that we may use. In some cases, reflection on conflict may lead to large-scale institutional changes, changes that would not even have been imagined had the exercise been confined to the provision of equal amounts of resources all round.[27]

These are some of the Aristotelian's arguments against the Rawlsian lib-eral. All have their basis in Aristotle's own arguments, as we have seen, and most of them are explicitly stated by Aristotle himself. But Aristotle's third opponent must now be confronted. This is, of course, the utilitarian, whose approach dominates much of the contemporary scene in economics and public policy.[28] The utilitarian agrees with Aristotle that resources are valu-able because of what they do *for people*. But she is a liberal, or a quasi-liberal, in wishing to leave the decision about goodness to each person. In particular, she wishes to make it a function of the satisfaction of desires or preferences that people happen, as things are, to have. She rejects the idea that any more objective account of good human functioning is either necessary or desirable.

The central difficulty with this proposal is one that is recognized both by the Aristotelian conception and by many liberal conceptions, including Rawls's.[29] It is the fact, frequently emphasized by Aristotle,[30] that desire is a malleable and unreliable guide to the human good, on almost any seriously defensible conception of good. Desires are formed in relation to habits and ways of life. At one extreme, people who have lived in opulence feel dis-satisfied when they are deprived of the goods of opulence. At the other extreme, people who have lived in severe deprivation frequently do not feel desire for a different way, or dissatisfaction with their way. Human beings adapt to what they have. In some cases, they come to believe that it is right that things should be so with them; in other cases, they are not even aware of alternatives. Circumstances have confined their imaginations. So if we aim at satisfaction of the desires and preferences that they happen, as things are, to have, our distributions will frequently succeed only in shoring up the status quo.[31]

The Aristotelian takes desire seriously as *one* thing we should ask about, in asking how well an arrangement enables people to live. But she insists that we must also, and more insistently, ask what the people involved are actually able to do and to be—and, indeed, to desire. We consider not only whether they are asking for education, but how they are being educated; not only whether they perceive themselves as reasonably healthy, but how long they live, how many of their children die, how, in short, their health *is*.[32]

In all of this, the Aristotelian approach understands the job of govern-ment to be, as we have said, both broad and deep. It takes cognizance of every important human function, with respect to each and every citizen. But now we must introduce an extremely important qualification. The conception does not aim directly at producing people who function in certain ways. It aims, instead, at producing people who are *capable* of functioning in these ways, who have both the training and the resources to so function, should they choose. The choice itself is left to them. And one of the capabilities Aristotelian government most centrally promotes is the capability of choosing: of doing all these functions in accordance with one's very own practical reasoning.[33] We shall see in the next sections that leaving this place for choice is an absolutely essential part, for the Aristotelian, of promoting truly *human* functioning, in every sphere. In short: the person who is given a clean public water supply can always put pollutants into the water she drinks. The person who has received an education is free, later on, to waste it. The person who has good recreational facilities may fail to take advantage of them. The government aims at capabilities, and leaves the rest to the citizens.[34]

Many questions need to be raised here; and we shall return to this issue. For now, we should simply notice how much this qualification narrows the gap between the Aristotelian and the liberal. For it was the liberal's desire to create a context of choice for individuals that made her stop with the thin theory of good. The Aristotelian's claim is that stopping with such a thin theory neither shows the point of those instrumental goods nor gives sufficient guidance to promote their truly human use. And we can now add that such a thin theory may actually not show the legislator how to produce the capability of choosing, a human function that has institutional and material conditions like any other.

Two examples will clarify this point and give a general illustration of the differences between the Aristotelian theory and its various opponents. Let us imagine, first, the worker whom Marx described in his *Economic and Philosophical Manuscripts of 1844*. This worker performs a monotonous task in a large industrial enterprise over which he himself has no control. He is not prosperous; in fact, he is needy. But material need is only one part of his problem. The other part is that, being removed from choice and control over his work activity, he has been alienated from the fully human use of the food he has, and of his senses more generally. "In his human functions," Marx writes, "he no longer feels himself to be anything but an animal."[35]

In assessing the situation of this worker, the utilitarian, the liberal, and the Aristotelian will all ask different questions. The utilitarian will ask how he feels about his life and what he desires. It certainly seems possible that if things are bad enough with him, he will turn out to be far less dissatisfied than he ought to be, given his situation. He may lack the energy of desire and imagination to conceive of a better way and aspire to it. This deformation of desire was, for Marx, one of the worst features of such situations.

So the utilitarian question will be unlikely to lead on to a radical criticism of his material situation, or to a redistribution aimed at giving him a very different one.[36]

By contrast, the liberal's questioning about resources or primary goods will be likely to go somewhat further. For the liberal will ask not just how he feels, but what resources he actually commands. And this will certainly lead, in the theories of both Rawls and Dworkin, to a strong criticism of the worker's material situation, insofar as he is deprived, and to a redistribution that is aimed at giving him a more substantial amount. On the other hand, it is less likely that this liberal questioning about resources will lead to any far-reaching criticism of the relations of production that are, according to Marx, the primary impediment to this worker's truly human functioning. If he has enough things, the liberal judges that things are well enough with him, and that he has received equal treatment. The liberal characteristically does not probe more deeply, looking for impediments to good functioning in the structure of the worker's daily modes of interaction with others, asking whether his life is such that he is capable of using the resources he is given in a truly human way.[37]

The Aristotelian, by contrast, asks, and asks in a very wide-ranging way: What is this worker able to do and to be? What are his choices? What are his modes of interaction with his work and with other human beings? What is he able to imagine and to enjoy? How is he eating and using his senses? And how do the institutional and work-related conditions of his life promote or impede these functionings? The job of government, on the Aristotelian view, does not stop until we have removed all impediments that stand between this citizen and fully human functioning. This job will, then, frequently involve a great deal more than reallocation of resources. It will usually involve radical institutional and social change.[38]

Take, again, the women in a village in Bangladesh, as described in the impressive study *A Quiet Revolution,* by Marty Chen.[39] These women had low status in their community, in every area. They were less well nourished than males, less educated, less respected. Let us consider their situation where just one question, the question of literacy, is concerned.

A desire-based approach, which has frequently been used in this and related cases, argues that if these women do not demand more education and a higher rate of literacy, there is no reason at all why government should concern itself with this issue. Polls are taken; women express satisfaction with their educational status; no further effort is made. As Chen's account makes clear, this approach looks very short-sighted once one considers the weight of the cultural forces pressing these women not to demand more education (and also not to *feel* that they want more); once one considers, as well, the absence, in their daily lives, of paradigms of what education could do and be in lives similar to theirs, the absence of any experience of the alternative they are asked to consider. Sometimes the combination of ignorance and cultural pressures actually prevents the formation of the desire for education; sometimes it prevents only the public expression of the desire. In both cases, a utility-based approach to public policy will be unable to criticize the status quo, no matter how unjust, on reflection about the full range of human possibilities.

As Chen describes the history of this problem, the next approach tried was, in fact, a liberal approach, practiced both by an international development agency and to some extent by the local government. This approach consisted in giving the women of the village ample educational resources, in the form of adult literacy materials. (Already, notice, this approach took a stand about what functions and what resources were the important ones for these people, giving them literacy materials rather than simple cash. In this sense it ceased to be a purely liberal approach. It also ceased to be a purely liberal approach when it gave these women more, on account of the special impediments they faced in functioning, than was given to males who lacked these impediments.) But this approach had little impact on the women's functioning. This was so because no attempt was made by the development agency to study their way of life in depth, asking what role literacy played and might play in it, how it might fit in with their other functions, and also what special impediments their current way of life created for the good use of educational resources. Merely handing some resources to the women did not go far enough. For example, it did not begin to address, or even describe, the many conflicts in functioning that a literate woman would be likely to encounter in that society.

The failure of this liberal project prompted a transition to what seems to be a more Aristotelian approach. The researchers began to look at the women's lives in greater depth, asking what, over all the major functions and over a complete life, the women were able to do. This led to a searching inquiry, carried out in women's cooperatives, in partnership between the local and the foreign women, into the role of education in their functioning, and its relationship to other valuable functionings. This brought about the beginning of many complex and interrelated transformations in women's role in the village, transformations involving the whole structure of gender relations and relations of production. The Aristotelian argues that this kind of inquiry is the only kind that goes deep enough.[40] Without such an inquiry into the goodness and full humanness of various functionings, and into the special obstacles faced by deprived groups, the most valuable sort of social change could not have begun. Simply making enough things available was not enough. But to do more we need a conception of the good.

The liberal argues that citizens have been treated as free and equal if they have been given equal amounts of all-purpose resources (Dworkin), or if inequalities can be justified as being for the good of the worst off (Rawls).

The Aristotelian also holds, as we have seen, that political rule is a rule of free and equal citizens. But she holds that citizens have been treated as free only if they have been given the necessary conditions for the exercise of choice and practical reason (among which will be education, political participation, and the absence of degrading forms of labor). And they have been treated as equals only if the whole life of each one of them has been considered with rich imagination[41] and, as a result, each one has been given whatever he or she needs in order to be in a position of capability to live a rich and fully human life, up to the limit permitted by natural possibilities.

THE THICK VAGUE CONCEPTION OF THE GOOD

But if we are to give priority to the good, we must have a conception of the good. And this is where the liberal becomes apprehensive. For it appears that any substantial notion of the good that might be used by political thought will be biased in favor of some projects that citizens might choose, and hostile toward others. Such a conception will, it seems, therefore be objectionably paternalistic in its tendency to support some ways of life rather than others. Liberals suspect, furthermore, that the Aristotelian's decision to base her substantial conception of the good on an account of the human being will import metaphysical elements that are controversial among the citizens, and thus will prove unable to ground a political consensus.[42] So the Aristotelian must show what her concept of the good is, how much determinate content it has, how (using what background concepts) it is derived, and what political work it can do.

The Aristotelian uses a conception of the good that is not "thin," like Rawls's "thin theory"—that is, confined to the enumeration of all-purpose means to good living,[43] but "thick"—dealing, that is, with human ends across all areas of human life. The conception is, however, vague and this in a good sense. It admits, that is, of many concrete specifications; and yet it draws, as Aristotle puts it, an "outline sketch" of the good life.[44] It draws the general outlines of the target, so to speak. And yet, in the vague guidance it offers to thought, it does real work. The Aristotelian proceeds this way in the belief that it is better to be vaguely right than precisely wrong; and that, without the guidance of the thick vague theory, what we often get, in public policy, is precise wrongness.

The thick vague theory is not, in the sense that worries liberals, a metaphysical theory. That is, it is not a theory that is arrived at in detachment from the actual self-understandings and evaluations of human beings in society; nor is it a theory peculiar to a single metaphysical or religious tradition. Indeed, it is (as I argue in HN) both internal to human history and strongly evaluative;[45] and its aim is to be as universal as possible, to set down the basis for our recognitions of members of very different traditions as human across religious and metaphysical gulfs. The theory begins, as we shall see, from an account of what it is to be a human being. But this account, far from being based on "metaphysical biology" (as some critics of Aristotle have held),[46] is actually based on the commonness of myths and stories from many times and places, stories explaining to both friends and strangers what it is to be human rather than something else. The account is the outcome of a process of self-interpretation and self-clarification that makes use of the storytelling imagination far more than the scientific intellect. In HN I describe this process as occurring within a single community whose members wish to clarify to themselves and to their children the meanings they have found in living as human beings. But an equally important part of such stories, as I try to show in NRV, is that they are recognitions of humanness across distance. Aristotle wrote, "One can see in one's travels to distant countries the ties of recognition and affiliation that link every human being to every other" (EN 1155a21–2). The vague thick theory is a set of stories about such ties. In this way, it is a most general and preliminary evaluative theory: for it recognizes that certain aspects of human life have a special importance. Without them, we would not recognize ourselves or others as the sort of beings we are; and they provide the basis for our recognition of beings unlike ourselves in place, time, and concrete way of life as members of our very own kind.

The basic idea of the thick vague theory is that we tell ourselves stories of the general outline or structure of the life of a human being. We ask and answer the question, What is it to live as a being situated, so to speak, between the beasts and the gods, with certain abilities that set us off from the rest of the world of nature, and yet with certain limits that come from our membership in the world of nature? The idea is that we share a vague conception, having a number of distinct parts, of what it is to be situated in the world as human, and of what transitions either "up" or "down," so to speak, would turn us into beings no longer human—and thus (since on the whole we conceive of species identity as at least necessary for personal identity) into creatures different from ourselves. Frequently this conception is elucidated (and perpetuated) by myths, especially myths of non-human yet anthropomorphic creatures, either bestial or godlike,[47] who force our imaginations to ask, "Why, if these creatures resemble humans, don't we count them as human?" In this way, we learn something about ourselves.[48]

Take, for example, the countless stories told by the ancient Greeks about the Olympian gods—beings who look like human beings, who have most of the same desires, but who are also immortal and, to a certain extent, invulnerable. Imagining them, we ask what our sense of the great gulf between their way of life and ours tells us about the role of certain natural limits in making us the beings we are. Take, again, the Cyclopes, beings who have human shape and form, but who live in isolation from community and who lack all sensitivity to the needs of others, all sense of commitment and affiliation. What do we learn about our own self-understanding, when we notice that our stories treat such creatures as nonhuman monsters?

This is the way the exercise proceeds. (In HN I develop in detail some concrete examples.) And the great convergence across cultures in such story-telling, and in its singling out of certain areas of experience as constitutive of humanness, gives us reason for optimism that if we proceed in this way, using our imaginations, we will have, in the end, a theory that is not only the parochial theory of our local traditions, but also a basis for cross-cultural attunement. In fact, it would be surprising if this were not so, since the question we are asking is: What are the features of our common humanity, features that lead us to recognize certain others, however distant their location and their forms of life, as humans and, on the other hand, to decide that certain other beings who resemble us superficially could not possibly be human? The question we ask directs us to cross boundaries.[49]

The list we get if we reflect in this way is, and must be, open-ended. For we want to allow the possibility that some as yet unimagined transformation in our natural options will alter the constitutive features, subtracting some and adding others. We also want to leave open the possibility that we will learn from our encounters with other human societies to revise certain elements in our own standing account of humanness, recognizing, perhaps, that some features we regarded as essential are actually more parochial than that. We must insist that, like most Aristotelian lists,[50] our working list is meant not as systematic philosophical theory, but as a summary of what we think so far, and as an intuitive approximation, whose intent is not to legislate, but to direct attention to certain areas of special importance. And the list is not only intuitive, but also heterogeneous; for it contains both limits against which we press and powers through which we aspire. This is not surprising, since we began from the general intuitive idea of a creature who is both capable and needy. We shall return to this point, showing how it affects our political use of the list.[51]

Here, then, as a first approximation, is a kind of story about what seems to be part of any life that we count as a human life.

Level A of the Thick Vague Conception:
The Constitutive Circumstances of the Human Being
(or: the Shape of the Human Form of Life)

Mortality

All human beings face death and, after a certain age, know that they face it. This fact shapes more or less every other element of human life. Moreover, all human beings have an aversion to death. Although there are many circumstances (varying among individuals and from culture to culture) in which death will be preferred to the available alternatives, it is still true that in general human beings wish to live and, like Lucretius's "first mortals" (prior to any culture) leave with fear and grief "the sweet light of life."[52] If we did encounter an immortal anthropomorphic being, its way of life would be so different from our own that we could hardly regard it as a part of the same kind with us. The same would be true if we encountered a mortal being that showed no tendency to avoid death or to seek to continue its life.[53]

The Human Body

We live our entire lives in bodies of a certain sort, whose possibilities and vulnerabilities do not as such belong to one human society rather than another. These bodies, similar far more than dissimilar (considering the enormous range of possibilities) are our homes, so to speak, opening us to some options and denying others. We are so used to our bodies that we tend to forget how different from other bodies and conceivable bodies (and from the condition of bodilessness) they are, how far and how deeply they demarcate our possibilities. The fact that any given human being might have lived anywhere and belonged to any culture is a great part of what grounds our mutual recognitions; this fact has a great deal to do with the general humanness of the body, its great distinctness from other bodies. The experience of the body is culturally shaped; but the body itself, not culturally variant in its requirements, sets limits on what can be experienced, ensuring a lot of overlap.[54]

There is of course much disagreement about *how much* of human experience is rooted in the body. Here metaphysics enters into the picture in a nontrivial way. So in keeping with the general nonmetaphysical character of the list I shall include at this point only those features that would be agreed to be bodily even by metaphysical dualists. I shall discuss the more controversial features (perceiving, thinking, etc.) as separate items, taking no stand on the question of dualism.

1. *Hunger and thirst; the need for food and drink.* All human beings need food and drink in order to live; and all have comparable, though varying nutritive requirements. Being in one culture rather than another does not make one metabolize food differently. Furthermore, all human beings have appetites that are indices of need. Appetitive experience is to some extent culturally shaped; and sometimes it is not parallel to the

body's actual level of need. And yet, we discover enormous similarity and overlap. Moreover, human beings in general do not wish to be hungry and thirsty (though they might choose to fast for some reason). Aristotle remarks that if we discovered someone who really did not feel hunger and thirst at all, or, feeling them, did not care about eating and drinking, we would judge that this person was "far from being a human being."[55]

2. *Need for shelter.* A recurrent topic in myths of humanness is the nakedness of the human being, its relative fragility and susceptibility to heat, cold, the elements in general. Stories that explore the difference between our needs and those of furry or scaly or otherwise protected creatures remind us how far our life is constituted by the need to find refuge from the cold, or from the excessive heat of the sun, from rain, from wind, from snow and frost.[56]

3. *Sexual desire.* Though less necessary as a need than the needs for food, drink, and shelter, sexual desire is a feature of more or less every human life. Aristotle includes it among the desires whose complete absence would be the sign of a being far from human. It is, and has all along been, a very strong basis for the recognition of others different from ourselves as human beings.

4. *Mobility.* We are, as the old story goes, featherless bipeds—that is creatures whose form of life is in part constituted by the ability to move from place to place in a certain way, not only through the aid of tools we have made, but also with our very own bodies. Human beings like moving about, and dislike being deprived of mobility. An anthropomorphic being who, without disability, chose never to move from birth to death would be hard to view as human; and a life altogether cut off from mobility seems a life less than fully human.

Capacity for Pleasure and Pain

Experiences of pain and pleasure are common to all human life—though once again their cultural expression and perhaps, to some extent, the experience itself, will vary. Moreover, the aversion to pain as a fundamental evil is a primitive and, apparently, unlearned part of being a human animal. A society whose members altogether lacked that aversion would surely be considered to be outside the bounds of humanness.[57]

Cognitive Capability: Perceiving, Imagining, Thinking

All human beings have sense-perception, the ability to imagine, and the ability to think, making distinctions and, as Aristotle famously says, "reach(ing) out for understanding."[58] And these abilities are regarded as valuable. It is an open question what sorts of accidents or impediments to individuals in these areas will be sufficient to make us judge that the form of life is not human, or no longer human. But it is safe to say that if we imagine a tribe whose members totally lack sense-perception, *or* totally lack imagination, *or* totally lack reasoning and thinking, we are not in any of these cases imagining a tribe of human beings, no matter what they look like.

Early Infant Development

All human beings begin as hungry babies, aware of their own helplessness, experiencing their alternating closeness to and distance from that, and those, on which they depend. This common structure to early life—which clearly is shaped in many and varied ways in different social arrangements—still gives rise to a great deal of overlapping experience that is of great importance for the formation of emotions and desires, and that is a major source of our ability to see ourselves in the emotional experiences of those whose lives are otherwise very different from our own. The merits of one or another psychoanalytical theory of infancy can be debated; that there is some general overlapping structure of deep significance cannot be. And the work of Freud on infant desire and of Melanie Klein on grief, loss, and other emotional attitudes has, despite the presence of *some* culture-specific material, still succeeded in mapping some part of the territory of our common humanity. If we encountered a tribe of apparent humans and then discovered that they never had been babies and had never, in consequence, had those experiences of extreme dependency, need, and affection, we would, I think, have to conclude that their form of life was sufficiently different from our own that they could not be considered part of the same kind.[59]

Practical Reason

All human beings participate (or try to) in the planning and managing of their own lives, asking and answering questions about what is good and how one should live. Moreover, they wish to enact their thought in their lives— to be able to choose and evaluate, and to function accordingly. This general capability has many concrete forms, and is related in complex ways to the other capabilities, emotional, imaginative, and intellectual. But a being who altogether lacks this would not be likely to be regarded as fully human, in any culture.[60]

Affiliation with Other Human Beings

As Aristotle claimed, all human beings recognize and feel a sense of affiliation and concern for other human beings. (Here the conceptual and the empirical are closely linked: we recognize other humans, and our concept of the human is shaped, in an open-ended way, by what we find ourselves able to recognize.) Moreover, we value the form of life that is constituted by these recognitions and affiliations—we live to and with others, and regard a life not lived in affiliation with others to be a life not worth living. (We may want to spell this out further: for it is Aristotle's view that we define ourselves in terms of at least two sorts of affiliation: intimate family relations and social or civic relations.)

Relatedness to Other Species and to Nature
Human beings recognize that they are not the only living things in their world: that they are animals living alongside other animals, and also alongside plants, in a universe that, as a complex interlocking order, both supports and limits them. We are dependent upon that order in countless ways; and we also sense that we owe that order some respect and concern, however much we may differ about *what* we owe, to whom, and for what reasons. Again, a creature who treated animals exactly like stones and could not be brought to recognize some problem with that would probably be regarded as too strange to be human. So, too, would a creature who did not care in any way for the wonder and beauty of the natural world. (Here, perhaps, we are in the process of watching some part of our kind become other than what a human being has usually been taken to be; perhaps we shall someday be called upon either to change our conception of humanness or to acknowledge a fundamental gulf in forms of life among humans.)[61]

Humor and Play
Human life, wherever it is lived, makes room for recreation and laughter. The forms play takes are enormously varied and yet we recognize other humans, across many and varied barriers, as the animals who laugh. Laughter and play are frequently among the deepest and also the first modes of our mutual recognition. Inability to play or laugh is taken, correctly, as a sign of deep disturbance in an individual child; if it is permanent the consequence may be that we will prove unable to consider the child capable of leading a fully human life. An entire society that lacked this ability would seem to us both terribly strange and terribly frightening. We certainly do not want a life that leaves this element out; and on the whole we want more of it than circumstances permit us to have.[62]

Separateness
However much we live for and to others, we are, each of us, "one in number," proceeding on a separate path through the world from birth to death. Each person feels only his or her own pain and not anyone else's. Each person dies alone. When one person walks across the room, no other follows automatically. When we count the number of human beings in a room, we have no difficulty figuring out where one begins and the other ends. These

obvious facts need stating, since they might have been otherwise; we should bear them in mind when we hear talk of the absence of individualism in certain societies. Even the most intense forms of human interaction, for example sexual experience, are experiences of responsiveness, and not of fusion. If fusion is made the goal, the result is bound to be bitter disappointment. And this is so no matter how much society may try to hold us together. Plato's *Laws* discusses the aim of doing everything possible, "by hook or by crook," to make "common even what is by nature private, such as eyes, ears, hands, so that they will seem to see and hear and feel in common." It never works.[63]

Strong Separateness

Because of separateness, each human life has, so to speak, its own peculiar context and surroundings—objects, places, a history, particular friendships, locations, sexual ties—that are not the same as those of anyone else, and in terms of which the person to some extent identifies herself. Though societies vary a great deal in the *degree* of strong separateness they permit and foster, there is no life, short of a life of total imprisonment, and perhaps not even that life, that really does fail to say the words "mine" and "not-mine" in some idiosyncratic and non-shared way. What I touch, use, love, respond to, I touch, use, love, respond to from my own separate point of view. The items I call "mine" are not exactly the same as those called that way by any other person. On the whole, human beings recognize one another as beings who wish to have some separateness of context, a little space to move around in, some special items to use and hold and cherish.[64]

This is an open-ended list. One could subtract some items and/or add others. (A comparison of this list with the list in NRV will show me doing this.) But it is a thick vague starting point for reflection about what the good life for such a being might be.

Notice that the list is already evaluative: it singles out some items, rather than others, as the most important items, the ones in terms of which we identify ourselves. We say that a life without these items or structures is not recognizable as human; and, given that any life we can coherently wish for ourselves or for others will have to be, at least, human (see HN),[65] it sets an outline around our aspirations. But it does this in two different ways. For, as I said and as we can now see, the list is composed of two different sorts of items: limits and capabilities. As far as the capabilities go, it is clear that calling them part of humanness is making a very basic sort of evaluation. It is to say that life without this item would be too lacking, too impoverished, to be human at all. *A fortiori*, it could not be a good human life. So this list of capabilities is a kind of ground-floor, or minimal conception of the good.

With the limits, matters are more complicated. For we insist that human life, in its general form, consists in a struggle against these limits. Humans do not wish to be hungry, to feel frustration or pain, to die. (Separateness is extremely complex, both a limit and a capability.) And yet, we should not assume that the evaluative conclusion to be drawn is that we should try as hard as possible to get rid of the limit altogether. It is characteristic of human life to prefer recurrent hunger plus eating to a life with neither hunger nor eating; to prefer sexual desire and its satisfaction to a life with neither desire nor satisfaction. And even where death is concerned, human beings probably do not, when they think most clearly, wish to lose their finitude completely; or, if they vaguely do so, it is at the cost of embracing a transition to a wholly different form of life, with different values and ends, in which it is not at all clear that the identity of the individual could be preserved. So the evaluative conclusion has to be expressed with much caution, in terms of what would be a humanly good way of countering the limitation.[66]

This brings us to the second stage of our thick vague conception. For now we are in a position to specify vaguely certain basic functionings that should, as constitutive of human life, concern us. We shall actually introduce the list as a list of the related capabilities, rather than of actual functionings, since we have argued that it is capabilities, not actual functionings, that should be in the legislator's goal.

Basic Human Functional Capabilities

1. Being able to live to the end of a complete human life, as far as is possible; not dying prematurely, or before one's life is so reduced as to be not worth living.
2. Being able to have good health; to be adequately nourished; to have adequate shelter; having opportunities for sexual satisfaction; being able to move about from place to place.
3. Being able to avoid unnecessary and non-useful pain, and to have pleasurable experiences.
4. Being able to use the five senses; being able to imagine, to think and reason.
5. Being able to have attachments to things and persons outside ourselves; to love those who love and care for us, to grieve at their absence; in general, to love, grieve, to feel longing and gratitude.
6. Being able to form a conception of the good and to engage in critical reflection about the planning of one's own life.
7. Being able to live for and to others, to recognize and show concern for other human beings, to engage in various forms of familial and social interaction.

8. Being able to live with concern for and in relation to animals, plants, the world of nature.
9. Being able to laugh, to play, to enjoy recreational activities.
10. Being able to live one's own life and nobody else's.
10a. Being able to live one's own life in one's very own surroundings and context.

This is a list of functional capabilities that are very basic in human life. The claim is that a life that lacks any one of these, no matter what else it has, will be regarded as seriously lacking in humanness. So it would be reasonable to take these things as a focus for concern, if we want to think how government can actually promote the good of human beings. The list provides a minimal theory of good. It is not meant to suggest that these are unrelated items; for in obvious ways they interact with one another, and interpenetrate one another. An example of interaction is the relationship between moving about and nourishing oneself. Aristotle notices that the two have to be looked at together, in the sense that our characteristic mode of nutrition, unlike that, for example, of sponges, requires moving from here to there. In this sense the two are made for one another. An example of interpenetration is the relationship between separateness and all of the others: whatever we do, we do as beings who are, each of us, "one in number," separate and distinct, tracing distinct paths through space and time.

At the same time, we must also notice that it is basic to the whole structure and motivation of the list that it is a list of *separate* components, components that may in principle conflict with one another as well as offering one another cooperation and mutual support. Concern for other species may or may not fit well with our efforts to feed ourselves, to be mobile, to be healthy. Our care for those close to us may or may not be harmoniously related to our cognitive self-development. The approach to the list through myths and stories promises that we will go on exploring the various items in many different imagined combinations, seeing how they support one another and where they conflict. And the whole approach being suggested here insists, throughout, on recognizing a plurality of good things, things distinct from one another in quality. The ethical and political situation the list puts us in is thus very much like the situation depicted in the polytheism of Greek religion. There are many divinities—that is to say, for our purposes, many areas of human life that claim our attention and reverence.[67] The quality of a life must be evaluated along all of these distinct dimensions. And yet the "gods" do not always agree—that is, one strand in our common humanness may not be harmoniously related to another, given the circumstances of life.

THE ARCHITECTONIC FUNCTIONINGS

We now notice a special case of interpenetration, one that is fundamental for our understanding of the list as a whole, and its political implications. Two of the human functions organize and arrange all of the others, giving them in the process a characteristically human shape. These two are: practical reason and affiliation. All animals nourish themselves, use their senses, move about, and so on—and all of this as beings one in number. What is distinctive, and distinctively valuable to us, about the human way of doing this is that all these functions are, first of all, planned and organized by practical reason, and, second, done with and to others.

These two functions are not simply two among others. They are the two that hold the whole enterprise together and make it human.[68] Human nourishing is not like animal nourishing, nor human sex like animal sex, because human beings can choose to regulate their nutrition and their sexual activity by their very own practical reasoning; and also because they do so not as solitary Cyclopes (who would eat anything at all, even their own guests), but as beings who are bound to other human beings by relationships of mutual attention and concern. We may sometimes find in a putatively human life activity that lacks this humanizing character. Of the worker in his example, Marx writes:

> It is obvious that the *human* eye gratifies itself in a way different from the crude, non-human eye; the *human* ear from the crude ear, etc. . . . The *sense* caught up in crude practical need has only a *restricted* sense. For the starving man, it is not the human form of food that exists, but only its abstract being as food; it could just as well be there in its crudest form, and it would be impossible to say wherein this feeding-activity differs from that of animals.[69]

But the point is that this life is less than human, *a fortiori* surely not a good human life. Practical reason is both ubiquitous and architectonic. It both infuses all the other functions and plans for their realization in a good and complete life. And the same is true of affiliation. We do whatever we do as social beings; and the kind of deliberative planning we do for our lives is a planning with and to others.

At this point, we should return to Rawls. For we find Rawls's liberalism partially converges with the Aristotelian conception at this point. In Rawls's account of the person and the person's moral powers, and in his stipulation that principles are being selected for a life that is going to be shared with others, we find an approximation to our own requirements that a human life should be according to practical reason and affiliation. Rawls, like the Aristotelian, is prepared to rule out the conceptions of the good that do not make room for choice and practical reason: in this sense, as he explicitly says, there is an element of perfectionism in his theory. His recent work spells this out in even more detail, in terms of the two distinct moral powers. And he insists, further, that the political conception chosen must be such as to support the development of the moral powers in the citizens. Where affiliation is concerned, once again Rawls is Aristotelian. For he stipulates that the conception must be one by which citizens can live together in community, and he imagines the citizens as sociable beings, beings whose fundamental interest is to live with and toward others.[70]

But then it appears problematic that Rawls stops where he does, and refuses to move further in the direction of the Aristotelian theory. For the Aristotelian claim (which Marx endorses and develops) is surely a plausible one: that powers of practical reason are powers that require, for their development, institutional and material necessary conditions that are not always found. One would then suppose that citizens who value the moral powers in themselves and in others, and whose aim it is to select a conception of justice by which they can live well together in community, would take thought for those conditions, and think of good political principles not simply as principles regulating the distribution of the instrumental "primary goods" but, instead, as principles for the adequate realization of these and other fully human capabilities in the citizens. And this approach, as we have suggested, would seem to lead in the direction of a more sweeping reconsideration of labor relations, educational institutions, and other aspects of the form of life of the citizens than is promised in Rawls's "thin theory" of the good.[71]

Rawls's failure to move further in this direction is perhaps explained by his Kantianism. Perhaps he really does not think of the moral powers as interdependent with circumstances in the world, and in need of support from the world.[72] This tendency to separate the realm of morality from the empirical world shows up, in fact, in Rawls's failure to bring together the "thin theory" of the good embodied in the enumeration of primary goods with the theory of good embodied in the account of the two moral powers, saying how and whether the primary goods are understood as providing support for the moral powers.[73] We will return to this topic. But in order to deal with it well, we need to pursue in more detail the Aristotelian conception of the task of politics.

THE TASK OF POLITICS, IN RELATION TO THE THICK, VAGUE CONCEPTION

The task of Aristotelian politics is to make sure that no citizen is lacking in sustenance.[74] With respect to each of the functionings mentioned in the thick vague conception, citizens are to receive the institutional, material, and educational support that is required if they are to become capable of functioning in that sphere according to their own practical reason—and functioning not just minimally, but well, insofar as natural circumstances permit. Politics examines the situations of the citizens, asking in each case what the requirements of the individual for good functioning are, in the various areas. Both the design of institutions and the distribution of resources by institutions is done with a view to their capabilities.

The Aristotelian aim should be understood along the lines of what has been called *institutional,* rather than *residual,* welfarism. That is, politics does not just wait to see who is left out, who fails to do well without institutional support, and then step in to bail these people out. Its aim is, instead, to design a comprehensive support scheme for the functionings of all citizens over a complete life. Aristotle's common meal plan, we recall, did not simply assist the poor. It subsidized the entire common meal program for all citizens, so that nobody could ever come to be in a situation of poverty with respect to that program. In a similar way, the Aristotelian conception (and Aristotle himself) promotes a comprehensive scheme of health care and a complete plan of public education for all citizens over a complete life,[75] rather than simply giving aid to all those who cannot afford private health care and private education. This way is defended as more equal and more just.

The Aristotelian uses the available resources to bring all citizens across a threshold into a condition in which good human functioning, at least a minimal level, can be chosen. In NFC, I give a more extensive account of this aim, in terms of levels of capabilities. To summarize briefly, the Aristotelian program aims at producing two types of capabilities: internal and external. Internal capabilities are conditions of the person (of body, mind, character) that make that person in a state of readiness to choose the various valued functions. External capabilities are internal capabilities plus the external material and social conditions that make available to the individual the option of that valued function. Internal capabilities are promoted, above all, by schemes of education, by health care, by appropriate labor relations. But over and above this the legislator must work to make sure that a capable individual has the chance to function in accordance with that capability: and this calls for another, slightly different, set of concerns with labor, and with the circumstances of personal and social life.[76]

In all of these areas, as I have said, treating citizens as free and equal means moving all of them across the threshold into capability to choose well, should the available resources at all permit this. The focus is always on getting more to cross the threshold, rather than further enhancing the conditions of those who have already crossed it. This is so for two reasons. First, because that is what it is to treat citizens as free and equal. Second, because, as we have noted, once a person has crossed that threshold, more is not necessarily better. The limit of money's usefulness in human life is set by its role in getting an individual across the threshold into good living; after that, more of it is not clearly better, and may well be worse. Good living may admit of degree: it may be that there are resources that will further enhance good functioning for someone already above the threshold. But, first of all, these are not likely to be found in the sphere of money and property, but, far more likely, in the sphere of education, and other goods that an individual who already has reached a certain level of capability can be expected to pursue on his or her own, given that capability. Thus if once the political structure makes available to each and every citizen education sufficient to bring them across the threshold—whatever we decide that ought to be—getting further still is something that they can reasonably be left to pursue on their own, and that they will be in a good position to pursue, given their already achieved capability level.

It should be noticed in what follows that the Aristotelian conception does not introduce a distinction corresponding to Rawls's distinction between the basic structure of society—in constructing which we are permitted to use only the thin theory of good—and the legislative stage, in which fuller information may be used.[77] For the Aristotelian, it would not be very clear how one might draw any such distinction, or what, in terms of it, ought to count as basic. Educational policy and structure, population policy,[78] a scheme of labor relations—all of these would presumably belong to a later legislative stage in Rawls's scheme; and yet for the Aristotelian they are absolutely basic, at least as basic, and perhaps more so, than the scheme of offices and concrete judicial and deliberative institutions. The Aristotelian finds choices in all of these areas important in making it possible for citizens to live well; and she sees no way of doing any of them well without consulting the entirety of the thick vague theory of good.[79]

If we now examine our list of basic capabilities, remembering that what we aim at in each sphere is the capability to function, in that sphere, according to both practical reason and affiliation, we can begin to imagine what the conception requires. It requires comprehensive health care; healthy air and water; arrangements for the security of life and property; protection of the autonomous choices of citizens with respect to crucial aspects of their medical treatment. It requires sufficient nutrition and adequate housing; and these are to be arranged so as to promote the choices of citizens to regulate their nutrition and their shelter by their own practical reason. (This would, for example, lead one to place emphasis on health education, drug education, and so forth.) It requires the protection of the capability of citizens to regulate their own sexual activity by their own practical reason and choice. (Here once again, support for educational programs would seem to play a crucial role.) It would require protection from assaults and other preventable pains. For the senses, for the imagination, and for thinking, it would require, beyond medical support, education and training of many kinds, aimed at the fostering of these capabilities; and the protection of the arts, as essential for the good functioning of imagination and emotion, as well as sources of delight. For practical reason, it would require institutions promoting a humanistic form of education, and the protection of citizen choices in all contexts, including the context of designing the political conception itself. For affiliation and the emotional life, it would require support for rich social relations with others, in whatever way it will emerge, through argument, that the institutional and political structures can best support and protect these relations. It would require reflective policies promoting due respect for other species and for the world of nature. It would require the provision both of recreational facilities and of forms of labor that permit the choice of recreation and enjoyment. And finally, for separateness, and for strong separateness, it would require protection of a sphere of non-interference around the person, larger or smaller, so that, according to practical reason and in relationship with others, each person can choose, in his or her own context, to lead his or her very own life.

The idea is that the entire structure of the polity will be designed with a view to these functions. Not only programs of allocation, but also the division of land, the arrangement for forms of ownership, the structure of labor relations, institutional support for forms of family and social affiliation, ecological policy and policy toward animals, institutions of political participation, recreational institutions—all these, as well as more concrete programs and policies within these areas, will be chosen with a view to good human functioning.

It would require more than one *book* to make arguments in each of these areas, saying what alternatives the Aristotelian would be likely to choose. But in order to give an idea of the depth at which the conception operates, designing the most basic things with a view to the good, we can make some preliminary comments about four areas: labor, property, political participation, and education. In each case I shall draw on Aristotle himself, who gives us a better idea than anyone else of what the Aristotelian conception requires.

Labor
Aristotle notices a fact that frequently gets obscured from view in discussions of this sort, including most liberal discussions. This is, that some forms of labor are incompatible with good human functioning. Because they are monotonous and mindless, and demanding in their time requirements, they leave the worker less than fully human, able to perform other functionings only at a less than fully human level. Aristotle may have had too extreme a

view about what forms of labor were like this (see NFC); but it is the beginning of progress to recognize that some in fact are. And Marx was especially indebted to Aristotle for his own reflections on this point.[80] Liberal discussion usually assumes that if we give people enough money and commodities, and guard against some especially flagrant abuses (abuses that count, for example, as diminutions of basic liberties), things will go well enough, and people will be able, at the close of the working day, to get on with their conceptions of the good, whatever they are. (This is especially true of liberal Kantianism, which tends, as we have said, to think of the moral personality as impervious to damage from the world.) The Aristotelian makes no such assumption.[81] The conception calls for a searching examination of the forms of labor and the relations of production, and for the construction of fully human and sociable forms of labor for all citizens, with an eye to all the forms of human functioning. Only that will count as treating people as both free and equal.

Property

Land, money, and possessions are just things, and have no intrinsic worth. Thus there is no absolute right to property in the Aristotelian conception. The claim citizens have is to sustenance in their various essential functionings: to being brought across the threshold into capability for good human functioning. And the question about property must simply be, what form or forms of ownership best promote this situation? Best promote, that is, not only good functioning but the equal distribution of good functioning, in the sense that every citizen is to move across the threshold. In addressing himself to this question, Aristotle never seriously considers the possibility that all ownership should be private. This he considers highly divisive, inimical to sociability, and subversive of the stability and security of the polity. He considers, as we have seen, various combinations of common and private ownership, schemes where some private ownership is combined with common use, and also (as the agrarian nature of his polity requires) schemes in which some of the commonly owned land is held by individuals who are in charge of developing it.[82] What he asks in assessing these various forms is, what makes human functioning best? Or to take his other way of putting the question, what is it to treat citizens as free and equal?

It is important to notice that in defending *common* ownership Aristotle is not defending *state* ownership. Common ownership is in a very real sense ownership by all the citizens in common, and not by some remote bureaucratic entity. The Aristotelian conception must take thought for this distinction and its practical realization, since it is especially difficult to foster common ownership under modern conditions of size and population; and yet especially important to foster it, insisting on this distinction.[83]

Although Aristotle barely mentions the idea that there should be no common ownership, he does take very seriously indeed the idea that there should be no private ownership. This idea had been defended, of course, by Plato; but it was obviously attracting interest in other quarters as well.[84] Aristotle argues against it. And his arguments are of interest to us: for they show us exactly what role property plays, and fails to play, in the Aristotelian conception. There seem to be two areas in which Aristotle believes that some private property-holding will promote fully human functioning. One is the area of strong separateness. Aristotle believes that it is a basic human good that each person should go through life surrounded by a context that is, in part, just his or her own, into which nobody else can interfere. Property is a part of that context. This argument derives from older Athenian traditions: for Athenians prided themselves on the fact that they enjoyed a certain latitude and non-interference in their private dealings.[85] What is worth noticing is that the support for private property provided by this argument is contingent and controversial. If someone can show the Aristotelian that the particular kind of context of non-interference that separate functioning really requires does not, in fact, include private ownership, then the defense of private property, thus far, collapses. And Aristotle's insistence on common use—that it ought to be possible for a needy person to help herself to your crops, without penalty and with good will—shows that in any case he did not defend private ownership in the form in which most contemporary thought defends it.[86]

His other argument connects property with sociability, through an observation about human psychology. In *Politics* II, criticizing Plato, Aristotle observes that the thought that something is all your own makes a person care for something, and take responsibility for it, far more and more intensely than the belief that the thing in question is owned by many. Thus including some private ownership in the city will be useful, as an incentive to concerned, responsible, and energetic activity. Just as in a household with too many servants taking care of the tasks no task gets done well (he observes), so in a Platonic city no socially valuable task will be well looked after.[87] Similar arguments for a measure of private enterprise have recently been advanced in some contemporary socialist and communist countries. Here again, as with the first argument, we see that private property is supported only through a contingent instrumental argument, which will fall if at some time its psychological premises prove false.

Political Participation
The Aristotelian conception is one in which all citizens share in ruling, as well as in being ruled. This is essential to the conception of what it is to treat citizens as both free and equal. More concretely, each citizen is a citizen in

virtue of having two sorts of capability in the political sphere: legislative capability and judicial capability (see NFC).[88] But we must now ask why this is so according to the conception we have described. A welfarist conception need not be democratic, clearly. And since the Aristotelian aims at producing capabilities to function humanly, rather than at protecting natural rights, we need to ask in virtue of what argument this form is arrived at.

Aristotle's arguments are rather direct, since planning the conception of the good that shapes a citizen's life is a job that goes on, in part, in the political sphere. The argument is then, first, that good functioning in accordance with practical reason requires that every citizen should have the opportunity to make choices concerning this plan.

Aristotle's second argument cannot be set out in full here. It is, that in setting out fully and adequately the list of basic functionings that constitute the thick vague conception, we need to divide sociability into two parts, requiring for fully good human functioning both close personal relationships (friendships, family relationships) and also relationships of a political kind, the function that is constituted by playing one's role as a citizen alongside other citizens. The arguments that support this are set out in detail in *The Fragility of Goodness*, ch. 12.[89] They have a particular poignancy, since Aristotle, as a resident alien at Athens, had personal friendships without having political relationships. He is then judging, in effect, that his own life lacks something that is essential for fully good human functioning.

Finally, Aristotle appeals to the conception of political rule as a rule of free and equal citizens.[90] They are not free if they are treated despotically by a ruler and have no share at all in rule. Nor are they treated as equals if they are relegated to subordinate functionings while some king lords it over them. This does not mean that there is no room in government for expertise; nor does it mean that citizens can never delegate functions of some sorts to experts. It does mean that citizens should be judged by citizen juries selected in some representative way; and it means that some sort of democratic legislative body, either direct or representative, should make the major decisions concerning the conception. Citizens are not forced or required to participate. They are given what Aristotle calls "empowerment" (*exousia*). In Athenian terms, their names are in the lottery, although when a name comes up the person can always decline the function. This is Aristotle's way of respecting practical reason in the design of specifically political institutions.

Education

No part of the political design occupies the Aristotelian as much as education. Education is required for each of the major functionings; and it is required, as well, for choice itself, as the Aristotelian insists. One distinctive sign of the Aristotelian conception, with its intense focus not only on functioning but also on truly human functioning within the various spheres of life, will be its tendency to make education a, perhaps the, central focus of planning, and to judge success in this aspect to be the hallmark of a successful political design (cf. *EN* II.1, *Pol.* VIII.1, and other refs. in NFC).[91]

The Aristotelian approach will be to specify vaguely certain capabilities that we wish to develop in citizens through education, and then, as Aristotle puts it, to behave like good doctors (*EN* X.9), looking responsively at the needs and circumstances of the varied groups of citizens and designing the structures of education in such a way as to bring them to those capabilities.[92] He envisages a combination of a more or less uniform public structure with a more flexible private education provided in and by the family. But there would be many other ways in which this combination of intimacy with community might be captured. The central point is that the Aristotelian will at each step look at what the citizens are actually able to do and be in virtue of their education, and will measure its success accordingly. It will not assume that merely providing resources for education is sufficient, especially where adverse circumstances exist, but will use imagination to design programs that will make it possible for disadvantaged groups to take full advantage of resources.

But the issue of education cannot usefully be discussed further without confronting, at least in a preliminary way, two of the most difficult issues it raises, issues on which the gap between the liberal and the Aristotelian appears to be especially wide. These are the issue of pluralism and the issue of choice.

PLURALISM AND CHOICE

The liberal's central motivation for operating without a "thick" conception of the good is to leave room for a pluralistic society, and to respect the equality of citizens as choosers of their own conceptions of the good, favoring no conception over any other. As we have noted, Rawls narrows the list of available conceptions considerably through his insistence on the two moral powers. But in the respects that are most important to someone thinking about the history of American democracy, Rawls's conception leaves the most divisive choices open. Citizens are not told what religion they must have, or even whether to have a religion. They are not told what forms of sexual conduct to adopt, or what professions to pursue, what recreations to enjoy. The liberal view about Aristotelianism is that it always involves opting for a single conception of good rather than a plurality; and that in the process it tells people what they should be, asking them (as Dworkin puts it) to live the life that a supremely wise man thinks would be best for them.[93]

This is actually to remove their moral autonomy, and thus, from the liberal's point of view, to treat them *unequally*.

There is no issue to which the Aristotelian should be more sensitive than this one, since her ability to convince contemporary citizens of the merits of her view depends very much on the way these charges are answered. The first thing she must insist on is that her conception of the good, while thick, is in fact vague. That is, it is designed to admit of plural specifications, in a number of different ways. First of all, the constitutive circumstances of human life, while broadly shared, are themselves realized in different forms in different societies. The fear of death, the love of play, relationships of friendship and affiliation with others, even the experience of the bodily appetites—these never turn up in a vague and general form, but always in some specific and historically rich cultural realization, which can profoundly shape not only the conceptions used by the parties in these areas, but also their experience itself, and the choices they will make. To take just one example, developed at length in NRV, the sexual appetite will be both differently talked about and differently experienced in a society that does not contain several of the salient beliefs around which sexual discourse and experience are structured in our society, such as the belief in the moral salience of the gender of the object, the belief that each person has an inner sexual orientation that is relatively permanent and morally assessable, and so forth.[94] Nonetheless, as NRV went on to argue, we have in these areas of our common humanity sufficient overlap to sustain a common discourse, focusing on a family of common problems. And frequently the common discourse will permit us to criticize some conceptions of the grounding experiences themselves, as at odds with other things human beings want to do and to be.

When it comes to choosing a conception of good functioning with respect to these problems, we can expect an even greater degree of plurality to become evident. And here the Aristotelian conception wants to retain plurality in two significantly different ways: what we might call the way of plural specification, and what we might call the way of local specification.

Plural specification means just what its name implies: that the political plan, while operating with a definite conception of the good at a vague level, operates with a sufficiently vague conception that, while much is ruled out as inappropriate to full humanity, there is a great deal of latitude left for citizens to specify each of the components more concretely, and with much variety, in their lives as they plan them.[95] Some conceptions of the good are indeed ruled out by the insistence on our list of functions. But many alternatives are left in. For corresponding to each of the vague functions there is an indefinite plurality of concrete specifications that may be imagined, in accordance with circumstances and tastes.[96] Many concrete forms of life, in many different occupations, display functioning in accordance with all the major capabilities. And once we have imagined forms of labor that are not (as Aristotle thought all manual labor must be) oppressive to humanity, we will be able to describe a wide and open-ended number of concrete forms of employment, recreation, and so forth, answering to varied talents and tastes.

Where religion is concerned, the Aristotelian conception follows the lead of Aristotle himself. For if we examine his list of the virtues and consider what, from the point of view of Greek traditions, is missing, we notice a very striking omission. The virtue of piety, and proper behavior toward the gods, receives no discussion at all.[97] I believe that this is closely connected with the political nature of the list: the point is, that the lawgiver is to take no thought for this virtue in the design of institutions, beyond, apparently some supporting of specifically civic festivals. In part this protects the separate choices of citizens in that sphere: this was already in some ways an Athenian tradition. In part as well, it protects the cross-cultural character of politics for the concerns of the lawgiver are to be those that are broadly shared and shareable, whereas religion is seen as a sphere of local particularity. Our Aristotelian conception then, makes no special provision for religion, regarding it as one of the ways in which citizens may choose to exercise their powers of thought, emotion, and imagination; it protects the separateness with which they do this, and fosters a climate of non-interference.

In education, the Aristotelian aims at the cultivation of certain powers of mind, but she realizes that these general powers are developed in many different ways, by many different concrete courses of study. Here she will be likely to allow students a certain flexibility, increasing as their capability for choice increases, and structured in accordance with the assessment of the background and needs of the students in each case.

This brings us to the way of local specification. Aristotelian practical reasoning is always done, when well done, with a rich sensitivity to the concrete context, to the characters of the agents and their historical and social circumstances. This means that in addition to the pluralism we have described the Aristotelian must also consider a different sort of plural specification of the good. For sometimes what is a good way of promoting education in one part of the world will be completely ineffectual in another. Forms of affiliation that flourish in one community may prove impossible to sustain in another. In such cases, the Aristotelian must aim at some concrete specification of the general good that suits, and develops out of, the local conditions. This sensitivity will help the Aristotelian to answer the charge of paternalism.[98]

And yet we insist that the Aristotelian does not simply defer to local traditions, for example, where gender relations are concerned. She assesses them against her vague conception of the good. Comparing the current conditions with the vague conception, she imagines a possible transition from the current ways to some specification of the vague conception that fits that history and those circumstances. This is, in fact, what happened in our example from Bangladesh. Once the parties abandoned the idea that they could realize the good in Bangladesh in much the same way they might have in Europe, they were able to join with the local women to assess the current situation, to compare it with a possible transformation of that situation in which the women would realize a greater scope and dignity of activity, and to imagine specific forms of education that would assist, in those concrete circumstances, the transition from the current state to the state of greater capability.

Here we have a case in which cultures with radically different traditions in the areas in question confronted one another, with excellent results. These results were possible because the parties (Western women and rural women) recognized one another as fellow human beings, sharing certain problems and certain resources, certain needs for fuller capability and certain possibilities for movement toward capability. They were possible, as well, because both parties approached one another with the resources of imagination, emotional responsiveness, and humor, not simply with scientific facts and calculations—making possible a fully human interaction. (The prose of Chen's account, with its rich descriptive and evocative character, manifests the characteristics of mind that the Aristotelian approach needs to use in order to be fully rational.) Perhaps, too, the results were possible because the women did not identify so deeply with their current ways of life that they refused the invitation to imagine something different. Dissatisfaction and reflection in this way support and increase one another. But above all the confrontation was possible because the Aristotelian approach is not a paternalistic approach, as Dworkin and others have alleged, one that simply tells distant people what wisdom requires. It is an invitation to participate in a reflective adventure. And the claim is that the "thick vague conception" is only as valuable and as lasting as its role in guiding such adventures. The parties are provided with a map of possibilities, or rather initiated into a dialogue about such a map—and then, after imaginative reflection, they are asked what they would choose.

Things will not always be so easy—though, indeed, it is not as if the issue of women's education is, in fact, a simple obvious issue, with a simple policy outcome. It is among the most divisive and the most urgent issues in the developing world, and it is great credit to the Aristotelian view if it can direct reflection about it. There will, however, be other questions that will prove still more deeply divisive, as traditions confront one another, and as each confronts its own internal diversities and conflicts. A society whose entire way of life rests upon adherence to policies that deprive members of a certain race, or class, or gender of the good human life will not be eager to endorse either the contents or the procedures of the Aristotelian list as essential for all human beings. Does this count against the Aristotelian conception?

Here the Aristotelian has three points to make. First, it can almost certainly be shown that the thick vague conception *is* endorsed by the opponent as central in his own life, and in other related lives for which he cares. He lives in such a way as to endorse it, even while he denies its importance, in debate, for others whom, by discourse and interaction, he implicitly recognizes as human beings. Second, the opponent's failure to endorse the full Aristotelian conclusion is (in this case of inconsistency, and in other related cases) explained by his failure to reflect and imagine, not by his successfully performing the Aristotelian procedure but arriving at different results. Sustained and searching reflection and imagining would have revealed the inconsistencies we have mentioned. And reflection, in modifying beliefs, would, sooner or later, modify the relevant emotions and desires. It should not count against the Aristotelian conception that people who fail to work through its procedures do not concur in its results (or, through it, agree with one another). Third, the conception is not intended to answer every difficult question. There will be many issues on which citizens disagree—especially when conceptions themselves are unclear or in process of evolution (as in the case of abortion)—where the Aristotelian list pronounces no decisive verdict for either side. The conception (as we shall see further below) directs government to protect the privacy of citizens in many areas. But it remains an open question, and one that should be settled in and through the evolution of reflective debate, how far and into what areas that protection extends.

There is much more to be said here, and most of it will have to be said concretely. But the claim is that the Aristotelian conception provides a richer and more promising starting point for further work on divisive social issues than do the thinner conceptions used by many liberalisms—and also than the fully determinate conceptions used by many forms of conservatism and communitarianism.

It is frequently charged that there is, in the kind of social democracy imagined in the Aristotelian conception, a deep tension between the value of well-being (and of public care for well-being) and the value of choice. As government more and more fully supports well-being, with a more and more comprehensive (if vague) conception of the good, it more and more removes from citizens the choice to live by their own lights. In much of the recent debate about the adequacy of welfarism in Scandinavia, for example, this tension is frequently alleged, and constraint on choice is assumed to be a result of the very structures that support functioning.[99]

The Aristotelian conception insists that this tension is, to a great extent, illusory. Human choice is not pure spontaneity, flourishing in spite of the accidents of nature.[100] The Aristotelian uses (and defends with argument) a more naturalistic and worldly conception of choice, according to which, as we have said, both the capability to choose good functioning within each sphere and the capability of choosing at all, quite generally, have complex social and material necessary conditions, conditions that are not likely to exist without strong government intervention. Marx's worker is not choosing to work as he works, even if he lives in a liberal capitalist democracy. Women in many, in fact almost all, parts of the world have not chosen the lives they lead, since frequently they have no conception, or a deficient conception, of alternatives and a confined list of possibilities. Choice is not only not incompatible with, but actually requires, the kind of governmental reflection about the good, and the kind of intervention with laissez-faire, that we find in Aristotelian social democracy.

In Aristotelian social democracy, citizens exercise choice in four ways. First, in every area of life, given the material and institutional provisions of the plan, they become capable of choosing to function well in that sphere (or not to, should they choose that). Second, given the political structure of social democracy, they also choose the plan: they are at every stage to feel not like sheep but like active participants. (This means that every effort should be made to dispel the idea that a large remote bureaucracy is doing the planning, and to encourage citizen participation. This is at the core of a certain disaffection with social democracy in Scandinavia; and we should guard against it.) Third, as we have said, citizens have choice in the sense of having many available options within the vague conception, given its vagueness.[101]

And finally, separateness and strong separateness have been read here to require the protection, around each citizen, of a sphere of privacy and non-interference within which what goes on will not be the business of political planning at all, though politics will protect its boundaries. What is in this sphere and how far it extends are matters for political argument; but the Athenian interpretation of this idea was that it included almost all speech, above all political speech, most of family and sexual life, and most, though not all, of one's dealings with personal friends.

An adequate account of this fourth sort of choice is absolutely essential, if the Aristotelian conception is to satisfy some of the strongest intuitions to which the liberal appeals. The conception needs a scheme of basic rights in order to give further definition to the concept of strong separateness. But we should notice that these rights will not be construed as the natural and more or less *a priori* starting point for political thought, as in some liberal conceptions (though not in all).[102] They will be justified with reference to the role they play in protecting a way of life that citizens have agreed to be good for them as human beings.

In this area the Aristotelian must diverge from Aristotle. For while Aristotle attaches significance to some parts of the Athenian tradition of citizen freedom—for example, to the privacy of the family and to the absence of restriction on political speech and participation—it must be admitted that the general question, "How far may government regulate people's daily lives, and in what ways?" had little interest for him.[103] He devotes to it no sustained analysis. Furthermore, some of his concrete recommendations are likely to horrify most liberals. Pregnant women are required to do exercise every day for their health. Abortions for population control are, in certain cases, not just permitted but required, as are certain types of infanticide. Ages for marriage and child-bearing are regulated by a stern scheme of incentives and disincentives.[104] It is all very well to point out that the urgency of problems of infant mortality and population control in his society explains these paternalistic injunctions; but this does not either explain or excuse the absence of sustained philosophical reflection on the limits of the law.

It seems to me that this type and this degree of paternalism are not intrinsic to the Aristotelian conception. In fact, I believe that a more consistent development of its basic intuitions about strong separateness and choice would be in the direction of a scheme of basic rights of the person. And I suspect that even Aristotle himself felt able to interfere so much in these cases because he was dealing above all with women, whom he did not admit as free and equal citizens, and with children, who did not yet have adult citizen rights. He himself recognized that the status of citizen called forth a greater restraint.

The issue of choice is deep. We cannot deal with it fully without a more extended account (part of which I have tried to provide elsewhere) of what it is to be an animal that chooses, and what it is to educate a child to become such an animal. But it seems to me clear that the issue of choice is not all on the side of the liberal, by any means. Indeed, the Aristotelian can turn the liberal's charge back against him, arguing that there is a deep tension between liberal *non*-intervention and the value of choice, since frequently the liberal does not permit himself to do enough restructuring to make people really capable of choosing.[105]

THE MEASUREMENT OF WELFARE IN SCANDINAVIA

I have already made certain comparisons between the Aristotelian conception and the Scandinavian social democracies. Now we can make the comparison more concrete by describing a fascinating convergence. For in fact the strategies by which both the Finnish and the Swedish governments have inquired into the well-being of citizens replicate or parallel, to a surprising degree, the Aristotelian approach and even the Aristotelian vague conception.[106]

The central intuition of the Scandinavian approach to welfare measurement is that the human being is an active being who pursues good functioning in a number of different areas. Each of these components is irreducible to any other; therefore any good measure of how well people are doing will be a plural measure. The quality of life will be assessed along all of these dimensions. Furthermore, what we look for when we look at the lives of citizens (argues Robert Erikson, a leading Swedish theoretician of the approach) is for their "capacity . . . to control and consciously direct (their) living conditions; i.e., the individual's level of living will be an expression of his 'scope of action'." In order to assess the lives of citizens in this way, government researchers "must take a stand on which the most central areas of human life are, the areas where it is most essential that the individual can direct his living conditions."[107]

This approach, as Erikson and others insist, is fundamentally opposed to what had been the dominant approach to the measurement of welfare prior to their work, namely an approach that measures quality of life by measuring the satisfaction of desires or preferences. Feelings of satisfaction, argues Erik Allardt, pioneer of the Finnish approach, are unstable and unreliable as measures of how well people are doing. What we should do instead, he insists, is to look at what they are actually able to do, what their functionings and choices actually are in many different areas. Allardt gave his major book on welfare measurement the active title *Having, Loving, Being* in order to indicate both the breadth of his concern and its active character.[108]

The list of components of good living used by the Swedish researchers included, as Robert Erikson reports the following items:[109]

Components	*Indicators*
1. Health and access to care	Ability to walk 100 meters, various symptoms of illness, contacts with doctors and nurses
2. Employment and working conditions	Unemployment experiences, physical demands at work, possibilities to leave the place of work
3. Economic resources	Income and wealth, property, ability to cover unforeseen expenses up to $1000 within a week

4. Knowledge and educational opportunities	Years of education, level of education reached
5. Family and social integration	Marital status, contacts with friends and relatives
6. Housing and neighborhood facilities	Number of persons per room, amenities
7. Security of life and property	Exposure to violence and thefts
8. Recreation and culture	Leisure time pursuits, vacation trips
9. Political resources	Voting in elections, membership in unions and political parties, ability to file complaints

(Erikson notes that in an earlier survey questions were asked about diet and nutrition; but Swedish citizens resented such questions as an intrusion on privacy.)

The resemblance of this list to the Aristotelian list is striking though not surprising, given what we have said about the universal character of the thick vague conception. (In fact, more or less identical conceptions turn up in assessments of quality of life currently being used in medical practice and medical ethics.) The list is, from our point of view, somewhat unrefined. Some of the indicators are actual functionings, some resources for functioning, some capabilities. Had Erikson examined these distinctions further, more clarity might have been achieved. (In some cases, however, he can justify the shift as the result of reflection on a problem. For example, he deliberately decided that, given the subtle obstacles to the political participation of minority groups and women, one could not be convinced that an individual had actually been rendered fully *capable* of participating except by the fact that he or she *did* participate.) Some components of interest to us are omitted. The parallel Finnish survey, for example, asked about the citizens' relationship to nature and to animals, and about a wider range of social interactions.[110] And some of the items included are of unclear relevance: for example, it is unclear in what direction marital status is supposed to be an indicator of quality of life! Finally, some of the questioning does not go deep enough. The full quality of labor relations cannot be ascertained by these questions; there is no attempt to ask whether the holding of private property is in fact always a positive indicator of quality of life. But despite these flaws, the survey surely has more power than many comparable measures to inform government of the really important things, the things with which its work is most centrally concerned.

The results of the survey were used in the way recommended by the Aristotelian conception. Where the data showed a lower level of capability in some area or areas for some identifiable subgroup of the population—women and elderly people figured prominently here—the government set to work to imagine a response, aiming at the fuller integration of these groups into good human living. Erikson concludes his study by contrasting Swedish social democracy with the liberalisms of other Western nations:

> I would suggest that poverty is the main welfare problem to social liberalism while inequality is the main problem to social democracy. . . . To social democracy state activities are not only a supplementary mechanism, but one on par with the market. In an institutional welfare state a redistributive model of social policy includes provisions to cover basic needs for all citizens.

This contrast is perhaps somewhat unclearly expressed; for liberalism is very much concerned with equality, in its own way. Erikson's point is perhaps better expressed by saying that liberalism and social democracy are concerned with equality in different ways.[111] Liberalism focuses above all on giving resources. (And, as Erikson notes, this is frequently connected with a willingness to rely on the market, except where poverty or severe hardship is produced.) In social democracy the concern for equality is a concern for equal capability to live well over a complete life. Government activity provides comprehensive and not just supplementary support, operating with a partially comprehensive conception of the good.

ARISTOTLE AND THE LIBERAL

This has been a sketch. And much more work remains to be done to elaborate its parts, and to show the relationship of each part to various claims made by different versions of liberalism. But instead of beginning that larger task here, I want instead, in concluding, to focus once again on the basic intuitive idea of the Aristotelian conception, contrasting it as clearly as possible with some of the intuitive underpinnings of Rawls's Kantian liberalism.

Rawls's Kantian constructivism uses an idea of the person that is in many respects a Kantian idea. The person[112] is characterized above all by the two moral powers and not, for example, by needs, or vulnerabilities. The basic structure of society is seen as an expression of the parties' moral personhood in the arrangement of the available resources. Persons are understood to need resources for the various things they do and choose; in this sense Rawls's Kantianism is empirical. But their need and their dependency is not exactly the focus of the conception's intuitive idea, nor of its account of the moral powers themselves. This interpenetration between person and nature is not imagined as going very deep, in the sense that once necessary things are to hand, all is well. No deeper consideration of the structure of relatedness between persons and things—or, indeed, persons and one another—is called forth by the Kantian idea of the person. For although Rawls's is indeed an empirical Kantianism, it retains some part of the Kantian tendency to separate the moral realm from the natural, and to think of moral personality as creating a realm of its own, a realm to some extent distinct from and independent of the natural realm. I am saying this vaguely, since it is only vaguely that I have been able to get at these intuitive features of liberal Kantianism. But I think that the Kantianism does important work here, and that we must focus on it if we are to understand at a deep level the difference between the two conceptions.

The Aristotelian conception, by contrast, begins from the intuitive idea of a being who is neither a beast nor a god. This being comes into the world (the single world there is, the world of nature) characterized both by certain basic powers and by amazing neediness—by rich neediness, we might say, borrowing a phrase from Marx, in the sense that the very powers of this being exist as needs for fulfillment and claim, for their fully human development, rich support from the human and the natural world. This being's good must always be pursued as a system of complex relations of dependence between the agent and unstable items in the world, such as friends, loved ones, food, water, a city of fellow citizens. Government is "a sharing for the sake of the good life,"[113]—that is, a complex series of cooperative stratagems devised to protect and support citizens in their eating, moving, loving, and choosing, so as to convert their basic powers into fully human capabilities for choices of functioning. Human activity always goes on in complex interdependence. The task of politics must be to imagine forms of interdependence that are human rather than slavish, and to forge those circumstances, where possible, in the world.[114]

POSTSCRIPT, 2001

This essay was written in 1989, while I was in residence at the World Institute for Development Economics Research, an institute located in Helsinki and affiliated with the United Nations University. The references to social democracy and the use of Scandinavian welfare data derive from my interest in a convergence I discovered between the concerns of Scandinavian social scientists and those of Aristotle. I still endorse many of the contentions of the essay, but my version of the "capabilities approach" has developed further; the fullest and most authoritative presentation of my views (as of now) can be found in my 2000 book *Women and the Human Development: The Capabilities Approach*. Four developments in particular should be observed.

First, I now endorse a form of "political liberalism" in the Rawlsian sense, rather than the apparently comprehensive conception of liberalism advanced in the present essay. That is, I see the list of central human capabilities as a list to be endorsed for political purposes by citizens who otherwise hold different comprehensive conceptions of the good, and I argue that they can be the object of an "overlapping consensus" among such citizens. This means, too, that I wish to present the capabilities in a way that is "free-standing": as a partial ethical conception that can be accepted by people who hold different metaphysical views and different views about human nature. So I would not ground them in a specifically Aristotelian conception of human nature, but rather in the simple ethical idea of what a sufficiently dignified human life requires. (Elsewhere I have argued that in any case Aristotle's conception of human nature is ethical rather than metaphysical, but that is a controversial interpretive claim, and if I am wrong about Aristotle I still wish the grounding of the capabilities to be ethical rather than metaphysical.)

This brings me to my second issue. In thinking about the capabilities in the present essay, I already introduce the notion of a fully human life. I would now like to enrich that notion by bringing in the idea of human dignity, and describing the political goal, where the capabilities are concerned, as that of a life worthy of the dignity of the human being. Thus a rather Kantian idea of respect for persons is combined with the Aristotelian idea.

Third, because liberal theories deriving from the Kantian part of the social contract tradition have exercised such an important influence on our political thought in recent years, I have felt it important to criticize one aspect of these views, namely, their picture of citizens as roughly equal in need and capacity, and relatively independent. In "The Future of Feminist Liberalism," *Proceedings and Addresses of the American Philosophical Association* 74 (2000): 47–79, I argue that such approaches cannot adequately conceptualize and address the needs people have for care in times of asymmetrical dependency: infancy, old age, and the entire lives of many people with disabilities. I argue that the capabilities approach can do a better job, because its political conception of the person sees human dignity as residing in animality, including neediness, rather than contrasting animality and neediness with rationality, as do all Kantian views. This emphasis is quite consistent with the present essay, and deepens its criticism of other liberal views.

Fourth, although I still think of the capabilities in connection with ideas of human dignity and a fully human life, I also think that the capabilities approach can be extended to address the ethical claims of non-human animals, in connection with related ideas of the characteristic form of flourishing of each creature. I broach this topic in "Animal Rights: The Need for a Theoretical Basis," in the March 2001 issue of the *Harvard Law Review,* and it will form an important part of my future work on the approach.

NOTES

This essay was originally published in *Liberalism and the Good,* edited by R. Bruce Douglass, Gerald M. Mara, and Henry S. Richardson (New York and London: Routledge Press, 1990).

1. On the distinction between ownership and use, see *Politics* II.5 as a whole; for an excellent discussion of the history of this distinction in Greek political thought, see Newman (1887), commentary on II.5.

2. *Pol.* 1332b25–7; cf. 1325b7, 1334a27–9.

3. It is not possible to make a sharp distinction between the ethical and the political in discussing Aristotle's views, since for him the task of politics is to secure to all the citizens the conditions of a complete good human life, and an essential element in the complete good life is political activity (see below). Thus Aristotle explicitly describes his ethical writing as a part of political inquiry. This is an important difference between his views and various forms of liberalism; we shall study its implications below.

4. Nussbaum (1988, 1990a, 1990c).

5. The institute is the World Institute for Development Economics Research (WIDER), Helsinki, a branch of the United Nations University. For the work that has been done so far in the project on defining the quality of life, see Nussbaum and Sen (1990).

6. Thus Rawls explicitly limits his discussion to the conceptions of "a modern constitutional democracy" (Rawls [1985] 224), and his discussion of the relevant historical issues focuses on the Enlightenment and debates over toleration—thinking clearly, above all, of the English and American versions of these debates, and not about the rather different histories of other European democracies, for example those of Scandinavia. Dworkin's discussion is even more explicitly American; in Dworkin (1985) he refers to many concrete examples from the current American debate, provisionally defining liberalism in terms of positions on these issues.

7. Rawls (1971) 8 ff. limits the discussion to the principles that should govern the basic structure of a single society; he opposes the application of the principles discovered in the original position to questions of justice between nations. In Rawls (1985) the scope of the discussion has contracted further, since now the results are said to hold only for the basic structure of society in a group of nations that share a certain history and certain traditions: "Whether justice as fairness can be extended to a general political conception for different kinds of societies existing under dif-.

ferent historical and social conditions, or whether it can be extended to a general moral conception, or a significant part thereof, are altogether separate questions. I avoid prejudging these larger questions one way or another" (225).

8. See Brundtland (1987) for an eloquent statement on this issue; on hunger see Dreze and Sen (1990); on women's issues, and on the general question of justice in relation to national boundaries, see O'Neill (1990).

9. Aristotle: cf. *EN* (*Ethica Nicomachea*) 1103b26–31, 1179a18–20, 1179a33–b4; for discussion and further references see Nussbaum (1986a). For Rawls's statements on this issue, see especially Rawls (1980) 516–19, 554 ff. See also Rawls (1971) 46–53.

10. *Politics* 1323a 17–19. For a full discussion, and other references, see NFC.

11. For textual references and discussion, see NFC and also Nussbaum (1988a). Cf. esp. *Pol.* 1323a17–19, 1324a23–5, 1325a7, *EN* 1103b2–6.

12. Rawls (1971) 396. For further development of the view of primary goods, see Rawls (1982) and (1988).

13. See especially *Politics* I.8, VII.1. On the excessive attention to wealth in Sparta, *Pol.* 1270a11 ff., where the large inequalities of resources produced by the Spartan system are also criticized. For a typical example of Aristotle's attitude to money—as necessary in order to avoid the constraints of poverty, but productive of excessive luxuriousness if present in too large a quantity, see *Pol.* 1266b24–6. It is interesting to note that *isotēs*, the Greek work for "equality," also means a "middle" amount; and when Aristotle says there should be *isotēs* of resources, he plays on this double meaning (1266b24), contrasting the "equal" with the deficient and the excessive.

For contemporary discussion of these issues, see Nussbaum and Sen (1990): especially the papers by Sen and Cohen.

14. On Phaleas, see *Pol.* 1266a39 ff., and for discussion see NFC.

15. See Dworkin (1981, 1985).

16. Rawls (1971) 396. Rawls (1982, 1988) refines and expands the list, making it far more heterogeneous and focusing less attention on wealth. Thus the latest version of the list in Rawls (1988) divides primary goods into five categories: (1) basic rights and liberties; (2) "freedom of movement and free choice of occupation against a background of diverse opportunities"; (3) "powers and prerogatives of offices and positions in the political and economic institutions of the basic structure"; (4) income and wealth; (5) the social bases of self-respect. Rawls suggests he is willing to add other goods, "for example, leisure time, and even certain mental states such as the absence of physical pain." On the one hand, this alteration of the list addresses some of the Aristotelian's criticisms, since it now includes a number of human capabilities that the Aristotelian, too, regards as basic human goods. But insofar as it does so, the new list seems to depart from the original notion of "primary goods," the notion of all-purpose means that are neutral among conceptions of the good. Rawls (manuscript) shows that he still wishes to maintain the original conception, against Sen's more Aristotelian proposal; thus there now seem to be considerable tension and ambiguity in the position. In NFC I discuss the original list proposed in (1971), criticizing it from an Aristotelian position.

17. See *Pol.* VII.1, and the discussion in NFC. Here the Aristotelian conception and Aristotle are explicitly and fully together.

18. See Sen (1980, 1987); I compare Sen's conception to Aristotle's in NFC.

19. Cf. *Pol.* VII.1. and note 13 above.

20. See especially *Rhet.* II.15–17, discussed in Nussbaum (1986) 339–40. The bad effects of wealth include insolence, arrogance, and a mercenary attitude to other valuable things.

21. On Milo, see *EN* 1106b3, and the discussion in "The Discernment of Perception" in Nussbaum (1990). For Sen's statements of similar points, see (1980, 1984, 1987). Aristotle discusses the nutritional and exercise needs of pregnant women at *Pol.* 1335b12 ff.

22. On women's capabilities and the support they require, see Sen (1984, 1985). The relationship between Sen's views and Aristotle is discussed in NFC. Aristotle does not take exactly this view of women, since he does not consider them at all capable of living a fully good human life under any circumstances; but he does say that they should have what is required for living the sort of good life that is open to them; and throughout the *Politics* he manifests concern for the nutrition and development of women. On children, he explicitly commits himself to the idea that each child should get whatever it, as an individual, needs in order to flourish—cf. *EN* 1180b7 ff., where this idea is used to defend the role of the family in education.

23. See Rawls (1988) and especially Rawls (manuscript).

24. On the moral powers, see Rawls (1980).

25. See Rawls (manuscript); Dworkin (1981).

26. Throughout *Politics* II, Aristotle repeatedly points to the many ways in which regimes, whether or not they have a *theory* of the good, nonetheless commit themselves, through their policies, to some definite conception of the good.

27. Here the Aristotelian view develops a point that Aristotle's own emphasis on the plural and noncommensurable nature of the components of the good life makes natural; and to some extent Aristotle himself recognizes the possibility of such conflicts—see Nussbaum (1986) ch. 11 and "Discernment of Perception" in Nussbaum (1990). But he does little with this point, and tends on the whole to believe that the claims of the different components will be in harmony. For some further observations on this point, see Nussbaum (1990b).

28. For ancient analogues to various aspects of the utilitarian position, see Nussbaum (1976) and (1986) ch. 4. Aristotle attributes to Protagoreans the view that all appearances are true (*Metaph* IV)—a view which, in the area of ethics, would have related implications.

29. See Rawls (1971) 258–65: "The upshot of these considerations is that justice as fairness is not at the mercy, so to speak, of existing wants and interests. . . . Both justice as fairness and perfectionism establish independently an ideal conception of the person and of the basic structure so that not only are some desires and inclinations necessarily discouraged but the effect of the initial circumstances will eventually disappear" (261–62). See also Rawls (1988).

30. The point is most frequently expressed as a criticism of the thesis that pleasure is identical with the good: cf. *EN* VII.11–14, X.1–4; cf. also the account of "bestial vice" and of desires malformed through bad experiences in *EN* VII.5, 1148b15 ff.

31. See Sen (1984, 1985, 1987), O'Neill (1990), and Allardt (1990). Speaking of the policies of the Finnish model of welfare research, Allardt writes: "To base the choice of welfare criteria entirely on the subjective views of the people themselves is therefore likely to lead to an unfruitful conservatism."

32. This question is not independent of desire (cf. NFC); for it is, in effect, to ask what they *would* desire if their education and knowledge of alternatives were above the threshold of what is required for practical reason and choice. Thus Dworkin (1985) is misleading when he suggests that a procedure of this sort asks what some ideally wise man would choose *for* others, as if this is a person they have no chance of being. In Aristotle's view, the good human life is in principle "common to many: for it is open to all who are not maimed with respect to excellence, as the result of a certain learning and concern" (*EN* 1099b18–20). It is up to politics to create the conditions in which this learning can take place.

33. For further discussion of Aristotle's views on this point, see NFC and HN, with further textual references; and cf. Sen (1985).

34. This does not imply that it is easy to draw the line between capability and actual functioning, or to tell when the absence of a function results from choice, rather than from the absence of a capability. On this problem, see Williams (1987).

35. Marx (1844), in Tucker, pp. 88–89: see the discussion in NFC. Another section of this passage is cited and discussed below. On Marx's debt to Aristotle during this period, see de Ste. Croix (1981) especially 69 ff.

36. See the related discussion in Marglin (1974).

37. See Rawls (1971), Dworkin (1981, 1985). A much discussed limitation of Rawls's account of distribution is his assumption that the subjects of distribution are "heads of households" who will act on behalf of the interests of their families. On the limitations of this position where women's issues are concerned, see Okin (1987). Dworkin, unlike Rawls, explicitly assumes that ownership of resources will be private: see Dworkin (1981) pp. 283, 290. One might also note that (again, unlike Rawls) Dworkin appears to rely on actual uncriticized preferences, leaving the market mechanism to do the screening. Thus his view is less likely than is Rawls's to ask certain critical questions.

38. On Aristotle's sweeping rejection of all manual labor from the lives of citizens, see below n.80 and accompanying text.

39. Chen (1986).

40. This example also shows how the Aristotelian approach insists on being sensitive to context and history, making judgments that suit all the particular features of the case and balancing an ongoing interest in the general conception with concrete perceptions. See "Discernment" in Nussbaum (1990) and the further discussion of Chen's example in Nussbaum (1990a). Both of these papers discuss Aristotle's own view about particular perceptions, with textual analysis and references.

41. On the faculties of the good legislator, see "Discernment" in Nussbaum (1990), and Nussbaum and Sen (1989).

42. Dworkin distinguishes his own view from a view that he finds both in Marxism and in various forms of conservatism, namely, the view "that the content of equal treatment cannot be independent of some theory about the good for man

or the good of life, because treating a person as an equal means treating him the way the good or truly wise person would wish to be treated" (1985, pp. 191–92). Although he does not explicitly name Aristotle here, the description certainly coincides with some versions of Aristotle that are frequently accepted, especially through the Catholic tradition. Rawls is more explicit, contrasting his view with the "perfectionist" views of both Plato and Aristotle (1988, pp. 254, 272–73, cf. also 1971, 25, 325). Admittedly, Aristotle's supporters frequently contribute to this situation, portraying his account of the good as metaphysical: see, in very different ways, MacIntyre (1981, though the view is different in 1987), Williams (1985). Williams's very interesting account of Aristotle on human nature is discussed in HN. For an example of the Catholic use of Aristotle to ground a sectarian metaphysical theory of the good, see Maritain (1943).

43. Note, however, that the theory has grown "thicker," and closer to Aristotle's; see above n. 16.

44. *EN* 1098a20–23; for full discussion of this passage, see HN.

45. For this terminology, see Charles Taylor (1989, 1990); compare the use of the idea of a "model of man" in Putnam (1987). It will be seen that the Aristotelian account of the human being, as I construe it, is closer to what Rawls calls a concept of the person than to what he calls a theory of human nature, in the sense that it is an evaluative conception, constructed within human society: see HN. But it is a conception of a being who is essentially embodied and dwelling in the world of nature—cf. below; in this way it is importantly distinct from Kant's conception of the moral agent.

46. See MacIntyre (1981), Williams (1985): both, in general sympathetic to Aristotle, find a serious difficulty for his account at this point.

47. On the role of reflection about beasts and gods in arriving at a conception of the human, see HN, Nussbaum (1986), and "Transcending Humanity" in Nussbaum (1990).

48. See HN for a further account of this procedure; on the way in which a sense of species identity sets bounds to aspiration and well-wishing, see *EN* 1159a8–12, 1166a19–23.

49. An obvious problem is that some agents who ask this question will arbitrarily exclude certain humans from humanity; and Aristotle himself is guilty of this, in his reflections on women and natural slaves. On how the Aristotelian approach can confront this difficulty, see HN; and also Nussbaum (1990b).

50. This is true of many lists that have sometimes been taken as closed and normative: for example, the list of the "four causes" in the *Physics*; usually Aristotle is explicitly open-ended about what his account has produced.

51. HN approaches the list by focusing on the two architectonic capabilities, and briefly describes the limits; NRV focuses on the limits, as they give rise to a unitary debate about the virtues. Here I try to put these pieces together.

52. Lucretius *De Rerum Natura* V. 989: cf. Nussbaum (1989).

53. Aristotle discusses mortality in *De Anima* II.4, and in the discussions of courage in the ethical works. See also Nussbaum (1989) and "Transcending Humanity" in Nussbaum (1990).

54. On the role of the body in the conception of the human being, see also NRV; and on Aristotle's view of the unity of soul and body, see Nussbaum and Putnam (1990).

55. *EN* 1119a7–10. NRV holds that appetitive desire is culturally shaped, and pursues the implications. On cultural invariance in nutritive need, however, see Gopalan (working paper). Aristotle recognizes the political importance of nutrition throughout the *Politics:* see NFC, and refs. above.

56. The need for shelter is a central theme in Greek myths about the "human condition": see, for example, Protagoras' speech in Plato's *Protagoras,* and Aeschylus' *Prometheus Bound.* Aristotle does not very much stress this feature, but he takes its importance for granted. His preferred definition of "house" is "a covering that prevents destruction from rain and wind and heat" (*De Anima* 403b3–4—he is not as happy with the attempt to define it as "stones and bricks and timber"). *Politics* VII.11 discusses the selection of the city's location with a view to the health of the citizens, asking what winds are healthy, etc., and pursuing the question of a healthy water supply.

57. NRV discusses a Stoic argument that holds the belief that pain is bad to be a cultural artifact; this view seems highly implausible, although one should certainly grant that *conceptions* of the painful and the pleasant are shaped by cultural learning. Rawls now is willing to add the absence of pain to the list of primary goods: see above n. 13.

58. *Metaphysics* I.1; see the discussions in NRV and HN. HN discusses Aristotle's view that not every child born of two human parents is human: in the absence of a certain basic level of capability (see NFC) the judgment of the species membership cannot be made, since being human is, as we have argued, an evaluative matter.

59. For a related account of the story of a human life, see Wollheim (1986); in NRV I discuss the views of Klein (1984) about the emotional life of the young child. According to all major ancient philosophers, Aristotle included, emotions are closely linked to belief, and can be changed by change of belief; in Aristotle's view they are partly constituted by beliefs. This being the case, there is a great deal of room for the cultural shaping of emotion, as Epicureans and Stoics were quick to point out. But given that all cultures hold some beliefs about the great importance of items external to the agent and difficult to control (i.e., there has never been a thoroughly Stoic culture), every culture will have some analogue of emotions such as grief, anger, love, and fear. On this see also Lutz (1988).

60. On practical reason and affiliation, see HN.

61. On this part of human life, see Allardt (1990), who convinced me that NRV had been defective in omitting it from the list. In one way, this element is very Aristotelian, since Aristotle insists throughout on thinking of the human being as an animal and a natural being among others, and on the beauty and interest of all natural creatures (see *Parts of Animals* I.5). On the other hand, it must be acknowledged that the ethical works do not take an interest in any ethical issues arising out of these facts; and the *Politics* tends to treat animals and plants as valuable only insofar as they subserve human ends. This seems to me an odd tension in Aristotle, perhaps to be explained by the early date of some parts of the *Politics,* before Aristotle's years

of biological research. See, however, *Pol.* I.5, where he briefly considers the animals' own interests.

62. Aristotle's emphasis on this element is striking: see *EN* IV.6–8. Few moral philosophers place so much emphasis on this. Rawls is now prepared to consider adding leisure time to the list of primary goods (above n. 13): and to this the Aristotelian would no doubt say that the time itself is valuable as a space for a certain sort of human activity, namely what Aristotle calls *diagogē meta paidias* and *homilia emmelēs* (passing the time with play, and harmonious association, *EN* 1127b33 ff.).

63. This is based on the general Aristotelian requirement that substances be "one in number" and "separate": cf. *Metaph* V.7, VII 1, etc. For an excellent account of the position and its intuitive credentials, see Wiggins (1980). The Plato reference is to *Laws* 739c.

64. "Strong separateness" is defended by Aristotle in his criticisms of Plato in *Politics* II: see Nussbaum (1980). The separateness of persons is fundamental to Rawls's critique of utilitarianism: cf. (1971) 554 ff.

65. Here I leave to one side the very difficult problems connected with Aristotle's defense of the contemplative life in *EN* X.6–8; in (1986) Appendix to ch. 12 I argue that this passage is in a number of important ways inconsistent with the overall argument of the *EN*. It is especially inconsistent, it seems to me, with passages that insist on circumscribing aspiration and well-wishing by considerations of kind membership, explicitly ruling out the transition to the divine (above n. 48).

66. On confronting the limits, see Nussbaum (1989) and "Transcending Humanity" in Nussbaum (1990).

67. See Nussbaum (1986) chs. 2–3, Nussbaum (1990b).

68. See HN.

69. Marx (1844) in Tucker, pp. 88–89, discussed in NFC.

70. See Rawls (1980, 1985, 1988).

71. Despite Rawls's expansion of the list of the primary goods, he is still clearly opposed to this idea: see especially the discussion of "civic humanism" in (1988) 272–73.

72. There are, of course, other motivations: above all, the desire to find a conception that can win an "overlapping consensus" from citizens of different religious and ideological backgrounds: see, for example, (1988) 256.

73. In a fairly obvious way, the basic rights and liberties provide support for the moral powers; but this element in the list of primary goods is logically not parallel to, for example, income and wealth: for it is itself a set of human capabilities, not a tool whose point is seen only in connection with the capabilities. What Rawls does not investigate, it seems to me, is the role of goods like income and wealth in making possible the development of a person who will have the capability of choosing a conception of the good.

74. On this task, see the further discussion in NFC.

75. The notion of the complete life is central in Aristotle's conception of *eudaimonia,* and in his thought about what a human being is generally. Its political influence can be seen in his concern to provide for functions that are specific to a particular time of life (see *Pol.* VII.14). Compare Rawls's notion of the citizens as "normal and fully cooperating members of society over a complete life" (1988, p. 270).

76. See NFC; the line between internal and external is difficult to draw, and it is always hard to say when a failure to function is due to external circumstance, when to absence of inner capability, and when to the individual's choice. (On this problem see Williams [1987].)

77. Rawls (1971) 195 ff.

78. Aristotle is very much concerned with population policy, and criticizes previous legislators for not devoting enough time to this: see for example *Pol.* 1266b8 ff. Aristotle's concerns with the issues that are faced today by development economists have in general been too little described and emphasized in the literature: in part, because philosophers tend not to be interested in these issues, in part because of the still prevailing tendency to think of ancient Greece as the ancestor of modern Europe, rather than as a developing country. (See NFC 170–71).

79. On the importance of considering the list as a whole, see NFC n. 30, and cf. Sen (1987).

80. For Aristotle's views about manual labor, cf. NFC; Marx's own emphasis on leisure for workers was certainly very much indebted to Aristotle. Aristotle's view was that neither farming nor any form of manual labor was compatible with the functions of the citizen. The Aristotelian conception should depart from Aristotle on this point, while not failing to press the Aristotelian question about the relationship between forms of labor and full humanity. Ancient Athenian political ideals contain a richer conception of the laborer: the plays of Aristophanes, especially, reflect a tradition that ascribes political value to the type of practical intelligence involved in the activities of the farmer and the craftsmen. In our own political tradition, the poems of Walt Whitman provide helpful models; I discuss Whitman's relation to ancient Greek democratic traditions in "Discernment," in Nussbaum (1990).

81. See Nussbaum (1986) chs. 11–12.

82. See esp. *Pol.* II.9–10, VII.10.

83. For example, by encouraging worker-owned businesses and other forms of worker control.

84. See *Pol.* II.3–7, and Newman's commentary.

85. On Athenian traditions in this regard (with particular reference to Thucydides' portrait of Periclean ideals), see "Discernment" in Nussbaum (1990). The insistence of Athenians on the integrity and separateness of the body is especially striking: see Halperin (1989).

86. One might fruitfully compare to this housing policies that have been adopted in some socialist and social-democratic countries, giving the homeless certain rights toward unoccupied or luxury housing.

87. *Pol.* 1262a32–40.

88. Cf. *Pol.* 1275a22–23, 1275b18–20, 1276a4–5.

89. Nussbaum (1986): cf. *Pol.* III.5, VII.9–10.

90. On the development of the ancient Athenian conception of freedom and the free citizen, see Raaflaub (1985).

91. On education, see further in NFC. Rawls (1988) 268 allows the state to take a limited interest in education, insofar as children are viewed as future citizens. But note that his conception of the citizen is more circumscribed than is Aristotle's, and

the state's concern with education will be correspondingly limited. (For example, the state will presumably not be able to concern itself with the role played by literacy and other forms of education in promoting nonpolitical types of functioning—although Rawls does allow it to take thought for the citizens' being "economically independent and self-supporting members of society over a complete life . . . all this from within a political point of view.")

92. In this connection, NFC discusses the approach to education embodied in Buck (1945).

93. See Dworkin (1985).

94. See Foucault (1984), Halperin (1989); the issue is discussed in NRV.

95. On the different types of further specification of ends, see NRV. Plural specification may be either individual or communal: societies too may choose among available options for instantiating a particular function. But very often the society's history, traditions, circumstances, and other ends will make the appropriate choice rather more circumscribed. This is how "local specification" (below) differs from "plural specification": in plural specification the idea is one of choosing from among a plurality of available options, in accordance with tastes; in local specification the idea is one of finding the appropriate way of instantiating a certain function, given awareness of one's traditions, circumstances, etc. Obviously the two interact and overlap in complex ways.

96. Here modern interests in individual self-discovery and self-expression move the contemporary Aristotelian away somewhat from Aristotle—but less than one might think, since Aristotle too values the contribution of diverse experiences of life (see *Pol.* III.15 on the analogy between deliberation and a public feast); and Aristotle, too, thinks of the good human life as a development and full expression of capabilities. On different ingredients of the modern sense of identity in this regard, see Taylor (1989).

97. Piety is typically one of the five main virtues in lists of virtues—along with courage, moderation, justice, and wisdom. See Plato's *Protagoras* for an example. But morality and religion are less distinct in Greece than they are for us, and there is little sense of the religious as a separate sphere of exalting spiritual experience. The gods protect spheres of value, and honoring the divine is above all acting so as to show respect for the valuable.

98. On education, see NFC and Buck (1945). For criticism of monolithic approaches to curricular planning, see Nussbaum (1987). For further discussion of local specification, see NRV.

99. See the essays in Graubard (1986).

100. See Nussbaum (1986) ch. 9.

101. It is especially important to notice that Aristotle believes it is possible to deliberate rationally not only about instrumental means to ends, but about the constituents of the end themselves—even about constituents of *eudaimonia,* the ultimate end. On this see Wiggins (1975), Richardson (1986).

102. Dworkin (1985), however, has an instrumental understanding of rights that comes closer to this aspect of the Aristotelian position.

103. See Barnes (1989).

104. See, for example, *Pol.* VII.16 on the regulation of marriage and pregnancy, VII.17 and VIII on the regulation of physical and cultural education. The issue is thoroughly discussed in Barnes (1989), with further references.

105. In this connection one might recall the well-known exchange on freedom between Margaret Thatcher and Neil Kinnock: she asserting that the policies of Labour would diminish citizens' freedoms, he replying that it was only on account of such policies that he and others like him had had the freedom to choose a university education.

106. See Allardt (1975, 1976, 1990), Erikson (1990), Erikson et al. (1987), Galtung (1980), Graubard (1986), Vogal et al. (1988).

107. Erikson (1990).

108. Allardt (1975), discussed in Allardt (1990). The Finnish approach places greater emphasis on the delineation of valuable types of personal affiliation than does the Swedish approach, and also includes consideration of the individual's relationship to animals and the world of nature. Procedurally, it employs both objective and subjective indicators, though, like the Swedish approach, it focuses on the former, asking above all how individuals are actually doing. Another important contribution of this approach is its (very Aristotelian) use of the concept of a threshold of good living in each of the various areas, below which no individual should be: see Allardt (1990).

109. Erikson (1990).

110. See Allardt (1990).

111. See Sen (manuscript).

112. Notice that even the fact that the basic notion is that of *person* rather than that of *human being* is significant: on this difference, see Wiggins (1980), Williams (1985a). Kant, at least, intended the rational to be a genus of which the human (the "animal rational") was just one species: and morality to be based on rationality rather than on our specific humanness, far less on our animality.

113. See for example *Pol.* 1328a37–8.

114. I am especially grateful to Henry Richardson for encouraging me to develop these ideas in the first place, and for giving me extensive and searching criticisms; thanks are also due to Gerald Mara and the others present at the Georgetown conference for their helpful comments. I am grateful to Amartya Sen for discussion of the issues. Much of this work was done at WIDER, Helsinki (see n. 5); I gratefully acknowledge the support of the Institute during the period of writing.

Bibliography

Allardt, E. 1975. *Att ha, Att Älska, Att Vara. Om Wälfärd i Norden. (Having, Loving, Being. On Welfare in the Nordic Countries.)* Borgholm: Argos, 1975.

———.1976. "Dimensions of Welfare in a Comparative Scandinavian Study." *Acta Sociologica* 19:227–40.

——— .1990. "Having, Loving, Being: An Alternative to the Swedish Model of Welfare Research." In Nussbaum and Sen, 1990.

Barnes, J. 1989. Paper presented to the 9th Symposium Aristotelicum on the *Politics*. Published in the Proceedings of the Symposium, ed. G. Patzig.

Brundtland, G. H. 1987. *Our Common Future*. Report of World Commission on Environment and Development.

Buck, P., et al. 1945. *General Education in a Free Society: Report of the Harvard Committee*. Cambridge, MA: Harvard University Press.

Charles, D. 1988. Comments on Nussbaum 1988. *Oxford Studies in Ancient Philosophy*, Supplementary Volume.

Chen, M. 1986. *A Quiet Revolution: Women in Transition in Rural Bangladesh*. Dhaka: BRAC.

Chodorow, N. 1978. *The Reproduction of Mothering*. Berkeley and Los Angeles: University of California Press.

Dalenius, T. 198-. *Privacy in Surveys: A Scandinavian Problem*.

Dreze, J., and A. Sen. 1990. *Hunger and Public Action*. Oxford: Clarendon Press.

Dworkin, R. 1981. "What is Equality? Part 2: Equality of Resources." *Philosophy and Public Affairs* 10: 283–345.

————. 1985. "Liberalism." In *A Matter of Principle*. Cambridge, MA: Harvard University Press: 181–204. Originally published in S. Hampshire, ed., *Public and Private Morality* (Cambridge: Cambridge University Press, 1978).

Erikson, R. 1990. "Descriptions of Inequality. The Swedish Approach to Welfare Research." In Nussbaum and Sen, 1990.

Erikson, R., E. Hansen, S. Ringen, and H. Uusitalo, eds. 1987. *The Scandinavian Model. Welfare States and Welfare Research*. London: M. E. Sharpe, Inc.

Foucault, M. 1984. *The History of Sexuality*, Vol. 2. Trans. R. Hurley. New York: Pantheon.

Galtung, J. 1980. "The Basic Needs Approach." In K. Lederer, ed., *Human Needs: A Contribution to the Current Debate*. Cambridge, MA: Oelgeshlager, Gunn, and Hain.

Gopalan, C. Forthcoming. "Undernutrition: Measurement and Implications." Paper prepared for the WIDER Conference on Poverty, Undernutrition, and Living Standards, Helsinki, July 1987. To appear in the Proceedings, ed. S. Osmani, Oxford: Clarendon Press.

Graubard, S. R., ed. 1986. *Norden: The Passion for Equality*. Oslo: Norwegian University Press. Original published in *Daedalus*.

Halperin, D. 1989. *One Hundred Years of Homosexuality and Other Essays on Greek Love*. New York: Routledge, Chapman and Hall.

Klein, M. 1975. *Love, Guilt, and Reparation and Other Works* 1921–1945. London.

————. 1984. *Envy, Gratitude, and Other Works* 1946–63. London.

Lutz, C. 1988. *Unnatural Emotions*. Chicago: University of Chicago Press.

MacIntyre, A. 1981. *After Virtue*. Notre Dame, Ind.: University of Notre Dame Press.

————. 1987. *Whose Justice? Which Rationality?* Notre Dame, Ind.: University of Notre Dame Press.

Marglin, S. 1974. "What Do Bosses Do? The Origins and Functions of Hierarchy in Capitalist Production," Part 1. *Review of Radical Political Economics* 6: 60–112.

Maritain, Jacques. 1943. *The Rights of Man and Natural Law*. New York: Charles Scribner's Sons.

Marx, K. (1844). *The Economic and Philosophical Manuscripts of 1844.* Trans. M. Milligan. In *The Marx-Engles Reader,* ed. R. C. Tucker, New York: 1978.

Newman, W. 1887. *Aristotle's Politics: Text and Commentary.* Oxford: Oxford University Press.

Nussbaum, M. 1976. "Consequences and Character in Sophocles' *Philoctetes.*" *Philosophy and Literature* 1: 25–53.

———.1980. "Shame, Separateness, and Political Unity: Aristotle's Criticism of Plato." In A. Rorty, ed., *Essays on Aristotle's Ethics.* Berkeley and Los Angeles: University of California Press, 395–435.

———. 1986. *The Fragility of Goodness: Luck and Ethics in Greek Tragedy and Philosophy.* Cambridge: Cambridge University Press.

——— .1986a. "Therapeutic Arguments: Epicurus and Aristotle." In M. Schofield and G. Striker, eds., *The Norms of Nature.* Cambridge: Cambridge University Press.

———.1987. "Undemocratic Vistas." A Review of Allan Bloom, *The Closing of the American Mind. The New York Review of Books:* November 5.

———.1988. "Nature, Function, and Capability: Aristotle on Political Distribution." *Oxford Studies in Ancient Philosophy,* Supplementary Volume: 145–183.

———.1988a. "Reply to David Charles." *Oxford Studies in Ancient Philosophy,* Supplementary Volume.

———. 1989. "Mortal Immortals: Lucretius on Death and the Voice of Nature." *Philosophy and Phenomenological Research:* December.

———.1990. *Love's Knowledege: Essays on Philosophy and Literature.* New York and Oxford: Oxford University Press and Clarendon Press.

———.1990a. "Non-Relative Virtues: An Aristotelian Approach." In Nussbaum and Sen, 1990. An earlier version published in *Midwest Studies in Philosophy,* 1988.

——— .1990b. "Reply to Onora O'Neill." In Nussbaum and Sen, 1990.

———.1990c. "Aristotle on Human Nature and the Foundations of Ethics." In J. Altham and R. Harrison, eds., a volume in honor of Bernard Williams. Cambridge: Cambridge University Press.

Nussbaum, M., and H. Putnam. 1992. "Changing Aristotle's Mind." In *Essays on Aristotle's* De Anima, ed. M. Nussbaum and A. Rorty. Oxford: Clarendon Press.

Nussbaum, M., and A. Sen. 1989. "Internal Criticism and Indian Rationalist Traditions." In M. Krausz, ed., *Relativism: Interpretation and Confrontation.* Notre Dame, Ind.: University of Notre Dame Press: 299–325.

Nussbaum, M., and A. Sen, eds. 1990. *The Quality of Life.* Oxford: Clarendon Press.

Okin, S. M. 1987. "Justice and Gender." *Philosophy and Public Affairs* 16: 42–72.

O'Neill, O. 1990. "Justice, Gender, and International Boundaries." In Nussbaum and Sen, 1990.

Putnam, H. 1981. *Reason, Truth, and History.* Cambridge: Cambridge University Press.

——— . 1987. *The Many Faces of Realism.* La Salle, Ill.: Open Court.

Raaflaub, K. 1985. *Die Entdeckung der Freiheit.*

Rawls, J. 1971. *A Theory of Justice.* Cambridge, MA: Harvard University Press.

——— . 1980. "Kantian Constructivism in Moral Theory: The Dewey Lectures 1980." *The Journal of Philosophy* 77: 515–72.

———. 1982. "Social Unity and Primary Goods." In A. Sen and B. Williams, eds., *Utilitarianism and Beyond*. Cambridge: Cambridge University Press: 159–86.

———. 1985. "Justice as Fairness: Political Not Metaphysical." *Philosophy and Public Affairs* 14: 223–51.

———. 1988. "The Priority of Right and Ideas of the Good." *Philosophy and Public Affairs* 17: 251–76.

———. Manuscript. "Reply to Sen." Now part of the revised Dewey Lectures.

Richardson, H. 1986. *Rational Deliberation of Ends*. Ph.D. diss., Harvard University.

de Sainte Croix, G. E. M. 1981. *The Class Struggle in the Ancient Greek World*. London: Duckworth.

Sen, A. 1980. "Equality of What?" In *Tanner Lectures on Human Values*, I, ed. S. McMurrin. Cambridge: Cambridge University Press. Repr. in Sen (1982).

———. 1982. *Choice, Welfare, and Measurement*. Oxford: Basil Blackwell.

———. 1984. *Resources, Value, and Development*. Oxford: Basil Blackwell.

———. 1985. *Commodities and Capabilities*. North-Holland.

———. 1987. *The Standard of Living*. Tanner Lectures on Human Values 1985, ed. G. Hawthorne. Cambridge: Cambridge University Press.

———. Manuscript. *Inequality Reexamined*.

Taylor, C. 1989. *Sources of the Self: The Making of Modern Identity*. Cambridge, MA: Harvard University Press.

———. 1990. "Explanation and Practical Reason." In Nussbaum and Sen, 1990.

Vogel, Joachim, et al. 1988. *Inequality in Sweden: Trends and Current Situation*. Stockholm.

Wiggins, D. 1975. "Deliberation and Practical Reason." *Proceedings of the Aristotelian Society:* 29–51. Repr. in Wiggins, *Needs, Values and Truth*, Oxford: Blackwell, 1987.

———. 1980. *Sameness and Substance*. Oxford: Basil Blackwell.

Williams, B. 1985. *Ethics and the Limits of Philosophy*. Cambridge, MA: Harvard University Press.

———. 1985a. "Hylomorphism." *Oxford Studies in Ancient Philosophy* 4: 189–199.

———. 1987. Comments on Sen, "The Standard of Living." In Sen, 1987.

Wollheim, R. 1986. *The Thread of Life*. Cambridge, MA: Harvard University Press.

CHAPTER THREE

Justice and the Dilemma of Moral Virtue in Aristotle's *Nicomachean Ethics*

SUSAN D. COLLINS

The current revival of Aristotle's political thought might seem to constitute a serious, even revolutionary challenge to liberalism, a tradition that has historically viewed Aristotle and Aristotelianism with no little suspicion. But in a remarkable effort to heal the breach between liberal thought and the tradition it supplanted, those who champion Aristotle today almost unfailingly present him as a friend and not a foe or even foreigner.[1] At the very least, Aristotle's present-day students argue that his thought sparks renewed awareness of the foundations and supports of liberal politics, as well as of its proper aims, because it challenges us to reconsider two matters that liberalism has too strictly ruled out of court: virtue and the human good or flourishing (*eudaimonia*).[2] The Aristotelian focus on virtue and human flourishing compels us to reconsider the foundations and aims of liberalism by asking whether there are virtues necessarily connected with the support of the liberal order, and whether liberal political life ought to foster the qualities and goods constituent of human flourishing. By illuminating matters of such fundamental importance, the Aristotelian perspective has much to contribute to our political education.

Notwithstanding the fact that neo-Aristotelians obviously follow Aristotle in focusing on virtue and the human good, the aim of this essay is to show that there is in Aristotle's thought a deeper and more radical investigation of these matters than they typically allow. In particular, I will argue that in his account of justice as a virtue in Book V of the *Nicomachean Ethics*, Aristotle presents a dilemma at the heart of moral virtue and that clarity about this dilemma is crucial for understanding the relation between virtue and human flourishing. Although a preoccupation with the foundation for justice is pervasive in current political theory, justice is a virtue about which even neo-Aristotelians have comparatively little to say.[3] This neglect is surprising especially on the part of neo-Aristotelians since justice is the culmination of Aristotle's investigation of the particular moral virtues and the clearest point of intersection between virtue as a quality of civic devotion and as a constituent of human flourishing.

A prefatory statement concerning this intersection and its significance in Aristotle's account of moral virtue is in order. Aristotle and his present-day students agree that virtue is necessary for both the support of any political order and human flourishing. Accordingly, they may be said to agree that virtue has dual roots. In their effort to address the problems of liberalism, however, neo-Aristotelians tend to emphasize one or the other of these roots, and thus either the qualities needed to support the liberal order—the civic or "liberal" virtues—or the qualities belonging to human flourishing that liberalism should foster. Aristotle, by contrast, treats the relation between the two roots of virtue more systematically and comprehensively. He shows, for example, how the requirements of the political order and those of human flourishing temporally and logically intersect, how the education of character is of significance for the happiness of both the community and the individual, and how virtue supports and is supported by law. In his account of justice in the *Nicomachean Ethics*, Aristotle presents most fully the intersection between our virtue as citizens and as flourishing human beings. Both general justice (the sum of the virtues in one) and particular justice (the characteristic with respect to gain that is a part of general justice) are presented as virtues that at one and the same time constitute our perfection simply and entail "the use of virtue with a view to the good of another."[4] Justice is like the other virtues in being a characteristic but "alone among the virtues" in being directed toward another and, in the broadest sense, the common good. In this way, justice promises to be a kind of perfect good: good for the one who is virtuous and for the community with a view to which the virtuous person acts. To speak from moral virtue's own perspective, justice is a peak and a completion because it is the most explicit and fullest expression of moral virtue's promise to be both noble and good (cf. 1099a22–31).

But Aristotle's subsequent examination of justice as a virtue leads us to question whether this promise can be fulfilled since the intersection in justice between virtue as devotion to the community and as human flourishing proves to involve a crucial dilemma. The obvious difficulty, of course, is that justice is different in different political orders or regimes and the requirements of justice can vary depending on the circumstances, whereas, as Aristotle himself would insist, human flourishing is a single thing. Yet the obvious difficulty is not in fact the most troubling one from moral virtue's own perspective, since this perspective can accommodate the thought that some circumstances are better for our flourishing than others (cf. Berkowitz 1999, 10–11; T. Smith 1999, 628–33, cf. 633–34; Yack 1993, 107–108, 262, 268). The most troubling difficulty, rather, is that even in the best case—in the best community under the best circumstances—justice may require concessions of moral virtue that on its own terms moral virtue can neither refuse nor accept.[5] As the use of virtue for the sake of the common good, justice is one completion and peak of moral virtue, and the end toward which it is directed may properly be said to govern the activity of moral virtue itself. Strictly speaking, however, moral virtue is not defined in terms of the common good—it is, rather, an end and a good in itself, which is chosen for its own sake and as the core of human flourishing. The question at hand, then, is whether in its orientation toward the common good, justice also fully comprehends moral virtue as a good in itself, or whether, as I will argue, in justice, moral virtue is confronted with a dilemma that it cannot on its own resolve. A sign that there exists a potential difficulty is suggested by Aristotle's identification of another complete virtue, magnanimity, which comprises all the virtues and each to the greatest degree, and which is the basis of the correct self-regard. But, as I will seek to show, the dilemma of moral virtue is most fully laid out in the discussion of justice itself.

In the first part of the essay, I provide an overview of how the questions of virtue and the human good have been treated by neo-Aristotelians and then argue that Aristotle's more thorough account sheds light on aspects of these questions that neo-Aristotelian treatments tend to obscure. In the second part, I follow Aristotle's discussion of general and particular justice to show how, even as he encourages our admiration of justice, he lays out the dilemma I have just sketched. By then concluding with a consideration of the significance of this dilemma, for Aristotle and for us, I hope to place in a new light the relation of his thought to the problems of liberalism. Although Aristotle is as eager as his students today are to bring virtue and the human good to the attention of politicians and political thinkers, his clarity about the relation between virtue's dual roots leads to a profound moderation in his hopes for politics. This moderation is born not of skepticism about the existence of a human good. It comes, rather, from long reflection on the possibility that virtue could constitute that good—a reflection that may represent Aristotle's deepest challenge to liberalism but also his most generous gift.

VIRTUE AND THE HUMAN GOOD IN NEO-ARISTOTELIANISM

Since virtue has two roots, it is possible to consider it from two vantage points or as an answer to two separate questions: What are the qualities needed for the support and stability of the political community? What are the qualities that constitute human flourishing? Against the "polemically charged distortions of Aristotle" in the early modern thinkers, as well as the overly perfectionist versions of his thought in contemporary scholarship, Peter Berkowitz insists that "from an Aristotelian perspective, the student of politics must take into account the virtues relative to the maintenance of the specific regime in question as well as the virtues relative to a human being's final end or perfection" (Berkowitz 1999, 11; see also p. 172). An Aristotelian, that is, is as much concerned with the maintenance of the regime in question as he or she may be with the idea of human flourishing. Because regimes differ, there will be "a specific set of virtues that are relative to the regime's particular needs and goals" (1999, 10). By this account, one need not pronounce on the human good as such when seeking to determine those qualities of character that are supportive of the institutions and practices of the political order. "However the question of human perfection is decided," Berkowitz observes, "no regime can long survive unless qualities of mind and character that support its specific principles and purposes and counteract its unwise tendencies are deliberately cultivated and regularly exercised" (1999, 12).

A more expansive but equally political way to conceive of the matter is to argue, as does William Galston, that every political community promotes and must defend an idea of the human good specific to its own regime. The argument undergirding this position is that liberalism itself is not neutral with respect to the good. Galston writes, "to pursue its understanding of justice and the human good, liberal societies have over time developed their characteristic institutions and practices: representative governments, diverse societies, market economies, zones of private action." Certain virtues are called forth by this good because "sustaining these institutions and practices, in turn, requires of liberal citizens specific excellences and character traits: the liberal virtues" (Galston 1991, 18).[6] Among the many recent works to give this view weight across ideological boundaries has been John Rawls's *Political Liberalism*, in which he lays out the view that at least a "thin theory of the good" is necessary for the support of liberal institutions and practices. Thus, "even though political liberalism seeks common ground and is neutral in its aim," Rawls suggests, "it is important to emphasize that it may still affirm the superiority of certain forms of moral character and encourage certain moral virtues" (Rawls 1993, 194; cf. Berkowitz 1999, 24–27). Liberalism may therefore promote "the virtues of fair social cooperation such as the virtues of civility and tolerance, or reasonableness and the sense of fairness" and the ideal that is affirmed in connection with the political virtues "characterize the ideal of a good citizen of a democratic state" (Rawls 1993, 194–95).

To be sure, arguments abound over how extensive or "thick" the liberal idea of the good is—how overarching an ideal and way of life, and so how exclusive of other ways of life. Nevertheless, there remains substantial agreement that certain "liberal virtues" are necessary to support "liberal purposes" (Galston 1991, 216).[7] It is important to note, however, that whether we bracket the question of the human good for the purposes of a political consideration of virtue, as Berkowitz suggests, or we argue with Galston that there is an ideal of the good that is a liberal ideal, the specification of the virtues is tied in both cases to the regime in question.[8] The political frame—the concern for the support of the regime—is primary, and thus virtue is first and foremost political virtue. In this sense, the virtues are instrumentally valuable rather than intrinsically so. The "challenge," as Galston observes, "is to give an account of individual virtue that supports rather than undermines liberal institutions and the capacious tolerance that gives liberal society its special attraction" (Galston 1991, 216). Yet, Galston also acknowledges, "the fact (if it is a fact) that the instrumental virtues are socially functional does not mean that they are individually advantageous" (1991, 220). Included among such virtues are some that would be fundamental to every political order: for example, courage as the willingness to defend one's country at the risk of one's life, loyalty to the core principles of the regime, and lawabidingness.[9] But depending on how neo-Aristotelians conceive of liberal politics, they enumerate a range of other virtues from familial piety to autonomy and self-reflectiveness. This range reflects differences in views about what the supports of liberalism are and what "goods" are inherent in liberal practices.[10]

Even for those who would focus on a strictly political and hence instrumental understanding of virtue, however, the question inevitably arises whether it is possible to leave the matter here. As Berkowitz observes, "it needs to be acknowledged that insofar as the link between the lesser virtues, which are exercised as a means to various ends, and the higher virtues or the virtues of human excellence, which are exercised for their own sake, is severed, virtue threatens to become a mercenary undertaking" (Berkowitz 1999, 172; see also Yack 1991, ch. 9; cf. Rawls 1993, 195). There are two ways to formulate the difficulty Berkowitz points to, though the first implies the second. The first formulation asks "whether there is a conception of the virtuous or excellent individual *linked intrinsically to liberal theory* and seen as valuable, not instrumentally, but for its own sake" (Galston 1991, 229, my emphasis). Do the virtues necessary for the support of the regime—for example, civility, tolerance, open-mindedness, reflectiveness—also constitute a distinctively liberal conception of the good human being, and is there a conception of the best way of life connected with liberalism's practices and educative forces?[11] This suggestion, however, only points to the second formulation of the problem: If there are virtues and a way of life promoted and fostered by liberal politics, do these constitute a truly flourishing life— a life judged, that is, by the standard of human flourishing and not by that of any specific regime? Indeed, among those neo-Aristotelians who emphasize the perfectionist rather than the strictly political aspects of Aristotle's thought, the primary question for virtue is not what qualities support the regime and are distinctively liberal virtues, but what qualities constitute human flourishing simply.

In its seeking to uncover a non-relative ground for human flourishing and thereby for the good community, this perspective is openly evaluative.[12] Accordingly, it proceeds by determining those features of the human good for which the good community ought to be responsible. Taking her lead from Aristotle, Martha Nussbaum observes, "it is obvious that he was not only a defender of an ethical theory based on the virtues, but also the defender of a single objective account of the human good, or human flourishing. This account is supposed to be objective in the sense that it is justifiable . . . from features of humanness that lie beneath all local traditions and are there to be seen whether or not they are in fact recognized in local traditions" (Nussbaum 1988, 33).[13] There is typically agreement among neo-Aristotelians that the study of political life has to begin from the sphere of the local, namely "common opinion" and tradition. The most important task of this study for those who emphasize the perfectionist aspects of Aristotle's thought, however, is to evaluate political life from the standpoint of the good—the flourishing, development, perfection, lower and higher needs or activities—of human beings as such.

From this standpoint, the virtues are properly understood not as the qualities that support the regime, but as "precisely those qualities the possession of which will enable an individual to achieve *eudaimonia*, and the lack of which will frustrate his movements toward that *telos*" (MacIntyre 1984, 137). The political task of institutions and education, accordingly, is to foster movement toward our *telos*, such that, as Galston observes, "a good community provides a way of life in which each individual realizes the human good to the greatest extent possible for that individual" (Galston 1980, 192).[14] This Aristotelian perspective on politics is concerned with the political community as a vehicle of human flourishing, and much less concerned about it in its own right. The good community fosters the virtues as the constituents of human flourishing, and acts, therefore, not with a view to its own advantage strictly speaking but with a view to the benefit of its members.

As the evidence they adduce from Aristotle's thought indicates, the dual concerns that "political" and "perfectionist" neo-Aristotelians bring to the questions of virtue and the human good—the support of the political order, on the one hand, and human flourishing, on the other—clearly draw sustenance from Aristotle's own approach. Yet in treating these two concerns as well as their intersection, Aristotle illuminates possibilities and difficulties that neo-Aristotelians tend to overlook. In particular, Aristotle confronts in a full and systematic way the questions on either side of virtue's coin. If the virtues required by the community are not in some fundamental sense good for the person who possesses them, why ought any particular individual choose to possess and act in accord with them? If the virtues of human flourishing are harmful to the community, why would the community be interested, or why ought it to be compelled to inculcate them? Aristotle confronts these questions because he never loses sight of virtue's dual roots, and indeed, his account of moral virtue presents itself as a reconciliation of the separate concerns connected with these two roots.

VIRTUE AND THE HUMAN GOOD IN ARISTOTLE

In the first book of the *Nicomachean Ethics,* Aristotle proposes that the human good is the final end in the realm of action (*praxis*) in accord with which we order all our actions. If there is such an end, we seek knowledge of it so that we may have the right "target" (*scopos*) to aim at (1094a18–24).[15] In answer to the question of which science or capacity we ought to turn to for this knowledge, Aristotle concludes that politics or the political art is the most authoritative and architectonic: "Since it uses the other sciences, and, further, legislates what people ought to do and refrain from doing, its end encompasses all the rest and would thus be the human good" (1094b4–7). Of course, it does not follow from the fact that politics is the "authoritative" voice with respect to the human good that it is the correct or true voice, and Aristotle's observation is intended as an observation of fact and not a prescription. He speaks here to the primacy of the political community in shaping our understanding of the good, a primacy which needs to be acknowledged even if it is later brought into question. This connection of the good to the political community is the reason why he will insist that the investigation of the good is "a kind of political investigation" (1094b10–11).

Nevertheless, Aristotle does not then undertake to discover the good by way of an examination of politics in the obvious sense or the good of the *polis* on its own terms. He takes his bearings first from what most people—the "many" and the "refined"—call the human good, which is happiness. Moreover, allowing for some disagreement about what happiness is, Aristotle is nonetheless able to point to a consensus that "being happy" is the same as "living well" and "acting well" (1095a17–20). The good life and good action at its core, then, become the focus of the investigation of the *Ethics*.[16] The political community may be primary in its authoritativeness, but it is not authoritative simply. That there is disagreement about what the good or happiness is and that the good can become an object of inquiry are enough to remind us of this fact. Aristotle thus makes us aware of the political character of the inquiry at the same time as he indicates that the question of the good cannot be settled on the basis of political authority alone.

Now, it is possible to bracket the many complications and digressions of Book I to note a few of its tentative conclusions. Since happiness requires good action (*praxis*), it entails the perfection and activity of that part of the soul, our "desiring and longing part," from which action proceeds (1102b28–31). The perfection connected with action is moral virtue, which disposes our desires and longings in conformity with reason and issues in "noble and good" deeds (cf. 1139a21–27, 1098a12–18, 1099a22–31). Since to live well is to act well, and to act well is to do so in conformity with moral virtue, moral virtue is clearly central to our happiness or flourishing. But because our desires and longings are not rational in themselves and so must be made "obedient" to reason, moral virtue requires education and training (1102b31–1103a2). This education is equally a concern of the political community and, indeed, originally defined by its authoritative voice: the "skilled politician" (*politikos*) is concerned with virtue above all because "he wishes to make the citizens good and obedient to the laws" (1102a7–10). Moral virtue is the sphere, then, in which the education necessary for the good of the community and that of the individual intersect. Or, to put this another way, we require moral virtue if we are to come to the perfection of our nature, and the legislator cannot be indifferent to the character of that perfection.

For this reason, the virtues must have the twofold character of being good for the community and for the one who possesses them. In the best case, the aim of the education to virtue will be to create good citizens who are also flourishing human beings. It is this conclusion or proposition that Aristotle takes into Book II of the *Ethics* and the discussion of moral virtue proper: good action issues from the perfection of our nature, which is a concern of both the political community and the individual, and the noble and good actions that constitute our flourishing as human beings also benefit (or surely do not harm) the community in which we live. To use Aristotle's famous phrase, we are "political animals" because the flourishing of human nature requires the community and law in both a rudimentary and a high sense. This, at least, is the promise of moral virtue that undergirds Aristotle's investigation and is given its fullest expression in his discussion of justice.

JUSTICE AS A CHARACTERISTIC

In the introduction to Book V of the *Nicomachean Ethics*, Aristotle observes that "everyone means by justice the sort of characteristic [*hexis*] on the basis of which people are made able [or fit] to do just things, act justly, and wish just things" (1129a3–11). He proposes that the investigation of justice take this opinion as its foundation, saying that in this way the investigation will follow the method used in the examination of the other virtues. Among other things, this method involved starting from common opinions about virtue with a view to clarifying them.[17] There are other matters connected with the investigation of justice, namely "the sort of actions with which justice and injustice are concerned, the sort of mean justice is, and the extremes of which the just is a mean" (1129a4–5). In taking our bearings from Aristotle, however, we must address these matters first within the context of justice as a characteristic or virtue.

The immediate significance of this starting point is indicated by Aristotle's corollary observations. Unlike capacities and sciences, characteristics do not apply to opposite things: medicine, for example, applies to both health and disease, and can produce either, whereas health produces only healthy acts. As characteristics, the virtues pertain only to their like—just as health produces only healthy actions, so the virtues produce only virtuous actions. In this way too, Aristotle's introductory emphasis on justice as a virtue is continuous with his treatment of the other moral virtues. Each of the virtues is a particular characteristic that makes its possessor disposed to act well, and this disposition and the good action issuing from it constitute health from the point of view of human flourishing.

It is also true, however, that justice is not in every way like the other virtues. As Aristotle noted when he introduced the particular virtues and now recalls, justice has more than one meaning (cf. 1108b6–9). To be more precise, the term "justice" is used in two different senses, though these are so close in meaning that the difference is not always noticed. On the one hand, Aristotle explains, "the lawbreaker is thought to be unjust," but so too is "the one who takes more than his share [or is grasping, *pleonektēs*] and is unfair [lit. unequal, *anisos*]" (1129a32–34). The "just," then, is thought of both as the lawful and as the fair, and the unjust, as the unlawful and unfair (1129a34–b1). Aristotle classifies these two meanings of justice—the lawful and the fair (or equal)—under the respective headings of general and particular justice.

In his elaboration of these two meanings of justice, Aristotle discusses first general justice, explaining its connection to law and its status as complete virtue, and second, particular justice as a characteristic and a part of general justice that accords with two forms of equalities, distributive and commutative. He concludes with a brief consideration of justice as reciprocity. These three discussions lay the ground for understanding how justice is a characteristic and how it presents a dilemma for moral virtue.

Before turning to the examination of general justice, however, Aristotle digresses briefly. His ostensible aim is to clarify what it is that those who are called "grasping" seek to obtain for themselves. They seek the "good things simply," which are the goods that are "subject to fortune" and that "human beings pray for and pursue" (1129b1–6). People who are grasping desire a greater share of these goods than they ought to have, and for this reason, they are considered unfair. Yet, Aristotle also interjects at this point, human beings typically err in their pursuit of the good, because the good things simply are "not always good for some people" (1129b3–4). What people ought to pray for, he advises, is that they will be the sort of human beings for whom the simply good things will actually be good, and they ought to choose the things that are good for themselves (1129b5–6). Aristotle thus prefaces his discussion of general and particular justice with a statement not only of the object of human grasping but of the standard by which one can judge how much and which of the good things one ought to pursue: the true benefit or harm to oneself. Whether this standard, which is obviously relevant to particular justice, is also consistent with the requirements of justice will eventually have to be clarified.

General Justice

Aristotle introduces his consideration of general justice by drawing out the connection between justice and law. On the basis of the definition of the unjust person as a "lawbreaker," he notes that "it is clear that all the lawful things are somehow just." They are lawful, that is, "in having been laid down by the lawgiver, and each of the lawful things we assert to be just (1129b11–14). The law is comprehensive in scope and aim: it "make[s] pronouncements on everything," and its aim is the common good—"the advantage for all in common or for the best or for those who hold power in accord with virtue or in some other such way" (1129b14–17). That the law as justice is connected with its securing of the common advantage is underlined by Aristotle's further conclusion that "in one sense, we call just those things that produce and preserve happiness and its parts for the political community" (1129b17–19). Indeed, the law's end entails its broad scope. In order to secure the common advantage and thus the happiness of the political community, the law commands the deeds of virtue and forbids acts that are bad or wicked (cf. 1138a5–7). In requiring that one not break the ranks in battle or flee or throw away one's weapons, for example, the law commands courage; in prohibiting adultery or outrage, moderation; and in forbidding the striking or slandering of another, gentleness (1129b19–24). This justice— the laws as they concern virtue and vice and are directed at the general advantage—is what Aristotle now calls "complete virtue" (1129b25–26).

The simplest sense in which justice as the lawful is complete virtue is that it comprises all the virtues. Quoting the proverb, Aristotle observes that "in justice, every virtue is summed up in one" (1129b29–30). Yet he then amends the proverb: justice is not complete virtue simply but complete as the sum of the virtues "directed toward another" (1129b26–27). Justice is thus identical with the "use (*chrēsis*) of complete virtue," and the person who is just in the complete sense "is able to use virtue with a view to another, and not only with a view to himself" (1129b32–33). The orientation of justice "toward another" constitutes its unique power, since many people are able to practice virtue in their own affairs but not in relation to another. For this reason, Aristotle also observes, "justice *alone* of the virtues is thought to be the good of another, because justice is directed toward another, for it does what is advantageous for another" (1130a3–5, my emphasis).

The tenor of Aristotle's account of general justice becomes clearer in light of the attack on justice to which this last statement alludes: the attack by the sophist Thrasymachus in Plato's *Republic*. Thrasymachus attaches blame to justice understood as the advantage of another, arguing that justice is simply the advantage of the stronger: the ruling group which establishes laws for its own advantage and then declares that it is just for the ruled to obey them (*Republic* 338c–339a). Aristotle, by contrast, celebrates the greatness of justice understood as "another's good." In its orientation toward others, justice as a virtue is essential both to citizenship and, in the most complete respect, to ruling since action in relation to the community as a whole is inherent in ruling. Aristotle thus recalls Bias's saying that "ruling will show the man [*anēr*]" (1130a1–2); it will show the man in the best sense as one who is "a guardian of the just" and not, as Thrasymachus recommends, as a tyrant (1134b1–8).[18] Far from condemning justice as the advantage of another, then, Aristotle highlights the praise that accrues to it for this very reason. As he reports, "justice is often thought to be the greatest (*kratistē*) of the virtues, and more wonderful than the evening or morning star" (1129b27–29). In this same spirit, Aristotle himself distinguishes between the best and worst human beings in a manner heavily weighted on the side of justice: "the one who uses wickedness both toward himself and toward his friends is the worst, but the best is the one who uses virtue not toward himself but toward another, for this is a difficult task" (1130a5–8). By identifying the best of actions with definitively just acts at the same time as he singles out the difficulty of such acts, Aristotle captures a side of justice that Thrasymachus's attack obscures. Justice does indeed require us to act with a view to another's good, and this is exactly why it is admired.

The general case with regard to justice may be stated in the following way. Citizenship in the community means that any action, including a virtuous action, has a dual aspect: it can be understood from the point of view either of one's own or another's good. In constituting the use of all the virtues with a view to another, general justice pertains primarily to the second aspect of virtuous action. By comparison, Aristotle has already identified another completion and peak of moral virtue connected primarily with the first aspect: Magnanimity, too, is the sum of the virtues, for it consists in the possession of every virtue to the greatest degree. Because of his perfection in virtue, the one who possesses magnanimity is worthy of honor and appropriately regards himself as so worthy. Magnanimity accordingly issues in self-honoring or pride, and in the few great actions proper to such a peak of virtue (1123b15–1124a4). Its completeness, in other words, does not depend on an orientation toward the good of another. On the basis of this account alone, however, it seems possible also to argue that justice represents the higher of the two peaks of moral virtue because it comprises both human perfection—all the virtues summed up in one—and this perfection turned toward the good of another. This is, indeed, the suggestion we are left with at the conclusion of the account of general justice. Justice is the "greatest of the virtues," "more wonderful than the evening or morning star," and the best human being is "the one who uses virtue not toward himself but toward another." General justice as complete virtue, it might be said, constitutes both our good and another's good. As Aristotle concludes, virtue and justice are the same, but "in their being [*to einai*]," they differ: in being in relation to another, it [the characteristic] is justice, but in being a certain characteristic simply, virtue (1130a10–13).[19]

Particular Justice

If general justice thus constitutes virtue entire, there is still another justice that belongs to it as part to whole. "Particular justice" is connected with the second sense of justice as "fairness." The unjust human being is unfair in "grasping" for more of the good things than is his or her share; the one who is just is disposed to take only what is fair or equal. When Aristotle turns to the discussion of particular justice, however, his first order of business is to prove that there is in fact a justice of this kind—one which is like the other virtues in being a characteristic and a part of general justice. Although his very efforts in this direction suggest that there may be room for doubt, he offers several pieces of evidence.

First, there is a "sign" that a particular vice exists that we identify specifically with graspingness and call injustice. A person can do an injustice as a result of a certain vice but not because he or she is "grasping." To use Aristotle's examples, it may be cowardice that causes a person to run away in the face of danger; anger that leads one to speak harshly; or stinginess that makes one begrudge financial help. Someone who is simply grasping, who wants more of the good things without consideration for others, acts not out of any or all of these particular vices but as the result of a vice we blame as injustice (1130a16–19). Indeed, the same wrongful act can issue from different vices: "one person may commit adultery for the sake of gain, winning this above all, whereas another does so out of desire, having to pay and incurring a loss" (1130a24–25). While the latter individual would appear to be licentious rather than unjust, the former would appear to be unjust but not licentious. Finally, we attribute all other injustices to particular vices—adultery to licentiousness; forsaking one's comrades in the line to cowardice; assaulting another to anger (1130a28–32). We attribute the desire to make a gain, however, to no other vice than injustice. The connection of injustice with the desire for gain, Aristotle thus insists, "makes it manifest that there is a certain injustice besides the whole of it, this other being a part" (1130a32–33).

Having made this case for particular justice as a characteristic, Aristotle can then clarify its relation to complete justice. Acknowledging that general and particular justice share the same name, he observes that they both also "possess their power in being in relation to another" (1130b1–2). General justice, however, pertains to "everything that is the concern of a serious person"—all the lawful things—whereas particular justice consists in the proper disposition toward the goods (money, honor, and security) of another (1130a32–b5). Particular justice stands to general justice as part to whole, then, in being the characteristic that pertains to the desire for gain. The just human being in this sense is disposed only to take what is fair or equal in relation to another's goods, the source of injustice being "the pleasure that comes from gain" (1130b4).

Aristotle's clarification of the relation between particular and general justice, however, immediately raises another question: If particular justice disposes a person to take only his or her equal share of the goods that human beings "pray for and pursue," what is this "equality" in accord with which the just human being is correctly disposed? The formal answer to this question is offered in Aristotle's discussion of the two forms of particular justice: distributive and commutative (or corrective) justice. Distributive justice is concerned with "equality" in the distribution of the common goods understood as "honor, money, or any of the good things of which there is a part for those who share in the regime [*politeia*]" (1130b30–32). Commutative justice pertains to exchanges or agreements and has the task of restoring equality when there has occurred an unfair loss and gain (1130b32). The question of the equal in particular justice, moreover, is linked with the question of justice as a mean. The fact that what is just corresponds to a certain equality, Aristotle observes, implies that there is a "more and a less" in relation to which it stands. Justice is a mean, then, with respect to these inequalities (1131a10–15). Since particular justice in both its distributive and commutative forms must determine the equality in relation to at least two persons, it involves at a minimum four terms: the shares of the good to be allotted and the persons among whom these shares are to be distributed (1131a15–20). Distributive and commutative justice, therefore, establish the mean with respect to the assignment of shares among individuals. Aristotle underlines the significance of justice in this sense by noting that "fights and accusations arise when those who are unequal possess and are assigned equal [shares], and when those who are equal possess and are assigned unequal [shares]" (1131a22–24).

Distributive justice establishes the mean in the distribution of the common goods according to the merit of the parties among whom the distribution is to be made. Because it establishes this mean in accord with merit, distributive justice must measure all the terms of the equation: the shares of the good to be distributed and the merit of the parties. It thus establishes the mean using a geometric proportion, and it accords with a principle with which "everyone" agrees: "the just in distributions ought to be in accord with a certain desert" (1131a25–26). The real problem is that people argue about what constitutes desert—"democrats say it is freedom; oligarchs, wealth; others, noble birth; aristocrats, virtue" (1131a26–29). But while Aristotle acknowledges this dispute, he leaves its resolution to his *Politics* (cf. *Politics* 1280a7ff.). It is apparently sufficient for the purposes of the *Ethics* simply to outline the formal principle undergirding distributive justice as a mean: Justice obtains when the distribution of goods accords with desert, and injustice when people possess and are assigned more or less of these goods than they merit.

Commutative justice pertains to the correction or rectification of harms in exchanges and agreements, both voluntary and involuntary (1130b33–1131a1). Voluntary transactions include all open exchanges and agreements, such as selling, buying, renting, or lending; involuntary transactions include anything covert such as theft, adultery, even assassination, or anything violent, such as assault, kidnapping, or murder. As a correction in cases where a harm or a loss has occurred, commutative justice seeks to restore the parties involved to the correct mean by imposing a penalty (or punishment, *zēmia*) on the wrongdoer (1131b32–1132a18).[20] Commutative justice assumes distributive justice since it accepts as just the original standard for the distribution of goods—money, honor, or security—and seeks only to rectify the loss or harm caused by an injustice in the case of exchanges and agreements. Because its task is simply this rectification, commutative justice is in principle blind to the differences between parties (but cf. 1132b28–30), and it therefore establishes the mean in accord with an arithmetic rather than geometric proportion.

The mean that is justice in the particular sense, then, accords with the equalities established by distributive and commutative justice. That this answer is a formal one is evidenced most clearly by the dispute over the question of merit in distributive justice.[21] Even though Aristotle does not resolve this dispute, his acknowledgment of it points to the primacy not only of distributive justice but more importantly of the regime (*politeia*) in establishing the mean in particular justice (cf. 1130b30–32). The regime is primary for particular justice in being the defining principle of the *polis:* the distribution of offices that is determined by the authoritative element of the city and by the end for the sake of which this element rules (*Politics* 1278b10–15, 1279a25–1279b10). Since all distributions and all law more generally are thus derivative of the regime, the mean or equality in accord with which one is just is relative to the regime of which one is citizen or subject.

Reciprocity, the Regime, and Justice as a Virtue

The significance of this connection between the regime and the mean for the question of justice as a virtue begins to become clear in Aristotle's discussion of reciprocity. Here Aristotle argues against the "Pythagorean" view that simple reciprocity—suffering what one has done to another—is justice. Nevertheless, he also acknowledges, a certain proportionate reciprocity is necessary if human beings are to come together in a political association; there must be, in other words, mutual exchange. This necessity of "exchange" applies to both evils and goods, since if people cannot requite evil for evil, they are regarded as slaves, and without an exchange of goods, there is no community (1132b31–1133a2). The regime thus figures in this most rudimentary sense: If the community as a community is to exist, there must be mutual exchange among free individuals, which requires in the first place equality in terms of a proportion among individuals composing the community. Indeed, this equality, however it is finally defined, is the very ground of law. As Aristotle will emphasize in his consideration of political justice, political justice exists in law, and law is natural only among those "for whom there is equality in ruling and being ruled" (1134b14–15).[22]

Once he has clarified the foundation of the political community in proportionate reciprocity, Aristotle brings the discussion of justice as a virtue to its conclusion. It is now clear, he claims, "that just action is a mean between doing injustice and suffering injustice, for the former is to get more and the latter to get less [than one's share]" (1133b30–32). On this score, however, Aristotle must acknowledge how justice as a mean is unlike the other virtues: it is not a mean with respect to two vices since suffering injustice is hardly a vice. Rather, justice "belongs to a mean" (1133b32–1134a1). It "belongs to a mean" because it is determined by the equality established by law in accord with the correct proportion, and the extremes with respect to which it stands are taking more than the established equality and receiving less. A person in whom the virtue of justice exists, then, is one whose "choice accords with the just" such that "in distributing between himself and another, or between two others, he does not assign more of the choiceworthy to himself and less to his neighbor, or the reverse of harm, but assigns equal shares in accord with proportion" (1134a1–6). The unjust human being, by contrast, seeks to secure "an excess of the simply beneficial and a deficiency of the harmful" (1139a9–11). As a characteristic and a part of general justice, then, particular justice disposes a person to abide by the equality established in law with a view to the common advantage. The law as law accords with the equality consistent with the regime and aims at the common advantage of those who "share in the regime."

THE DILEMMA OF MORAL VIRTUE

In light of the conclusion that the just choice accords with the mean established by law and more fundamentally the regime, we may now ask about the status of particular justice with respect to the standard for choice that Aristotle articulated in his preface to general and particular justice. This standard, as we saw, was the good in the best sense, the true benefit or harm to oneself. The good in this sense is not what most human beings pray for and pursue; as it was defined by Aristotle, rather, the true human good is the possession of good character. One must choose what is good for oneself in order to become "the sort of human being for whom the good things simply are also good for one" (1129b5–6). According to this standard, then, one ought to take of the good things those that are necessary for one's flourishing. But from the point of view of the law, the requirements of the good—taking what is needful for one's flourishing—would inevitably entail injustice. For the law must meet another standard: it must care for the common advantage and therefore require that we abide by the mean established by distributive and commutative justice for the sake of the common advantage. Justice accords with human flourishing or the good order of the soul, then, only inasmuch as that order preserves or contributes to the common good. By this account, however, we may start to wonder how, from the point of view of moral virtue itself, justice is a virtue and in what sense we are bound by its requirements.

One resolution of the problem would appear to be the suggestion Aristotle offered in his discussion of particular justice. Justice is the perfection that pertains to the desire for gain. To choose in accord with the just and the law, therefore, is to act in accord with the characteristic that constitutes the healthy disposition with respect to the desire for gain. In being this disposition, justice itself is our true good or flourishing. But the difficulty here is one Aristotle pointed to when he indicated that there may be some doubt concerning justice as a characteristic. For in the course of providing evidence that there is a characteristic we identify with particular justice, Aristotle reminded us that there are other characteristics pertaining to the desire for gain. The most obvious of these is liberality (cf. 1130a16–19). If particular injustice is to be identified with action for the sake of gain and due to the pleasure that comes from gain, then it is difficult to distinguish injustice from the vice Aristotle has identified as stinginess and also associated with the desire for gain (1121b31–1122a3, 1122a7–13, cf. 1122a3–7). One important difference between stinginess and injustice would appear to be that stinginess is directed solely toward money while injustice is directed toward all the goods human beings pray for and pursue. On the other hand, Aristotle has also identified magnanimity and courage as the specific virtues pertaining to the other goods, honor and security, that he associates with particular injustice. In light of these other virtues, then, how can it be said that justice as a virtue constitutes the perfection pertaining to gain?

One way to address this question is to recur to the view suggested by the discussion of complete justice, and to say that as a part of complete justice, particular justice constitutes the proper mean pertaining to gain in relation to the common good. This is one reason why Aristotle paused in his discussion of particular justice to reiterate its relation to complete justice (1130b10–13). For particular justice as the "equal" is a part of the lawful, and the aim of the laws is to "produce and preserve happiness and its parts for the political community" (1129b17–19). Particular justice as a virtue is the perfection with respect to gain, then, that has as its aim the common good of the political association. Yet, this solution to the question of justice's status as a characteristic is again problematic precisely because justice differs from the other virtues in this very decisive respect. To repeat, the mean in the case of justice is established not by reference to the good condition of the individual concerning the desire for gain—not, that is, by the standard Aristotle pointed to at the outset of the discussion of particular justice (1129b1–11)— but by reference to an equality or proportion established by law concerning parties who are contending for the good things. If in its connection with law, particular justice is not a mean with respect to two vices, then by this very fact it is also not an "extreme in accord with what is best and good" (cf. 1107a6–8). Just action accords with law and what is fair or equal, and not with what is choiceworthy by any other standard.

Indeed, this problem, as it is presented in the case of particular justice, mirrors the problem for justice also in the general sense, since in being oriented toward the common good, the virtues necessarily take their bearings from an end other than moral virtue itself. The most striking instances of the dilemma that this presents for moral virtue occur when the good of the community and the activity of moral virtue are not compatible: for example, when the common good requires surrender rather than noble action in battle; when a generous or magnificent action would involve unjust taking; when the defense of the country calls for deception or fraud; when justice demands punishments at which reason balks; or when service to one's country entails the betrayal of a friend. But these instances only point to the more general problem that the orientation of justice toward the common good is not an orientation toward moral virtue for its own sake. To be most precise, this is the dilemma of moral virtue: as justice, it looks to the good of the community, and as virtue, it looks to the good of the virtuous individual, yet these are different ends and different perfections. Accordingly, when Aristotle cautions early in his discussion of justice that the education of the good citizen (the education "with a view to the community [koinon]") may not be the same as the education of the good man (anēr) simply (1130b25–29), he is pointing not to a tension between moral virtue and some other possibility, but in the first place to a dilemma within moral virtue itself.

Now, the resolution of the dilemma of moral virtue might still seem to be found in the proposition that in the best case—in the best political community under the best circumstances—the good citizen will be the same as the good human being. But this resolution would have to grapple with the argument of this essay that in light of justice's connection with law and the common good, its requirements are not the same as those of moral virtue as an end and a good in its own right: Understood as human flourishing, moral virtue is not defined by the requirements of the common good, whereas for the political community as such, justice has to be the highest virtue. Thus, while justice may be a peak of moral virtue, it is a peak which also marks the limits of the political community, even or especially for those who would be devoted to it as the locus of morally serious action.

Conclusion

In a work whose purpose is to investigate the best life, Aristotle's treatment of justice may be said to reflect his political realism. His realism does not begin, however, from the supposition that self-interest is the fundamental principle of human nature. To the contrary, in being "for the sake of another," justice is the greatest of the moral virtues and, as such, cannot be captured within the terms of simple self-interestedness. Justice is properly understood, rather, in terms of the admirable self-concern of a virtuous person to be noble and good. In this respect, the deftness with which Aristotle deflects the Thrasymachean criticism of justice belongs naturally to his effort in the Nicomachean Ethics to give moral virtue its full due. To live well—to flourish—is to act well, and moral virtue is the perfection of the desiring and longing part of the soul from which good action issues. Accordingly, as the virtue that orients the individual toward the common good, justice reflects the longing of the virtuous person to act nobly and well and so to flourish in the true sense. Even if, as I have argued, the peak of moral virtue represented by justice also marks the limit of the political community with respect to such flourishing, it marks this limit in accord with moral virtue itself.

In Aristotle's thought, moreover, the recognition of this limit points the way not to "the self" and self-interestedness as most fundamental but to friendship. For the longing of the virtuous person for noble and good action is best satisfied in friendship with another who is virtuous. As Aristotle famously notes in his introduction to friendship in Book VIII of the *Ethics*, "when people are friends, they have no need of justice, but those who are just need friendship in addition" (1155a26–27). Justice is not needed between friends because there exists "the just in the fullest sense": friends have all things in common, and each wishes the other's good (1159b29–32). A virtuous person in particular most loves and takes pleasure in good character and action, and in the case of two virtuous friends, these are the things for which each loves the friend and wishes the friend's good. In loving their friend in this way, accordingly, the virtuous at one and the same time wish the good of their friend and their own good (1157b33). Indeed, it is with a view to the good in this best sense that, at the other peak of virtue, the one who is magnanimous is described as being "unable to live toward another, except a friend" (1124b31–1125a1). In accord with moral virtue itself, then, and not some other standard or good, the community of friends can be seen to be superior to the political community.

By this account, it is possible to say that Aristotle is at one with liberalism in marking a sphere outside of the political that might be called private. On the other hand, the very different ground upon which he does this reflects a long and careful investigation of virtue as the human good, and this is an investigation liberalism may need but cannot fully embrace. For, however much liberalism may admit the necessity of virtue for its own support, it must always leave unanswered the question of what the good is. From liberalism's point of view, the life of virtue as the life of noble and good actions can only be one possibility among many possible pursuits of happiness.[23] Aristotle's thought is foreign and so a serious challenge to liberalism on this question, but for that very reason it may also provide light in some dark corners. Most importantly, Aristotle may be able to provide a much clearer view of political action itself because he can account for the noble as opposed to merely self-interested ground of that action, and thus he can account for a motive that remains active in us, whatever liberal theorizing may say. By making qualitative distinctions among pursuits of the good, moreover, Aristotle may offer a firmer defense of a sphere separate from the political because he can both mark the limits of politics and justify them. In these matters also, nevertheless, it would be important to ask how far down the road of virtue liberalism can go without surrendering the principles that are dearest to it.

NOTES

I wish to thank the Earhart Foundation for their generous support during the preparation of this essay.

1. One is tempted to say that liberalism has a distinguished history of Aristotle-bashing from Thomas Hobbes to Stephen Holmes. But compare T. Smith (1999, 634): "Ironically, Aristotle is sometimes vilified as hostile to liberalism, but liberal practice may require the kind of resources Aristotelian theory provides"; Berkowitz (1999, 22): "There is more antiquity in modernity than is commonly supposed. Virtue is an element of this neglected antiquity within liberal modernity, and as such, I shall argue, it constitutes an important resource for liberals today" (see also p. 17); and Salkever (1990a, 264): "This Aristotelian understanding of the function of political philosophy is not only compatible with the contemporary liberal regime; it is in fact needed to sharpen our sense of what liberalism is for, and the ways of life this regime aims at supporting."

2. "Flourishing" as a translation for *eudaimonia* or "happiness" has its source in G. E. M. Anscombe's "Modern Moral Philosophy," and is preferred by many neo-Aristotelians because it distinguishes the full sense of *eudaimonia* in Aristotle— its connection with virtue and the perfection of our character or nature—from happiness understood as mere sentiment. I will use the terms "human good" and "human flourishing" interchangeably.

3. This is a complaint echoed by Bernard Yack (1993, 150) and David O'Connor (1988, 417), whose work constitute exceptions to the rule. Yack notes that the disregard of justice as a virtue is especially true in the case of general justice, even though "it seems likely that we will seriously misunderstand [Aristotle's] account of justice unless we devote some attention to his concept of general justice" (1993, 158).

4. As O'Connor argues, justice in Aristotle's terms is not properly understood as altruism in the modern sense. Rather, for Aristotle, virtue can be viewed from two perspectives, which O'Connor calls simple and relational virtue: "the perspective of simple virtue focuses on what sort of psychic state (*hexis*) a particular virtue is, while the perspective of relational virtue focuses on how a given psychic state manifests itself in community life with other people" (1991, 138). Justice is both a characteristic (general justice is the possession of all the virtues in this sense) and relational, to use O'Connor's terms. The problem for justice, accordingly, is not instilling altruism or overcoming egoism, but orienting individuals toward the shared life of the community. See also T. Smith (1999, 628), who follows O'Connor

in arguing that justice is a reorientation of the individual toward a satisfying common life.

5. Compare, for example, Yack: "Aristotle sums up the basis for moral conflict in ordinary political life in his famous distinction between the good man and the good citizen (*Pol.* 1276b–78b). Only in the best regime will the good man and the good citizen have exactly the same virtues (*Pol.* 1278b)" (1993, 262). I will have more to say about the problem for virtue even in the best regime later in this essay. Yack's suggestion is the orthodox view, but is at odds both with other suggestions by Aristotle and, I think, with Yack's own cogent analysis of moral conflict (1993, ch. 9). Thomas Smith details clearly and without compromise the political limits of the common good, but suggests that in the best case—when individuals are properly oriented toward the good—the problem of the common good can in principle at least be solved. He supports this suggestion by treating relationships of *philia*, the family and friends, as "analogical communities" to the political community. In an important footnote, however, he observes, "Drawing similarities between family and political life obscures as much as illuminates. Most obviously, the political community lacks filial ties of natural affection. In addition, Aristotle thinks that most fathers do not care about the formation of their children (NE 1108a29), and politicians fare even worse in his estimation (NE 1180a25, 1180b28–1181a13). If it is difficult to strive for a harmonious family, then how much more problematic would it be to strive for a harmonious political community" (1999, n. 15). My argument will be that in sketching the limits of justice with respect to the activity of moral virtue itself—our flourishing in the deepest sense—Aristotle shows us also the absolute limits of the political community. Friendship may be an answer to this problem, but an answer outside the bounds of politics strictly speaking. See Dobbs (1996) for a discussion of the relation of the family (*oikos*) to the political realm (*polis*) in which he argues that Aristotle's view is that the pursuit of human excellence is actually better supported "in a regime of constitutional pluralism, where the integrity of the household is preserved and the polis plays its indispensable supporting role" (88).

6. There have been attacks from all sides on liberalism's claims concerning its neutrality, well known among which is Sandel's *Liberalism and the Limits of Justice* (1982). The view of the neo-Aristotelian skeptics concerning liberalism's neutrality is summed up in a statement by Steven Smith: "The Aristotelian eudaimonist will, however, respond that the neutral state is a contradiction in terms anyway. Every society, no matter how wide and diverse its territory and population, tends to promote one or at most a few human types and classes whether this be the soldier, the priest, the aristocrat, the warrior, or the common man. Since we cannot opt for a society that respects literally every type, it is best to be clear about what type or classes deontological liberalism really favors" (1986, 7).

7. The interest in virtue crosses many ideological boundaries. As Shelley Burtt observes, "In recent years, political philosophers across the ideological spectrum have rediscovered virtue. In fact, the idea of reinvigorating public life with suitable doses of citizenly devotion has proved so compelling to theorists in recent years that we can identify a range of politics of virtue on offer today, each with its own problems and possibilities" (1993, 360).

8. In emphasizing Aristotle's "realism" or political perspective, Berkowitz's and Yack's efforts balance overly perfectionist versions of Aristotle by reviving aspects of his thought, for example, Books IV through VI of his *Politics*, that tend to get overlooked in these versions. Galston highlights, in order to refute, liberalism's claims of neutrality concerning the good. All of these scholars would agree, however, that the liberal virtues, whatever they may be, do not exhaust the human good; at most, they are a limited specification of that good.

9. Galston notes further that "not every citizen must possess these virtues but, rather, that most citizens must. The broad hypothesis is that as the proportion of nonvirtuous citizens increases significantly, the ability of liberal societies to function successfully progressively diminishes" (1991, 220).

10. Compare, for example, Galston's list of liberal virtues (1991, 213–327) with that of Macedo (1990, 265–77). See also Berkowitz's discussions of Hobbes, Locke, Kant, and Mill (1999, chs. 1–4), and Salkever (1990b, 178–90).

11. See Salkever 1990a, chs. 5–6 and 1990b; Macedo 1990, 265; Galston 1991, 228–37; Berkowitz 1999, 179–92. From this point of view, the most compelling defense of liberalism is that it fosters and supports individual flourishing defined in liberal terms. For a far-reaching articulation of a liberal "way of life," see Stephen Macedo's *Liberal Virtues* (1990). Macedo argues, "Liberal politics does not insulate the private sphere from the public sphere; even in the absence of litigation, public values penetrate and partly constitute private relations. . . . Liberal political norms have a private life: they help shape and structure the private lives of liberal citizens. To a greater extent than liberals usually allow, freedom is a way of life" (265).

12. For an account of the evaluative character of Aristotelian social science, see Salkever, 1990a, ch. 1 and 1990b; also Nussbaum 1992, MacIntyre 1984, 56–59. Cf. Yack 1993, 281–82.

13. Nussbaum goes on to note, "And one of Aristotle's most obvious concerns is the criticism of existing moral traditions, in his own city and in others, as unjust or repressive, or in other ways incompatible with human flourishing. . . . Aristotle evidently believes that there is no incompatibility between basing an ethical theory on the virtues and defending the singleness and objectivity of the human good. Indeed, he seems to believe that these two aims are mutually supportive" (1988, 33–34).

14. "The evaluation of a human community" from the standpoint of human flourishing is the focus of Galston's earlier work *Justice and the Human Good;* his defense of distinctively liberal virtues as necessary to the support of the regime, the focus of his later *Liberal Purposes*. See also Nussbaum (1992, 223–37). Even Yack, who emphasizes the political aspect of the virtues, also acknowledges "the polis exists for the sake of *human* flourishing (*eudaimonia*); human beings do not exist for the sake of the polis's own flourishing (1993, 97, his emphasis). He nevertheless is critical of separating Aristotle's "science of ethics" from his "science of politics" (18). The question of the human good in relation to a liberal community and, more broadly, to modernity as a historically self-conscious age presents several difficulties for those Aristotelians who wish to emphasize the perfectionist aspects of Aristotle's thought. Thus, for example, Nussbaum seeks to make a non-relative virtue-ethics also "context-sensitive" (1992, 32–36) and MacIntyre insists that the

good is properly understood as embedded in a coherent tradition (1988, chs. 10–11 and 21; see Salkever's helpful critique, 1990a, 30–36). Others, such as Salkever and Galston, either conclude that there is no final resolution to the question of the good that transcends specific circumstances or insist on a range of possibilities for human beings (see, for example, Salkever 1990a, chs. 2–3 and Galston 1980, 56–58 and 1991, ch. 8).

15. Citations of Aristotle's *Nicomachean Ethics* and *Politics* are to the Oxford Classical Texts editions. Translations are my own.

16. On how much of the *Nicomachean Ethics* is given over to this question, especially in light of the fact that Aristotle finally identifies the life of contemplation as the best life, compare Yack (1993, ch. 9) with Cropsey (1977, 252–53).

17. It is important to note one change in Aristotle's method of investigation. In Book I, he advises that we begin our study from "what is known to us," and for this reason, "the one who is to be a competent audience concerning the noble and just things, and, in general, the political things ought to have been nobly raised in habits" (1095b3–6). For the discussion of justice, however, Aristotle would appear to expand his frame of reference in beginning from "everyone's" opinion concerning justice.

18. See also 1125b11–14 as well as *Republic* 359b1. As Aristotle notes, the ruler is thus the "guardian of the just," but as a result, "there seems to be nothing left for him" (1134b1–3).

19. This is a notoriously difficult statement in the *Nicomachean Ethics*. For further discussion of the interpretation I follow, see Stewart (1892, I.401) and O'Connor (1991, 141) (see also O'Connor's argument against Aquinas's view on pp. 145–46).

20. On the question of the assessment of this penalty, see Burnet (1988, 218–19). The mathematical character of commutative justice follows, of course, from the presentation of the mean in mathematical terms, but for this reason, the discussion has a very odd quality. As David Ross notes, "The problem of 'rectificatory justice' has nothing to do with punishment proper" (Ross 1925).

21. Since Aristotle reserves the investigation of this dispute to his *Politics*, it could be said that while his treatment of justice in the *Nicomachean Ethics* illuminates an aspect of justice the Thrasymachean attack obscures, it also obscures what the Thrasymachean attack illuminates.

22. For a discussion of the relation between law and politics, see Yack 1993, 194–208, and of political justice more generally, chs. 5–6. Particularly helpful on the question of law and the regime is Yack's observation that "Aristotle's final reason for promoting a disposition to lawfulness is the least familiar but probably the most important. As mentioned above, a disposition to lawfulness is for him a necessary and essential condition for the establishment and maintenance of political community" (205). Yack cites both *Nicomachean Ethics* 1134b13, and *Politics* 1292a32, which notes that where "laws do not rule, there is no regime." See also Bodéüs's discussion of the relation of natural right and the common good (1999, 79–86).

23. When Aristotle speaks of human flourishing in connection with moral virtue, he means just this, the life of noble and good action. He does not speak, that is, in terms of a "rational life plan" or project, as, for example, Rawls does or even some neo-Aristotelians (see Yack's criticism of contemporary philosophy on this

question [1993, 281–283] as well as Smith's observation concerning neo-Aristotelians [1999, 630]). One of the great tasks of the *Nicomachean Ethics* is to articulate and explore the life of virtuous action as the best possible life for a human being: first, to say what the best life in terms of moral virtue is and then to investigate that life's claim to be best simply. What is at stake in this investigation—what the claims of moral virtue are to be the best life and whether it is such, even by its own standards—is one of the most important reasons why the question of what this life is cannot finally be left open.

BIBLIOGRAPHY

Anscombe, G. E. M. 1958. "Modern Moral Philosophy." *Philosophy* 33 (January): 1–19.

Aristotelis. 1988. *Ethica Nicomachea.* Edited by I. Bywater. Oxford: Oxford University Press.

———. 1986. *Politica.* Edited by W. D. Ross. Oxford: Oxford University Press.

Berkowitz, Peter. 1999. *Virtue and the Making of Modern Liberalism.* Princeton, N.J.: Princeton University Press.

Bodéüs, Richard. 1999. "The Natural Foundations of Right and Aristotelian Philosophy." Translated by Kent Enns. In *Action and Contemplation: Studies in the Moral and Political Thought of Aristotle,* edited by Robert C. Bartlett and Susan D. Collins. Albany, N.Y.: State University of New York Press.

Burnet, John, ed. 1988. *The "Ethics" of Aristotle.* London: Methuen. 1900. Reprint, Ayer.

Burtt, Shelley. 1993. "The Politics of Virtue Today: A Critique and A Proposal." *American Political Science Review* 87 (March): 360–68.

Cropsey, Joseph. 1977. *Political Philosophy and the Issues of Politics.* Chicago: University of Chicago Press.

Dobbs, Darrell. 1996. "Family Matters: Aristotle's Appreciation of Women and the Plural Structure of Society." *American Political Science Review* 90 (March): 74–89.

Galston, William. 1980. *Justice and the Human Good.* Chicago: University of Chicago Press.

———. 1991. *Liberal Purposes: Goods, Virtues, and Diversity in the Liberal State.* Cambridge: Cambridge University Press.

Macedo, Stephen. 1990. *Liberal Virtues: Citizenship, Virtue, and Community in Liberal Constitutionalism.* Oxford: Clarendon Press.

MacIntyre, Alasdair. 1984. *After Virtue: A Study in Moral Theory.* 2nd ed. Notre Dame, Ind.: University of Notre Dame Press.

———. 1988. *Whose Justice? Which Rationality?* Notre Dame, Ind.: University of Notre Dame Press.

Nussbaum, Martha C. 1988. "Non-Relative Virtues: An Aristotelian Approach." In *Midwest Studies in Philosophy* 13, edited by Peter A. French et al. Notre Dame, Ind.: University of Notre Dame Press.

———. 1992. "Human Functioning and Social Justice: In Defense of Aristotelian Essentialism." *Political Theory* 20 (May): 202–46.

O'Connor, David. 1988. "Aristotelian Justice as a Personal Virtue." In *Midwest Studies in Philosophy* 13, edited by Peter A. French et al. Notre Dame, Ind.: University of Notre Dame Press.

———. 1991. "The Aetiology of Justice." In *Essays on the Foundations of Aristotelian Political Thought,* edited by Carnes Lord and David O'Connor. Berkeley: University of California Press.

Rawls, John. 1993. *Political Liberalism.* New York: Columbia University Press.

Ross, David. 1925. *Ethica Nicomachea.* Oxford: Oxford University Press.

Salkever, Stephen G. 1990a. *Finding the Mean: Theory and Practice in Aristotelian Political Philosophy.* Princeton, N.J.: Princeton University Press.

———. 1990b. " 'Lopp'd and Bound': How Liberal Theory Obscures the Goods of Liberal Practices." In *Liberalism and the Good,* edited by R. Bruce Douglass, Gerald R. Mara, and Henry S. Richardson. New York: Routledge.

Sandel, Michael J. 1982. *Liberalism and the Limits of Justice.* Cambridge: Cambridge University Press.

Smith, Steven B. 1986. "Goodness, Nobility, and Virtue in Aristotle's Political Science." *Polity* 19:5–26.

Smith, Thomas W. 1999. "Aristotle on the Conditions for and Limits of the Common Good." *American Political Science Review* 93 (September): 625–36.

Stewart, J. A. 1892. *Notes on Aristotle's "Ethics."* 2 vols. Oxford: Clarendon Press.

Yack, Bernard. 1993. *The Problems of a Political Animal: Community, Justice, and Conflict in Aristotelian Political Thought.* Berkeley: University of California Press.

PART TWO

VIRTUE

CHAPTER FOUR

MacIntyre and Aristotle on the Foundation of Virtue

ARISTIDE TESSITORE

In the decades prior to the end of the Cold War the most vociferous critics of modern liberalism came from the political left; liberal democracy was haunted by the specter of communism. Since the collapse of the Soviet Union and the demolition of the Berlin wall, liberalism is without serious political rivals; it is not, however, without serious critics. Among them is Alasdair MacIntyre, perhaps the most prominent neo-Aristotelian in America. MacIntyre has managed to elicit vehement criticism from both the left and the right while, at the same time, drawing often begrudging acknowledgment of the seriousness of his critique. Unfailingly erudite, MacIntyre's writing gives expression to an important voice in both contemporary and ancient philosophy, one whose influence will continue to make itself felt for the foreseeable future.

The first part of this essay provides a sympathetic overview of MacIntyre's project as a whole and especially its relationship to the thought of Aristotle. In the second part, I bring to light key differences separating the teaching of Aristotle from that of MacIntyre. I draw on an understanding of Aristotle largely influenced by the work of Leo Strauss and, in so doing, bring into dialogue two traditions of Aristotelian inquiry that have remained relatively aloof from each other. The essay concludes with a critical appreciation of the significance of MacIntyre's neo-Aristotelianism as it might appear from an Aristotelian perspective. This discussion puts into question the problematic relationship between nature and history as it bears on the foundation of human virtue.

MacIntyre's Project and the Turn to Aristotle

Triumph and Decline

The idea that the West is in a state of decline is not new. Indeed, the intellectual world of Weimar Germany was gripped by a pervasive sense of crisis that profoundly shaped participants and those coming of age during this period.[1] At its center was the relationship between theory and practice or, more generally, between science and politics. Max Weber's addresses on the bifurcation of science and politics as vocations (1918, 1919) became touchstones for a diagnosis of the (still unresolved) problem of practical reason. During the 1920s Oswald Spengler's bestseller, *Decline of the West*, gained intellectual credibility. Forty years later, Leo Strauss, a German émigré profoundly affected by the Weimar conversation, began the published version of the Page-Barbour lectures by speaking of a crisis in the West that manifest itself in a weakened sense of purpose and consequent moral-political bewilderment among its citizens.[2] With the publication of *After Virtue* in 1981, MacIntyre took his place among the most recent and influential contemporary thinkers to maintain that the West is in a state of grave moral decline.

MacIntyre claims that contemporary moral discourse has become fragmented and incoherent because it has been uprooted from the cultural soil that had given it birth and nourishment. It is not that denizens of the modern world are less likely to appeal to moral standards, but that these very appeals conceal the extent to which the standards have been eroded. The peculiar modern problem is not only that moral discourse has become fundamentally unintelligible but that those who employ moral arguments are typically unaware of the problem. The impoverishment of moral thinking in the modern world is exacerbated by the absence of self-knowledge on the part of those most infected by it.

One symptom of this impoverishment is interminable debate on moral issues that, MacIntyre argues, are incapable of resolution under current conditions. Ethical argument in either its academic or political contexts has become a modern tower of Babel in which participants speak past one another because they lack a common language that could make any resolution possible. The reason for this predicament is, that although each participant may deploy arguments that derive in a consistent and logical way from antecedent premises, the various premises are fundamentally incommensurable. As a consequence, different positions are incapable of rational evaluation since there is no overarching framework within which competing standards can be compared and ranked. The ungrounded character of first principles means that the adoption of a particular framework of moral discourse is essentially arbitrary. The problem is only obscured, not dissipated, by the fact that interlocutors in modern debates continue to invoke liberal standards that are only *apparently* neutral (e.g., rights, universalizability, or utility) in their attempt to mediate ethical disputes.

The most telling symptom of the modern crisis can be seen in an uncritical and pervasive acceptance of "emotivism," the doctrine that all moral judgments are *nothing but* expressions of preference, attitude, and private feeling.[3] Notwithstanding MacIntyre's contention that this view fails on theoretical grounds and that several philosophers in the analytic tradition are arrayed against it, the inability of these philosophers to agree among themselves regarding the rational principles by which to adjudicate moral issues furnishes no convincing escape from emotivism and, worse, inadvertently provides additional grist for its mill. This impotence in analytic philosophy, together with the impact of philosophies arising in Germany and France (especially Nietzsche and Sartre) that concede in different ways the substance of the emotivist doctrine, suggests the pervasive influence of this viewpoint. As MacIntyre expresses it, the profoundly changed circumstances framing moral discourse in contemporary society are reflected in the fact that,

> to a large degree people now think, talk and act *as if* emotivism were true, no matter what their avowed theoretical stand-point may be. Emotivism has become embodied in our culture.[4]

The claim that emotivism is embodied in contemporary culture is a sociological one. MacIntyre fleshes out this contention with recourse to the notion of "character," a concept in which social roles and psychological types are fused in such a way as to embody the distinctive moral and metaphysical claims of a particular society. The characters who most embody contemporary emotivist culture are the aesthete, the bureaucratic manager, and the therapist. All three types view human beings as means to other ends but consider questions about the ends themselves beyond the scope of rational or objective assessment. Whether one views people as potential objects for personal satisfaction (aesthete), resources to be organized with a view to maximum efficiency and effectiveness (manager), or a welter of neurotic symptoms that need to be channeled into socially useful energy (therapist), the comparative worthiness of these ends (personal satisfaction, efficiency, effectiveness, and social usefulness) are never called into question and evaluated. Rather, they furnish the arbitrary starting points from which an unconsciously fragmented sense of ethical standards is drawn. As a result, an individual in the process of working out an identity is continuously thrown back upon the "unencumbered self" (Michael Sandel's now famous phrase)[5] since the particular social roles or practices that typify modern life furnish no moral compass by which to orient one's life. Hidden behind the standard of professionalism and the various techniques it generates is a prior choice to embrace a particular profession or life-style which is itself incapable of rational scrutiny because it is the result of an arbitrary and private preference, attitude, or feeling.

The Enlightenment, Aristotle, or Nietzsche

For MacIntyre the pervasiveness of emotivism is no accident. The emotivist fabric of liberal society has been two hundred years in the making; it is the result of the Enlightenment or, more precisely, the failure of the Enlightenment. The aim of the Enlightenment project in its French, Scottish, and German incarnations was to articulate universal moral principles by appealing to an ahistorical conception of rational justification against what was felt to be the tyranny of tradition. Although MacIntyre acknowledges the vast differences that separate figures such as Diderot, Hume, Smith, and Kant, they all attempted but failed to formulate a ground for morality that would be available and compelling to all human beings *qua* rational persons. Although these thinkers agreed to a surprising degree on the content of the morality they were attempting to justify (something that MacIntyre attributes to a shared historical background), that content actually belonged to an earlier tradition of moral discourse ultimately traceable to Aristotle through the medium of its various medieval appropriations.

MacIntyre succinctly characterizes the three elements required for the Aristotelian scheme: "man-as-he-happens-to-be," "man-as-he-could-be-if-he-realized-his-essential-nature," and the moral precepts that enable him to pass from one state to the other.[6] The Aristotelian understanding of morality presupposes both a conception of untutored human nature and the notion of a human *telos* or end. The conflict between these two states is the field wherein ethical precepts are generated. Although Aristotle draws from an earlier Homeric tradition of morality, he significantly reforms it by detaching the Homeric conception of virtue from any immediate connection with a particular social role. Aristotle does retain a functional notion of human excellence, but attaches it to the very notion of human being itself. Development of the virtues is essential to the proper performance of the human function because human beings possess an essential nature and therefore an essential purpose. As such the practice of these virtues is not merely a means toward the achievement of some further end, but a necessary and central part of a complete human life lived at its best.[7] Moreover, human virtue cannot be exercised outside the political community but attains its fullest development among citizens engaged in the common project of living well.

It was the deliberate rejection of any notion of a human *telos* on the part of Enlightenment thinkers that ensured the failure of that project. The abandonment of the view that human beings have an essence that defines their true end left a fragmented moral scheme composed of the remaining two elements: (1) a set of moral injunctions now bereft of their teleological context, and (2) a view of human nature in all its untutored splendor. The succession of attempts to find a rational basis for shared moral beliefs by deducing them from an understanding of human nature (or reason) proved to be a Sisyphean task for it sought to bring together "a set of moral injunctions on the one hand and a conception of human nature on the other which had been expressly designed to be discrepant with each other."[8] Abandoning the central functional concept of Aristotelian moral discourse in either its Greek or medieval versions deprived morality of any rational or objective basis.

Over the last 200 years, Enlightenment thinkers have appealed to one of several conceptions of rights, universalizability, utility, shared intuitions, or some combination of these as an objective ground for morality. The result has been a history of continually unresolved disputes; no uncontested account of tradition-independent morality has emerged and consequently, no neutral set of criteria is available to adjudicate the claims of rival and contending traditions.[9] The interminability of debate over moral principles has itself become a leading feature of modern liberalism. Although it has been embraced by at least some liberals as a kind of virtue, MacIntyre maintains that, judged from the standpoint of the Enlightenment itself, the failure to bring about rational consensus on moral issues signals the failure of the project as a whole. Nor is that failure without serious consequences for the fabric of liberal society. The erosion of community and elevation of egoism, the loss of salutary authority and concern for a common good, and a more or less explicit fear that irrationalism lies at the basis of commitment, contribute to many of the social and political dislocations characteristic of contemporary society.

Nietzsche's unwelcome but penetrating critique of Enlightenment thinking revealed the fault lines hidden beneath its appealing but unattainable goal. The impossibility of deriving moral imperatives ("ought") from some descriptive statement about human nature or function ("is") was pointed out by Hume and hardened in the fire of Kant's critical philosophy. Kant attempted to thwart moral relativism by appealing to the a priori and universal standards of practical reason governing an autonomous human will. Nietzsche revealed the core problem with this effort by asserting not only the priority of the will, but its essential irrationality as well. Consensus about reason is itself derivative, arising from a culturally bound and historically rooted will to power. Nietzsche brought to the surface a cancer hidden within the liberal project. Lying beneath a superficial and naive consensus about the rules of reason and progress in history is an ugly truth about the irrationality of all traditions and moralities, including that of the Enlightenment (despite its disavowal of tradition). "Nietzsche's historic achievement [was] to understand more clearly than any other philosopher . . . not only that what purported to be appeals to objectivity were in fact expressions of a subjective will, but also the nature of the problems that this posed for moral philosophy."[10] Emotivism contains the seeds of nihilism; the Enlightenment necessarily issues in post-modernism; and despair about the possibility of providing any rational ground for moral judgment leads to the invention of the distinctively modern self—the individual.

The failure of the Enlightenment project is in some large measure due to its explicit rejection of a moral tradition for which Aristotle provided the intellectual core. Nietzsche's compelling diagnosis of the failure of this project is therefore a diagnosis of the failure of the historical sequel to the rejection of the Aristotelian tradition. It is this fact that leads MacIntyre to look to pre-liberal society and especially to the ethical teaching of Aristotle to see whether it might be possible to reconstruct something like Aristotle's ethical teaching within the framework of modern culture. In MacIntyre's words: "The key question does indeed become: can Aristotle's ethics, or something very like it, after all be vindicated."[11] For MacIntyre, the dramatic choice facing contemporary moral philosophy is a choice between the diagnosis of Nietzsche[12] and the teaching of Aristotle, between post-modern skepticism and pre-liberal virtue.

MacIntyre on Practice, Narrative Unity, and Tradition

MacIntyre attempts to provide a reconstructed version of Aristotle's ethical teaching, one that cedes central place to the virtues and the communal context necessary for living the good life. It is a reconstruction rather than a return to Aristotelian teaching because Aristotle's notion of a human *telos* was drawn from a now discredited metaphysical biology, his understanding of community relied upon the Greek polis, and he inherited from Plato a jejune belief in the unity of individual and political virtue. MacIntyre attempts to make the needed transposition by developing three core notions: (1) practice, (2) narrative unity, and (3) tradition.

A practice is a complex form of socially established human activity that leads to the attainment of a good internal to the activity at issue.[13] MacIntyre illustrates with respect to the game of chess which brings with it the possibility of excellence in chess playing. Without fully developing MacIntyre's nuanced account, it suffices to note that a practice escapes the subjectivity of emotivism precisely because the internal good to which it directs its participants requires that any given individual subordinate his or her personal preferences, tastes, and attitudes to the authoritative standards that currently define the practice in question. Even the attempt to reform a particular practice presupposes the development of excellence in accordance with the canons by which that practice has been shaped. These very standards provide an overarching and authoritative framework within which argument is meaningful, that is, capable of resolution at least in principle.

If judgments within practices escape the charge of subjectivity, the same cannot be said in determining the relative value or worth of the practice itself given the multiplicity of practices and the different virtues necessary to secure their internal goods. For example, the virtues necessary to secure the internal goods of parenthood are not the same as those needed to achieve the goods of any number of careers, which are again different from those necessary to acquire excellence in the leisure activity of chess. MacIntyre attempts to avoid the emotivist pitfall of subjectivity by appealing to a rehabilitated version of the human *telos,* something that he derives from the narrative unity of a human life. Particular practices exist within the larger story of a specific life. Despite various constraints that are beyond human control and the unpredictability that contributes to the shape of a human life, MacIntyre observes that the present is always informed by some image of the future which presents itself in the form of a *telos.*

> Unpredictability and teleology therefore coexist as part of our lives; like characters in a fictional narrative we do not know what will happen next, but nonetheless our lives have a certain form which projects itself towards our future.[14]

The notion of a *telos* derives not from some biologically grounded understanding of human nature but is located in the historical narrative of a particular human life. Confronted with the conflicting and irreconcilable demands of competing practices, it is not necessary (or in MacIntyre's view even feasible) to ask which practice is best for human beings as such, but rather which most helps to preserve the unity, depth, and coherence that a particular life has begun to develop. The discovery of such a unity presupposes a willingness to question, reflect, and seek. This kind of quest is a continuing form of education with respect to the nature of the various ends sought and, more importantly, it is an education in self-knowledge. It is in this way that MacIntyre arrives at a provisional and Socratic-sounding conclusion about the good life for a human being.

[T]he good life for man is the life spent in seeking for the good life for man, and the virtues necessary for the seeking are those which will enable us to understand what more and what else the good life for man is.[15]

It is because the narrative unity of a particular human life is always located within a larger historical context that MacIntyre turns to the idea of tradition. A tradition is constituted by a set of practices and a particular understanding of their importance and meaning. It is by no means static; indeed, vital traditions "embody continuities of conflict."[16] For MacIntyre there is no ahistorical, timeless mode of reasoning accessible to human beings. All humans find themselves in a particular tradition and as such the narrative unity of an individual human life is embedded in a larger historical and social matrix that provides the resources by which an individual quest for the good is understood, evaluated, and criticized.

Given the multiplicity of traditions confronting citizens of the modern world, individuals must evaluate the relative worth of one tradition over another. Since the only means of making these crucial determinations are themselves part of a particular tradition, MacIntyre attempts to stave off the charge of relativism by speaking of the "rationality of traditions." His controversial claim is that choices between traditions can be rationally made, not by an appeal to some non-existent standard of reason as such, but by a kind of "robustness test"; that is, the historically demonstrated capacity to overcome what he calls "epistemological crises" and continue in a more vital form.[17] MacIntyre's paradigm, one to which his more recent books have increasingly moved, is found in Aquinas's ability to negotiate an epistemological crisis by forging a synthesis of the Aristotelian and Augustinian traditions in the thirteenth century.[18] MacIntyre finds in Thomism an Aristotelian tradition with resources for its own enlargement, one that stands as the most serious rival to the genealogical tradition inaugurated by Nietzsche and taken over by post-modernism.[19] MacIntyre's own project might be understood as doing for the Aristotelian tradition in the twentieth century what Aquinas succeeded in doing in the thirteenth. Although he never explicitly says so, MacIntyre's notion of "the rationality of traditions" attempts to establish a delicate balance between Nietzsche's insight into the historicity of all truth claims without surrendering the Aristotelian argument for an objective order, a larger truth to which and by which our efforts are and must be measured. In the face of post-Enlightenment relativism and perspectivism, MacIntyre affirms the possibility and importance of rational theorizing, but this can only be a work of and within a tradition. The Enlightenment attempt to stand outside of tradition proves chimerical. The continued attempt to find some neutral Archimedean point on which to ground moral discourse does not reveal a rational concern for fairness, but

blindness to the hidden and, in part for this very reason, irrational prejudices of the dominant if decaying liberal tradition.

Aristotle on MacIntyre

MacIntyre notes especially three areas in Aristotle's account that endanger
the whole Aristotelian enterprise: (1) belief in a unity of virtue that views
conflict (*stasis*) as *the* problem to be avoided; (2) facile dependence upon
the contingent and now extinct structure of the polis; and (3) a conception
of teleology that relies on a properly discredited metaphysical biology.[20] The
distinctively un-Aristotelian elements in MacIntyre's project result from the
attempt to redress precisely these limitations.

MacIntyre maintains that, at root, Aristotle's ahistorical approach to the
study of ethics and politics is shaped far more than he realizes by an insufficiently critical acceptance of the historical contingencies characteristic of
ancient Greek culture. His use of the category of nature, viewed from the
vantage point of historical hindsight, has become fundamentally suspect.
As a result, the categories, beliefs, and at least some of the virtues presented
by Aristotle as universal are now seen to be historically contingent. Aristotle's analysis of human nature appears to be merely one expression, albeit
a powerful one, of the particular prejudices of a historical moment. Mac-
Intyre's novel solution attempts to relocate the essential structure of Aristotle's thought within a dynamic historical tradition. By supplying the
historical consciousness that Aristotle lacks, MacIntyre draws from the Aristotelian tradition a bracing critique of the limited and symptomatically
foundationless character of the post-Enlightenment world. This section
assesses each of the particular and related problems in Aristotle's thought
as they are identified by MacIntyre and strives to do so from Aristotle's point
of view.

Authoritative Practice and the Unity of Virtue

Aristotle would certainly accept the notion of authority implicit in practice as it is developed by MacIntyre. Indeed, he illustrates and clarifies his
teaching about ethical virtue in precisely this way. One need only think of
his often repeated appeal to the authoritative standard provided by the
morally serious person (*spoudaios*) or his insistence that one becomes virtuous by adhering to the authoritative standard furnished by *orthos logos*.
MacIntyre, however, underestimates the extent to which Aristotle questions
authority, albeit respectfully, in his ethical and political studies with the consequence that he overstates Aristotle's emphasis on the unity of virtue. In

MacIntyre's reading, Aristotle inherits from Plato a "belief in the unity and harmony of both the individual soul and the city-state."[21] The most relevant and debilitating consequence of this inheritance is that it renders Aristotle blind to the centrality of opposition and conflict in human life and thus deprives him of an important resource for human learning. But is this really Aristotle's view?

In fact, Aristotle's notoriously problematic teaching on the relationship between ethical and intellectual virtues has elicited a variety of rival interpretations, and is still among the most debated questions in Aristotelian studies today. One of the deepest rifts lies between those who maintain that Aristotle argues for some combination of moral and intellectual excellence and those who maintain that his endorsement of contemplative excellence is separable from, and perhaps even incompatible with, his teaching on moral virtue.[22] Although it is not possible to enter into all the nuances of this debate, the persistence of controversy itself—particularly one that concerns the central teaching of his ethical treatises—is an initial indication of Aristotle's tendency to preserve rather than dispel tensions in his account of the good life for a human being.

A careful assessment of the *Nicomachean Ethics* reveals that responsibility for these competing interpretations must be laid squarely on Aristotle himself; his most famous study of ethics presents both positions (generally referred to as the "inclusivist" and "intellectualist" ideals) without attempting to reconcile fully the conflict between them. Since Aristotelian scholars typically divide between partisans of the inclusivist and intellectualist interpretations of Aristotle's position, I include a brief exegetical analysis from the final book of the *Nicomachean Ethics* (where Aristotle offers a comparative consideration of ethical and philosophic lives as they bear on the all-important question of human happiness) as initial evidence of Aristotle's deliberate ambiguity on this point.[23]

Excursus: Nicomachean Ethics, Book X
Aristotle's concluding teaching on the surpassing happiness of the philosophic life is supported by six arguments (10.7.1177a18–b26): (1) Contemplation is the best (*kratistē*) activity because it involves the best thing in us. (2) It is the most continuous activity in which human beings can engage. (3) It is held to contain pleasures of marvelous purity and permanence. (4) It is the most self-sufficient activity, for the wise need not depend upon others in order to contemplate. (5) It is loved for its own sake and produces no result beyond itself. (6) It is an activity of leisure par excellence. On the basis of these six arguments, Aristotle concludes that contemplation is the highest activity in accordance with virtue and, consequently, that complete human happiness consists in a life of study.

On the one hand, the similarity between philosophic and ethical excellence is suggested by the particular arguments used to establish the superior happiness of the contemplative life. All six of these arguments apply, to some extent at least, to ethical excellence as well. With respect to the six propositions enumerated above, one should consider the following Aristotelian assertions: (1) Justice is considered the best (*kratistē*) of the virtues (5.1.1129b27–28). (2) Friendship, based on the practice of moral virtue, facilitates the continuous activity characteristic of happiness (9.9.1170a5–11). (3) Pure and liberal pleasures are found in the activities of virtue and intelligence (10.6.1176b18–21). Less broadly, generosity in particular and virtuous action in general are accompanied by pleasure (4.1.1120a24–31). (4) Self-sufficiency is characteristic of the magnanimous person (4.3.1125a11–12). (5) The repeated insistence that noble actions are desirable for their own sake is one of the leitmotifs of the *Nicomachean Ethics* (e.g., 3.7.1115b11–13, 4.1.1120a23–25, 4.2.1122b6–7, 10.6.1176b6–9). (6) Justice and moderation are cited as activities appropriate to leisure (*Pol.* 7.15.1334a11–34). The point here is that the very arguments used by Aristotle to substantiate the superiority of the theoretical life simultaneously suggest a similarity between philosophic and moral excellence. The philosophic life is happier than the moral life not because it is radically different from it, but because it offers to a greater and more perfect degree the very things that decent persons both seek and enjoy for themselves, a kind of argument that supports the "inclusivist" interpretation of Aristotle's teaching.

On the other hand, it is important to note that although Aristotle does not emphasize dissimilarity or dissonance in the relationship between ethical and theoretical virtue in Book X, neither does he deny it. Indeed, Aristotle weaves into the argument of this book three striking indications of persistent tension: (1) the unanswered question of whether life is for the sake of pleasure (10.4.1175a18–19); (2) the suggestion that the practice of the greatest and most noble moral virtues impedes the highest human excellence (10.8.1178b1–5); and (3) the apparently insignificant character of moral virtue in light of divine activity (10.8.1178b7–23).

(1) In the course of his reconsideration of pleasure in Book X, Aristotle raises a crucial theoretical question: Is life for the sake of pleasure or pleasure for the sake of life? At issue is nothing less than the fundamental standard for gauging a flourishing human life: Is it a certain experience of pleasure(s) or a life characterized by noble disregard for questions of this sort? The disturbing character of Aristotle's failure to resolve this question in the concluding book of his study is augmented by the fact that he had earlier cited with apparent approval the belief that nothing prevents pleasure from being the supreme good (7.13.1153b7–8), a view that implies that life is for the sake of pleasure.[24] Without going so far as to suggest that Aristotle

advocates a kind of philosophic hedonism, it is sufficient to observe that the unanswered question about pleasure in Book X, together with the arguments from Book VII (11–14) which it recalls, evidences the continuing presence of a perspective that challenges the teaching on ethical virtue for which the *Ethics* is rightly famous.

(2) In his final discussion of happiness, Aristotle suggests that the external equipment necessary for great and noble actions may constitute an impediment to the life of study (10.8.1178b1–5). Although he does not elaborate the problem here, it is easily clarified in light of his earlier discussions. Peak moral virtues such as magnificence and magnanimity presuppose an abundance of external goods, something that in turn requires attentiveness to the economic and political circumstances that make these virtues possible and appropriate. A preoccupation with these concerns and with the constantly shifting circumstances from which they arise reduces both suitability and appreciation for a life given over to study of the unchanging beings of nature or, at least, the unchanging problems that delimit the natural contours of a human life.

(3) In the course of his final assessment of ethical virtue, Aristotle turns to the question of divine activity (10.8.1178b7–23). It is here that the problematic relationship between ethical and intellectual virtue becomes most apparent. In what does the happiness of the gods consist? It would be ludicrous to try to conceive of them as practicing moral virtue, since all forms of virtuous conduct are "trifling and unworthy" (*mikra kai anaxia*) of gods (10.8.1178b17–18). The only possible activity appropriate to deities is some form of contemplation. This description of the gods, one that echoes the earlier account in Book VII (7.14.1154b26–31), is Aristotle's most severe and most explicit criticism of the human tendency to project a concern for ethical virtue onto the divine. He argues instead that happiness is coextensive in its range with contemplation (10.8.1178b28–32). Given the essentially political character of human beings, human imitation of divine indifference toward moral virtue would be reprehensible. Nevertheless, an appropriate human approximation of divine detachment might express itself in the cultivation of ethical virtue as a means to the godlike activity of contemplation, rather than as an end in itself. In both cases ethical virtue remains important; however, it possesses a profoundly different character among those who cultivate it as a means to one's true happiness and those who embrace ethical virtue for its own sake.

By way of contrast, the happiness associated with ethical virtue is limited, not only by a need for those external goods necessary for the practice of moral virtue, but because the most sublime happiness turns out to belong to another kind of activity. Aristotle's depiction of divine disinterestedness, together with his identification of human happiness and the godlike activity

of contemplation, points to the existence of a still unresolved tension between ethical and philosophic excellence. This problem is exacerbated by
Aristotle's further undeveloped suggestion that the activity of *nous,* more
than anything else, constitutes the identity of a human being (10.7.1178a5–8),
a suggestion that undercuts his earlier insistence on the composite nature
of human being as the most salient aspect of human identity and therefore
happiness.[25]

A harsh expression of this so-called "intellectualist argument" is found
in *Magna Moralia,* where ethical virtue is reduced to the status of a household manager who attends to daily necessities so that the lord of the house
might enjoy the freedom and leisure necessary to engage in philosophic
thought (*MM* 1.34.1198b9–20; see *EE* 8.3.1249b4–25). The difference between
this account and the one given in the *Nicomachean Ethics* is instructive.
Although both discussions clearly affirm the superiority of the philosophic
life, in the *Nicomachean Ethics* moral virtue is said to be subordinate to, but
never the servant of, philosophic contemplation. Whereas the latter view
suggests that ethical virtue is ultimately devoid of intrinsic dignity, the argument of the *Nicomachean Ethics* is distinctive precisely for its insistence on
an independent status for ethical virtue. Indeed, Aristotle's often-repeated
assertion that moral acts are undertaken for their own sake comes as close
as any single line to constituting a refrain for the entire book. In the *Nicomachean Ethics* Aristotle subordinates the life of ethical virtue to the philosophic way of life while at the same time retaining a sense of its importance.
The life of ethical virtue, unlike the life of slavery, does result in substantial human happiness. Nevertheless, a still greater possibility exists for those
who are able to take their bearings from the supremely happy activity of
philosophic contemplation.

The continuing controversy over Aristotle's teaching on the precise relationship between moral and theoretical excellence is well grounded in the
text. This (all too) brief excursus into the *Nicomachean Ethics* is intended
to show that the ambiguity of Aristotle's treatment is due, at least in part,
to the fact that he provides two different accounts of this relationship. Nevertheless, I believe it would be a mistake to conclude that Aristotle's teaching on the best life is inconsistent. The deeper consistency is reflected in his
refusal to simplify the question of the best way of life. Aristotle's depiction
of ethical virtue is faithful to the phenomenon of ethical virtue as it appears
in the lives of its best exemplars. At the same time, his account of philosophic activity preserves, without emphasizing, a sense of the inevitable
controversy that accompanies a life of radical inquiry. Theoretical and
practical matters vie for the attention of human intelligence and, given the
very different and necessarily limited capacities of human beings, the full

development of one can lessen appreciation for the importance of the other.[26] Aristotle consistently resists the temptation to try to reconcile completely two elevated ways of life that cannot be in every respect reconciled.

Indeed, a close reading of the *Nicomachean Ethics* reveals that the entire account is shot through with tensions that are never fully resolved: between magnanimity and justice, prudence and wisdom, justice and friendship, continence (*enkrateia*) and ethical virtue, as well as different and conflicting evaluations of pleasure in Books VII and X.[27] Against MacIntyre's view that Aristotle inadvertently codifies an existing and authoritative Greek tradition of class-based morality,[28] his account in the *Nicomachean Ethics* in fact preserves and reveals, rather than dispels, a wide range of persistent tensions that necessarily characterize human attempts to live well. Nor does he suggest any easy harmony between individual and civic excellence. This problem is suggested by his incomplete and open-ended consideration of the relationship between a good citizen and a good human being simply (*Pol.* 3. 4), as well as the preface for his sketch of a best regime which turns out to be an unresolved dispute about the best life for a human being (*Pol.* 7.1–3). Moreover, even the best regime is unable to accommodate fully the legitimate claims of all who contribute something essential to the political partnership. The use of slaves or resident aliens in the "regime to be prayed for" of *Politics* VII–VIII fails to balance the legitimate and conflicting goods of political virtue and political participation.[29]

Greater attentiveness to the unresolved character of a range of key problems in Aristotle's ethical and political writings reveals that his own expectations about unity are less sanguine than the idealized standard of individual and civic excellence attributed to him by MacIntyre. Although it is certainly true that Aristotle relies on culturally embedded opinion (*endoxa*) as starting points for his considerations, he is in no way constrained by them. The crucial distinction between nature and convention remains fundamental to Aristotle's mode of analysis, although it is true that his generally sympathetic account of conventional opinion sometimes obscures this fact.[30] If Aristotle's profound awareness of the essentially political character of human action and thinking leads him to be especially solicitous of authoritative opinion, an adequate encounter with the radical character of Aristotelian inquiry requires that we at least entertain the possibility that his seeming endorsement of certain conventional viewpoints might be part of an effort to accommodate himself to a prevailing ethos rather than an adequate expression of the limitations of his own thought. To entertain this possibility does not, of course, absolve Aristotle from any and every mistake; nor does it deny that his thought, and the thought of every writer, arises from and is shaped by a particular cultural context. It is to hold open the more modest, though still rare, possibility that a human being might—to some extent at least—see beyond the limitations that any given political culture imposes upon its inhabitants.

MacIntyre's emphasis on the unity of virtue both within individuals and with reference to political life inadvertently diminishes his appreciation for the open-ended, unresolved character of Aristotelian ethical inquiry. The absence of any fully just regime ensures the persistence of tension and factional strife in any and every political association. The permanence of such tensions, although politically dangerous (in significantly varying degrees to be sure), simultaneously encourages critical scrutiny of authoritative practice. The always incomplete unity and imperfect justice of the polis act as a catalyst for the full development of both practical and theoretical excellence. Both prudence and the capacity for political philosophy are permanent political needs. These two distinct kinds of excellence are logically prior to the notion of political authority in Aristotle's thought; indeed, they provide the ground by which the authoritative good held out by the polis is established and evaluated (consider *Pol.* 3.4.1277b25–30; *NE* 7.11.1152b1–3; *Pol.* 7.3.1325b16–23).

The Greek Polis versus Tradition

A second and related problem raised by MacIntyre concerns a relationship of dependency that attaches Aristotle's ethical teaching to the structure of the now defunct polis. According to MacIntyre, a good deal of Aristotle's understanding of ethical virtue is unintelligible apart from a political context that no longer exists. Aristotle "did not understand the transience of the polis because he had little or no understanding of historicity in general."[31] This leads MacIntyre to wonder whether it is possible to be an Aristotelian and, at the same time, look upon the polis from a historical perspective; that is, as merely one in a series of social and political forms within which it is possible to exemplify human excellence.[32]

Although it is certainly the case that Aristotle is not characterized by "historical consciousness" in any way that approximates present-day meanings of the term, his putative lack of awareness about the transience of the polis is open to question. MacIntyre himself draws attention to the key fact when he writes, "Aristotle who saw the forms of social life of the city-state as normative for essential human nature was himself a servant of that Macedonian royal power which destroyed the city-state as a free society."[33] Aristotle lives and writes at a time when the fragile association of the polis is being swallowed up by larger and more powerful empires.[34] In addition to the experience of empire, he writes of the household, village, and tribe. It may well be that Aristotle demotes these forms of association in his study of politics for the same reason that he turns away from empire as a site for sustained political investigation. It is characteristic of Aristotle's approach to the study of nature that he takes his bearings from a specimen in its prime, not necessarily in its final stages of development. It may well be the case that the fortuitous set of circumstances that gave rise to the development of the Greek polis becomes the locus classicus for Aristotle's study less out of cultural bias, and more because it offers the most transparent window from which to view the ethical capacities and problems of political animals.[35] The point here is not that human nature changes in a fundamental way under alternative modes of association (something that Aristotle would deny), but that it may become more distorted and therefore more difficult to see. If eighteenth- and especially nineteenth-century thinkers could boast of an insight into the historicity of all knowledge, Aristotle's deepest challenge to modern and post-modern modes of thought arises from a series of insights afforded by the fleeting arrangements and proportions of the Greek polis.

MacIntyre's emphasis on tradition corresponds in part to Aristotle's insistence that ethics is part of the study of politics and that education is always embedded in a regime; that is, a particular political form of association that carries its own limitations and possibilities. The absence of a perfectly just political arrangement (as evidenced in *Politics* VII–VIII) means that the particular and authoritative moral code embodied in any given political association (whether polis, nation-state, or empire) will always be found wanting at least to some degree. Rather than provide a perfectly rational basis for morality, Aristotle acknowledges the existence of a persistent irrationality in ethical practice while, at the same time, attempting to render ethical inquiry more consistent with itself and, to that extent, more rational. Whereas the political (or in MacIntyre's terms, historical) context for ethical practice means that the practice of ethical virtue is invariably problematic from the point of view of reason, Aristotle also directs readers to a kind of theoretical excellence that transcends in a particular way the political context from which it arises.

To be sure Aristotle does not invoke a Platonic "idea of the good" or a Kantian notion of a priori categories deduced from reason itself. Rather, beginning with the inescapably political condition within which humans find themselves, his own inquiries reveal a constant sifting of authoritative opinions so as to render them increasingly consistent with themselves and one another. Based, however, on the number of issues that remain unresolved, it would be more accurate to characterize Aristotle's "philosophy of human affairs" (*NE* 10.9.1181b15), not in terms of final conclusions, but as an attempt to delineate the natural parameters of enduring problems that accompany human attempts to live together and to live well. Indeed, the dialectical process exhibited in Aristotle's political investigations suggests a much more *zetetic* understanding of the human good than is typically attributed to him. This point is partially recognized by MacIntyre,[36] but is at odds with his belief that Aristotle's ethical teaching reflects an insufficiently critical dependence on existing canons of Greek practice as they have been shaped by the polis. MacIntyre's historical perspective underestimates the extent to which Aristotle combines genuine solicitude for authoritative opinion (*endoxa*) with critical scrutiny of those same opinions. Aristotle, unlike the thinkers of the Enlightenment, does not attempt to cut reason free from the moorings of tradition but is open to the possibility that one can distill from the always contingent character of political practice, universal standards of human goodness that apply to human beings as such. If Aristotle's teaching about human nature emerges from critical examination of the authoritative practice of the Greek polis, it is, nevertheless, a nature that embraces all human beings regardless of the particular historical circumstances that impinge upon the narrative unity of any given life. In this regard, Martha Nussbaum's attempts to sketch the essential attributes of a human life regardless of political culture or historical era seem to capture an essential aspect of Aristotle's persistent challenge and contribution to contemporary debate.[37]

Metaphysical Biology versus Narrative Unity

MacIntyre maintains that the teleological conception upon which Aristotle builds his notion of virtue rests upon an untenable metaphysical biology. The rejection of that biology renders his account of human flourishing vulnerable by depriving it of a *telos* that could justify his teaching on virtue as it is confronted by rival and incompatible beliefs about human flourishing. As a result, any adequate Aristotelian account of human virtue requires a new teleology, one that MacIntyre develops out of the notion of narrative unity. The most relevant questions to be raised here are whether Aristotle's ethical teaching in fact presupposes a metaphysical biology in the sense in which MacIntyre understands it and, if not, how Aristotle's biology compares to MacIntyre's notion of narrative unity as the most promising locus for a credible teleology.

Aristotle is famous for beginning the *Metaphysics* with the statement that all human beings naturally desire to know. As he develops this idea in his study of ethics, it leads to a no less famous elevation of *theōria* as the key activity of a flourishing human life. The best life for a human being is one lived in accordance with the almost divine activity of *nous*. This amounts to asserting that human beings are by nature metaphysical animals, a teaching that, MacIntyre notes, stands in some tension to Aristotle's equally famous claim that human beings are by nature political animals.[38] Aristotle's elucidation of human nature is framed by two poles which together delimit the sphere of distinctively human activity: human beings both live together with others in political communities and are capable of some kind of theoretical awareness of nature as a whole. Both ends of the human spectrum build upon some notion of human biology and, as is so often the case in Aristotle's writing, each stands in tension with the other.[39]

Stephen Salkever has done much to recover a genuinely Aristotelian notion of teleology by showing that it is not derived from his metaphysics.[40] Speaking of Aristotle's use of teleology in the "social sciences," Salkever explains that Aristotle begins with a sense of nature or biological inheritance that is neither determinative of nor irrelevant to human action. Since our biological inheritance includes a number of impulses not all of which are compatible, with no master impulse or structure of drives to control human life, political life cannot be reduced to either biological drive or ethical ideal. Politics arises neither spontaneously nor in opposition to biological inheritance, but as the unintended result of attempts to live securely. At the heart of the political problem is a tension among conflicting needs that does not admit of precise practical or theoretical resolution. Consequently, Salkever argues that Aristotelian political science is guided by a set of questions that define the task of social science: namely, how particular communities can best solve the problems of living, living together, and living well, which, as problems requiring simultaneous resolution, make human experience unique.

Aristotle combines two only apparently contradictory premises: (1) that there is an intelligible human good that holds universally, and (2) that appropriate responses to particular political questions vary from one context to another. No general rule or system can be derived directly from an adequate theoretical understanding of the human good. Indeed, the greatest political dangers arise from those who ignore theory and those who think it can be applied directly to politics. The human situation both requires and makes possible the development of two distinct kinds of intellectual virtue of paramount importance. Theoretical reason gropes toward some understanding of the whole of which human beings are a part, and practical reason seeks to apply that understanding to the specific circumstances within which particular human beings find themselves. Aristotle does not derive his ethical teaching from a set of metaphysical commitments; rather his metaphysical assertions arise from unresolved conflicts at the core of politics. As such they are always, at least in principle, available.

MacIntyre's alternative to Aristotelian teleology is found in the notion of the narrative unity of tradition. Notwithstanding the acknowledgment of ruptures or crises within and by which traditions grow, MacIntyre's emphasis on narrative unity underplays the profound dislocations that characterize the unfolding of a historical tradition. This becomes evident in his willingness to analyze both Aristotle and Aquinas as representatives of the concept of tradition. The amorphous character of what MacIntyre calls "the Aristotelian tradition" proves to be a two-edged sword. On the one hand, the fluidity of any particular tradition enables it to live beyond its original historical epoch but, on the other, it necessarily burdens that tradition with historical accretions that blur the distinctive contributions of its most remarkable thinkers—in this case, *either* Aristotle *or* Aquinas.

MacIntyre would, of course, be the first to acknowledge the revolutionary character of Aquinas's transformation of Aristotelian inquiry. His analysis attributes to Aquinas the establishment of a new paradigm, one that transcends the two rival and incommensurable schemes of inquiry and belief found in Aristotle and Augustine, by reconstructing the thought of each within the framework of a unified metaphysical theology.[41] MacIntyre attempts to sustain a delicate balance: on the one hand, his recognition of the revolutionary character of Aquinas's achievement emphasizes the discontinuity between Aquinas's teaching and that of Aristotle (or Augustine for that matter) but, on the other, his deployment of the historical notion of narrative unity points to the continuity between Aristotelian and Thomistic inquiry. In one sense this is clearly a reasonable position since, however deep the divide between them, Aquinas took over much of the language and thought of Aristotle and it is largely through the power of his synthesis that Aristotle has been preserved in the Christian West. What is more problematic is the extent to which MacIntyre's conscious effort to place the categories of history into the forefront of his project effectively blurs the distinction between—to use MacIntyre's own language—two rival traditions of inquiry. MacIntyre wants to have it both ways. While he maintains that Aquinas's transformation of Aristotle constitutes a paradigm shift, he also subsumes these differences under the single concept of tradition. The latter, which provides the fundamental conceptual framework for MacIntyre's project as a whole, effectively undercuts the force of the former.

The problems with this mode of analysis are manifest in subtle but important ways. The first problem has already been anticipated in the previous two sections but can now be described as a tendency to allow the historical triumph of Aquinas's appropriation of Aristotle to color MacIntyre's reading of Aristotle himself. This is perhaps most apparent in MacIntyre's interpretation of Aristotle's account of practical rationality. MacIntyre quickly dismisses the "intellectualist" reading of Aristotle and settles the controversy concerning the relationship between ethical and intellectual virtue in a way that appears closer to Aquinas than Aristotle. For example, in *Whose Justice? Which Rationality?* MacIntyre maintains that, *for Aristotle,* the life of the mind "is impossible" without moral and political virtue, and that "all rational practical activity has as its ultimate final cause the vision, so far as it is open to human beings, of what God sees."[42] This is consistent with the position that MacIntyre maintains in *After Virtue,* where he contends that both Aristotle and Aquinas are committed to a strong thesis concerning the unity of the virtues, notwithstanding the different grounds (polis and *civitas Dei*) that, he acknowledges, underlie each position.[43] As I have already argued, MacIntyre's emphasis on the unity of virtues in Aristotle ignores some of the crucial and unresolved ambiguities characteristic of his treatment of politics. This may or may not derive from a tendency to read Aristotle through the optic provided by Aquinas, but it is, in any case, more compatible with the metaphysical unity grounding Aquinas's approach than with the kind of open-ended investigations characteristic of Aristotle's writing.

Secondly, MacIntyre too readily dismisses the extent to which Aristotle's own inquiry might provide the most searching challenge to prevailing historical sensibilities. To his credit, MacIntyre insists that Aquinas does not merely supplement Aristotle's reliance upon the categories of nature, but offers a radical critique of it.[44] In Aquinas's view, the defective character of Aristotle's treatment turns out to reflect a defect in the natural human order of which he provides an account. This leads Aquinas to draw upon the Augustinian understanding of fallen human nature in order to explain the limitations in Aristotle's argument. Aquinas is in this way able to "improve" upon Aristotle by inserting his understanding of practical rationality and virtue into a Pauline and Augustinian framework. The magnitude of Aquinas's accomplishment consists precisely in showing how the comprehensive natural and political science of Aristotle could in fact be reconciled with the grace of the gospels; a reconciliation that inevitably and profoundly transformed what MacIntyre calls the Aristotelian tradition. The thought of both Aristotle and Aquinas can be characterized as "foundational," but in fundamentally different ways. Whereas Aristotle sought to ground his understanding by moving toward some biologically informed conception of *nature,* Aquinas anchored his appropriation of Aristotle on the authority of grace as it has been revealed in *history.*[45]

It may well be the case that Aquinas improves upon Aristotle but this would not, in any obvious way, be the position of Aristotle himself. MacIntyre seems too quick to assign the victory to Aquinas without providing an equally compelling analysis of the way in which Aristotle would put into question the theological underpinnings of the alternative he provides. Presumably, Aristotle could claim that Aquinas's arguments for the existence of God are unconvincing and that whatever limitations inhere in his own account, they are preferable to the leap of faith required by Aquinas's reliance on the biblical tradition.[46] In principle, there is room in MacIntyre's analysis for such an articulation, but he seems uninterested or unwilling to provide one. This follows from his historicist analysis of Aristotle, one that makes it impossible for the foundational elements in Aristotle's thought to have applicability outside the polis or, more generally, ancient Greek culture without undergoing the kind of radical transformation embodied in the writing of Aquinas.

I can only suggest the underlying issue here, one that points to what may be the deepest difference between what MacIntyre and Strauss each learn from their study of ancient political philosophy. For MacIntyre, it appears that the discontinuity between the Enlightenment project on the one hand and the pre-modern ancient *or* medieval versions of Aristotle on the other is most telling. Although Strauss also emphasizes the profound divide separating ancient and modern understandings of politics, he gives much greater weight to differences that arise from the philosophic perspective (in either its ancient or modern expressions) and those that arise from a perspective that is grounded in biblical faith.[47] MacIntyre's willingness to speak of Aristotle and Aquinas as representatives of a single, albeit transformed, historical tradition pushes into the background one of the deepest and most fruitful controversies in the West.

It is possible to sketch this controversy by delineating the key difference between Aristotle and Aquinas, one that is necessarily de-emphasized by MacIntyre's reliance on the historical concept of tradition. Notwithstanding the brilliance of the Thomistic synthesis, Aquinas necessarily subordinates Aristotle's conception of nature to the more authoritative standard imparted by divine revelation; that is, the relative priority given to nature and authority in Aristotle is reversed by Aquinas. Aquinas is, of course, at pains to demonstrate the extent to which the natural order sought in Aristotelian philosophy is harmonious with the datum of revelation. From the point of view of theology, this is perfectly sensible since the God of revelation is at the same time the author of creation. Hence, any discrepancy between the findings of natural science and the teachings of biblical revelation can only be a temporary impasse, the result of either or both insufficient scientific understanding of the natural world or a mistaken appropriation of the truth of revelation. In principle—that is, theological principle—there can be no conflict between the order of grace and that of nature since they both arise from and are sustained by the same inexhaustible source. For Aquinas, the historical and authoritative biblical tradition provides the touchstone against which to sharpen and complete a conception of nature.

By way of contrast, it is characteristic of Aristotelian inquiry that traditions based on authority—even the highest authority—are subordinated to critical scrutiny as a way of distinguishing conventional authority from a more universal notion of nature (within which authority still holds a proper but subordinate place). The point here is that MacIntyre's notion of tradition does not apply equally or adequately to both Aristotle and Aquinas. Whereas Aquinas grounds his inquiry in a tradition of faith that leads him to build his understanding on a fundamental and non-negotiable truth about God's existence, there is and can be no comparable notion of authoritative tradition in Aristotle. If theology views philosophy as its handmaiden, a tool to help clarify the deposit of faith, philosophy is necessarily suspicious of claims that cannot be made transparent to reason but rest instead upon an authority that purports to be higher than reason. Each claims final authority for itself and the absence of some higher ground recognized as such by each side of the dispute means that this conflict cannot be resolved.[48] A vital and irreducible conflict between philosophy and revelation lies buried beneath MacIntyre's historical notion of the unity of a narrative tradition.

For Aristotle, the discovery of nature is driven by critical examination of the most authoritative opinions. This is in the first place a negative project regarding the most pervasive cultural paradigms of politics and morals. Aristotle's project is also positive, but this dimension of his teaching is often misunderstood in no small measure because of a tendency to overestimate the continuity within what MacIntyre takes to be the Aristotelian tradition. It is more appropriately understood as positive in the open-ended way it attempts to delineate the natural parameter within which one might fruitfully investigate the enduring problems of an animal at once both political and metaphysical.

ARISTOTLE ON MACINTYRE'S TURN TO HISTORY

MacIntyre brings to the surface ethical fault lines partially concealed beneath the unprecedented political and economic successes of modern liberalism. As we have seen, the peculiar predicament characteristic of contemporary political debate is brought about by the absence of any undisputed notion of nature or reason to adjudicate disagreements about the human good. One immediate consequence of the contemporary situation is that the value of Aristotle's perspective can only come to light as a debate between rival and conflicting versions of moral inquiry. MacIntyre aptly identifies the manner in which such a debate could be carried out.[49] It is first necessary to identify and characterize limitations and failures in rival traditions of inquiry as judged by that tradition's own standards. The ability to explain and understand those limitations and failures in some precise way, together with a rival version's inability to do the same, would demonstrate the rational superiority of a particular viewpoint without presupposing any shared horizon. In *Three Rival Versions*, MacIntyre brilliantly engages both the enlightenment and genealogical perspectives in exactly this way as part of his attempt to reveal the superior intellectual resources of what he calls the Aristotelian tradition, but what might more accurately be called the Thomistic appropriation of Aristotle.

If this sort of engagement is well calculated to demonstrate the continued fruitfulness of a certain kind of Aristotelianism in a post-modern world, it is hard to imagine that it is a sufficient account of the hold it exercises over MacIntyre himself. Though he never says so, I suspect that MacIntyre embraces Thomistic Aristotelianism, not because of its ability to survive epistemological crises, but because he simply believes it to be true; in the contemporary situation, the former provides a necessary propaedeutic to the latter. MacIntyre succeeds in winning a hearing for his views (at least in part) by presenting them as one side in an ongoing debate, the winner of which will be determined by the verdict of history.

MacIntyre's pedagogical strategy, if it may be called that, is inseparable from the immense influence he has had on contemporary ethical debate, saturated as it is with methodological and historical self-consciousness. The apparently fatuous character of Aristotle's invocation of nature does not result merely from the kind of self-evident stature imputed to the most pervasive aspects of consciousness within a particular historical epoch. Rather, the turn from nature to history is a long and complex story involving both the rise of biblical consciousness (which elevates history as the realm in which God acts) and the constructive project of modern philosophy (which deliberately sets itself the task of overcoming the strictures of nature). The historical categories of thinking that result from the problematic relationship between these two dynamic sources of modern consciousness constitute the necessary starting points for contemporary discourse, and it is here that MacIntyre begins his own efforts to criticize both the extravagant hopes of the Enlightenment project and the equally extravagant despair that accompanies its failure.

MacIntyre's halfway house is the notion of the unity of narrative tradition. It is, however, a halfway house that floats on the undulating sea of history (notwithstanding the ballast of tradition) rather than nature. Ironically, MacIntyre's attempt to give a certain kind of historicist defense of the Aristotelian tradition as it is found in Aquinas obscures the deepest challenge that each of these thinkers presents to current sensibilities.

MacIntyre rightly emphasizes the unfinished character of Aquinas's version of inquiry, a characteristic reflected in his use of the "disputed question." But in MacIntyre's account of the rationality of traditions, the unfinished character of the Thomistic project is given an un-Thomistic emphasis. Confrontation with rival traditions necessarily brings with it the possibility of discovering a more rationally acceptable alternative. The problem with this view arises from the fact that it makes adherence to tradition conditional since, to be rational, adherence depends upon continual success in supplying an account of rival traditions superior to those which they are able to offer on their own behalf. Further, there is no way of ruling out ahead of time the possibility that some other tradition could furnish a more rational account than that to which one had been provisionally attached. While philosophically consistent, both the conditional character of adherence to tradition and the authority given to reason in this analysis are deeply at odds with the position of Aquinas.

Aquinas maintains the superiority of his position, not because of its ability of survive an epistemological crisis, but because of its truth. For Aquinas truth is not in the least affected by the verdict of human history or the powers of human rationality since it rests upon the unassailable ground of divine revelation. Whether it is accepted or not, the definitive (if still unfolding) truth about the nature and destiny of human beings has inserted itself into human history with the result that any engagement with a rival tradition of inquiry is both constrained and bolstered by this fact. Christians live not by what can be made transparent to human reason, but by faith in what remains in some crucial sense unseen. Moreover, their adherence to the tradition of faith is not conditional but assured, drawing from a hope that is not confined to human rationality or to the changing currents of human history, but whose source springs from the City of God. Paradoxically, MacIntyre's historicist defense of the superiority of the Thomistic perspective is unable to account for the heart and soul of the very version of inquiry he upholds as the example par excellence of the rationality of tradition. It is for this reason, I suggest, that MacIntyre's rendition of Thomism might best be understood as a pedagogical strategy, perhaps in some sense analogous to the place occupied by the wager in Pascal's defense of Christianity.

However one might assess the resources of the Thomistic tradition with which MacIntyre has associated himself, the paradoxical character of his analysis is deepened by the fact that it causes him to rule out the most radical challenge to contemporary sensibilities, one that comes not from Thomas but from Aristotle. Notwithstanding the profound differences separating the Thomistic tradition from the modern paradigms of encyclopedia and genealogy, there is one respect in which all three versions of inquiry have more in common with each other than with Aristotle—all are imbued with some form of the historical consciousness that informs MacIntyre's own analysis. The Thomistic, or more generally biblical, tradition elevates history as the locus of divine revelation and lives from a hope that is directed to the City of God.[50] The encyclopedic tradition looks to a secularized version of Christian hope, one that will be fully achieved in history based on the gradual and steady progress of science. The genealogical perspective registers disappointment at the loss of Enlightenment hopes for rational progress, unmasking all claims to larger purpose as disguised expressions of the will to power. MacIntyre's critique of contemporary sensibilities is circumscribed by the historical consciousness from which it arises. If this enables him to engage contemporary thinkers on their own terms, it simultaneously deprives him of the full force of Aristotle's challenge to the most pervasive (and therefore most hidden and most unquestioned) sensibilities of modern or post-modern consciousness.

It is possible to articulate Aristotle's radical challenge to prevailing sensibilities as a claim: The peculiarities of ancient Greek politics offer a privileged insight into the essential and defining problems of human nature, a nature that, although currently eclipsed by the pervasive influence of historical consciousness, cannot be altogether snuffed out. An Aristotelian perspective holds that the most profound truths (including those involving human beings) are grounded in nature; what is new, distinctive, or historically unique is important, and even crucially important, but ultimately as part of an always imperfect effort to disclose the unchanging ground of being from which these variations arise. But this is also to say that variations in politics, religion, and history are themselves subordinate—despite their authority or charm—to the fundamental category of nature. The effort to understand Aristotle in his own terms proves more radical than the attempt to clarify his thought from a perspective allegedly superior to that of Aristotle himself. It yields an account of human nature that is free from both the hopes and disappointments entangled in historical consciousness.

MacIntyre's effort to transpose Aristotle into a contemporary key, particularly his attempt to rescue the notions of *telos* and political community by deriving them from the categories of narrative unity and tradition conceals, or at least partially conceals, despair about the possibility of rational inquiry as Aristotle understands it. Whereas MacIntyre gives history the final word (the rationality of a tradition is gauged by its ability to survive an "epistemological crisis"), Aristotle evaluates particular historical traditions in light of an understanding of nature—an understanding of the human good that includes, among other things, an awareness of the irreducibly political character of human being and rational inquiry. MacIntyre actually cedes more to Nietzsche's diagnosis of the historicity of all truth claims than he wishes, and for this reason finds it difficult to furnish an adequate theoretical ground upon which to resist the very forces of perspectivism and relativism that he seeks to subvert. To his credit, the very contradiction in MacIntyre's thought—his attempt to win a hearing for the perspective of nature from within the categories of history—poignantly reflects the contemporary predicament and does so with a brilliance and erudition that rivals the best contemporary thinkers.

Aristotle's alternative to MacIntyre's neo-Aristotelianism may, of course, be wrong but this cannot be known ahead of time. It could only be concluded on the basis of a genuine and sympathetic engagement with the most serious alternative he poses to the modern project and its aftermath. In this regard the work and legacy of Leo Strauss and, from a sympathetic but different point of view, the writing of Pierre Manent are marked by precisely this sort of engagement.[51] The writing of both Strauss and Manent emerges from within the ambit of Heidegger's profound meditations on the changing manifestations of Being in history. It is an encounter that leads them to recognize and examine in the classical accounts of the unchanging character of being(s), the radical alternative to Heidegger's thought. To the extent that MacIntyre insists on the fundamental importance of looking at Aristotle through the lens of history, he disallows Aristotle to put into question the most pervasive sensibilities of modern and post-modern consciousness, sensibilities that MacIntyre himself wishes to subject to critical examination. This is in no way to deny the importance of either historical inquiry or historical consciousness, both of which are essential facts of modern life. It is, however, to put into question the *fundamental* character of historical consciousness as an unassailable, virtually a priori, basis for the activity of philosophic investigation itself. Aristotle's inquiry into the nature of a political and metaphysical animal frames persistent tensions that characterize the human effort to live together and to live well, tensions that continue to give rise both to the need for and possibility of human virtue.

Notes

1. John Gunnell's *The Descent of Political Theory* (Chicago: University of Chicago, 1993) deftly brings into view and traces the lasting influence of the Weimar conversation on the history of political theory, particularly as it bears on the contemporary practice of social science in the United States.

2. Leo Strauss, *The City and Man* (Chicago: University of Chicago Press [1964] 1977), 1–3.

3. Alasdair MacIntyre, *After Virtue*, 2nd ed. (Notre Dame, Ind.: University of Notre Dame Press), 11–12.

4. Ibid., 21.

5. Michael Sandel, "The Procedural Republic and the Unencumbered Self," *Political Theory* 12, no. 1 (February 1984): 81–96.

6. MacIntyre, *After Virtue*, 52.

7. Ibid., 140.

8. Ibid., 55.

9. Alasdair MacIntyre, *Whose Justice? Which Rationality?* (Notre Dame, Ind.: University of Notre Dame Press, 1988), 334–35.

10. MacIntyre, *After Virtue*, 113.

11. Ibid., 117–18.

12. Strauss argues that the radical historicism of Heidegger is prepared in a decisive way by Nietzsche's attack on nineteenth-century historicism. Although Nietzsche preserves a kind of classical ambiguity or complexity that Heidegger abandons, Strauss maintains that Nietzsche nevertheless adopted "the fundamental premise of the historical school" (*Natural Right and History* [Chicago: University of Chicago Press (1953) 1968], 26–27, n. 9).

13. For MacIntyre's development of the notion of "practice," see *After Virtue*, 187ff.

14. Ibid., 216.

15. Ibid., 219.

16. Ibid., 222.

17. MacIntyre, *Whose Justice?* 349–69.

18. This is especially true of *Whose Justice? Which Rationality?* and *Three Rival Versions of Moral Enquiry: Encyclopaedia, Genealogy, and Tradition* (Notre Dame, Ind.: University of Notre Dame Press, 1990).

19. *Whose Justice?* 402–403; *Three Rival Versions*, 196–215.

20. *After Virtue*, 162–63. In his most recent work, MacIntyre reaffirms the need to repudiate "important elements in Aristotle's biology," although he now acknowledges the impossibility of rendering ethics completely independent of biology. He sets himself to this task in *Dependent Rational Animals* (Chicago and La Salle: Open Court, 1999), see esp. p. x. MacIntyre does not, however, go so far as to withdraw or qualify the notion of the narrative unity of tradition as the proper locus for a defensible notion of teleology.

21. *After Virtue*, 163.

22. Among the most influential of the many scholars who have debated this question, W. F. R. Hardie's "Aristotle on the Best Life for a Man," *Philosophy* 54 (1979): 35–50 and Richard Kraut's *Aristotle on the Human Good* (Princeton, N.J.: Princeton University Press, 1989) have argued the former position whereas J. L. Ackrill's "Aristotle on *Eudaimonia*," in *Essays on Aristotle's Ethics*, ed. A. Rorty (Berkeley: University of California Press, 1980) and John Cooper's *Reason and Human Good in Aristotle* (Indianapolis: Hackett, [1975] 1986) the latter.

23. The following discussion of the concluding book of the *Nicomachean Ethics* is an abridged version of an argument I have made more fully in *Reading Aristotle's Ethics: Virtue, Rhetoric and Political Philosophy* (Albany, N.Y.: State University of New York Press, 1996), especially in chapter five.

24. René Gauthier and Jean Jolif point out that the decision to put this question aside as inappropriate in the present context has occasioned a great deal of comment on the part of those who are uncomfortable with Aristotle's willingness to turn away from such a crucial issue. They observe that most major commentators (Alexander of Aphrodisias, Michael of Ephesus, St. Albert, St. Thomas, et al.) have not been able to resist the temptation to try to resolve a question that the text leaves in suspense. See *L'Éthique à Nicomaque*, ed. René Gauthier and Jean Jolif, vol. 2 (Louvain: Publications Universitaires, 1970), 843–44.

25. The tension between ethical and philosophic virtue preserved in these three arguments in Book X is augmented by Aristotle's earlier treatment in Book VII. Although only alluded to here, I have argued that Aristotle's new beginning in Book VII reveals a radical dissonance between ethical and philosophic excellence, a dissonance that is softened but not retracted in his final comparative evaluation in Book X. See *Reading Aristotle's Ethics*, ch. 3.

26. This formulation is influenced by Thomas Nagel's discussion of the competition between theoretical and practical reason, although we emphasize different aspects of the contest. "Aristotle on *Eudaimonia*," in *Essays on Aristotle's Ethics*, ed. A. Rorty (Berkeley: University of California Press, 1980), 257–58.

27. For a systematic analysis of each of these tensions, see *Reading Aristotle's Ethics*.

28. MacIntyre's sharpest expression of this view is found in *A Short History of Ethics* (New York: Macmillan, 1966), esp. 66–68 and 78–80. Although he softens the harshness of this critique in subsequent books, the same fundamental point continues to find expression. Consider the general dependence of Aristotelian virtue upon the social structure of the polis in *After Virtue* (discussed below) and fainter echo with respect to the virtue of magnanimity in *Dependent Rational Animals*, 127.

29. For realistic assessments from different points of view of continuing conflicts in Aristotle's best regime, see Bernard Yack, *The Problems of a Political Animal* (Berkeley: University of California Press, 1993) and Robert Bartlett, "The 'Realism' of Classical Political Science: An Introduction to Aristotle's Best Regime," in *Action and Contemplation*, ed. Robert Bartlett and Susan Collins (Albany, N.Y.: State University of New York Press, 1999).

30. Strauss maintains that Aristotle is "the discoverer of moral virtue," something that, from Plato's point of view, "is a kind of halfway house between political or vulgar virtue which is in the service of bodily well-being . . . and genuine virtue which, to say the least, animates only the philosophers as philosophers" (*The City and Man*, 27).

31. *After Virtue*, 159.

32. Ibid., 163.

33. Ibid., 159.

34. Ronald Beiner, writing about Gadamer's Aristotelian insight into the primacy of *ethos*, observes that Aristotle may have composed the *Ethics* "from within an awareness that the essential force of this *ethos* had already exhausted itself"; that is, "he was describing an ethical culture that had been, since the emergence of the Sophists, in the process of losing its sway" ("Do We Need a Philosophical Ethics?" in *Action and Contemplation*, ed. Robert Bartlett and Susan Collins [Albany, N.Y.: State University of New York Press, 1999], 42).

35. Consider Strauss's remarks on the extent to which Aristotle's understanding is circumscribed by the limitations of the Greek polis in *City and Man*, 30–35.

36. *After Virtue*, 219.

37. See especially Martha Nussbaum's "Human Functioning and Social Justice: In Defense of Aristotelian Essentialism," *Political Theory* (May 1992): 202–246 and "Non-Relative Virtue: An Aristotelian Approach," *Midwest Studies in Phi-*

losophy 12 (1988): 32–53. The political implications of this approach to ethics are developed in "Aristotelian Social Democracy," included in the first part of this volume.

38. *After Virtue,* 158.

39. David O'Connor observes that just as contemplation is natural in the beginning of the *Metaphysics* and mere sociality in the beginning of the *Politics,* so the enjoyment of rhythm and mimesis is said to be natural at the beginning of the *Poetics.* Not only philosophy, but its two chief rivals—politics and poetry—first come to light as natural. I take this occasion to acknowledge O'Connor's helpful critique of an earlier version of this essay.

40. Salkever provides a full argument for this position in *Finding the Mean: Theory and Practice in Aristotelian Political Philosophy* (Princeton, N.J.: Princeton University Press, 1990). This paragraph is especially indebted to his summary statement on p. 103. The contemporary relevance of Aristotle's insistence on the biological basis for ethics is developed in a systematic way by Larry Arnhart in *Darwinian Natural Right: The Biological Ethics of Human Nature* (Albany, N.Y.: State University of New York, 1998).

41. MacIntyre is especially forthcoming about the revolutionary character of Aquinas's transformation of Aristotelian thought in chapter 10 of *Whose Justice? Which Rationality?* Cf. *Three Rival Versions,* esp. 122.

42. *Whose Justice? Which Rationality?* ch. 8, p. 143.

43. Cf. *After Virtue,* 180 and *Whose Justice? Which Rationality?* 181.

44. Consider especially *Whose Justice? Which Rationality?* 205, 181–82.

45. MacIntyre alludes to the crucial role of the Bible in generating historical consciousness in his discussion of medieval Aristotelianism. He writes, "It is the linking of a biblical historical perspective with an Aristotelian one . . . which is the unique achievement of the middle ages in Jewish and Islamic terms as well as in Christian" (*After Virtue,* 180).

46. Charles Griswold makes a similar point in his review of *Three Rival Versions. Political Theory* 19 (August 1991): 465–66.

47. Consider Leo Strauss's "The Mutual Influence of Theology and Philosophy," *Independent Journal of Philosophy* 3 (1979): 111–18.

48. This problem is given its sharpest articulation in Leo Strauss's "The Mutual Influence of Theology and Philosophy."

49. This is spelled out with greatest clarity in *Three Rival Versions,* 181.

50. This is not to imply that Aquinas is thinking in historical categories in the way that adherents of the encyclopedic or genealogical traditions do. Like Aristotle, Aquinas thinks in terms of nature but, unlike Aristotle, it is a nature that has been illuminated by the events of biblical history and will be seen most clearly when human history ceases.

51. Consider especially Strauss's *Natural Right and History* and Manent's "Strauss and Nietzsche" and "On Historical Causality," in *Modern Liberty and its Discontents,* ed. and trans. Daniel J. Mahoney and Paul Seaton (Boston: Rowman & Littlefield, 1998), 199–214.

CHAPTER FIVE

Leo Strauss's Aristotle and Martin Heidegger's Politics

DAVID K. O'CONNOR

In 1933, Martin Heidegger assumed the rectorship of the University of Freiburg. His inaugural address, "The Self-Assertion of the German University," called for a spiritual and institutional revolution at the university that would complement the larger political revolution occurring through National Socialism. The peroration of this infamous Rectoral Address suggests that Heidegger at that moment had a much greater appreciation of the risks he was running than is sometimes ascribed to him by either defenders or critics. Referring to the National Socialist revolution, but also to the philosophic revolution opened up by his own path of thinking, he invoked Plato's *Republic*, the great blueprint of philosophic revolution:[1]

> We fully understand the splendor and greatness of this revolutionary beginning [*Aufbruch*] only when we carry within ourselves that profound and far-reaching thoughtfulness that gave ancient Greek wisdom the word: *Ta megala panta episphalē*. 'All that is great stands in the storm [*Sturm*].' (Plato, *Republic* 497d9) (Rectoral Address, 480)

Heidegger's version of his concluding quotation from the sixth book of the *Republic* is not a simple translation of the Greek, which more literally says, "All that is great risks a fall." Though many have roundly criticized Heidegger's version as a misappropriation of Plato's text,[2] it is in fact a splendid compression of the entire section of which this passage is the conclusion. The section begins when Adeimantus sets philosophy a terrible dilemma about its relationship to politics: "Of all those who start out on philosophy—not those who take it up for the sake of getting educated when they are young and then drop it, but those who linger in it for a longer time—most become quite queer, not to say completely vicious; while the ones who seem perfectly decent, do nevertheless suffer at least one consequence of the practice you are praising—they become useless to the cities" (*Republic* 6, 487c6–d5, Bloom trans.). In the first case, philosophy becomes subservient to the more action-oriented ambitions of power and politics, a ready source of excuses and rationalizations. In the second, philosophy is simply discontinuous with the serious business of adult life, an idle amusement. The more disdainfully philosophy cocoons itself in idleness from the serious world, the more indulgent and irrelevant it seems; but the more resolutely it "takes direction" from the serious world and cares for it, the more philosophy threatens to become a tool of partisan political projects.

Socrates concedes that much is true about Adeimantus' dilemma. In the first place, those with the natural endowments for philosophy are most exposed to the temptations of despotism: the potential philosopher is also the potential tyrant (*Republic* 6, 491e1–492a5). Only if some stroke of luck keeps these talented people from being carried away by political ambition can they remain uncorrupted; Socrates cites here the example of his *daimonion*, the divine sign that has always turned him away from political engagement (*Republic* 6, 496c3–5). But even if a genuine philosopher should somehow arise, he cannot safely exercise political power in any actual city, since he is in the position of a knowledgeable pilot stranded on a ship of fools (*Republic* 6, 488a1–489a2). "He keeps quiet and minds his own business—as a man in a storm, when dust and rain are blown about by the wind, stands aside under a little wall" (*Republic* 6, 496d6–8, Bloom trans.). As a result, the retiring philosopher will miss out on the opportunity political leadership could provide for him to grow more himself and to save the common good along with his own (*Republic* 6, 497a3–5). Nevertheless, Socrates takes up the challenge to show "how a city can take philosophy in hand without being destroyed" (*Republic* 6, 497d8–9), and it is at this point that Socrates gives Adeimantus the very warning Heidegger gave his colleagues and students: "*Ta megala panta episphalē*." Like Socrates, Heidegger decides to run the risk of stepping out from behind the wall into the storm.

Leo Strauss studied classical political philosophy always with an eye on Adeimantus' dilemma. This emphasis made the center of gravity of his own writing on Aristotle quite different from that of interpreters who read the *Ethics*, *Politics*, and *Rhetoric* looking instead for, say, models of community or political deliberation or political discourse. Strauss's emphasis here was a sound one by his own criterion: it reflects well Aristotle's own preoccupations, so Strauss's focus opens us to understanding Aristotle as he understood himself. The existential choice between the political life and the philosophic life informs all of Aristotle's investigations of political affairs.[3]

But Strauss's Aristotle interpretation, prominent in his writings for two decades, from the mid-1940s to the mid-1960s, also had a purpose beyond understanding Aristotle in himself. It became the central vehicle through which Strauss worked out his own complicated appropriation of and resistance to Martin Heidegger.

The continuing importance of the question of the relation between philosophy and politics has been revealed to all by Heidegger's intimacy with National Socialism. But unlike many commentators, Strauss did not leave things at finding in Heidegger an example of the political naivete or presumption to which intellectuals are prey. Strauss took with complete seriousness Heidegger's claim that his own reconception of philosophy was a return to the essence of Greek philosophy, and particularly of Aristotle's philosophy. When Strauss proposed his own distinctive account of Aristotle, he was at the same time trying to rechannel the intellectual energies of Heidegger's appropriation of him, an appropriation central to Heidegger's own philosophic revolution. Strauss felt a special urgency to resist Heidegger's attack on the Aristotelian dichotomy between politically engaged practical reason and detached or disinterested theoretical reason, since Strauss saw this attack as the precondition of Heidegger's replacement of virtue in Aristotle with resoluteness in his own thought. But at the same time, Strauss was deeply indebted to Heidegger's account of philosophy's responsibilities to prephilosophic experience. In the first section, I will sketch Heidegger's philosophical position as Strauss saw it, and make clear what Strauss wished to appropriate and what to resist in this position. In the second, I show how Strauss's exchange with Alexandre Kojève reveals that a number of Strauss's distinctive ideas about the relation between philosophy and politics are covert responses to Heidegger. Finally, we will consider how Strauss's Aristotle has been constructed to contribute to this implicit polemic, examining Strauss's interpretation of a few crucial texts from the *Politics* and *Nicomachean Ethics*.

Leo Strauss's Heidegger:
Philosophy as Practical and Patriotic

As a first approximation, we can say that two related themes of Martin Heidegger's thought in the 1920s were to be particularly important for Leo Strauss's work: the essential involvement of theoretical reason with decision and resolute commitment, and the continuity between philosophic and prephilosophic understanding. Strauss's problem with Heidegger, one might say, was how to preserve the benefits of the second without the pernicious costs of the first.

Heidegger's Early Aristotle Lectures and *Being and Time*

Strauss's first contact with Heidegger was in 1922, at Freiburg. A new holder of a doctoral degree, Strauss had come primarily to hear and meet Edmund Husserl, but came away most deeply impressed by what he understood of Heidegger's Aristotle ("A Giving of Accounts," 461).[4] These early Aristotle lectures contain much that received its definitive statement in *Being and Time* (1927). Strauss made special mention of Heidegger's interpretation of the famous first sentence of the *Metaphysics:* "All men by nature desire to know." In this and related lectures from the same period, Heidegger sought to strip away the traditional understanding of this sentence, which reduced it to a statement of the naturalness of idle and disinterested curiosity. Instead, Heidegger interpreted "desire to know" through his central concept of "care," blurring the sharp line between the practical and the theoretical.[5] Most crucially for Strauss, Heidegger's approach brought philosophic thinking back within the context of the temporally located decision making characteristic of practical wisdom. The theoretical could not be simply assumed to be separate from the interests of and demands on practical thinking. One was suddenly forced to think about, even to justify anew, the old Aristotelian verities that had established philosophy's independence of and superiority to the passionate engagements of politics. Impressed as he was by Heidegger's reformulation of theoretical thinking, Strauss resisted one defining feature of it: he "could not stomach" the central place of resoluteness ("A Giving of Accounts," 461). In a lecture from the 1950s he never published, Strauss gave an especially clear summary of what was so hard to swallow:[6]

> To be authentic means ... to risk oneself resolutely, despising sham certainties (and all objective certainties are sham). Only if man *is* in this way do the things in this world reveal themselves to him as they are. The concern with objectivity necessarily narrows the horizon. . . . . To live dangerously means to think exposedly. . . . . Commitment can only be understood by an understanding which is itself committed. . . . No human life that is not mere drifting or shallow is possible without a project, without an idea of existence and dedication to it: "idea of existence" [in Heidegger's thinking] takes the place [that is, especially the place held in Aristotle's ethics] of "respectable opinion of the good life." But "opinion" points to knowledge, whereas "idea of existence" implies that in this respect there is no knowledge possible, but only what is much higher than knowledge, that is, knowledge of what is: project or decision. ("An Introduction to Existentialism," 36, 37, 45; I have inserted the bracketed expansions.)

Finding the Heidegger of this period morally indigestible, Strauss later claimed he "ceased to take any interest in him for about two decades" ("A Giving of Accounts," 461).

Strauss's interest returned, it seems, by 1945, when he published the first version of his own distinctive Aristotle interpretation in the essay "On Classical Political Philosophy." Here and in later essays, Strauss emphasized the continuity between the concepts and interests of actual political life and the theorizing of authentic political philosophy. His development of this conception of political science, and his critique of approaches to political science modeled on the natural sciences, was deeply indebted to Heidegger's radicalization of Edmund Husserl's phenomenology. Heidegger argued that Husserl had not really lived up to his own slogan "Back to the things themselves," since Husserl began from an experience of the world already transformed by philosophy and its theoretical prejudice. Heidegger's phenomenological recovery of the truly natural world in *Being and Time* took as its starting point the world as made up of things ready-to-hand (that is, of what the Greeks would call *pragmata,* objects of our interest, engagement, and care) rather than of things merely present-to-hand (that is, *ousiai,* objects neutralized for our theoretical inspection). Strauss appropriated this *"pragmata*-ism" of Heidegger to develop his own view of how the political philosopher respects and refines what is valued by politics. It is this direct contact with the concepts and interests of everyday politics, Strauss argued, that allows the philosopher to be politically useful and responsible. This ascent from everyday political conceptions is fundamentally different from purportedly "scientific" methods in the study of politics. Politics cannot be understood, it can only be caricatured and distorted, by theorizing that does not take its bearings from the prephilosophic concerns and talents of engaged political actors.[7]

The challenge Strauss faced, then, was this: the very continuity he so much valued between prephilosophic politics and authentic political philosophy seems to invite Heidegger's claim that thinking as much as politics requires resolute engagement with destiny and fate. Strauss's most pointed statement of the problem focused on Heidegger's "improvement" on Nietzsche:[8]

> The radical historicist [that is, Heidegger] refuses to admit the transhistorical character of the historicist thesis. At the same time he recognizes the absurdity of historicism as a *theoretical* thesis. He denies, therefore, the possibility of a theoretical or objective analysis ... of the various comprehensive views.... The theoretical analysis of life is noncommittal and fatal to commitment, but life means commitment.... If not Nietzsche himself, at any rate his successors [especially Heidegger]

deny the possibility of theory proper and so conceive of thought as essentially subservient to, or dependent on, life or fate. (*Natural Right and History*, 26, emphasis added)

The prephilosophic starting points, to which philosophy must open itself, threaten to infect philosophy with the very aspects of willfulness, passion, and partisanship that made Heidegger's view of philosophy distasteful to Strauss. To see things as they are, Heidegger suggests, is impossible while approaching them in the cool detachment the tradition has taught us to seek in the philosopher.

The depth of Strauss's difficulty can be seen immediately when one considers how close Strauss's Aristotle comes to sharing this sentiment. For example, Strauss says in a critique of positivism, "Aristotelian political science necessarily *evaluates* political things; the knowledge in which it culminates has the character of categoric advice and of exhortation" ("An Epilogue," 207, emphasis added).[9] And when he characterizes the sort of political philosophy exemplified by Aristotle's *Politics,* he says: "Political things are by their nature subject to approval and disapproval, to choice and rejection, to praise and blame. It is of their essence not to be neutral but to raise a claim to men's obedience, allegiance, decision, or judgment. *One does not understand them as what they are,* i.e., as political things, if one does not take seriously their implicit or explicit claim to be judged in terms of goodness or badness, of justice and injustice, i.e., *if one does not measure them* by some standard of goodness or justice" ("What Is Political Philosophy?" 12, emphasis added).

I suggest that the interpretation of specific aspects of Aristotle's political science became one important way Strauss faced the challenge of preserving philosophy's *interest in* politics without letting philosophy become entangled in a Heideggerian *engagement with* politics. We can get a more precise sense of what in Aristotle is especially relevant to Strauss's strategy by considering Heidegger's most public and uncompromising statement about the involvement of philosophy in politics, the notorious Rectoral Address.

Heidegger's Rectoral Address

When he became rector in 1933, Heidegger hoped his own philosophizing would *give* direction *to* as well as *take* direction *from* the commencement of the National Socialist revolution. But from Heidegger's point of view, the needed revolutionary philosophizing was also a *return,* to "the revolutionary beginning [*Aufbruch*] of Greek philosophy" (Rectoral Address, 471). The address is thus a precious document for Heidegger's view of the political implications of his appropriation of Greek philosophy, and particularly of Aristotle. So, at least, seems to have been the opinion of both Heidegger and Leo Strauss. For present purposes, we can pass over the scholarly controversy about the extent to which in this address Heidegger was or was not consistent with his earlier philosophizing. I think there can be no question that the address represents Heidegger as Strauss understood him, and it may in fact be one of the primary documents on which Strauss based his view of Heidegger.

A letter from Strauss to Alexandre Kojève of January 16, 1934, indicates that Strauss looked up a passage in the address for Kojève soon after it was published.[10] (Perhaps Strauss's stomach for Heidegger in the 1930s had been a bit stronger than he later recalled.) As it happens, that passage is the very section of the address that Heidegger himself later regarded as its essence ("Facts and Thoughts," 498). In this section, Heidegger discussed how he saw the relation between his own revolutionary thinking and Greek philosophy. He insisted on two points. First, the distinguishing mark of Greek philosophy was not, as the tradition might seem to imply, its merely theoretical and self-satisfied character, for it always maintained its link to craft knowledge, *technē*.[11] "Theory" was already for the Greeks "awed perseverance in the face of what is" (Rectoral Address, 474). Such thinking was not at all a detached contemplation of the world, but a passionate engagement with the world in all its recalcitrant necessity. It was—and here Heidegger used Aristotle's term[12]—an *energeia*, a being-at-work, and so "the highest realization of genuine practice." Second, this science could not do its work merely by affecting consciousness or awareness; it was a power that permeated human existence [*Dasein*] as a whole, something that formed people rather than merely informing them. Thus "for the Greeks science is not a 'cultural good,' but the innermost determining center of the totality of national and political existence [*des ganzen volklich-staatlichen Daseins*]" (Rectoral Address, 472–73).[13] In other words, the work of philosophy was already with the Greeks essentially formative of nation and state, rather than merely one cultural good among others, only accidentally related to this or that part of the inhabitable earth.

Philosophy conceived as an *energeia*, then, is in the first place essentially continuous in its motives and satisfactions with *praxis* or action, especially with the paradigmatic actions of politics. I will summarize this point by saying that for Heidegger philosophy is essentially "practical," in the sense of being *praxis*-like. But besides being action-oriented, philosophy so conceived is essentially "patriotic," if we may use that word in its etymological sense. For as Heidegger describes philosophy in the Rectoral Address, it has an inescapable responsibility to and for the *patria*, the fatherland; it is *volklich-staatlich* or perhaps *vaterlaendisch*. Heidegger seems to have characterized his own thinking as an even more "energetic" embodiment, an intensification, of the practical and the patriotic aspects of Greek philosophy.

First, Greek philosophy's "active perseverance" in the face of science's "impotence before fate" (473) must be made even more radical, more self-conscious, if human existence is now to give an authentic response to "the forsakenness of modern man" heralded by Nietzsche's announcement of the death of God. Such an authentic response requires, says Heidegger, "completely unguarded exposure to the hidden and uncertain," i.e., the questionable. Questioning is then no longer a preliminary step, to give way to the answer and thus to knowledge, but questioning becomes itself the highest form of knowledge (Rectoral Address, 474). Such questioning knowing, such zetetic philosophy, will express itself as "knowing resoluteness toward the essence of Being" (Rectoral Address, 474). "This knowledge," Heidegger declared, "is not the settled taking note of essences and values in themselves; it is the most severe endangerment of human existence [*Dasein*] in the midst of the overwhelming power of what is" (Rectoral Address, 477). Resoluteness raises to a new level of activity and energy the awed perseverance of the Greeks. This intensification is made possible, it seems, by Nietzsche and Heidegger's more penetrating understanding and experience of "the uncertainty of the totality of what is" (Rectoral Address, 474), an understanding and experience that flows from their appreciation of the historicity and contingency of human values. What the Greeks experienced simply as a necessity and a fate beyond the reach of science, Nietzsche and Heidegger reveal as historical destiny, to be embraced rather than merely accepted or endured.

Second, Heidegger also intensifies the national and political aspect of Greek philosophy. Indeed, the address abounds with invocations of the German nation or people [*Volk*] and their political organization in a state [*Staat*]. "The very questionableness of Being," Heidegger says, "drives the nation [*Volk*] to its work and its struggle, and makes it into a political entity [*Staat*]" (Rectoral Address, 477). Heidegger indicates that the student body, by virtue of its intimacy [*Mitwissenschaft*] with nation and state, plays the very important role of keeping their professors more patriotic than they might otherwise be, just as the faculty keeps the students more disciplined and scientific (Rectoral Address, 478–79). He seems to believe that the state is the privileged vehicle for the expression of the German people's historical destiny and mission. One might say that for Heidegger in the Rectoral Address, politics is treated as superior in dignity to any entity either subpolitical (for example, the family or the university) or superpolitical (for example, the German language); blood and earth send down their deepest roots only when expressed through sovereignty.

Heidegger's thinking after 1933 moved away from these two positions. Roughly speaking, the action orientation or spontaneity described by resolute questioning shifted toward the receptivity described by *Gelassenheit,* a sort of philosophic listening; while the "patriotism" of nation and state shifted toward a rootedness (*Bodenstaendigkeit*) that no longer privileged the political. Strauss's attitude to these shifts can be gauged by this caustic comment:[14]

> One is inclined to say that Heidegger has learned the lesson of 1933 more thoroughly than any other man. Surely he leaves no place whatever for political philosophy.... These fantastic hopes [of Heidegger's later philosophy are] more to be expected from visionaries than from philosophers. ("Philosophy as Rigorous Science and Political Philosophy," 34)

Strauss, after all, shared to some extent the Rectoral Address's view rather than the later view of two important points. First, Strauss's own conception of political science was "patriotic" insofar as it insisted on the privileged importance, the defining importance, of politics in human existence. "Political philosophy rests on the premise that the political association— one's country or one's nation—is the most comprehensive or the most authoritative association" ("What Is Political Philosophy?" 13). Second, we will see that Strauss shared a version of the Rectoral Address's account of the basic structure of philosophy as a commitment to *active* questioning rather than to a sort of receptive listening. Heidegger's two intensifications of Greek philosophy in the Rectoral Address are, then, a better guide than later Heidegger to Strauss's Aristotle interpretation, which takes its orientation from Adeimantus' dilemma about the relation between philosophy and politics. The structure of this implicit polemic against Heidegger's twin traps of resolute engagement and patriotism is closest to being explicit, that is, is most exoteric, in Strauss's debate with his old friend Alexandre Kojève.

Esotericism as a Response to Heidegger: Strauss and Kojève

Strauss's method of responding to Heidegger through interpretations of Greek philosophy is always discreet, but it is nowhere more open than in his exchange with Alexandre Kojève over Strauss's book *On Tyranny.* This book is ostensibly a commentary on Xenophon's *Hiero,* a beautiful interrogation of the relative value of the life devoted to politics and the private life, presented in the form of a fictional dialogue between the poet Simonides and the tyrant Hiero. But our goal is not to evaluate Strauss's reading of Xenophon, so we will focus less on the commentary itself than on Strauss's subsequent elaboration of its themes. I believe Strauss's commentary, published in English in 1948, describes, in a rather indirect and muted fashion, Xenophon's Simonides as a more extreme paradigm of the model of the philosopher's relation to politics implicit in Strauss's Aristotle.

Kojève as Heidegger's Surrogate

At Strauss's urging, Kojève published in 1950 a French review of On Tyranny, "L'action politique des philosophes," in which he made much more explicit than Strauss himself had the main themes implicit in the original commentary. In 1954, a French edition was published of Strauss's commentary, and also included an expanded version of Kojève's review, now titled "Tyrannie et Sagesse" ("Tyranny and Wisdom"), and a French translation of Strauss's response to this expanded review. Strauss gave his response the title "Restatement on Xenophon's Hiero" (hereafter "Restatement"), and he later reprinted this response in its original English version in 1959, in What Is Political Philosophy? This response to Kojève's review of the book not only makes Strauss's account of Xenophon more explicit than the commentary itself, it also brings more into the open Strauss's polemic with Heidegger.

For Strauss, Kojève was a kind of amiable surrogate for Heidegger. "With the exception of Heidegger," Strauss had written to Kojève, "there is probably not a single one of our contemporaries who . . . made the case for modern thought in our times as brilliantly as you."[15] He was very pleased Kojève had responded to the Xenophon book in detail: "I am glad that finally someone represents the *modern* position intelligently and in full knowledge—and without Heidegger's cowardly vagueness" (Correspondence September 4, 1949, original emphasis). Of the many fascinating themes in this exchange, especially important for our purposes is Kojève's argument that philosophy fails in its own orientation toward the truth when it is essentially utopian and detached rather than revolutionary and engaged. Though Kojève's own rhetoric and thought in his review tend toward Hegelian and Marxist/Stalinist categories, there are abundant signs that Strauss saw their exchange as focused on the example of Heidegger's relation to Hitler. Neither Strauss nor Kojève mentioned this example explicitly, that is, exoterically. But in one especially revealing passage, Kojève claimed Xenophon was unacquainted with the new modern type of tyranny "exercised in the service of truly *revolutionary* political, social, or economic ideas . . . with a *national, racial,* imperial, or humanitarian basis," a lightly veiled allusion to Hitler as well as Stalin ("Tyranny and Wisdom," 139, emphasis added). Strauss's original response to this passage ("Restatement," 188–89) apparently did make explicit reference to Hitler, as the published version does to

Stalin, but he removed the reference from the published version at Kojève's request.[16] As we will see shortly, this was not the only place where Strauss concealed the extent to which his reflections on Xenophon and Kojève were the vehicle of his reflections on Heidegger. I believe this concealed focus accounts for the comment Strauss made to Kojève when he first asked him to write a review of the book: "I know no one besides yourself and [Jacob] Klein who will understand what I am after (I am one of those who refuses to go through open doors when one can enter just as well through a key-hole)" (Correspondence, August 22, 1948). He expected Kojève and Jacob Klein, two old friends both deeply influenced by Heidegger, to detect his own involvement as well.[17]

Kojève's Defense of Philosophy as Practical and Patriotic

The issue of whether philosophy must be practical and patriotic in the Heideggerian senses of these terms first emerges in a playful way in the niceties of mutual admiration in which Kojève and Strauss indulge at the beginning of their essays. "In a brilliant and impassioned book, but in the guise of a calmly objective work of scholarship," Kojève began, "Strauss lays bare great moral and political problems that are still ours" ("Tyranny and Wisdom," 135–36 note; compare Heidegger's critique of unworldly objectivity, Rectoral Address, 477). Strauss returned Kojève's compliment: "Kojève belongs to the very few who know how to think and who love to think. He does not belong to the many who today are unabashed atheists and more than Byzantine flatterers of tyrants for the same reason for which they would have been addicted to the grossest superstitions, both religious and legal, had they lived in an earlier age. In a word, Kojève is a philosopher and not an intellectual" ("Restatement," 185–86). Kojève calls Strauss's book "impassioned" to indicate that Strauss's own thinking has value precisely because of its engagement with "timely" issues; it does not and should not live up to the ideal of politically disinterested contemplation Strauss defends in his book;[18] its calm objectivity is merely a guise. Strauss calls Kojève a philosopher rather than an intellectual to suggest that Kojève's own thinking is not "timely" and engaged, but simply in the service of the truth.[19] In short, Kojève suggests Strauss is in his own philosophizing more of a Heideggerian than he admits, Strauss that Kojève is less of one than he claims.

Kojève raises the fundamental issue of the engagement and patriotism of philosophy in earnest later in the essay. "At first sight," Kojève says, "the philosopher [as Strauss represents him] will renounce all *action* properly so-called." This "Epicurean" attitude inspired the popular image of the philosophical life. According to this image, the philosopher devotes all his time to the quest for "truth," which is pure "theory" or "contemplation" with no necessary connection with "action" of any kind ("Tyranny and Wisdom," 150). Kojève offers two independent arguments for rejecting what he calls the "Epicurean" view of the detached philosopher, one that is *ontological*, one that is *epistemological*. He then argues from these critiques of "Epicureanism" for a broadly *ethical* conclusion, based on the shared pedagogical interests of philosophers and political men. All of these three arguments bring up aspects of Heidegger's two intensifications of Greek philosophy in the Rectoral Address, so that Strauss's response to them is at the same time his response to Heidegger's practical and patriotic conception of philosophy. It is true that Kojève's own development of the political implications of these ideas is in two ways quite different from Heidegger's, as one would expect from Kojève's Hegelian and Marxist tendencies: he sees a clearer end to history, and so demands less of a resolute openness to an unknown destiny; and he tends to be rather more "internationalist" than patriotic in the Heideggerian sense. But most of Strauss's response to the fundamental issue of philosophy's relation to politics is unaffected by these differences.

Kojève's *ontological* argument is based on the historicity of Being, which makes purely contemplative, unworldly philosophizing impossible:[20]

> The Epicurean attitude [depends on the assumption] . . . that Being is essentially immutable in itself and eternally identical with itself, and that it is completely revealed for all eternity in and by an intelligence that is perfect from the first; and this adequate revelation of the timeless totality of Being is, then, the Truth. . . . But if one does not accept this *theistic* conception of Truth (and of Being), . . . if Being creates itself ("becomes") in the course of History, then it is not by isolating oneself from History that one can reveal Being. . . . The philosopher must, on the contrary, "participate" in history, and it is not clear why he should then not participate in it *actively*, for example by advising the tyrant. . . . The "sectarian" life . . . is strictly unacceptable for the philosopher who . . . acknowledges that reality (at least *human* reality), is not given once and for all, but creates itself in the course of time. . . . The members of the "sect," isolated from the rest of the world and not really taking part in public life in its historical evolution, will, sooner or later, be "left behind by events." ("Tyranny and Wisdom," 151–52, 155; original emphasis)

Kojève's argument clearly is akin to Heidegger's intensification of the action orientation of Greek philosophy, its practical aspect, into resolute engagement. Authentic philosophy is an *energeia* or *praxis*, not mere contemplation. It is essentially active, so there can be no in principle objection to its action being directly political. Indeed, insofar as the most important "events" in "historical evolution" just *are* political events, political participation will be essential. Once one has given up the theistic conception of Being, one's philosophizing becomes essentially worldly. The death of God is the life of politicized philosophy.

Kojève's *epistemological* argument is independent of this rejection of theistic ontology. It is based on the difficulty isolated, unengaged philosophers have in testing the value of their convictions and avoiding a smug and narcissistic elitism. Kojève begins with the completely isolated, allegedly self-sufficient philosopher:

> The Epicurean attitude is open to criticism even allowing the theistic conception of Being and Truth. The isolated philosopher necessarily has to grant that the necessary and sufficient criterion of truth consists in the feeling of "evidence" that is presumably prompted by the "intellectual intuition" of the real and of Being. [This criterion] is invalidated by the simple fact that there is madness. The Epicurean philosopher, living strictly isolated in his "garden," could never know whether he has attained Wisdom or sunk into madness, since it is only by seeing our ideas shared by others or accepted by them as worth discussing that we can be sure of not finding ourselves in the realm of madness. ("Tyranny and Wisdom," 152–53)

The classical solution to this problem is a theory of philosophic friendship. Strauss, says Kojève, believes such a group of talented friends can provide all the intersubjectivity one could need to distinguish mere subjective certainty from objective knowledge:

> The Epicurean . . . does not live in complete isolation, and he receives philosophical *friends* in his "garden" with whom he engages in discussion. . . . But [an Epicurean "garden" is] populated by a small "elite" with a marked tendency to withdraw into itself. . . . Strauss seems . . . to justify this kind of behavior. . . . The philosopher will therefore have recourse to *esoteric* (preferably oral) instruction which permits him, among other things, to select the "best" and to eliminate those of "limited capacity" who are incapable of understanding hidden allusions and tacit implications. ("Tyranny and Wisdom," 154, original emphasis)

If with Kojève one gives up one's faith in utterly individualistic intuition as the criterion of knowledge, one is led to some sort of intersubjective confirmation. Strauss, interpreting Xenophon, intimates that an esoteric mode of philosophizing, intersubjective but still essentially private rather than political, can respond to this need.

Kojève denies that this esoteric model of philosophy is adequate, and the form of his denial brings him to the heart of Strauss's own conception of philosophy. The demand for intersubjectivity has no principled reason to rest satisfied with such a closed group of friends. As Kojève says, while the sect does manage to exclude *madness*, it also tends to foster *prejudices* ("Tyranny and Wisdom," 154–55). The logic of the criterion of intersubjectivity pushes the philosopher in principle to seek recognition from the widest possible group. This finally entails, as one might put it, that the philosopher passes from being a merely social to being a fully political animal:[21]

> If one does not want to leave it at the merely subjective criteria of "evidence" or of "revelation" (which do not exclude the danger of madness), one cannot be a philosopher without at the same time wanting to be a philosophical *pedagogue*. And if the philosopher does not want artificially or unduly to restrict the scope of his pedagogical activity (and thereby risk being subject to the prejudices of the "sect"), he will necessarily be strongly inclined to participate, in one way or another, in the total direction of public affairs, so that the State be organized and governed in such a manner that the philosopher's philosophic pedagogy be possible and effectual. ("Tyranny and Wisdom," 163, original emphasis)

Here, too, we see in Kojève's position a reflection of Heidegger's conception of philosophy, specifically of his "patriotism." Philosophy's orientation toward truth drives it toward engagement with the larger community in the most intensified manner available, through political action as such. Driven by the engine of recognition, philosophy by its very nature is formative of a state.

Strauss's Esoteric Defense of Esotericism

Kojève's ontological and epistemological critiques of the esoteric model of philosophy prepared his broadly ethical critique of "Epicurean" philosophy's desire to remain apart from political interests and entanglements. We have also seen that these critiques defend a conception of philosophy akin to Heidegger's practical and patriotic one. The most straightforward way to oppose Kojève and Heidegger would be to reject their historicist ontology in favor of an Aristotelian cosmology, that is, to defend the doctrines of the *Metaphysics* against those of *Being and Time*. Strauss himself saw no prospects for this, and the alternative strategy he adopted for opposing Heidegger's intensifications of Greek philosophy is the key to understanding his Aristotle interpretation.

When Strauss's "Restatement" was originally published in French translation in 1954, Strauss took up the ontological issue in its final paragraph.

Strauss removed this crucial paragraph when he reprinted the essay in English in 1959, apparently with the intention of keeping the extent of his engagement with Heidegger esoteric.[22] Strauss begins by contrasting the ontological presuppositions of classical political philosophy to Kojève's, but concludes with a gesture toward the contrast between Heidegger's political engagement and the moderation he and Kojève shared:

> Philosophy in the strict and classical sense is quest for the eternal order or for the eternal cause or causes of all things. It presupposes then that there is an eternal and unchangeable order within which History takes place and which is not in any way affected by History.... This presupposition is not self-evident. Kojève rejects it in favor of the view that "Being creates itself in the course of History." ["Tyranny and Wisdom," 152] ... On the basis of Kojève's presupposition, unqualified attachment to human concerns becomes the source of philosophic understanding: man must be absolutely at home on earth, he must be absolutely a citizen of the earth, if not a citizen of a part of the inhabitable earth.[23] On the basis of the classical presupposition, philosophy requires a radical detachment from human concerns: man must not be absolutely at home on earth, he must be a citizen of the whole. In our discussion, the conflict between the two opposed basic presuppositions has barely been mentioned. But we have always been mindful of it. For we have both apparently turned away from Being to Tyranny because we have seen that those who lacked the courage to face the issue of Tyranny, who therefore "*et humiliter serviebant et superbe dominabantur,*" were forced to evade the issue of Being as well, precisely because they did nothing but talk of Being. ("Restatement," 212)

The reference to Heidegger's National Socialist involvement, and particularly to his willingness to wield undemocratic power as rector under the direction of the party, is obvious in the last sentence. Strauss's Latin quotation comes from a particularly revealing passage of Livy:

> The nature of crowds: *the mob is either a humble slave or a cruel master.* As for the middle way of liberty, the mob can neither take it nor keep it with any respect for moderation or law. Moreover, there is seldom a lack of men to minister to its savage passions and drive to bloodshed those who already are all too eager to inflict death and torture. (Livy 24.25.8, Selincourt translation)

The philosopher as minister of savage and murderous passion: Strauss's bleak vision of where Heidegger's practical and patriotic path must lead.

Strauss comes close to suggesting in the final sentence of this suppressed paragraph that he and Kojève can leave open the fundamental ontological question while still reaching agreement on the broadly moral claim that philosophers cannot decently become resolutely engaged with tyrannical power. As a provisional interpretation, we can say that Strauss's response to the "atheistic" conception of Being is not primarily ontological, but prudential.[24] The political restraint and decency, the respect for moderation and law, that the "theist" reaches by the "Epicurean" path of absolute devotion to the eternal order and "cosmopolitanism," the "atheist" must reach while still "absolutely a citizen of the earth, if not a citizen of a part of the inhabitable earth," say, of Germany in 1933. The pressing question Strauss faces, then, is how to respect the political *Bodenstaendigkeit* of a worldly philosophy without falling into the savage passions of Heidegger's resolute action.

Strauss's response to Kojève's *epistemological* critique of "Epicureanism" is complex. He attempts to construct his own model of how philosophy can be more worldly and less "cosmological" than the "Epicurean theism" Kojève rejects, while still remaining more dispassionate or detached than Kojève's practical and patriotic historicism. He begins simply by suggesting that the requirement of intersubjectivity does not, *pace* Kojève, drive the philosopher to the widest possible group. It may well be that wider groups, especially the political community, are more susceptible to prejudice than the "esoteric" group of philosophical friends:

> Much as we loathe the snobbish silence or whispering of the sect, we loathe even more the savage noise of the loudspeakers of the mass party. . . . If we must choose between the sect and the party, we must choose the sect. ("Restatement," 195)

Strauss concedes to Kojève that intellectuals ancient and modern have always been susceptible to the reassurance, not to say flattery, provided by the small group of fellow believers. But he thinks the philosopher is no less likely to have his prejudice reinforced by the greater sophist of the state than by the lesser of the clique.

This undermines part but not all of Kojève's case for philosophy's "patriotism" as opposed to its "esotericism." The desire for recognition, in Kojève's opinion, drives both philosophers and statesmen to become universal pedagogues, that is, to aspire to formative influence on political communities. This *motive* may still be potent, even if we doubt that it has all the beneficial epistemological consequences Kojève ascribes to it, and this is the more fundamental level of Strauss's response. "Patriotism" of the philosopher's kind, a particular type of political ambition, may be intrinsic to the motives and talents that make of one a philosopher.

Strauss responds to this problem, the heart of his disagreement with Kojève, by stages. His strategy is to give a richer account than Kojève has done of why the philosopher's interest in other human beings will be very limited, focused only on the small class of fellow philosophers or potential philosophers. The philosopher will not feel the attraction to political action Kojève alleges; his attractions will be essentially private. Strauss begins with an exoteric account that depends on "theistic" premises:

> The philosopher's dominating passion is the desire for truth, i.e., for knowledge of the eternal order, or the eternal cause or causes of the whole. As he looks up in search for the eternal order, all human things and all human concerns reveal themselves to him as paltry and ephemeral. . . . He is as unconcerned as possible with individual and perishable human beings and hence with his own "individuality," or his body, as well as with the sum total of all individual human beings and their "historical" progression. . . . The political man must reject this way altogether. He cannot tolerate this radical depreciation of man and of all human things. . . . He must "care" for human things as such. ("Restatement," 198)

That Strauss has Heidegger on his mind here is suggested by the quotation marks he puts around "care" in the last sentence. Strauss indicates that a political man may well be characterized by care for the merely human and historical, but not the philosopher. The passage harks back to the very first theme from Heidegger that so impressed the young Strauss in 1922: Heidegger's interpretation of Aristotle's "desire to know" in terms of "care." Strauss is opposing, then, the view of philosophy as *energeia* so prominent in the Rectoral Address. But the lack of "care" he here opposes to the political man's attitude is worthy of philosophers as "impractical" and cosmological as Thales or Anaxagoras.[25] If this were his only response to the "worldly" philosopher, he would clearly be relying too much on exactly the point at dispute. Strauss needs to justify esoteric detachment to the philosopher who, if he does not find man the highest thing in the cosmos, at least finds him the most interesting. To put the point in Heidegger's terms, Strauss needs to leave the philosopher open to political "care" without letting him be consumed by resolute engagement.

Strauss first offers an exoteric account of the philosopher's "care" for at least some other human beings, an account that is exoteric or "popular" exactly because it depends on theistic premises:

> We shall try to explain this in a *popular* and hence in an unorthodox manner. . . . The souls of men reflect the eternal order in different

degrees. A soul that is in good order or healthy reflects it to a higher
degree than a soul that is chaotic or diseased. . . . The philosopher therefore has the urge to educate potential philosophers simply because
he cannot help loving well-ordered souls. ("Restatement," 200–201,
emphasis added)

According to this account, philosophers are truly and directly in love with
the cosmos and its eternal order, and so indirectly love certain human beings
who embody the fact that man is a microcosm. It becomes clear immediately that Strauss saw the complete insufficiency of this exoteric description
of the philosopher. He moves from this insufficient exoteric account to a
more sufficient and esoteric account to explain why philosophers of such
"Epicurean" detachment yet have philosophical friends. Strauss concedes
that the theistic assumption is not necessary for philosophy; all that is necessary is a dedication to the quest for knowledge, even if such knowledge is
not held to be of an eternal cosmic order:[26]

The most important thing for us, or the one thing needful, is *quest* for
knowledge of the most important things, or philosophy. In other words,
we realize that only by philosophizing can man's soul become well-
ordered. . . . One does not have to make [the assumption that the
well-ordered soul is more akin to the eternal order than is the chaotic
soul] to be a philosopher, as is shown by Democritus and other pre-
Socratics, to say nothing of the moderns. ("Restatement," 201, emphasis added)

But once one has given up the ordered cosmos and its reflection in the
microcosm of man, how will one explain how philosophers take other philosophers or potential philosophers as objects of their care? Kojève had
suggested that all philosophers, "theist" and "atheist" alike, would seek philosophical friends because of their epistemological need for intersubjectivity
and recognition. Strauss says "it seems" one will be "forced" into such an
explanation if one gives up the theistic assumption, and he suggests there
is something lacking in such an explanation: "We must leave open whether
one can thus explain . . . the *immediate* pleasure which the philosopher
experiences when he sees a well-ordered soul [that is, a soul committed to
the quest for knowledge] or the *immediate* pleasure which we experience
when we observe signs of human nobility." Strauss goes on to contrast the
"mercenary" love rulers have for their subjects and the "nonmercenary" love
philosophers have for their friends ("Restatement," 201–202, emphasis
added). The clear implication, it would seem, is to shift the source of the philosopher's delight in a questing soul from its epistemological benefit to the

philosopher to the *intrinsic* nobility of resolute openness to questioning. The philosopher's love for his philosophic friends, and *only* for them, is non-instrumental; in particular, his practical interest in his fellow citizens is indeed mercenary (see especially "Restatement," 199).

Strauss is most explicit about what is at stake in this reorientation of philosophy from the eternal order to a "quest" earlier in the essay:[27]

> Philosophy as such is neither dogmatic nor skeptic, and still less "decisionist," but zetetic (or skeptic in the original sense of the term). Philosophy as such is nothing but genuine awareness of the problems, i.e., of the fundamental and comprehensive problems. . . . The evidence of all solutions is necessarily smaller than the evidence of the problems. ("Restatement," 196)

It turns out, then, that the well-ordered soul, the one that attracts the philosopher's eros, is primarily the questioning soul; and the questioning soul may or may not take its bearings from eternity rather than worldliness, since "the evidence of all solutions is necessarily smaller than the evidence of the problems."[28] Philosophers cannot take the problems seriously without being "inclined to a solution," and thus inclined to becoming sectarians. But philosophic friendship can often be closer among those who "incline" to different solutions than among those who incline to the same solution: one's zetetic friends may be quite different from one's fellow sectarians ("Restatement," 196). One understands in this light the general significance of Strauss's particular comment that "the nascent shock" of the way Kojève takes atheism and tyranny for granted "is absorbed by . . . the knowledge of long standing that Kojève belongs to the very few who know how to think and who love to think" ("Restatement," 185).[29] Zetetic philosophy works wonders of reconciliation. There seems to be in principle no reason Strauss could not have felt the same affection for the author of the following passage: "Questioning is then no longer a preliminary step, to give way to the answer and thus to knowledge, but questioning becomes itself the highest form of knowledge" (Rectoral Address, 474).

One is driven to the following provisional conclusion: just as Kojève believed the Epicurean attitude was open to criticism for its elitist recourse to esotericism, *even allowing the theistic conception of Being,* so Strauss believed the Epicurean recourse to esotericism, that is, its rejection of "patriotism," was defensible, *even without commitment to the theistic conception of Being.* To put the point another way, Nietzsche could be an authentic Platonist, or in Kojève's language an "Epicurean," as far as the morality of esotericism goes, even while differing metaphysically from Platonism in as radical a way as is imaginable.[30] The moral law of esotericism, not the starry

heaven of eternity, is indispensable to classical political philosophy. This esotericism guarantees that whatever "care" a philosopher takes for political
affairs will not need a "practical" embodiment. The only political involvement essential to the philosopher is purely instrumental, aimed to guarantee
the tolerance of the political community for the philosopher's "attempts to
convert young men to the philosophic life," that is, to gain philosophical
friends: "There is no necessary connection between the philosopher's indispensable philosophic politics [of convincing the political community that
philosophers] are not subversives . . . but good citizens and even the best of
citizens . . . and the efforts which he might or might not . . . undertake with
a view to establishing the best regime or to the improvement of the actual
order" ("Restatement," 205–206). The care of questioning will be kept
entirely separate from the resolute engagement of political action properly
so-called, because the philosopher will not desire, *pace* Kojève, "to participate, in one way or another, in the total direction of public affairs, so that
the State be organized and governed in such a matter that the philosopher's
philosophic pedagogy be possible and effectual" ("Restatement," 205, quoting "Tyranny and Wisdom," 163). In a more Aristotelian vocabulary, the philosopher who takes an interest in politics will ultimately do so only as an
exercise of theoretical rather than practical reason. Strauss will bring his
Aristotle as close as possible to this esoteric, politically interested, but politically uninvolved philosopher. This Aristotle has given up reliance on the thesis that man is not the highest thing in the cosmos, and so becomes a kind
of synthesis between Kojève's utterly unworldly "Epicurean" and the utterly
"patriotic" and "practical" Heideggerian.

LEO STRAUSS'S ARISTOTLE: MAKING PHILOSOPHY "IMPRACTICAL" AND "UNPATRIOTIC"

Strauss's Aristotle is characterized by a systematic dichotomy between an
exoteric doctrine directed toward and preservative of the decency of ordinary political men, and an esoteric doctrine directed toward the true philosophic eros of those whose talent and taste fits them for a life of fundamental
questioning. This dichotomy allows Aristotle to address the politically involved man without inflaming political *passion,* and to address the erotic
philosopher without inflaming *political* passion. An uncharitable critic
might think Strauss's interpretation makes Aristotle fulfill on the intellectual plane the male sexual fantasy of the lover who is both the madonna and
the whore: sober decency in public, manic eroticism in private. "Thought
must not be moderate, but fearless, not to say shameless; but moderation is a virtue controlling the philosopher's speech" ("What Is Political

Philosophy?" 32). But with more justice one could say Strauss's fantasy opens up a profound perspective for understanding the human motives that create Adeimantus' dilemma, and that led to Heidegger's entanglement in it. Adeimantus had charged that the unworldly or otherworldly philosopher became useless in the serious man's world of politics, but this unworldliness was comic and contemptible; only the worldly philosopher became threatening and vicious. On Strauss's view, Heidegger had interrogated more boldly and consistently than anyone else Nietzsche's announcement to the philosophers of the future that God is dead, or that unworldliness has become motivationally inert. The comic age of philosophy, of Thales and his well, of Socrates and his wife, had come to a close; *incipit tragoedia*.[31] From this moment, philosophy must run the risk of worldliness, of falling onto Adeimantus' horn of political involvement with its deadly seriousness and passionate resoluteness. Strauss accepted this great risk, since he judged that otherworldliness had become merely "popular," that is, part of an exoteric defense *of* philosophy rather than of an esoteric invitation *to* it.

Because Strauss takes on this risk, Strauss's achievement in his Aristotle interpretation does not really conform to his own slogan of understanding the thinkers of the past exactly as they understood themselves. Strauss's center of gravity cannot be in the same place as Aristotle's. What he accomplished is better understood, in direct competition with Heidegger's interpretations of Aristotle, as a penetrating intensification of certain aspects of Aristotle's thought, tailored to answer Strauss's own philosophic concerns. What must philosophy look like once man has become, if not the highest, then at least the most interesting object of the philosopher's care? Strauss's interpretation of Aristotle is intended to reveal and systematize Aristotelian resources for addressing this most unAristotelian of questions. Not unlike Heidegger, Strauss will find certain tensions in Aristotle's teaching about the relation between philosophy and practice and philosophy and patriotism. These tensions reveal two competing (or perhaps complementary) tendencies in Aristotle's thought, one broadly "Epicurean" and one broadly Heideggerian. Strauss will then emphasize and in some respects intensify the "Epicurean" tendency into a general teaching, resulting in an appropriation of Aristotelian resources that is systematically opposed to Heidegger's appropriation. In other words, Strauss arrives at his Aristotle only by *resolving* certain tensions that Aristotle's texts leave open, or at least do not explicitly resolve. Strauss uses the distinction between the esoteric and the exoteric to justify his resolutions as genuinely Aristotelian. His general strategy is to elevate the Epicurean tendency to the status of Aristotle's final or philosophic position, relegating the opposing tendency to the status of a politic accommodation to the requirements of civic life. The more Heideggerian tendencies in Aristotle, then, become aspects of a political horizon that Strauss's Aristotle transcends utterly, though discreetly.

I believe Strauss's general strategy of applying the esoteric/exoteric dichotomy produces a discontinuity between philosophy and politics too unambiguous to be Aristotle's own conception. Aristotle does not resolve his tensions between, for example, moral and intellectual virtue and between practical and theoretical wisdom with the definitiveness Strauss produces. The Heideggerian tendencies have as much right to be called Aristotelian as the Epicurean tendencies Strauss emphasizes. In this particular respect, one might call Strauss's interpretation a kind of minimizing distortion of the practical and patriotic tendencies in Aristotle. But this distortion is not the result of an interpretive error so much as it is a response to the almost inhuman difficulty of maintaining a purely zetetic stance in the face of the fundamental problems. "The danger of succumbing to the attraction of *solutions*," that is, of what I have called *resolutions* of Aristotle's tensions, "is essential to philosophy which, without incurring this danger, would degenerate into playing with the problems" ("Restatement," 196, emphasis added). Where Aristotle hovered between detachment from and involvement in politics, Strauss's philosophic seriousness (like Heidegger's) succumbed to the desire to find one's feet.

The next two sections explore how Strauss uses his general distinction between exoteric and esoteric dimensions of Aristotle's thought to resist the Aristotelian tendencies Heidegger was to intensify into resolute engagement and patriotism. I conclude with a brief account of why considerations about the nature of piety prevented Strauss from ultimately identifying even with his intensified Aristotle.

Strauss's Intensification of the "Impractical"

We can illustrate Strauss's minimizing distortion of Aristotle's practical tendency by considering Aristotle's rejection of the Platonic conception of the good-in-itself (*Nicomachean Ethics* 1.6). This passage provides a basis for Heidegger's intensification of Aristotelian philosophy in the direction of practice (that is, of being *praktikos* or action-oriented). Aristotle sets out to calm those who, "realizing their own ignorance, are impressed by those who claim happiness is some great thing that transcends us [*hyper autous*]." To bring them back to earth, Aristotle must criticize "some who think that besides all the other good things there is something else good in itself, which is also the cause of all the other things being good" (*Nicomachean Ethics* 1.4, 1095a25–28). He defends a less transcendent account of the "good-in-itself":

> What sort of things should one place among [things good] 'in themselves'? Is it just those that are pursued even all alone, such as thinking [*phronein*] and seeing and some pleasures and honors? For even if we also pursue these *for the sake of something else*, nevertheless one would

place them among things *good in themselves*. (*Nicomachean Ethics* 1.6, 1096b16–19, emphasis added)

Aristotle is arguing here against the Platonic notion that only the idea of the good is truly good in itself. Once we acknowledge that such things as thinking, seeing, and certain pleasures and honors are pursued even if nothing comes from them, we also must concede that they are good in themselves *even if* we also pursue them *for the sake of something else*. After stating this foundational programmatic principle, Aristotle puts forward an important Platonic objection to it, stated as a rhetorical question:

If these things [such as thinking, seeing, and some pleasures and honors] as well as [the idea of the good] are among things good in themselves, the account of the good will have to turn out to be the *same* for all of them, just as the account of whiteness is the same for snow and white lead. But the accounts by virtue of which honor and thought and pleasure are goods are *different* and distinct. So the good is not something *common* in accord with a single idea. But then how *is* [the good] to be said of things? For surely it is not like the case of things that share a name merely *by accident*. (*Nicomachean Ethics* 1.6, 1096b21–27, emphasis added)

Aristotle imagines the Platonist arguing that *no* account can be given of some common ground on which both the highest good, whatever it is, and such goods as thinking and being honored are all understood to be good, that is, good in themselves. Aristotle's reply reveals his strategy for justifying his programmatic principle:

Don't good things share a name by virtue of *deriving from one thing* [*aph' henos*] or by all *being referred to one thing* [*pros hen*], or rather *by analogy* [*kat' analogian*]? For as sight is in a body, mind is in a soul, and similarly for other cases. But perhaps these topics should be put aside for now, since to consider them with precision would be more proper to a different philosophic inquiry. (*Nicomachean Ethics* 1.6, 1096b27–31, emphasis added)

Without pursuing this "different philosophic inquiry" into the general structure of analogy,[32] we can say this about how Aristotle's programmatic principle is justified by the concept of analogy: something will count as good in itself to the extent that its goodness derives from or is analogous to the paradigmatic case of goodness. This is why it is illegitimate to infer from "For person *P*, good *X* is more choiceworthy than good *Y*" to "For person *P*, good *Y* is not choiceworthy in itself." There may be some common ground on which good *Y* can be seen as an imperfect analogue of good *X*, rather than, for example, as a mere means to obtaining good *X*. In the crucial case of the comparison between the philosophic and political lives, the exact nature of this common ground will depend on how one describes the analogical relation between the paradigmatic good of theory and the secondary good of practice.[33]

The significance of this programmatic principle for Aristotle's investigation of the best way of life is clear: even if philosophic virtue *is* higher than moral virtue, even if it is *the* paradigm case of virtue, moral virtue will still be choiceworthy for itself. Furthermore, the exercise of practical wisdom would be choiceworthy for its own sake even if no practical effect followed from it, simply as an excellence of one part of the rational soul.[34] This programmatic principle gives all the appearances of being presented as definitive and foundational, a fine example of the way "Aristotle opposes the divine madness of Plato . . . in the spirit of his own unrivaled sobriety" (*Natural Right and History*, 156). The madness of Plato reduced all virtue not grounded in philosophic knowledge to merely vulgar or popular virtue,[35] whereas Aristotle defends the autonomous dignity of morality and politics. But Aristotle's tendency to radically depreciate politics relative to philosophy, most prominently in *Nicomachean Ethics* 10.7–8, could well be thought inconsistent with this programmatic defense of moral virtue. I can only assert without argument here that one can reasonably interpret these passages consistently with the programmatic principle. Such passages could be seen simply to articulate in detail what the principle should have led us to expect in general: the political life is a relatively less perfect analogue of the paradigmatic life, the life of contemplation. But the very existence of the analogy required by the principle could be taken to establish an underlying common ground between the theoretical and the practical. This common ground opens a path toward Heidegger's practical intensification. Heidegger can find in practice something "the most severe endangerment" that constitutes philosophic questioning (Rectoral Address, 474) will bring to an even higher level of self-consciousness and resoluteness. This path becomes especially tempting once one has lost one's faith in a cosmos whose eternity and divinity guarantee the superiority of thought directed toward it to all thought directed toward what is historical and merely human.

In resisting the Heideggerian intensification of this common ground between theory and practice, Strauss intensifies instead the philosophic perception of the "secondary" status (*Nicomachean Ethics* 10.8, 1178a9) of merely political action. This intensification is especially bold in Strauss's formulation of classical political philosophy's harsh conclusion about the ultimate status of moral virtue:

If striving for knowledge of the eternal truth is the ultimate end of man, justice and moral virtue in general can be fully legitimated only by the fact that they are required for the sake of that ultimate end or that they are the conditions of the philosophic life. From this point of view the man who is merely just or moral without being a philosopher appears as a *mutilated* human being. (*Natural Right and History*, 151, emphasis added)

In the process of intensifying the *imperfection* of the political life relative to the philosophic life into *mutilation*, Strauss removes any possible starting point for Heidegger's competing intensification of philosophy's analogical relationship to practice. But this attempt to close off Heidegger's path might seem to have denied altogether the common ground Aristotle's programmatic principle establishes between theory and practice. It would be tempting, for both Strauss's critics and his supporters, to say that Strauss probably thought the programmatic principle itself *exoteric*, so that *Nicomachean Ethics* 1.6 would prove to be merely propaedeutic for the more esoteric revelations of moral virtue's lack of intrinsic worth in *Nicomachean Ethics* 10.7–8. But this would be a very desperate measure. Strauss may have come "dangerously close to implying that *all* technical discussions are exoteric,"[36] but Aristotle's extended polemic with Platonic ontology is surely the worst candidate imaginable for such treatment. Moreover, such a reading would leave Strauss with no basis for a doctrinal distinction between his Aristotle and his Plato. Their only difference would be Aristotle's comparative discretion and gentleness in mounting essentially the same critique of popular virtue. But Strauss gives an account of the tension between Aristotle's defense of moral virtue and his radical depreciation of politics that retains an important distinction between Aristotle and Plato.[37] Therefore, though Strauss nowhere cited or discussed Aristotle's defense of the intrinsic value of moral virtue in *Nicomachean Ethics* 1.6, I propose to read his account as a description of precisely how the analogy works between the practical and the theoretical. In effect, this description of the analogy turns out to be Strauss's alternative account of the common ground exploited by Heidegger's practical intensification.

We start from the perception that there are two natural ends by reference to which the choiceworthiness of moral virtue could be understood most fully: the perfection of the individual or the harmony of the community (Strauss refers especially to *Politics* 3.6, 1278b21–24). But Strauss argues that neither end can establish a perspective from which the analogous goodness of moral virtue becomes visible. First, philosophy is the perfection of the individual. According to Strauss, Aristotle claimed that "the highest end of man by nature is theoretical understanding or philosophy and this perfection does not require moral virtue as moral virtue, i.e. just and noble deeds as choiceworthy for their own sake. . . . Actions resembling moral actions proper . . . are intended by the philosopher as mere means toward his end" (*The City and Man*, 26–27).[38] The philosopher performs what look like moral actions from prudential motives rather than moral motives as such; therefore such actions are not "moral actions proper." He is not *interested in*, he has no *care for* such actions in themselves, and so does not perform such actions in the way a man of moral virtue does. So starting from the philosopher's view, we cannot see any useful analogy between moral virtue and philosophic virtue. Starting from man's social end is also no help, but for the opposite reason: the city is for the sake of the virtue of its individual citizens, so we do not appreciate more fully moral virtue itself by looking to the flourishing of the city. (We may, of course, understand more fully the attractiveness of the common good by considering its relation to individual virtue.). "Moral virtue is then not intelligible as a means for the only two natural ends which could be thought to be its end." From this point of view, "moral virtue, it seems, must be regarded as an 'absolute'," or perhaps we could say, as *sui generis* (*The City and Man*, 27).[39] It seems that no analogical relation to other things good in themselves serves to illuminate its choiceworthiness.

Another way to describe this "absolute" character of moral virtue with regard to philosophy is to say that "the sphere ruled by prudence is *closed* since the principles of prudence . . . are known independently of theoretical science" (*The City and Man*, 25, emphasis added). This closure has the useful function of preventing sophists and other intellectuals of dubious moral character from unsettling the decency and prudence of political men. Revolutionary fervor cannot easily breach the firewall between moral sobriety and philosophic madness. But it also shields philosophers from the intrusion of specifically political modes of caring about human life. In particular, the philosopher as such does not look toward political leadership with appreciation, let alone with envy, for he sees in it nothing bearing a fruitful analogy to his own precious activity. These are the exoteric terms of the peaceful co-existence Strauss's Aristotle proposes between philosophy and politics.

But this exoteric point of view is not the full story. It is consistent with Aristotle's programmatic principle insofar as it respects the intrinsic goodness of more than just the paradigmatic good of philosophy, but it goes overboard in this direction. For it does not exploit the principle's suggestion that our appreciation of what is intrinsically good can be enhanced by seeing the analogy between the most perfect good and non-paradigmatic goods (for example, between intellectual and moral virtue). The exoteric view respects the diversity of goods at the cost of forgetting their hierarchy and

community. Strauss suggests that Aristotle's discreetly communicated esoteric view provided the missing reminders:

> Moral virtue shows that the city points beyond itself but it does not
> reveal clearly that toward which it points, namely, the life devoted to
> philosophy. . . . When the philosopher Aristotle addresses his political
> science to more or less perfect gentlemen, he shows them as far as pos-
> sible that the way of life of the perfect gentleman points toward the
> philosophic way of life; he removes a screen. . . . The gentleman is by
> nature able to be affected by philosophy; Aristotle's political science is
> an attempt to actualize this potentiality. . . . The moral-political sphere
> is then not *unqualifiedly* closed to theoretical science. (*The City and
> Man*, 28, emphasis added)

The political man, at least if he is a gentleman, can learn to appreciate his
own virtue fully by learning to appreciate philosophy even more. This re-
spectful openness to appreciating philosophy, as distinct from a truly erotic
openness to living as a philosopher, is the work done by the analogy between
philosophy and politics. It changes the self-image of the political man. At
the same time, the analogy does nothing at all to the self-image of the philosopher. The political man sees his better self reflected in the philosopher,
but the philosopher sees nothing of himself in the mirror of politics. The
fact that the relevant analogy works only in one direction allows Strauss not
only to block access to, but to deny the very existence of the common ground
between philosophy and politics that Heidegger tried to occupy.

We should try to understand this "one-way street" analogy a bit more
to see how Strauss's intensification of the "impractical" responds to Heidegger's intensification of the practical. Strauss and Heidegger implicitly
have different models of what is common between the two objects of the
analogy. For Strauss, there is no truly common ground between philosophy
and politics, no independently accessible dimension along which the choiceworthiness of philosophy can be measured against politics. Philosophy does
not simply do better or perfectly something politics does in an inferior way.
Here Strauss could appeal to Aristotle's own suggestion that the analogy of
goodness is closely related to the analogy of being (*Nicomachean Ethics* 1.6,
1096a23–29). Aristotle did not believe there was some common or neutral
dimension of being such that some things simply had more of it while others
had less. For example, a frog and its greenness both have being, but the frog
has being in a primary way (as a substance), while its greenness has being
only in an analogical or derivative way that can be fully understood only
in light of the paradigmatic way a substance has being. But for Heidegger
there is such a common dimension. He seeks to find it by getting behind the

distinction between theoretical and practical reason, to a more primordial sense of thinking. Here Heidegger could appeal to Aristotle's so-called function argument, which identifies actualization (*energeia*) as the fundamental dimension of happiness (*Nicomachean Ethics* 1.7, 1097b22–1098a18). This common ground allows us to compare the lives devoted to philosophy and to politics by asking which is more fully "energized." Aristotle's statement of his methodology in *NE* 1.6 seems to be with Strauss, while his practice often seems more on Heidegger's side. Both have resolved something Aristotle seems to have left in tension.

Strauss's model does not require that there be no commonality at all between philosophy and politics, nor does Heidegger's model require this common dimension to be as definite as a shared material substratum. Consider the way someone with a taste for meat compares the choiceworthiness of four pairs of grocery items: sixteen ounces of hamburger and twelve ounces of hamburger; a hamburger and a turkeyburger; a hamburger and a veggieburger; and a hamburger and a picture of a hamburger. The meat-eater ranks more hamburger as *simply* more choiceworthy than less; a hamburger as a more choiceworthy *meat* than a turkeyburger; and a hamburger as a more choiceworthy *food* than a veggieburger. As for the last pair, we cannot even understand what the picture of the hamburger is, cannot even see that it is a *representation* or image of something choiceworthy (without being choiceworthy in itself), except by reference to a real hamburger. In the first case, the hamburger to hamburger comparison, there is an undifferentiated, shared substratum to provide the common dimension of the comparison, so that the comparison is simple or unqualified. The inferior member of the pair is choiceworthy in exactly the same *way*, though not to the same *extent*, as the superior member. No analogy is required to make the comparison. In the fourth case, of the hamburger and its picture, there is no common dimension at all (unless one calls "grocery item" a common dimension). We can learn nothing about why the superior member of the pair is choiceworthy by studying the inferior member; the analogy is only informative in one direction, from the top down. We might say there is no real relation between the hamburger and its picture.

Strauss and Heidegger have models of the analogy between philosophy and politics less like these two extreme cases and more like the two middle cases. Neither of the common dimensions in the middle comparisons—meat and food—can be understood without some sort of analogy. Yet the sense in which one can understand the inferior member of each pair to be an imperfect version of "the same thing" as the superior member is quite different in the two cases. In Heidegger's model, philosophy is like the hamburger and merely moral virtue the turkeyburger: the red meat of fearless philosophic thinking feeds in a purified and intensified mode the same taste for resolute confrontation with destiny as authentic politics. Strauss sees politics and moral virtue more like the way the meat-eater sees the veggie-burger: something perhaps necessary to support mere life, but only a chastening reminder of the stuff of living well. But perhaps we must leave these questions aside before we begin pursuing a "different philosophic inquiry."

The qualified openness of moral and political virtue to philosophy, then, is not allowed by Strauss to reveal a "practical" or *praxis*-like aspect of philosophy. What work does this openness do? Strauss's most explicit statement about how moral virtue reflects philosophic virtue suggests that the idleness of philosophy, its tendency toward rest rather than motion, becomes informative for the political man, even though at first blush this tendency appears utterly anti-political:

> [Taking] the *philosophic* life . . . [as] the highest subject of . . . *political* philosophy, . . . however absurd it seemed to common opinion, was nevertheless "divined" by pre-philosophic political life: men wholly devoted to the political life were sometimes popularly considered "busybodies," and their *unresting* ways were contrasted with the greater freedom and the higher dignity of the more retired life of men who were "minding their own business. ("On Classical Political Philosophy," 91, emphasis added)

The passages from Aristotle that Strauss cites to support this observation do not in fact unambiguously value "the more retired life" for its idleness. They emphasize instead that the philosophic life is more self-sufficient in its actualization (*energeia*) than the political life.[40] Being a "busybody" seems more a matter of being too wrapped up with *other people* than of being too wrapped up with *praxis*. Whether philosophy's self-sufficiency is also a manifestation of its distance from *praxis* depends on the relation between *praxis* and *energeia*, which these passages leave open.

The Aristotelian tension between "rest and motion" is, it seems, resolved by Strauss in favor of rest. Where Aristotle hovers between a more *praxis*-oriented view and a less, Strauss finds an exoteric defense of the decent political man pointing toward an esoteric completion in "impractical" philosophy. The most striking illustration of this sort of resolution is magnanimity. Strauss seems to suggest that "the *full* phenomenon of magnanimity" shows that this virtue, the perfection of moral and political life as such, must be understood in light of what transcends political life, that is, the philosophic life (*The City and Man*, 27, emphasis added).[41] It is true the magnanimous man seems torn between two poles of excellence, one of rest and one of motion:[42] "He stays away from what is commonly honored, and from areas where others lead; he is idle and dilatory, except when there is some great honor or task at stake, so he devotes his actions to few things, but to great and renowned ones" (*Nicomachean Ethics* 4.3, 1124b23–26).[43] But to see how much "practical" orientation Strauss must resolve away, we need only consider the tension between benefaction (*euergesia*) and magnanimity. The magnanimous man prefers actively benefiting others to being passively benefited:

> [The magnanimous man] is the sort to be a benefactor [*eu poiein*], though he is ashamed to be a beneficiary [*euergetoumenos*], since superiority belongs to the first, but subordination to the second. He also reciprocates more benefits [*anteuergetikos*] than he receives, so that the one repaid will both owe him something and be the receiver [rather than the agent] of benefaction. Magnanimous men seem to remember the benefits they confer, but not the ones they receive, since the one who receives a benefit is subordinate to the one who confers it, and the magnanimous man wants to be superior. . . . It belongs to the magnanimous man to ask for nothing, or at least to ask with great reluctance, but to give aid eagerly. (*Nicomachean Ethics* 4.3.1124b9–14, 17–18)

So potent is the magnanimous man's attachment to his image of himself as active that he becomes something of an ingrate about the favors he has received, and something of an embarrassment in the favors he lavishes. Aristotle explains these tendencies in his treatment of friendship and benefaction:

> Benefactors [*euergetai*] seem to love their beneficiaries more than those who receive a benefit love those who do it. . . . Here is the cause of this: Being is choiceworthy and lovable for everything; we have being insofar as we are in activity [*energeia*] (i.e., in living and acting [*prattein*]); the agent of some work [*ergon*] is in a way in activity in that work; and so the agent loves the work as the agent loves his being. This [attachment] is natural, since what the agent is in potency [*dunamis*], the work manifests in activity [*energeia*]. (*Nicomachean Ethics* 9.7.1167b17–18, 1168a5–9)

This intense devotion to benefaction is the *inter*personal expression of the magnanimous man's *intra*personal devotion to fully "energizing" his self. Indeed, this extension of self into the action of others through benefaction seems to be the fullest expression of the political man's self-love (*Nicomachean Ethics* 9.8, 1169a11–13); it is the way in which the political man energizes his true self (*touth' hekastos estin*), which is mind (*nous*) (*Nicomachean Ethics* 9.8, 1169a2, 17–18).

This suggestion that beneficent magnanimity is a privileged way to energize the true self does indeed appear to set up a most interesting analogy with the philosophic life, whose characteristic *energeia* was singled out as superlatively divine, continuous, pleasant, self-sufficient, choiceworthy, and leisured, all in the service of energizing the true self (*einai hekastos touto*), mind (*nous*) (*Nicomachean Ethics* 10.7, 1177a12–b31). Perhaps this striking agreement is the highest manifestation of the openness of the political horizon to the philosophic life. But does the openness also threaten (from Strauss's point of view) to work in the other direction, so that philosopher's "self-devotion" will contain the seeds of a similar desire for benefaction? To put this in more political terms, has Aristotle here established the common ground on which Kojève stakes his claim that the philosopher will necessarily become a pedagogue, and so desire to be formative of nation and state? This question about magnanimity is the transition from Strauss's resistance to the practical aspects of philosophy to the issue of patriotism.

Strauss's Intensification of the "Unpatriotic"

Strauss clearly saw there were aspects of Aristotle's attitude toward politics that made it difficult to avoid Heidegger's patriotic intensification. The basic orientation of political science toward evaluation, and its continuity with politics as it is understood by the politically engaged, would seem to give the philosopher a strong tendency toward practical involvement. The point of Aristotelian political science, after all, is to be good, not merely to know the good, and it is a short step from the practical interest in being good oneself to the pedagogical interest in helping others to be good. Strauss's most striking recognition of this tendency in Aristotle even concedes that benefaction (and so magnanimity) on the highest political level appears as divinizing as contemplative activity as such:

> That Zeus-like man who has the highest natural title to rule ... is the man of the highest self-sufficiency who therefore cannot be part of a city: is he not, if not the philosopher, at least the highest political reflection of the philosopher? (*The City and Man*, 37)

Strauss's problem is to show that the patriotism of the philosopher's reflection in the statesman is an artifact of the mirror of politics, rather than a true representation.

In response to Alexandre Kojève's account of the inescapable attraction of political pedagogy to the philosopher, Strauss constructed a philosopher who had only the most tenuous of practical interest in human beings in general, though an intensely erotic interest in potential philosophers. One might say Strauss privatizes the motivating force of magnanimous benefaction. It is true that Strauss did not see the philosopher's "privacy" as absolute. There must be some motive, after all, for Simonides to give the tyrant Hiero advice that would moderate the tyranny, and not all of that advice, and perhaps very little of it, can be understood as recruiting or protecting potential philosophers. But Simonides' motive, it turns out, cannot be understood as a species of political engagement. His "care" is directed elsewhere. What he does for his fellow creatures when he tries to make Hiero a somewhat better and less oppressive ruler is better seen as mere philanthropy, based on the natural human affection for human beings as such, rather than on any specific attachment to politics, let alone to a specific political community. Simonides gives only *humanitarian* aid to Hiero's subjects. In a contemporary context, Strauss's philosopher would be more likely to find himself involved with organizations ameliorating world hunger or environmental degradation than as an adviser to a head of state, let alone as a minister playing midwife to the birth of the Common Market.

This reduction of the philosopher's specifically *political* ambition to a detached, cosmopolitan, and perhaps somewhat bemused philanthropy is a regular feature of Strauss's accounts of classical political philosophy. Indeed, it is literally Strauss's last word on the topic: "On Classical Political Philosophy," Strauss's first statement on this theme (1945), and his last in the essay on Aristotle's *Politics* in *The City and Man* (1964), both conclude with reflections on the detachment of the philosopher from political care. Strauss's general strategy for blocking Heidegger's patriotic intensification of Aristotle is to intensify two tendencies that complement each other to move the philosopher away from the temptations of political pedagogy. First, Strauss suggests that despite the political philosopher's respect for the evaluative engagements of political men, his ultimate concern with political affairs is not practical after all.

> The question of the *nature* of political things ... is the limit of political philosophy as a *practical* discipline: while essentially practical in itself, the question functions as an entering wedge for others whose purpose is no longer to guide action but simply to understand things as they are. ("On Classical Political Philosophy," 94)

In the ascent from political things, the philosopher must move through the air of the values and commitments that constitute the phenomena to be studied, but he finally escapes altogether the atmosphere of action for the ethereal realm of contemplation. Politics becomes an object present to hand for inspection, rather than an affair requiring resolute engagement. As Strauss puts this point in *The City and Man*, "The '*human things*' [toward which

Socrates turned philosophy's attention] are not 'the *nature of man*'. . . . Within . . . the sphere of all *human things* . . . prudence is supreme . . . since the principles of prudence are known independently of *theoretical* science. . . . The *natural end of man* . . . becomes genuinely known through *theoretical* science" (13, 25, 26, emphasis added). Strauss here introduces (without drawing attention to) a systematic distinction between "the human things" and "the nature of man" that is not explicit, to say the least, in Aristotle's texts. It turns out, then, that the Straussian philosopher will appropriate Aristotle's practical works in a way that does not require political action for its completion. "Knowledge of the human soul" rather than the practical wisdom of a Pericles is "the highest political art" ("What Is Political Philosophy?" 39). And since the philosopher's concern with political things does not intrinsically seek a practical completion (though it has some remnants of merely human interest through philanthropy), it need not be, indeed it cannot be, partial to any particular fatherland or *patria*.

This is an unusually bold intensification of the scattered indications of a purely theoretical interest in Aristotle's practical works. Strauss has a difficult task to counterbalance the many passages that display Aristotle's practical intention, and that indeed make his practical works, in a sense opposed to Strauss's, "the highest political reflection of the philosopher." In effect, Strauss tries to hold onto theory's disconnection from action while giving up Aristotle's insistence that theory is inactive because the objects of its interest are eternal and unchangeable. Once human beings become, if not the highest then the most interesting objects of theory, it is much harder to guarantee this result.

But Strauss has another and more powerful suggestion for why the political philosopher will not succumb to patriotic engagements:

> We conclude with a remark about a seeming self-contradiction of Aristotle's regarding the highest theme of his *Politics*. He bases his thematic discussion of the best regime on the principle that the highest end of man, happiness, is the same for the individual and the city. . . . The difficulty arises from the fact that the highest end of the individual is contemplation. He seems to solve the difficulty by asserting that the city is as capable of the contemplative life as the individual. Yet it is obvious that the city is capable at best only of an analogue of the contemplative life. Aristotle reaches his apparent result only by an explicit abstraction, appropriate for a political inquiry strictly and narrowly conceived, from the full meaning of the best life of the individual; in such an inquiry the trans-political, the supra-political—the life of the mind in contradistinction to political life—comes to sight only as the limit of the political. (*The City and Man*, 49)

It should surprise no one that the author of *Persecution and the Art of Writing* finds the key to Aristotle's intention in "a seeming self-contradiction." Aristotle states exoterically that contemplation can be "at home on earth," and more particularly can be a part of the life of "a citizen of a part of the inhabitable earth," that is, of a particular political community. But, Strauss suggests, he also indicates esoterically that "the full meaning of the best life of the individual" is the life of the stranger without any patriotic attachments. The best life is essentially cosmopolitan, the life of a "citizen of the whole" ("Restatement," 212). For support, Strauss cites the following passage:

> Two questions need to be investigated, however. First, which life is more choiceworthy, the one that involves taking part in politics with other people and participating in a city, or the life of a stranger [*bios xenikos*] cut off from the political community? Second, and regardless of whether participating in a city is more choiceworthy for everyone or for most but not for all, which constitution, which condition of the city, is best? This second question, and not the one about what is choiceworthy for the individual, is a task for political thinking and theory. And since that is the investigation we are now engaged in, whereas the former is a further task, our task is the second question. (*Politics* 7.2, 1324a13–23)

Aristotle has abstracted from the cosmopolitan possibility because he wanted to open the political horizon to the dawn of philosophy without scorching it with the direct noon of philosophy's ultimate rejection of patriotism. This defense of the stranger's life is Strauss's replacement for the otherworldliness of Aristotle. In this respect, Strauss's Aristotle is the direct equivalent of Xenophon's Simonides and of Plato's stranger from Elea: "The precise relation between the philosopher and the political man (i.e., their fundamental difference) is the thematic premise, not of the *Republic* and the *Gorgias* in which Socrates as citizen-philosopher is the leading character, but of the *Politicus* [*Statesman*] in which a stranger occupies the central position" (*On Tyranny*, 87). The stranger is a teacher of legislators, but his political isolation guarantees his merely theoretical interest in politics; his pedagogy will not be distorted by patriotic passion or more generally by an entanglement in what Strauss liked to call "the here and now." And this theoretical and cosmopolitan attitude to politics is what ultimately explains and justifies the philosopher's distance from moral virtue as such: "The 'practical science' of . . . the teacher of legislators . . . differs from prudence in all its forms because it is free of that involvement the dangers of which cannot be averted except by moral virtue" (*The City and Man*, 29).

Many have criticized Leo Strauss for what they see as his elitist, anti-democratic conception of politics and philosophy. But I hope I have shown why Strauss's defense of esotericism is poorly understood in these terms. What from one perspective is philosophy's indulgent egoism is from another its disciplined resistance to the patriotic temptation of becoming essentially formative of nation and state. "Since the wise man does not need human beings in the way in which, and to the extent to which, the ruler does, his attitude toward them is free, not passionate, and hence is not susceptible of turning into malevolence or hatred" (*On Tyranny*, 91). Strauss's defense of what he himself called the "selfishness" of philosophy so conceived (*On Tyranny*, 125, n. 59) can be appreciated only when one has a clear view of what he saw as the alternative: philosophy in the service of worldly and revolutionary politics. That this esoteric stance runs important moral risks was as least as clear to Strauss as to his critics. But he saw no way of retrieving Aristotle from Heidegger that would altogether avoid the sting of Adeimantus' dilemma. Hiding behind a wall, it seems, exposes the philosopher to storms of its own, storms Strauss was willing to endure for the sake of his great project: *Ta megala panta episphalē.*

Aristotle's Silent Impiety: Why Strauss Was Not an Aristotelian

I would like to conclude by returning to my suggestion (see note 24) that Strauss's own attachment to the "Epicurean" model of philosophy he ascribes to Aristotle (and to Xenophon's Simonides) is provisional or conditional. Strauss's Aristotle is an experiment to see the extent to which one can, without refuting Heidegger's basic ontological premise, still escape from Adeimantus' dilemma. The Aristotelian philosopher as Strauss reconstructs him is politically interested without being politically involved, and his esotericism prevents him from undermining the decency and moderation of politics with the passions of philosophy. But Strauss also pursued another vision of philosophy, one he thought of as Socratic.

This Socratic ideal of philosophy would confront Heidegger's phenomenology directly. Strauss sometimes suggests that one could challenge Heidegger's understanding of the starting points of philosophic ascent in something like the way Heidegger himself challenged Husserl. Heidegger argued that Husserl had truncated and washed out the human experience of the prephilosophic world, transforming *pragmata*, that is, objects of caring engagement, into *ousiai*, that is, objects of mere theoretical inspection. Strauss suggests that Heidegger in turn truncates prephilosophic experience by overlooking or removing our experience of something external cutting across our grain, "a kind of divination that not everything is permitted" (*Natural Right and History*, 130). One might say that Heidegger's exaggeration of our spontaneous powers in a world of things "ready-to-hand" is equal and opposite to Husserl's exaggeration of our receptive powers in a world of things indifferently present. Heidegger's waiting for the arrival of the gods is a mistake, for man as man is unintelligible without his awareness of sacred restraints. The gods are always already here in the natural consciousness, a consciousness from which philosophic thinking must ascend, but which it can never simply escape.[44] Radical resoluteness can be arrived at, then, only by failing to respect or by utterly rejecting a crucial part of the phenomenological "datum" from which one is supposed to start. This, I believe, is the point Strauss had in mind when he said of his exchange with Kojève, "We have both *apparently* turned away from Being to Tyranny because we have seen that those who lacked the courage to face the issue [of *tyranny*] . . . were forced to evade the issue of *Being* as well" ("Restatement," 212, emphasis added). To consider tyranny is only *apparently* to turn from Being because Being cannot be fully understood without an accurate phenomenology. The failure to respect the natural recoil of decent men to the prospects of revolutionary violence, for example, is an evasion of an indispensable part of the phenomena being considered. To steel oneself to Machiavellism is not to untrammel one's mind, but to close it.[45]

To put this point another way, the city in its "natural," prephilosophic self-understanding is a sacred city, not a secular city (see *The City and Man*, 240–41, the concluding paragraph of the book). Aristotle's silent exclusion of piety from the list of the virtues and his demotion of shame are aspects of his implicit rejection of this self-understanding.[46] Receptive openness to "the evidence of those simple experiences regarding right and wrong which are at the bottom of the philosophic contention that there is natural right" (*Natural Right and History*, 32–33), not to say unquestioning obedience to God's commandments, is the foundation of piety as it is normally understood, the piety of the believer. For Strauss's Aristotle, on the other hand, it appears that such "evidence" cannot be built upon. The rejection of the evidentness or givenness of such experiences means that the ascent from the simple experience of sacred restraints results in a rupture or a discontinuity between anything the decent political man could recognize as piety and anything the erotic man could recognize as philosophy. Obedience is the piety of belief; but for Strauss's Aristotle, questioning is the piety of thinking.

Strauss ultimately did not identify with this Aristotelian and Simonidean view, though it is beyond our power to discuss here how he distanced himself from it. One might say Strauss intensified Aristotle's commitment to starting from decent opinions. The continuity Strauss requires philosophy to retain with religious belief is more controlling than the continuity his Aristotle demanded between philosophy and respectable moral opinion, which after all philosophy ultimately transcends utterly. Strauss also makes it clear that "the citizen-philosopher Socrates" represents for him an alternative to Simonides' and Aristotle's "Epicurean" ideal. This ideal is characterized by its "atheism" (in Kojève's sense), its unerotic egoism, and its suitability for a political stranger. By contrast, Socrates is characterized by his piety, his eroticism, and his attachment to his fatherland, his *patria*. Perhaps the Socratic combination of Heideggerian patriotism and anti-Heideggerian piety was seen by Strauss as a superior alternative to his Aristotle. However that may be, Strauss did indicate in the concluding sentence of his commentary on the *Hiero* where one must turn to find his analysis of these questions: "a comprehensive and detailed analysis of Xenophon's Socratic writings" (*On Tyranny*, 105, last sentence of the book). Strauss's late works devoted to this project are protected by a much denser veil of esotericism than any of the covert engagements with Heidegger of Strauss's middle period with which we have been concerned. Rather than "reflect[ing] a diminution of power,"[47] this denser veil reflects Strauss's judgment that the question of piety is ultimately the deepest human question, deeper than any political question properly speaking. "Only by beginning [with this prephilosophic piety of the city] will we be open to the full impact of the all-important question which is co-eval with philosophy although the philosophers do not frequently pronounce it—the question *quid sit deus*" (*The City and Man*, 241, last sentence of the book). Even here, Strauss's greater reserve about piety than tyranny reflects his sense of kinship with Simonides. Though willing to stoop to the morally dubious business of advising a tyranny without preaching against it, Simonides "is said to have repeatedly postponed and finally abandoned the attempt to answer the question which Hiero had posed to him, What is God?" (*On Tyranny*, 104–105). These two invocations of "the all-important question," nearly two decades apart, indicate as gracefully as one could wish Strauss's own sense of both the focus and the limit of his middle period engagement with Heidegger: he could not understand Being without facing tyranny, and could not understand tyranny without facing God.

Notes

1. Page references to the Rectoral Address and to Heidegger's 1945 reflections on the address and the rectorship more generally, titled "Facts and Thoughts," refer to Karsten Harries's translation in *Review of Metaphysics* 38 (March 1985): 467–502, which I have sometimes altered. The German text is *Die Selbstbehauptung der Deutschen Universitaet* and *Das Rektorat 1933/34: Tatsachen und Gedanken* (Frankfurt:

Vittorio Klostermann, 1983). There is something misleading about calling Heidegger's *Aufbruch* a "revolutionary beginning" as I have, since he understood it to be a return to something primordial. This sense of revivifying potencies lying dormant would perhaps be captured better by a word like "renewal." Heidegger sees his renewal of the Greek experience of Being as something like the "break out" involved in a spring thaw.

2. In an influential article, "Die grossen Worte des Rektors Heidegger: Eine philologische Untersuchung," *Frankfurter Allgemeine Zeitung*, March 2, 1984, 25, Dolf Sternberger has harshly criticized Heidegger's use of the passage from the *Republic*. Sternberger starts from Karl Jaspers's comment that Heidegger's translation was "willful" and the image of the storm "empty pomp and sentiment" (*Gebaerde und Pathetik*). But Sternberger sees more than bad taste in the use of "in the storm," and suggests three ways in which Heidegger's usage is morally unacceptable. First, the rhetorical effect of Heidegger's concluding sentence would have been quite different, and decidedly less Nazi, if he had translated *episphalē* in a standard way, say by using Schleiermacher's "classic" translation (which, it should be noted, is in fact rather inaccurate) *bedenklich* or a more neutral translation like *zum Fallen geneigt*. These translations, Sternberger suggests, would have left open the thought that the Nazi regime had within itself the seeds of its own degeneration, whereas the "storm" image acknowledges only external threats. Second, by using "in the storm," Heidegger introduces a "heroic vocabulary" that has played an "allegorical role" for war in "German patriotic poetry." Third, Sternberger insinuates that Heidegger's use of "storm" bears a sinister relationship to the "storm troopers" of the Nazi S.A., that is, the *Sturm-Abteilung*, who were a strikingly visible part of the audience at the Rectoral Address. He does not bother to specify what this relationship is, but he seems to think Heidegger was identifying with or pandering to the S.A.

None of these charges makes much sense. Heidegger did not use a "standard" translation because he was not simply translating the passage, but adumbrating the entire section of which it is the conclusion. And though it is true enough that "storm" had in Heidegger's speech many military resonances, it was a word with a long history in German reflection on cultural and spiritual crises, reaching back at least to the *Sturm und Drang* of Goethe's time. No doubt Heidegger did intend to play on the prominence of "storm" as well as other terms prominent in Nazi jargon, but the words hardly belonged to the Nazis, who themselves were taking up a more general Weimar language of cultural crisis and renewal. As I read the Rectoral Address, Heidegger appropriates this culturally available language for his own project rather than merely echoing or pandering to the specifically Nazi use of the terms. Indeed, the immediate response of some Nazi Party officials to the Rectoral Address was to grouse about Heidegger's merely "private National Socialism"; they saw him as trying to usurp for his own purposes, and with doubtful orthodoxy, some of their own themes. Simply put, at least some of the Nazis in the audience were irritated that Heidegger had twisted their own favorite words. That Heidegger in the Rectoral Address was involved in something of a competition for control over a culturally potent vocabulary seems not to have been considered by Sternberger and critics who have followed him. At any rate, Sternberger shows no awareness of the context of the original passage in the *Republic,* nor of its significance in the context of the themes concerning Greek philosophy in Heidegger's address.

Sternberger's charges against Heidegger's use of "in the storm" have gotten themselves established in the secondary literature. Sternberger is the ultimate source for four prominent critiques of the Rectoral Address. None of these critics realizes the offending line comes from the conclusion of Socrates' response to Adeimantus' challenge. Bernd Martin praises Sternberger's "outstanding even if also polemical" interrogation of the Plato citation, in "'Alles Grosse ist gefaehrdet'—Der Fall Heidegger(s)," in *Martin Heidegger und das "Dritte Reich": Ein Kompendium,* ed. Bernd Martin (Darmstadt: Wissenschaftliche Buchgesellschaft, 1989), 3, n. 4. Martin says Heidegger used the *Republic* passage (the Greek of which is quoted inaccurately in the first sentence of the article) "in a distorting [*sinnentstellter*] form," and characterizes the quotation as "this willful, fundamentally false version [*Diese einwillige, im Grunde falsche Uebertragung*]." He also seems to have Heidegger playing to the storm troopers in the audience (3), though he reports an eyewitness's recollection that the S.A. men were bored by Heidegger's speech and did not regard him as one of their own (4).

Tom Rockmore, *On Heidegger's Nazism and Philosophy* (Berkeley: University of California Press, 1992), in a passage that cites Martin as its authority, says that Heidegger "deliberately distorts the passage from Plato" (71). But Rockmore's discussion of the Rectoral Address is superior to Sternberger's and Martin's insofar as he sees that the Rectoral Address should be read in light of the *Republic*'s account of the relation between philosophy and politics (54–72). But he assumes a trivial reading of the *Republic* in which Plato has nothing but unmixed enthusiasm for the prospect of philosophers wielding political power.

More extreme in its inflation of Sternberger's original charges is Richard Wolin, *The Politics of Being* (New York: Columbia University Press, 1990). Sternberger is cited by Wolin (86, n. 49), though oddly enough for a minor point rather than for these major philological charges. But Wolin seems to follow Sternberger closely. He repeats Sternberger's insinuation about "storm troopers," and adds to it the further insinuation that Heidegger was calling to mind the notorious Nazi propaganda journal *Der Stuermer* (91). Like Sternberger, he contrasts Heidegger's version to "standard" translations (albeit to English rather than German translations). Finally he follows Sternberger, indeed Sternberger's subtitle, in characterizing his harshest charge as "philological." (Oddly enough, Wolin leaves off Sternberger's subtitle in his citation, and misreports it in his own bibliography, replacing 'philologische' with 'philosophische,' which effectively obscures his indebtedness.) Wolin calls Heidegger's translation of the passage an act of "philological apostasy," a "willful misreading," and a "deliberate falsification" (90). There is no evidence in Wolin's discussion that before venting this philologist's outrage he had taken into account the somewhat basic philological requirement to read the passage in the *Republic* from which Heidegger took the quotation.

Finally, Johannes Fritsche, *Historical Destiny and National Socialism in Heidegger's Being and Time* (Berkeley: University of California Press, 1999), uncritically repeats Wolin's charges (221–22). He does at least note, as does Rockmore, that the context of the *Republic* is relevant; but his account of this context (223, n. 22) is so vague as to be useless.

3. I discuss Aristotle's focus in his political writings on the existential choice between philosophy and politics, and emphasize how this focus has been obscured in the interpretive paradigm dominant in Anglo-American analytic circles, in "The Ambitions of Aristotle's Audience and the Activist Ideal of Happiness," in *Action and Contemplation: Studies in the Moral and Political Thought of Aristotle,* ed. R. Bartlett and S. Collins (Albany: SUNY Press, 1999).

4. Reprinted in *Jewish Philosophy and the Crisis of Modernity,* ed. K. H. Green (Albany: SUNY Press, 1997).

5. For the themes of Heidegger's 1922 Aristotle lectures, the best source is Heidegger's October 1922 plan for a book, recently discovered and now translated as "Phenomenological Interpretations with Respect to Aristotle: Indication of the Hermeneutical Situation," trans. Michael Bauer, *Man and World* 25 (1992): 355–93. Theodore Kisiel, *The Genesis of Heidegger's Being and Time* (Berkeley: University of California Press, 1993), 238–40, gives an account of precisely the lecture on the *Metaphysics* to which Strauss refers. For the fullest development of Heidegger's reinterpretation of the relation between practical and theoretical reason in Aristotle, see the lecture course of 1924/25 published as *Plato's* Sophist, trans. R. Rojcewicz and A. Schuwer (Indianapolis: Indiana University Press, 1997).

6. Published in *The Rebirth of Classical Political Rationalism,* ed. T. Pangle (Chicago: University of Chicago Press, 1989). In accord with his usual avoidance of so much as mentioning Heidegger's name, it appears Strauss titled the lecture, "An Introduction to Existentialism," Pangle changed the title to "An Introduction to Heideggerian Existentialism" (p. xxix).

7. See especially three essays in *What Is Political Philosophy?* (Chicago: University of Chicago Press, 1988 [1959]): "On Classical Political Philosophy," 78–79 (the direct relation between classical political philosophy and political life); "Political Philosophy and History," 74–75 (classical political philosophy started from the natural consciousness); "What Is Political Philosophy?" 23–25 (positivism's mistaken contempt for the prephilosophic) and 27–28 (the abstractness of modern political philosophy compared to the naturalness of classical political philosophy); and two later autobiographical reflections: "Philosophy as Rigorous Science and Political Philosophy," 31, in *Studies in Platonic Political Philosophy,* ed. T. Pangle (Chicago: University of Chicago Press, 1983), and "A Giving of Accounts," 461 (Heidegger's radicalization of Husserl, that is, his "*pragmata*-ism").

8. See also "Relativism," 26, in *The Rebirth of Classical Political Rationalism.*

9. In *Liberalism Ancient and Modern* (Chicago: University of Chicago Press, 1995 [1968]).

10. An English translation of the Strauss-Kojève correspondence is in *On Tyranny,* revised and expanded edition, ed. and trans. V. Gourevitch and M. Roth (Chicago: University of Chicago Press, 2000).

11. For Heidegger's discussion of *technē*'s relation to *phronēsis* and *theoria,* see the texts mentioned in note 5.

12. For Aristotle's general view of happiness, and so of philosophy, as *energeia,* see especially *Nicomachean Ethics* 1.7, 1097b22–1098a18, the *ergon* ("function") argument; for the assimilation of philosophic *energeia* to *praxis,* consider *Nicomachean Ethics* 10.8, 1178b33–1179a29.

13. I have followed Strauss in translating *Volk* with "nation." See *The City and Man* (Chicago: University of Chicago Press, 1978 [1964]), 33, n. 46.

14. See also Strauss's letter to Kojève of June 26, 1950, apparently about Heidegger's *Holzwege:* "Heidegger's position is the last refuge of nationalism: the state, even "culture", is done with—all that remains is language—of course with the modifications that became necessary as a consequence of 1933–45."

15. Correspondence August 22, 1948, referring to Kojève's *Introduction to the Reading of Hegel.*

16. See the correspondence of September 19 and 28, 1950: Strauss removed three sentences apparently referring to Hitler, in part, he says, to respect the "exoteric" character of Kojève's exposition. Kojève certainly did conceive of Hitler as a tyrant of the new, revolutionary type; see his reference to "the democratization of imperial Germany (by way of Hitlerism)," *Introduction to the Reading of Hegel,* ed. A. Bloom, trans. J. Nichols (Ithaca: Cornell University Press, 1980 [1969]), p. 160 note, quoted by Gourevitch and Roth, p. xv.

17. Strauss regarded Jacob Klein's work as indispensable for understanding how "classical philosophy originally acquired the fundamental concepts of political philosophy by starting from political phenomena as they present themselves to the . . . pre-philosophic consciousness" ("What Is Political Philosophy?" 75 with n. 4). Strauss's comment "I am one of those who refuses to go through open doors when one can enter just as well through a keyhole" may well be an allusion to Nietzsche. Poem 42 among those prefaced to the second edition of *The Gay Science* uses this very image in its third and fourth lines (my translation):

Grundsatz der Allzufeinen	*Basic Principle of the Over-Refined*
Lieber auf den Zehen noch	Rather even on tiptoe
Als auf allen Vieren!	Than on all fours!
Lieber durch ein Schluesselloch	Rather through a keyhole
Als durch offne Tueren!	Than through open doors!

Nietzsche surely invites the interpretation that he is one of the over-refined, and Strauss would be doing the same with his allusion. Both would be making the point that their writing is discreet and has an esoteric dimension. (The German expression "batter an open door" means to belabor an obvious point or to make a show of something that goes without saying.)

18. See especially *On Tyranny,* chapter V, "The Two Ways of Life," 90: "The specific function of the wise man is not bound up with the individual political community: the wise man may live as a stranger."

19. Compare the conclusion of "Tyranny and Wisdom," 176: "In general terms, it is history itself that attends to 'judging' (by 'achievement' or 'success') the deeds of statesmen or tyrants, which they perform (consciously or not) as a function of the ideas of philosophers, adapted for practical purposes by intellectuals."

20. I have throughout substituted Strauss's "sect" for the Gourevitch/Roth "cloister" as the translation of Kojève's *chapelle*.

21. I have substituted Strauss's translation from "Restatement," 205, from "to participate" to the end, for the Gourevitch/Roth version.

22. Gourevitch and Roth, p. xxii, offer the hypothesis that Strauss omitted this 1954 passage because by 1959 "he had decided to speak out about Heidegger explicitly and at length, and . . . wished his public comments to be suitably modulated." I believe this vastly underestimates the "length" of Strauss's implicit engagement with Heidegger in his publications before 1959; and I know of no text Strauss published after 1959 that fits their description of an explicit and lengthy treatment. For those who may find incredible the notion that Strauss could try to suppress his engagement with a philosopher as famous as Heidegger, it may be worth noting that the first major work of Heidegger translated into English, *An Introduction to Metaphysics*, appeared in 1959, and *Being and Time* only in 1962.

23. Notice how Strauss is here somewhat more "nationalist" than "internationalist," reflecting his emphasis on Heidegger and Hitler rather than Marx and Stalin.

24. This is only provisional because it does not take into account Strauss's suggestion in the last sentence that evasion of the problem of tyranny entails a truncated appreciation of Being itself. I will have more to say on this point in the final section, when I discuss piety in Strauss's Aristotle.

25. Aristotle uses both Thales and Anaxagoras as examples of philosophers who pursued theoretical wisdom to the exclusion of practical wisdom; see especially *Nicomachean Ethics* 6.7, 1141b3–8.

26. See also Strauss's comment on Simonides' attitude toward nature and the gods: "Hiero and Simonides mention 'the gods,' but there is no apparent connection between what they say about 'nature' and what they say about 'the gods.' It is possible that what they mean by 'the gods' is chance rather than 'nature' or the origin of the natural order" (*On Tyranny*, 105, from the chapter "Piety and Law"). Strauss thus suggests that the model of the philosopher's relation to politics he finds implicit in Simonides' relation to Hiero, centered on esotericism, does not depend on the "theistic" premise.

27. See also "What Is Political Philosophy?" 38–39: "Socrates viewed man in the light of the mysterious character of the whole. . . . He viewed man in the light of the unchangeable ideas, i.e., of the fundamental and permanent problems."

28. See also "What Is Political Philosophy?" 40: "Philosophy is characterized by the gentle, if firm, refusal to succumb to [the charm of] . . . absolutizing either knowledge of homogeneity or knowledge of ends. . . . It could appear as Sisyphean or ugly, when one contrasts its achievement with its goal [of total knowledge]. Yet it is necessarily accompanied, sustained and elevated by *eros*. It is graced by nature's grace."

29. Gourevitch and Roth, p. xviii, note the allusion of p. 196 to Strauss's friendship with Kojève.

30. See *Studies in Platonic Political Philosophy*, "Note on the Plan of Nietzsche's *Beyond Good and Evil*," 175: "The graceful subtlety as regards form, as regards intention, as regards the art of silence are in the foreground in *Beyond Good and Evil*. . . .

In other words, in *Beyond Good and Evil*, in the only book published by Nietzsche in the contemporary preface to which he presents himself as the antagonist of Plato, he 'platonizes' as regards the 'form' more than anywhere else."

31. See Strauss's claim that for classical political philosophy the relation between philosopher and the city is not tragic, responding to Kojève's claim that for the historicist it is tragic ("Restatement," 206, responding to "Tyranny and Wisdom," 166).

32. Can a *pros hen* relationship be understood on the model of a paradigmatic and an imperfect exemplification of some trait? Christopher Shields, *Order in Multiplicity* (New York: Oxford University Press, 1999), 118, suggests *Metaphysics* 4.2, 1003b2–3 could perhaps be read in a way that supports this idea. He says the passage may indicate that things standing in a *pros hen* relationship can be related as a trained physician is related to a talented folk healer who is naturally suited (*euphues*) for medicine: the healer exemplifies the form of being medical "*incompletely* or *inchoately*, or at any rate differently from the way a trained physician manifests it" (emphasis added). This example would fit my way of reading *NE* 1.6, but I believe this passage cannot be read in this way. Aristotle is contrasting three levels of actualizing medical science (1003b1–3): the state of having learned medicine (*exein*), the state of being able to learn medicine (*euphues einai*), and the state of actually practicing medicine (*ergon*). Compare *NE* 6.13, on the relation between inborn or natural virtue and virtue in the definitive sense (*kuria*): one has natural virtue when one is naturally suited (*euphues*) for definitive virtue, which is present only when the agent also has practical wisdom (1144b34–1145a2). In both cases, the naturally suited person does not have an incomplete version of the complete medical science or virtue so much as an undeveloped version of it. This developmental model does not fit the relationship between (fully developed) political virtue and philosophic virtue that is at question in *NE* 1.6–7. Something like the developmental model is also Shields's preferred reading (112, n. 10).

33. For simplicity, I will use "analogy" to name whatever relationship holds between a more paradigmatic good and a less paradigmatic good. At the end of this section I will consider two competing models of this relationship. This critique of the Platonic conception of the good-in-itself is put to work in Aristotle's outline of the highest good in the following chapter, *Nicomachean Ethics* 1.7. This outline in effect provides some detailed guidelines for the investigation of claims for various goods and activities to be good in themselves, and emphasizes that for something to be good in itself is not an all-or-nothing affair, but instead admits of degrees. See the characteristics of the highest good enumerated in *NE* 1.7, 1097a22–24 (finality), 1097a28–30 (completeness), 1097b14–20 (sufficiency), 1098a16–18 (actualization or *energeia*): Aristotle consistently leaves open the question of whether some one activity or virtue is superlatively final, complete, sufficient, and actualizing, always maintaining that even if there is one superlative virtue or activity, the others do not lose their status as final, complete, choiceworthy, and actualizing. I take this as strong confirmation of my reading of 1.6.

34. See *NE* 6.12, 1144a1–3, 6.13, 1145a2–4; *Pol.* 7.14, 1333a24–30.

35. See for example *The City and Man*, 27, n. 34.

36. Stanley Rosen, "Hermeneutics as Politics," in *Hermeneutics as Politics* (New York: Oxford University Press, 1987), 121, original emphasis. This is a stimulating

essay. I disagree with Rosen's view that Strauss was committed, as an act of will, to the "theistic" premise of an eternal order. I am trying to show that Strauss's interpretation of Aristotle, and the *Hiero*, is meant to address even those who hold to a Heideggerian ontology.

37. "Aristotle is the founder of political science because he is the discoverer of moral virtue. For Plato, what Aristotle calls moral virtue is a kind of halfway house between political or vulgar virtue which is in the service of bodily well-being (of self-preservation or peace) and genuine virtue which, to say the least, animates only the philosophers as philosophers" (*The City and Man*, 27).

38. In support of this and the parallel passage of *Natural Right and History* (Chicago: University of Chicago Press, 1953) at 151 with 152, n. 26, Strauss cites *NE* 10.7, 1177a25–34 (the superior pleasure and self-sufficiency of theory), 1177b1–8 and 16–18 (the superior leisure and choiceworthiness for itself of theory), and 10.8, 1178a9–b21 (the superior independence and divinity of theory). Both passages also cite the whole of the last chapter of the *Eudemian Ethics*. The first part of this chapter contains a treatment of *kalokagathia*, roughly synonymous with magnanimity. It criticizes the Spartans for not choosing moral virtue for its own sake so much as for the advantages, especially in war, that flow from it. The second part gives an account of contemplation of god as the target at which practical wisdom aims. (This part provides the same sort of example as *NE* 10.7–8; it parallels closely *NE* 6.13, 1145a6–11, which Strauss cites (*The City and Man*, 25) to support his claim that "practical wisdom is lower in rank than theoretical wisdom . . . and subservient to it.") Thus the structure of the chapter as a whole mirrors Strauss's idea that magnanimity reveals that virtue has "two entirely different roots" (*Natural Right and History*, 151), one pointing toward concern for the common good, the other to the perfection of the individual, neither of which fully explains what is so attractive about magnanimity.

39. In a parallel passage, Strauss says "justice and moral virtue in general can be *fully legitimated* only by the fact that they are required for the sake of that ultimate end or that they are the conditions of the philosophic life" (*Natural Right and History*, 151, emphasis added). He does not seem to have made the relatively simple mistake of thinking the mere fact that moral virtue might be a means to something else, in particular to theoretical virtue, would show moral virtue was not choiceworthy in itself. Otherwise he would also be committed to saying the common good is not choiceworthy in itself, since he says the city is for the sake of moral virtue. In other words, these two passages do not require Strauss to reject Aristotle's programmatic principle. Strauss argues that philosophers will be *uninterested* in moral virtue as such; he does not and does not need to argue that it is *structurally* impossible for them to value moral virtue in itself merely because they value philosophy more.

40. Strauss cites *NE* 6.8, 1142a1–2 with 10.7, 1177a25ff, and *Metaphysics* 1.2, 982b25–28. But a passage more suggestive for Strauss's purposes is *Eudemian Ethics* 1.8, 1218a15–24. Aristotle there advises those who want to argue that the good in itself is something eternal and unmoving to start from agreed examples of noble things, rather than from controversial ones like numbers. For example, one could start from such uncontroversial noble things as "health and strength and moderation," and

argue that "the noble is even more present in unmoving things [*akinēta*]." Aristotle describes how to move from the nobility of health, strength, and moderation to the superior nobility of the eternal and unmoving in a way that supports Strauss: "[Health, strength, and moderation] are kinds of order and rest [*ēremia*]; but granting this, unmoving things are even more like this, since order and rest are more present in them."

41. Strauss cites the following passage to support this claim: "Perhaps one would suppose this [that is, virtue] rather [than honor] to be the end of political life" (*Nicomachean Ethics* 1.5, 1095b30–31). Strauss's thought seems to be that to move from a concern with honor—the basic defining characteristic of magnanimity—to a concern with virtue is to become open to seeing the ultimately apolitical perfection of virtue in philosophy. But in the immediate sequel, Aristotle says virtue is also too incomplete to be the end of political life; the end must be the *praxis* of virtue, not just the having of it. He then explicitly puts off discussing the theoretical life (1095b31–1096a5). The move from honor to virtue to *praxis* is clear; perhaps there is a suggestion of a further move to theory. But it is quite unclear that theory is here to be *contrasted* to *praxis*.

42. See also the contrast between Alcibiades and Socrates as exemplars of magnanimity: *Posterior Analytics* 2.13, 97b16–25. Aristotle is describing how to seek a common definition of a term that has more than one sense, and uses magnanimity as his example. Alcibiades (along with Achilles and Ajax) exemplifies the "motion" pole of magnanimity, characterized by intolerance of insult and a tendency to take revenge; Socrates (along with Lysander) exemplifies the "rest" pole, characterized by indifference to good and bad fortune. Alas, Aristotle does not say here whether he thinks there is in fact some common aspect unifying the concept of magnanimity, or whether magnanimity simply has two distinct meanings.

43. See also *NE* 9.8, 1169a32–34: "It is even possible [for the morally serious person] to give up actions for a friend, since becoming the cause of a friend's action is nobler than acting oneself."

44. Laurence Berns, "The Prescientific World and Historicism: Some Reflections on Strauss, Heidegger, and Husserl," 169–81, in *Leo Strauss's Thought: Toward a Critical Engagement*, ed. Alan Udoff (Boulder, Colo.: Lynne Rienner Publishers, 1991), gives a brief but very useful account of these aspects of Strauss's thought in relation to Heidegger.

45. See especially "What Is Political Philosophy?" 43: "Machiavelli's teaching . . . seems to have opened up a depth from which the classics, in their noble simplicity, recoiled. . . . [But as a matter of fact, in this teaching] an amazing contraction of the horizon presents itself as an amazing enlargement of the horizon." See also the beginning of Strauss's commentary, *On Tyranny*, 22–24.

46. See "On Classical Political Philosophy," 94; *The City and Man*, 28. See also *On Tyranny*, 130 n. 2 to p. 103, which indicates Strauss understood Aristotle's silent demotion of piety to be of a piece with the silence of Simonides and Hiero about piety. See also note 26 above, which shows that Strauss thinks Aristotle arrives at the same "practical" view of piety's irrelevance as one would arrive at by accepting an atheistic cosmology. Strauss might well have pointed out that Aristotle "defends" tragedy in the *Poetics* in part by implicitly denying that man's relationship to the

gods is its true theme. One must qualify the sense in which for Strauss Simonides or even Xenophon arrive at the "same" view as Aristotle about how philosophy transcends politics, morality, and piety. Simonides is willing in his own voice to give advice for improving tyranny without raising explicit doubts about the legitimacy of tyranny; Xenophon is at least willing to give such advice a voice, though only through a dialogue that prevents this voice from being his own; Aristotle gives his advice only grudgingly, always keeping the indecency of even the best tyranny on the surface. All three may hold, according to Strauss, essentially the same esoteric view of philosophy, but they differ in their willingness to expose this view to public scrutiny. Needless to say, Machiavelli goes much further than even Simonides, since he not only gives tyrants advice in his own voice, but does not even try to improve them. See Strauss's contrast between the Aristotelian and the Machiavellian view of natural right, *Natural Right and History,* 161–62.

47. S. Rosen, "Hermeneutics as Politics," 133.

CHAPTER SIX

Liberalism's Need for Virtue and Christian Theology

CHARLES R. PINCHES

SHALL LIBERALISM AND VIRTUE EMBRACE?

I am a Christian theologian, and not necessarily a liberal. In my theological writings I have frequently found myself using Aristotle. The main reason for this, I suppose, is that I can find no more compelling account of the Christian moral life than that given by St. Thomas Aquinas in the second part of his *Summa Theologiae;* and of course that text, indeed any and all of Aquinas's writing about ethics, is suffused with wisdom gleaned from Aristotle's ethics and politics.

Now Aquinas transforms Aristotle as he uses him. He is run through the mill of Christian theology, becoming so thoroughly ground up with Augustine or the biblical writers that the specific view we find in Aquinas of what is good, what the human life is to be lived towards, benefits more from Aristotle by way of contrast rather than by way of extension. What remains, of course, is a certain structure that is indispensable for both thinkers: that we must begin ethical reflection with a discussion of happiness, the end for human beings; that one attains this end by act; that the virtues are necessary both to know what are good acts and also to do them; that the moral life is not to be lived alone but with friends; etc. Aristotle's arguments about these things are appropriated and built upon by Aquinas, and it is always instructive to return to them. Moreover, Aquinas did not return to Aristotle simply because he needed a dissertation topic but because of the power of the account and its capacity to display what is true about human beings, even if not all that is true.

Lately we are witnessing a return to Aristotle by another group besides antiquarian philosophers or theologians. These are modern liberal intellectuals. What is going on in this return? After all, compared with the likes of Kant, Locke, or Mill, Aristotle has hardly been a central figure in moral and political discussion among liberals. However, as Peter Berkowitz tells us in his recent book *Virtue and the Making of Modern Liberalism*, lately a new brand of liberal has arisen.

> For quite a while leading academic liberals and their best-known critics formed an unwitting alliance, promulgating the view that liberal political theory, on the one hand, and theories of politics that dealt with virtue, the common good, and the ends of political life, on the other hand, represented rival and incompatible frameworks. Despite the staying power of this view in many precincts of the academy, over the last decade innovative writings by a new generation of liberal thinkers have made clear that without violating, indeed in accordance with the dictates of, its own principles, liberalism may affirm that good government depends on the exercise of specific virtues by citizens and their representatives.[1]

Berkowitz does not mention Aristotle in this passage, but of course he does mention virtue. And Aristotle is associated with virtue. Indeed, the one place where Berkowitz pauses in his book to lay out an account of virtue *per se* is in a section in his introduction entitled "Aristotle's Account of the Virtues." In this section Berkowitz tells us something more about what he wants to do with Aristotle and virtue. Well, actually, he qualifies his return to Aristotle and the virtues in an important way since he realizes that Aristotle's shoes cannot simply be leapt back into. Indeed, Berkowitz helpfully poses certain objections to his project before he begins it.

> The familiar objection remains that [Aristotle's] catalogue of the virtues in the *Ethics* reflects the particular and contingent sensibilities of the ascendant class in fourth-century Athens. To this objection it is easy to reply that we need not follow Aristotle in every respect, that we are not bound to endorse only those or all those virtues which Aristotle discusses. . . . But even after these replies have been accorded their due weight, a thorny issue persists: by invoking the notion of a human being's characteristic activity or function and the idea of the greatest good, Aristotle's account of virtue, if only at its peak, appears to depend upon a discredited metaphysical biology and a refuted speculative cosmology.[2]

Berkowitz's way of getting around these problems is simply to set the deep questions aside. If he does not want precisely Aristotle's, what sort of virtues does Berkowitz want? What is their relation to some general view of the good life? What sort of vision of the human being does he propose if not that based on the discredited Aristotelian biology? Well, reasons Berkowitz, instead of trying to settle such matters, it is certainly true that

> in ordinary language and everyday experience we still distinguish good from bad lives, and . . . we still invoke virtues such as courage, generosity, integrity, toleration, decency, delicacy, and the capacity for love and friendship in order to characterize and evaluate both ourselves and others. This is all that one needs, from an Aristotelean perspective, to commence the investigation of virtue and take the question of the political significance of virtues seriously.[3]

Since we began with mention of Aquinas, it is perhaps helpful at this early stage quickly to mark a contrast between Berkowitz and Aquinas. Like Aquinas, Berkowitz does not want much to do with Aristotle's particular virtues. But unlike Aquinas, he hopes to get around them not by proposing a new way of understanding the moral life grounded in a different view of human nature, but merely by looking around here and there in our discourse to find what we think are virtues, and go from there.

What are we to say of this approach to Aristotle and the virtues from the new brand of liberal that Berkowitz himself represents? For myself, it is not without disappointment that I shall have to say I believe the project will founder, necessarily. Indeed, I believe a closer look at Berkowitz's proposal cannot but lead to the conclusion that the older liberals were likely right after all: liberalism is indeed adverse to virtue. It remains a very hard thing to hold a liberal polity and the moral virtues, any list of them at all, together in firm embrace.

Unless. Unless, that is, liberalism can become robust in a way not yet displayed in the writings either of the old liberals or the new ones of Berkowitz's ilk. Unless it can mark itself as a genuine way of life with a story of its own, and with corresponding virtues. Unless, in short, it can become something like a religion. As I shall seek to point out, there is promise for this in the work of self-proclaimed "reformist liberal" Richard Rorty, although of course it remains to be seen from which perspective Rorty's new vision can be thought promising. In this essay we will look beyond Berkowitz to Rorty, and beyond Rorty once again to Aristotle and also Aquinas, although now more separate than together. But first to Berkowitz and the liberal return to virtue.

OLD HABITS: VIRTUE MOTIVATIONALIZED

The argument of Berkowitz's book is substantially based upon a series of historical points that, I believe, are generally correct. He sets out early to show how much more common was the language of virtue in four thinkers foundational to liberalism: Thomas Hobbes, John Locke, Immanuel Kant, and J. S. Mill. Berkowitz shows plainly that each believed that a liberal polity needed "virtue" among its citizens for its health and sustenance. And, as Berkowitz implies, it has become far less clear that modern liberals believe this.

However, if we are to advance beyond these historical points, an important question must be addressed: Can we assume that what the founding liberals wanted when they called for "virtue" to sustain their liberal regimes was the same sort of thing that more classical thinkers had in mind when they spoke of virtue, thinkers such as Aristotle and Aquinas for whom virtue was absolutely central in any coherent account of ethics? Perhaps we should be wary of being swept away by the mere historical fact that the term "virtue" was used more commonly by earlier liberals than it is used by contemporary liberals such as John Rawls. Do we know that when they used the term "virtue" the early liberals pointed to the same thing that the classical thinkers and/or Christian thinkers had in mind as they used the term?

One does not have to work very hard to show that this is a question worth considering. As Berkowitz himself notes, Kant, almost indisputably the most consistent and probing of the four thinkers Berkowitz focuses upon in his book, quite explicitly set about to adjust the meaning of the term "virtue." Berkowitz writes,

> In the *Doctrine of Virtue,* Kant understands by virtue only that which serves a moral end and perfects the highest or best part of us, our rational nature. Virtue is necessary because, as rational beings who are finite and situated in the natural world, human beings are constantly tempted, even while recognizing its authority, to break the moral law. Since executing the moral law because it is the moral law involves a perpetual struggle to resist and conquer powerful passions, virtue is "moral strength of the will." Such strength is expressed through qualities of mind and character that enable one to subdue the inclinations deflecting one from taking the concept of duty as the incentive for carrying out the moral law. It is also expressed in qualities enabling one to perform actions that respect humanity in oneself and in others. As in the works of Hobbes and Locke, the virtues in Kant's thought can be understood as the qualities that enable human beings to act in accordance with the dictates of reason, but the dictates of reason for Kant are laws of morality and not prudence.
>
> To clarify the difference between his own understanding of virtue and the traditional or Aristotelean understanding, Kant insists that virtue is not mere habit or aptitude but, rather, a set of inner dispositions rooted in firm, reflectively held, and purified principles.[4]

Notice that Kant believed that his view of virtue deviated importantly from Aristotle's. In connection with Berkowitz's project, it seems this point will need discussion, particularly since, as we have seen, Berkowitz himself wishes to avoid giving any sort of substantive definition of virtue in relation to some general view of the good life. Put in relation to Berkowitz's more historical points, for anything like a return to "virtue" in modern liberalism to make sense, we need to know more about what is the "virtue" to which we are returning, particularly because liberalism has a history of working outside classical understandings of the term.

Consider in this regard some of the alterations in the meaning of the term "virtue" this brief discussion of Kant seems to require. Notoriously, Kant thought that in order to act morally, i.e., in Kant's sense of moral "without qualification," one needs to act from duty alone—and duty was defined by him in distinction from inclination.[5] Since the inclinations could not function as the seat of (purely) moral motivation, if virtue was to play a role in morality, its role with respect to the inclinations would need to be described not as a shaping of these (as, for instance, virtue shapes the passions in Aquinas's thought) but rather as a "subduing," as Berkowitz's brief comments rightly mark. Or, unlike Aristotle, for whom moral virtue "comes as a result of habit,"[6] or Aquinas, who quite willingly goes on record as holding that "virtues are habits,"[7] Kant shifts his understanding of virtue away from habit toward "inner disposition," however that might be understood.

As he goes on to tell us, Berkowitz does not entirely agree with Kant's understanding of virtue.

> Kant puts forward a nonprudential account of virtue: he moralizes virtue making morality and virtue synonymous. Hobbes develops a purely prudential account of virtue: he drains much of the morality out of virtue, transforming it into enlightened self-interest. A third approach, one that is beholden neither to the restrictive metaphysical assumptions compelling Kant to equate virtue with morality nor to the restrictive metaphysical assumptions requiring Hobbes to reduce virtue to rational self-interest, can recognize virtues relative to human perfection as well as virtues relative to the preservation of political society.[8]

For Berkowitz, this more promising view, free of "restrictive metaphysical assumptions," is exemplified by Mill, whom he treats last among his four founders of liberalism. I must confess, however, that I am not much interested in this next step with Mill, for it seems to me that in his criticism of Kant, Berkowitz has failed to note the key change in virtue that Kant brings. This is a change yet detectable in virtually any liberal account of the virtues, including Berkowitz's: according to liberalism, one does not need to be good (be virtuous) to know the good. Or, put more in Kant's terms, the virtues function to motivate us to do what we know to be good by some other means, rather than to form us to know the good as we could not have known it without the virtues.

This is what I shall call liberalism's motivationalization of the virtues. Once motivationalized, while the virtues might be thought important instruments to get people to do the good or to make society run smoothly, they can no longer be the focal point of inquiry into what is righteous or good, and this is a substantial change from classical accounts such as Aristotle's or Aquinas's. Consider the following quote from William Frankena, a liberal moral philosopher thought generally to be quite friendly to the return to virtue thinking in modern moral philosophy. "It does strike me that, if the only thing an ethics of virtue can tell me is to do that act which . . . I will be doing from a certain motive, then it cannot do what is needed. One can hardly go about looking to see what motive he will be acting from . . . as a way of determining what to do."[9] Frankena knew where to draw a line. Virtues are wonderful as they help me to do the right thing, but they do no direct work in identifying what the right thing to do is.

Berkowitz by and large ignores these issues, which are essentially epistemological, but also quite practical since they involve not only what the moral life is, but how living it shapes us. In absence of any careful reflection, Berkowitz simply follows the liberal convention of motivationalizing or instrumentalizing the virtues. Returning to Kant, those parts briefly summarized by Berkowitz, we see this convention at work. It is most graphically displayed in the use of the term "prudence" to mean what is advantageous or useful to the attainment of the goals that suit us or me.

To repeat, Berkowitz notes (above) that "the virtues in Kant's thought can be understood as the qualities that enable human beings to act in accordance with the dictates of reason, but the dictates of reason for Kant are laws of morality and *not prudence*" (emphasis added). For Kant the laws of morality rest on the only true moral law, the categorical imperative, which we know not through training in any particular history or community but *qua* rational beings. And this is the key difference. For understood as a virtue in the classical sense, prudence plainly rests upon and arises within such a history and community. Indeed, for Aquinas it is the crown of the virtues precisely because it arises out of and completes training in the cardinal virtues. As he holds, "no moral virtue can be had without prudence."[10]

Once prudence is displaced by Kant's laws of morality, what does it become? Consider again Berkowitz's further use of the word (above), now packed in the term "prudential account." "Kant puts forward a *nonprudential account* of virtue . . . [whereas] Hobbes develops a purely *prudential account* of virtue: he drains much of the morality out of virtue, transforming it into enlightened self-interest" (emphasis added). Here prudence is actually *contrasted* with morality, and appears to mean something like shrewd selfish thinking. Very quickly, we have come a long way from Aquinas.

Josef Pieper believes the change in prudence we have here witnessed is indicative of modernity. "To the contemporary mind, prudence seems less a prerequisite to goodness than an evasion of it. The statement [from Aquinas] that it is prudence that makes an action good strikes us as well-nigh ridiculous. Should we hear it said, we tend to misunderstand the phrase, and take it as a tribute to undisguised utilitarianism. For we think of prudence as far more akin to the idea of mere utility."[11] In contrast, prudence for Aquinas is perfected practical reason. As Pieper expresses it, it has two sides, perceiving and acting. "Perceptively it is turned toward reality, 'imperatively' toward volition and action."[12] Importantly, then, it is by prudence that we come to see what is good—not, for Aquinas, the Platonic form of "the good," but rather the particular goods of and in specific situations. Of course, how we see these realities has everything to do with how we will act toward them. So it is, says Pieper, that the perceptive or "cognitive aspect is prior and sets a standard."[13]

Aquinas's (and Pieper's) view of prudence relates directly to Aristotle's view of practical wisdom, which is for him the "eye of the soul." For Aristotle, practical wisdom is to be distinguished from mere cleverness which is "to be able to do the things that tend towards the mark we have set before ourselves, and to hit it."[14] Far exceeding cleverness, practical wisdom for Aristotle requires that the mark we aim at is noble. And we know what is noble as we have been trained up into the virtue of practical wisdom.

Not surprisingly, this spot in Aristotle has troubled thinkers like Kant, for if we believe that practical wisdom is necessary to see and know the good, and practical wisdom, like other virtues, is learned, then morality seems to begin from a markedly contingent (historical) starting point. In fact, Aristotle says as much.

> [T]his eye of the soul acquires its formed state not without the aid of virtue . . . for the syllogisms which deal with acts to be done are things which involve a starting-point . . . and this is not evident except to the good man; for wickedness perverts us and causes us to be deceived about the starting points of action. Therefore it is evident that it is impossible to be practically wise without being good.[15]

Aristotle's position here reminds us of another he strikes in the *Nicomachean Ethics*, that a bad start in life makes virtue well-nigh impossible. "It makes no small difference, then, whether we form habits of one kind or of another from our very youth; it makes a very great difference, or rather all the difference."[16] It is in this context that we can see how thoroughly intertwined is a community's life of virtue with its vision of the good. And we can appreciate all the more what Kant intended to do when he set about to sever the connection between the moral law and any particular community who might speak of it. Communities would still produce virtues, perhaps quite specific ones, but those virtues could now be seen as motivating its members to do what was specified by the moral law, rather than shaping them to see it.

In the end, this is almost precisely how Berkowitz hopes to use what he calls the "extra-liberal reservoirs"[17] of virtue. And it is very much a *use* since, as he expresses his particular project, a "crucial task for liberal theory is to determine how the virtues necessary to the preservation of liberalism may be sustained."[18] As a good liberal, in other words, Berkowitz continues to treat virtues as instruments. He wants to use them to shore up a liberal polity that, apparently, we already know to be good quite apart from our having (or not having) the virtues.

Buying Virtue from the Christians

In the forgoing analysis we have suggested that despite his apparent concern to get back to the virtue ethics of thinkers such as Aristotle, Berkowitz perpetuates certain key liberal presumptions about virtue that are foreign to that thinking, these best summed up in the instrumentalization or motivationalization of the virtues. Another way to see the force of this point is to mark how Berkowitz's project trades mainly in metaphors of economic exchange and production, which we can (somewhat shamelessly) extend.

Liberalism as a political system has a need for virtue among its citizens if it is to be sustained. Put bluntly, liberalism is in need of virtue capital. Berkowitz's program for attaining this capital is made all the more difficult by the older, more doctrinaire view held by the current board of directors of liberalism that it doesn't need virtue to keep its place in the world. Berkowitz, a young, forward-thinking employee in the company, writes this book as an appeal to his fellow liberals to agree to tap into these extra-liberal reservoirs of virtue, appealing to views expressed by the company's founders (e.g., Kant, Locke, Mill) that liberalism requires virtue to thrive.

We can imagine the company's production manager at this point asking: where primarily are these virtue reservoirs located? Where might Berkowitz and his fellow liberals go to buy the instrumental virtues they need for the sustenance of the corporation of liberalism? On this score, Berkowitz has learned the most from Tocqueville.

It is . . . useful to understand the logic of Tocqueville's argument, and the links he illuminates between democracy, virtue, and the non-governmental institutions that have in the past fostered the virtues on which the well-being of democracy depends. What has changed since Tocqueville wrote is not the need of liberal democracy in America for the virtues that, according to his observations, were once fostered by associational life, family life and religious belief. What has changed is our capacity to satisfy that need.[19]

The invocation of Tocqueville's analysis establishes Berkowitz as one of those liberals who puts stock in "the value of religion." Unlike earlier observers of American society such as Crèvecoeur, Tocqueville saw the importance of religion, particularly local Christian churches, for upholding a public life, and hedging out the most corrosive effects of individualism.[20] While he notes that the religious sources of virtue are somewhat diminished from Tocqueville's time, Berkowitz gives us the distinct impression that he would welcome renewed help from these sources when, at the end of his book, he calls for the "recovery of the old sources of virtue or the development of new ones."[21]

In the light of this appeal, it is appropriate for those of us who call ourselves "Christian" to ask what we are to make of this. (I should think the same question should apply to Jews or Muslims although I shall not be answering for them.) One response, as old as Bishop Eusebius, intimate friend of the Emperor Constantine, is to be rather flattered that society at large is interested in what the church can do for it and to set about to look for ways to accommodate the request.

To Berkowitz's credit, he is not altogether full of sweet talk. The market metaphor, as opposed to the metaphor of earthly power and authority for which Eusebius fell, actually helps here, since it is plain that the churches are of use only insofar as they continue to produce the virtues liberalism needs. A lengthy quotation from Berkowitz on the thinker who seems his favorite from among the four founders, namely Mill, makes this clear.

Mill's appeal to the virtue-fostering role of citizenship, voluntary association, the family and education was not his last word on the sources that sustain virtue. It was to religion, or, better, religion rightly understood, that Mill assigned the task of perfecting the soul of modern man. . . . Mill argues for the need to promulgate a new religion to replace Christianity. More precisely, Mill wished to overcome organized Christianity, or the rituals, ceremonies, institutions, and dogmas through which Jesus' teachings have been handed down—and, in Mill's view, deformed. Mill conceded that in the past virtues—courage, cleanliness, sympathy, self-control, veracity, justice, and even the "most elevated sentiments of which humanity is capable"—resulted from an "artificial discipline" and an "artificial education" that was largely religious. This, however, was due not to religion's "intrinsic force" but to the advantage that religion enjoyed from having at its disposal traditional authority, monopoly over early education, and the weight of public opinion. Moreover, having lost its capacity to educate, Christianity, Mill argued, had lost its utility. Not only, in Mill's view, were its dogmas no longer believable, but its teachings, he judged, enfeebled the intellect, extirpated the passions, and made men selfish and weak.

The new religion Mill envisaged, the "Religion of Humanity," would take its cue from Jesus, whom Mill regarded as a man of "sublime genius" and "the pattern of perfection for humanity." Although the Religion of Humanity, as Mill expounded it, does not deny the existence of God, its teachings do render him all but irrelevant to the life of man.[22]

Mill's view that "Christianity had lost its utility" should remind Christians that if they wish to take advantage of the recent demand for virtue on the market proclaimed by the new liberals, they must prepare for the day when the virtues Christians provide are no longer the virtues liberalism wants. Berkowitz himself never directly comments on Mill's proposal for the "Religion of Humanity," but clearly Christians who might hope to strike a deal with contemporary liberals for virtue cannot let it pass. If one sees "religion" principally as a useful resource for producing virtues, Mill's aspirations for a new religion as providing the foundation for a new set of virtues, and his concomitant distaste for the virtues (or, to him, vices) he imagines the Christianity of his time to have produced, seem to imply a plan to establish a competitor virtue-producing religion. Christians may find themselves at odds with this humanistic faith, whatever form it ends up taking. As a first clue, they will almost certainly need to dispute Mill's appropriation of Jesus as a man of sublime genius.

In the end, in the open market for virtue it is hard for the Christian church to see Berkowitz's overture to the extraliberal sources of virtue—of which, no doubt, it is one—as terribly attractive. Were theologians like financial advisors, they should advise that this is a deal the church can do without. But it is not necessary to refuse the offer so directly and impolitely, for, as we argued earlier, virtue is not the sort of thing that can be exchanged on the open market, precisely because particular virtues are not detachable from the way of life, the history and tradition, indeed, the claims to the truth about what is the best and most complete human life in which those virtues arise. In short, the virtues are not instruments by means of which we motivate ourselves to live rightly; they are necessary not only for us to live rightly, but even to know what "living rightly" amounts to.

If Christians somehow have failed to learn this lesson about what the virtues are from within their own tradition, they can learn it from Aristotle. To be in further conversation with liberals who also profess an interest in Aristotle, they shall need to see that these liberals have learned it as well. From a theological standpoint, then, the promise in the recent return to Aristotle and virtue among liberals lies precisely in that reading him will teach them this lesson. If Berkowitz is a test case, the lesson appears to be a quite difficult one to learn.

RETELLING LIBERALISM'S STORY: RORTY'S ALTERNATIVE

We have argued that Berkowitz treats the virtues as instruments, and that this amounts to a mistake about virtue. The mistake, however, does not blunt the force of two other points Berkowitz presses, namely that (however they are understood) virtues are necessary to sustain a polity such as liberalism is, and that the relative strength of the virtues (whichever ones might be named) is waning in our contemporary Western social and political environment.

Berkowitz expresses these two points actually in the context of what I have marked as his most incontrovertible claim, namely that the makers of modern liberalism talked more of virtue than their late twentieth-century successors.

> In various ways the makers of modern liberalism derive the necessity of virtue from the logic of politics and derive from the logic of a state based on natural freedom and equality the conclusion that government has a very limited role in protecting or promoting virtue. This limitation was less of a liability when liberalism could confidently rely upon extra-liberal or nongovernmental sources of virtue. The weakening or exhaustion of these sources does not bring about a weakening of liberalism's need for virtue; it only weakens liberalism's capacity to satisfy its need.[23]

It is in this connection that we can see the practical force of Berkowitz's book. If they are increasingly in short supply, where will liberalism get its requisite virtues? As we have noted, Berkowitz's preference is that they be "outsourced," perhaps to such communities as the Christian church. Yet here is where our arguments about the noninstrumentality of the virtues, their necessary connection to a way of life that, as it trains us in the virtues, trains us also to see the good as we could not otherwise have seen it (as in the virtue of prudence), make this both a less promising and also more dangerous strategy for thinkers like Berkowitz whose chief concern is to sustain a liberal polity. It is less promising because the virtues are not so easy to buy on the open market as Berkowitz's instrumentalized view of the virtues suggests, and it is more dangerous since liberals may find that if they turn their young ones over to extraliberal sources of virtue such as churches or synagogues, they may end up abandoning the liberal vision.

It is at this point that we cannot but return to the suggestion already marked in Mill: why doesn't liberalism turn itself into a religion? Speaking as a Christian theologian, I should like to recommend this. When he thinks about establishing something like a liberal religion, Mill bites off a chunk of Jesus. I think he is radically mistaken about Jesus, of course, but I know what it is to argue with him about Jesus. One could imagine a similar squabble between Jews and Christians on Jesus, or Moses. One of the difficulties I find in engaging with liberalism is that it is both ubiquitous and amorphous. It is hard to find a liberal who will speak confessionally, largely because the presumption is that we all sort of believe what liberals believe, which saves us from having to say what that is, and why it is worthy of belief.

Of course there is a liability in this for liberalism, for it currently has the luxury of imagining itself to be above the religions, not one of them. Indeed, this very view is part of liberalism's success since it has been able to tame religions by privatizing them. But if Berkowitz is correct on the points just mentioned, namely that liberalism needs virtues to survive, that liberalism itself is not supplying these, and that the extra-liberal sources of these virtues are waning, then privatization may be precisely one of the "luxuries" he refers to that once were available to modern liberalism's makers, but are no longer. With respect to the virtues and their historical sources in "religion," liberalism, as Berkowitz plausibly suggests, may be the victim of its own success.[24]

This notion that liberalism should consider becoming a religion is intriguing when placed next to the following comments from Alan Ryan:

> [Richard Rorty's] *Achieving Our Country* is an appeal to American intellectuals to abandon the intransigent cynicism of the academic, cultural left and return to the political ambitions of Emerson, Dewey, Herbert Croly, and their allies. What Rorty has written—as deftly, amusingly, and cleverly as he always writes—is a lay sermon for the untheological.[25]

The idea that *Achieving Our Country* is a sermon and Richard Rorty a preacher[26] seems to me particularly apt, not the least because much of this book reads as if it was written on the plane on the way into the airport. In a word, Rorty has written more substantial books. Yet this one is particularly revealing about what Rorty hopes for, as not uncommonly a believer's sermons reveal his hopes and dreams much more clearly than do his academic tomes. And these hopes and dreams include his belief that liberalism needs to takes its own religion seriously. Indeed, Rorty excoriates fellow liberals who have lost the faith, falling victim to an academic negativism and cynicism that cannot but poison liberalism's future. Consider the following extensive quote from Rorty's "sermon" as a call to return to liberalism's true faith.

> Leftists in the academy have permitted cultural politics to supplant real politics, and have collaborated with the Right in making cultural issues central to public debate. . . . The academic Left has no projects to propose to America, no vision of a country to be achieved by building a consensus of the need for specific reforms. Its members no longer feel the force of James's and Croly's rhetoric. The American civic religion seems to them narrow-minded and obsolete nationalism.
>
> Whitman and Dewey were among the prophets of this civic religion. They offered a new account of what America was, in the hope of mobilizing Americans as political agents. The most striking feature of their redescription of our country is its thoroughgoing secularism. In the past, most of the stories that have incited nations to projects of self-improvement have been stories about their obligations to one or more gods. For much of European and American history, nations have asked themselves how they appear in the eyes of the Christian God. American exceptionalism has usually been a belief in special divine favor, as in the writings of Joseph Smith and Billy Graham. . . .
>
> Dewey and Whitman wanted Americans to continue to think of themselves as exceptional, but both wanted to drop any reference to divine favor or wrath. They hoped to separate the fraternity and loving kindness urged by the Christian scriptures from the ideas of supernatural parentage, immortality, providence, and—most important—sin. They wanted Americans to take pride in what America might, all by itself and by its own lights, make of itself, rather than in America's obedience to any authority—even the authority of God.[27]

We shall in our final section consider the interesting matter, broached at the end of this quote, about what to say regarding Rorty and sin. I think Rorty is wildly wrong about sin, of course, since I believe, with St. Paul, that "all have sinned and fall short of the glory of God." But, as when Mill confessed a new Jesus, Rorty's repudiation of sin can help us see our disagreements and their significance more clearly. In effect, in this slender book, Rorty does us the favor of confessing liberalism. And, as we can tell, he has little sympathy for those in the church of liberalism, the "academic Left," who have been seduced—and, to wit, are seducing others—with what amounts to false doctrine.

As he combats the heresy of the academic Left, Rorty appeals to "American National Pride." Indeed, in his defense of his own orthodox liberalism, Rorty is prepared to speak of a particular history of a specific people, Americans. So for Rorty, liberalism is not merely a set of universal ideas about rights and freedom, but an actual history that has been lived and nurtured in a particular land by people we can name. Specifically, for Rorty, Dewey's and Whitman's writings and vision are root sources of authority. What members of the academic Left have neglected is the hope and positive vision for action that these men sought to give to their generation of liberals and pass on to subsequent generations. Liberalism was for Dewey and Whitman a secular religious vision.[28] As such they knew that for liberalism properly to compete against the religious visions it opposed, especially the American Christian vision, it must retell the story of America in secular terms. Americans need to understand themselves as an exceptional people, but not because they are God's chosen people or have some special divine calling, but because of their various achievements, however it is that Rorty wants to mark these.[29] This story, then, will become a proper basis for pride, which can move us together toward hopeful action, faithfully extending the great tradition of American liberalism as its earlier heroes conceived it.[30]

According to Rorty, the chief problem with members of the academic or "spectatorial" Left is that they have not sufficiently broken free from the Christianity that preceded them in America. Especially since the Vietnam War there has been among liberals a lack of faith in humanism which includes a "failure of nerve which leads people to abandon secularism for a belief in sin . . . [an urge] which Dewy hoped Americans might cease to feel. Dewey wanted Americans to share a civic religion that substituted utopian striving for claims to theological knowledge."[31] In effect, the great fault of the academic Left is that they have fallen into sin, which is not so much to say that they have sinned, but that they have fallen back into the grasp of the Christian notion of sin—the very idea that there is such a thing as sin. Plagued by sin, proper national pride is stultified and new, genuine action and achievement is cut from its life source.

Rorty mentions Aristotle not once, but I wish to suggest that his argument about liberalism is a good deal more Aristotelian than Berkowitz's. First, Rorty returns to pride, which is for Aristotle the crown of the virtues: "Now the proud man, since he deserves most, must be good in the highest degree; for the better man must be good. . . . Pride, then, seems to be a sort of crown of the virtues, for it makes them greater, and it is not found without them."[32] As Nietzsche saw, having the benefit of the Christian history lying between himself and Aristotle, proper pride matches its good achievements not against evil or sin, but against weakness and failure: good vs. bad rather than good vs. evil.[33]

But perhaps most importantly, Rorty is Aristotelian precisely because he begins his rethinking about where we should head and what we should do *from somewhere*. Rorty embraces his particular location as an American "reformist liberal" at the turn to the twenty-first century, and he invokes a story and praises the heroes of the American liberal past whose ideas he—and, as he adds, "people like us"[34]—embrace. Similarly, Aristotle presumed the setting of the *polis* in fourth-century Greece. Such social location clearly informed his now somewhat embarrassing portrait of what virtue should look like in a person, or, perhaps as Aristotle might have added, in "men like us." As he tells us, virtue reaches its apex in the magnanimous man who is slow of gait, with "a deep voice and a deliberate way of speaking."[35] Moreover, it was in the setting of the *polis* that Aristotle presumed training in the virtues would take place, novices being drawn up by well-seasoned men of magnanimity into the noble way of life of the virtuous community.

This recalls what is profoundly un-Aristotelian about the attempt to return to virtue recommended by Berkowitz since it assumes a disjunction between the training in virtue and its subsequent exercise in the nation state. This is true in practice—since, on Berkowitz's admission, liberalism lacks the resources, i.e., the specific stories, people, practices, and communities, to train up its young people in the virtues it needs to survive—and in theory, since the new virtuefied liberalism can in the end give nothing but an instrumental account of virtue. Whatever one makes of the power of Rorty's sermonizing, and however much (or little) one is compelled by his stories of the greatness of Dewey and Whitman, Rorty is plainly attempting to raise a virtuous army of liberal souls. He is trying to train American liberals to think, act, and be like him.

CHRISTIAN VIRTUE AND THE REALITY OF SIN

This is not the place to give a full account of the Christian virtues as they oppose Aristotle's magnanimity, Rorty's American liberal pride, or even whatever virtues liberals such as Berkowitz suppose are necessary to sustain a national liberal polity.[36] We can, however, offer some summary comments about the path this essay has taken, noting where it leaves us with respect to any further attempt to consider virtue theologically as opposed to untheologically, or, for that matter, untheologically as opposed to theologically. We have argued that the concerns articulated by Berkowitz—that liberalism is in need of virtue, that it avoids serious discussion of it to its peril, and that this discussion was more prevalent in its earlier days—may indeed be correct. However, when in his attempt to address these problems Berkowitz turns to the "extra-liberal reservoirs" of virtue, he betrays a deeply ingrained tendency of liberalism, namely, the motivationalization or instrumentalization of the virtues. As we have argued, this profoundly alters how virtue is understood, a point we can see most clearly when considering how prudence or practical wisdom is understood. The Aristotelian account of the virtues, upon which Aquinas builds, assumes that virtue is essential if the good is to be known and done. Hence, any account of the good is inseparable for the virtues that open it to us. The liberal presumption that its vision of the proper layout of our social and political lives can be had and articulated separately from this, and then extra-liberal resources drawn upon to uphold this vision, is naive both about virtue and about how training in virtue within particular communities forms us into people who see the good in a particular way.

Rorty, we have suggested, is less naive. Drawing upon suggestions in Whitman and Dewey (and, as we discovered, also in Mill), Rorty attempts in word and action—in his preaching, storytelling, and fiery accusations of heresy—to mark liberalism out as a secular religion. Established as a particular people with a set of heroes, a unique history in America, and a vision for the future, the liberal community to which Rorty appeals can begin to specify its virtues. We may need to wait to see this Rortian form of liberalism come to full flower as it works to specify its vision, develop its creedal formulations, and articulate its unique virtues. However, Rorty goes far enough in *Achieving Our Country* to make it clear to Christians, and perhaps also to other religious communities, that his liberal community's virtues and vision of a common life do not match very closely with Christianity's.

Speaking as a Christian, I must confess ambivalence about which sort of liberalism I prefer, Berkowitz's or Rorty's. Plainly Berkowitz's is the more friendly to the existence of the Christian church; indeed, when he speaks of the extra-liberal reservoirs of virtue that he hopes will serve to uphold liberalism, the first concrete institutions that spring to mind are church and synagogue, I suspect not only for those Jews and Christians who read him, but for Berkowitz himself. Yet as we have suggested, Christians (or Jews) must be wary of invitations from liberalism to become the suppliers of virtue, not only because the very notion of a virtue market runs counter to virtue as we have described it, but also because liberalism, at present somewhat unclear about precisely which virtues it wants since it has survived for so long thinking itself immune from the need to articulate a specific vision of what is good, may in the future decide that the virtues "supplied" by the churches may not be the ones it needs.[37] By no means do we need to decide that different communities of virtue (Christian, Jewish, liberal, etc.) will always disagree about particular virtues. But agreement or disagreement between communities on such matters is simply not possible until each is prepared to say what it believes.

This is where Rorty's liberalism, despite its unfriendliness to Christianity, is preferable to Berkowitz's. As mentioned earlier, Rorty is explicit that his key difficulty with the heretical liberalism he opposes is its failure clearly to expunge, thoroughly to anathematize, the notion of sin. Rorty's clarity on this point is helpful. For we Christians are challenged in response to say something about sin and how it relates to our understanding of the good human life.

So it is that I conclude this essay with a brief set of comments on the theological connection between sin and virtue, and do so by contrasting Christian thought with that of both Aristotle and Rorty. I begin with a distinction between a conceptual understanding of sin and the knowledge of sin itself. With respect to the particular story Christians tell and the communal life to which they are called, it is important to maintain that we must be taught our sins. This is what occurs in the Christian practices of confession, prayer, and worship around which a great deal of Christian common life is built. Apart from these practices, it is not possible to specify what sins are. Indeed, like the virtues, sins come with training, as a way of life is grown up into. Reinhold Niebuhr, who is known to have been fond of calling original sin the one clearly self-evident Christian doctrine, was on this point overzealous. To be sure, Christians hold that we must become convicted about our sins, but this point itself attests to the need to be taught, somehow or other, that we are sinners and about how we have sinned. God surely has other ways of convicting us of our particular sins than by Christian confession, but, in any case, it is something we must learn, not something that stands before us as a self-evident truth.

Christianity, therefore, is itself a certain kind of training in sin, including not only the knowledge of what our sins are, but also that we are sinners. Hence, in response to the rejection of sin by Richard Rorty, Christians need not suppose he is being disingenuous in this rejection. Rorty, like everyone on the Christian account, is truthfully a sinner. It is not, of course, the task of theological argument to convince him of this. Rather, what argument can do in this context is mark out conceptually what follows in the Christian account of the moral life when it begins with an affirmation of the reality of sin—as opposed to an account which, like Rorty's (and also Aristotle's), does not grant this reality.

Nowhere is this made more plain than in the second part of the *Summa Theologiae*. There the specific nature of sin is directly tied to what are called virtues. This is true in a certain sense in Aristotle's *Ethics*, since, as he holds, virtues are to be found as a mean between two vices. However, vices are not identical with sins. Both hold us captive but, importantly, the captivity of sin is both deeper and also more hopeful.

As we have noted, Aristotle remarks that the training of the young in virtue makes "all the difference." He demonstrates with this remark an accurate sense of the close relation of virtue to a way of life rooted in the habits and practices of a people. Virtue cannot be lifted out of this context, and therefore neither can vice. Yet conceptually this gives Aristotle some difficulty, since it brings us face to face with the troubling matter of how a person who is trained in vice can be thought responsible for his vicious character. In response, Aristotle merely maintains that we are "somehow part causers of our states of character."[38] This implies that the vicious man who was raised in vice could have done something to cause his character to be otherwise, to break the power of vice, although what this thing is cannot be clearly known.

By contrast, according to St. Paul and to Augustine, there is nothing we can do to break the power of sin in our lives. (Importantly, for both of these Christian thinkers sin is not merely our misdeeds, but the state we inhabit after the fall. Sin, then, is inherited, or as Rorty's maternal grandfather Walter Rauschenbusch emphasized, it is structural.[39]) Employing the words of the apostle, Augustine laments his state of sin at a time just prior to his conversion in the Milanese garden:

> It was in vain that "I delighted in Thy law according to the inner man, when that other law in my members rebelled against the law of my mind and led me captive in the law of sin that was in my members." For the law of sin is the fierce force of habit, by which the mind is drawn and held even against its will, and yet deservedly because it has fallen willfully into the habit. "Who then should deliver me from the body of this death, but Thy grace only, through Jesus Christ our Lord?"[40]

Measured against Aristotle's trained vices, sin is more crushing. Like Augustine, we are all powerless to break it. But it is also more hopeful precisely in that, not only as vice but also as sin, our unfortunate state of captivity is subject to God's grace that frees us. So it is that the virtues take the form, for Christians, not of achievement but of gift. This is the key reason Aquinas insists that the theological virtues of faith, hope, and charity, which transform the life of virtue particularly as they transform prudence, are "infused" rather than "acquired." It is also intrinsically connected to the reason why Christians mark pride in our achievements as one of the greatest sins rather than as the crown of the virtues.

Paul's seminal treatment of sin in Romans has another feature that distinguishes it profoundly from an Aristotelian view. For Paul, that we are sinners is the basis for our essential equality. Again, the news is not good: we all suffer in our sins, for we all are sinners, and "there is no partiality with God" (Rom. 2:11). As he details so graphically in the earliest chapters of Romans, whoever we are, Jew or Gentile, we are "without excuse" (Rom. 2:1). In short, our equality resides in that we are all equally condemned by a righteous God.

Now it is plain enough that Aristotle knew nothing of such ideas, nor was he concerned to know, since for him the inequality of human beings was apparent. Indeed, virtue accented what began as a natural inequality of human capacity; the high-minded man who had added virtue to natural strength rightly held himself aloof from what David Ross translates as "the middle class," his superiority to them was plain and therefore appropriately marked by his behavior.[41]

Aristotle's attention to the details of actual social relations in the community in which the virtues are practiced and formed reminds us of the fact that his (and anyone's) view of virtue has temporal and political location. Any extraction of particular virtues from this context—what I have argued the liberalism of Berkowitz attempts—forgets this. Rorty is bolder, and more insightful, since he means to nourish a world of "people like us." Conceptually, the return in Rorty to the language of American pride without sin makes good Aristotelian sense. After all, confession of sin, which Rorty maintains the "spectatorial Left" is yet obsessed with, is a Jewish or Christian addition; Aristotle knew nothing of it. Moreover, pride is rightly held in particular achievements in history that can be told and retold by a people, whether *polis* or nation, who extend the way of life inherited from their forebears.

However, there is something puzzling in this. The close fit of Rorty's American agenda with Aristotelian pride cannot but make us wonder how it will maintain its allegiance to the values of equality that are, Rorty continues to believe, hallmarks of liberalism. After all, as we have suggested in our brief foray into St. Paul's account of sin, notions about our equality arise historically in conjunction with the view that we stand as sinners before a God who both judges and loves us all equally. In short, given Rorty's view, why should we suppose, as he apparently does, that it is good for a people to "protect the weak from the strong?"[42] Freed from the Christian story of our sin and God's grace, the story by means of which Aristotle was so thoroughly transformed by Aquinas, why should Aristotle's account of natural inequality not also reemerge with a return to the moral centrality of pride? If Rorty means to think historically, he may need to ask whether his secular faith is as free from the residual influences of Christianity as he seems to hope it is.

These questions take us inside the logic of liberalism, and I have attempted to speak in this essay from outside it, from the perspective of a Christian looking on. Yet questions of what is or ought to be going on inside the logic of liberalism, particularly as it returns to Aristotle and the virtues, in the end are more pressing for liberals than for Christians. I have made frequent gestures to Aquinas in this essay as one who fundamentally transformed Aristotle's ethics. As I hope is plain in this final section, Aquinas was able so to transform Aristotle's vision of the virtuous life, retaining much of its formal properties while almost completely replacing its content, precisely because of his allegiance to this fundamentally Christian theological vision.

This leads us again to the fact that the virtues Christians like Aquinas uphold are tied intrinsically to the moral vision expressed in Christian life and belief. They cannot be plucked from the vine like ripe grapes and put to use in the production of a new wine. Or, to return to Jesus's metaphor, it is foolishness to fill old wine-skins with new wine, for they will burst and the new wine will go to waste. As Rorty seems to understand, it may indeed be time for American liberalism to recognize that it can no longer be contained within older theological talk of sin and grace. It needs instead to be poured into the new skins provided by the likes of Whitman and Dewey and their thoroughly secularized faith. As I have suggested in this essay, however, a question for Rorty and other liberals who return to Aristotle, skirting his Christian transformation in Aquinas and others, is how the new wine will taste when placed in those new wineskins. This new liberal wine of American national pride may be of another vintage altogether, perhaps pressed from grapes newly sprung from an ancient Grecian vine. No longer will this new wine hold the flavor of the Christianity inhering in the old skins. As such, I suspect we will discover its various virtues are altogether different.

Notes

1. Peter Berkowitz, *The Making of Modern Liberalism* (Princeton, N.J.: Princeton University Press, 1999), 170. Berkowitz says less about Aristotle through the course of the book but treats his understanding of the virtues in the introduction (pp. 7–14). There is no other account of virtue given, and it is virtue—the need for it and the presumption of it by liberalism's founders—that animates the entire book. Berkowitz clearly means to revive virtue for modern liberal thought, and since his only discussion of virtue itself is undertaken in relation to Aristotle, we can infer that he is an Aristotelian reviver.

2. Berkowitz, *Making*, 12.

3. Ibid., 13.

4. Ibid., 119–20.

5. See for instance the famous opening pages of the first section of *Foundation of the Metaphysics of Morals*.

6. *Nicomachean Ethics* 1103a5.

7. *Summa Theologiae* I–II, 55,1.

8. Berkowitz, *Making*, 132.

9. William Frankena, "Pritchard and the Ethics of Virtue," in *Perspectives on Morality: Essays by William Frankena*, ed. K. E. Goodpaster (Notre Dame, Ind.: University of Notre Dame Press, 1976), 158.

10. *ST* I–II, 65,1.

11. Josef Pieper, *The Four Cardinal Virtues* (Notre Dame, Ind.: University of Notre Dame Press, 1966), 4.

12. Ibid., 12.

13. Ibid., 12.

14. *NE* 1144a23.

15. *NE* 1144a32.

16. *NE* 1103b25.

17. Berkowitz, *Making,* 6.

18. Ibid., 177.

19. Ibid., 189.

20. For elaboration on this point, see Robert Bellah et al., *Habits of the Heart* (1984), 37.

21. Berkowitz, *Making,* 192.

22. Ibid., 159.

23. Ibid., 32.

24. As Berkowitz insightfully notes, "The very actualization of liberal principles and exercise of liberal virtues can wither liberalism's roots and erode the soil on which liberalism's principles and virtues rely for their nourishment.... [This is the] anxious predicament in which liberalism finds itself today, a predicament in which liberalism has become the victim of its own successes and instigator of its own excesses" (ibid., 174–75).

25. Alan Ryan makes these comments on the dust jacket of Richard Rorty's *Achieving Our Country* (Cambridge, Mass.: Harvard University Press, 1998).

26. This reference to Rorty as a secular preacher is intriguing in a book in which we are told (p. 59) of his blood connection to one of the great American preachers of all time, namely Walter Rauschenbusch, Rorty's maternal grandfather, Baptist pastor and the author of many books including one strikingly entitled *Christianizing the Social Order.* Rauschenbush wrote another book entitled *Prayers of the Social Awakening* in which we find a prayer concerning "those who come after us." There Rauschenbush prays for "those who come after us, for our children and the children of our friends, and for all of the young lives that are marching up from the gates of birth, pure and eager with the morning sunshine on their faces.... Help us to break the ancient force of evil by a holy and steadfast will and endow our children with purer and nobler blood and nobler thoughts. Grant us grace to leave the earth fairer than we found it; to build upon it cities of God in which the cry of needless pain shall cease; and to put the yoke of Christ upon our business life that it may serve and not destroy. Lift the veil of the future and show us the generation to come as it will be blighted by our guilt, that our lust may be cooled and we may walk in the fear of the Eternal. Grant us a vision of the far off years as they may be redeemed by the sons of God, that we may take heart and do battle for thy children and ours" (quoted from Walter Rauschenbusch, *Selected Writings,* ed. Winthrop S. Hudson [New York: Paulist Press, 1984], 229).

Besides causing us to reflect wistfully about this Christian pastor praying, in essence, for his thoroughly secularized grandson, this quote reminds us that an attempt to ground a liberal political agenda in Christianity has already been made in America, and reveals why it will not be made again. Rauschenbusch's prayer may be quite beautiful, and it is thoroughly and demandingly Christian, including such a request as that the yoke of Christ be placed on our business life. However, even if the social conservatives win their liberal battle (i.e., with liberal ideas championing both sides) for prayer in public schools like those in Texas, Rauschenbusch's prayer is not the sort that will be prayed there. What remains of Christian-piety-at-large in America plainly lacks anything like Rauschenbusch's social vision.

27. Rorty, *Achieving*, 14–16.

28. This religion is rightly called secular since, as Rorty notes, "Whitman thought there was no need to be curious about God because there is no standard, not even a divine one, against which the decisions of a free people can be measured. Americans, he hoped, would spend the energy that past human societies had spent on discovering God's desires on discovering one another's desires. Americans will be curious about every other American, but not about anything which claims authority over America" (ibid., 16). America, in other words, self-consciously replaces the authority of God with no other authority than itself.

29. I must confess to having little sense, really, of why Rorty thinks America is so good after all, and what, really, he means by "good" anyway—or why whatever it is that he thinks is good is truly good. But perhaps this is a difference in religious language.

30. Rorty makes it quite plain in his rhetoric that the vision he is setting out is for a particular community. This is especially clear when he uses the first person plural. For example, consider the following quote: "The job of people like us will be to make sure that the decisions made by the Inner Party are carried out smoothly and efficiently. It will be in the interest of the international super-rich to keep our class relatively happy" (*Achieving*, 87).

31. Ibid., 38.

32. *NE* 1123b28–30.

33. See for instance parts five and six of *Beyond Good and Evil*. Ironically, the structure of the argument I am giving bears close resemblance to Nietzsche's, as it seems to me Rorty's does as well. What remains somewhat puzzling to me is how Rorty will keep the new humanistic religion democratic. For as Nietzsche quite convincingly argued, "the democratic movement is the heir of the Christian movement" (*Beyond Good and Evil*, trans. Walter Kaufmann [New York: Vintage Books, 1989], 116).

34. Rorty, *Achieving*, 87.

35. *NE* 1125a12.

36. For such an extended account see Stanley Hauerwas and Charles Pinches, *Christians among the Virtues: Conversations with Ancient and Modern Ethics* (Notre Dame, Ind.: University of Notre Dame Press, 1997).

37. To build on pieces of Berkowitz's historical thesis, which owes much to critics of liberalism such as Alasdair MacIntyre (in *After Virtue* [Notre Dame, Ind.: University of Notre Dame Press, 1981] and elsewhere), the appearance of this immunity from the need to specify the good resides in the historical fact that liberalism was largely built atop a Christianized society. However, with the weakening of this foundation in practice, narrative structure, and community, liberalism is no longer exempt from having to articulate a particular vision of the good for human beings.

38. *NE* 1114b22.

39. See, for instance, *A Theology for the Social Gospel* (Nashville: Abingdon Press, 1987), 57–68.

40. *Confessions,* Bk. 8, chap. 5, trans. F. J. Sheed (Indianapolis: Hackett, 1993), 136. Quotations are from Paul's Letter to the Romans 7:22–25.

41. See Aristotle's whole discussion of how the high-minded or proud man should behave socially (*NE* 1124b1–1125a36, in Ross's translation [New York: Oxford, 1980], 92–95).

42. Rorty, *Achieving,* 43.

PART THREE

LAW, ECONOMICS, AND POLITICS

·

CHAPTER SEVEN

The Middle Way

What Contemporary Liberal Legal Theorists Can Learn from Aristotle

MIRIAM GALSTON

American legal theorists have long been preoccupied with questions about method and truth in legal and moral reasoning. Their inquiries have focused on whether and how theorists, citizens, lawmakers, judges, and other public officials can attain truth, correctness, or certainty in their legal and moral pronouncements.[1]

Until the last decades of the nineteenth century, American legal theory was dominated by formalist views, which saw legal reasoning in the ideal case as a closed, deductive system based upon a finite number of foundational principles and rules. By the beginning of the twentieth century, formalism as an ideal was under attack by adherents of legal realism and sociological jurisprudence.[2] Members of the latter two schools of thought argued that the legal system was in fact and of necessity uncertain and imprecise, assessed by such measures as the lack of predictability of judicial decisions and the absence of a unique, correct solution to particular legal questions. The source of legal uncertainty was explained by members of these schools of thought in terms of one or more of the following circumstances. For some, the law's foundational principles, statutory and common law rules, and specific judicial decisions do not form a coherent whole. Therefore, reliance on them can yield inconsistent, even contradictory results. Others argued that the human and commercial situations to which law applies are themselves constantly changing. As a result, legal structures will have to be altered (deliberately or otherwise) on a more or less continuous basis to fit the reality they purport to govern. Alternatively, the uncertainty of legal determinations was seen as attributable to the fact that applying general rules to specific fact patterns is rarely mechanical. This makes moral and legal determinations a question of judgment and enables, if not encourages, judges to look to considerations outside what is explicit or clearly implicit in precedent to adjudicate concrete cases. Finally, some of the critics of the formalist ideal emphasized that people who engage in moral and legal reasoning—whether as theorists, lawmakers, judges, or citizens—will necessarily be influenced by personal, class, or cultural biases that affect the manner in which they interpret or apply existing legal materials.

For some of the challengers to formalist legal theory, the fluid nature of law and the indeterminate nature of legal reasoning were seen as defects, i.e., as departures from an ideal of perfectly syllogistic and certain reasoning that, consciously or unconsciously, they shared with the formalists.[3] For others, the uncertainty of the law is, at least in part, a consequence of the law's need to respond to complex and evolving "social, industrial and political" realities and, hence, it is a primary cause of the law's "immense social value."[4]

The desire of legal theorists to determine whether and how reasoning about human affairs can attain correct outcomes has continued to the present day. In the last several decades, these epistemological concerns have been expressed differently than in the early part of the century. At one end of the contemporary legal theory spectrum, there is renewed interest in formalist-type theories, such as neo-Aristotelian natural law theory.[5] However, the earlier natural law ideal of searching for unchanging truths about human nature and human affairs that are in principle universally binding and should be used to evaluate the correctness of particular moral and legal determinations has given way to alternative notions of natural law, some of which are free of unitary interpretations of human nature and morality.[6]

At the other end of the spectrum are schools of thought—such as critical legal studies ("CLS"),[7] critical race theory,[8] some feminist approaches,[9] law as narrative,[10] different voice scholarship,[11] and poststructuralism[12]—that celebrate what Suzanna Sherry calls "nonrational epistemologies,"[13] such as relativism,[14] subjectivism, "radical particularism,"[15] radical social constructivism,[16] decisionism,[17] and nihilism.[18] The doctrines at this end of the legal theory spectrum explicitly challenge the possibility of rational legal and moral discourse at the same time that they repudiate the substantive bodies of thought connected with traditions of such discourse.

Between the two extremes are numerous contemporary legal theorists who have attempted to mark out territory that is neither objectivist or formalist, on the one hand, nor subjectivist or relativist, on the other. These authors, whom I call theorists of the middle way, reject the idea that knowledge must be absolute and unchanging to be worthy of the name. Aristotle provides theoretical grounds for their intuition: at the beginning of the *Nicomachean Ethics* he observes that

precision cannot be expected in the treatment of all subjects alike. . . .
[W]hen the subject and basis of a discussion consists of matters that
hold good only as a general rule, but not always, the conclusions reached
must be of the same order. . . . For a well-schooled man is one who
searches for that degree of precision in each kind of study which the
nature of the subject at hand admits . . . [19]

For Aristotle, in other words, rejection of the formalist ideal of reasoning demonstratively to a determinate conclusion is not a practical conces-
sion to the limitations of human cognition.[20] Nor does it mean that the
results of inquiry about matters not amenable to precision must be anything
less than the truth.[21] Aristotle's epistemological observations thus call into
question the dichotomy between universal knowledge and everything else
on the ground that it reflects a misunderstanding of the relationship between knowledge and its object in connection with human affairs. Rather
than being apologetic about the limits of their understanding, legal theorists should seek to understand why much of human conduct is not and cannot be captured by absolute, universal rules.

Although precision may be neither possible nor appropriate when
reasoning about certain aspects of human affairs, there are nonetheless
standards to guide or issue from such inquiries. Middle-way theorists, by
definition, assume such standards because their theories agree that such
reasoning is not simply arbitrary or ad hoc. Two distinct approaches of contemporary liberal legal theory of the middle way that can learn from Aristotle will be discussed in this essay.[22] The first is characterized by a reluctance
to have recourse to substantive moral and political principles that exist independently of a particular legal order. The second approach, in contrast, is
characterized by a willingness to recognize and incorporate such principles into reasoning about human affairs to some extent. Because of the resistance of theorists of the first type to legal reasoning that has recourse to
substantive standards—other than standards embedded in a constitution,
statutes, and judicial precedents—this approach relies to a much greater
degree than the second on the process of communal deliberation and on
various structural, procedural, and related devices constraining deliberation
to reach decisions about human values and conduct.

THE PROCESS-ORIENTED MIDDLE-WAY APPROACHES

Liberal legal theorists of the middle way who are reluctant to impose or even
propose external substantive standards to guide the legal reasoner have

developed approaches to moral and legal reasoning that depend upon theories of practical reason understood as wholly or mostly independent of universal principles and rules, yet not arbitrary or ad hoc.[23] Their wariness about developing external substantive standards as part of a theory of practical reasoning stems in large part from one or more of four beliefs: that we do not in fact know definitively which goals and values are superior; that we cannot attain such knowledge even if we try; that our ability to evaluate goals and preferences correctly is in any event politically irrelevant because the goal of public life should be to ensure the conditions of the private pursuit of life plans rather than to encourage people to pursue one or more publicly designated life plans, whether that restriction is for the sake of reducing political conflict or to make possible the autonomy of individuals; and that the content of human happiness or the common good is not unitary or uniform.

Arguably all of these reasons are epistemological at bottom. Although it is true that at present the contemporary liberal legal commitment to diversity and autonomy seems to be based upon a belief in the intrinsic value of these objectives, it is possible that this commitment originally came into being as a result of, and is currently reinforced by, the more basic belief that human reason is incapable of proving definitively the superiority of one or more conceptions of the human good.

Because of the preceding considerations, many contemporary middleway theorists with a process orientation share the belief that government actors and institutions should not favor the goals and values of one subgroup of the larger community over another, regardless of whether they originate in religious, moral, or cultural concerns of the sub-group.[24] Relatedly, the task of legal theory is to describe the structural, procedural, and related conditions that must exist so that individuals or communities can themselves understand which values they should hold, what outcomes they should pursue, and how to pursue them. It is characteristic of these theories to describe some form of group discourse as the best vehicle for making practical decisions with respect to values or actions.[25] The conclusions reached and consented to in the group discussions envisioned by these theories are seen as both valid and validated because of the qualities of the participants in the reasoning process, in particular, because of their equality as participants, their being informed or becoming informed (through the group discourse) before reaching conclusions, their seriousness about the process, the respect they accord one another, and their willingness to learn and grow from the give-and-take among the participants.[26] For such theorists, substantive standards are the product, not the precondition, of communal deliberation.[27]

AN ARISTOTELIAN APPRAISAL OF THE
PROCESS-ORIENTED MIDDLE-WAY APPROACHES

The attempt to avoid the extremes of objectivism and subjectivism without relying upon extra-legal substantive standards can be illuminated and, in some respects, refined by turning to Aristotle's observations about moral theory and *phronēsis* or practical reason. Four features of the thought of process-oriented middle-way theorists are especially worth examining from an Aristotelian perspective: (1) the preference for communal debate over individual investigation, (2) the importance for self-governance of consent by an individual to rules he has participated in creating, (3) the aspiration to self-government and transformative political participation, and (4) the insistence on ideal speech conditions as a precondition for legitimate communal debate.

Communal Reasoning

The preference on the part of contemporary liberal legal theorists for reasoning about human affairs in a communal setting is grounded, among other reasons, in the belief that when people put their opinions forward in a public forum in an attempt to persuade others, the communal scrutiny that results is likely to weed out obvious errors and increase the range and depth of information bearing upon the topic at hand. The result of deliberative encounters, according to this view, should be sounder, more informed beliefs or decisions than would be possible if individuals reason in isolation.

There is a substantial amount of support for the usefulness of communal inquiry in Aristotle's writings. It is a hallmark of his own investigations to begin with a review of what others have said on the topic under discussion and to weigh what appear to be the strengths and weaknesses of these points of view.[28] In addition to canvassing the opinions of experts, living and dead, Aristotle can be said to consider the opinions of the reader and others living in Athens, since he frequently tests the opinions of other authorities against "what people think" or what "seems to be the case." Aristotle thus makes use of the opinions of individuals and groups, past and present, along with other analytical tools to put the most likely alternatives on the table for evaluation.

The theoretical justification for Aristotle's method is contained in his *Topics,* where he discusses the nature and mechanics of dialectical reasoning. Dialectical reasoning, according to Aristotle, reasons in a strict syllogistic fashion from generally accepted opinions.[29] Because the logical structure of dialectical reasoning is syllogistic, if two dialectical arguments reach con-tradictory conclusions, the source of the contradiction is in the premises, not the form, of the argument. As a consequence, dialectical reasoning can help people identify two generally accepted opinions only one of which (at most) can be true. It thus focuses attention on the likely locus of error, enabling the reasoner to examine the suspect opinions more closely.[30] Gen-erally accepted opinions, for Aristotle, are those that seem to be right "to all or to the majority or to the wise—that is, to all the wise or to the majority or to the most famous and distinguished of them."[31]

Aristotle's explanation of the reason why playing the opinions of some people off against those of others can facilitate the search for truth thus sup-ports some aspects of the beliefs of contemporary legal theorists about the importance of communal inquiry. It departs from them in important ways, however. First, Aristotle appears to equate the effectiveness of face-to-face encounters among living people with imagined encounters among dead people or people living but not present at the discussion.[32] Readers of Aris-totle's books, for example, are expected to learn about the topic discussed by having a conversation with its author.[33] This raises the question of what the contemporary legal thinkers under discussion believe face-to-face dis-cussions contribute as a result of the physical proximity of the participants.

Second, Aristotle and these legal theorists assign different weights to the opinions of individuals. For Aristotle, only generally accepted opinions can serve as the basis of dialectical (as opposed to rhetorical or sophistical) argu-ment. Since opinions are said to be "generally accepted" either if all or most people hold them or if they are held by one or more wise people,[34] the im-plication is that Aristotle equates the force of the opinion of one wise man with the opinion held by all or most people. As a theoretical matter, then, generally accepted opinions carry weight for Aristotle because they are a promising source for true opinions rather than because they command widespread support. They serve as the basis of dialectical inquiry because they are presumptively, although not necessarily, correct.[35] In other words, it seems that the relatively high place Aristotle accords to the opinions of all or most people derives from his insight that the breadth of agreement can serve as a proxy for wisdom.

Self-Governance and Consent

This difference between middle-way, process-oriented legal theorists and Aristotle is also related to their differing views about the importance of con-sent. These legal theorists rely on agreement by participants to the results of group decisionmaking to legitimate law for several reasons. For some, the dominant purpose of consent is to promote the values of autonomy and self-governance. Although Aristotle did not talk about "autonomy" *per se,* a discussion of the importance of being able to govern oneself (and be governed by others) finds pride of place in his philosophy. In the best case, he argues, the good man has the knowledge and virtue necessary to author the rules that guide his life, and not just to accept them on the authority of others.[36] This is possible if, and only if, a person possesses practical wisdom or prudence.[37] In contrast, the virtue of a citizen who lacks the capacity for ruling is "true opinion."[38] Aristotle thus differs from contemporary legal theorists in identifying self-governance with the active exercise of reason rather than the initiation of, participation in, or assent to rules by which a person is governed. In this regard, as was the case in connection with the importance for Aristotle of communal inquiry, agreement by those affected is only a rough approximation of the core value—reason—upon which correct decisions and self-governance rest.[39]

For other legal theorists, confidence in consent as the hallmark of successful deliberative outcomes derives primarily from their uneasiness, mentioned above, at the distance they see between the method of practical reason and that of scientific or syllogistic reasoning. Even theorists who maintain that the lack of determinacy or predictability on the part of practical reasoning does not imply that the insights arrived at by such reasoning are arbitrary feel greater comfort when deliberations are open and participatory. On the face of it, their justification seems to be that, if agreement can be reached by people with different views and objectives, the result must be more comprehensive, hence more likely to be correct, than a result reached by a single individual or small group. Thus, communal reasoning culminating in consent is sought in the name of both autonomy and correct outcomes.

Finally, for some process-oriented legal theorists, the possibility of consent makes deliberative encounters attractive as a solution for the peculiar and destabilizing problems of a pluralistic and liberal legal order, namely, the existence of diverse, sometimes irreconcilable values and visions of the best way to live. Given the reluctance of these theorists to impose on a population of adult individuals a unitary idea of the best course of action in particular situations much less a single account of human happiness or the common good, they place their faith in voluntary processes designed to foster a spirit of respect, cooperation, and compromise among those who participate. The attitudes thus inspired, it is hoped, will enable people to agree to solutions that they would not otherwise agree to, given their different beliefs and goals they initially hold.

From an Aristotelian perspective, it is curious to employ the practice of rational discourse to create what Aristotle would view as moral virtues,[40] rather than to develop moral attitudes and behaviors to facilitate the cultivation of reason. First, Aristotle would undoubtedly favor instilling moral virtues in people directly, i.e., through habituation, on the ground that the process of becoming moral is more likely to be successful if begun when a child is young.[41] Thus, for him habituation of children through rote imitation of the moral qualities upon which social cooperation depends would be preferable to persuading adults of the importance of such qualities, since adults may already have entrenched habits tending in a different direction. Second, as I have argued elsewhere, for Aristotle, a person needs certain moral qualities to be capable of exercising her rational faculties or being reasonable in the first place.[42]

Self-Governance and Transformative Political Participation

A third feature of deliberative encounters according to the theorists under consideration is the potential transformative effect they can have on the individuals who participate. This effect is sometimes explained in terms of enabling people to develop some aspect of their mental capacities, to become moral agents, or to become fully responsible, autonomous human beings.[43] Understanding deliberative encounters as transformative in this way can be seen as based, explicitly or implicitly, upon the Aristotelian dictum that man is by nature political.[44] Process-oriented middle-way legal theorists have a tendency to reject Aristotle's dictum if it is construed to mean that a life of engagement in politics is essential to human happiness. Rather, they argue that such a life is one, but not the unique avenue to the realization of human potential.[45] Alternatively, such theorists assume that human beings' political nature should be understood as synonymous with their social nature and, thus, as consistent with many fundamentally private ways of life or membership in groups.[46]

Aristotle would almost certainly reject treating engagement in political life as interchangeable with engagement in social life or membership in groups in general. For Aristotle the boundary between the political community and any other type of community is well defined and meaningful. In Book I of the *Politics*, he explains what is distinctive about each type of community or human association (*koinōnia*), whether political or sub-political, in terms of the end that each pursues. The end of the association of man and woman is reproduction; that of master and servant, survival; that of the household, the necessities of daily life; and that of the village, daily needs that are not necessities.[47] The end of the city or political community, in contrast, is the good life, or living well.[48] To accomplish these differing objectives requires different faculties and skills. As a consequence, Aristotle warns the reader against imagining that fitness to govern any one type of association can be generalized to fitness to govern any other.[49]

Based upon Aristotle's analysis, it would also be mistaken simply to assume that the human fulfillment derived from involvement in interpersonal relationships characteristic of one type of community or association is the equivalent of the human fulfillment from involvement in relationships characteristic of any of the others. The only way, then, to determine whether Aristotle's dictum can be translated into a statement about human sociality would be, first, to determine what he meant by a political community and which aspects of participation in such a community he believed actualized human nature and, second, to make a parallel investigation of social association and interpersonal relations of the type intended by contemporary legal theorists to determine if the latter can perform the same function as the former.[50]

While such a task goes beyond the scope of this essay, I believe it is fair to say that, at the very least, Aristotle would deny the equation of human nature as political and human nature as social unless the end of social association is the good life or living well. The measure to be used in an inquiry of this kind would thus be whether the end of social association is a partial good—as is the case with couples, master-servant relationships, households, and villages—or a complete good. Students of Aristotle have long wrestled with his concept of "living well."[51] On a high level of generality, Aristotle indicates that living well is characterized by self-sufficiency, and he suggests that it consists in acquiring and exercising the moral and deliberative virtues.[52] On a more concrete level, however, Aristotle is much clearer about what happiness is not than about what it is. What is uncontested is that Aristotle rejects the popular beliefs that pleasures of the senses and/or material acquisitions make up the core of happiness.

The failure to distinguish sharply between people's social and political natures thus has consequences for contemporary liberal legal theory. Among other things, it makes possible the view expressed by some writers that intermediate associations are significant forums for the development and exercise of civic virtue. Cass Sunstein, for example, has argued that labor unions, religious associations, women's groups, civil rights organizations, and charitable organizations may serve an important function in fostering civic virtue among their members.[53] Frank Michelman expresses a belief in the desirability of active involvement in associations and other activities "outside the major, formal channels of electoral and legislative politics."[54]

The view that participation in pre- or sub-political associations will create or maintain civic virtue has obvious appeal. Given our enormous and diverse country, it may well be that intermediate associations bear a closer resemblance to certain aspects of the classical city than our nation as a whole ever can. In particular, such associations permit the homogeneity and personal knowledge among members that the classical republicans extolled among citizens.[55] Such associations, however, appear to differ from the classical concept of the city in a decisive respect, namely, by aiming at the good of their members rather than the common good. In that event, the "civic virtue" encouraged by such associations would actually reinforce private preferences without attempting to scrutinize those preferences prior to placing them on the public agenda.[56] Cass Sunstein anticipates this objection: he asserts that intermediate organizations will scrutinize existing practices critically and encourage the exercise of civic virtue, understood as the pursuit of goals other than self-interest, narrowly conceived.[57] However, he gives no explanation of why this will be the case, and his conclusion seems to be contradicted by the way such organizations in fact operate.

Ideal Speech Conditions and Communal Discussion

The fourth feature of certain process-oriented middle-way legal theorists is the practice of laying down specific preconditions for communal deliberation to assure the legitimacy of the deliberations and their outcomes.[58] These preconditions, which are patterned after the conditions of Jürgen Habermas's ideal speech situation,[59] require that all who are affected by decisionmaking be permitted to participate and that the input of all participants receive equal consideration. To achieve the latter objective, the rules require each participant to have an equal opportunity to speak, question, and express his or her point of view freely. Any form of compulsion, whether direct or indirect, is prohibited.[60] Deliberative discourse is seen as successful when, despite initial disagreements, consensus is reached on a rational basis either about matters of policy or its implementation. The hallmark of the ideal speech situation is thus that it aims at understanding through rational and voluntary discourse, rather than at consensus based upon compromise, barter, or manipulation.[61]

From an Aristotelian perspective, once again contemporary liberal legal theorists are attempting to do indirectly what they might be more successful doing directly. Although the ground of consensus when the ideal speech situation is achieved is rational persuasion, the rational element is expected to enter into and ultimately permeate the discourse because of the equality, honesty, and openness of the participants. This assumes that all participants (and thus, in principle, that all people) will recognize the truth of a particular point of view after an exhaustive screening process.

This assumption, however, seems to require other, arguably untenable assumptions. First, it assumes that by positing certain structural constraints on the conversation (equality, honesty, openness), the participants will exhibit certain moral qualities. In particular, it assumes that they will forgo, or cease to experience, the desire to pursue their own self-interest at the expense of the interest of others and the larger community when these interests collide. Aristotle would find this expectation questionable on the basis of his belief that moral virtue must be internalized to be reliable.[62] Yet he would be the first to concede that without the ability to control one's passions, deliberation is impossible.[63] As was the case with the second feature of this approach discussed above, Aristotle would undoubtedly advocate instilling moderation, honesty, and a spirit of cooperation in people starting in childhood to ensure that the adult participants in a deliberative conversation will be willing to judge the opinions put forward without exclusive regard to their personal circumstances.

Second, the belief that a rational consensus can be reached in this manner seems to assume as well that all reasoning about human affairs, including moral and political reasoning, can ultimately be justified by deductive or empirical means; without this assumption, it is difficult to understand how a deliberative discourse can issue in rational persuasion of all parties. But the notion that all of the results of deliberation can be justified logically or empirically should be objectionable to theorists who emphasize practical reason (as contrasted with deductive argument) as the path to a certain kind of practical knowledge. For Aristotle, some, including some of the most important, determinations reached in such situations can be known only through prudence or practical wisdom, a rational process that often defies logical or empirical justification. The possessor of practical wisdom may well be guided to a large degree by precepts of a kind that can be tested and refuted. In many instances, however, the decisive variables are so numerous, complex, and interdependent that the process of reasoning cannot be broken down into a succession of linear arguments. If this is correct, the ideal speech situation would be doomed in principle unless, first, all participants possess or can come to possess practical wisdom through discussion and, second, the practical wisdom of all of them will operate identically. This is extremely unlikely, if for no other reason than the circumstance that practical wisdom appears to derive in large part from experience (and from the way in which individuals perceive and learn from their experiences).[64] Thus, the ideal speech situation, which is premised upon equal respect for the individual participants and their differences, would be unable to reach its goal unless, when the layers are peeled back, each participant's mind is revealed to work in an identical fashion. Yet this possibility would also seem to be objectionable to theorists for whom respect for people's distinctiveness is paramount.

Aristotle would deal with this dilemma by challenging the belief that practical wisdom is a capacity that all possess (or can learn) to an equal degree. It is interesting that he embarks upon his definition of practical wisdom by studying the people to whom we attribute practical wisdom[65] rather than more abstractly, as he does in the case of some other mental faculties. His approach may suggest that practical wisdom is not a generic capacity and that its workings are inseparable from the person who exercises or possesses it. Aristotle also distinguishes practical wisdom from other mental faculties that resemble it, such as shrewd guessing, calculation in the service of partial or evil ends, having correct opinions, and good sense.[66] Practical wisdom thus resembles a talent that is developed through experiences of a certain kind, but it also depends in part on a natural or intrinsic core capacity of the individual. If this is the case, communal inquiries may not be able to replicate the mental process of a single person with a natural capacity and suitable experiences to actualize it.

THE MIDDLE-WAY APPROACHES OPEN TO EXTERNAL SUBSTANTIVE STANDARDS

Numerous other legal thinkers who believe that reasoning about moral or legal issues can achieve correct or non-arbitrary results in the absence of logical or empirical proof adopt an approach that combines substantive and procedural elements.[67] These thinkers tend to identify the rational faculty involved in this type of reasoning as "practical reason," "practical wisdom," "prudence," or "judgment." In reaching decisions, judgments, or conclusions, the person exercising practical reason relies on some combination of tradition, history, formal instruction, observation, experience, and reflection.[68] So understood, the person engaged in practical reasoning resembles a doctor who relies upon the totality of her book and life learning to arrive at decisions in individual cases. The person engaged in moral or legal reasoning, however, faces a subject matter of far greater complexity and much less regularity than the subject matter of the medical arts.

Contemporary legal thinkers of the middle way who believe in the possibility of moral philosophy or moral truth[69] disagree about the extent of its relevance for legal reasoning, especially the reasoning of judges or public officials. The most preeminent legal theorist who argues for independent substantive standards guiding (as well as issuing from) legal reasoning is Ronald Dworkin. His writings elaborate a theory that explains how it is possible for judges and others[70] to arrive at "right answers" in hard cases, i.e., in the absence of legal principles, rules of law, or legal precedents that dictate specific conclusions.[71] For Dworkin, in such cases judges first have, and should have, recourse to established legal materials (such as rules, principles, statutes, regulations, and previous judicial decisions) and the principles implicit in those materials. To prevent judges from relying on intuition or "making decisions that seem right in isolation" when they turn to principles implicit in established legal materials,[72] Dworkin requires them to determine which principles are consistent with each other and with the body of settled legal materials thought to be right.[73] To establish a comprehensive theory of this kind a judge may have to prefer some of the legal materials or principles over others.[74]

Dworkin argues that, whenever the result of this process fails to account satisfactorily for established legal materials, including the principles implicit in them, or it produces more than one comprehensive theory, the comprehensive theory that best fits existing legal materials will be the one that "is superior as a matter of political or moral theory."[75] It is at this stage, then, that Dworkin advocates having recourse to sources external to the law. A judge is nonetheless obliged to render decisions that defer to existing law as much as possible, consistent with the obligation to maintain the law's integrity. Moral and political philosophy are thus not free to determine the direction or content of the law except insofar as is required to enhance its integrity.[76]

In two recent articles, Ken Kress argues that Dworkin's methodology produces suboptimal results because it presumes that the legal theory adopted by judges who rely on external sources must aim at a high degree of fit with established legal materials. This requirement, according to Kress, is never adequately defended,[77] and it prevents judges from reaching as morally correct a theory as would be possible if a less rigorous fit were required.[78] Kress concedes that the jurisprudence elaborated by Dworkinian judges will improve from the standpoint of morality over time, but he argues that such a result is inadequate for a "legal system that aspires to do justice."[79] At the same time, Kress acknowledges that judges have differing capacities for what he calls "critical moral truth" and that, as a consequence, the real question is not which legal theory is absolutely best in the abstract, but which theory we would want judges to adopt given their views about critical moral matters as compared with their views about the dominant ideology embedded in the settled law.[80] He concludes that in the best case, i.e., when judges are well equipped to think critically about moral matters, some version of natural law theory will produce better decisions than a theory heavily tied to established legal precedents. But he leaves open whether such judges exist now or will likely exist in the future.

Anthony Kronman also recognizes the possibility of standards of moral truth or justice independent of a legal system, but he is wary of judges substituting moral truth or a philosophic theory of justice for existing law. Kronman argues that judges do need to engage in moral reflection to fill gaps in existing law for several reasons.[81] Yet he also urges that this aspect of the judicial function be limited to infrequent occasions and that judges resist the temptation to treat law as a "subfield of morality" or a text for philosophic exegesis.[82] Instead, Kronman endorses Alexander Bickel's doctrine of prudence or "good practical wisdom" as a judicial virtue.

According to Bickel, judges must resist moral imperatives, cultivate the ability to "live with the disharmony between aspiration and historical circumstance," and look for "opportunities that permit the marginal and evolutionary reconciliation of our principles and practices."[83]

Kronman[84] identifies the occasions on which judges should have recourse to moral principles with the educational role of courts, that is, their responsibility to "instruct and elevate, to bring out the best in us and show us where our own convictions lead."[85] But the courts also have a responsibility to respect the democratic principle of the consent of the people and to promote peace through compromise. In his view, therefore, to be effective in their role as educators, the courts must assess and accommodate the environment in which they render decisions rather than operate as philosopher-kings.[86]

Christopher Eisgruber also believes that there are independent standards of justice and morality that the Constitution of the United States does not embody. Unlike Kronman or Dworkin, however, he believes that judges should completely refrain from importing these values into judicial decisions. He reasons that Constitutional norms already reflect a commitment to justice, albeit imperfect, and this level of justice is superior to philosophic norms from a political point of view, i.e., because it reflects standards that can realistically gain the consent of the people over the long term. For Eisgruber, then, Constitutional norms are desirable from a moral point of view because they are substantively good (as well as attainable). Prudent judges should therefore pursue a fuller realization of Constitutional norms rather than try to modify them in light of external standards.[87]

AN ARISTOTELIAN APPRAISAL OF THE MIDDLE-WAY THEORIES OPEN TO EXTERNAL STANDARDS

Despite their differences, these theories echo important aspects of Aristotle's understanding of the way values and actions should be understood and ranked. All of the legal theorists discussed in the preceding section envision a form of practical reasoning that can be employed in deciding difficult legal questions in the absence of clear answers based upon established legal materials. Their descriptions of the reasoning process share with Aristotle's an expectation that practical reason arrives at judgments taking into account a combination of principles, rules of varying degrees of generality, and particular features of individual situations.[88] These theorists contemplate, as does Aristotle, the possibility of a single individual capable of deliberating well. And they appear to agree with him that practical wisdom is not possessed by human beings equally.[89]

The legal theorists discussed in the preceding section appear to regard the consent of people to the laws governing them as important primarily because of the necessity in a democracy of ensuring voluntary support for and obedience to the laws. This necessity is practical, i.e., to avoid civil disobedience, lawlessness, or excessive coercion to uphold the law, but it is based as well on part of the core meaning of democratic government. Aristotle would agree that consent of the people is desirable to secure voluntary obedience to laws. He would, however, emphasize more than most theorists today the role of habit in assuring consent and voluntary obedience as well as for instilling in people a sense of the goodness of their laws.[90] Aristotle would find that the theorists discussed in the preceding section (with the exceptions of Kronman and, possibly, Eisgruber) overestimate the ability of people in general to conduct themselves in accordance with beliefs that are not supported by corresponding habits. Consent, Aristotle would argue, is not sufficient to ensure lawabidingness unless reinforced by compatible character traits.

Finally, all of the theorists discussed in the preceding section except Eisgruber agree that there are situations in which the practical wisdom of judges cannot operate successfully without recourse to disciplines external to the law, in particular, moral and political philosophy. In the writings of Aristotle, in contrast, the source of the moral insights of the person possessing practical wisdom is less certain. In many places in his writings, it is the moral virtue of the person who exercises practical wisdom that seems to provide a moral compass to guide his decisions.[91] Elsewhere Aristotle suggests that some kind of cognitive knowledge of the end of human action would be useful for guiding individuals in their pursuits, and he asserts that law is the product of "some sort of practical wisdom and intelligence."[92] But Aristotle never claims that philosophy can or should direct the practical reasoning of lawmakers, even though he intends his *Politics* as an aid to the development of practical reason in the reader.[93] Aristotle thus has less confidence than the contemporary theorists discussed in the ability of theoretical reason to direct human affairs absent the virtues of character, just as he believes practical reason and deliberation will fail to attain practical wisdom in their absence.

CONCLUSION

Several themes have emerged through the preceding sketch that should give pause to contemporary liberal middle-way legal theorists. First and foremost is the strong connection between deliberative excellence and character that Aristotle elaborates at length. Each, in his view, presupposes the other to be fully realized. Aristotle's understanding stands in stark contrast to contemporary middle-way theory, which tends to view moral questions as fundamentally private matters, to be decided by each individual in accordance with his or her conscience. His understanding challenges this contemporary understanding by raising the possibility that insistence on a strong separation between moral education and education more generally will prevent the emergence of truly deliberative communities and leaders with practical wisdom.

Second, this sketch has brought to the fore fundamental assumptions of middle-way theorists about human equality and inequality. Political equality is a central tenet of a liberal constitutional democracy, yet that fact does not and need not necessitate a comparable equality in every aspect of human life. For Aristotle, the capacity for practical reasoning appears to be unevenly distributed among the population, especially in the form of practical wisdom, which is limited by its very definition to people possessing a high degree of experience and commitment to "living well" in the Aristotelian sense, as contrasted with those adept at pursuing one or more partial goods.[94] The legitimacy of Aristotle's insight is admitted tacitly in the writings of those authors who focus exclusively or disproportionately on the practical reasoning of judges, at the expense of other public officials and the population in general. Aristotle's ideas thus expose a conceptual difficulty at the core of theories of liberal constitutional democracy.

Finally, it is characteristic of liberal legal thought to be more comfortable investigating, discussing, and disagreeing about questions of method than about issues of human nature. The first book of the *Nicomachean Ethics,* in contrast, contains a powerful assertion of the inseparability of these two: all inquiry and knowledge about human affairs must take into account the complexity of the human soul and the consequences of that complexity for the possibilities of human conduct. This leads Aristotle to warn that it is inappropriate to expect the precision of mathematics in human inquiries. Wisdom about human affairs combines an appreciation of the reality of human commonality and the reality of human particularity with a sense of how these interact. It is thus part of the wisdom of middle-way theorists to be unsatisfied with those who would assimilate law to science or relegate it to complete subjectivity. And it is part of their wisdom to locate their project in the area between science and subjectivity because this is where the realities of human nature and human conduct reside. Theirs is the task of understanding and responding to the persistent conflicts between the rule of law and the pull of human particularity, between claims of right and the requirements of justice. In negotiating these extremes and what lies between, they would do well to turn to Aristotle both for support and enlightenment.

Notes

1. To some extent, these questions depend for their answers upon parallel questions raised by other disciplines, such as moral and political philosophy. As is discussed in this essay, the degree to which a legal theorist or public official should address issues of moral truth from an extra-legal perspective as part of the process of reasoning to legal conclusions is controversial.

2. On legal formalism, see Ernest J. Weinrib, "Legal Formalism: On the Immanent Rationality of Law," 97 *Yale Law Journal* 949, 952 (1988). On legal realism, see the essays in William W. Fisher III, Morton J. Horwitz, and Thomas Reed, ed., *American Legal Realism* (1993). On sociological jurisprudence, see Roscoe Pound, "The Scope and Purpose of Sociological Jurisprudence," 25 *Harvard Law Review* 489 (1912). See also G. Edward White, "From Sociological Jurisprudence to Realism: Jurisprudence and Social Change in Early Twentieth-Century America," 58 *Virginia Law Review* 999 (1972).

3. See Morris R. Cohen, *Law and the Social Order* (New York: Harcourt, Brace, 1933), 192–97.

4. See Jerome Frank, *Law and the Modern Mind* (Gloucester: Peter Smith, 1930), 6–8, 10–11; Roscoe Pound, "The Scope and Purpose of Sociological Jurisprudence," *supra* note 2.

5. Other important theoretical perspectives that can be considered formalist in inspiration are the law and economics movement and analytical positivism, such as H. L. A. Hart, inspired by John Austin, developed.

6. The major figures associated with the modern turn to natural law in legal theory are Lon Fuller, Lloyd L. Weinrib, Russell Hittinger, John Finnis, and Michael Moore. See Robert P. George, ed., *Natural Law Theory: Contemporary Essays* (Oxford: Clarendon Press, 1992); Charles Covell, *The Defense of Natural Law: A Study of the Ideas of Law and Justice in the Writings of Lon L. Fuller, Michael Oakeshott, F. A. Hayek, Ronald Dworkin, and John Finnis* (New York: Oxford University Press, 1992).

7. See generally Andrew Altman, *Critical Legal Studies: A Liberal Critique* (Princeton, N.J.: Princeton University Press, 1990); Mark Kelman, *A Guide to Critical Legal Studies* (Cambridge, Mass.: Harvard University Press, 1987); John Stick, "Can Nihilism Be Pragmatic," 100 *Harvard Law Review* 332, 333 n.2 (1986) (arguing that CLS encompasses both nihilists and non-nihilists and that the nihilists "tak[e] nihilist critical arguments to state general truths," whereas the non-nihilists merely use nihilist arguments to "point . . . out local flaws in particular arguments").

8. Critical race theory is an approach to the study of law that examines the racial (and racist) history and racial (and racist) consequences of seemingly race-neutral laws. The method of critical race theory emphasizes the experiences and subjective interpretations of individuals of color, makes use of interdisciplinary (e.g., social science) studies of race and racism, and it aims at clarifying the conditions of and obstacles to meaningful legal reform. For the literature by and about critical race theorists, see Richard Delgado and Jean Stefancic, "Critical Race Theory: An Annotated Bibliography," 79 *Virginia Law Review* 461 (1993) and

Delgado and Stefancic, "Critical Race Theory: An Annotated Bibliography 1993, A Year of Transition," 66 *University of Colorado Law Review* 159 (1995). Although critical race studies are dominated by works by and about black and Afro-American experiences, there is a burgeoning critical race movement by and about Asian-American and Latino authors. See, e.g., Robert S. Chang, "Toward an Asian American Legal Scholarship: Critical Race Theory, Post-Structuralism, and Narrative Space," 81 *California Law Review* 1241 (1993).

9. See, e.g., Lucinda M. Finley, "Breaking Women's Silence in Law: The Dilemma of the Gendered Nature of Legal Reasoning," 64 *Notre Dame Law Review* 886 (1989). Feminist jurisprudence encompasses a broad range of attitudes toward the possibility and desirability of political truth. On the methods of different types of feminism, see Tracy E. Higgins, "By Reason of Their Sex: Feminist Theory, Post-Modernism, and Justice," 80 *Cornell Law Review* 1536, 1592 (1995) (arguing that feminists are not necessarily relativists; properly understood, "antifoundationalism undercuts both objectivism and relativism"); Janet Radcliffe Richards, "What Feminist Epistemology Isn't (and the Implications for Feminist Jurisprudence)," 1 *Legal Theory* 365 (1995); Joan C. Williams, "Deconstructing Gender," 87 *Michigan Law Review* 797, 802–806 (1989). See also Catharine MacKinnon, "Toward Feminist Jurisprudence," 34 *Stanford Law Review* 703 (1982).

10. See, e.g., William N. Eskridge, Jr., "Gaylegal Narratives," 46 *Stanford Law Review* 607 (1994); see also Symposium, "Legal Storytelling," 87 *Michigan Law Review* 2073 (1989); Robin West, "Jurisprudence as Narrative: An Aesthetic Analysis of Modern Legal Theory," 60 *New York University Law Review* 145 (1985). For criticism of storytelling as a source of legal standards, see the authorities cited in Eleanor Marie Brown, "Note: The Tower of Babel: Bridging the Divide between Critical Race Theory and 'Mainstream' Civil Rights Scholarship," 105 *Yale Law Journal* 513, 516 n.11 (1995).

11. See Stephen M. Feldman, "Diagnosing Power: Postmodernism in Legal Scholarship and Judicial Practice (With an Emphasis on the *Teague* Rule against New Rules in Habeas Corpus Cases)," 88 *Northwestern University Law Review* 1046, 1102–04 (1994) (including critical race theory and feminism among different voice approaches to scholarship and noting that the classification of different voice scholarship as a type of postmodernism can undermine the uniqueness and effectiveness of that scholarship).

12. The term "poststructuralism" is often equated with the term "postmodernism." Postmodernism can, however, be seen as a broader term, encompassing poststructuralism as well as other movements. See Gary Minda, *Postmodern Legal Movements: Law and Jurisprudence at Century's End* (New York: New York University Press, 1995), 229–32 (dividing postmodernism into poststructuralism and neopragmatism); Peter C. Schanck, "Understanding Postmodern Thought and Its Implications for Statutory Interpretation," 65 *Southern California Law Review* 2505, 2514–15 (1992).

13. Suzanna Sherry, "The Sleep of Reason," 84 *Georgetown Law Journal* 453, 465, 472 (1996) (criticizing those who repudiate the priority of reasoned argument over other modes of knowing and suggesting "parallels between religious beliefs and the alternative nonrational epistemologies offered by the critical scholars"). See also Martha C. Nussbaum, "Skepticism about Practical Reason in Literature and the Law," 107 *Harvard Law Review* 714 (1994) (characterizing the views of several

prominent legal and political theorists as "attack[ing] certainty and justification rather than belief and commitment").

14. I use "foundationalism" or "objectivism" on the one hand and "relativism" or "subjectivism" on the other to refer to the two outer poles of the epistemological continuum. Good working definitions of these terms are given by Richard Bernstein, *Beyond Objectivism and Relativism: Science, Hermeneutics, and Praxis* (Philadelphia: University of Pennsylvania Press, 1983), 8. According to Bernstein, relativism views concepts as "relative to a specific conceptual scheme, theoretical framework, paradigm, form of life, society, or culture . . . there is no substantive overarching framework or single metalanguage by which we can rationally adjudicate or universally evaluate competing claims of alternative paradigms." Objectivism assumes that "there is or must be some permanent, ahistorical matrix or framework to which we can ultimately appeal in determining the nature of rationality, knowledge, truth, reality, goodness, or rightness." *Id.* Contrast Owen Fiss, "Objectivity and Interpretation," 34 *Stanford Law Review* 739, 748–49 (1982) (arguing that objectivity in judicial interpretation is different from correctness insofar as interpretation is objective if it is "constrained by disciplining rules," whereas correctness is a more rigorous standard).

15. The term "radical particularism" comes from Margaret Jane Radin and Frank Michelman, "Commentary, Pragmatist and Poststructuralist Critical Legal Practice," 139 *University of Pennsylvania Law Review* 1019, 1046, 1049 (1991) (referring to pragmatic and feminist thinkers who dismiss the meaningfulness or utility of rules altogether).

16. The term is from Suzanna Sherry, "The Sleep of Reason," *supra* note 13, at 458, 472–73.

17. Frank Michelman, citing Drucilla Cornell, also uses the term "decisionism," defined as "the conviction that moral choice proceeds not from publicly certifiable grounds of reasoning, but from the inexplicable private impulses of individuals, objectively unfounded and rationally unguided." Frank I. Michelman, "The Supreme Court, 1985 Term—Forward: Traces of Self-Government," 100 *Harvard Law Review* 4, 25 (1986).

18. On nihilism as it pertains to legal theory, see Joseph W. Singer, "The Player and the Cards: Nihilism and Legal Theory," 94 *Yale Law Journal* 1 (1984); Stick, "Can Nihilism Be Pragmatic?" *supra* note 7. Singer distinguishes nihilism from irrationalism: the nihilist despairs of living a meaningful life, while the irrationalist does not. Singer, "The Player and the Cards: Nihilism and Legal Theory," at 4 n.8. Singer identifies himself with the latter view: rational truth and objectivity are unavailable, but we can nonetheless live a life of goals, caring, and commitment. His deepest criticism of traditional legal thought maintains that the dichotomies of rationality and irrationality, or objectivity and subjectivity, do not adequately describe our moral and epistemological choices.

19. Aristotle, *Nicomachean Ethics* 1.3 1094b12–25 (all translations of the *Nicomachean Ethics* are those of Martin Ostwald). See also *id.* 6.5 1140a33–b3 ("things whose starting points or first causes can be other than they are do not admit of demonstration").

20. For discussion by legal theorists about the character and significance of indeterminacy in legal reasoning, see Brian Leiter, "Legal Indeterminacy," 1 *Legal*

Theory 481 (1995): John Hasnas, "Back to the Future: From Critical Legal Studies Forward to Legal Realism, or How Not to Miss the Point of the Indeterminacy Argument," 45 *Duke Law Journal* 84 (1995); Ken Kress, "Legal Indeterminacy," 77 *California Law Review* 283 (1989).

21. See Aristotle, *Nicomachean Ethics* 6.5 1140b4–7 (practical wisdom "is a truthful characteristic of acting rationally in matters good and bad for man"). See also *id.* 6.2 1139b11–13 ("truth is the function of both intellectual parts [of the soul]," i.e., the theoretical and the practical).

22. The following discussion does not exhaust the types of contemporary liberal legal theory nor the important individual representatives of the two approaches discussed. These omissions are a consequence of space limitations.

23. See Daniel Farber and Philip Frickey, "Practical Reason and the First Amendment," 34 *University of California at Los Angeles Law Review* 1615, 1645–47 (1987); Cass R. Sunstein, *Legal Reasoning and Political Conflict* (New York: Oxford University Press, 1997), ix, 45–46, 56–58, 99.

24. As others have noted, however, liberal theorists have a tendency to promote values such as tolerance, cooperation, neutrality, and autonomy, which, though themselves substantive values, are thought to be structural or minimal conditions to enable individuals to pursue their own life plans as they conceive them. See Stephen Gardbaum, "Liberalism, Autonomy, and Moral Conflict," 48 *Stanford Law Review* 385 (1996) (criticizing this tendency and arguing that, correctly understood, liberalism should promote choice and autonomy as substantive values).

25. See, e.g., Michael J. Perry, "Toward an Ecumenical Politics," 60 *George Washington Law Review* 599, 607, 610 (1992); Robin West, "Liberalism Rediscovered: A Pragmatic Definition of Liberal Vision," 46 *University of Pittsburgh Law Review* 673, 673–74, 680–83 (1985); Bruce Ackerman, *Social Justice in the Liberal State* (New Haven, Conn. and London: Yale University Press, 1980).

26. See, e.g., Michelman, "Traces of Self-Government," *supra* note 17, at 4; Cass R. Sunstein, "Beyond the Republican Revival," 97 *Yale Law Journal* 1539 (1988); Bruce Ackerman, *We the People. Vol. I, Foundations* (Cambridge, Mass.: Harvard University Press, 1991), 272–74.

27. See, e.g., Frank I. Michelman, "Law's Republic," 97 *Yale Law Journal* 1493, 1524–29 (1988) (the participants in a communal decision-making process create the normative standards through the discussion); Suzanna Sherry, "Civic Virtue and the Feminine Voice in Constitutional Adjudication," 72 *Virginia Law Review* 543, 548 (1986); West, "Liberalism Rediscovered," *supra* note 25, at 673–74, 680–83 (the nature of the good life can only be known through the process of communal inquiry).

28. See, e.g., Aristotle, *Nicomachean Ethics* 1.5–6.

29. Aristotle, *Topics* 1.1 100a18–20, 100a30–b18. Although Aristotle does not mention practical reason in his account of the functions of the art of dialectic, it seems that the method could be used to evaluate moral beliefs and certain practical decisions as well as to test the ultimate principles of the sciences. See *id.* 1.2 101a36–b3.

30. See Aristotle, *Topics* 1.2 101a34–36 ("For the philosophic sciences it is useful, because, if we are able to raise the difficulties on both sides, we shall more easily discern both truth and falsehood on every point").

31. Aristotle, *Topics* 1.1 100b21–23.

32. Aristotle certainly sees the usefulness of face-to-face encounters. Aristotle's account of dialectical encounters for the sake of training (which appears to aim at beating one's opponent as opposed to seeking the truth) would seem to require live encounters to be effective.

33. The arguments in Aristotle's writings are almost exclusively dialectical, which is not what one would expect from the first philosopher to write systematically about the nature of syllogistic and demonstrative reasoning.

34. See *supra* note 31.

35. Not coincidentally, the Greek word for "generally accepted opinion" (*endoksa*) is sometimes translated as "probable opinion."

36. See Aristotle, *Politics* 3.4 1277a27–28; see also *id.* 1277b13–30 (when the city is made up of people who are equal and free, the good man has the capacity to rule and be ruled both).

37. Aristotle, *Politics* 3.4. 1277b25–26.

38. Aristotle, *Politics* 3.4 1277b29–30.

39. Some middle-way legal theorists emphasize the quality of assent as well as the fact of assent. See *infra*, p. 242.

40. Although liberal legal theorists of the kind under discussion are often opposed to society imposing its (particular) understanding of good character on individuals, they almost uniformly assume or attempt to create a cluster of moral virtues supportive of the basic features of a liberal society. See the discussion in Miriam Galston, "Taking Aristotle Seriously: Republican-Oriented Legal Theory and the Moral Foundation of Deliberative Democracy," 82 *California Law Review* 331, 361–69 (1994). A critical difference between their approach and that of Aristotle is that they seek a voluntary situation in which such virtues are likely to arise spontaneously.

41. Aristotle believed that moral virtue was a result of habit in the first instance. As a consequence, it is easier to acquire moral habits if one does not have to first "unlearn" bad habits.

42. See Galston, "Taking Aristotle Seriously," *supra* note 40, at 372–76.

43. See Perry, "Toward an Ecumenical Politics," *supra* note 25, at 614–15; Lawrence Byard Solum, "Freedom of Communicative Action: A Theory of the First Amendment Freedom of Speech," 83 *Northwestern University Law Review* 54, 79–80 (1989) (describing and criticizing the theory of self-realization through speech).

44. Aristotle, *Politics* 1.2 1253a.

45. See, e.g., Ackerman, *We the People, supra* note 26, at 230–31; Michelman, "Traces of Self-Government," *supra* note 17, at 22–23.

46. Among those who fail to make a sharp distinction between the political and the social are Fred Dallmayr, "Nature and Community: Comments on Michael Perry," 63 *Tulane Law Review* 1405 (1989); Mark Tushnet, *Red, White, and Blue: A Critical Analysis of Constitutional Law* (Cambridge, Mass.: Harvard University Press, 1988), 10; Solum, "Freedom of Communicative Action: A Theory of the First Amendment Freedom of Speech," *supra* note 43, at 54, 80; Michael J. Perry, *Morality, Politics, and Law* (New York: Oxford University Press, 1988), 11; Ronald R. Garet, "Communality and Existence: The Rights of Groups," 56 *Southern California Law Review* 1001, 1070–71 (1983). Some contemporary legal theorists have recognized

the special meaning that Aristotle attributes to the term "political." See, e.g., Stephen M. Feldman, "Republican Revival/Interpretive Turn," 1992 *Wisconsin Law Review* 679, 689–90.

47. Aristotle, *Politics* 1.2 1252a–b.

48. Aristotle, *Politics* 1.2 1252b29–30 (the city comes into existence for the sake of living, but it exists for the sake of living well); see also *id.* 3.9 1280b38–1281a10 (contrasting the goal of living together, which is the aim of subpolitical associations, with that of living well, acting nobly, and acquiring political virtue, which are the object of political association).

49. Aristotle, *Politics* 1.1 1252a.

50. My criticism of the confusion between "social" and "political" would not apply to the term "social" when used in a comprehensive manner such as in the phrase "social science." According to Stephen Salkever, the contemporary term "social science," which includes political science, anthropology, sociology, psychology, economics, and history, appears to be what Aristotle meant by "political science" as the term is used in the *Politics* and the *Nicomachean Ethics*. See Stephen G. Salkever, *Finding the Mean: Theory and Practice in Aristotelian Political Philosophy* (Princeton, N.J.: Princeton University Press, 1990), 59–60.

51. The literature is vast. See John M. Cooper, *Reason and the Human Good in Aristotle* (Cambridge, Mass.: Harvard University Press, 1975).

52. See Aristotle, *Politics* 1.2 1252b27–30 (self-sufficiency), 1253a7–18 (human beings are the most political of all gregarious animals because they have reason [*logos,* or "speech"], which makes possible perception of good and evil, just and unjust).

53. Sunstein, "Beyond the Republican Revival," *supra* note 26, at 1573.

54. Michelman, "Law's Republic," *supra* note 27, at 1531. Michelman's list includes social or recreational clubs; schools; management, directorates, and leadership groups of all types of organizations; workplaces and shop floors; and public events and street life as well as the more traditional town meetings and civic and voluntary organizations mentioned by Sunstein.

55. These characteristics are often rejected by liberal legal theorists today. See Kathleen M. Sullivan, "The Supreme Court, 1991 Term: Foreword: The Justices of Rules and Standards," 106 *Harvard Law Review* 21, 68 (1992); Robin West, "The Supreme Court, 1989 Term: Foreword: Taking Freedom Seriously," 104 *Harvard Law Review* 43, 61 (1990).

56. For a critique of this kind, see Kathryn Abrams, "Rainbow Republicanism," 97 *Yale Law Journal* 1713, 1714 (1988) (suggesting that informed decisionmaking in clubs, workplaces, and other associations will not provide an experience equivalent to engagement in political life). The comments in the text do not necessarily apply to participation in local government, although such activity may be viewed as involvement in intermediate associations. See Richard Briffault, "Our Localism: Part II—Localism and Legal Theory," 1990 *Columbia Law Review* 346, 393–99.

57. Sunstein, "Beyond the Republican Revival," *supra* note 26, at 1573. His claim about obtaining a sense of community and an opportunity to participate in deliberative activities through such organizations is more credible. But the strong bonds that people form within these partial communities may well increase the assurance on the part of the members of the rightness of their parochial interests and, as a con-

sequence, make it more difficult for them to consider fairly the demands of the public interest, which sometimes requires self-sacrifice. This problem is accentuated by Sunstein's recommendation that private or intermediate associations be insulated from the state, although he also says that without government regulation such organizations may be a source of "oppression" and lead to "intolerable results." *Id.* at 1574.

58. See Solum, "A Theory of the First Amendment Freedom of Speech," *supra* note 43, at 96–99; Michelman, "Traces of Self-Government," *supra* note 17, at 31–32; cf. Frank I. Michelman, "Family Quarrel," 17 *Cardozo Law Review* 1163 (1996) (discussing his reliance upon and disagreement with the theory of communicative action of Jürgen Habermas).

59. See Jürgen Habermas, "What is Universal Pragmatics?" in *Communication and the Evolution of Society*, trans. T. McCarthy (Boston: Beacon Press, 1979), 1–5; *The Theory of Communicative Action*, Vol. I: *Reason and the Rationalization of Society*, trans. T. McCarthy (Boston: Beacon Press, 1984), 25; *Moral Consciousness and Communicative Action*, trans. C. Lenhardt and S. Nicholsen (Cambridge, Mass.: MIT Press, 1990), 86–94, 198.

60. See Solum, "A Theory of First Amendment Freedom of Speech," *supra* note 43, at 97.

61. When the conditions are less than optimal, there is the risk that real persuasion and consensus are not reached, even if the participants arrive at a unanimous result. For example, those who are more articulate or present arguments based upon better factual premises will sound more authoritative. Indicia of power on the part of some speakers, such as their education, dress, or social and professional positions, may intimidate others or make them persuasive for the wrong reasons. Some people may agree to join the consensus out of a desire to achieve group harmony. For all their promise, deliberative encounters may fail in their aspirations even if no person or persons deliberately attempt to manipulate the conversation toward their own preferences.

62. In addition, imposing these structural conditions amounts to imposing a moral code in the guise of neutral ground rules, thus admitting through the back door what would be rejected at the front.

63. Aristotle, *Nicomachean Ethics* 6.5 1140b11–19.

64. See Aristotle, *Nicomachean Ethics* 6.8 (noting that young men do not display practical wisdom because they lack experience, an essential ingredient).

65. Aristotle, *Nicomachean Ethics* 6.5 1140a24.

66. See Aristotle, *Nicomachean Ethics* 6.5–9, 11.

67. The generalizations expressed in this paragraph are based upon numerous thinkers whose views differ in many important respects, although they share the attributes discussed in the text in common. Thinkers of this kind are mentioned in the text and notes that follow.

68. For a useful summary of the views of such thinkers and citations to their writings, see Sherry, "The Sleep of Reason," *supra* note 13.

69. See, e.g., the essays by David Brink, Joseph Raz, and Philip Pettit in Brian Leiter, *Objectivity in Law and Morals* (Cambridge: Cambridge University Press, 2001). The following authors imply that some form of moral truth is possible and discuss the extent to which moral philosophy or moral truth should have a role in

shaping the lives of individuals or legal regimes: Ken Kress, "Why No Judge Should Be a Dworkinian Coherentist," 77 *Texas Law Review* 1375 (1999); Anthony T. Kronman, "Response: The Value of Moral Philosophy," 111 *Harvard Law Review* 1751 (1998), "Living in the Law," 54 *University of Chicago Law Review* 835 (1987); Christopher L. Eisgruber, "Justice and the Text: Rethinking the Constitutional Relation between Principle and Prudence," 43 *Duke Law Journal* 1 (1993); Joseph Raz, "Liberalism, Skepticism, and Democracy," 74 *Iowa Law Review* 761 (1989); Ronald Dworkin, *Law's Empire* (Cambridge: Belknap Press, 1986), *Taking Rights Seriously* (Cambridge, Mass.: Harvard University Press, 1977).

70. Dworkin also believes that political officials should justify their decisions in terms of such a theory. Dworkin, *Taking Rights Seriously, supra* note 69, at pp. 87, 106 (arguing that if a member of Congress votes to prohibit abortion, he should vote on all relevant issues to uphold the sanctity of life). However, he recognizes that this is unlikely for politicians, citizens, and political commentators most of the time. Ronald Dworkin, *A Matter of Principle* (Cambridge, Mass.: Harvard University Press, 1985), 184, n. 1. This essay refers to judges only, since these theorists seem to have them in mind most of the time.

71. According to Dworkin, there are often or generally right answers in cases where there is not a clear, dispositive precedent or rule. See Dworkin, *Taking Rights Seriously, supra* note 69, at 143, 279, 365. Although Dworkin's theory has evolved, I believe that the core concept has remained fundamentally the same, namely, that judges who make decisions within a legal system should rely on a mixture composed of established legal materials and moral or political philosophy when confronting situations not controlled by settled law. See Ronald Dworkin, *Freedom's Law: The Moral Reading of the American Constitution* (Cambridge, Mass.: Harvard University Press, 1996), 1–12. For the view that Dworkin's thought has changed significantly, see Joseph Raz, "Dworkin: A New Link in the Chain," 74 *California Law Review* 1103, 1116 (1986).

72. For the difference between "principles," "policies," and "goals," see Dworkin, *Taking Rights Seriously, supra* note 69, at 22–23, 90; *A Matter of Principle, supra* note 70, at 2–3, 11, 69. He advocates using principles implicit in established legal materials to reach legal judgments because of his conviction that the moral, political, and social values from which legal rules and precedents derive are themselves an integral part of law. *Id.,* at 29–30.

73. Dworkin, *Taking Rights Seriously, supra* note 69, at 87.

74. Dworkin, *Taking Rights Seriously, supra* note 69, at 87.

75. Dworkin, *A Matter of Principle, supra* note 70, at 107–108, 143, see also *id.* at 161, *Taking Rights Seriously, supra* note 69, at 113.

76. Thus, for Dworkin the path to truth in judicial reasoning does not follow a formula and disagreements about which practical decisions are correct are possible and even likely.

77. Ken Kress, "Coherentist Methodology Is Morally Better Than Either Its Proponents or Its Critics Think (But Still Not Good Enough)," 12 *Canadian Journal of Law & Jurisprudence* 83, 94 (1999) (explaining that Dworkin insists on a high level of fit with settled law in order to maintain a high degree of consensus among people governed by the law).

78. Kress, "Coherentist Methodology Is Morally Better," *supra* note 77.

79. *Id.*, pp. 94–95, Kress, "Why No Judge Should Be a Dworkinian Coherentist," *supra* note 69, at 1392, 1415.

80. Kress, "Why No Judge Should Be a Dworkinian Coherentist," *supra* note 69, at 1420.

81. These are: to preserve the law by understanding the "background conditions that give laws their meaning, purpose, and aspirational force"; to articulate the collective values and commitments embodied in law; and to diminish the extent of moral conflicts by promoting a regime of tolerance. Kronman, "Response: the Value of Moral Philosophy," *supra* note 69, at 1761–63.

82. Kronman, "Response: the Value of Moral Philosophy," *supra* note 69, at 1761–62.

83. See Anthony T. Kronman, "Alexander Bickel's Philosophy of Prudence," 94 *Yale Law Journal* 1567, 1570 (1985). Kronman again defers to Bickel in "Response: the Value of Moral Philosophy," *supra* note 69, at 1761.

84. Kronman gives the impression in his 1985 article that he largely concurs with the views that he attributes to Bickel.

85. Kronman, "Alexander Bickel's Philosophy of Prudence," *supra* note 83, at 1580–81.

86. See Kronman, "Alexander Bickel's Philosophy of Prudence," *supra* note 83, at 1570–71.

87. See Eisgruber, "Justice and the Text," *supra* note 69, at 2, 14, 15–18.

88. See Aristotle, *Nicomachean Ethics* 6.8 1141b–1142a.

89. See Aristotle, *Nicomachean Ethics* 10.9 1180b25–26. Dworkin is the clearest example of a contemporary legal theorist who sees this ability as rare: he calls the judge who can get right answers in hard cases "Hercules," to indicate the extraordinary character of the task he has to perform. In contrast, in his writings, Kronman appears to recommend that individuals in general, and lawyers in particular, should (and, by implication, can) work at developing their practical reasoning faculties. See Kronman, "Living in the Law," *supra* note 69, "Response: the Value of Moral Philosophy," *supra* note 69, at 1753, 1755–59, 1761–64.

90. See Aristotle, *Nicomachean Ethics* 2.1 1103a–b5, 3.1 1109b34, 10.9 1179b20–1180a18.

91. See Aristotle, *Nicomachean Ethics* 6.12 1144a, 6.13 1145a; but see *id.* 10.8 1178a (stating that the principles of practical wisdom are *in accordance with* the moral virtues and correctness in morals is in accordance with practical wisdom) (emphasis added).

92. See Aristotle, *Nicomachean Ethics* 1.1–2, 10.9 1180a18–19. The ambiguity in Aristotle's writings referred to in the text is discussed in Galston, *Taking Aristotle Seriously, supra* note 40, at 372–75.

93. See Aristotle, *Nichomachean Ethics* 10.9 1180a18–25, 33 (a person who seeks to help others to live well needs to know "something about legislating"—the topic elaborated by Aristotle in the *Politics*). See also *id.* 1180b13–25 (suggesting that knowledge of general rules is typically useful although not absolutely necessary).

94. See especially Aristotle, *Nichomachean Ethics* 6.12 1144a23–30, see also *id.* 6.8 1142a11–16.

CHAPTER EIGHT

Integrating Public Good and Private Right

The Virtue of Property

JILL FRANK

Most political thinkers—past and present—agree on the necessity of private property for a political life.[1] A more precise form of this claim, evident in current political theory and political science as well, is that private property is necessary to a specifically liberal-democratic political life. Consider two examples. Robert Putnam, among others, has argued that trust or social capital plays a central role in "making democracy work."[2] This is because trust generates (even as it emerges from) the reciprocal bonds among members of a polity to which these members and their political institutions are accountable. Studies conducted by scholars of social capital show trust to be more or less absent from regimes adopting systems of collective ownership. Although nothing is made of this point, these studies imply that the social capital necessary for democracy presupposes some form of private capital.[3] Scholars of eastern European countries in transition reach a similar conclusion: it is important, they maintain, to study the transition from a command to a market economy alongside the transition from one-party domination to democracy because these transitions mutually reinforce one another. Like the scholars of social capital, these scholars presume that, by somehow linking individual citizens to the polity as a whole and private interests with a common good, private property is necessary for successful democratization.[4]

How? Private property as described in most contemporary legal and political theory is an individual right to the possession, use, and disposition of material things. Key to individual liberty, independence, and security, it protects against arbitrary exercises of governmental power and against interferences from neighbors. It encourages efficient economic activity by setting up zones of sovereignty within which private owners may effectively do as they will with what is theirs. Liberal-democratic politics, however, depends not only on privacy but on reserves of public goods; it depends not only on individual autonomy and independence but on some form of collective action and interdependence; and it depends not only on protection against arbitrary redistribution but on equality. The dominant contemporary theorization of property seems to put private property distinctly at odds with liberal-democratic politics.

What form of private property might more successfully integrate private right and public good and so facilitate rather than obstruct the practices integral to liberal-democratic politics? Against the dominant paradigm of property in contemporary legal practice and political theory that defines property in terms of exchange value, I argue that we ought to treat property not simply in terms of exchange value but also as an activity of use bound to the practices of citizenship. I find traces of this understanding in contemporary legal practice and political theory, and in the writings of Thomas Jefferson and James Madison. For its most complete development, I return to Aristotle and to his ancient understanding of "property."[5] Thinking outside the constructions of the reigning paradigms, with their restrictive assumptions about the nature of property, opens possibilities for a liberal-democratic politics intent on integrating private right and public good.

The Value of Property

David Lucas owned two lots on the Isle of Palms in the coastal zone of South Carolina that he bought in 1986 to build a residential development. Two years later, South Carolina enacted the *Beachfront Management Act (BMA)* to prevent hazardous conditions from eroding the coastal zone and also with a view to environmental preservation. The *BMA* prevented Lucas from building the residential development. He sued the South Carolina Coastal Council demanding compensation for what he claimed was a taking of private property under the fifth amendment to the U.S. Constitution, the relevant part of which reads: "no one shall be deprived of life, liberty or property without due process of law nor shall private property be taken for public use without just compensation." The *Lucas* case went to the U.S. Supreme Court.[6] The issue before the Court was whether the *BMA* amounted to a taking of private property that required compensating Lucas. The Court decided in favor of Lucas. Justice Scalia, writing for the majority, held that regulatory prohibitions, like the *BMA,* that totally extinguish the value of property should be compensated, unless the uses being limited by the regulation are already prohibited by nuisance or property law. As Scalia put it: "Any limitation so severe cannot be newly legislated or decreed (without compensation), but must inhere in the title itself, in the restrictions that background principles of the State's law of property and nuisance already place upon land ownership."[7]

This case opens a host of interesting questions. Central for my purposes are the ways in which Scalia's opinion reflects and reinscribes the contemporary dominant paradigm of property. That Scalia takes property use to be primarily a matter of the relations between private individuals who can be named in a lawsuit underscores the privatizing and individuating aspects of the dominant conception of private property. That he takes property use to be governed by private law protects property use from legislative regulations which might effect redistribution in the name of a common good, and so safeguards the exclusionary privilege that attaches to private ownership. By rejecting the relevance of public law—including zoning ordinances—in his determination of how property use may be regulated, Scalia defines the public good as that which already is protected by private right. If private property has any public aspect at all on Scalia's understanding, it is via public nuisance which treats the public as the aggregation of particular private individuals.[8]

It is not the case that all environmental legislation would fail under Scalia's test. His test would likely prohibit property uses that produce air pollution, cause dangerous erosions of land, or have other similarly adverse consequences, when these uses harm particular identifiable individuals. But seeing the protection of the environment as a matter of private law leaves no room for the argument that the environment should be protected for the common benefit it brings to the members of a political community as a whole, now or in the future.[9] It leaves no room for conceiving of the environment as a public good, a good to be enjoyed and preserved for common use, unless such use is already protected by protecting private property rights between individual citizens, those who can be identified and hence individuated.

Underpinning Scalia's account of property is the idea that the use of private property is determined by its economic value: any "deprivation of all economically beneficial use" constitutes a compensable taking.[10] If a diminution in the value of property is a diminution in property itself, then the extinction of the economic value of Lucas's land is tantamount to the extinction of his property altogether. In what has been dubbed "a Bill of Rights for Property Owners," Congress has encoded Scalia's understanding of property in the *Omnibus Property Rights Act of 1995*. This *Act* [by section 204 (a) (D)] expands Scalia's economic account of property by insisting that any diminution in the value of property by 33 percent constitutes a compensable taking.[11]

Economic efficiency analysis—the dominant paradigm for understanding property in contemporary Anglo-American legal and political theory—echoes these treatments of property by the Supreme Court and Congress. Economic analysis treats private property as a fungible good determined by its exchange value.[12] Private property, so understood, depends on exclusive ownership since it is only under exclusive ownership that an owner—as the one who stands to gain or lose—will be motivated to use her property efficiently. Excludability, in this way, internalizes the external costs associated with diffuse ownership or control.[13] Property is, in short, the power to hold, to withhold, and to exclude.[14] Understanding property wholly in terms of exchange value delimits the use of property to the domain of economic life, leaving little sense of how property might be central, let alone relevant, to a public or political life. Understood as a principle of exclusion, as that which separates and protects individuals from one another, private property may be seen to thwart rather than to enable common action and therefore to be inimical to the social coalition integral to the practices of democratic politics. Property is political, by the lights of this paradigm, insofar as it secures the separateness of members of a political community, and insofar as it secures within a polity the withdrawal of its members from their collectivity.

Contrasting democracy to the traditions of aristocratic patronage, Alexis de Tocqueville associates the rise of this sort of property *with* democracy. In democracies, he claims, people spend more time and energy meeting their private interests. They become ambitious for material wealth and economic prosperity rather than for honor and heroic virtue. Ties between individuals erode and this gives rise to individualism, egoism, and, ultimately, to the withdrawal from political life.[15] It may be true that democratic conditions, such as, for example, democracy's guarantee of individual rights, make possible the rise of this sort of property. At the same time, democratic politics itself seems to depend on a different practice of property. I turn next to accounts which treat property not only as a matter of exchange value but also as an activity of use.

THE USE OF PROPERTY

Dissenting in *Lucas*, Justice Blackmun claims that the majority understands property incorrectly when they say that the *BMA* renders Lucas's lot valueless. It is true that Lucas may not build residentially on his lots but he can still do other things, like "picnic, swim, camp in a tent, or live on the property in a movable trailer."[16] The regulation may render Lucas's land less valuable in terms of what it can get on the market but, Blackmun insists, property must be understood not just in terms of its exchange value but in terms of its use-value as well. Blackmun also rejects the idea that property use should be treated solely as a private relation between individuals. Private property does not only set up boundaries of exclusion between individuals or act only as a guardian against governmental action. Because its use necessarily has what some legal scholars have called "spillover effects," private property engages individuals in activities which connect them with other members of a public at large.[17] Blackmun's opinion suggests that property use simultaneously affects individual private interests and the interests of a community as a whole.

If, on the economic conception, property is a moat, carving out a private sphere in which one can do with it what one wills, implicit in Blackmun's approach is the idea that property also operates as a bridge. A table may physically separate those who sit around it, but, as Hannah Arendt pointed out, it also gathers those around it to chat or share a meal.[18] Good fences make good neighbors not just because fences separate neighbors but also because they connect them to one another. Like the table, or like any border—national or neighborly—property works simultaneously to separate and to relate people. Property may individuate, privatize and exclude, but it also underscores our potential mutuality by engaging us in interdependent activities of use.

From Blackmun's opinion also emerges the idea that there can and should be public good limits on private property use. For Blackmun, the job of delineating and enforcing these limits belongs not only to the private law of property and nuisance but to the legislature since only it can properly protect the welfare of the polity as a whole. The legislature's role is as much educative as it is protective. Part of its job is to teach citizens that along with the rights associated with property ownership come correlative duties— duties in regard to property use—which belong to the practice of citizenship. Although Blackmun does not speak in precisely this way, by giving the legislature an educative role he implies that the duties associated with property ownership and use are as much internal to the practice of property as they are to be imposed on property users by coercive rules and regulations. In this way, Blackmun's dissenting opinion orients inquiry away from property only as a matter of right to the duties associated with property as well, and away from property's fungibility to property as an activity of use bound with citizenship.

Advocates of personality theories of property—both contemporary and historical—make much of these ideas, arguing that private property, through its use, is necessary for developing moral personality, for developing character relating to individual choice and freedom, and, most especially, for cultivating the virtues of good citizenship.[19] Personality theorists tend, however, to subordinate the use-value of property to the virtue of personality, reducing the activity of use to, as Jeremy Waldron puts it, following Hegel, "the wilful satisfaction of material need."[20] In so doing, they tend to underemphasize, as do the economic analysts, the more public or political aspects of the activity of use. Thomas Jefferson's and James Madison's remarks on property make more of property's public or political aspects. Notwithstanding important differences between them, both Jefferson and Madison take property to be bound to good citizenship via its use.

JEFFERSON ON THE PUBLIC GOOD OF PROPERTY

In a letter to Madison, written on September 6, 1789, Jefferson claims: "the earth belongs . . . to the living." Society as a whole, he says, makes rules for the appropriation of its lands. Private property is a social creation, a product of these laws, and it is subject to redefinition by each generation. It is up to the present generation, this suggests, to do with the earth as it wills. As Jefferson puts it, "the dead have neither powers nor rights over it."[21] The dead may have no power or rights over the earth, which is to say, no obligations *to the past* constrain the present generation, but it is not the case that the living have no obligations at all. Specifically their obligation, as it was the obligation of the generation before them, is not to adversely affect future generations. Jefferson makes this point by criticizing future debts. And he makes it also through the idea of the usufruct.

Although this point is infrequently discussed, Jefferson says that "the earth belongs *in usufruct* to the living."[22] Usufruct, derived from Roman law and still in effect in civil law jurisdictions today, works like the legal device of a trust. It gives the beneficiaries of the trust the right to draw from the trust's capital "all the profit, utility and advantage which it may produce." And it attaches to this right an obligation: that the beneficiaries must hand the trust over to the next set of trustees "without altering the substance of the thing."[23] In Jefferson's example, each generation must receive the earth as free of debts and encumbrances as possible *and* they are obligated to pass it on in that way. The earth, in other words, is held by each generation in trust for the common use of the individual members of society at the time and for future generations. This is a public trust that is determined by the polity as a whole and safeguarded by the positive laws of the legislature, reviewed, as Jefferson would have it, every nineteen years.

In language that foreshadows Blackmun, Jefferson insists that duties correlate with rights in the matter of property use, and that private property rights, properly understood, are governed with a view to the common good of the polity as a whole. Jefferson demonstrates his commitment to property's proper use in other writings as well. In an 1813 letter to John Adams, for example, he insists on the necessity of property for good citizenship even as he rejects an aristocracy of wealth in favor of one based on natural talents and virtue.[24] By the lights of the economic paradigm, Jefferson's distinction has a paradoxical quality: how can he be for property but against wealth? One way to make sense of the difference is by way of the threefold typology Jefferson introduces in his *Notes on the State of Virginia* and elsewhere that distinguishes among feudal, agrarian, and commercial property arrangements.[25] With feudal property and commercial wealth, Jefferson associates corruption and unfreedom. Feudalism, he maintains, cultivates dependence and servility since users of property do not own the property they use. Since commerce allows for and encourages the accumulation of wealth unlimited by use, this sort of property gives rise to privilege and hierarchy. Commercial wealth, Jefferson insists, creates a society in which a corrupt few—namely, the manufacturers—have a monopoly of economic and political power.[26] Agrarian property-holders, by contrast, are "the most precious part of the state," as he puts it in a letter to Madison.[27] Their property, via its use, anchors their independence and freedom, and it allows them to cultivate the virtues necessary for self-governance, good citizenship, and the pursuit of the common good.[28] What exactly is the connection between property and virtue? Jefferson does not say. But his remarks leave us with a sense of the distinctive role of use and of the importance of the duties associated with proper use both for the cultivation of individual virtue and for the pursuit of the public good.

Jefferson also leaves us with the following questions: how to square his celebration of the virtues conducive toward *self*-governance that he associates with agrarian property, with the exclusively external public good limits on private use he offers in his "earth belongs to the living" proposal? If, as that proposal suggests, private property rights are entirely determined by society as a whole, indeed if society as a whole holds the property of the earth in common ownership, what is to safeguard the rights of particular individuals? Safeguarding individual property rights was precisely Justice Scalia's worry in *Lucas*. It is also James Madison's.

MADISON ON PROPERTY AND PRIVATE RIGHT

Madison rejects Jefferson's claim that private property is a product of positive laws, merely a social creation. Treating property instead as a pre-political right, he underscores property's connection to individual liberty and identity. In an article called "Property" that appeared in the *National Gazette* in 1792,

Madison writes about property in two senses. There is property in the narrow sense which includes merchandise, money, and land. And there is property in a second, broader, and, in his word, "juster" sense which includes a person's opinions and faculties, his labor, leisure and time, and his liberty of conscience.[29] Property in this broader sense embodies and represents who we are as well as what we own. In Madison's view, these two senses of property depend on one another. Private property must be protected not only because of its economic value but also because it is somehow constitutive of civic identity. Where property in the broad sense is protected, Madison argues, the means for acquiring property in the narrow sense must be protected as well. The inequalities such protection produces may be a source of political conflict, indeed, in Madison's words "the most durable and common source" of conflict.[30] But, as Madison explains in *Federalist 10*, the effects of these inequalities can only be controlled; they cannot be eradicated since to do so would be an utter abrogation of freedom.[31]

Note that, at least in its broad sense, Madisonian property involves activity, specifically the activity of use. It is using one's faculties that connects property in the narrow sense to individual liberty. And, insofar as the use of one's faculties relates individual owners to society at large, there is, through the activity of use, a public aspect to Madisonian property as well.[32] It is, arguably, this understanding of property that Madison wrote into the Fifth Amendment, one that looks quite different from Scalia's. The right of property, on this reading, is private, and, because the right is exercised through its use and has a public or political component, it is governed by public good considerations as well. For Madison, as for Jefferson and for Blackmun, property, through its use, defines our freedom *and* our obligations.

Both Madison and Jefferson suggest that proper property use is bound to the virtues necessary for good citizenship, but neither explains exactly what the relation between the two might be. From Jefferson, we get a robust conception of the duties of citizenship and of the public good limits on private property. From Madison, we get a robust conception of the rights of citizenship and of the private right limits on the public good. I turn next to Aristotle to explore more deeply the relation between property and virtue, and, through it, to bring together Jefferson's primary commitment to the public good of property with Madison's commitment to property as primarily a matter of private right.[33]

THE VIRTUE OF PROPERTY

Aristotle spends most of the first two books of the *Politics* discussing property arrangements in different venues: in the home, among friends and neighbors, in existing polities, and under his preferred constitutions. He argues that property in all these venues should be "in a certain sense common, but as a rule private" (*Pol.* 1263a25, 40).[34] Most readers treat this as an endorsement of private property as the economic paradigm understands it.[35] But a literal translation from the Greek suggests otherwise. Aristotle advocates *idias ktēsis, chrēsis koinas,* "holding things as one's own for common use" (*Pol.* 1263a25, 40).

Some of the arguments Aristotle offers in defense of this mode of owning—specially those he levels against systems of collective ownership—resonate with our contemporary economic ones. Echoing what economists call the tragedy of the commons, Aristotle argues in favor of holding land privately on the ground that people will care less about land that is shared, allowing it to go to waste (*Pol.* 1263a25–27). Yet Aristotle rejects the reduction of property to mere fungible items of exchange. In language we might find in Jefferson's writings, Aristotle decries as improper and corrupting modes of exchange he calls retail trade (and Jefferson calls manufacturing), modes of use he calls barbarian which require use without actual ownership (what Jefferson calls feudalism), and modes of owning which allow for acquiring and accumulating (or holding) without use.[36] In language we might find in Madison's "Property" essay, Aristotle insists that property is bound to individual identity.

What is it to "hold as one's own for common use"? Aristotle offers the following examples: we use properly things like clothes and food when we take them in the home for immediate use (*Pol.* 1257a7–14); we use properly things like land and crops when we hold them as our own and give them over to our neighbors to use when they need provisions on a journey (*Pol.* 1263a37); and we use properly things like political offices when we hold them as our own to the common good of all the citizens of a polity, in the manner of stewardship (*Pol.* 1279a29–33, 1309b7). As these examples indicate, there are substantial continuities between the so-called private practices of the home (the *oikos* in the Greek, the root of our word, "economy") and the practices of social and political life (*Pol.* 1260b14–20).[37] Property in all venues and in all its myriad forms is held as one's own for use. With the transition from household to polity, individual and immediate use becomes a using with others, which is to say, common use. Property, this suggests, is both private and inherently political or public. Aristotle's commitment to this dual capacity of property may be seen throughout the *Politics:* from the central role he accords property in enabling the polity to be a unity of the different (against Plato's defense of common property among the guardian class) (*Pol.* II.2, 3, 5); to his claim that a well-ordered polity should have common meals open to all citizens (*Pol.* 1330a3–5); to his recommendation that in a good polity land should be divided into two parts—one public, the other private—and that each citizen should have lots in each part for reasons of justice and fairness, and to inspire concord among citizens in case of border wars (*Pol.* 1330a11–20).

Property's apparently paradoxical quality—its capacity to integrate private and public—can be explained and, more importantly, preserved, by the relation I take Aristotle to develop between property and virtue. Put briefly, it is by treating property as a site of the practice of virtue that we can, I believe, make sense of property's capacious duality. Virtue, Aristotle says, is a matter of acting well, of using what one has; for, however good his dispositions may be, man does not demonstrate virtue if he does not act well, and only by acting well can he come to have a good disposition in the first place (*NE* 1103b23). In Aristotle's words:

> Of virtue (*aretē*) there is the activity (*energeia*) according to it. But it makes no small difference whether we place the chief good in holding (*ktēsis*) or in using (*chrēsis*), in habit (*hexis*) or in activity (*energeia*). For habit takes it in itself not to bring a good to completion, even when the habit lies there as a ruling principle (*archē*). But activity (*energeia*) not so; for the activity (*energeia*) will of necessity be acting (*praxis*) and acting well (*praxis*). (*NE* 1098b31–1099a4)[38]

Were habit alone taken to be the mark of virtue then virtue would simply be a matter of having certain capacities. It would not matter whether these capacities were ever used in action. If good habit alone does not amount to virtue, neither does action by itself. Actual deeds may or may not be evidence of the doer's character (*Rhet.* 1367b32), but it is impossible to act well without having the appropriate habits (*NE* 1103b24). Indeed, were action alone to be the mark of virtue, then no one could ever be said to have skill or anything like a capacity. If a person does something but does not do it out of the appropriate habit or disposition, he may be acting in conformity with some principle or other, but the action is not freely his own. A stable disposition to act well is thus necessary for acting well to be preferred; acting well and preferring good acts both depend on good habit.[39] Habits change out of action and actions change with changes in habit. Habit is, then, a formation of one's possibilities out of one's past actions, such that one "has" it in oneself to act a certain way:

> [W]e become just by doing just actions, and temperate by doing temperate actions and brave by brave actions . . . and in a word, habits are formed out of activity (*energeia*) in like ways. (*NE* 1103b15–21)

Action seizes upon a possibility opened up by habit. Acting justly, temperately, bravely, in short, acting well, depends on properly discriminating what needs to be done—good judgment—and such discrimination depends on being properly habituated. There is, then, a reciprocal and dynamic relation between the elements that co-constitute virtue: acting well depends on good habits and good habits are formed by acting well. I become brave by acting bravely. And I act bravely only insofar as I am in the habit of so acting.

The language Aristotle uses in his discussion of virtue is striking: He speaks of habit as a kind of holding or possession and action as a mode of use. He speaks of virtue, in other words, in terms of property. And he does so in two ways at once. There is, on the one hand, an analogy between property and virtue: just as virtue calls not for action alone but rather for action out of the appropriate habit, so too does owning properly call not for using alone but for use out of proper holding; and just as good habits emerge from acting well, so too does holding well depend on proper use. Like habit and action, then, holding and using belong together by way of a reciprocal and dynamic relationship.[40] At the same time, in Aristotle's definition of virtue, the words connoting property, "holding" and "using," and the words signifying virtue, "habit" and "action," stand in for one another: "[I]t makes no small difference whether we place the chief good in holding (ktēsis), or in using (chrēsis), in habit (hexis), or in activity (energeia)" (NE 1098b31–33). This suggests that habit is a kind of holding and that holding is a matter of habit. It also suggests that action is a mode of use and that using is a matter of action, ideas we have already seen in the writings of Madison, Jefferson, and Blackmun.

Putting these points together, we can see that good habit, as a matter of holding properly, depends on using properly what is held, that is, acting well. And we can see that acting well, as a mode of proper use, depends on holding properly what one has as one's own, hence ownership.[41] As the practice of holding and using things properly, property, like any activity, already calls for good habit conjoined with acting well, that is, virtue. And, as the practice of holding and using habits properly, virtue calls for property. It is by understanding property as a verb and not strictly as a noun, as an activity of use and not strictly as a fungible thing, that property is bound to, is indeed a site of, virtue. And it is by understanding virtue as a verb and not strictly as a noun, as an activity and not strictly as a thing, that virtue is a kind of property.

Property, on this reading, is both an external good and a characterological good or a good of the soul. Aristotle, however, appears to distinguish these categories of goods (Pol. VII.1, NE I.8). Identifying the end of a good life—eudaimonia—with virtuous activity of the soul, he claims, for this reason, that it falls among the goods of the soul and not among external goods (NE 1098b18–20). Apparently limiting the goods of the soul to the virtues of intellect and character, he cites as external goods, by contrast, good children, fine birth, and beauty, as well as wealth, political power, and friends (*NE* 1099a31–b6). That property is properly categorized as an external good is evident in Aristotle's definition of wealth as that which

> consists in an abundance of coin and land; the possession of agricultural land and the possession of moveables, cattle and slaves, distinguished in number, magnitude and beauty. And these are all owned (*oikeia*), secure, free, and useful. (*Rhet.* 1361a13–16)

Wealth is the abundance of what is owned for use. Therefore, commentators conclude, it is an instrumental external good.[42]

A few sentences later, however, Aristotle summarizes his account of wealth as follows:

> All in all, wealth consists in using things rather than having acquired them. It is really the activity (*energeia*) of using things that constitutes wealth. (*Rhet.* 1361a24–25)

Wealth, this means, is not only what is owned for use. It is also the activity of use itself. Plato insists on this understanding of wealth as well in the *Euthydemus*, the dialogue that Aristotle cites when he distinguishes among kinds of goods (*NE* I.8). Speaking about the good of wealth, Socrates asks whether we should be happy by the presence of good things. We would, he says, but only if they benefited us. Would they benefit us if we only had them but did not use them? No. Happiness requires not only possessing good things but also using them. And, not just using them any old way, Socrates adds, but rather using them rightly (*Euthydemus* 280a–e). Benefiting, literally "bringing goodness," involves virtue, for a thing can benefit an owner only if the owner excels at its proper use. Socrates concludes that property brings *eudaimonia* by way of proper use, that is, virtuous activity. Aristotle says the same. To distinguish categorically instrumental from intrinsic goods or external from characterological goods, this suggests, is to miss Aristotle's fundamental point that, at least in the case of the good of wealth, property is as much a practice or an activity as it is a tool or instrument and, more specifically, that properly practiced, property calls for virtuous activity of the soul.

Aristotle's account of liberality and its excess—prodigality—underscores this relation between external and characterological goods. Aristotle defines prodigality as ruining oneself by "wasting one's substance" (*NE* 1120a1). Wasting one's substance is not simply recklessly giving away too many things to the wrong people, for the wrong reasons, and at the wrong times, although it is that too. One's "substance" (*ousia*), derived from the verb "to be" (*einai*), is, at the same time, that by virtue of which somebody "is" a somebody. Wasting one's substance is, in this sense, "losing oneself" (*NE* 1120a3–4). One has as one's substance what one holds as one's own for use. And one "has" as one's substance one's habits, and these constitute who one is. What is owned for proper use—things or habits—is what is "proper to one" (*ta oikeia*). As what is owned for use in both senses, property brings "well-being" (*eudaimonia*) through use or well-doing. Aristotle may distinguish external goods from goods of the soul but, in so doing, he marks not only their difference but the degree of their interrelation.

Like Madison, then, Aristotle insists upon two senses of property and he too thinks they depend on one another. Property, in the narrow sense, is the stuff of the home, and also land, crops, and, perhaps strangest to modern ears, political offices. It is what one holds for immediate use and for use with other members of a polity. There is also the property that one holds as one's own for use in a more basic sense: the habits which constitute who one is. Habit, we saw, is the formation of one's possibilities out of one's past actions, such that one "has" it in oneself to act a certain way. If what is proper to one is who one is, and what is proper to one is property, then, in this sense, what one has is who one is. One has as one's own what one holds as one's own for use whether this is property in the narrow sense, or the habits, faculties, talents, and opinions that constitute who one is and relate one, through their use, to others.

Virtue, on this reading, is not mapped onto property relations from the outside but rather emerges within the practice of property. It emerges in the presence of a proper ordering of the soul, even as the practice contributes to that proper ordering. Read with a view to the double or bi-directional sense of the word "of," this is the "virtue of property." This connection between property and virtue allows us to make more explicit than did Jefferson why property conduces, through its proper use, to the public good. It also allows us to make more explicit than did Madison how the activity of proper use, in virtue of its dependence on proper holding, requires a defense of private right. Finally, it allows us to see the necessary connection between the public good and private right of property. It is insofar as property is a matter of possession and use, of good habits and acting well, that it is a site of the cultivation of the individual virtues associated with *both* self-governance and the pursuit of the common good. By providing an account of property which, through its relation to virtue, links inextricably and in a reciprocal and dynamic way private holding with common use, Aristotle bridges the tensions between public good and private right left unresolved by Jefferson and Madison.

Conclusion

What is democratic about this account of Aristotelian property? Even the proper practice of Aristotelian property, it could be argued, will have the effect of institutionalizing disparities among those with a lot of property, those with less, and those without any at all. Even if property is reconceived as the power to hold things for use with others, this power may still be withheld. And even if things held for use are given away, property may simply reinscribe social hierarchies by producing patronage relations.[43] The problem with private property—in its Aristotelian or in its contemporary economic version—is that it establishes and safeguards social inequalities inimical to democratic politics. Aristotle, indeed, explicitly criticizes the leveling effects of equality, defending instead a property qualification for citizenship and celebrating differential property ownership among citizens as characteristic of a well-constituted polity (*Pol.* 1266a39–b33).

While it is true that wealth in Athens afforded citizens the opportunity for self-display, increased their public profiles, and bolstered their political power, displays of wealth were also public services which occasioned the practice of large-scale community patronage.[44] And, while it is true that Aristotle argues against the kind of property equalization advocated in Phaleas' constitution, for example, he also insists that "by friendly consent there should be common use of property and that no citizen should be in want of subsistence" (*Pol.* 1330a1–3). Aristotle objects to property equalization, I think, for the same reason many present-day liberal-democratic theorists do, namely, because it treats everyone as equals without regard to their distinction.[45] This is most productively read not as a rejection of democracy in the name of inequality, but as an argument against a particular kind of democracy, specifically a democracy associated with strict, or, to use Aristotle's term, arithmetic equality.

Arithmetic equality abstracts from all particularity that might distinguish persons from one another. It is the kind of equality Aristotle associates with the corrective principle in transactions where

> [i]t makes no difference whether a good man has defrauded a bad man or a bad one a good one, nor whether it is a good or a bad man that has committed adultery; the law looks only at the nature of the damage, treating the parties as equal, and merely asking whether one has done and the other suffered an injustice, whether one has inflicted and the other sustained damage. (*NE* 1132a2–7)

In corrective justice, equality is numerical, which is to say, it is the mean between greater and lesser (*Pol.* 1301b30). Aristotle disfavors this sort of

equality not only as a way of determining the proper distribution of property in a polity, but as the criterion for the just distribution of any goods in
a polity, including power. Democracies based on this sort of equality may
have *some* element of justice, he says, but, taking numerical equality to be
wholly determinative, they take equality on the basis of freedom to mean
that citizens are entirely equal. In so doing, they "strip away the qualifications of the persons concerned and judge badly" (*Pol.* 1280a9–11). One
might argue that Aristotle rejects democracies ruled by decrees for much
the same reason. Decrees, determined by aggregating the votes of citizens who
are individuated and equated on numerical grounds alone, do not respect
qualitative or, in Aristotle's words, proportional or geometric individuation.

In order to be just, distributions of power, property, and other goods
must both recognize differences among people *and* compare those differences under a common measure. As Aristotle puts it: "For persons who are
equal the shares must be equal. For those who are unequal the shares must
be unequal" (*Pol.* 1282b20–21). In other words, just distributions (and well-
ordered polities more generally) must accommodate both equality and distinction.[46] Aristotle, this suggests, rejects equalization of property for the
same reason Madison and, indeed, Jefferson did: namely, because it levels
differences that come about through the exercise of diverse habits, talents,
and faculties or, in Jefferson's words, "natural affections of the mind."[47]
Stripping away the qualifications of the persons concerned, strict equalization neglects differences that reflect and produce individuality.

Assuming that the best form of democracy is committed to an equality
hospitable to individual distinction or plurality, let me conclude by un-
derscoring the ways in which the connections Aristotelian property has to
individual distinction or virtue also mark its democratic, indeed its liberal-
democratic, promise. Like Scalia's account of property, Aristotelian property individuates and distinguishes. But as the site of proper and common
use, it also integrates members of a polity into webs of interaction. Insofar
as it depends on ethical habituation and also on integrated human activity,
Aristotelian property reflects liberal democracy's dual commitment to individuation and collective action. Dependent upon the self-generated good
will of those who hold and use, acting within the constraints set by the idea
that property is a public trust, Aristotelian property models liberal democracy's dual commitment to freedom and responsibility. As a practice which
produces reciprocal obligations among members of a polity, Aristotelian
property ensures the accountability of members of a polity to one another
through their activity. Linking individual holding to common use, Aristotelian property integrates private right and public good. Liberal-democratic
politics calls for individuation, initiative, autonomous action, as well as
membership, a recognition of interdependence, acting well with others.

Aristotelian property calls for holding things as one's own, being an owner, hence individuation, as well as use together, hence, collective activity. Treating property as a site of virtue reveals property's liberal-democratic potential by disclosing the ways in which the practice of property, bound as it is to the habits and actions of political agents, can produce a self-governing collectivity that preserves individual distinction.

NOTES

For their contributions to this essay, my thanks go to Amittai Aviram, Keith Bybee, Peter Euben, Larry Glickman, Gerald Mara, Sara Monoson, Arlene Saxonhouse, Aristide Tessitore, and to participants at the 1997 Annual Meeting of the American Political Science Association, to members of the Philosophy Department at the University of Alberta, Edmonton, and to participants in the Walker Institute Faculty Research Seminar Series at the University of South Carolina, Columbia, where earlier versions of this essay were presented. I am especially grateful to the University of South Carolina's generous support in the form of a CLASS award.

1. Although not, of course, about what its proper distribution ought to be.

2. Robert Putnam, *Making Democracy Work: Civic Traditions in Modern Italy* (Princeton, N.J.: Princeton University Press, 1993). See also John Dunn, "Trust and Political Agency," in *Interpreting Political Responsibility: Essays 1981–1989* (Princeton, N.J.: Princeton University Press, 1990), 26–44; John Dunn, "Trust," in *The History of Political Theory and Other Essays* (Cambridge: Cambridge University Press, 1996), 91–99; Barbara Misztal, *Trust in Modern Societies* (Cambridge: Polity Press, 1996). For an account of trust more concerned with prosperity than with democracy, see Francis Fukuyama, *Trust: The Social Virtues and the Making of Prosperity* (New York: Free Press, 1995).

3. The omission of any discussion of private property is especially surprising in the case of Dunn, "Trust and Political Agency," at pp. 34–41, who locates the source of his account of trust in the writings of John Locke. An exception is Richard Rose, "Postcommunism and the Problem of Trust," in *The Global Resurgence of Democracy,* 2nd ed., ed. Larry Diamond and Marc F. Plattner (Baltimore: Johns Hopkins University Press, 1996), 251–63.

4. For works that address the role as well as the dangers of private property, see David Stark and Laszlo Bruszt, *Postsocialist Pathways: Transforming Politics and Property in East Central Europe* (Cambridge: Cambridge University Press, 1998); M. Steven Fish, "Russia's Fourth Transition," in *The Global Resurgence of Democracy,* 2nd ed., ed. Larry Diamond and Marc F. Plattner (Baltimore: Johns Hopkins University Press, 1996), 264–75; Clauss Offe, "Capitalism by Democratic Design? Democratic Theory Facing the Triple Transition in East Central Europe," *Social Research* 58 (1991): 865–92, esp. at pp. 874–81. See also Cass Sunstein, "On Property and Constitutionalism," *Cardozo Law Review* 14 (1993): 907–35.

5. I put property in quotation marks because there is no word for property, as we know it, in Greek. That said, I will drop the quotation marks for the rest of this essay. Aristotle's writings on property are too often overlooked by political theorists. There are two exceptions: Fred D. Miller, *Nature, Justice, and Rights in Aristotle's Politics* (Oxford: Clarendon Press, 1995), ch. 9; and Robert Mayhew, "Aristotle on Property," *Review of Metaphysics* 46 (1993): 803–31.

6. *Lucas* v. *South Carolina Coastal Council,* 112 S. Ct. 2886 (1992).

7. *Lucas,* p. 2900. Again, at p. 2900: "A law or decree . . . must . . . do no more than duplicate the result that could have been achieved in the courts—by adjacent land owners (or other uniquely affected persons) under the State's law of private nuisance, or by the State under its complementary power to abate nuisances that affect the public generally, or otherwise." As Richard Epstein points out, Scalia "gives a narrow reading to the term 'otherwise.'" See "*Lucas v. South Carolina Coastal Council:* A Web of Tangled Expectations," *Stanford Law Review* 45 (1993): 1369–93, at p. 1379 n.39.

8. For helpful discussion of Scalia's treatment of what he calls the "background principles of nuisance and property law" (*Lucas,* p. 2901), see Joseph Sax, "Property Rights and the Economy of Nature: Understanding *Lucas v. South Carolina Coastal Council,*" *Stanford Law Review* 45 (1993): 1433–55, at pp. 1440–42.

9. A case recently heard by the U.S. Supreme Court restricts even further the possibilities for regulating property in the name of a common good, arguing that "because waterfront owners in Rhode Island historically enjoyed the right to fill wetlands on their property without governmental regulation, the state could not curb that freedom today, *even for landowners who acquired the land with knowledge of the regulations,* without paying compensation for a taking" [my emphasis]. See *Palazzolo* v. *Rhode Island,* No. 99–2047, discussed by Linda Greenhouse, "Supreme Court Roundup: Justices Press for Clarity in a Property Rights Dispute," *New York Times,* February 27, 2001, p. A18.

10. *Lucas,* p. 2893. Although Scalia notes (p. 2894 n.7) that "the rhetorical force of [that rule] is greater than its precision . . . ."

11. S. 605, 104th Congress, 2d Session, March 1, 1996. For a discussion of this legislation, along with state legislation geared to protect property owners "without regard to the public interest," see Joseph Singer, *Entitlement: The Paradoxes of Property* (New Haven, Conn.: Yale University Press, 2000), 2.

12. Lawrence C. Becker, *Property Rights: Philosophic Foundations* (London: Routledge & Kegan Paul, 1977), ch. 2; Robert Cooter and T. Ulen, *Economic Analysis of Law* (Ill.: Scott, Foresman, 1988); Harold Demsetz, "Toward a Theory of Property Rights," *American Economic Review, Proceedings and Papers* 57 (1967): 347–59; and Richard A. Posner, *Economic Analysis of Law* (Boston: Little, Brown, 1986).

13. Demsetz, "Toward a Theory of Property Rights," 351–53.

14. Excludability is a feature shared by other noneconomic accounts of property too. See Stephen R. Munzer, *A Theory of Property* (Cambridge: Cambridge University Press, 1990), 89; Jeremy Waldron, *The Right to Private Property* (Oxford: Clarendon Press, 1988), 5–12; Robert Nozick, *Anarchy, State and Utopia* (New York: Basic Books, 1974), 171.

15. Alexis de Tocqueville, *Democracy in America,* trans. George Lawrence (New York: HarperPerennial, 1988), Vol. II, Part IV, ch. 6, pp. 690–95.

16. *Lucas*, p. 2909.

17. *Lucas*, pp. 2910–11. I take the phrase "spillover effects" from Joseph Sax, "Takings, Private Property and Public Rights," *Yale Law Review* 81 (1971): 149–86, at p. 154.

18. Hannah Arendt, *The Human Condition* (Chicago: University of Chicago Press, 1958), 52.

19. See Waldron, *Right to Private Property*; Margaret Jane Radin, "Property and Personhood," *Stanford Law Review* 34 (1982): 957–1015; Peter Stillman, "Hegel's Analysis of Property in the *Philosophy of Right*," *Cardozo Law Review* 10 (1989): 1031–72.

20. Waldron, *Right to Private Property*, 366.

21. Thomas Jefferson, Letter to James Madison (September 6, 1789), in *The Republic of Letters*, vol. I, ed. James Morton Smith (New York: Norton, 1995), 631–36.

22. For a very helpful discussion of the place of property in early American republican politics generally and of Jefferson's position in particular, see Gregory S. Alexander, "Time and Property in the American Republican Legal Culture," *New York University Law Review* 66 (1991): 273–352, esp. at pp. 282–83.

23. *Black's Law Dictionary*, 5th ed. (St. Paul, Minn.: West, 1979), citing *Civ. Code La*. Art. 533.

24. Thomas Jefferson, Letter to John Adams (October 28, 1813) in *The Papers of Thomas Jefferson*, ed. J. Boyd (Princeton, N.J.: Princeton University Press, 1958).

25. Thomas Jefferson, *Notes on the State of Virginia*, ed. W. Peden (Chapel Hill, N.C.: University of North Carolina Press, 1955), Query 19, pp. 164–65 for a discussion of the differences between agrarian and commercial property; and Thomas Jefferson, "A Summary View of the Rights of British America" (1774) in *The Papers of Thomas Jefferson*, vol. 1, ed. J. Boyd (Princeton, N.J.: Princeton University Press, 1958), 121ff., for Jefferson's criticisms of feudal property.

26. Thomas Jefferson, Letter to John Jay (August 23, 1785) in *The Papers of Thomas Jefferson*, vol. 8, ed. J. Boyd (Princeton, N.J.: Princeton University Press, 1958), 426.

27. Thomas Jefferson, Letter to James Madison (October 28, 1785) in *The Papers of Thomas Jefferson*, vol. 8, ed. J. Boyd (Princeton, N.J.: Princeton University Press, 1958), 681–82.

28. Jefferson's idea here is that property gives a stake in community. Our contemporary policies demonstrate the continued relevance of this idea: encouraging locally owned businesses in urban centers; allocating actual ownership rights—not just rental benefits—in public housing; tax breaks for homeowners.

29. James Madison, "Property," *National Gazette*, March 29, 1792 in *The Writings of James Madison*, vol. 6, ed. G. Hunt (New York: G. P. Putnam's Sons, 1906), 101.

30. *The Federalist Papers*, No. 10, ed. Clinton Rossiter (New York: Penguin, 1961), 79.

31. Ibid., 78.

32. For a similar conclusion about Madison, see Alexander, "Time and Property in the American Republican Legal Culture," 331–32; and Laura Underkuffler, "On Property: An Essay," *Yale Law Journal* 100 (1990): 127–48, esp. at pp. 133–37.

33. Though Aristotle would not recognize rights as an organizing principle of politics. See, for discussion, Leo Strauss, *Natural Right and History* (Chicago:

University of Chicago Press, 1953), 182–83; Alasdair MacIntyre, *After Virtue* (Notre Dame, Ind.: University of Notre Dame Press, 1981), 66–67; Richard Kraut, "Are There Natural Rights in Aristotle?" and Malcolm Schofield, "Sharing in the Constitution" both in *The Review of Metaphysics* 49 (1996): 755–74 and 831–58 respectively. For a different view, see Miller, *Nature, Justice, and Rights in Aristotle's Politics,* ch. 4.

34. In what follows, I supplement translations of Aristotle's *Politics* by H. Rackham (Cambridge, Mass.: Harvard University Press, 1977) and Benjamin Jowett, ed. Stephen Everson (New York: Cambridge University Press, 1996) with my own.

35. For example, Richard Schlatter, *Private Property: The History of an Idea* (New York: Russell & Russell, 1951), 16; Waldron, *Right to Private Property,* 6; Becker, *Property Rights,* 62; Munzer, *Theory of Property,* 128–29.

36. *Politics* Book I, chs. 9–10; Book II, ch. 5.

37. *Contra* Hannah Arendt, *The Human Condition,* ch. 2. For discussion of the relation between private and public in fourth-century Athens, see David Cohen, *Law, Sexuality, and Society: The Enforcement of Morals in Classical Athens* (Cambridge: Cambridge University Press, 1991), ch. 4. For the "political economy of the ancient household," see William James Booth, *Households: On the Moral Architecture of the Economy* (Ithaca, N.Y.: Cornell University Press, 1993), ch. 2.

38. I supplement translations of Aristotle's *Nicomachean Ethics* by H. Rackham (Cambridge, Mass.: Harvard University Press, 1982), and David Ross, revised by J. L. Ackrill and J. O. Urmson (Oxford: Oxford University Press, 1980) with my own.

39. See, for discussion of *hexis,* Stephen G. Salkever, *Finding the Mean: Theory and Practice in Aristotle's Political Philosophy* (Princeton, N.J.: Princeton University Press, 1990), 79–81.

40. *Pace* John Hare, "*Eleutheriotes* in Aristotle's *Ethics,*" *Ancient Philosophy* 8 (1988): 19–32, esp. at pp. 20–25, who claims that liberality, the virtue of property, actually signifies two different virtues—"good stewardship" (proper holding) and "generosity" (proper use)—which are in tension with one another.

41. This insight is at the heart of Aristotle's rejection, in Book II of the *Politics,* of common ownership. It explains why the argument of Terence Irwin, "Generosity and Property in Aristotle's *Politics,*" *Social Philosophy and Policy* 4 (1987): 37–54 that the virtue of liberality can be exercised in the absence of private ownership is wrong.

42. For the distinction between external goods that are instrumental to happiness and those that are intrinsic, see Martha Nussbaum, *The Fragility of Goodness* (Cambridge: Cambridge University Press, 1986), 327–28; Nancy Sherman, *The Fabric of Character* (Oxford: Clarendon Press, 1989), 125–26; and John Cooper, "Aristotle on the Goods of Fortune," *Philosophical Review* 94 (1985): 173–97.

43. Paul Veyne, *Bread and Circuses* (London: Butler and Tanner, 1980), 70ff.

44. Moses I. Finley, *Politics in the Ancient World* (Cambridge: Cambridge University Press, 1983), 35ff., and Sitta von Reden, *Exchange in Ancient Greece* (London: Duckworth, 1995), 74.

45. Most liberal-democrats do not argue for strict egalitarianism and the reasons they give often resonate powerfully with those of Aristotle: see, for example, John Rawls, *A Theory of Justice* (Cambridge, Mass.: Harvard University Press, 1971);

Ronald Dworkin, "What is Equality? Part 2: Equality of Resources" *Philosophy and Public Affairs* 10 (1981): 283–345; and George Kateb, "Democratic Individuality and the Claims of Politics," *Political Theory* 12 (1984): 331–60.

46. See Jill Frank, "Democracy and Distribution: Aristotle on Just Desert" *Political Theory* 26 (1998): 784–802.

47. Thomas Jefferson, Letter to James Madison (October 28, 1785) in *The Papers of Thomas Jefferson,* vol. 8, ed. J. Boyd (Princeton, N.J.: Princeton University Press, 1958), 681–82.

CHAPTER NINE

Aristotelianism, Commerce, and the Liberal Order

DOUGLAS J. DEN UYL &
DOUGLAS B. RASMUSSEN

Aristotelianism has not been philosophically defeated. Indeed, these days, at least in ethics, it has come into something of a revival. The revival does not, however, include many efforts to use Aristotle to ground a classical liberal to libertarian political theory. Rather, to employ somewhat anachronistic modern language, Aristotle has served to support forms of conservatism, moderate welfare statism, and liberalism of a more modern variety.[1] There are undoubtedly a number of reasons why Aristotle appears to be better suited to these political theories than to classical liberalism or libertarianism. We cannot explore all those reasons here. But we suspect that one of the main reasons is his antipathy to commerce, or at least his antipathy to attitudes toward commerce found among a number of classical liberals. Consequently, Aristotelianism and commerce will be the focus of this essay. Aristotelianism seems to us to demand that attention first be given to metaethical and metaphysical issues, but these are topics that cannot be engaged here. We have made some modest efforts to address them elsewhere.[2] We do draw upon our own materials here also, but at the level of social and political theory.[3] We do not accept the view that political philosophy can successfully be divorced from the more fundamental areas of philosophical inquiry, but we do accept the practical realities involved in writing a single essay.

It is not part of our intention to attempt to show that Aristotle somehow *really* was a classical liberal or lover of commerce. What then do we mean when we speak of our "Aristotelian" sympathies? When we use the terms *Aristotelian* or *Aristotelianism* to describe our position or approach to certain issues, it will be primarily in what James Collins called a "recurrent-thematic-classificatory-polemical sense." That is to say, we are making novel use of positions that are clearly inspired by Aristotle, but without necessarily being historically linked with Aristotle or working within Aristotle's framework and method. Thus, our work is more schematic than historical, more argumentatively dictated than based on any independent examination of Aristotle's texts.[4] It is in this sense that we can say on the one hand that we are not out to turn Aristotle into a classical liberal, and on the other hand claim that what we do say is Aristotelian.

THE NATURE OF RIGHTS

Since "rights talk" is at the center of classical liberalism, some discussion of it seems in order. Rights are an ethical concept, but they differ from other ethical concepts. They have a unique function. They are not directly concerned with either achieving the moral good or obtaining right conduct. Rather, rights are *meta-normative* principles; that is to say, they are concerned with establishing a political/legal context that protects the condition for the possibility of self-perfection among others.

The fundamental principles of a polity's legal system must have some normative basis, if it is ultimately to have authority; and so the attempt to make law entirely independent from morality is a mistake. But it is also a mistake to reduce the moral concepts that underlie a polity's legal system to those moral concepts that provide guidance for individuals in the conduct of their daily lives. What, then, is the fundamental difference between normative and meta-normative principles, and how are they connected? An examination of the character of human moral well-being, as conceived by a certain account of neo-Aristotelian ethics,[5] will provide answers to these questions.

Human moral well-being—or as many neo-Aristotelian ethicists call it, "human flourishing"—is concerned with choices that necessarily involve the particular and the contingent. Knowledge of the moral virtues and true human goods may tell all of us what abstractly speaking we ought to do. But in the real world of individual human conduct, where all actions and goods are concrete and where human well-being takes a determinate form, what the moral virtues and human goods involve cannot be determined from the philosopher's armchair. A successful moral life is, by its very nature, something that is highly personal. For example, having a career, an education, a home, friends, and medical care are goods which, when considered from an abstract perspective, are good or appropriate for all human beings. They ought to be created or achieved. Yet, this claim is not too helpful in providing guidance to the individual in a concrete situation. None of these goods exist in an abstract or generic manner. How are they to be created or achieved? What kind of job, education, home, and medical care does one need? Who will be one's friends? To what extent and in what amount are these to be pursued? How is the achievement of one of these goods to be related to the achievement of other goods? What is the proper "balance" or "mix"?

This view of human flourishing could correctly be described as entailing a "moral pluralism" regarding human values. The human good is something real, and it is individualized and diverse. But there is something at the concrete level that is really common to all the various forms of flourishing and indeed must be. It is the essential core of practical wisdom itself, and this essential core has another name—self-direction.[6] The act of exercising reason, of using one's intelligence, is not something automatic. It is something that the individual human being needs to initiate and maintain. Thus, self-direction pertains to the very essence of human flourishing—it is the formal essence—and thus is common to all forms of flourishing, regardless of how diverse.

Self-directedness is, therefore, both a necessary condition for self-perfection and a feature of all self-perfecting acts at whatever level of achievement or specificity. This is another way of saying that the phenomenon of a volitional consciousness[7] is both a necessary condition for, and an operating condition of, the pursuit and achievement of self-perfection. The absence of self-directedness implies the absence of self-perfection, although the presence of self-directedness does not necessarily imply the presence of self-perfection.

None of this, of course, is to say that any choice one makes is as good as the next, but simply that the choice must be one's own and must involve considerations that are unique to the individual. One person's moral well-being cannot be exchanged with another's. The good-for-me is not, and cannot be, the good-for-you. Human moral well-being, then, is something objective, self-directed, and highly personal. It is not abstract, collectively determined, or impersonal.

This last point is crucial because it allows us a way to determine the unique moral function of rights. According to our theory, rights are concerned to protect the condition under which self-perfection can occur among others. Obviously securing the condition for the possibility of self-perfection is logically prior to and distinct from the pursuit of self-perfection directly or even the establishment of contexts promotive of self-perfection. Securing the condition for the possibility of self-perfection must be understood as essentially "negative," if we are correct that self-directedness does not imply or guarantee self-perfection and that one's self-perfection is not exchangeable with another's. In other words, we are not trying with our theory of rights directly and positively to secure self-perfection, but rather to protect, and thus prevent encroachments upon, the condition under which self-perfection can exist. Our aim is thus to protect the possibility of self-perfection, but only through seeking to protect the possibility of self-directedness.

The single most common and threatening encroachment upon self-directedness and consequently self-perfection is the initiation of physical force by one person (or group) against another. We therefore need a principle which will, to borrow a phrase from Robert Nozick, allow "moral space" to each person—a sphere of freedom whereby self-directed activities can be exercised without being trampled by others or vice versa.

The aim of our theory of rights is thus to secure politically and legally the possibility of self-direction. However, why is self-direction taken as the condition to be protected? Are there not many other conditions that are also necessary for the possibility of self-perfection? Why should not securing these conditions be a political and legal concern?

THE NEED FOR A META-NORMATIVE PRINCIPLE OF RIGHTS

The individualized character of human flourishing creates a need for another type of ethical principle, once we realize that human moral well-being is only achieved with and among others. We are social beings, not in the Hobbesian sense of merely needing others to get what we want, because we are powerless on our own, but in the sense that our very maturation as human beings requires others.[8] Indeed, a significant part of our potentialities is other-oriented. If this is true, however, there is a difficulty. If one person's particular form of well-being is different from another's and may even conflict with it, and if persons can prevent others from being self-directed, then certain interpersonal standards need to be adopted if individuals are to flourish in their diverse ways among others. An ethical principle is needed whose primary function is not guiding a person to well-being or right conduct, but providing a standard for interpersonal conduct that favors no particular form of human flourishing, while at the same time providing a context for diverse forms of human flourishing to be achieved. Such a principle provides the needed context by protecting what is necessary to the possibility of each and every person finding fulfillment, regardless of the determinate form virtues and human goods take in their lives. Thus, it is very important that there be such a thing as a meta-normative principle.

Self-directedness is the only feature of human flourishing upon which to base a meta-normative principle because it is the only feature in which each and every person in the concrete situation has a necessary stake. Also, self-directedness is the only feature of human flourishing whose protection is consistent with the diverse forms of human flourishing. We cannot have a meta-normative principle that will structurally prejudice society more toward some forms of self-perfection than others. To do that would be, in effect, to act against the requirement that our theory supports self-perfection. So, the principle we arrive at must be universal in the sense of being equally applicable to all individuals.

In addition, the universality requirement necessitates that we center our principle on that characteristic present in all forms of self-perfection (or its pursuit); otherwise, we will again prejudice the situation in favor of some forms of self-perfection over others. So-called "generic goods"—for example, food, clothing, shelter, knowledge, friendship, artistic appreciation, and love, or even central virtues like integrity, courage, and justice—will not suffice as our standard here.[9] Even though they are universal in the sense of helping to define the meaning of self-perfection for all individuals, their particular form or application is given by the individual. This means that while, for example, artistic pursuit or appreciation may be necessary for anyone's self-perfection, the particular form it takes will differ widely. Our principle must apply to both the particular and general in the same way and in the same respect, or we will be back to an a priori slanting of the situation in favor of some forms of self-perfection over others.

On the basis of what we have said so far, it is clear that the only type of rights we possess that are consistent with protecting the condition necessary for the pursuit of any form of self-perfection are rights of equal liberty, where no one is allowed to take an action toward another that threatens or destroys that other's self-directedness. The basic rights we possess are thus principles of mutual non-interference. This translates socially into a principle of maximum compossible-and-equal freedom for all. The freedom must be equal in the sense that it must allow for the possibility of diverse modes of flourishing and, therefore, must not be structurally biased in favor of some forms of flourishing over others. The freedom must be compossible in the sense that the exercise of self-directed activity by one person must not encroach upon that of another.

Because we are not directly concerned with the promotion of self-perfection itself, but only the condition for it, it is not the consequences per se that will determine encroachment. What is decisive is whether the action taken by one person toward another secures that other's consent or is otherwise a function of that other's choices. For one may violate another's rights and produce a chain of events that lead to consequences that could be said to be to that other's apparent or real benefit, or one may not violate another's rights and produce a chain of events that lead to one's apparent or real detriment. Yet, since the purpose here is to structure a political principle that protects the condition for self-perfection rather than leading to self-perfection itself, the consequences of actions are of little importance (except insofar as they threaten the condition that rights were designed to protect in the first place). Our concern here is not with how acts will turn out, but rather with setting the appropriate foundation for the taking of any action in the first place.

THE NATURAL RIGHT TO PRIVATE PROPERTY

In the Lockean tradition of liberalism the natural right to private property is arguably its most controversial component. Our purpose here is not to start applying our theory to particular rights that have been traditionally associated with the Lockean tradition. Rather, we seek to outline some implications of our theory of rights in this controversial area and to further indicate the meaning of our foregoing arguments.

Ayn Rand has written that "the right to property is a right to action . . . it is not the right to *an object*, but to the action and the consequence of producing or earning that object."[10] We take this statement to be the essence of the correct approach to thinking about property rights. This statement contrasts nicely with the usual understanding reflected in a statement like: "a property right is, roughly, a right which a person has with respect to a specific thing,"[11] where there is nothing that refers to the essence of a property right as an action. This traditional way of thinking of property rights in terms of things is not completely avoided by those who define property in terms of ownership.[12] "Ownership" is less "object" or "thing-oriented" than many approaches, but it is still a derivative concept from what must be first said about action.

The relationship people have toward things or objects, whether in terms of possession or ownership, is a function of human action. The central question about property rights, therefore, is how one's theory fits into what one says in general about rights and human action. Our own position can be summarized by noting that human beings are material beings, not disembodied ghosts, and being self-directed is not merely some psychic state. Self-directedness pertains to actions in the world, actions employing or involving material things at some place and at some time.[13] And it is not objects *per se* that the individual needs to have property rights to, as if any random distribution were acceptable.[14] Human beings need to have property rights to things that are the result of their own productive efforts. For individual human beings to flourish they need to maintain control of what they have produced. Since judgments are themselves not simply psychic states, a person's choices and judgments cannot be said to have been respected if the material expression of those judgments is divested from the individual.

The notion that production is a highly individualized affair is perhaps our first indication that Locke was mistaken in his contention that God or nature has given mankind a stock of objects (in common or otherwise) from which we must devise a set of rules for just distribution (or even, as we shall see, for original ownership). The most nature offers is the potential opportunity for the transformation of the material world. A theory of property rights will, therefore, concern itself with legitimate exploitation of opportunities, not with things or objects. *Ownership* will be the legal expression of the legitimate exploitation of opportunities. Notice that this way of looking at the issue does not rule out ownership in or property rights to that which is not a thing or area of land, such as electromagnetic fields. This way of looking at the issue also does not begin with the essentially collectivist assumption that there is a common stock of goods that everyone must equally regard as "wealth." Property, wealth, and any object qua object are not beings *in rerum natura*—that is, things that exist "out there" independently and apart from human cognition and effort. Rather, they are essentially a function of the intellectual and physical efforts of individual human beings.[15]

It is quite illegitimate to regard anything as wealth that is not the product of man's mind or action. This claim follows from our general denial of non-relational value, from our assertion about the primacy of human thought and action in production, and from experience. The relatively impoverished continent of Africa is no less generously endowed with natural assets than is North America, but the former is clearly less wealthy than the latter. We believe that a significant part of the reason for this has to do with encumbrances placed upon the exploitation of opportunity. In any case, our point is that wealth is a concept relative to productive acts and interests, so each new existential state of the material world is simply a new field of opportunities just as the previous state was. This is true for all existential states considered apart from human action.

When one thinks of opportunities, one does not think first of objects but rather of actions whose end may be to secure objects. But if we are correct in saying that objects themselves are productions or creations, then even objects cannot be the end of an action, but a feature of the actions themselves; and traditional moral wisdom has had plenty to say about the mistake of treating objects as ends. Two points appear to follow from this: (1) the objects or possessions one has must be considered an extension of what one is (assuming no dichotomy between oneself and one's actions) and not as items contingently attached to oneself; and (2) the concept of "opportunity" must be a function of the general right to action (as specified above) if there is to be a natural right to property.

We have seen that our natural rights consist in a set of meta-normative principles that define a set of compossible moral territories. We also argued that individuals are in a significant sense value creators, each of whose eu-daimonic fulfillments is unique to the individual. Rights remain abstract and negative in order to accommodate the truth of individualism. Now since rights define moral territories, they circumscribe areas within which the individual is free to act. Having freedom of action within certain bound-aries is nothing less than having an opportunity for action within those same boundaries. Since the extension of the opportunity is equivalent to the extension of the boundaries, the first point we learn about the natural right to property is that it is simply another name for the freedom to act and, hence, to live according to one's own choices. To put the point another way, the natural right to property is a natural right and shares the central fea-tures of any natural right.

To distinguish a natural right to property from other natural rights we need a differentia. *Opportunity* functions more like a genus because it would be present in all other natural rights as well (for example, free speech being the opportunity to communicate what one wishes within permissible bounds). The differentia for property comes with respect to the concept of exploitation. We understand *exploitation* to be the attempt to transform one's legitimate opportunities into consequences that accord with one's values. Since actions and consequences generally have a material dimension, the act of transformation involved here usually incorporates something tan-gible. This must certainly be true with respect to drafting positive law in this area; for even intellectual property rights must have a tangible embodiment (such as books, articles, and works of art) if they are to have the protection of law. But at this stage it is enough to note that property rights will concern allowable acts of transformation of the material world. Throughout this dis-cussion, *allowable, legitimate,* and similar terms will refer to actions that do not cross the borders of another's moral territory without permission.

The right to transform the material world is little else than the right to act, since actions occur in the material order. The second component in the natural right to property, therefore, is equivalent to saying that one has the right to act. What becomes controversial is the extent to which one has the right to retain the consequences of one's actions. But how does one go about solving such a problem? The first issue, we believe, concerns a "bur-den of proof" argument. With respect to property rights, the burden of proof could go in either of two directions: (1) the individual must show why he must be allowed to keep the consequences of his actions, or (2) others must show grounds for interfering with the retention of those consequences. It is clear from the theory of rights presented in the last section that the bur-den of proof is the latter. Exercising a natural right is not something one is obligated to justify to others. What *retaining the consequences* means has not yet been examined.[16]

Discussions of property are off to a wrong start if the central rights question requires that the individual justify retention of the consequences of his actions in the absence of any evidence of a border crossing. Another way of putting the same point is that a discussion of property rights is off to a wrong start if the first question is taken to be "How much of what a person produces should he or she be allowed to keep?" For us, the question ought to be the reverse: "When, if ever, can some people interfere with the productive acts of others?"

Secondly, since property is created or produced through an act of transformation, the Lockean proviso that there must be "enough and as good" left for others in cases of original acquisition is moot. For there can never be "enough and as good" left for others if every action issues in a unique transformation. If an action transforms the material order, there can be no other forms of property like it, until a similar action accomplishes the same result. Picking an apple from a tree should not be judged in terms of the numbers of apples left, but in terms of the action that transformed the tree into a useful commodity. All this follows, of course, from our claim that there is no such thing as pre-existing (in other words, pre-transformed) wealth.

One may wish to argue that one is obligated to leave equivalent *opportunities* for others to perform the same act of transformation. But apart from questions of scarcity, it is not clear why one has this obligation. This is because one's act of transformation in no way deprives another of what he had transformed. Nor is it the case that opportunities are as similar to each other as the apples on the tree, since they are highly dependent on the individual's circumstances, interests, and abilities. Finally, opportunities are essentially matters of judgment and thus in no way common. Even with apples one may judge them ready to eat while another predicts they will make one sick by being too green or too ripe. Mavrodes claims that the act of transformation deprives another of his rights, because one is acting upon something one had no right to (the unowned object).[17] But this fails, "to distinguish between depriving another of their rights and depriving them of an opportunity."[18] The former is clearly illegitimate while the latter is not, and acts of transformation under conditions of original acquisition are clearly not violating rights because (virtually by definition) no one has rights to the pre-transformed objects in question, since in the relevant sense they are not yet objects.

From all this, it follows that a correct theory of the natural right to property will recognize that no one has a right to the acts of transformation of others, since there can be no pre-existing claims to that which does not yet exist (the transformed entity).[19] Yet, since we are speaking of rights, we are speaking of meta-norms applicable in a social context. The social context requires that the acts of transformation be compossible. Now *compossible* here does not issue simply in "ambiguity clarification," for any system of rules will clarify ambiguities about who can do what (provided the rules are clear and practicable). *Compossible* here must refer to a set of rules or principles that are consistent with the general theory of natural rights we developed in the opening part of this essay. We believe that there is in principle a wide latitude of acceptable rules that would satisfy the compossibility requirement. We do not believe, however, that the latitude is completely open.

Since we are at a general level of discussion here, the restrictions upon the latitude of acceptable rules must themselves be general. Here we follow the lead of F. A. Hayek in requiring that the limitations upon the latitude of acceptable rules be universality and negativity. Universality is uncontroversial because all rights are supposed to have this characteristic. In this context *negative* means (1) boundary setting in nature and (2) exclusionary; (1) makes (2) possible, and (2) is justified by our previous discussion of the burden of proof and our conception of eudaimonia as requiring moral territories. Both jointly capture the concept of "negative" because natural rights are essentially obligations of restraint, and because there is a lack of a pre-existing obligation not to engage in opportunity deprivation (since no rights are being violated in the process).

Perhaps some examples would help clarify our point. Mavrodes, in his discussion of the original acquisition of a tree, states that a number of rules would be possible in such a case and lists the following:

1. Everyone has the right to fell any standing tree, and he who does so thereby becomes the owner of the fallen tree.
2. Everyone has the right to fell any standing tree and to trim off its branches, and he who does so is the owner of the resulting log.
3. Everyone has the right to mark any unmarked tree by painting his initials on it, and he thereby acquires ownership of it.
4. Everyone has the right to claim any unowned tree by marking it and then offering a sacrifice on top of Mt. Cloudpiercer. He who does so owns the tree.
5. Everyone has the right to claim any unowned set of trees by posting, in the village square, a notice of his claim which defines the set, such as "I claim all of the trees which now stand, and which shall stand in the future, in the valley of the Broad River from its source in the mountains to its mouth at the edge of the sea." Whoever does so thereby comes to own all of the trees so specified.
6. Everyone has the right to claim any unowned tree by marking it and then giving a feast for all of his fellows. He who does so comes to own the tree.
7. Everyone has the right to claim any unowned tree by marking it and then giving each of his fellows a useful tool, such as an axe or a saw. He who does so comes to own the tree.

Mavrodes argues that since there is no "ready metaphysical principle" to decide which of these is appropriate, they are all possible. We mostly agree. Universality and negativity are "metaphysical" limitations, but ones that do not significantly pare down Mavrodes's list. Specifically, rules 1–3 and 5 seem possible on our theory, but 4, 6, and 7 are not acceptable.[20] These three violate our negativity requirement by making one's right contingent upon paying off others. Negativity is required to ensure that property rights are *initiated* by individuals. In addition, 4, 6, and 7 seem to require the presence of the state in a way that the other rules do not. Requiring that individuals perform ceremonies, give banquets, or give gifts would seem to suppose the presence of a third party who defines the extent to which one must give or perform to qualify as an owner. But Mavrodes may simply be saying that some overt act may be required as a sign of ownership, and with that we would generally agree. Our point however is that one must distinguish recognizing an exploited opportunity from the actual exploitation itself. The former may involve third parties but must arise in *response* to the latter.

Our general point here is that in specific situations and social settings, how to cash all this out in terms of positive law and rights will be difficult and beyond the purview of abstract moral and social theory. A community of artists might settle upon criteria of visual perspective in their society (for example, you own what you can see) in cases of original acquisition. We find it highly improbable that these criteria would command consensus, but then it is also unlikely that the Puritanical idea that one owns what one can physically labor upon would be the only acceptable principle of original acquisition.

People will come to discover they have different values than those they may have held at the time of the original acquisition, so as property gets exchanged the overall look of holdings will alter. A would-be artist who gained a large holding under the terms of original acquisition mentioned in the last paragraph might discover he has no talent for art. His own form of flourishing might be best served by divesting himself of part of his land in exchange for other goods (perhaps even rights of use on the lands of others). It is the essence of the individualist position that we cannot settle an appropriate value system for diverse individuals a priori. Rules of original acquisition are often less a matter of morality than they are a matter of getting co-operative society off the ground.

Unrestricted voluntary transfer of goods is a feature of property rights that follows from the negativity requirement and the primitive moral proposition that choice is respected through consent in a social context. Consent is the means by which the integrity of moral territories is maintained interpersonally. And property is nothing other than the material expression of one's moral territory. In order to be able to carry our moral territories with us across time and in compossible fashion with others, others must restrain themselves from crossing into our territory unless given permission.

Much of what we have said depends upon the validity of the first principle mentioned earlier and to which we promised to return, namely that the "objects" or "possessions" that one has must be considered extensions of what one is. Since we have already shown that persons have natural rights to their pursuit of eudaimonia, if it is the case that property is simply an extension of self, we would have the natural right to property as well; for then, the natural right to property—appropriate to a certain context—is essentially a restatement of the basic natural rights for which we have already argued.

As living things, human beings have no choice about being related to other things in existence. Yet human beings do have much to say about what they will be related to and the manner by which they will be related. Further, human beings have the responsibility for creating relationships that will enable them to flourish. We are beings that create relationships, and these relationships—be they logical, loving, or productive—are the means by which humans know, care for, and control their environment. They are both the means and the constituents of human flourishing. Thus as a being whose conceptual powers allow it to create, control, and use relationships, the exploitation of opportunities in the world is a fundamental expression of what and who an individual human being is.

Taking control of another's property against their wishes can now be seen to be nothing less than taking control of one of the central relationships that constitute a human being's life. There is and can be no dichotomy between a human being's natural right to liberty and a human being's natural right to private property. The latter is the expression of the metaphysical fact that human beings are material things that flourish through the exploitation of opportunities in the material world.

The acceptance of this basic natural right does not preclude the possibility that what one does within the legitimate boundaries of one's moral territory has "undesirable" neighborhood effects upon others. Such effects *may* be of interest to moralists, but they do not necessarily imply unethical action and certainly do not imply the presence of a rights violation. If A produces a better product than B, then the consequences to B will be "undesirable"; but A has not necessarily done anything "wrong" and has not violated B's natural rights. One is not by nature obligated to provide others with a stream of favorable consequences. One is only obligated to restrain one's actions in such a way that the moral territories of others are not penetrated without permission. But this brings us back full circle to our initial thesis about the concept of natural rights.

The idea that the right to property is a function of the right to action and thus grounded in agency is certainly consistent with the sort of Aristotelianism with which we have allied ourselves. Our defense of private property is, however, not exactly the same as Aristotle's own, which has a much more utilitarian flavor to it (*Politics* 1263aff). Still, a defense of private property is within the confines of standard Aristotelianism and only goes part of the distance in showing how Aristotelianism can undergird classical liberalism or libertarianism. What seems more troublesome is to show how Aristotelianism can be engaged to support what seems more directly contrary to it, namely, commerce. To that task we now turn.

COMMERCE AND FRIENDSHIP

To accomplish our end, we shall concentrate mainly on the concept of Aristotelian friendship. As John Cooper points out, nearly one-fifth of the *Nicomachean Ethics* is devoted to the issue of friendship. Moreover, friendship forms a significant part of Aristotle's political theory through the concept of civic friendship. We intend to concentrate mainly on "friendships of utility," or what Cooper more properly calls "advantage-friendships." We shall argue that advantage-friendships are the basis of commercial orders, and properly so. Moreover, efforts to model social orders on any other form of friendship are bound to fail and are contrary to the implications, and often the text, of Aristotle's social theory. Our examination of advantage-friendships should not only vindicate liberalism from the charge of being incompatible with Aristotelianism, but also indicate the proper place of such relationships within an Aristotelian natural-rights perspective

Aristotle clearly takes character-friendships to be the paradigm case of friendship. Character friendships are those based upon virtue. This raises the question of whether, and in what sense, advantage-friendships are really forms of friendship. In this connection we believe it is most instructive to look at Cooper who, on the one hand, takes relationships of utility or advantage to be a form of friendship under certain conditions while, on the other, eschews most commercial transactions as qualifying as advantage-friendships. In Cooper's interpretation of Aristotle, friendships exist only when "the friend will wish his friend whatever is good, for his own sake, and it will be mutually known to them that this well-wishing is reciprocated."[21] In friendships of utility or advantage-friendships, the good wished is to be benefited. This is a lower order good from the one wished for in character-friendships. Thus the type of good involved, rather than the character of the personal relation, demarcates the type of friendship. This is because all forms of friendship, according to Cooper, must wish another good for *his own sake*. Personal relations that treat the other as means to one's own good do not qualify as friendships of any type.

Although Cooper claims that Aristotle emphasizes the altruistic ingredient of friendship, Cooper more properly and commonly employs *unself-interested* to refer to the wish that one's friend achieve a type of good for his own sake. Therefore, to form a friendship there must be an unself-interested concern for the other person's good. This would seem to preclude all advantage-friendships (certainly commercial ones), because one person's concern for another seems to be purely instrumental—that is, one takes an interest in the other for one's own sake and not for the sake of the other. It should be noted that Cooper does not require that the unself-interested concern for the other be the only concern, nor apparently the primary one. Nevertheless, such a concern must be present for a relationship to qualify as a friendship.

Although commercial relationships seem to be precluded by Cooper's insistence on the presence of unself-interested good will, he allows that certain forms of commercial relationships do qualify as advantage-friendships. Consider the following:

> Friends of all three types . . . wish for their friend's well-being out of concern for the friend himself. This is as true of a businessman who, through frequent profitable association, becomes friends with a regular customer, as it is of a husband and wife or two intimate companions who love one another for their characters. Such a businessman looks first for mutual profit from his friendship, but that does not mean that he always calculates his services to his customer by the standard of profit. Finding the relationship on the whole profitable, he likes this customer and is willing to do him services otherwise than as a means to his own ultimate profit. So long as the general context of profitability remains, the well-wishing can proceed unchecked; the profitability to the well-wisher that is assumed in the well-wishing is not that of the particular service rendered (the particular action done in the other person's interest) but that of the overall fabric of the relationship. Here, then, one has a complex and subtle mixture of self-seeking and unself-interested well-wishing and well-doing.[22]

This passage is instructive because it shows (a) that merely having an advantageous relationship with someone does not thereby produce an advantage-friendship, and (b) that commercial relationships can carry with them a mutually unself-interested concern for the other, provided the context of profitability remains. Notice, however, that commercial transactions that do not possess the "regular-customer" feature would not qualify as advantage-friendships.

It is our view that Cooper's interpretation of Aristotle on advantage-friendships is mistaken both as an interpretation of Aristotle and as a theory of advantage-friendships in general. First, Cooper's interpretation fails to explain the phenomena. Consider the case of the businessman cited above. In this case the businessman, after repeated associations, comes to *like* his customer (or vice versa) and may occasionally go out of his way to do something special for him, even though that special favor may not have been necessary. Notice, however, that it is not advantage that matters here, but rather the personal qualities of the parties involved. Presumably on Cooper's account there would be no friendship if the businessman had decided, as a matter of good business practice, to give regular customers special treatment simply to keep them as regulars. Consequently, the advantages involved become a contingent factor in the relationship this businessman now has to his customer. Cooper has described not what advantage-friendships are, but how a higher form of friendship can grow out of contexts that originated for mutual advantage.[23] In essence, Cooper treats all forms of friendship as more or less complete versions of character-friendships. The advantages being received are incidental (or becoming so) to what is essential about the friendship (namely, the unself-interested relationship now being formed). It is our view that Cooper has gotten the matter entirely backward. Advantage-friendships are only incidentally character-friendships, but are essentially defined by the advantage each person self-interestedly seeks to gain by the association. Under Cooper's interpretation the reverse is the case. In this connection Aquinas saw the matter correctly:

> [O]f those who love one another for the sake of utility, one does not love the other for the sake of the other but inasmuch as he receives from the other some good for himself. . . . Thus they do not love their friend for what he is in himself but for what is incidental to him, his utility or pleasantness. Therefore, friendships of this sort plainly are not friendships essentially but incidentally. . . .[24]

If Aquinas is correct, the door is open to seeing advantage-friendships as a type of co-operative association, but one that lacks the essential ingredient of a true friendship. Since our purpose here is not to examine character-friendships, we will allow Cooper that wishing another good for their own sake is that essential ingredient. The other types of friendships would involve ingredients found in the essential kind, but would lack the essential component in its full sense (see below).

It is also our contention that commercial relations can be considered paradigmatic forms of advantage-friendships, and in this connection Cooper has a most interesting footnote.[25] In that footnote he discusses Aristotle's contention that there are two types of advantage friendships: one governed by explicitly agreed-upon exchanges, and the other by the characters of the two parties to the exchange. An example of the former might be a signed contract. An example of the latter might be a handshake. We need not dwell on this distinction here because we bring it up again below. Cooper's thesis is that the former type of friendship (call it an "L-friendship," for legal friendship) is a purely commercial transaction and thus no friendship at all, "not even an advantage-friendship." L-friendships lack the element of mutual unself-interested good will. The second type (call them "C-friendships," for character friendships) can have elements of good will and be a type of friendship. The *Nicomachean Ethics,* therefore, removes essentially commercial transactions from the realm of friendships.

The *Eudemian Ethics,* on the other hand, offers a different conclusion. Consider these remarks by Cooper:

> The *EE* begins by marking off the same two types of advantage-friendship (1242b31–32) . . . But as the argument proceeds it becomes apparent . . . that this division is provisional only; the latter type is really a confused relationship, in which the parties cannot decide whether to treat one another as real friends or as advantage-friends. . . . Thus, in this passage Aristotle actually implies that it is only where an association is purely commercial that it can count as an advantage-friendship. . . .[26]

Cooper goes on to suggest that the *NE* and not the *EE* should be taken as the final word on the subject; but even Cooper admits that Aristotle "refuses to abandon completely the earlier ideas which are causing the trouble."[27]

If Cooper is correct in noting a shift of doctrine between the two treatises, we believe Aristotle got it right in the *EE*. We are not, however, persuaded that the differences between the two treatises amount to anything other than a slightly more ambiguous treatment in the *NE*—not a substantive shift of doctrine. The *EE* is more forthright in proclaiming that there is no single or defining element that pervades all three forms of friendship. Consider, for example, the following passage:

> Therefore to confine the use of the term friend to primary friendship [i.e., character-friendships] is to do violence to observed facts, and compels one to talk paradoxes; though it is not possible to bring all friendship under one definition. The only remaining alternative, therefore, is, that in a sense the primary sort of friendship alone is friendship,

but in a sense all sorts are, not as having a common name by accident and standing in a merely chance relationship to one another, nor yet as falling under one species, but rather as related to one thing. (*EE* 1236b20–27)

What Aristotle means by "related to one thing" is that all forms of friendship have a relationship to the primary form (character-friendships) but are not reducible to it. In other words, the other forms of friendship cannot be *defined* in terms of the primary form, nor do they stand to it as instances to their species; rather, the different forms of friendship stand in different relationships to the primary form while exhibiting one or more of the attributes of that primary form. Yet, since the relationship between the various types of friendships is not "accidental" or "by chance," we would also expect there to be a general conceptual framework for the term *friendship*. It is somewhat difficult to know for certain, given the ambiguity of the texts, what that framework might be. But we would suggest that Martin Ostwald's rendering of *philia* is closest to correct, provided it too is not understood in the mistaken way of attempting to define all forms of friendship in terms of the primary one: *philia* "designates the relationship between a person and any other person(s) or being(s) which that person regards as peculiarly his own and to which he has a peculiar attachment."[28]

It seems to us that the attempt to define all forms of friendships in terms of unself-interested good will restricts the range of friendships and logically functions in a genus-to-species form. This violates the message of the preceding passage from the *EE*. However, we also admit that Aristotle's discussion, especially when both treatises are considered, is not without ambiguity. In the end, therefore, the logical and textual ambiguities in Aristotle open the way for alternative interpretations. Given what we have argued above, our approach will be to consider commercial transactions as paradigm forms of advantage-friendships. We believe this interpretation, especially in light of Ostwald's understanding of *philia*, can be adopted without doing an injustice to the spirit of Aristotle's doctrine.

Part of the problem in regarding commercial transactions as forms of friendship, however attenuated they may be, is that such relationships are clearly self-interested. In our culture, as Webster's dictionary shows, *self-interested* means "selfish" which in turn means "without consideration for others." We shall argue that selfish behavior is possible in commercial transactions, but not essential. What is essential for commercial relationships is described in the following passage from Adam Smith.

Man has almost constant occasion for the help of his brethren, and it is in vain for him to expect it from their benevolence only. He will be more likely to prevail if he can interest their self-love in his favor, and show them that it is for their own advantage to do for him what he requires of them . . . and it is in this manner that we obtain from one another the far greater part of those good offices which we stand in need of.[29]

What this passage shows is that market transactions require an interest in others. It is true that this interest is a means to satisfying one's own interest, but it is an interest in others nonetheless. Suppose then, following Ostwald, that what all friendships have in common is an interest in others. Some of these (the highest types) have this interest in a way that considers the other for his or her own sake, what Cooper calls being "unselfinterested." Other types, however, carry a genuine interest in others, but not for their own sake. Market exchanges require a genuine interest in others, because one's own success depends upon getting others to see one's own interest as their interest; in other words, as sharing an interest.

Oddly enough, command economies (e.g., socialism) do not require an interest in others, for obedience, and not persuasion, is their mode of eliciting cooperation. Command structures can, and often do, embody selfishness (understood as lack of concern for the interests of others) in a pure form, since those issuing the commands need pay no heed to anyone's interests but their own. Voluntary market transactions, on the other hand, will not occur if both parties do not see the relationship as mutually advantageous. This shared interest and advantage, at least for the duration of the transaction, embodies several features that can be found in higher forms of friendship: mutual advantage, mutual interest, co-operation, unity of purpose, and even good will.

If we take the simple case of a two-person, two-commodity, voluntary exchange, all the features of friendship just mentioned can be found. Mutual advantage is obvious, and mutual interest is demonstrated by what Smith rightly perceived to be necessary for voluntary exchange to occur. Co-operation is manifested by the conclusion of the exchange. Only unity of purpose and good will remain. The first is more easily understood if we posit a third-party interference in the transaction. If we assume that the third party wishes to prevent the transaction by force and not by offering a more advantageous trade to one of the parties, then it is evident that both the original parties share a unity of purpose in their desire to complete the transaction. Both would see the third party as a threat to what the two of them wish to accomplish jointly (the trade), and it is this sense of joint accomplishment that expresses their unity of purpose.

The case of "good will" is more problematic than the other characteristics. For example, Aristotle claims that mutually recognized good will is

necessary for friendship (*NE* 1156a5). However, he also claims that advantage-friendships do not contain good will (*NE* 1167a12). Cooper's arguments
demonstrate that good will (understood as wishing the other well for his
own sake) can be part of advantage-friendships, but our argument implies
that this kind of good will is not essential to advantage friendships and does
not characterize the most common feature of such friendships. In this connection, two avenues of discussion are open to us: (1) refrain from using the
concept of good will in advantage-friendships, but employ a more rudimentary form of the term; and (2) recognize that there is an abstract sense
of the term that underlies advantage-friendships, but which factors in only
obliquely in any specific case. The second of these will be discussed during
our discussion of civic friendship below.

If we cannot characterize advantage-friendships as possessing good will
because each party does not wish for the other's good for the other's own
sake, then perhaps there is something *like* good will present here. We believe
that what is present is simply "wishing the other's good." In any voluntary
trade, one wants the other to obtain what he believes good, because it is the
means to achieving what one desires for oneself. This is the means by which,
at least during the specific transaction, one comes to regard the other as "peculiarly his own and to which he has a peculiar attachment." If this wishing for the other's good is mutually recognized, as it would be if the trade
occurs, then an advantage-friendship is present. What is absent here is the
wishing for good for *the sake of* the other. Nevertheless, it is the wishing for
another's good that forms the basis of good will proper. Furthermore, we
believe that it is this idea of merely wishing another good that is tacitly understood by Aristotle to keep relations of mutual advantage in accord with
the "friendliness" exhibited by the primary form of friendship. And just as
good will by itself does not imply a friendship (because one might have good
will toward someone who does not know of it), neither does merely wishing for another's good imply an advantage-friendship, for we can also wish
for the good of someone we do not know. Therefore, advantage-friendships,
like the primary form, do depend upon mutually recognized wishing for the
other's good. A wants B to get what he wants so A can get what A wants. This
explains the incentive business people have to get *satisfied* customers.

In many respects, then, advantage-friendships share components found
in character-friendships. Of course, as Aristotle points out, these friendships
are prone to disputes (*NE* 1162b5–20) and break down easily, because utili-
ties change (*NE* 1156a22). But they belong in the category of friendships because of the similarities to the highest form just mentioned. In addition to
what we have argued above, we would add that advantage-friendships have
a range of forms that more or less approximate character-friendships. At the
top of the range are transactions like those described in Cooper's example

of the regular customer. Here one is not sure whether it is real friendship or advantage-friendship that binds the two together (*EE* 1242b35–40). At the lowest end of the scale would be those transactions in which one party plays upon the weaknesses of the other to gain a quick trade. Here the high-pressure salesperson comes to mind and the transaction exists on the border of co-operation and exploitation. At the center, however, are the normal voluntary transactions that result in mutually recognized "gains from trade" for both the parties. These central cases are the essence of commercial relationships, for too much of the high end of the scale would lower trading volume and too much of the low end would breed distrust and destroy the conditions of trade themselves.

As a final distinction under the current heading, we would like to argue that advantage-friendships fall into two basic categories: formal and personal. This distinction is founded upon Aristotle's distinction between moral and legal friendships of utility (i.e., "C-friendships" [character type friendships] and "L-friendships" [legal type friendships] mentioned earlier, *NE* 1162b23–37). In the legal type of friendship the terms are made explicit, whereas the moral type relies on some element of trust. For Aristotle, trust in a commercial setting means that an advantage would be returned at some future time, rather than immediately upon receipt. The one party therefore trusts the other to return the favor. Aristotle seems to associate the legal form more directly with commercial transactions where payment is given at the time the benefit is received. Yet Aristotle's limited experience with types of commercial relationships, when compared to our own, somewhat restricts the usefulness of his discussion of his own distinction. We have therefore chosen to use different terms, which bear a resemblance to Aristotle's own terms, but which do not require an adherence to Aristotle's own discussion.

Formal friendships of advantage are those relationships governed by clearly understood legal, contractual, or customary rules. One's contractual relationship with one's employer would be an example, as would most shopping trips to the local mall (since prices are marked and both parties know reasonably well what their roles are). Personal friendships of advantage, on the other hand, are transactions not grounded essentially upon explicit formal rules. Attending a garage sale or swapping collector's items might be examples here. Many small businesses, when they first get started, are grounded in personal friendships of advantage among the founding partners. In our society, although most noncommercial friendships of advantage would fall under the category of personal, most commercial transactions come under the category of formal.

Even though Aristotle correctly identifies an important distinction, he fails to draw a connection between them and seems to place a higher value on the moral (personal) types of advantage-friendships. Nevertheless, the connection between the two can be accounted for within Aristotle's theory, and this connection considerably lessens the reasons for giving a higher value to the personal form. What Aristotle fails to realize is that the personal forms of advantage-friendships inevitably transform themselves into the formal variety if they are sustained over a period of time. Aristotle notes that advantage-friendships are prone to dispute and misunderstanding. There are strong incentives, therefore, to formalize the transaction so that both parties know what to expect and what their responsibilities are. Moreover, economists are correct to note that the increased certainty and clarity of responsibility makes transactions more efficient, leading to increasing gains and advantages for all. In other words, it is simply more advantageous for all concerned if trading for mutual advantage is predominantly formal. A further important incentive to formalize advantage-friendships must also be noted: since, as Aristotle points out (*NE* 1157a17), bad people can form advantage-friendships as well as good, and since it is often difficult to determine the character of someone else, formalized transactions reduce the risk and information costs characteristic of dealings with relatively unknown persons.

It might be argued that Aristotle is right to attach a higher value to personal friendships of advantage, since these are more like true friendships by possessing more human and "friendly" qualities. Yet formal friendships of advantage are like true friendships also: they are more stable and less prone to dispute than their personal counterparts. In addition, the explicit terms allow for future planning and co-operation that is difficult with purely personal forms of advantage-friendships. The problem with holding that personal friendships of advantage are more friendly—truer friendships—than formal friendships of advantage is that it assumes that character-friendships are a species (a universal notion) and that advantage-friendships are but instances of this kind of relationship. Consequently, all advantage-friendships turn out to be little more than poor cases of the primary sort. Such an assumption misconstrues the way Aristotle understands *friendship*. As we have seen (*EE* 1236b20–27), there is no way to bring all cases of friendship under one definition, and so there is no theoretical reason to attach a higher value to personal friendships of advantage than formal ones. It is in any case clear that the evolution of commercial systems indicates that people find it more advantageous to associate on explicit terms. Saying this in no way implies that the human qualities more evident in personal advantage-friendships are not to be valued, even at times more highly valued than impersonal qualities that may attend the formal type. Rather, it is to say only that since it is advantage that is being sought, formal relationships more effectively secure that advantage.

CIVIC FRIENDSHIP

Aristotle claims that lawgivers are more concerned to foster friendship among their citizens than they are with promoting justice (*NE* 1155a2324). This claim raises the question of the kind of friendship Aristotle is speaking of here. *Civic friendship* is the term used by Aristotle, but is this form of friendship a fourth kind or a version of one of the three main types? As we shall see, Aristotle considers civic friendship as falling under one of the three main types—friendships of advantage. Locating civic friendship under the category of advantage-friendships implies that civic associations are not, and cannot be, associations of character-friendships. There is a temptation to interpret Aristotle's political writings as requiring, in an ideal sense, a community where all are friends of virtue. After all, Aristotle says that although states may be founded out of need, they continue "in existence for the sake of the good life" (*Politics* 1252b30). And he also states "the same things are best both for individuals and for states, and these are the things which the legislator ought to implant in the minds of his citizens" (*Politics* 1333b36–37). Therefore, if character-friendships are at least part of what it means to live a good life, then the best states will be those whose citizens associate for the sake of virtue.

It seems to us quite mistaken to try to read Aristotle as holding that citizens should hope to associate with one another as friends of virtue. As Aristotle himself notes (*EE* 1245b20–25), it is neither possible nor desirable to have many friends of this type. True friendships must occur in circles much smaller than those that characterize a state. In both the *Nicomachean* and *Eudemian Ethics* Aristotle claims that civic friendships are versions of friendships of advantage (*NE* 1159b2–1160a30; *EE* 1241a32–1243b35 passim). In many respects, however, the *Eudemian Ethics* is clearer on this question than the *Nicomachean*. Consider the following passages:

> Civic friendship on the other hand is constituted in the fullest degree on the principle of utility, for it seems to be the individual's lack of self-sufficiency that makes these unions permanent—since they would have been formed in any case merely for the sake of society. (*EE* 1242a5–9)

> Civic friendship is, it is true, based on utility, and fellow-citizens are one another's friends in the same way as different cities are . . . nor similarly do citizens know one another, when they are not useful to one another. (*EE* 1242b23–26)

> Civic friendship looks to equality and to the object, as buyers and sellers do. . . . When, therefore, [friendship] is based on definite agreement, this is civic and legal friendship. (*EE* 1242b33–36)

Notice that these passages clearly see civic friendships as friendships of advantage. Furthermore, these passages suggest a more accurate understanding of the relationship between individuals and groups in society than would a theory modeled after character-friendships.

It would be mistaken, however, to believe that the *Nicomachean Ethics* offers us no support for our argument (e.g, *NE* 1155a23–27, 1160a11–15). Friendships can take priority over justice because there is a practical necessity "in achieving a peaceful social order." Citizens need to "get along" with one another, for if they do not, the attainment of higher virtues is an impossibility. The first step in achieving a peaceful social order is to get the members of society to see the political framework as being to their mutual advantage: "a city is said to be in concord when [its citizens] agree about what is advantageous" (*NE* 1167a27–29). This, of course, raises the question whether it is their real or perceived advantage that should be secured. It is evident from these passages that at least perceived advantage is a necessary condition for peaceful co-operation or concord.

Many modern readers balk at the idea that civic orders can be founded and maintained on advantage, because their understanding is informed by Enlightenment social-contract theory. In such theories advantage is understood as a form of self-interest defined as the unprincipled gratification of desire. If the civic association does not satisfy enough of one's personal desires, one will seek to abandon it unless kept in check by the Leviathan. The alternative seems to be using character-friendships as the central concept and then judging societies in terms of their conformity to that model. All highly pluralistic and commercial cultures fail to live up to this standard, because the overwhelming percentage of one's dealings with others is on an advantage basis. Moreover, the institutions that arise in such cultures are predominantly formal (some would say "impersonal"), further removing people from the "personal" qualities that seem to be necessary for friendships. The result, then, is a choice between hardheaded Hobbesian egotism or pollyannaish hopes for citizens who love and care for each other as good friends do.

There is, however, an Aristotelian mean between these extremes. If individuals can see their advantage in terms of general rules that make those advantages possible, then the mean between Hobbesian atomism and character-friendships is found.[30] Just as two traders can mutually value the context of profitability that makes their trade possible, so too can citizens who associate with one another come to value the principles that give rise to and regulate their mutually advantageous association. We need not suppose that the association for mutual advantage is devoid of an appreciation for how the advantages themselves depend upon the existence of rules designed to secure those advantages. Nor must we suppose that the parties involved can only co-operate with one another if they will another's good for his own sake.

As economist James Buchanan has shown, the existence of formalized rules themselves is advantageous,[31] and this truth is undoubtedly appreciated by most members of a relatively stable community. Civic friends are linked by virtue only if the rules they see as mutually advantageous are just ones. They are not, and will never be, friends of virtue in the sense of having a selfless interest in the good of other citizens for their qualities as virtuous persons. This explains why theories of right and justice are more philosophically significant than theories of political organization or friendship. It also confirms our view, not always or necessarily shared by Aristotle himself, that the attainment of the good life is an individual quest.

By this time it has perhaps occurred to the reader that our argument in favor of an Aristotelian foundation for commercial societies has ignored what is most significant about Aristotle's works—his criticism of those features most common in commercial societies: unlimited acquisition, usury, industrialism and technocracy, and the undisciplined pursuit of the satisfaction of desires. These are common themes used by opponents of liberal commercial orders to criticize such societies. We have examined some of these criticisms in detail[32] and cannot do so here for reasons of space. It is not, in any case, necessary that we do so. Having argued that Aristotle's theory of friendship can be plausibly interpreted so as not to contradict, and indeed to support directly, commercial orders is enough. That Aristotle was not an advocate of many of the features characteristic of commercial orders does not, in itself, prevent the possibility of a defense of commercial societies on Aristotelian grounds. Indeed, the main point of our analysis in this section has been to claim that commercial relations are paradigmatic of advantage-friendships in the Aristotelian sense.

CONCLUSION

We have argued in different books and various essays that a neo-Aristotelian ethics supports a version of natural rights classical liberalism. That is to say, an ethics that conceives of self-perfection or human flourishing as the ultimate moral standard upholds a political / legal order that sees protection of individual liberty as its chief aim. Contrary to many contemporary liberal and conservative theorists, we contend that an ethics of self-perfection does not require a perfectionist politics. The aim of politics is not virtue, but peace and order (as defined by our basic, negative natural right to liberty).

We have in this essay provided only a sketch of this overall argument, because we have had a different goal. We wanted to show the importance of our neo-Aristotelian conception of human flourishing to a defense of both the right to private property and the liberal commercial order. We sought to justify the right to private property in terms of the right to liberty, which is itself dependent on our neo-Aristotelian conception of human flourishing. Our argument appealed to many features of human flourishing, one of which is natural sociality. One of the things our argument for the natural right to private property acknowledged is the important role for custom and convention in determining the specific contours of property claims. Justifying the right to private property thus does not require that one assume "a state of nature."

We also sought to use Aristotle's notion of advantage-friendship in order to provide a new way to conceive of the commercial order. When it comes to explaining the typical relationships found in a liberal commercial order, our aim was to offer a middle ground between Hobbesean egotism and character-friendships. Aristotelian advantage-friendships offer that ground.

Overall, we contend that here, as well as elsewhere, neo-Aristotelian ethical thought has much to offer when it comes to defending the liberal order. There is much to be considered.

NOTES

1. Writers as diverse as Jacques Maritain, Henry Veatch, William Galston, Alasdair MacIntyre, and the like have all appealed to Aristotle, arrived at diverse political conclusions, and shunned classical liberalism.

2. See Douglas B. Rasmussen and Douglas J. Den Uyl, *Liberty and Nature* (La Salle, Ill.: Open Court, 1991); idem., *Liberalism Defended: The Challenge of Post-Modernity* (Cheltenhan, UK, and Lyme, US: Edward Elgar, 1997); idem., "'Rights' as MetaNormative Principles," in *Liberty for the 21st Century,* ed. Tibor R. Machan and Douglas B. Rasmussen (Lanham, Md.: Rowman & Littlefield, 1995), 59–75. See also Douglas B. Rasmussen, "Human Flourishing and the Appeal of Human Nature," *Social Philosophy and Policy* 16 (Winter 1999): 1–43; and Douglas J. Den Uyl, *The Virtue of Prudence* (New York: Peter Lang, 1991).

3. Specifically, *Liberty and Nature,* chs. 4 and 5.

4. See James Collins, *Interpreting Modern Philosophy* (Princeton, N.J.: Princeton University Press, 1972), 54–55, for a discussion of the different ways of using a philosopher's thought. Collins developed this classification for application to modern philosophers generally, but it can be applied to any philosopher. We have applied it to Aristotle.

5. Human flourishing is on this account objective, inclusive, individualized, agent-relative, self-directed, and social. See "Human Flourishing and the Appeal to Human Nature" and *The Virtue of Prudence* for a discussion of these features and how they interrelate.

6. It is important to realize that by "self-directedness" in this context we do not mean full-blown Millean autonomy or the directedness of the perfected self where

one is fully rational. Instead, we mean simply the use of reason and judgment upon the world in an effort to understand one's surroundings and to make plans to act within or upon it. Self-directedness as just described is still true of the actions of the most self-perfected of individuals, but nothing in this description requires or implies such individuals or even successful conduct. The protection of self-direction in this sense does not favor one form of human flourishing over any other because it is the act of exercising practical reason that is being protected, not the achievement of its object. Further, self-direction is not something disconnected from an individual's own good, but a necessary component of its achievement.

7. See *Liberty and Nature,* 34, 70–75, and 92–96, and Douglas B. Rasmussen and Douglas J. Den Uyl, "Reply to Critics," *Reason Papers* 18 (Fall 1993): 120–21. Also see Douglas J. Den Uyl, *The Virtue of Prudence,* 181–86. The term "volitional consciousness" is taken from Ayn Rand, but the concept is as old as Aristotle. See *De Anima* II, 5.

8. Although human sociality is always manifested in some particular family, group, community, culture, and society, it is not thereby limited to those particular manifestations. It is not confined to some select group or pool of humans but is, in principle, open to *any* human. There is no a priori limitation regarding with whom one may have a relationship. To claim, then, that one's flourishing or moral maturation is impossible without sharing values with others does not mean that sociality is confined to only those currently existing relationships and sets of values. Human sociality allows for openness to strangers or human beings in general. Indeed, human flourishing is possible only if people can be open to relationships with others with whom no values are *as yet* shared.

9. See our discussion of the concept of justice in "Rights as MetaNormative Principles."

10. Ayn Rand, "Man's Rights," in *The Virtue of Selfishness* (New York: New American Library, 1961), 94.

11. Allan Gibbard, "Natural Property Rights," *Nous* 10 (1976): 77.

12. Lawrence C. Becker, *Property Rights* (London: Routledge and Kegan Paul, 1977), 18–20, especially note 11, p. 120.

13. See George Mavrodes, "Property," in *Property in the Humane Economy,* ed. Samuel Blumenfeld (La Salle, Ill.: Open Court, 1974), 183.

14. David Kelley, "Life, Liberty, and Property," *Social Philosophy and Policy* 1 (Spring 1984): 112.

15. If this individualistic perspective is correct, it seems to follow immediately that we need not consider the mere existential condition or arrangement of material assets as necessarily indicative of any particular moral proposition. In other words, we need not consider, as for example Becker does (*Property Rights,* 109–111), the mere presence of resource depletion or inequity in holdings as indicative of anything of moral interest.

16. See Robert Nozick's famous "tomato juice" example in *Anarchy, State, and Utopia* (New York: Basic Books, 1974), 175.

17. Mavrodes, *Property,* 189, 195, passim.

18. Gibbard, "Natural Property Rights," 78. Mavrodes implicitly endorses an idea of a positive right to an opportunity to acquire property. It should in general

be noted that we understand the concept of "equal opportunity" to signify that the basic natural, negative right to property is legally protected and implemented for all members of a political community. This does not involve "an equal distribution of opportunities" in the sense of requiring the distribution of goods and services in accordance with some principle of equality.

19. The only way out, at this general level, is to take the collectivist premise seriously and argue that *all* of one's actions have attached to them obligations to serve the interests of others such that *no* actions are ever really one's own. We need not comment here about how contrary such a position is to our neo-Aristotelian conception of human flourishing.

20. Notice that this is different from what we say in *Liberty and Nature.*

21. John M. Cooper, "Aristotle on the Forms of Friendship," *Review of Metaphysics* 30 (June 1977): 631.

22. Ibid., 638–39.

23. These may not yet be friendships of character, but that is only because Cooper has arrested the development of the friendship before it reached that state and not because Cooper has explained advantage-friendships.

24. Aquinas, *Commentary on the Nicomachean Ethics* (Chicago: Henry Regnery, 1964), vol. II, p. 714. See also *NE* 1156a10–20 for a clear statement on Aristotle's part of what Aquinas is saying.

25. Cooper, "Aristotle on Forms of Friendship," 639.

26. Ibid.

27. Ibid.

28. Martin Ostwald, "Glossary of Technical Terms," in *Nicomachean Ethics,* trans. Martin Ostwald (Indianapolis: Bobbs-Merrill, 1962), 311–12. We wish to thank Henry Veatch for pointing this out to us.

29. Adam Smith, *Wealth of Nations* (Oxford: Oxford University Press, 1916; Liberty Press/Liberty Classics edition), 26.

30. We owe the basic insight into our argument at this point to Bernard Yack, "Community and Conflict in Aristotle's Political Philosophy," *Review of Politics* (1985): 92–112.

31. James Buchanan, *The Limits of Liberty* (Chicago: University of Chicago Press, 1965), ch. 2.

32. *Liberty and Nature,* 206–19.

PART FOUR

THE FOUNDATIONS OF MODERN POLITICS

CHAPTER TEN

The Culture of Democracy
Aristotle's Athēnaiōn Politeia *as Political Theory*

GERALD M. MARA

LIBERALISM'S CULTURAL TURN

Perhaps the most significant recent development in liberal political phi-losophy is its recognition of the importance of political culture. This goes beyond liberal theory's need to consider how different social influences may further or frustrate its normative goals.[1] Rather, this perspective argues that support for liberal institutions should not be based on any supposed meta-physics of the person, but on a recognition of the priorities of liberal cul-ture. According to this view, liberal theory's task is to identify which political and social institutions are compatible with the basic tenets of liberal society. In so doing, liberalism can strengthen the arguments for some contem-porary democratic practices (the constitutional protection of equality of opportunity) and criticize political arrangements (campaign financing laws which privilege the influence of powerful economic interests) or economic policies (welfare reform strategies which threaten the human potential of children born to disadvantaged parents) that fail to respect the priorities that shape a liberal community.

The most important recent statement of this position is John Rawls's *Political Liberalism.* For Rawls, the problem of securing reasonable com-mitments to liberal institutions is both posed and solved by the complex nature of liberal society. "A modern democratic society is characterized not simply by a pluralism of comprehensive religious, philosophical and moral doctrines, but by a pluralism of incompatible yet reasonable comprehensive doctrines. No one of these doctrines is affirmed by citizens generally. Nor should one expect that in the foreseeable future one of them, or some other reasonable doctrine will be affirmed by all, or nearly all, citizens."[2] Political liberalism responds to incompatible comprehensive doctrines about the good by decoupling the public justification of liberal institutions from comprehensive doctrines of any sort. Instead, the basic stability of liberal society should depend on an overlapping consensus among a broad, though hardly limitless, range of comprehensive commitments.[3]

From one perspective, the cultural turn in *Political Liberalism* is compatible with Rawls's thought experiment in *A Theory of Justice*.[4] An appreciation of the fact of reasonable pluralism can help to filter the considered judgments that are central to the process of reflective equilibrium.[5] Yet from the less settled perspective of postmodern liberals such as William Connolly, Rawls's cultural turn opens liberal theory to an indeterminacy which rejects permanent solutions to political problems. "[T]his cultural sojourn of Rawlsian thought is not the consummation of liberalism: it prepares liberalism to engage the debate between those who think a benign hermeneutic can continue to revolve within the established parameters of traditional liberal assumptions, demands, and faiths and those who think that this shift prepares Rawlsian theory for its next set of debates."[6] Connolly welcomes the reliance of liberal theorizing on changes within liberal culture because it widens the space for democratic politics (characterized as a kind of agonistic pluralism).[7] Since liberal cultural tenets are shaped and reshaped by the outcomes of political competitions, they cannot exert the limiting influence that Rawls imagines.

Grounding a social contract or rational choice approach to political theory in cultural interpretation avoids the abstraction that distances so many of these presentations from social realities. Reinforcing the importance of politics reminds us that culture is a fluctuating and not a fixed set of meanings. Yet tracing theory to culture and ultimately to politics also diminishes the intellectual resources that are needed when the limits of culture and the hazards of politics are most apparent. One of the implications of liberalism's cultural turn is that the justification of liberal institutions is something that is possible only for those who already accept liberal principles as compelling. However, the reliance on liberal culture is more problematic if those principles themselves need justification. This becomes more than a philosopher's obsession when liberal states confront cultures or subcultures over practices that liberalism finds abhorrent, from ethnic cleansing in Kosovo to clitoridectomy in Togo.[8] Absent reasonable arguments, attempts to oppose or eliminate such practices may look like nothing more than exercises of power. This same dilemma arises in societal contexts where liberalization and democratization are incomplete. If theory depends on settled cultural resources, on what theoretical/cultural grounds can we endorse liberalization in Singapore or democratization in Iran?

A second problem with the dependence of political theorizing on cultural commitments or democratic processes is the resulting impact on possibilities for self-criticism. If the critical capacity of liberal theory is guided by the priorities of liberal culture or entwined with the practice of democratic politics, it is limited in its ability to assess these priorities and practices in critically distant ways. Eventually, this framework threatens to dismiss all such criticisms as illiberal or anti-democratic,[9] constraining sympathetic and constructive efforts to explore the possibilities and hazards of liberal democratic life.

Epistemologically, this perspective sees practical rationality as a cultural or political, rather than a natural or anthropological possibility. While both Rawls and Connolly would celebrate the post-metaphysical or antifoundational maturity of this position, its intellectual contributions are compromised by its own antimetaphysical rhetoric. Richard Rorty's non-political philosophy blithely dismisses both the possibility of and the need for any public form of rationality beyond the culturally sanctioned.[10] The more politically serious analyses of Habermas and Rawls rely on forms of procedural rationality that provide appropriate contexts for determining collective actions. Yet in so doing both positions also confront the question of *why* such procedures should be normatively privileged and neither seems capable of answering that question without either retreating to contingent cultural agreements (this is the form of public rationality that we accept) or recreating a post-metaphysical metaphysics of the person (this is the form of public rationality that respects our rights and dignities as equal moral beings). Furthermore, the exclusive focus on procedure leaves both positions incapable, in principle, of providing substantive criticisms of outcomes that have been determined in procedurally correct ways.

This essay argues that Aristotle offers a different and preferable perspective on the uses of political culture within political philosophy. I try to make this case by reading Aristotle's *Athēnaiōn Politeia* (*Constitution of the Athenians*) as a critical and reconstructive assessment of the political culture of democracy. This work is interpreted, not simply as a historical or descriptive account, one of the many constitutions "collected" by Aristotle or his students, but as an examination of how one particular democratic society could be improved so as to strengthen its potentials and diminish its pathologies. In crafting this discussion, Aristotle relies on an appreciation of positive and negative possibilities within democratic regimes themselves. However, those cultural characteristics cannot be fully examined without involving a critical rationality whose scope and categories extend beyond the boundaries set by democratic culture. Thus, this exercise of practical rationality points toward the importance of questions that Rawls dismisses (wrongly) as metaphysical, treating rationality and justice as anthropological and not simply cultural possibilities. This examination of democracy in the *Athēnaiōn Politeia* is circular in that it focuses on the enhancement of democratic possibilities, but it is non-circular in that it assesses these possibilities in light of a rationality that aspires to cross-cultural validity. Paralleling the democratic regime itself, the *Athēnaiōn Politeia* invites, rather than demands or supplies that exercise of critical reason. In so doing, the work acknowledges the possibility of a rational critique of democratic culture that is not simply anti-democratic in nature.

THE *ATHĒNAIŌN POLITEIA* AS A CULTURAL INVESTIGATION

Interpreting the *Athēnaiōn Politeia* (*AP*) as practical political theory means taking a controversial position on genre and authorship. Neither of these questions can be settled by external or linguistic evidence separable from interpretations. The author of the most extensive commentary on the *AP*, P. J. Rhodes, doubts that it was composed by Aristotle, in part because he sees little connection between its perspective and categories and the rest of Aristotle's political philosophy.[11] Since Aristotle's attitude toward democracy, particularly Athenian democracy, was negative, "the Athenian constitution may not have seemed particularly important to him."[12] Consequently, the *AP* should be read as a synoptic history and analysis of one *politeia* among many, probably composed by one of Aristotle's associates. More recently, Josiah Ober has agreed with Rhodes's attributing the work to one of Aristotle's students, though he does not deny the possibility of Aristotelian authorship.[13] John Keaney, on the other hand, makes a convincing evidentiary and interpretive case that the work is authentically Aristotle's, positioning the *AP* within the Aristotelian corpus as an exploration of how the institutional power of the *dēmos* orders the regime's entire political identity.[14]

I share Keaney's conclusion about the genuineness of Aristotle's authorship, but I do so on the basis of a different reading of the work's genre and significance. In spite of their many differences, neither Rhodes nor Keaney is inclined to award the Athenian constitution any special importance as the object of political investigation, in part because both tend to stress the theoretical aspects of Aristotelian political science.[15] As Keaney notes in a slightly different context, the *AP* includes a large number of "seems" (*dok-*) constructions, implying a degree of tentativeness, perhaps even inadequacy, as compared with more scientific investigations into the structures and purposes of political communities.[16] Yet Aristotle's political science is richly nuanced and its concerns are as much practical as theoretical. Aristotle's political works also have a certain audience in mind,[17] composed primarily not of political scientists or political philosophers, but of actual or potential practitioners who can affect the quality of public life. These people do not come to this discussion devoid of beliefs and interests. The *AP* is thus written against the backdrop of partisan treatments of Athens' political controversies.[18] Ober is more appreciative of the *AP*'s political contextualization, but I do not share his conclusion that "[t]he problem of 'how to criticize Athenian democracy' has . . . simply dissolved into the much simpler project of narrating the historical development of democracy and describing Athens' current governmental and legal arrangements."[19] My treatment relies on a more extended, though less intense, notion of criticism and sees more connections between the *AP* and the *Politics.*

Thematic and rhetorical continuities between the *Politics* and the *AP* are suggested by the short transition to the political writings found at the end of the *Nicomachean Ethics.* Aristotle notes that the collection of constitutions (*tōn synēgmenon politeōn*) will be of use in considering (*theōrein*) "those things that save or destroy both cities [generally] and individual regimes and the particular causes through which some are governed well and others the opposite" (*NE* 1181b15–20).[20] Both the more focused discussion of the *AP* and the broader comparisons of the *Politics* can be interpreted as resources for fostering both stability (or civility) and quality (or improvement). The connection between these two priorities is suggested in *Politics* 5.9 when Aristotle considers the meaning of an education *pros tēn politeian* (with a view to the regime). A healthy political education does not overbreed the citizens in the regime's specific character, but instead fosters moderation, nourishing both civility and a decent way of living. "[T]o be educated with a view to the *politeia* is not to do the things that please the oligarchs or those who want democracy but those that will enable oligarchic or democratic governance. . . . [I]n democracies thought to be most democratic, the opposite of what is advantageous has happened. The cause of this is that [the democrats] define freedom badly" (1310a20–5).

The significance of improving instead of reconfiguring regimes is reinforced by the fact that the comparison of regimes in *Politics* 3.6–7 is only a sketch. While certain general regime types are correct (*orthotēs*) or deviant (*parekbasēs*), there are broad empirical ranges within each. Democracies, particularly, are diverse, both in sociological and economic compositions and in institutional arrangements. Some democracies are thus markedly better (more civil and more decent) than others (*Politics* 4.4–5). Within the real world of Greek politics there are particular reasons for Aristotle to care very much about prospects for improving democracies. In *Politics* 3.15, he comments that the increasing size of cities (which I take to mean population density and urbanization) makes it unlikely that any regime will come into being without substantial democratic components (1286b20). While political theory cannot simply be restricted to democratic theory, political philosophy cannot be really political without engaging the question of how democratic decencies can be enhanced and democratic dangers avoided or diminished.

An examination of the Athenian democratic *politeia* is particularly instructive due to the regime's complex political and cultural identity. In some respects, Athens is a striking example of the most radical and most dangerous democracy, a popular regime with a (relatively) urban base which exercises its rule not by law but by decree (cf. *Politics* 4.4). Near the end of the *AP*'s discussion of the sequence of regime changes undergone by Athens, Aristotle comments, "the *dēmos* has now made itself sovereign (*kurios*) over everything, and it controls everything by votes (*psēphismata*) and in the law courts (*dikastēria*) in which the *dēmos* are the rulers; even those matters [formerly] judged by the [Areopagus] Council have now come to the *dēmos*" (41.2). In the *Politics*, this form of democratic rule is said to be the one most likely to be tyrannical (1292a15–20). In the *AP*, Aristotle traces the errors made by the regime to the influence of the demagogues, particularly with respect to the rule of the sea (41.2). From this perspective, the historical development of the Athenian constitution would seem to offer a striking picture of democratic abuses.

Yet the *AP* also comments on a very different characteristic of the Athenian regime, a gentleness or mildness that could be extended into a certain kind of moderation. This characteristic is notably displayed in the amnesty and reconciliation that help to conclude the anti-democratic rule of the Thirty Tyrants. In crafting these arrangements, the Athenians "seem distinct from all others in responding to misfortune, by behaving most nobly and most politically in private and public" (40.2–3). They agreed to pay the Thirty's debts to the Spartans out of public funds, "believing that this was the first beginning of concord (*homonoia*), whereas in other cities those who have established democratic control not only do not hand over their own, but also make efforts to divide the land anew" (40.3). Aristotle's Athens is simultaneously the most and the least typical, the worst and the best, of democracies. Reflections on its *politeia* are particularly appropriate for practical efforts to enhance democratic possibilities and to diminish democratic abuses.

If one of Aristotle's goals in the *AP* is to encourage pragmatic reflection on the political culture of a complex democracy, then the use of a large number of "seems" constructions need not indicate the work's inferior intellectual status as measured against a more scientific treatment of political institutions. Instead, this language may signal a discussion characterized by mutuality, a relative absence of contentiousness, and an openness to improved levels of understanding. The initial recognition of a seeming truth (that Athens was well governed during the period of the five thousand) can help to establish provisional agreements on the part of Aristotle and different members of his audience. At the same time, by refraining from presenting this seeming truth as evident or obvious (*phaneron*)[21] (that Athens *was* well governed at this time) Aristotle invites observations that might challenge or correct what seems to be the case. While frequent seems constructions may diminish the conclusiveness of the *AP*, they compensate by increasing possibilities for interactive conversations and reflective discoveries.[22]

This conversation involves at least three central themes within the *AP*. The first concerns the central principles of the regime, those priorities or commitments which make the democracy a *politeia* of a certain sort (*Politics* 3.8). The *AP* examines these priorities, freedom and equality, not as abstract principles but as institutionalized practices. In particular, this examination suggests that democratic regimes benefit when institutions moderate political activism. The second theme concerns the appropriate content of democratic collective action, the purposes or functions that the democracy characteristically pursues or performs. The *AP* considers collective action inspired by two very different psychocultural characteristics, a boldness that endangers and a gentleness that safeguards the quality of life in a democratic culture. The third theme involves cultural examples that help to construct a complex portrayal of models of democratic political activity. The *AP*'s assessment of significant historical figures within Athens' political history underscores the requirements, abuses, and vulnerabilities of democratic citizenship.

INSTITUTIONALIZING FREEDOM AND EQUALITY

The principles that inform a democracy's institutions and culture (cf. *Politics* 2.11) are freedom (*Politics* 3.8; 5.9) and equality (*Politics* 3.1,9; 5.9). The well-being of democratic communities is significantly influenced by how these principles are understood and institutionalized (cf. *Politics* 6.2,3). In the *AP*, the two democratic principles are examined as institutional and cultural conditions that have emerged historically within a particular regime context.[23] In addition to narrating their development and analyzing their functions, Aristotle also tries to assess their contributions to the qualities of civility and decency within the democratic regime.

The historical development of freedom and equality in Athens begins with conflicts over power. The early structure of Athens' *politeia* was severely oligarchic; it invested sovereign (*kurios*) power in the Areopagus Council, "which ordered the greatest number of and the most significant affairs in the city and punished and fined all wrongdoers authoritatively" (3.6). The many (*hoi polloi*) "found themselves so to speak having no share in anything" (2.3). Draco's ordinances (4.1–4) modified and routinized a number of institutional arrangements, but did not change the "completely oligarchical" (2.2) nature of the *politeia* and the virtually complete enslavement (*doulōein*) of the many to the rich or the few (2.2,5.1), visible particularly in the practice of securing monetary loans on the liberty of the borrower (2.2,4.4). Eventually, these abuses initiated a confrontation (*antestē*) of the notables by the people (*dēmos*), beginning a continued *stasis* (factional conflict) (2.1–2) that was not moderated until Solon's reforms. The process of radical democratization within Athens was thus spawned by the domination of the oligarchs. By moving from the enslavement of *hoi polloi* to the resistance of *ho dēmos,* Aristotle implies that the many's identity as a political force has been organized if not created by oligarchic oppression.[24] The Athenian *dēmos* thus strove for the condition which was the opposite or other (*heteron*) of enslavement, freedom (*eleutheria*) (6.1,12.4).[25]

This process of democratic liberation begins when Solon eliminates the practice of securing loans by personal liberty, achieving the so-called "shaking off of burdens" (*seisachtheia*) (6.1–2) which Aristotle calls the most democratic of Solon's reforms (9.1). By the end of the historical narrative, the *dēmos* has freed itself in a more active way, changing its political condition from powerlessness to having sovereign or controlling (*kurios*) authority (41.2). In its connection with the collective action of the *dēmos* this more active form of freedom has also become a political and social category created and regulated by a particular arrangement of power.

Aristotle thus begins the institutional portion of the *AP* with a statement of the contemporary conditions for and implications of an Athenian citizen's being free. "Sharing in citizenship are those born of citizen parents on both sides, they are enrolled in their demes when they become eighteen. When they are registered, the demesmen decide about them according to oaths, first, whether they seem to be of legal age, and if they are not held to be so, they go back to the boys, and, second, whether they are free (*eleutheros*) and have been born according to the laws. If they are deemed not to be free, they can appeal to the law court and the demesmen elect five men from among themselves as accusers. If he does not seem to have a just claim to be recorded, the city sells him, but if he wins the demesmen are compelled to record him" (42.1–2). Thus characterized, freedom is not a protected private sphere but a political status which provides access to institutional offices, responsibilities, and powers. Keaney's insight that one of the central narrative strands in the *AP* is the replacement of the Areopagus Council by the *dēmos* as sovereign authority in the city thus also traces changes in the Athenian understanding of freedom. In addition to serving this ordering function, however, this development can also raise pragmatic questions about the nature, implications, and even dangers of democratic freedom.

In the pre-Solonic and Solonic chapters, freedom opposes the abuses of sovereign power; the enslavement of the many creates an abiding suspicion about power that is *kurios,* a sense that is reinforced in the chronicle of the

Thirty's terrorization of the city (35.1). Witnessing the transformation of freedom in the radical democracy into one of the instruments of authoritative power can both draw upon and reinforce that suspicion, especially in cases where those who unsuccessfully appeal the deme's decision not to record them as "free and born according to the laws" are sold. Whereas oligarchic oppression had earlier created a consciousness of the masses' lack of freedom, the *dēmos'* control over the category of freedom now also confers the power to enslave. Implicating active political freedom with power that is *kurios* can serve as a cautionary warning against an abusive exercise of that freedom. Yet in a democratic culture only democratic limitations on sovereign power can be accepted as legitimate. Where might such limitations be found?

The *AP* suggests that one source is the institutionalization of a certain kind of equality. Eventually, equality before the law emerges as a basic condition for civility, the protection of difference, and social trust. Legal equality is also capable of tempering active political freedom's excessive use of sovereign power. Democratic freedom and equality play their most positive political roles when boundaries between their institutional expressions are maintained. The health of the democracy is threatened when those boundaries begin to erode.

Legal equality begins to be institutionalized in the Athenian regime by the reforms of Solon. Aristotle comments that Solon could have responded to the conflict between oligarchs and democrats opportunistically, becoming tyrant by siding with either group against the other. Instead "he chose to save the country and legislate for the best" (11.2). Solon himself defends this legislation as an attempt to create a condition in which each of the contending parties is equal before the law (12.3–4). By implying that the alternative to political equality is a kind of tyranny, Aristotle reinforces the observation that political ruling and being ruled involves a certain kind of equality among the parties (*Politics* 1132b25). Solon's reforms do not so much make Athens more democratic as make it more political (9.2).

Solon attempts to negotiate factional quarrels over inequality through two basic institutional strategies. The first eliminates economic and political practices that enslave the poorest class and deprive it of any share in political decision. Solon not only protects impoverished debtors against enslavement but also opens membership in the assembly and the law courts to the poorest citizens (7.3–4; 9.1–2). By making some political institutions accessible to every class of citizen Solon maintains the political relevance of economic distinctions while refusing to disenfranchise any citizen completely on the basis of poverty.

Second, Solon makes the regime's legal structures into frameworks that manage conflict, rather than into strategic weapons for use within power contests. Solon's own poetic account of his political activity underscores the

importance of making both good and bad (or noble and base) equally subject to the law (12.3–4).[26] By creating a structured framework for regulating
interaction and resolving conflict, Solon encourages political agreement or
mutuality (*homoion*) among citizens and constrains the use of force according to the rules of justice (12.1,4). In obvious ways, the institutionalization
of political equality represents an alternative to the arbitrariness of the oligarchs. The punitive functions of the Areopagus Council are now limited by
its constitutional function of guarding the laws (*nomophylakein*). For many
of the same reasons, the legal equality of noble and base can also impose
limitations on the otherwise sovereign exercise of democratic power. Just as
legal equality prevents the notables from abusing the many on the basis of
their lower social or economic status, it also prevents the many from despoil-
ing the notables because of their wealth or family histories. The kinds of
institutional reform initiated by Solon thus seem particularly appropriate
for a socially differentiated culture. Solon does not attempt to homogenize
difference by creating a common civic ethos which would make social
distinctions either irrelevant or pernicious. While the institution of legal
equality makes the social differences between noble and base irrelevant from
the point of view of justice, in another sense it maintains respect for differentiation among social classes since class positioning cannot justify social
aggression.

As the Athenian democratic regime develops, however, the boundaries
between active political freedom and equality before the law tend to diminish. The principal institutional cause of this change is the eventual vesting
of sovereign power in the assembly and the law courts, "for when the *dēmos*
is sovereign (*to kurion*) over the vote, it becomes sovereign over the *politeia*"
(9.1–2). Equality is now institutionalized primarily in the use of the lot to
determine the holders of virtually all political offices and in the use of os-
tracism to remove those "who might seem to be great" (32.6). This change
involves more than simply the removal of economic barriers to political
office or even the replacement of the Areopagus Council by the assembly
and the law courts as authoritative political institutions. What also arises is
the dangerous belief that constitutional or institutional limitations on democratic bodies are themselves anti-democratic. The roots of this opinion are
explored more fully in the *Politics* (5.9), when Aristotle reflects on the con-
flation of the meanings of equality and freedom. "Two things are thought
to define democratic rule, that the multitude should be authoritative and
freedom. Justice is thought to be equality (*to ison*), equality [supports] the
authority of the majority's opinion, and freedom [means] doing whatever
one wishes" (1310a25–30). The influence of equality comes not in a respect
for boundaries that might limit the exercise of political freedom, but in the
aggregation of individual desires which determine decisions that are at once

free and *kurios*. The principal political consequence of conflating freedom and equality is the disappearance of any difference between law and votes or decrees, for the only legitimate limits on democratic decisions are those that democratic bodies set for themselves.[27] Yet while eliminating boundaries between freedom and equality might maximize the possibilities of political freedom, it also tends to threaten the conditions for mutuality, respect for difference, and social trust that should hold a democratic community together. In answer to the question raised in *Politics* 3.10, "if the poor through their greater numbers divide [among themselves] what belongs to the rich, is not this unjust?" comes the polemical answer, "By Zeus! This was determined justly by those holding control" (*tō kuriō dikaiōs*).

Though the worst sorts of democratic behavior were not practiced by the Athenians even on the occasion when it seemed most excusable, the dangers of rule by decree are hazards to which Athens is continually vulnerable. One of the challenges facing concerned democratic citizens is how to avoid the forms of recklessness that could endanger the democratic goods enabled by equality before the law. Present-day deliberative democrats recommend adopting appropriate institutions that create boundaries between democratic deliberation and political decision and action.[28] Aristotle's reliance on equality before the law suggests a basic sympathy with this strategy.[29] At the same time, he apparently does not believe that institutional solutions are by themselves sufficient. Solon's institutional reforms were not in the end successful in preventing civil *stasis*. In the third book of the *Politics* Aristotle offers an implied criticism of the incomplete nature of the sorts of reforms initiated by Solon. Arrangements which attempt to instill civility through legal protections "assure [the possibility of citizens making] just claims on one another, but are not such as to make the citizens good and just" (1280b10).

The *AP* seems to depart most dramatically from the *Politics* over the issue of political education. In the *Politics*' sketch of the best regime, Aristotle begins to develop the outline of a political education that strives to nurture human beings who are able to choose well at leisure (*Politics* 7.14; 8.5). In the *AP*, however, Aristotle is generally silent about the cultural practices that might develop this kind of capacity in the Athenian regime. Since a democracy endorses the principle of being able to live as one likes (*Politics* 5.9), it is not easily positioned to conduct this sort of common education. Thus, the *AP*'s focus on culture is very different from Xenophon's in the *Constitution of the Lacedaimonians* (*LP*). While Athens clearly regulates citizen behavior across a variety of spheres, Sparta attempts to form the very core of the citizens' identities by eliciting civic republican virtues through a highly invasive enculturation (cf. Xenophon, *LP* 6.1–2). In the *Nicomachean Ethics* (10.9), Sparta is noted as the only regime that takes the

moral education of its citizens seriously. Eventually, however, this reputation turns out to be undeserved. Since Spartan education focuses exclusively
on fostering warlike virtue, it altogether neglects any preparation for living
well at leisure (*Politics* 2.9). Moreover, because the regime values warlike
virtue for the success it brings, its culture turns virtue into an instrument.
For all of these reasons, Athens' tentative and diffuse possibilities ultimately
seem preferable to Sparta's conclusive and concentrated realities. Since
Athenian culture "allows each to care for the education of his own in whatever way he thinks fit" (*Politics* 8.1), the educational alternative of encouraging reflection on the benefits and dangers of freedom, equality, and their
associated political practices is not a democratic cultural necessity but it may
be a democratic cultural possibility.

The Competing Paths of Boldness and Gentleness

In the *AP*, a reflection on democratic purposes is implicit in the consideration of two competing Athenian psychocultural characteristics, boldness
(*tharros*) and gentleness (*praotēs*).[30] These conditions are cognate to the two
very different conceptions of political action which Aristotle examines in a
more general way in *Politics* 7.3. The context of that discussion concerns
whether the best life is that of activity in the city or "rather that of a stranger,
disconnected from sharing in political things" (1324a15–20). Aristotle implies
that the dominant contemporary conception of political action focuses on
success in power competitions. "For happiness is practice, so the practices
of the just and the sensible have the end of achieving many things that are
noble. And indeed because of these determinations one might quickly
suppose that the best thing of all is to be sovereign (*kurios*) over all, that
one might have control over the greatest number and noblest of actions"
(1325a30–5). For Aristotle, this opinion is compromised by distorted notions
of *praxis* and nobility (*to kalon*). Against accepted conceptions of active
nobility, Aristotle denies that "the active life is . . . necessarily [one that is
directed against] others, the way some people believe." Thus, "cities are not
necessarily inactive (*apraktein*) just because they are off by themselves and
determine to live this way, for their parts can be active, since the parts of a
city have many common relations with one another" (1325b20–5). Aristotle
thus concludes book seven by replacing aggressive activity and its associated
warlike virtues with conceptions of civic action and the noble that foster
educational or cultural practices supportive of the peaceful virtues (7.14–15).[31]

    In the *AP*'s historical narrative, conspicuous assertiveness characterizes
Athens' political development from the end of the Persian wars through the
consolidation of the democracy after the defeat of the Thirty. Aristotle chal-

lenges the value of this form of collective action by calling the rule of the sea an error (*hamartia*). He supports this charge not through an explicit condemnation of the empire but through a treatment of Athenian domestic priorities that draws attention away from the empire and war to the peaceful activities that (defensive) war can protect and enable. This examination of Athenian domestic politics during the city's imperialistic expansion indicates how the impulses and practices that contributed to the empire also threatened the democratic regime itself.

Athens' imperialism both expresses and reinforces the regime's underlying potential for boldness. The emboldening of the regime begins after the Persian wars under the leadership of the Areopagus Council. Aristotle comments that the city was well governed (*epoliteuthesan . . . kalōs*) during this time because of the practice of military things by the populace, the winning of esteem or reputation (*eudokimesai*) among the Greeks, and the achievement of leadership (*hēgemonia*) over the sea against the wishes of the Lacedaimonians (23.2). This puzzling assessment seems at odds with the later criticism of the rule of the sea as one of the city's great errors. Rhodes and Keaney disagree over the significance of Aristotle's positive evaluation of this period of Athens' constitutional history. Rhodes believes that it is a repetition of the views of some other commentator, similar to the way in which the evaluation of the regime of the five thousand (33.2) seems to repeat the favorable judgment of Thucydides (8.97, 2–3).[32] Keaney claims that the difference between the two statements (the Athenians seem to have been well governed under the five thousand, whereas they were well governed under the influence of the Areopagus Council) emphasizes that the views on the Areopagus regime are Aristotle's own.[33] Both interpretations leave residual questions. Rhodes's view requires us to ignore any potential differences implied by the presence or absence of the "seems" construction and, in general, to take less seriously the distinctive voice of the *AP*'s text. While Keaney's analysis of the text's structure supports reading the *AP* as deliberately crafted composition, it also makes the differences between the explicit praise of the Areopagus-led regime in 23.2 and the eventual harsh condemnation of the rule of the sea in 41.2 even more puzzling. The linguistic similarity between the two statements strengthens the possibility of a deliberately crafted thematic connection. It would be utterly implausible to read the second statement as a deconstruction of the first, showing how wrong it would be to see Athens as *truly* well governed at the time when the rule of the sea began. To the extent that the positive assessment of Areopagus regime is sincere, Aristotle implies that Athens acted properly in developing its military capacity after the Persian wars, perhaps out of a need to maintain its own security in the face of continuing Persian threats and abusive Spartan behavior (23.4; cf. Thucydides 1.96,1). Though justifiable, however, this policy leads eventually to a condition which is itself the source or cause of a great *hamartia*. The continuing emphasis on the emboldening of the regime makes it unlikely that Aristotle's favorable verdict in 23.2 simply endorses a moderate imperialism under the Areopagites that was dangerously radicalized by the democrats. If we read these comments as part of a larger pedagogical project that encourages critical reflection on the regime's priorities, they suggest a need to examine carefully the regime consequences of even the most necessary public policies, to be conscious of the fine line that separates defense against aggression (a prudent gentleness) from aggressiveness itself (boldness).

As the historical narrative progresses, the emboldening of the regime is tied more closely to its democratization. The strongest voice in the early development of the empire is that of Aristeides, who combines support for Athenian rule over the sea with championing the cause of popular rule. "Now that the city was emboldened (*tharrousēs . . . tēs poleōs*) and a great deal of money had been collected, [Aristeides] counseled [the people] to take hold of the leadership and to come away from their farms and live in the city, telling them that there would be maintenance for everybody, for some through service in the army, for others through guarding, for others through managing common affairs. Thus persuaded and taking over the rule (*archē*), they treated the allies more despotically" (24.1–2). Thus, while Aristotle does not suggest that the empire is the cause of Athens' growing democratization,[34] he does indicate that Athens' boldness toward other cities and the *dēmos*' boldness within the *politeia* are reciprocally related. Under, first, Ephialtes and, then, Pericles, the *dēmos* comes to assume ever more of the power of the Areopagus Council. Pericles, in particular, "vigorously encouraged the city toward [being a] naval power, and, thus emboldened (*tharrēsantes*), the many came together to take all of the regime under its own control" (27.1–2).

For the Pericles of Thucydides' funeral speech, boldness asserted through the empire is the source of Athens' power and reputation. "Summing up, I say that our city educates all of Greece . . . and that this is not boastful speech for the moment but is instead the factual truth is signalled by the power of the city which we gained though these [accomplishments]" (Thucydides 2.41,1–2). Aristotle's assessment is far more critical. While he is not as openly confrontational as the Platonic Socrates of the *Gorgias*, he introduces considerations that call the wisdom and desirability of the empire into serious question. His first strategy is to treat the events associated with the war as important principally because of their impacts on Athens' *politeia*. This reverses Thucydides' treatment which positions all examinations of Athenian domestic politics within the narrative of the war, that event which was "great and worthy of discourse beyond all those which had gone before" (1.1). From the perspective of the *AP*, Aristeides is a more significant figure than Themistocles. And the most important consequence of the war in this context is its contribution to the increasing democratization of the regime. "Forty-eight years after the naval battle at Salamis . . . the war against the Peloponnesians began . . . and the *dēmos* in part voluntarily, in part involuntarily, came to the point where they ordered the regime themselves" (27.2). Aristotle thus implies that wars need to be understood in light of the domestic activities that they defend or support.[35] In changing the focus from war to domestic politics, Aristotle makes possible a renewed appreciation of the value of gentleness, the regime characteristic that can facilitate the political good of civic friendship (40.2–4; cf. *Politics* 2.4, 3.10; *NE* 8.1). Thus, to the degree that boldness compromises prospects for regime gentleness, it threatens to undermine those activities that are most politically worthwhile.

Aristotle's second challenge to the value of boldness subtly reminds the Athenians of the foreign and domestic political ills that were directly attached to the boldness of the city.[36] The emboldening of the many is followed immediately by the beginning of the war, which is chronicled as a series of Athenian defeats. The exhilarating victory at Salamis is followed by Sicily (29.1), Eretria (33.1), Euboea (33.1), Deceleia (34.1–2), and Aegospotami (34.2–3). Pylos is notable only in connection with its being retaken by Sparta (27.5). The sole Athenian victory mentioned is the very costly success at Arginusae (34.1). In both of these last cases, resulting domestic abuses are underscored. Anytus bribed the law court to gain acquittal against charges that he was responsible for losing Pylos. Blinded by anger, the *dēmos* used an unconstitutional procedure to condemn the Arginusae generals for failing to rescue the sailors. The narrative instantaneously associates the defeat at Aegospotami, the occupation (*kurion*) of Lysander, and the establishment of the Thirty (34.2–3). Though Athenians may be drawn to the fruits of boldness as events most worthy of being talked about, the fruits of gentleness or restraint (the amnesty and the reconciliation) seem more worthy of emulation.

POSSIBILITIES AND HAZARDS FOR DEMOCRATIC CITIZENSHIP

In the *Politics*, the examination of the city itself (*ti estin hē polis*) requires a substantive consideration of the citizens (3.1). This extends beyond the institutional question of who governs to a treatment of culture and education, for "whatever the preeminent element holds in honor will necessarily be followed in the opinions of the other citizens" (1273a40). Consequently, how a culture narrates the accomplishments and identities of its most exemplary citizens is both a sign of and a resource for civic education.[37] One of the distinctive features of Athens' diverse political culture is the range of men whose practices and identities continue to play influential symbolic roles. At times, there is widespread agreement about these people (Pericles is generally regarded as a prudent man—*NE* 6.5), but more commonly there is controversy (Solon's responsibility for the radical democracy is unclear—*AP* 9.1–2; *Politics* 2.12—and opinions about Theramenes' character are highly disputed—*AP* 28.5). Often, judgments about these figures are driven by political allegiances; aristocrats are inclined to blame Solon for contributing to the regime's democratization and strong democrats are the ones most likely to hate Theramenes. While Aristotle's own standard for judging these people is political, it is not associated with any form of intense partisanship. Instead, he assesses political figures in light of contributions made to the well-being of the city as a whole. By making the nature of good citizenship into an issue or a problem, Aristotle implies that it cannot be simply a matter of pursuing the competitive interests of one's own community or faction. And by indicating that this question requires thoughtful attention, he underscores the importance of critical judgment for constructive political action.

Solon and Democratic Rationality

The examination of Solon's contributions to the regime engages a fundamental debate within the political culture. Initially this concerns Solon's influence on the developing democratic order, specifically through allowing appeals to the *dikastēria* in cases where the law is ambiguous (9.1–2). The *Politics* (2.12) states that a number of people blame Solon for establishing the democracy by thus empowering the law courts. The narrower debate about Solon is thus contextualized by the broader debate about the merits and deficiencies of democracy. Since the parties to the debate are the same factions that Solon tried to reconcile, his efforts to harmonize the city were not altogether successful. At the same time, the persistence of these factional quarrels means that a review of Solon's attempt to moderate Athenian politics is of more than historical interest.

Solon is praised for refusing to align himself with either the oligarchs or the democrats. "[W]hen he could have subjected one or the other and thus tyrannized over the city, instead he incurred the hatred of both [factions], valuing nobility and the safety of the city much more than his own immediate gain (*pleonexia*)" (6.2). With regard to good citizenship, Aristotle's clear and (at one level) noncontroversial observation is that being a good citizen involves resisting the urges toward *pleonexia* (trying to grab more than one's share or preferring one's own interests to those of the community). What may be less recognizable, however, is that radical partisan-ship on either side of class conflict is a consolidation of *pleonexia*. Demo-cratic partisans easily recognize the coordinated injustice of the oligarchs and Solon himself traces all of the blame for the preceding *stasis* to the love of money (*philaguria*) and the arrogance (*hyperēphania*) of the rich (5.3). Yet as a partnership among continuous equals, the city would not be notice-ably better off if oligarchs and democrats simply reversed roles, for the pur-suit of either partisan agenda can lead to tyranny. From this perspective, one of the central requirements for good citizenship is the ability to understand that what is good for the community as a whole is not simply reducible to the interests of any single economic, social, or cultural class.

Yet there are other dangers to civic harmony beyond the desire to have more and one may be the moral passion for strict justice. If Solon had been so motivated, the just thing to do could well have been to punish the oli-garchs for their abuses, if not by disenfranchisement and redistribution, then through the creation of a form of democracy which replaced dichoto-mous inequality with radical equality. In this instance, there would be a troubling similarity in outcomes between the selfish desire to have more and the passion for justice. Solon's alternative approach is to reconstruct vari-ous forms of inequality to make them less devastating for those having less and more conducive to civic harmony and stabilization. Thus, one of the most critical abilities for the good citizen would be the capacity to balance the love of justice with a concern for the well-being of the community as a whole or with a certain degree of forgiving moderation.[38]

Yet Solon's good citizenship requires intellectual virtues as well. The complicated place of a certain kind of rationality within good citizenship is suggested by Solon's similarly complicated relationship to politics as a way of life. Keaney points to the "three lives" of Solon, politician, economic agent, and intellectual, noting that these three aspects of Solon's identity seem to be remarkably in balance.[39] Aristotle's emphasis on Solon's measured (*metrion*) character plays an interesting role within the more focused ethi-cal debate on the content of the best life in the *Nicomachean Ethics*, where the testimonies of Solon and Anaxagoras support the choiceworthiness of a moderate life that resists an obsession with politics (the desire to be ruler of land and sea) in light of an appreciation of a way of life (the contemplative or philosophic) which goes beyond it.[40] In the more political context of the *AP*, this characterization of Solon as balanced or measured highlights a form of rationality that represents an alternative politics rather than alternative to politics.

A sort of rationality that informs politics even as it extends beyond political immediacies is displayed within the fragments of Solon's poetry quoted in the *AP*. The quoted portions of the poem outline the political challenges faced by Solon and explain the reasons behind his political choices. By representing partisan and pragmatic concerns in a poetic context, Solon effectively encourages the reader to adopt a perspective of critical distance and to engage in a kind of political theorization. Solon's poetry is thus a pragmatic acknowledgment of a political rationality extending beyond the strategic, for it communicates Solon's own priorities and justifications to his fellow citizens, not simply to mobilize support, but to provide enlightenment and to encourage further examination.

In spite of Solon's praiseworthy motives and abilities, however, his success at constitutional reform is limited. During his ongoing presence within Athens, he faces challenges and criticisms that reflect persisting political tensions. Partially in reaction, Solon left Athens for the purposes of trade and observation (*theōria*) in Egypt, telling the Athenians that during his absence "each one should do as he had written" (11.2). After his departure, the city experiences repeated disturbances culminating in a renewed *stasis* (13.1–2). Yet even though Solon's reforms may be compromised, there is no express suggestion that he could have crafted better laws. The unintended consequences of his empowerment of the law courts stem not from any deviousness or incompetence on his part, but from "the impossibility of specifying what is best in universal language" (9.2) or the gap that always exists between what is said and what is done. At one level, appreciating the inadequacy of universal language for political guidance makes Solon's parting instructions to the city seem naive. While he deserves respect for resisting the opportunity to tyrannize, there is also a sense in which his particular departure from Athens may represent a failure of political leadership, one of the drawbacks of Solon's balanced life. However, it would be equally naive to expect even the best leadership to correct completely the human condition of irrationality. The urge to take more than one's share and the passion for unrelenting justice are expressions of avarice and anger, not simply dictates of a misguided rationality. Thus, if Solon's poetry points by implication to the need for rationality, his imperfect success signals its limits. It seems necessary for good citizens to understand both.

Interrogating the Peisistratids and the Tyrannicides

The *stasis* that follows Solon's efforts eventually leads to the tyranny of Peisistratus. The experience of the city with the Peisistratid family has created the most stirring model of democratic civic devotion. The institutional origins of the current democracy might be traced to the reforms of Cleisthenes (21.1–6; 22.1–2), but the emotional foundations are preserved in the storied deeds of the martyred tyrannicides, Harmodius and Aristogeiton, who are popularly associated with the end of the Peisistratid tyranny.[41] As the democratic citizens who gave their lives to preserve civic freedom, they are not simply behavioral models but objects of religious devotion (58.1–2). Yet the cultural opinions about the Peisistratids are not uniform, for Aristotle notes that "one might hear many [say] that the tyranny of Peisistratus was the golden age of Cronos" (16.7). On the surface, Aristotle would seem to take the anti-democratic side. In reality, his assessment is ambiguous, with more nuanced implications for good citizenship in a democratic political community.

Peisistratus should draw critical scrutiny because he was seldom what he seemed. Early in the *AP*, it is twice stated that Peisistratus "seemed to be most democratic [in loyalties and purpose] (*dēmotikōtatos einai dokōn*)" (13.5;14.1), even as he was aiming at creating a tyranny. Gaps between the seeming and the real Peisistratus persist throughout the story of his political career. Strategically, he succeeds through a number of particular deceptions: wounding himself to create the impression that he needs a bodyguard (14.1–2), cooperating with Megacles to manipulate a return from his first exile by enlisting a woman to masquerade as Athena (14.4), and disarming the populace through the use and misuse of *logos* in the assembly (15.4–5). He seemed to rule in a way that was *politikōs* and *praōs,* but his influence diminishes Athens' politicality (15.5) and much of the language that describes his accession to power refers to control and force (15.2–3). He may have avoided processes of legality by appearing to obey them (16.8–9). In this light, the widespread belief that Peisistratus' tyranny was the golden age (already represented in language which acknowledges exaggeration) seems mistaken. At the same time, the legend surrounding the tyrannicides is shown to be fundamentally wrong in virtually all of its significant claims. The truth about the Peisistratids needs to be pried loose from romanticizations on all sides.

Initially, Peisistratus does precisely what Solon refuses to do, taking advantage of a civil *stasis* to establish a tyranny. Yet in the exercise of that tyranny, Peisistratus' behavior partially mirrors Solon's, for he does not "in any respect give himself more than his share (*oudemian eautou pleonexian didous*)" (16.8). This assessment must be confined to the distribution of (broadly) economic goods because Peisistratus did take more than his share in the obvious case of the distribution of political power. Consequently, the belief that Peisistratus' rule was more political than tyrannical needs refinement. He ruled politically when he respected the well-being and property of those whom he ruled, but not when he prevented any sharing or rotation in the offices on the part of those who are generally equal (*Politics* 7.14). Peisistratus' most significant political cultural goal was to turn the citizens in the direction of "managing their own private affairs, leaving the care of all of the common things to himself" (15.5). If Solon made Athens more political, Peisistratus made it in a way more domestic.[42]

In the *Politics*, Aristotle calls a democracy based on an agricultural society the best democratic regime, in part because of the limitations which circumstances place on the scope and intensity of political activity (1318b5–10). This could be read as support for Peisistratus' policy of depoliticization. Yet as a positive institutional model for democratic reform, Peisistratus' policy is severely limited. Demographic changes and urbanization have concentrated the dispersed agricultural population that this sort of democracy requires. Moreover, while Aristotle's preference in the *Politics* describes an alternative democracy, Peisistratus' policy was an alternative to democracy. The surface similarities between Peisistratus' depoliticized society and the agricultural democracy therefore pale in light of their extensive differences with regard to the presence of law. Whereas the predominance of an agricultural population in a democracy makes the regime more likely to be ruled by laws, rather than decrees, the presence of the same population in a tyranny facilitates tyrants' standing above the laws.

The dark consequences of the absence of law are apparent in the truth behind the tyrannicide legend. According to the story, Harmodius and Aristogeiton lost their lives to free Athens from the control of Peisistratus' tyrant son, Hippias. Like Thucydides, Aristotle offers an alternative account that indicates that the deeds of the tyrannicides neither arose from public motives nor achieved a salutary public outcome. The cause of the conspiracy was an erotic quarrel between Harmodius and one of Peisistratus' other sons, Thettalus. The conspirators did not remove Hippias from power (instead, they killed another brother, Hipparchus) and in fact caused the tyranny to become harsher (19.1–2). Yet simply to draw anti-democratic implications from this exposé would be erroneous, for it is also relevant that the act that prompted the conspiracy was a private erotic aggression committed by a tyrant's son who was bold and insulting in his mode of life (18.2; *Politics* 1311a35).[43] Attempted tyrannicide was provoked by an action that failed to keep erotics separate from politics or private things from public things. The absence of such separations is one hallmark of tyranny, so that one-person rule often resembles a dysfunctional family.[44] In a sense, tyrannicide is provoked by tyranny itself.

Though the legend also says that the tyranny was put down by the freedom-loving Athenians, Aristotle, again like Thucydides,[45] claims that the overthrow was accomplished by the Spartans (19.2–3). However, it would be mistaken simply to read this correction as an attempt to embarrass democratic enthusiasts. Instead, the Peisistratus narrative could be interpreted as instructing democratic citizens on the political hazards of both certain forms of withdrawal and certain forms of aggression. The dangers of withdrawal are illustrated by the ease with which both the notables and the people place a care for the common things under Peisistratus' exclusive control (16.9–10). Whereas both parties had earlier agreed to Solon's political arrangements that at some level included them all, they later accept Peisistratus' anti-political arrangements that virtually exclude them all. What underlies this willingness is an excessive readiness to occupy oneself exclusively with one's own affairs, a tendency exposed by Solon's unheeded objections to Peisistratus (14.2–3).[46] Thus, the deceptions surrounding Peisistratus also involve broader deceptions about tyrants, for the Athenians failed to recognize that even tyrants who naturally conduct themselves with the greatest nobility (16.1–2) are dangerously positioned above law and institutions. The philanthropy of Peisistratus will be no safeguard against the insulting arrogance of Thettalus or the fearful vengeance of Hippias (19.1–2).

At the same time, the dangers of aggressiveness are underscored by the actions of the tyrannicides. Harmodius and Aristogeiton respond to a public abuse over a private matter with a conspiracy that has devastating public consequences. The tyrannicides compounded the damage done by Thettalus by allowing their passions to intrude into and to threaten the stability of public life. Thus, Aristotle may be less concerned with the absence of a burning civic devotion on the part of the tyrannicides (sincere public motives can be similarly destructive) than with the apparent lack of thoughtful consideration about the public consequences of their anger. Both Thettalus and Harmodius acted out of a boldness which blinded them to the wide damages they caused. The belief that Peisistratus' rule was a golden age is thus fostered by a comparison with the harsher tyranny that followed, something for which both the tyrant and the tyrannicides bear responsibility.

Pericles and Democratic Assertiveness

To the extent that a political community attempts to establish boldness as a public principle, it threatens to consolidate and intensify recklessness. It is Pericles, more than any other politician, who is associated with boldness as a public principle. It is helpful to consider Pericles' appearance in the *AP* in light of the exemplary role which Aristotle gives him in the *Nicomachean Ethics*. In book six (the book on intellectual virtue) Pericles is identified as the symbol or image of *phronēsis* (practical wisdom). "Those like Pericles are thought to be practically wise because they are able to see (*theōrein*) what is good for themselves as well as [what is good] for [other] human beings. That is our idea of a household manager or a statesman" (1140b5–10). While Aristotle goes on to challenge the Periclean conception of practical wisdom, he does not dispute Pericles' preeminence as a cultural and political figure. This pride of place is reinforced in Thucydides' assessment of the Athenian regime during the Periclean period. "Although in speech (*logos*) a democracy, Athens in fact (*ergon*) came to be ruled by the foremost man" (2.65.9). This Pericles is the democratic leader who is most associated with the calculated imperialism that leads eventually to the war (1.140,1–2; 141,1; 2.36,3–4) and who is the most eloquent proponent of a life of conspicuous daring as best for both individuals (2.40; 2.43.2–4) and cities (2.64,3–6).

By comparison, Pericles' role in the *AP* is subdued. If Keaney is right to say that Aristotle's treatment of Pericles is deconstructive,[47] part of his criticism subtly reduces the impression of Pericles' distinctiveness. In the *AP* he is one of a series of democratic politicians who contributes (after Aristeides and Ephialtes) to the growing democratization of the city and (after Themistocles and Aristeides) to the increasing development of naval power (27.1–2). By downplaying the conspicuousness of Pericles, just as he downplays the distinctiveness of the war, Aristotle responds to boldness by refusing to be overly impressed by it.

Paralleling the discussion of the war, the discussion of Pericles also focuses on how Pericles' policies affected the Athenian domestic regime. Pericles' most notable contribution to the power of the democracy was to institute pay for service in the law courts. He rather than Solon was most responsible for democratizing the regime through a manipulation of the *dikastēria* (cf. *Politics* 2.12). Extending this comparison, Aristotle also implicitly distinguishes between the public motives of Solon and the personal agenda of Pericles. Pericles is said to have initiated the policy of paying the dicasts in order to compete more successfully with his notable and rich rival Cimon. Since Pericles had no resources of his own, "he gave the many their own [resources] by establishing pay for the law courts" (27.4), a policy that has damaging public consequences. The payment for jury service eventually blurs the distinction between the private (remunerative) and public (adjudicative) activities of the citizens and facilitates the practice of bribing juries (27.5).

Aristotle nonetheless seems to echo Thucydides' assessment that public affairs were managed better under Pericles than under the popular leaders who followed him (28.1–2; Thucydides 2.65.6–7).[48] Yet the relationship between Pericles and his successors in the *AP* is ambiguous. In appearance, Pericles, like most of his predecessors, was more acceptable to the notables, whereas Cleon's manner marked him as the first of the demagogues (28.3). However, Aristotle's own assessment of the damage done by Cleon and his successors (they were all "most willing to be bold and to gratify the people with a view toward immediate popularity") (28.4) suggests similarities with Pericles as well. Pericles' projects of democratization and empire embolden the many further (27.1–2) and the desire to gratify for purposes of popularity is a reasonable description of Pericles' motives for paying the dicasts. In this respect, as in others, Pericles is very different from Solon, who voluntarily endured hatred in order to moderate civil *stasis*. Ultimately, Aristotle's treatment of Pericles seems less an attempt to eliminate all references to famous men than an effort to clarify the reasons why famous men deserve respect and emulation. The deconstruction of Pericles has a culturally reconstructive side.

Theramenes and Political Ambiguities

Aristotle raises expressly the issues of respect and emulation in a context that is openly controversial. It concerns the standing of Theramenes, whose reputation is as tarnished as Pericles' is shining. Theramenes was instrumental in establishing the oligarchies of 411 and 404 (32.2; Thucydides 8.64,4; 89,2–3; Xenophon, *Hellenica* 2.3,2). In both instances, he eventually broke with the extremists. He helped to moderate the oligarchy of 411 (33.2; Thucydides 97.1–2), but ended by being tried and executed by the Thirty under the manipulation of Critias (36.1; 37,1–2; *Hellenica* 2.3,15–56). The *AP* and other sources (e.g., Lysias, *Against Eratosthenes* 12.74–8) suggest that opinions about his character were bitterly split, with the more intense democrats inclined to see him as a political criminal (*Against Eratosthenes* 12.62–4).[49] Aristotle's treatment of Theramenes in the *AP* thus singles him out as the historical figure who was most controversial. His response to this controversy occasions one of the very few general claims made in the work, focusing on the proper activity or function (*ergon*) of a good citizen (28.5). Why might Aristotle explicitly address this question here?

The most damaging criticism of Theramenes is that he was "a destroyer of all regimes" (*pasas tas politeias kataluein*), for he twice contributed to the subversion of the democracy and subsequently turned on both oligarchies. Theramenes' later career parallels the unstable character of Athenian domestic politics in the last years of the Peloponnesian War. If his behavior provides any sort of example for democratic citizens it will be particularly relevant for those living under conditions of severe regime stress. According to critics, Theramenes used this period of stress opportunistically, supporting or abandoning regimes as it suited his interests (cf. Aristophanes, *Frogs,* 534–41; 967–70). Aristotle disputes this by reinterpreting his activities as attempts to discourage each of the regimes under which he lived from conducting its affairs *paranomōs,* against the laws or unjustly.[50] Aristotle thus finds Theramenes' most constructive political contribution in his efforts to move democratic and oligarchic regimes away from conditions of extremism. In different ways, the stories of Solon and Peisistratus suggest that the intersection of regime stress and political opportunism can lead to tyranny. By contrast, the job or task of the good citizen (*agathou politou ergon*) is to attempt to make the stressed regime respect lawfulness and reject violence, while behaving lawfully or politically (*politeuesthai*) under all of them.[51] To this extent, the *AP* expands the range of possibilities for being a good citizen "with a view to the regime" beyond displaying commitment to the regime's priorities (*Politics* 3.4).[52] And the congruence of the good citizen and the good man (*Politics* 3.4) may be possible in roles which are more assumable than ruling in the best regime.

In this connection, there are interesting parallels, noted also by Keaney, between the activities of Theramenes and Socrates' self-described mission in the *Gorgias*.[53] While Socrates normally denies that he is political in any institutional sense (cf. *Apology* 31c5–8), in the *Gorgias* he says he is the only statesman (*politikos*) in Athens because he tries to improve rather than simply to gratify his fellow citizens (521d6–8). Socrates calls this project of civic improvement "the only task of a good citizen" (*monon ergon . . . agathou politou*) (517c1–2). Both Theramenes and Socrates attempt to make the regimes in which they find themselves less unjust and both are eventually executed at the hands of extremists.[54]

Yet the differences between Theramenes and Socrates are as important as the similarities. Socrates' institutional non-politicality (his behavior during the Arginusae trial was compelled by circumstances—*Apology* 32b1–c3) distinguishes his practices from Theramenes' highly public attempts to affect the character of the Athenian regime. Theramenes' response to the injustices of the Thirty is both more confrontational and more structural than that of Socrates, who simply resists complicity in injustice (*Apology* 32c8–d4). What Socrates calls *politikē* in the *Gorgias* is part of what he often calls philosophy, investigating in conversation the advantages and deficiencies of different life choices (*Apology* 37e3–38a7; *Phaedrus* 230d4–7; *Charmides* 154e9–155a8).[55] Socrates' practice thus highlights by comparison the intensely political nature of Theramenes, the figure in the *AP* who comes closest to being purely civic. Unlike Solon he seems to have no other lives. Unlike Peisistratus he does not attempt to exercise domestic rule in a political context. Unlike Pericles he is not engaged in a competition with others over personal preeminence. Though Cleisthenes' reforms may have significantly democratized both political institutions and social categories (21.1–6), his motives are traced to his need to prevail over Isagoras in a struggle for influence (20.1–2). Theramenes can model the work of the good citizen because he is, in some respects, a quintessential citizen. Precisely because of this characteristic, his exemplary practice helps also to reveal the hardest edges of politics. This hardness is not shown simply by Theramenes' death, for death is also the consequence of Socrates' philosophy. There are, additionally, certain forms of moral hardness or risk that seem inevitably associated with intense citizenship. Theramenes may be more aggressive than Socrates in his responses to the Thirty's outrages, but he also shares responsibility for their crimes. Even if he is not a political opportunist, he is proactive in efforts to subvert the democracy (34.3). If Solon's fondness for alternative ways of life prevents him from confronting persistent forms of political irrationality, Theramenes' intense citizenship ensnares him in political violence. There is, therefore, an inevitable ambiguity about Aristotle's use of a controversial political figure associated with anti-democratic violence to underscore the point that "political participation in the current lawful regime is simply the mark of good citizenship."[56] For all of Aristotle's clarifications, Theramenes remains controversial, not simply on account of his own behavior, but because of what he reveals about politics itself.

The Continued Ambiguities of Democratic Citizenship

The complexities of Aristotle's treatment of this range of cultural figures suggest that he is not offering a single, well-defined model for democratic civil behavior. Instead, he encourages more nuanced appreciations of the demands and complexities, the potential achievements and pitfalls of democratic political life. This supports a view of democratic citizenship as thoughtful moderation, a characteristic that both draws upon and strengthens the regime's potential for gentleness. So, when Aristotle moderates the views that blame Solon as a radical democrat and condemn Theramenes as an opportunist, he does not attempt to replace them with truer, but equally simple opinions. Instead, his examinations of both figures identify fundamental and instructive ambiguities not only in their individual careers, but in democratic politics itself.[57]

  This ambiguous view of democratic politics is broadened within the final assessment of the emergent democracy that ends the *AP*'s historical narrative. The conclusion that the *dēmos* has made itself sovereign over everything is not followed by a lament that Athens degenerated from being ruled by Solon's laws to being ruled by the assembly's decrees. Instead, Aristotle comments that the *dēmos* seems (*dokousi*) to have acted correctly (*orthōs*) in taking power, for the many (*polloi*) are less corrupted by gain (*kerdes*) and favors (*charisin*) than the few (*oligoi*). The democracy is preferable to its most common alternative because of the corruption that it avoids. The historical narrative of the *AP* thus ends as it begins, with the abuses of the oligarchs. Yet the summary of the series of *politeiai* which marked Athens' democratic development pointedly leaves out the regime of the five thousand or that arrangement under which the Athenians seem to have been well governed. It is this same regime that Thucydides says was the best that existed in Athens during his time because of its moderate (*metria*)

blending of the many and the few (8.97, 2–3). In the *AP* Aristotle emphasizes that the rule of the five thousand was of very short duration, bracketed
by the oligarchy of the four hundred and the radical democracy (33.1–2;
34.1). The summary of regimes thus obscures the five thousand in favor of
its oligarchic predecessor and democratic successor (41.2). By absorbing the
five thousand into the four hundred, Aristotle provides more evidence of the
perfidy of the oligarchs who simultaneously hid behind and obstructed a
much more beneficial political arrangement. By implication, the unrealized
rule of the five thousand also provides an alternative to the relatively correct or just assumption of rule by the *dēmos*. Thus, Aristotle's use of the
"seems" construction in judging the correctness of the many's rule implies
both acknowledgment and tentativeness. The many's sovereign control is
juster than the corrupt rule of the oligarchs, but Athens' political development enclosed what seems to have been a preferred alternative as a largely
unrealized possibility.

THE INTERPRETATION OF CULTURE AND CRITICAL RATIONALITY

Read as a work of practical political education, the *Athēnaiōn Politeia* encourages its audience to think more critically and constructively about the
Athenian regime and, by extension, democratic political culture, generally.
This engagement moves beyond a Rawlsian analysis of liberal culture in
three respects. First, Aristotle's complex treatment suggests that the current
turn toward liberal culture is oversimplified theoretically. Rawls's focus on
reasonable pluralism, Habermas's concentration on communicative structures, and Connolly's identification of incipient contests over identity and
difference all focus on one dominant societal characteristic that needs to be
given pride of place in the sociology of liberal culture.[58] Within Aristotle's
treatment, democratic political culture is inherently strained and inconsistent, with its most striking structural (the institutionalizations of freedom
and equality), psychocultural (boldness and gentleness), and symbolic
(Solon, Pericles, Peisistratus, and Theramenes) features exerting potentially
opposing influences. The reason for this is not that democracy is a deviant,
contradictory regime but that democratic society is the most differentiated
and varied of political cultures.[59] Thus, Keaney's suggestion that the *AP*
traces the consistent structural influence of the sovereignty of the *dēmos*
should be moderated by the work's more nuanced treatments of the varie-
gated possibilities within the Athenian constitution. Similarly, the present
focus on liberal culture can be challenged for not taking cultural complexities seriously enough. Second, Aristotle cannot (therefore) treat the basic
priorities of democratic culture as supplying altogether adequate parame-

ters for normative political judgments. While appreciative in a number of respects, his analysis is also sensitive to the shortcomings of democratic culture, as illustrated by the critical questions surrounding democratic principles, purposes, and civic exemplars. As applied to the liberal culture that surrounds Rawls, an Aristotelian cultural analysis would focus on the drawbacks, as well as the goods, of reasonable pluralism and the incompletenesses, as well as the contributions, of proceduralism. Finally, because democracy is complex and problematic, Aristotle's examination requires the contributions of a critical rationality that is not simply constituted by cultural meanings. While both the possibilities and the dangers of the Athenian polity are expressed in culturally familiar terms, a full consideration of their import involves a rationality that is not culturally circumscribed. The *AP*'s need for this sort of theoretical supplementation is signaled by its own incompleteness. The strengths and limitations of Solon's attempt to establish legal justice among the noble and the base can be understood more comprehensively from a perspective that is suspicious of culturally determined categories of nobility and baseness and that appreciates the possibilities of a regime that attempts to make its citizens good and just. Potential criticisms of democratic political practices need to appreciate that equality is not simply a democratic commitment, but a condition of political life. Eventually, the examination of democratic culture needs to take seriously the possibility that some political cultures are (more or less) according to or against nature (*Politics* 1.2; *NE* 5.8).

This transcultural perspective is not, however, founded on a disconnected metaphysics. Rather, it emerges as rational discourse partners attempt to clarify ethical meaning (*sēmainein*) (cf. *Metaphysics* 1006b5–10) for purposes of identifying better and worse public choices. While this resembles Habermas's endorsement of procedures that allow the reaching of understanding, there are two important differences. First, Aristotle sees rational discourse partners as individuals who practice substantive intellectual and moral virtues and not simply as participants in a conversation structured in certain ways. Some procedurally correct agreements are in principle impossible if the discourse partners are truly rational and the presence of such agreements signals substantive irrationality.[60] Second, while this form of critical rationality requires enabling and supportive institutions, Aristotle does not attempt to identify a separately differentiated space that would correspond to and institutionalize its practice. For Aristotle, this form of critical rationality is a possibility that accompanies institutionally controlled democratic discourses of all sorts.[61]

The premise that rationality and justice are intelligible anthropologically grounds the comprehensive investigations of both the *Nicomachean Ethics* and the *Politics*. Yet it is also implicit within the pragmatics of cultural interpretation itself. If culture is a network of shared meanings that can help to make sense of practices or guide choices, then any cultural interpretation potentially offers an alternative way of understanding and arranging common forms of life. When Aristotle interprets the Athenian constitution in the *AP* or the Spartan constitution in the *Politics*, he does so in the belief that the rational scrutiny of these regimes can make some difference to the political choices of his audience. The *AP* problematizes the very core of the Athenian *politeia*, the *kurios* of the *dēmos*. The critique of Sparta is important because some of the individuals in Aristotle's audience apparently see the Spartan alternative as a better way of arranging Athenian public culture (cf. *Politics* 2.6; *NE* 7.14).[62] Rawls's reliance on an interpretation of liberal culture in *Political Liberalism* fits this description as well. A clearer understanding of the premises underlying our political and economic institutions must eventually lead to reconceptualizations of the requirements of social justice.

A second relevant premise underlying cultural interpretation is that the questions and categories employed cannot be supplied by any single cultural source. The attention to alternative forms of cultural life, represented by subcultures within our own society or by cultural forms which are more distant, suggests potential disquiet with dominant practices and meanings.[63] Yet the need to reconstitute other meanings as templates for cultural change implies that such meanings cannot be simply adopted without further intellectual criticism and reformulation. For example, Clifford Geertz's call for cultural translations that read "one sort of [cultural] sensibility in terms of those characteristic of another"[64] cannot simply rely on categories exclusive to either of the cultures being compared. Such translations also require principles of selection supplied by a more independent form of practical judgment.[65] Thus, in the *AP*, the alternative to boldness is a gentleness which emerges as a good, not only of democracy, but of political life itself. The critique of the Spartan regime in the *Politics* is not offered by a more open culture that views Spartan education with alarm, but by a critical rationality that asks what the political support for human virtue would really involve.

Recognizing the partiality or inadequacy of any single cultural vocabulary thus extends the interpretation of culture in the direction of a rationality that is, to adapt Paul Rabinow's contemporary term, more cosmopolitan in nature.[66] Here, cosmopolitanism implies not superiority or separation but involvement in a practical investigation that treats individual cultural forms as provisionally and imperfectly commensurable, comparable through cross-cultural categories (for example, the best regime for which one would pray) that are themselves always in the process of being worked out. Eventually, both Rawls's cultural turn and Connolly's invigoration of democratic politics also point toward this kind of cosmopolitanism. Rawls appeals to the priorities of liberal culture in order to do without metaphysics. Yet if "metaphysics" designates any conclusions that are taken to be universally true, Rawls's attempt to avoid them is unsuccessful. His sociological identification of reasonable pluralism as the most significant liberal cultural fact seems to rely not on a description of the contemporary cultural landscape, but on a prior normative understanding of a healthy political culture.[67] Within Connolly's agonistic politics the need to provide reasons for preferring some course of action over others transforms power contests over interest claims at least partially into rational interactions over meaning (the common ground of the *Gorgias,* the *AP,* and the *Politics*). From an Aristotelian point of view, then, positions like those of Rawls or Connolly confuse the priorities of political liberalism or the dynamics of agonistic pluralism with the structure of political thought.

As a work of political theory, the *AP* simultaneously points beyond itself to a more theoretical political discourse and makes the point of political theorization clearer. Here, theory should not be understood as a set of systematically related concepts, but as a kind of attentive regard which considers the full range of possibilities and problems facing people living together in a democratic regime. By inviting a theoretical examination of democratic institutions that is neither required nor forbidden by democratic culture, the *AP*'s text parallels the shortcomings and the possibilities of that culture itself. Yet it also reinforces the fact that political theory is a resource for practical choices, rather than the derivation of political norms from abstract rational or moral principles. Viewed within the context of the *AP,* the *Politics* emerges as a work designed to educate its audience in ways that may foster better political choices. In serving as this kind of bridge to the *Politics,* the *AP* emphasizes both the practical context of political theorizing and the reliance on theory which is embedded within thoughtful practice. This same bridging function assumes an important continuity between cultural and philosophical discourse. Political theory is neither dismissive of nor bound by the cultural priorities and political processes of decent, yet flawed regimes. For us (and there is no reason to believe that Aristotle would disagree) that decent, flawed regime is liberal democracy. We may be better positioned to appreciate both its decencies and its flaws by supplementing liberalism's cultural turn with Aristotelian insights.

NOTES

The basic argument of this essay was developed in connection with a course on classical democratic theory that I taught for the Classics Department at Georgetown in

1993. It has been refined and changed in courses ever since. I have profited enormously from the helpful comments and criticisms of earlier drafts provided by Aristide Tessitore, Jill Frank, and Alexander Sens.

1. This is the sort of normative or reconstructive sociology that informs Habermas's recent work in *Between Facts and Norms,* trans. William Rehg (Cambridge, Mass.: MIT Press, 1996), especially chs. 7 and 8.

2. John Rawls, *Political Liberalism* (New York: Columbia University Press, 1993), xvi.

3. Ibid., 15.

4. Ibid., xiv–xvi.

5. John Rawls, *A Theory of Justice* (Cambridge, Mass.: Harvard University Press, 1971), 20–21; *Political Liberalism,* 95–96.

6. William Connolly, "Identity and Difference in Liberalism," in *Liberalism and the Good,* ed. R. Bruce Douglass, Henry Richardson, and Gerald Mara (New York: Routledge, 1990), 66.

7. William Connolly, *The Augustinian Imperative* (Newbury Park, Calif.: Sage, 1993), 155–58; *The Ethos of Pluralization* (Minneapolis: University of Minnesota Press, 1995), xviii.

8. Cf. the exchange between Martha Nussbaum and Yael Tamir on the West's policy toward cultures where clitoridectomy is accepted (*Boston Review,* 21.3,5). Nussbaum's conclusion that "we should be ashamed of ourselves if we do not use whatever privilege and power had come our way to make [the practice] disappear forever" both implies and calls for a moral argument. I am grateful to Bradley Holst for calling this debate to my attention.

9. This may be one of the unforeseen negative consequences of Mark Warren's speaking of a war between foundationalism and democracy. See "Nonfoundationalism and Democratic Judgment," *Current Perspectives in Social Theory* 14 (1994): 151–82 at 153. I discuss more positive points of connection between the Platonic version of "foundational" political philosophy and democratic theory in *Socrates' Discursive Democracy* (Albany, N.Y.: State University of New York Press, 1997), 1–4, 251–59.

10. Rorty's claim (*Contingency, Irony and Solidarity* [New York: Cambridge University Press, 1989], 86–88) is based on the highly dubious assertion that most people can be commonsense non-metaphysicians, just as they are commonsense non-theists. In suggesting that this form of common sense is all that the bourgeois inhabitants of postmodern liberal communities want or need in order to make sense of the world and select public priorities, Rorty's naivete is matched only by his condescension.

11. P. J. Rhodes, *Commentary on the Aristotelian* Athēnaiōn Politeia (Oxford: Clarendon Press, 1981), 63.

12. Ibid., 62.

13. Josiah Ober, *Political Dissent in Democratic Athens* (Princeton, N.J.: Princeton University Press, 1998), 352.

14. John Keaney, *The Composition of Aristotle's* Athēnaiōn Politeia (New York: Oxford University Press, 1992), 12–14, 39–40.

15. Rhodes, *Commentary,* 7–8; Keaney, *Composition,* 24.

16. Compare *AP* 41.2–3 with *Politics* 1274b35.

17. For alternative views of the audiences of Aristotle's political works, see Mara, "Interrogating the Identities of Excellence," *Polity* 31 (1998); Thomas Smith, "The Audience of Aristotle's *Nicomachean Ethics*," *Journal of Politics* 62 (2000); and Aristide Tessitore, *Reading Aristotle's Ethics* (Albany, N.Y.: State University of New York Press, 1996). For all of their differences, all three see the rhetoric and the content of Aristotle's political works as intertwined.

18. Rhodes (*Commentary*, 15–28) provides an extensive discussion of how the *AP* might engage the various Atthidographers, though he limits his examination to the *AP*'s originality and reliability as a historical source. This is not an unimportant question, but it should not overly constrain views about the *AP*'s genre. For example, Aristotle's continuing use of the seems construction stands against the contentious Attidographic tendency to present highly controversial interpretations of Athenian history and culture as statements of plain fact. To this extent, the *AP* encourages a multivocality that many of these other works exclude.

19. Ober, *Dissent*, 363.

20. Translations are generally my own, but I have been guided by the Rhodes (Penguin) translation of the *AP*, the Ostwald (Bobbs-Merill) translation of the *Nicomachean Ethics*, the Lord (Chicago) translation of the *Politics*, and the Rackham (Loeb Classical library) translation of all three works. The Greek texts are those provided in the Loeb editions.

21. One could argue that Aristotle's use of *phaneron* in *Politics* 3.9 (1280b5–10) is a rhetorical sign of and response to the contentiousness of the context, disagreement over the just way to assign shares in political offices. In the next two chapters, what is said to be *phaneron* in 3.9, that the city must pay attention most of all to the presence of political virtue in allocating shares in the offices, is shown to be inadequate as a standard for determining how political offices should be distributed in actual regimes. Dishonoring those left with no shares would threaten to create "a city filled with enemies" (1281b30). Just as what is evident (in the *Politics*) is complicated by what follows, what seems to be the case (in the *AP*) can be clarified and nuanced by what follows. In both cases, Aristotle would seem to depend on thoughtful contributions and questions on the part of his audience. I am grateful to Charles Prince for calling my attention to the questions associated with the use of *phaneron* in *Politics* 3.9.

22. Rhodes (*Commentary*, 37) discourages overly subtle readings of the *AP* on the grounds that the author could make points more obviously. In response, Keaney (*Composition*, 62) offers a nice passage (a fragment from Theophrastus) which underscores the role which audience involvement plays in persuasive speech. Keaney (*Composition*) thus offers reasonable evidence that reading the *AP* in light of its intended effects on a political audience is not anachronistic. My reading attempts to work from the text to determine what some of Aristotle's persuasive goals might be.

23. Consequently, I am not as strongly inclined as Ober (*Dissent*, 352) to interpret the emergence of democracy in the Athenian context as a species of "teleological naturalism," a process within which Ober also discovers ambiguities (p. 355).

24. Keaney (*Composition*, 156–64) likewise sees a systematic variation in Aristotle's use of the terms *plēthos* and *dēmos*. There are also interesting parallels with

some current literature on the formation of political identities as responses to coercion. See, e.g., Michel Foucault, *Discipline and Punish,* trans. Alan Sheridan (New York: Vintage, 1979), 57–69, and John Borneman, *Belonging in the Two Berlins* (New York: Cambridge University Press, 1992), 254–62.

25. Orlando Patterson suggests that the development of a consciousness of freedom among the Greeks was tied directly to experiences with slavery, a practice that Patterson believes expanded after the *seisachtheia* (*Freedom,* vol. 1 [New York: Basic Books, 1991], 66–72). Whatever the complications of historical causality, the practice of slavery provides a vocabulary through which the relationship between the oligarchs and the many can be described (cf. *Freedom,* vol.1, 82–83). In employing this vocabulary, Aristotle thus places the historical narrative within a context intelligible to his contemporaries. It also provides a resource that allows Aristotle to problematize an association of democratic freedom and power which can effectively enslave those who are identified as unfree. Elsewhere, I argue that Aristotle's treatment of slavery itself is similarly problematizing ("The Near Made Far Away," *Political Theory* [1995]: 280–303 at 281–87).

26. Rhodes (*Commentary,* 174–76) argues persuasively that the meanings of good and bad or noble and base in this context are largely social; the bad and the base are those who fall outside of the *kaloi kagathoi.* In a way, the *AP*'s treatment of notable Athenians problematizes this category, rather than taking it for granted.

27. For a compelling illustration, see Xenophon's (not unbiased) account of the debate on the trial of the Arginusae generals. Confronting procedural objections to trying them collectively, "the majority cried out that it is outrageous (*deinos*) if the *dēmos* are not allowed to do what they wish" (*Hellenica* 1.7,12–13).

28. See Habermas, *Between Facts and Norms,* 311–14.

29. This is also reflected in the distinction between the legislative and political functions of politics in *NE* 6.8. I am grateful to Jill Frank for making this connection explicit.

30. I borrow the term 'psychocultural' from Marc Ross, *The Culture of Conflict* (New Haven, Conn.: Yale University Press, 1993). "Psychocultural dispositions are shared response tendencies acquired through mechanisms spelled out in both psychodynamic and social learning theories. . . . Dispositions are fundamental orientations vis-à-vis the self and others and include culturally learned and approved methods for dealing with others both within and outside one's community" (p. 51). Ross's intent is to use psychocultural variables to help explain why some societies are more conflictual than others (pp. 1–2). The use of modern social science categories to describe cultural characteristics of fifth- and fourth-century Athens may seem awkward, but it does help to reinforce the real social presence of such characteristics and their developmental connections with cultural education.

31. The educational purposes of the last two books of the *Politics* are discussed more fully by Carnes Lord, *Education and Culture in Aristotle's Political Philosophy* (Ithaca, N.Y.: Cornell University Press, 1982). Notable among the peaceful virtues is philosophy. Lord understands philosophy as intellectual culture, yet it might also include a kind of critical judgment.

32. Rhodes, *Commentary,* 290.

33. Keaney, *Composition,* 124.

34. Josiah Ober (*Mass and Elite in Democratic Athens* [Princeton, N.J.: Princeton University Press, 1989], 23–24) is skeptical of attempts to trace the development of the strong democracy to the empire. Aristotle's treatment in the *AP* suggests that both the empire and the radical democracy are expressions of the psychocultural disposition of boldness and that they are associated in ways that turn Athens into a certain kind of democratic regime.

35. In a sense, the same sort of movement seems at work in Socrates' shifts from "war stories" to an inquiry about philosophy in the *Charmides* (153a1–d5). So, while Aristotle does not romanticize the past, he does not ignore it.

36. A contemporary parallel is perhaps the moderation of the Spanish regime in the face of reminders of the devastating consequences of the Spanish Civil War. See Peter McDonough, Samuel H. Barnes, and Antonio Lopez Pina, *The Cultural Dynamics of Modernization in Spain* (Ithaca, N.Y.: Cornell University Press, 1998). "By the 1970s the characterization of Spanish politics as a battleground of principles and a charnel house of visionaries had not only become wearisome; it was also recognized as a dangerous fiction, a self-fulfilling prophecy that might perpetuate the cycle of anarchy and despotism" (p. 82).

37. On historical figures as cultural metaphors see Clifford Geertz, *Islam Observed* (Chicago: University of Chicago Press, 1968), 25, and Robert Bellah et al., *Habits of the Heart* (New York: Harper and Row, 1985), 28. Neither Geertz nor Bellah fully explores the possibilities of problematizing such figures.

38. This resembles the behavior of the equitable person who "does not stand on precise rights" (*NE* 5.10). Once again my thanks go to Jill Frank for pointing out this connection.

39. Keaney, *Composition*, 56–58.

40. For a development of this reading of the *Ethics*, see Mara, "Interrogating the Identities of Excellence," 301–329 at 317–22.

41. My understanding of the cultural importance of the tyrannicides has been greatly enhanced by the work of Sara Monoson. See *Plato's Democratic Entanglements* (Princeton, N.J.: Princeton University Press, 2000), ch. 1.

42. Comparing his tyranny to the age of Cronos is similarly revealing, owing to the absence of any politics in the so-called golden age. For a discussion of Plato's treatment of this golden age in the *Statesman,* see Mara, "Constitutions, Virtue and Philosophy in Plato's *Statesman* and *Republic,*" *Polity* (1981): 364–67, and Michael Kochin, "Plato's Eleatic and Athenian Sciences of Politics," *Review of Politics* (1999): 75–76.

43. In Thucydides' account (6.54–9) of the story behind the tyrannicide legend, the abuses of Thettalus are ascribed to Hipparchus. The variation in the *AP* (whatever its historical origins and whatever the intent) makes Hipparchus more of a victim and underscores the recklessness of the assassination. It also allows Aristotle to comment pointedly on the insulting arrogance of Thettalus (whereas Hipparchus was simply erotic, playful, and a lover of music). In either case, however, what prompted the attack was an abuse of power, something that Aristotle makes explicit within the much shorter account of the assassination in the *Politics* (1311a35).

44. Whatever the intent, there are multiple ironies when Aristotle (*NE* 8.11) points to Agamemnon as a model of kingly beneficence and care toward his people,

much as a shepherd "cares for and does well toward . . . his sheep." This conception of rule turns the human community into a herd and makes the king's concern for its welfare at the very least ambiguous. Aristotle then adds that the father relates to the child (Iphigenia?) in the same way. This provocative treatment of kingly friendship is developed more systematically in the *Politics* (3.14–16) when Aristotle considers the similarity of absolute kingship to household rule and the particular need to restrain kings through laws.

45. Thucydides emphasizes that most Athenians knew the truth about Spartan involvement (6.53.3). In the particular context which surrounds the retelling of the story (the witch hunts that followed the mutilation of the Hermae), knowing the truth heightens rather than restrains collective paranoia, suggesting that how we respond to the facts is at least as important as knowing what the facts are.

46. Cf. *NE* 6.8. This portion of the *Ethics* rejects both political activism (*polupragmon*) and political disconnection (*apragmon*) as appropriate understandings of "managing one's own affairs." Since what it means to manage one's own affairs well is not simply clear, one of the marks of practical wisdom may be the ability to determine the appropriate level of one's own politicality in light of personal and political circumstances.

47. Keaney, *Composition*, 58.

48. While Thucydides is often read as emphasizing the differences between Pericles' concern for the city and his successors' selfishness (e.g., Kagan, *The Archidamian War* [Ithaca, N.Y.: Cornell University Press, 1974], 26–29; Steven Forde, *The Ambition to Rule* [Ithaca, N.Y.: Cornell University Press, 1989], 32; Ober, *Dissent*, 96–98; Monoson, *Plato's Democratic Entanglements*, ch. 7), there is also an unsettling continuity implicit in Thucydides' verdict. Pericles having been first, his successors fought over who would be foremost next.

49. As Ober observes (*Dissent*, 361), intense oligarchs would be likely to condemn his defection from the oligarchic movements of 411 and 404. Yet Lysias' verdict clearly represents condemnation from the democratic side.

50. *Paranomos* can be read as illegal (the Arginusae trial) or as more generally unjust. Aristotle associates generally just actions with lawfulness in *NE* 5.1, but there are reasons to suspect that this is in need of substantial qualification (cf. Mara, "Interrogating the Identities of Excellence," 311–13; Tessitore, *Reading Aristotle's Ethics*, 35–42). In light of Aristotle's clear awareness that the qualities of the laws vary with the qualities of regimes (cf. *Politics* 1282b5), it is unlikely that he would see the true *ergon* of the good citizen as behaving lawfully in the narrow sense. It seems more likely that the task of the good citizen is to discourage injustice in the broader sense without being subversive of the regime. Theramenes' efforts to turn the oligarchy of the four hundred into the governance of the five thousand could be so described.

51. To the extent that Aristotle employs the example of Theramenes in this way, he departs from Thucydides' more pessimistic conclusion that human nature emerges in its clearest manifestation under conditions of civil conflict (3.82.2). For Aristotle, the crimes caused by civil stress are hazards, but not inevitabilities.

52. This especially true in light of the expanded reading of what it means to contribute to the regime's preservation at *Politics* 5.9.

53. Keaney, *Composition*, 147–48; "A Source / Model of Aristotle's Portrait of Theramenes," *Classical Journal* 75 (1979): 40–41.

54. Though Socrates' own extremism appears to be partially responsible for the death sentence. I discuss this more fully in *Socrates' Discursive Democracy*, 31–32, 58.

55. I try to develop this argument at greater length in chapter one of *Socrates' Discursive Democracy*.

56. Ober, *Dissent*, 363.

57. Thus, while there are a number of important parallels between Theramenes and Solon, I'm not sure that I would go as far as Keaney and call Theramenes "Alter Solon" (*Composition*, 147–48).

58. For example, Habermas's definition of the lifeworld as "a network composed of communicative actions" (*Between Facts and Norms*, 354) serves as a valuable corrective of systems theory, but it courts partialities of its own, drawing attention to some aspects of the lifeworld while obscuring others.

59. The parallel Platonic observation is at *Republic* 557c2–d9.

60. As in the treatment of different forms of moral ignorance (*agnoia*) in *NE* 3.1: "Every wicked man is ignorant of what he ought to do and ought to let alone and on account of this error (*hamartia*) injustices and all evils come into being. But an ignorance of the advantageous ought not to be spoken of as involuntary. Ignorance in choice is not the cause of involuntariness but of wickedness" (1110b25–30). A similar focus informs the introductory discussion about goods in *Politics* 7.1 where "no one would say that a human being is blessed who has no share of courage, moderation, justice or prudence" (1323a25).

61. Supported by the various forms of critical rationality expressed in the different sections of the *Politics*.

62. I suggest (*Socrates' Discursive Democracy*, 137–39) that this may also be the case for Socrates' treatment of the timocracy in book eight of the *Republic*.

63. Suggested by the otherwise very different anthropological projects of Ruth Benedict, *Patterns of Culture* (Boston: Houghton Mifflin, 1934), ch. 8, and Borneman, *Belonging in the Two Berlins*, 303–304).

64. Clifford Geertz, *Local Knowledge* (New York: Basic Books, 1983), 218.

65. In this case, the activity of translation arises from the need for a certain kind of cross-cultural civility in the presence of increasing cross-cultural contention (*Local Knowledge*, 224). The perspective of the cultural interpreter who reads one cultural sensibility in terms of another is not simply one voice among many (p. 234).

66. Paul Rabinow, *Essays on the Anthropology of Reason* (Princeton, N.J.: Princeton University Press, 1996), 24–25.

67. In spite of Rawls's admirable attempt to distinguish the senses in which political liberalism is and is not neutral (*Political Liberalism*, 174–211), it is unlikely that any robust form of Rawlsian neutralism can be convincingly defended. For a range of criticisms see William Galston, *Liberal Purposes* (New York: Cambridge University Press, 1991), 151–53 and Stephen Macedo, *Liberal Virtues* (New York: Oxford University Press, 1990), 50–69.

CHAPTER ELEVEN

The Deliberative Model of Democracy and Aristotle's Ethics of Natural Questions

STEPHEN S. SALKEVER

I. The Problem to Which Deliberative Democracy Is a Solution

This essay is an Aristotelian look at the theory of "deliberative democracy," a neo-Kantian way of thinking about what makes a good democracy that has gained wide academic support and may now be the most influential alternative to the model of constitutional or liberal democracy. As a model for evaluating democratic politics it has outstripped participatory democracy on the one hand and communitarianism on the other. While its most distinctive expression is in Jürgen Habermas's "discourse ethics,"[1] the label has also been adopted by John Rawls and his followers.

What sort of a normative concept is deliberative democracy? R. G. Collingwood famously remarked that one good way to understand an unfamiliar phenomenon is to reconstruct the question to which it appears to be an answer. Collingwood's "logic of question and answer," revised by Strauss and Gadamer,[2] is a good point of entry here, since my own position as an Aristotelian is not that of Rawls and Habermas (though I want to show that their deliberative model is not necessarily incompatible with Aristotelianism), and since I want to assume no particular familiarity with this sort of political theory on the part of my readers. I would say then that the problem to which deliberative democracy is a solution is this: *Find a model or an analogical metaphor to clarify our sense of what democratic poli-*

tics is and should be. In crafting this idealizing model or metaphor, you must stress liberty and equality, and you must not rely on any particular tradition of revealed religion." The deliberative model's answer to this question is that democracy is like a shared deliberation or discussion among friends about matters of mutual concern calling for action. It stands as a rival to other solutions to the same problem: the liberal metaphor that ideal democracy is like a contract or bargain among individuals to protect our attempt to live our own lives; the metaphor of participatory democracy, that ideal democracy is like a progressive revolutionary movement; the metaphor of communitarianism, that ideal democracy is like a family or band, or perhaps even an individual.

Politics needs idealizing metaphors, and the deliberative model has much to recommend it over the existing alternatives.[3] Moreover, given the contingency of human affairs, we will always be in need of new clarifying metaphors of this kind. Constructing them is one of the appropriate tasks of political theory or philosophy. Aristotle acknowledges this at the beginning of *Politics* 4 in saying that one of the things the science of politics must study is the question of what the best regime might be given certain assumptions about the best regime. My argument here is that model building should not be treated as the whole of political philosophy, because to work well a model must be set against the background of philosophy understood as inquiry into the permanent[4] questions, not only about politics but about the best way of life. It needs the support of more comprehensive philosophizing to be self-aware, to know what it is doing. Without such background inquiry, the model or metaphor is likely to undergo depersonalizing routinization into overly precise technical jargon and imitation science— its advocates will, in other words, cease to appreciate it as a model and instead treat it as a final solution to the question of the best regime. Such has been the fate of the deliberative model as presented and defended by John Rawls and Jürgen Habermas.

Both major proponents of the deliberative model deny that any more comprehensive philosophizing is necessary or possible. Yet at the same time Rawls and Habermas rely on conceptions of "public reason" and "moral freedom" that depend upon one such comprehensive philosophy for their meaning. That philosophy is a Kantian one, insofar as Kant follows the Rousseau of the *Social Contract* in identifying humanity as the natural species whose dignity lies in its transcendence of mechanical nature, in moral freedom, in obedience to laws it gives itself. This is especially the Kant of the 1784 essay, "An Answer to the Question: 'What Is Enlightenment?'" By reconsidering the deliberative model from the perspective of a very different comprehensive philosophy, Aristotle's ethics of natural questions, we can understand two central problems of the deliberative model more clearly:

its failure to deal adequately with the role of the emotions relative to reason and deliberation in political life and in human life generally, and its undefended commitment to the human good as the highest of all goods intelligible to philosophical reflection. My argument in the last two sections of the essay will be that Aristotle on emotion and on our relation to other beings provides a more plausible basis for a deliberative model of democracy than Kant.

I hope to avoid two pitfalls common to this sort of outsider's view. I don't want to claim that Aristotle is an early adherent of deliberative democracy. Aristotle sees deliberation as a virtue of human individuals rather than a characteristic of a regime as a whole.[5] The notion of a "public reason" linked with "moral" freedom, so crucial to the current deliberative model, has no Aristotelian equivalent, and he would probably deny that the most deliberative democracy is generally the best democracy,[6] although he might well agree that some form of democracy is the best possible regime today as in his own time. On the other hand, I do not claim that an appreciation of Aristotle proves the worthlessness of deliberative democracy theory. We need metaphors and models that suit the times, and Aristotle cannot supply those for us. The deliberative model is in several respects a clear improvement over other prominent contemporary models of democracy. Besides calling attention in a promising way to the question of the quality of the speech and thought that informs contemporary politics, it suggests the need to reconsider ways of thought that are built into the increasingly global economy and our nearly worldwide commitment to modern technology. As an alternative to liberal "rights talk," the deliberative model gives us a way to avoid the communitarian's exaggeration of the reality of the idea of "culture," both as a motive power in the world and as a central human need. The deliberative model seems truer to the insight[7] that the modern world is uniquely a place of unstable and complex identities, replete with both opportunities and threats for those serious about living well.[8] The model also allows us to question, without simply endorsing existing liberal democracy, the mysticizing valorization of "activism" and "the political" or "the people" or "democracy" all too typical of friends of the participatory model of democracy.[9] The model's strength lies in its valorization of a certain kind of reason in politics, but the critical power of the model is severely limited, I argue in section II, by the modelers' reluctance to take seriously the problem of giving a justificatory account of the conception of reason that defines their model.

My argument in sections III and IV is that by their ill-informed rejection of Aristotle as either an "essentialist" or a "civic republican,"[10] deliberative theorists rule out the possibility of bringing Aristotle usefully into conversation with the new model. This exclusion covers up important questions that deliberative democrats can and should address both about the role of political theory relative to democratic politics and about the substance of democratic theory itself. In particular, Aristotle casts his political theory in a style that is neither dogmatic and context-less essentialism nor a Rawlsian or Habermasian idealization of what the theorist takes to be the best in existing democratic practices—an either/or assumed by proponents of the modern deliberative model. Aristotle's view of the way theory informs practice is thus a plausible third alternative to these two horns of the modern theorist's dilemma. His ethics of natural questions proposes the idea that theory's role is to point out a way of interrogating those leading opinions he calls the *endoxa,* the reputable opinions that set the prevailing terms for discussion in a particular society. In section V, I argue that the substance of Aristotle's theory supplies a more accurate way of thinking about the relation of deliberation to emotion than the current deliberative model, a way that the deliberative model could incorporate without violating any of its core premises.[11] To see this, particular attention will need to be paid to the meaning of two of Aristotle's significant coinages or near-coinages, *prohairesis* (thoughtful choice) and *orexis* (desire). In section VI, I conclude with a few comments about why modern democrats should consider an Aristotelian alternative to the anthropocentrism (or perhaps even androcentrism) of the modern deliberative model.

II. THE DELIBERATIVE MODEL:
JOHN RAWLS AND JÜRGEN HABERMAS

Rawls and Habermas have differed over the question of liberalism and its relation to democracy. Rawls refers to his theory of justice as "political liberalism"; Habermas has in the past endorsed Marxian and republican critiques of liberalism, and still regards his version of democratic theory as distinct from both the liberal and the republican paradigms or models of democracy.[12] By now, however, both agree that a good democracy will endorse liberal individual rights yet somehow incorporate a richer sense of citizenship. Thus Rawls and Habermas share the idea that a good democracy must be more than a Lockean protector of rights and more than an efficient utilitarian distributor of subjective values. This something more is the claim that the best democracy will be a *reasonable* democracy, where *reason* is understood in a noninstrumental or nonutilitarian sense. This stress on reason as a central norm distinguishes the deliberative model from the communitarian and participatory alternatives. For deliberative theorists, the best democracy will encourage solidarity and the active pursuit of the public good, but it will not rank these goods at the top of its table of values. It reserves that place for reason. But reason is itself a contested term, and so we must ask what conception of reason the deliberative model invokes. Negatively, it is clear that reason is to be understood here neither as an instrumental capacity for obtaining subjectively determined ends, nor as the ability to discover true things about the world and our interests. Thus the deliberative model's version of rationality follows neither Hobbes and Hume on the one hand nor Plato and Aristotle on the other. It answers neither the utilitarian question of how I can get what I want at the lowest possible cost to myself, nor the Socratic question of what sort of life built around what sorts of desires will be most in my interest. What then does the Habermasian and Rawlsian conception of reason connote? The question reason answers for deliberative democrats like Habermas and Rawls is the one developed in the line of political philosophy beginning with Rousseau and refined in different directions by Kant, Hegel, and Marx: How can I be free?

One way to articulate this shared commitment to a particular notion of freedom is to note that both Rawls and Habermas have always had (and claimed to have) Kantian elements in their theorizing.[13] Lately, however, these elements have become more prominent in each. Habermas, persuaded by history, has moved away from Marxian and Hegelian historicist themes and gestures; and Rawls is less a Lockean or Humean rationalist than he was in *A Theory of Justice,* in which he asserted (1971, 16) that moral and political philosophy as a whole should eventually be subsumed under a grand theory of rational choice. The Kant that matters for them is the Kant of the essay "What Is Enlightenment?"[14] in which he describes the emergence of "public reason" as the central element of the Enlightenment, and defines that reason not in terms of cognition, but rather (following Rousseau's idea of moral freedom, briefly mentioned in Book 1, Chapter 6 of *The Social Contract*) as the obedience to general laws we as a people have prescribed to ourselves. It is this public reason that lifts us as individuals out of slavish dependence on appetite or desire alone.[15] This Kantian Enlightenment is thus the movement from self-imposed (through our own laziness and cowardice) childhood to maturity, emerging from mechanical nature and from accepting the rule of traditional authorities to give ourselves principles by which we live. The deliberative model achieves a certain philosophic depth and power by attaching democracy to the modern project of enlightenment and autonomy understood in this way.

This attachment also opens a range of questions about the accuracy and implications of the concept of public reason relative to other ways of thinking about who we are. But in the immediate rhetorical context of contemporary political theory, the focus of the deliberative model is reactive and negative: it is a critical response to liberal theory on the contract model.

Thus it continues even while significantly modifying the familiar debate between individualist and "civic republican" or communitarian models. According to the deliberative model, democratic politics should not be conceived in terms of resolving conflicts among competing interests through aggregative procedures such as regular and contested free elections.[16] Democratic politics instead should be to some extent transformative, aiming to convert interest-bearing individuals into at least part-time citizens. Rawls expresses this in his claim that a good democracy rests on a certain "overlapping consensus" substantively expressed in his principles of justice. For Habermas, a good democracy is one in which "discursive will formation" or the development of the basic terms and materials of public policy approximates the results of a consensus-oriented conversation in an "ideal speech situation," one in which speakers respect one another as *moral* equals,[17] and only the better argument has weight. As Iris Young (1996, 121) puts it, "the model of deliberative democracy conceives of democracy as a process that creates a public, citizens coming together to talk about collective problems, goals, ideas, and actions."

Democratic politics is thus understood as the means for such transformative citizenship—this involves rejecting a rational choice market model and requiring that citizens adopt a civic standpoint, an orientation toward the common good and hence to moral freedom, when they consider political issues in the public forum. As Young (1998, 1) says, "the theory of deliberative democracy conceptualizes democratic politics primarily as a process in which citizens work out problems and resolve conflict by discussion that leads to decisions. Voting and other means of registering preference, on this account, are only a small moment in a larger democratic process which consists of public discussion about the issues, both among citizens and political officials, where participants aim to persuade one another about the best policies and actions." The deliberative model goes farther than this, however, in claiming that democratic decisions must reflect some sort of *public* reason: "Deliberative democrats insist that deliberation must be public in a radical sense—only reasons that can be embraced by all of us are truly public, and hence justificatory" (Gaus 1997, 205). This is the distinctively Kantian element in deliberative democracy, and what distinguishes it from participatory democracy and communitarianism, its two predecessors, as an alternative to the model of Lockean liberalism. What is required for a praiseworthy democracy is not only active participation in political life or widespread commitment to a set of basic moral values, but *rational* participation under a certain non-instrumental interpretation of the meaning of "rational" as universal, public, and autonomous. Sparta might appeal to communitarians or civic republicans, but not to deliberative democrats. Rawls moves toward this position from a Lockean beginning, Habermas from a communitarian or republican one. Rawls regards Locke's liberalism as insufficiently political, while Habermas rejects the Rousseauan and republican traditions (as well as Hegelian and Marxian historicism) as involving "ethical overload" on democratic citizens. The central principle of the model of deliberative democracy can thus be understood as an updating domestication of Kant's elaboration of Rousseau's briefly defined "moral freedom" in the *Social Contract*—freedom and reason coalesce as obedience to laws we have self-consciously given ourselves.

Thus deliberative democracy rejects the radical, anti-representation stance of "participatory" or "strong" democracy.[18] It also rejects the stress on the ontological or psychological priority of the community asserted by communitarian theorists such as Charles Taylor and Robert Bellah. The stress on a strong meaning of rationality also puts deliberative theorists in opposition to postmodernists or deconstructionists. The positive element of the model is an image of a public or political realm that needs to be made rational—where reason means a certain universality and a certain uniquely human freedom, the freedom to choose or create the principles under which we live. Deliberative rationality acquires meaning in opposition to both an instrumental capacity for obtaining subjective ends *and* to the Platonic-Aristotelian rationality which is the ability to discover true things about the world and our interests, things that may contradict rules and principles we have freely adopted or created.

The core of the theory of deliberative democracy as understood by both Habermas and Rawls, then, is that the heart of modern democracy is a "public space" or "constitution" in which agreements can be reached among moral equals concerning the future of the polity. The Rawls / Habermas differences are important, but they are matters of detail within this broad agreement that what makes democracy normatively itself is the practice of public reason. For Rawls, public reason operates or should operate within politics ordinarily understood—in elections, legislatures, executives, and courts. Reasoning in such places becomes public when it proceeds from a shared view of justice, the one articulated in the two principles. For Habermas, the key site of democratic deliberation is not in government at all but in the non-state and non-market associations designated by the term "civil society"—reasoning there is public when it conforms to the rules of an ideal speech situation[19] and results in an agreement on the terms in which the polity will respond to policy issues. Habermas (1996, 27) wants a "decentered" society,[20] Rawls wants greater separation between political life and the surrounding institutions; Habermas's model is procedural, Rawls's substantive. But both agree that what is central to democracy as an aspiration is a public realm or realms in which equal citizens settle basic issues by deliberation, rather than by instrumental reasoning, or by compromise, or by majority rule, or by reference to a traditional or otherwise superior authority.

Tellingly, the major criticism each levels against the other is for theoretical immodesty that is insufficiently self-detected: Habermas tells Rawls that his theory presupposes opinions about the good life, while Rawls responds that all decision procedures, including Habermas's ideal speech situation, favor some substantive conclusions over others.[21] Both criticisms seem correct. But there is a deeper problem with accepting this sort of modesty as a norm for political theory, something akin to a problem with "middle-range theory" in the social sciences: theoretical modesty is misleadingly attractive (or attractively misleading) because it conceals (from the writer as well as the reader) theoretical choices that decisively affect the results of the inquiry. The deliberative model thus carries along with it an intentionally unexamined commitment to a profound conception of what it means to be a human being relative to the other beings in the cosmos—a commitment that calls for examination because it accords to humanity so extraordinarily lofty a place in the configuration of the universe. This self-enclosure blocks discussion not only of what it means to be a human being, but of the key terms of the model as well. By regarding reason and moral freedom and public space as normative givens, the model violates what Habermas and Rawls most value in the modern liberal polity—its willingness to submit its first principles to deliberative scrutiny and critique (Habermas 1987, 336–37). Thus it lessens the chances of what Habermas himself calls "philosophical enlightenment" (1971b, 7–8).[22] The deliberative model founders on a paradox: uniquely committed to rationality as a standard for good politics, it refuses without sufficient reason to acknowledge the possibility of plausible conceptions of rationality different from its own.

III. The Aims and the Style of Political Philosophy: The Problem with Ideal Modeling

Because of his emphasis on the centrality of deliberation to a well-lived human life, Aristotle is often cited by theorists of deliberative democracy as a distant ancestor. But deliberative theorists see the connection as remote because of Aristotle's supposedly anti-democratic elitist bias. Bohman's (1997, 324) comment is typical: "Some philosophers think that the exclusion of the many is desirable, since it improves deliberation. Aristotle and even Madison avoided such difficulties simply by assuming that deliberation should be restricted to those who are already wise, virtuous, and well-off." Aristotle appears here as a proponent of deliberation but not of democracy, or as someone unable to detach his conception of deliberation from the parochial structure of Greek social life.[23] Thus Aristotle is in effect classified as pre-philosophic as well as pre-modern.

Moreover, both Rawls and Habermas explicitly rank Aristotle with Plato as a dogmatic essentialist natural law teacher who is at the end of the day anti-deliberation.[24] This criticism, not necessarily consistent with the first, marginalizes Aristotle by treating him as an essentially "religious" or "metaphysical" thinker. The rhetorical strategy, by now so commonplace as to require no intention at all, is to patronize Aristotle as either a typical Greek aristocrat or as a narrow Thomist. The effect of these two highly questionable and never-defended interpretive judgments—that Aristotle is hostile to democracy, and that Aristotle is a dogmatic natural law theorist—is to exclude Aristotle along with Plato from the tradition or canon of political philosophical texts Rawls and Habermas see themselves as interpreting and developing.[25] As Athenian medievals, the Greek philosophers are doubly pre-modern and hence can be left outside the limits of philosophy properly understood. This practice of exclusion makes it difficult for Rawls and Habermas to take up the sort of rational self-criticism each sees as central to the process of inquiry.

One serious and generally unremarked consequence of this marginalization of Greek philosophy is that deliberative theorists assume that a political philosopher properly so-called will build a model that accurately depicts the normative core of contemporary beliefs about democracy. For these theorists, the only imaginable mode of political philosophy more comprehensive than model-building is the discredited pre-modern search for a model or a set of laws embedded in a reality outside of our settled convictions or the historical project of the modern European Enlightenment.[26] The fact that the Greek texts do not correspond to the caricatures of abstract universalism blended with ethnocentric prejudice upon which Habermas and Rawls rely for their dismissal of Plato and Aristotle is thus of more than antiquarian interest:[27] their exclusion means that the adoption of model-building as an approach to practical philosophy has no rivals and so goes undefended.

A symptom that such defense is required is the tension between Rawls's and Habermas's praise of deliberation and the rebarbatively technical and impersonal character of their prose. I don't think this tension is an accident or a superficial difficulty, but something that flows quite readily from excessive commitment to avoiding ambiguity wherever possible. Model-building is an attempt at clarifying simplification. The good physicist or economist has a knack for separating out what is crucial in a set of phenomena from what is mere noise—modeling is always an act of exclusion as well as of indicating an order where none was apparent before. Moreover, even in the most mathematical of the physical sciences, modeling is linked to metaphor and analogy.[28] But how can we judge the adequacy of a model, how can we tell whether the exclusions were intelligently made or not? In the modern natural sciences and the social sciences that follow them, precision, objectivity, and predictive power are important indicators. The styles of Rawls and Habermas seem to bow in the direction of these standards, and necessarily, since there are no others in their theory.[29] Yet at the same time, Rawls and Habermas are utterly opposed to imposing these standards on political talk and thereby reducing deliberation to technological or utilitarian calculation. Perhaps this is no inconsistency: perhaps it is reasonable that the style of philosophizing about political discourse should be different from the style of political discourse. But even so, the following questions need to be discussed: Should political philosophy aim at modeling a tradition—or is this approach implicitly too systematic and too much concerned with precision or the appearance of precision to aid our understanding and action? Should that modeling be subject to standards similar to those that govern the modeling of physical systems? The same questions that can be raised about rational choice models must also be raised about deliberative models; and to raise them well, we can profit greatly from a consideration of an alternative non-modeling and non-dogmatic natural law approach to the question of how philosophy should approach political traditions.

For Rawls and Habermas, the role of political or "public philosophy" is to supply "mediating propositions" that link general constitutional principles "to the specific situation and problems we face today, given the kind of people we are and are likely to remain." This is William Galston's (1998) formulation; Galston draws Aristotelian support for it by referring to the statement at the beginning of *Politics* 4 that the true political scientist must be able to determine the best regime given a hypothetical principle. But Galston neglects the context of this remark in the *Politics:* that the same person who discusses the best democracy or oligarchy or tyranny must also be able to discuss the best regime simply. He also neglects the remark at the beginning of *Politics* 7 (1323a14–16) that in order to discuss the best *politeia* we must give some thought to the question of the best way of life, though necessarily not an unambiguous answer to that question.

Thus from an Aristotelian point of view, the deliberative model claims both too much and too little. Too much, in that it attempts to articulate a normative stand sufficient to guide political practice—like modern natural law or modern rational choice theory rather than ancient natural right. It is legislative rather than critical in its intention, and treats its basic principles as necessary, not subject to deliberation, but as the starting point for all deliberation. Too little, in that it brackets metaphysical and psychological questions, either treating political philosophy as "freestanding" or autonomous (Rawls),[30] or treating its own requirements as only procedural, leaving those who follow the procedures free to choose whatever they like as a

rule of justice (Habermas). In Richard Rorty's (1996, 333) apt characterization, deliberative models are to be understood as "reminders" of particular
features of our practices, rather than as appeals beyond our practices—as
"idealizations" rather than "foundations." But this risks erasing any meaningful distinction between philosophy and systematic ideology, something
acceptable to postmodernists like Rorty, but presumably not to Habermas
and Rawls. Can political philosophy and political science do something
other than idealize or model an existing tradition of thought and practice?
Does any attempt to do more fall into the trap of abstractly universal dogmatism? This is where Aristotle comes in.

IV. The *Endoxa* and the Ethics of Natural Questions

There is a deep implicit agreement about the relationship between style and
objectivity uniting the followers of Descartes and Hobbes on the one hand
and of Nietzsche and Heidegger on the other: that propositions containing
objective truth must be clear and precise. If no such propositions can be
found, there is no objective truth about the world; if there is truth about the
world, then our clearest and most precise statements embody it. Clarity and
precision, absence of ambiguity, are the modernist marks of theoretical
authority, just as the explosion of pretensions to clarity and precision are the
hallmarks of postmodernist deconstruction. Plato and Aristotle violate, in
effect, this modern/postmodern theoretical agreement by setting forth the
view that true and false propositions about the world are distinguishable
from one another, but that such truths can never be stated in a clear and precise way. In Plato's dialogues, this is achieved by having Socrates question
his own apparently favored doctrines by calling attention to their incompleteness, as in the *Republic* and *Phaedo* on the status of the "forms," or by
explicitly refuting them, as in his assertion of the identity of the good and
the pleasant in the *Protagoras* or his dismantling of the view that knowledge
is right opinion plus *logos* about causes in the *Theaetetus* (see Desjardins,
1990). In Aristotle, the same combination of commitment to rational inquiry with acknowledgment of the inevitable imprecision of all such inquiry
is indicated in several ways: by his assertions of the need for different levels of precision in different kinds of discourse (*NE* 1, 1094b11–27), by his frequently calling attention to the "outline" or provisionally sketchy character
of his practical discourse (*NE* 2, 1103b34–1104a5), and by his acknowledgment that the key terms of his analysis, like nature (*Physics* 2, 193a4–9) and
good (*Metaphysics* 12, 1075a–1076a) and potentiality/actuality (*Metaphysics* 9, 1048a35–b6) are not demonstrably real entities no matter how real
they seem to him or to us.

The conclusion Aristotle seems to draw from his implicit rejection of the modernist link between precision and objectivity is not the postmodern premise that reality is relative to or constructed by the observer or the culture, but rather the idea that all claims to objective truth must be open to examination if our investigation into reality, a project whose value neither Plato nor Aristotle ever seem inclined to doubt, is to achieve as much truth as possible. The outcome of this is to privilege questions over answers in both moral/political and scientific inquiry in a way that is utterly absent from the modernism/postmodernism disagreement, and yet entirely compatible with the emphasis on continual critique the parties to that disagreement profess to value greatly. Before returning to the deliberative model of democracy, it will be useful to outline the general shape of Aristotle's political philosophizing, noting how both the style and the substance of his inquiry embody this non-relativistic privileging of question over answer.

Aristotle's *Nicomachean Ethics* and *Politics* together comprise a course in ethics and politics, a course intended as an element in the liberal education of young Greeks.[31] The aim of this course, he says in the first book of the *Ethics*, is action (*praxis*) rather than knowledge (*NE* 1, 1095a4–6); he adds in Book 2 that the inquiry is undertaken not to acquire theoretical knowledge, but in order to become good (*NE* 2, 1103b26–30). But what sort of a work is this, since it doesn't correspond to any modern sense of what a philosophical work in ethics and politics looks like? It is neither a systematic statement and resolution of central ethical and/or political issues (as in Hobbes, Locke, or Mill), nor is it an attempt to articulate one specially favored community's deepest or best insights about such things (as in Hegel or Dewey or Rawls or Habermas). Aristotle does not try to supply the theoretical foundation for a set of universally binding ethical principles or rules; nor does he give a coolly disinterested *wertfrei* account of the place of such principles or rules in human life. What then is the character, what is the rhetorical or pedagogical intent, of these theoretical discourses which aim at *praxis* rather than wisdom but which culminate (in Book 10 of the *NE* and Book 7 of the *Politics*) in the praise of impractical theorizing as the most choiceworthy way of life for human beings?

I believe the work embodies two pedagogical projects, the first more universal than the second, each with important implications for the other, and each of much interest to us today. The first is the attempt to establish the plausibility of a theoretical framework, built around a conception of nature (*phusis*) in general and of the nature of human beings in particular, for criticizing, rather than idealizing or epitomizing, the most widely respected ethical and political beliefs or values (the *endoxa*, the highly esteemed or reputable or generally approved opinions)[32] of any human community.

The second is a sustained and subtle critique of the *endoxa* of one such community, the one in which Aristotle teaches, the Greek and especially the Athenian regime, preserved for us in Pericles' Funeral Oration in Thucydides. That community is based on an understanding of virtue as virility or manliness, deeply suspicious of tyranny, vulgarity, effeminacy, and philosophy, and drawn to a life of memorable deeds crowned by honor and greatness of soul.[33] Aristotle's dual project continues the work of his teacher Plato, and does so in an indirect and undogmatic style much closer to Plato's than the traditional distinction between Plato's dialogues and Aristotle's "treatises" allows.[34] My central contention is that, for Aristotle, the core project of pre-philosophic moral education or character (*ēthos*) development is not to instill duty or responsibility[35] (though these are necessary conditions for good character) but to develop a certain kind of practical rationality; and that the business of moral and political philosophy is not to anchor character in theoretical certainty,[36] but to supply us with a set of questions and standards for examining our own characters and regimes and those of others.

Thus Aristotle's practical philosophy, like Plato's, is both naturalist and zetetic rather than transcendental and dogmatic—a preparation for self-critical inquiry, rather than a defense or explication of a principle or model. But this is not to say that it is merely skeptical or agnostic. Just as Socratic knowledge of ignorance is not simply ignorance but, in Leo Strauss's (1959, 38–39) phrase, knowledge of the elusive character of the whole, Aristotle's stress on questions itself reflects a definite sense of what human nature and human excellence or virtue are, a particular collection of tasks and abilities that, properly understood, suggests what I will call natural questions, rather than natural laws or principles. These natural questions have to do with the extent to which the customs and habits that form our characters promote the capacity for thinking and speaking in a distinctively and specifically human way, the hard to translate quality that Aristotle calls *prohairesis*. The word is hard to translate and to understand because it joins together two qualities, independence and reflectiveness, in a way that is unfamiliar to us (and not only to us, but to Aristotle's contemporaries as well—*prohairesis* is probably not a term taken from ordinary language, but an artful combination of *hairesis*, choice, and *pro-*, before).

Thus Aristotle does not intend only to puzzle or to encourage inquiry without advancing substantive positions of his own. Two Aristotelian propositions, both in Book 6 of the *Nicomachean Ethics*, express his bedrock understanding of the good human life, of practical reason or *phronēsis*, and of political science or philosophy. The first delineates the relationship between two intellectual virtues: "Political science (*politikē*) and *phronēsis* are the same *hexis* [capacity], but their being (*to einai*) is not the same"

(1141b23–24). That is, in context, you cannot be fully either a political scientist or a phronetic person without also being to some degree the other as well, though political science is directed toward universals and *phronēsis* toward particular actions. For Aristotle, moral education and the development of *phronēsis* call for the study of *politikē; politikē* is not a sufficient condition for *phronēsis,* but it comes close to being necessary.[37] To be good and to act well we need as clear a sense as possible of who we are as human beings, as well as who we are as Athenian or American democrats. To achieve such self-knowledge we need to pass a moment wondering about what exists beyond ourselves, and so Aristotle's ethical and political theory culminates, in Book 10 of the *NE* and Book 7 of the *Politics, not* in a series of basic principles or natural laws, but in difficult and practically unresolved questions (that is, with respect to the actions we will undertake after considering them) about our relationship to beings superior to us, to Aristotle's gods.[38]

The second key proposition is Aristotle's teleological definition of humanity mentioned above, his account of what it is among all the things we do and suffer that makes us who we are. This definition gives chief place to *prohairesis,* not merely "choice" or "intentional choice," and certainly not "free will," but the ability and the inclination to think through the options available to us and then to act on the basis of those deliberations: "*Prohairesis* is either understanding combined with desire or desire combined with thought; and what originates [movement] in this way is a human being (*anthrōpos*)" (1139b4–5).[39] This *prohairesis* is the quality that makes a human being a human being, for better or worse: "It is by prohairesing (*tōi prohairesthai*) that we are such as we are, and not by opining" (*NE* 1112a1–3).[40] Having a virtuous character is difficult, not because one needs a strong will or excellent genes to overcome pleasurable temptations, but because discerning the right thing to do in a particular situation, finding the mean, in Aristotle's typical metaphor, is very hard to do (1109a24–32). To be sure, we also are shaped in a preliminary way by our inborn biological potential for character of a certain kind, and even more by the habits we develop as children before we become capable of extensive deliberation (1103b23–25). We become just and moderate, etc., by performing just and moderate actions. Thus political people and others interested in character education and instilling ethics must pay careful attention to the habits we acquire as children, and especially to the kinds of songs and stories children become accustomed to (*Politics* 8). But primarily we are individuated as human beings by neither our habits, nor our actions, nor our desires, nor our beliefs, but by the way we think—which includes (paradoxically for us, but not for Aristotle) the way we feel.[41]

Aristotle's philosophical ethics is thus separate from though continuous with political education ordinarily understood. Both aim at forming better human beings, but in different ways: the latter habituates young people to respond in approved ways to feelings and circumstances, the former assumes such habituation and teaches a way of questioning and inquiry that lets us be critically aware of and, as far as possible, in control of our character.[42] Those questions have to do with the relationship between the habits and institutions we experience and a conception of natural problems and standards. It is not hard to state what Aristotle wants his audience, his students, to learn to do: We are to learn to treat ethical practices not simply as the *endoxa* they are, but as if they were criticizable solutions to problems posed by our inherited biological nature under various distinct circumstances, problems concerning how the prohairetic life can best be realized.

Teaching a way of questioning requires a different pedagogy from teaching a set of law-like rules. For one thing, Aristotle's pedagogy in the *NE* and the *Politics* acknowledges the particular beliefs, the *endoxa*, that form the moral horizons of its audience—just as Plato's Socrates or the Eleatic or Athenian Strangers of the dialogues must speak to the particular situation of the souls of each of his interlocutors. Aristotle's lectures are of necessity (because of their relatively impersonal lecture format) less subtle in this respect than Plato's dialogues, but it seems to me clear that he assumes a culture of the kind described above, and adapts his speech accordingly. One of the key problems of reading Aristotle (or Plato) well now is to imagine how the texts might read if the audience and its habits were not, as we are not, shaped by the virilist *endoxa* of the classical polis—even if we assume, as I think we can, that Aristotle's conception of the structure of potentiality and actuality that distinguishes human nature is in general outline perfectly believable.[43] Something like this exercise of imagination would be the starting point for an Aristotelian discussion of present-day democracy.

V. Reason and Emotion in Deliberative Democracy

How can this reprise of Aristotle's political philosophy improve the deliberative model? One of the charges raised most tellingly against the model by feminist theorists among others is that it ignores the emotions and is thus guilty of a narrow rationalism. Defenders of the model could respond that it does not ignore emotion: consider Rawls on "the two moral powers" ("the capacity for a sense of justice and the capacity for a conception of the good") and the "reasonable moral psychology" that can be derived from them (1996b, 81–84), and consider Kant himself, who presents the Enlightenment as a dramatic and impassioned quest for moral freedom. In the deliberative model, the emotions seem not to be ignored so much as stereotyped: the only emotions that count as positive are those that help public reason separate us from mechanical nature. Similarly, proponents of the liberal contract model, such as Hobbes, Locke, and Hume, have typically believed that the emotions to be cultivated if we want to achieve civil peace, the *telos* that defines liberal democratic politics, are calmness and lack of zeal, the "interests" rather than the "passions" (see Hirschman 1977). The deliberative model doesn't overlook the emotions in favor of cold reason, but it does regard the problematic of the emotions as straightforward and by now so obvious as to need no explanation or defense: We must learn to *dare* to be wise,[44] and all else will follow. The emotions are seen from the perspective of the task of unleashing public reason: emotions either aid or resist reason's emancipation as the guide to human life. Given this task, courage is preeminently good, cowardice and laziness particularly bad.[45] But is this implausible concept of nature as machine to be overcome by the courageous deployment of public reason one we want to carry forward in our political theorizing about democracy?

The background vision that sets democracy in the context of the inspired emergence of the autonomously human from the twin shadows of nature and superstition is pervasive in modern Western political philosophy, not only among those who follow in the line from Rousseau and Kant through Hegel and the Romantics. Achieving emancipation is difficult and perhaps impossible, but for a wide range of modern theorists the goal that gives meaning to our humanity is simple and clear. John Stuart Mill, who in general refuses to take Rousseau and Kant seriously, says this in Chapter 3 of *On Liberty* (1989, 60): "Human nature is not a machine to be built after a model, and set to do exactly the work prescribed for it, but a tree, which requires to grow and develop itself on all sides, according to the tendency of the inward forces which make it a living thing." Marx (1978, 160), in the *German Ideology,* stresses the need to overcome the "natural" division of labor so that we can gain control over our labor and develop it in any way we please.

The most influential twentieth-century democratic theorist, John Dewey (1927, 149), provides yet another formulation of this same view of emotion and reason in the light of the grand historical project of emancipating humans from nature through the establishment of democratic communities: "Regarded as an idea, democracy is not an alternative to other principles of associated life. It is the idea of community life itself. . . . Wherever there is conjoint activity whose consequences are appreciated as good by all singular persons who take part in it, and where the realization of the good is such as to effect an energetic desire and effort to sustain it in being just because it is a good shared by all, there is in so far a community. The clear consciousness of a communal life, in all its implications, constitutes the idea of democracy." A few pages later (151), Dewey adds the following distinction between *associations,* which are merely natural, and *communities,* which are decisively human and "moral": "Associate or joint activity is a condition of the creation of a community. But association itself is physical and organic, while communal life is moral, that is emotionally, intellectually, consciously sustained." Democracy is the grand and somehow necessary project in which human passion and reason combine to produce a new realm, distinct from the mechanical and meaningless nature from which we spring.

To a striking degree, these themes are already fully present in Kant's 1784 essay. Once we have developed the germ of free thought implanted in us by nature, human individuals organized as a people rather than a mere aggregate of individuals become increasingly able to act freely and responsibly: "Eventually, it [that is, "man's inclination and vocation to *think freely*"] even influences the principles of governments, which find that they can themselves profit by treating man, who is more than a machine, in a manner appropriate to his dignity" (Kant 1991, 59–60, italics in text). The deliberative model that flows from this Kantian source thus both presupposes and conceals, and so transmits without opportunity for reflection, an animating drama of the emancipation of humanity from the mechanical nature that frames and severely limits our understanding of the relationship of emotion and reason. Most notably, the drama teaches us that the interplay of emotion and thought in particular human lives and in the process of growing up are not matters of serious theoretical concern; they are displaced by the grandeur of the vision of emergent and universal moral freedom.

Aristotle's understanding is quite different and at least conceivably superior, particularly in the way he draws the line between human beings and other animals so as to open the way to a more nuanced understanding of thinking and emotion. The key terms in Aristotle's vocabulary here are *orexis* and *prohairesis. Orexis,* generally translated as desire, signifies not a passive or mechanical response to external stimuli or to internal "instincts," but an active and focused reaching out toward something in the environment, something we lack or need.[46] This is not a unique human feature—all living things reach out, desire, in characteristic and intentional ways that define their natures. Animals are not machines—or rational choice style reproductive fitness maximizers—but sets of potentials and insufficiencies that vary from species to species. It is true that Aristotle often refers to human beings as the peculiarly rational animals—but animals without the capacity for *logos* are emphatically endowed with qualities we ordinarily associate with 'reason,' such as discrimination, focus, memory, and the ability to learn and to choose. The line separating reason and feeling in Aristotle is less clear than it seems to us because he uses terms like desire (*orexis*) and perception (*aisthēsis*) to describe intentional activities rather than passive machine-like reactions to external stimuli (as is the case with post-Cartesian accounts of the line between human beings and other animals).[47] Voluntariness and responsibility are not the exclusive property of humans, and hence cannot be identical with our special ability to live by *logos* or according to *prohairesis*. *Prohairesis* may mean many things, but one thing it does *not* mean is bare 'choice'—which is *hairesis. Hairesis* is something we indeed do, but something that is also done by many other animal species.[48] It makes no Aristotelian sense to elevate voluntary or autonomous activity to the level of highest aspiration. *Prohairesis,* instead, refers in the *NE* and the *Politics* to our ability to make choice after deliberation (*bouleusis*) and reflection on our life's goals and on the options open to us.[49] But it does not mark a separation of thought from desire or emotion—just the reverse, since *prohairesis* is either *orexis dianoētikē* or *nous orektikos,* a "mixture" (itself a metaphor for a composite that cannot be formulated with any more precision) of thought and desire which can be thought of either as thought modified by desire or desire modified by thought. And it is this mixture that marks the specifically human way of life: "*Prohairesis* is thought that desires or desire that thinks, and such a starting point is a human being" (*NE* 6, 1139b4–5).

But achieving *prohairesis* and a prohairetic life is for Aristotle neither spontaneous in each individual nor a matter of historical necessity. It is instead an achievement that demands careful attention to the development of character in each of us. No single emotion, certainly not courage, the least distinctive and the easiest of the moral virtues according to Aristotle, can be associated with the development of the capacity for living prohairetically— but neither is this life in any way a separation of the mind from desire.

The key idea here is character, *ēthos,* another word for which we have no precise equivalent.[50] The notion of character combines emotion, desire, and reason in summing up an individual's "nature," an identity formed initially by habituation on the basis of biologically transmitted potentials, but gradually in the course of education becoming active, a motive force in an individual life.[51] In modern philosophy, the semantic content of *ēthos* is unfortunately drained away by two different ideas—the concept of "culture," and the concept of the "moral," or the "moral realm," a place in our lives where we obey laws we give to ourselves. Next to *culture,* character seems insufficiently precise and scientific; next to the "moral," character seems too "natural," insufficiently lofty and transcendent to capture our unique human dignity. Several centuries of reflection on *culture* and *the moral* have generated a number of familiar philosophical problems: Is *culture* a truly *moral* realm—or is morality universal and cosmopolitan, rather than local and parochial?

One major difference between Aristotle's philosophy-with-character and the modern philosophy-with-culture/"the moral" is that the latter can be made much more precise and systematic, since it points toward a single comprehensive human good to which all other particular goods can be subordinated in practice (or at least in politics at the level of idealizing models) as well as in theory. This may help account for the stiff impersonality of Rawlsian and Habermasian prose: they can reasonably aspire to expressing the perfectly correct model of human action or justice, in a way Aristotle cannot. There are two consequences of this that are troublesome in practice and, I think, avoidable in theory: the tendency to ignore or bracket the problem of education, of individual development, and the tendency to treat the achievement of full and self-governing humanity as an end in itself. The deliberative model might sacrifice theoretical self-assurance if it seriously entertained the Aristotelian alternative outlined here, but it would gain not only theoretical perspicacity but a richer and less distant position relative to the particulars of the ethical and political life around us.[52]

VI. The Horizon of the Deliberative Model

Finally, in the absence of any wider philosophizing to set the context and limits of the deliberative model, Rawls and Habermas are anthropocentric, and perhaps androcentric as well (since they stress a certain kind of courage or virility as the emotional quality powerful enough to lift us out of nature). They celebrate deliberative democracy as part of the story of the enlightenment, where enlightenment is understood in Kant's way as the creation of a new non-natural human "moral" reality. For Habermas, the drama of world history is the story of the change from traditional antirational societies, through the incomplete "rationalization of the lifeworld" that has resulted in a disenchanted (in Weber's sense) modernity, to a present in which the systems of instrumental rationality (market economics and technology) that dominate society are themselves not chosen by us rationally and deliberately, but control our lives in a way that betrays the emancipatory promise of modern critical reason. This is not unlike Foucault's critique of modernity as the substitution of invisible disciplinary regimes for visible traditional power. But Habermas (1981) thinks reason can reclaim its emancipatory potential—and that this reclamation is the descriptive and normative background that gives the deliberative model its life and appeal. This is a human-centered drama, one that sees no higher good than the realization of human potential, or of human "moral powers," in Rawls's phrase. For Aristotle, this might reflect a mistaken belief that nothing is effectively better than the human good or the good human life. It may even reflect the notion that the best life is one that involves realizing our moral powers by overcoming natural resistances to them, by displaying the kind of courage and energy that Kant saw as the moral virtues central to individual enlightenment.

This is rationalism, but of a curious sort, one which stresses publicity and universality and forswears the possibility of inquiring into the truths that lie outside of human practices. What matters is "moral" freedom and not persistent inquiry. Thus perhaps Richard Rorty is right in suggesting that the deliberative model implies a decisive though indirect commitment to Jerusalem over Athens: the paradoxical fate of the modern Enlightenment may be to transform itself into a new more enlightened, and quite godless, pre-enlightenment tucked comfortably within the limits of its own horizons. This general view reveals one deep connection between the stoutly modernist theorizing of Habermas and Rawls and Rorty's shrugging Postmodernism.[53] All three long for a comfortably consensual and rational community, and all see the task of philosophy as articulating (for the modernists) or at least (for postmodernists) pointing to the models through which the conflicts that threaten social solidarity can be resolved.

But for Plato and Aristotle, the aim of philosophy is neither to settle once and for all the questions of philosophy *nor* to show that these questions are fundamentally misconceived: foundationalism and anti-foundationalism are alternatives in modern philosophy, but Plato and Aristotle would accept neither position as definitive of the task of philosophy. They want a third thing: to assert what they take to be true answers to the problems of philosophy while at the same time showing reasons for questioning those answers and for continuing to ask and re-ask the questions. Aristotle, like Plato, aims not at lasting consensus, but at agreement sufficient for the purposes of action yet provisional enough to keep the questions alive. This makes his thought radically at odds with the spirit of modern and postmodern philosophy, but quite congenial to the spirit of modern liberal democracy.[54] In excluding the Aristotelian alternative without justification, the theorists of deliberative democracy tacitly and needlessly diminish the role of philosophy in both political life and political science.[55] The proponents of the deliberative model care too much about agreement and too little about deliberation. This is by no means a reason to reject the model as a useful guide to contemporary political judgment. What it shows is the importance of recognizing the model's need for a foundation, a need it shares with all other useful theoretical models. I offer a negative and a positive suggestion about how that need should be met. The negative one is that the deliberative model needs a better foundation than that supplied either by the *endoxa* of a hypostatized "democratic tradition" or by Kantian ontological dualism. My positive suggestion is twofold. First, one substantive or ontological foundation deliberative democrats should consider is the Aristotelian conception of nature and human nature. Second, whatever one ends up thinking about Aristotle's ontology and psychology, the ongoing debate about fundamental questions that is political philosophy provides an absolutely indispensable *discursive* foundation for deliberative democrats. To seek to narrow this debate for the sake of constructing a self-standing normative model, as Rawls and Habermas have done, is in effect to yield to the same spirit of modern technological reason that deliberative theorists want so much to oppose.

NOTES

1. For a good introduction to the model, see the essays by Seyla Benhabib, Joshua Cohen, and Iris Young in Benhabib (1996) and the essays in Bohman and Rehg (1997). For a Rawlsian approach to deliberative democracy, see Gutmann and Thompson (1996). For a sharp critique of the model in general and Gutmann and Thompson in particular, see Peter Berkowitz (1996). Rawls comments on his relationship to Habermas in his "Reply to Habermas" (a response to Habermas 1995). For an interesting application of Habermas's position to the issue of constitution-making in Canada, see Simone Chambers (1998). The term "deliberative democracy" seems to have been first used in its current sense by Joseph Bessette (1980). Bessette's approach here and in his *The Mild Voice of Reason* (1994) is more Aristotelian and less overtly theoretical than others are. For a theoretically sophisticated and explicitly Aristotelian discussion of how to evaluate the quality of deliberation in legislatures, see Uhr (1998). Abramson's book on the jury in American politics is a fine study of the extent to which juries are deliberative in the Aristotelian manner: "Long ago, Aristotle suggested that democracy's chief virtue was the way it permitted ordinary persons drawn from different walks of life to achieve a 'collective wisdom' that none could achieve alone. At its best, the jury is the last, best refuge of this connection among democracy, deliberation, and the achievement of wisdom by ordinary persons" (Abramson 1994, 11). Abramson is especially good at bringing out the ways particular questions about how juries should work, such as the issues of jury nullification and the need for unanimity, indicate the complex tensions between deliberation and other public goods, such as the need for a stable rule of law and the need to protect local minorities. Tulis's study (1987) of presidential rhetoric is another fine Aristotelian consideration of the relationship between presidential style and the deliberative character of American public debate.

2. Their revision consists largely in eliminating Collingwood's crudely historicist assertion that all thoughts and deeds reflect "absolute presuppositions" that are mutually unintelligible. See Gadamer (1990, 370–75).

3. Models and metaphors are necessary to make sense of complex hard to see phenomena like politics. As Aristotle says after using physical health as a metaphor for human virtue, "it is necessary to use visible witnesses for invisible things" (*NE* 2, 1104a13–14). Metaphor is especially invaluable as an instrument of education: "For learning easily is by nature pleasant to all, and words signify something, so that words that make us learn something are the most pleasant . . . and metaphor does this especially" (*Rhetoric* 3, 1410b10–13). On Aristotle's assessment of the place of metaphor in reasoning, see Arnhart (1981, 172–76).

4. "Permanent" is an exaggeration, but I haven't found an appropriate word or short phrase to convey my meaning. These questions are those that seem to us to be ones that arise from or accompany our nature, the problems and possibilities that human beings bring into the world. I will call them "natural" questions later, but they are natural only given an Aristotelian understanding of nature, which is very different from the modern understanding of nature as a machine. Speaking in an Aristotelian way, to say that these questions are natural is to say that they are questions about how best to promote successful or flourishing human lives. There is no single set of such questions, and because of this variation they aren't "permanent" questions. Moreover, any claim about the questions we should ask about the good life now, in this time and place, must be controversial—these questions are not a clearly intelligible bedrock foundation.

5. Though see Susan Bickford's (1996, 41–53) excellent discussion of the way Aristotle's *Rhetoric* provides an outline for thinking about deliberation as a public practice in ways that go beyond the modern deliberative model.

6. In *Politics* 2, 1268b–1269a, in his discussion of Hippodamus the great innovator, Aristotle argues that laws, traditions, and habits should often be treated as more authoritative than reason. Moreover, the best democracy according to *Politics* 6 (1318b) will be one in which the *dēmos* votes for officials and audits their conduct, as well as judging in the law courts, but does not always rule directly by deliberation. Similarly he praises farming democracies because the *dēmos* composed of farmers will often prefer to let the old laws stand. Much deliberation over many topics among many people is not the mark of the healthiest Aristotelian democracy.

7. I'm thinking here primarily of Appiah's (1994; 1997) critiques of Charles Taylor's communitarianism and identity-constraining varieties of multiculturalism.

8. There are some important objections to be made against the model as a model. It lacks the connection to the human desire for legality and justice that the contract model stresses, and the link to a desire for a strong identity evoked by the republican model and by nationalism generally. Compared with these models, deliberation as a standard sounds thin. Its proponents may rely too much on habits of mind that flourish in colleges and universities more than elsewhere.

9. Interestingly, one unique feature of the modern world that deliberative democracy seems wholly unable to grasp is the rise in the importance of religion in people's lives during the last half of the twentieth century. Neither Rawls nor Habermas is of much help in sorting through the complex relation between religions on the one hand and the deliberative ideal on the other. This deficiency might flow from the "neo" in their neo-Kantianism.

10. As far as I can tell, civic republican is a fairly new category, and seems to mean classical republicanism minus the classical republicans' relish for the invigorating character of war and military service in general.

11. On the connection between the emotions and deliberative rationality in Aristotle, see Garver (1994, ch. 4), Nussbaum (1995, ch. 3), Koziak (2000), and Bickford (1998).

12. Habermas (1996) presents a clear succinct statement of these distinctions.

13. Rawls from the start presented his theory of justice as a kind of Kantian contract theory, and said that in his opinion Kant's primary focus was on developing the

Rousseauan conception of freedom: "Kant's main aim is to deepen and to justify Rousseau's idea that liberty is acting in accordance with a law that we give to ourselves" (1971, 256). Habermas in works like *Knowledge and Human Interests* (1971a) attempted to blend a Kantian transcendental deduction of the fundamental human interests in freedom and reason with a modified dialectical materialist account of human history as a progressive self-formation of the human species.

14. Rawls in *Political Liberalism* says that he takes the concept of public (as opposed to private) reason from Kant's "What Is Enlightenment?" though he means something else by it. Rawls defines public reason as follows: "Public reason is characteristic of a democratic people; it is the reason of its citizens, of those sharing in the status of equal citizenship. The subject of their reason is the good of the public: what the political conception of justice requires of society's basic structure of institutions, and of the purposes and ends they are to serve. Public reason, then, is public in three ways: as the reason of citizens as such, it is the reason of the public; its subject is the good of the public and matters of fundamental justice; and its nature and content is public, being given by the ideals and principles expressed by the society's conception of political justice, and conducted open to view on that basis" (1996b, 213).

15. Of Kant's response to Rousseau, Susan Shell (1996, 5) says this: "Not cognition but virtuous self-mastery becomes man's badge of honor—one that lifts him beyond nature's abysmal fluctuations into direct community with the divine or holy will. At the heart of this moral economy lies human freedom . . . a freedom that consists in both making and submitting to universal law. As a power of original causation, moral will (albeit viewed from a practical point of view) borrows something of the aura of divine creation."

16. Bohman and Rehg (1997), xiii: "Deliberative theorists are in general agreement on at least this: the political process involves more than self-interested competition governed by bargaining and aggregative mechanisms."

17. The word "moral" obviously bears considerable weight in this formulation, and just as obviously makes sense only in a context in which we, like Kant, assume the existence of a separate moral "realm" or space defined by our rights and duties rather than our interests. Rawls (1996b, 279–80) articulates this idea of moral equality as follows: "Within a Kantian view there is no place for the idea of an individual's contribution to society that parallels that of an individual's contribution to associations within society. Insofar as we compare the worth of citizens at all, their worth in a just and well-ordered society is always equal." He explains moral equality further in a footnote to this sentence: "The worth of citizens in a well-ordered society is always equal because in such a society everyone is assumed to comply with just institutions and to fulfill their duties and obligations moved, when appropriate, by a sufficiently strong sense of justice. Inequalities do not arise from unequal moral worth; their explanation lies elsewhere" (280, n. 16).

18. Habermas (1996a, 27) describes his position as follows: "In agreement with republicanism, it gives center stage to the process of political opinion and will-formation, but without understanding the constitution as something secondary; rather it conceives the principles of the constitutional state as a consistent answer to the question of how the demanding communicative forms of a democratic opinion and will-formation can be institutionalized. Discourse theory has the suc-

cess of deliberative politics depend *not on a collectively acting citizenry* [my emphasis] but on the institutionalization of the corresponding procedures and conditions of communication." It is important to note that during the 1980s Rawls and Habermas each studied jurisprudence and legal philosophy and was decisively influenced by it, such that for Rawls *the* prime exemplar of public reason is the Supreme Court engaged in judicial review (1996b, 231–40). This is a long way from his claim in *A Theory of Justice* (p. 16) that all moral and political philosophy, or at least the theory of justice, would eventually be subsumed under the theory of rational choice (Rawls "corrects" this "error" in 1996b, 53, n. 7). On Habermas's recent legal education, see his preface to *Between Facts and Norms,* pp. xl–xliii. Still, for Habermas the rule of law is not an end in itself, but a procedure to be used for the purposes of public reason: "Law can be preserved as legitimate only if enfranchised citizens switch from the role of private legal subjects and take the perspective of participants who are engaged in the process of reaching understanding about the rules for their life in common" (1996b, 461). Habermas's antagonism to a traditional liberal understanding of individual rights is much greater than Rawls's; I can't imagine the latter saying this: "To the extent that we become aware of the intersubjective constitution of freedom, the possessive-individualist illusion of autonomy as self-ownership disintegrates" (Habermas 1996b, 490).

19. A situation in which the parties are committed to reaching agreement through communication and in which the only thing that counts is the force of the better argument.

20. "Proceduralized popular sovereignty and a political system tied in to the peripheral networks of the political public sphere go hand-in-hand with the image of a *decentered* society [Habermas's emphasis]."

21. For Habermas, Rawls cannot sustain his claim that the Rawlsian theory of justice is only "political" and not derived from any "comprehensive" view of the good life. According to Rawls, Habermas's insistence that he is more modest because his principle is procedural rather than substantive is untenable because an ideal speech situation can only be conceived once we specify the kinds of claims that can be made in it—it cannot be a purely open procedure, since at the very least it contains an intention: communicative action is or depends on the use of language oriented to mutual understanding—that is, to a substantive goal. See Rawls 1996b, 424–27, and Habermas 1996b, 18.

22. "One of the consequences of academic disciplinarity is that we no longer have any particular field of study whose role is to insist on self-examination, on reflection on the presuppositions and paradigms that guide our work: In relation to the sciences, philosophy today can not claim an institutionally secured position of privilege, but *philosophizing* [my emphasis] retains its universal power in the form of the self-reflection of the sciences themselves. . . . Philosophy, having become circumscribed as a specific discipline, can legitimately go beyond the area reserved to it by assuming the role of interpreter between one specialized narrow-mindedness and another. Thus I consider it philosophical enlightenment when doctors learn from sociological and psychoanalytic studies to appreciate the influence of the family environment in the genesis of psychoses and thereby also learn to reflect on certain biologistic assumptions of the tradition of their discipline. I consider it philosophical enlightenment when sociologists, directed by professional historians,

apply some of their general hypotheses to historical material and thereby become aware of the inevitably forced character of their generalizations. . . . I consider it philosophical enlightenment when philosophers learn from recent psycholinguistic investigations of the learning of grammatical rules to comprehend the causal connection of speech and language with external conditions and in this way learn to reflect on the methodological limits to the mere understanding of meaning. These are not examples of interdisciplinary research. Rather, they illustrate a self-reflection of the sciences in which the latter become critically aware of their own presuppositions."

23. "The concept of practical reason as a subjective capacity is of modern vintage. Converting the Aristotelian conceptual framework over to premises of the philosophy of the subject had the disadvantage of detaching practical reason from its anchors in cultural forms of life and sociopolitical orders. It had the advantage, though, of relating practical reason to the "private" happiness and "moral" autonomy of the individual. That is, practical reason was thenceforth related to the freedom of the human being as a private subject who could also assume the roles of member of civil society and citizen, both national and global" (Habermas 1996b, 1).

24. Here is Rawls 1996b, 134–35: "Plato and Aristotle, and the Christian tradition as represented by Augustine and Aquinas, fall on the side of the one reasonable and rational good. Such views hold that institutions are justifiable to the extent that they effectively promote that good. . . . By contrast, we have seen that political liberalism supposes that there are many conflicting reasonable comprehensive doctrines with their conceptions of the good, each compatible with the full rationality of human persons, so far as that can be ascertained with the resources of a political conception of justice." And Habermas 1996b, 95: "The classical primarily Aristotelian doctrine of natural law . . . as well as Thomas Aquinas' remodeled Christian version . . . clamped the different social orders together . . . In the train of the developments I interpret as the rationalization of the lifeworld, this clamp sprang open." Aristotle is powerfully defended against this pervasive misreading by Martha Nussbaum's (1990) "Aristotelian Social Democracy." Nussbaum argues that what she calls Aristotle's "thick but vague" conception of the human good is superior to Rawls's "thin theory" in that Aristotle recognizes *both* the plurality of human goods on the one hand, and the underlying universality of human problems or needs in relation to human possibilities or functionings on the other.

25. Habermas 1996b, Preface, p. xi: "After a century that, more than any other, has taught us the horror of existing unreason, the last remains of our essentialist trust in reason have been destroyed. Yet modernity, now aware of its contingencies, depends all the more on a procedural reason, that is, on a reason that puts itself on trial. The critique of reason is its own work; this double meaning, first displayed by Immanuel Kant, is due to the radically anti-Platonic insight that there is neither a higher nor a deeper reality to which we could appeal—we who find ourselves already situated in our linguistically structured forms of life."

26. An exception to this is Seyla Benhabib, whose criticism of Aristotle gets closer to a genuine difference between Aristotle on the one hand and Rawls and Habermas on the other. In a response to Martha Nussbaum's argument for "Aristotelian social democracy," Benhabib (1995, 255) says this: "What I find lacking in the Aristotelian account of human capabilities is the space, both in theory and in

practice, which allows one's understanding of the 'human condition' in Aristotelian terms to be translated into actively generated moral insight on the part of human actors. By contrast, discourse ethics claims that only those norms and normative institutional arrangements are valid which all those affected would agree to in a situation of practical discourse; likewise for the Rawlsian principle of justice, it is crucial that they would be chosen by the agents in the original position behind the 'veil of ignorance.'" But what Benhabib sees as a lack is a central part of Aristotle's overall theoretical argument about the relationship of theory and practice. Basic principles are not to be chosen on the basis of abstract and universal theoretically generated situations, but rather via continuing thought and deliberation about the particular *nomoi* and circumstances of a given *polis*. I know of no way of being certain that Aristotle is right about this, but the possibility that he is more right here than Rawls and Habermas should be taken seriously.

27. On Plato and deliberative democracy, see especially Mara (1997) and Saxonhouse (1998).

28. Helen Longino (1996, 274–75) comments as follows on the "semantic" theory of scientific explanation, set forth by Mary Hesse and others, that holds that scientific theories are not simply sets of propositions, but propositions embedded in orienting models: "Models are proposed as models of some real world system on the basis of an analogy between the model and the system, that is, the supposition that the model and the system share some significant features in common. Models often have their start as metaphors. Examples of such metaphoric models are typical philosophers' examples like the billiard ball model of particle interactions or the solar system model of the atom."

29. In the modern physical sciences (and in modern economics), a model is "an idealized system which is defined by a set of equations" (Kellert 1993, 86). A successful idealizing model in physics is one that yields hypotheses that can be tested against real world data. On model building as the essence of contemporary economics, see Robert M. Solow (1997). Solow (p. 43) says this about models: "A model is a deliberately simplified representation of a much more complicated situation. . . . The idea is to focus on one or two causal or conditioning factors, exclude everything else, and hope to understand how just these aspects of reality work and interact. There are thousands of examples; the point is that modern mainstream economics consists of little else but examples of this process."

30. For Rawls, political philosophy is like a module that can be slipped into any number of metaphysical and ethical theories (1996b, 387).

31. And perhaps also those not so young, if we believe Carnes Lord's attractive conjecture that the *Politics* were the basis for a program of adult education (Lord 1984, 10–11). The interpretation of Aristotle presented in the rest of this section is taken from Salkever (2000), where it is developed and applied in several ways. On the audience of the *Ethics* and *Politics*, historical and implied, see also Aristide Tessitore (1996), Richard Bodéüs (1993), and Thomas W. Smith (1994; 1999).

32. "The *endoxa* are opinions about how things seem that are held by all or by the many or by the wise—that is, by all the wise, or by the many among them, or by the most notable (*gnōrimoi*) and endoxic (*endoxoi*, most famous) of them" (*Topics* 100b21ff.). Aristotle's critical distance from the *endoxa*, like Plato's, is

signaled by the fact that each avoids using words like *gnōrimos* and *kalosk'agathos* as terms of genuine praise, preferring instead the less familiar *spoudaios* (serious) and *epieikēs* (equitable, decent).

33. For a clear and wide-ranging discussion of the critical character of Aristotle's political writing, see Gerald Mara (1995).

34. There are substantive differences between Plato and Aristotle, but they are not ethical and political ones. In a letter to Alexandre Kojève, Leo Strauss (1991, 279) identifies a key difference: "[T]he difference between Plato and Aristotle is that Aristotle believes that biology, as a mediation between knowledge of the inanimate and knowledge of man is available, or Aristotle believes in the availability of universal teleology, if not of the simplistic kind sketched in *Phaedo* 96."

35. Unlike the Rousseau of the *Social Contract.*

36. Unlike Kant.

37. Although experience is sometimes enough. *NE* 6, 1143b11–14.

38. But Aristotle's *politikē* does tell us that human beings are far from the best, most fully actual or switched-on beings in the cosmos, and that it would therefore be absurd to think that either *politikē* or *phronēsis* is the most excellent or serious (*spoudaiōtatē*) intellectual virtue.

39. The meaning of *prohairesis* is perhaps most revealingly indicated in the *Eudemian Ethics* (*EE* 2, 1227a3–5) where he speaks of it as more than the sum of wish plus belief: "As for *prohairesis*, it is neither simply wish nor simply opinion, but opinion and desire (*orexis*) when these follow as a conclusion of deliberation." For discussion of this passage, see Nancy Sherman (1989, 67).

40. Terence Irwin's (1985, 61) translation of this passage is: "It is our decisions to do what is good or bad, not our beliefs, that make the characters we have."

41. For Aristotle, the virtuous person is a self-lover, and possesses a certain kind of integrity: "The *spoudaios* (serious person) is in agreement with himself, and desires the same things according to his whole *psuchē*. . . . He wishes himself to live and to be preserved, especially that by which he thinks (*phronei*). For being is good to the *spoudaios,* and each person wishes good things for himself" (*NE* 9, 1166a13–20). That is to say, people are identical with their practical reason, their *phronēsis.*

42. The nearest Platonic analog to this Aristotelian distinction is the two kinds of moral education described by the Eleatic Stranger in the *Sophist* (229e–231b): The paternal way of direct exhortation and admonition, and the Socratic way of the practitioners of the "well-born" type of the sophistic art, who take pupils who think they know and through *elenchos* perform a sort of katharsis, making their student-patients dissatisfied with themselves rather than with others.

43. At any rate, considerably more plausible than Hegel's History or Kant's Reason. See Iris Murdoch (1985, 47): "Kant believed in Reason and Hegel believed in History, and for both this was a form of a belief in an external reality. Modern thinkers who believe in neither, but who remain within the tradition, are left with a denuded self whose only virtues are freedom, or at best sincerity, or, in the case of the British philosophers, an everyday reasonableness."

44. This is the Horatian motto Kant proposes we adopt in "What Is Enlightenment?" (1991, 54): "The motto of the Enlightenment is therefore: Sapere *aude!* Have courage to use your own understanding!"

45. "Laziness and cowardice are the reasons why such a large proportion of men, even when nature has long emancipated them from alien guidance, nevertheless remain gladly immature for life" (Kant 1991, 54).

46. My discussion of *orexis* owes much to Martha Nussbaum's in *The Fragility of Goodness* (1986, ch. 9). Speaking of Aristotle on the motion of all animals, ourselves included, Nussbaum says this: "Neither inert objects nor perfected gods, neither simply pushed around from without or spontaneously self-moving, we all reach out, being incomplete, for things in the world. That is the way our movements are caused" (289).

47. For philosophically informed discussion of the relevant and sometimes contradictory passages in Aristotle, see Richard Sorabji (1993, 112–16 and chs. 7 and 9).

48. Three Aristotelian distinctions are crucial to understanding the difference between Aristotle's "gradualist" line between human beings and other animals and the sharper and deeper Cartesian mechanical-beast / voluntary-man gulf that has been adopted without apparent reflection by the deliberative model: animal voice, *phōnē* (which allows individuals to signify pleasures and pains) and human *logos* (which allows us to become clear and articulate about our interests); animal *hairesis* and human *prohairesis;* and animal memory, *mnēmē* (which allows individuals to learn and to act upon that learning) and human recollection, *anamnēsis* (which allows us to search through our memories ourselves). He connects the latter two differences in *History of Animals* 1, 488b: "For human beings alone among the animals are deliberative (*bouleutikon*). Many share in both memory and teachability, but none except human beings have the power to recollect."

49. He does, however, use *prohairesis* to refer to some movements of *all* animals in *De Motu Animalium* 701a4–6.

50. Aristotle links *prohairesis* and *ēthos* when speaking of narrations that reveal character in the *Rhetoric* 3, 1417a17–19: "The narrative must be of character, and this will occur if we know what constitutes character (*ēthos*); one way to do this is to make the *prohairesis* clear—*ēthos* is such as it is by virtue of such a *prohairesis*, and the *prohairesis* is what it is by virtue of its end (*telos*)."

51. Aristotle's way of thinking about "nature" is very different from the idea of nature as system of necessity, the antithesis of autonomy, the conception of nature asserted by early modern physics and taken over by modern philosophy. But Aristotle's nature as an internal principle of individual activity turns up, without attribution, in a variety of quite modern texts, such as neurologist Antonio Damasio's (1994, xv) recent critique of the Cartesian separation of mind and body: "by nature I mean both the nature we inherited as a pack of genetically engineered adaptations, and the nature we have acquired in individual development, through interactions with our social environment, mindfully and willfully as well as not."

52. For arguments that "deliberative" or "participatory" democracy can be a good way to revitalize the necessary authority of collective institutions, see two recent articles by Mark Warren (1996a; 1996b). Warren's central point is reminiscent of a claim Aristotle makes about the role of popular election and oversight of officials in chastening the authority of even the most virtuous rulers: "These [the *epieikeis* who rule in farming democracies] will not be ruled by others who are their inferiors, and they will rule justly on account the fact that others have authority over the audits (*to tōn euthunōn einai kurios heteros*). For to be under constraint and

unable to do anything one might resolve to do is advantageous. The license to do what one wishes cannot defend against the *phaulos* (wretched) element in every human being" (*Politics* VI, 1318b36–1319a1). For an application of a very Aristotelian framework to modern politics, see the "capabilities" approach of economist Amartya Sen (see Salkever 1999). Sen admits (1987, 34) that capabilities' calculations, while not indeterminate or utterly relative, can never be as precise and conclusive as those produced by a theory that asserts a single good as the basis for measurement—like wealth or utility or choice or need. This means that precision has to be sacrificed here for the sake of "relevance" or "richness." But Sen is opposed to aggregating everything into a single measure, like GNP or average income, since such aggregation distorts our view of reality. In this case, he says, he prefers to be "vaguely right" rather than "precisely wrong"—because the goal of social science as he understands it is practical rather than theoretical, improving the capabilities for human functioning of real people in the real world, rather than building a systematic model to represent that world. For that reason getting it right is more important than being precise.

53. "The problem faced by us antifoundationalists is how to get rid of the idea that democracy is somehow enfeebled unless such shared premises exist. I think that the best solution to our problem is to play down the Greek idea that what makes us clever, language-using animals special is our ability to know, conceived as our ability to rise above the contingencies of culture and history. We antifoundationalists should try to substitute the idea that what makes us special is our ability to feel for, cherish, and trust people very different from ourselves. We should think of language as a tool for breaking down people's distrust of one another rather than as one for representing how things really are. To make this substitution, we have to persuade people to desert Athens for Jerusalem. We have to get them to appreciate Kierkegaard's suggestion that, *pace* Hegel, the whole point of Christianity was that God wanted lovers rather than knowers" (Rorty 1996, 335).

54. Understood in Leo Strauss's formulation as the *Weltanschauung* that tolerates indefinitely many *Weltanschauungen*.

55. Consider the anti-utopian and vaguely theist liberalism of Vaclav Havel (1996; 1997). The philosophical basis of Havel's liberalism is the sense that humans are part of a cosmos of ordered wholes, that we are not the best of beings within this cosmos, that the character of the order as a whole is both knowable in outline and unknowable with precision, and that such an awareness of the whole is essential to good politics even though not a source of action-guiding natural law. Havel is thus an Aristotelian, and it is unsurprising that mainstream political theorists have not remarked the importance of his thought.

BIBLIOGRAPHY

Abramson, Jeffrey. 1994. *We, The Jury: The Jury System and the Ideal of Democracy.* New York: Basic Books.

Appiah, Kwame Anthony. 1994. "Identity, Authenticity, Survival: Multicultural Societies and Social Reproduction." In *Multiculturalism: Examining the Politics of*

Recognition, ed. Charles Taylor et al., 149–63. Princeton, N.J.: Princeton University Press.

———. 1997. "The Multiculturalist Misunderstanding." *New York Review of Books* 44 (October 9): 30–36.

Arnhart, Larry. 1981. *Aristotle on Practical Reasoning*. DeKalb, Ill.: Northern Illinois University Press.

Benhabib, Seyla. 1995. "Cultural Complexity, Moral Interdependence, and the Global Dialogical Community." In *Women, Culture, and Development: A Study of Human Capabilities*, ed. Martha C. Nussbaum and Jonathan Glover, 235–55. Oxford: Clarendon Press.

———. Ed. 1996. *Democracy and Difference: Contesting the Boundaries of the Political*. Princeton, N.J.: Princeton University Press.

Berkowitz, Peter. 1996. "The Debating Society." *New Republic* 215 (November 25): 36–42.

Bessette, Joseph. 1980. "Deliberative Democracy: The Majority Principle in American Democracy." In *How Democratic Is the Constitution?* ed. Robert. A. Goldwin and William A. Schambra, 102–16. Washington, D.C.: American Enterprise Institute.

———. 1994. *The Mild Voice of Reason: Deliberative Democracy and American National Government*. Chicago: University of Chicago Press.

Bickford, Susan. 1996. *The Dissonance of Democracy: Listening, Conflict, and Citizenship*. Ithaca, N.Y.: Cornell University Press.

———. 1998. "Beyond Reason: Political Perception and the Political Economy of Emotion Talk." Paper presented at the APSA meetings, Boston.

Bodéüs, Richard. 1993. *The Political Dimension of Aristotle's Ethics*. Translated by Jan Edward Garrett. Albany, N.Y.: State University of New York Press.

Bohman, James. 1997. "Deliberative Democracy and Effective Social Freedom: Capabilities, Resources, and Opportunities." In *Deliberative Democracy: Essays on Reason and Politics*, ed. Bohman and Rehg, 321–48.

Bohman, James, and William Rehg, eds. 1997. *Deliberative Democracy: Essays on Reason and Politics*. Cambridge, Mass.: MIT Press.

Chambers, Simone. 1998. "Contract or Conversation? Theoretical Lessons from the Canadian Constitutional Crisis." *Politics & Society* 26 (March, 1998): 143–72.

Damasio, Antonio R. 1994. *Descartes' Error: Emotion, Reason, and the Human Brain*. New York: Avon Books.

Desjardins, Rosemary. 1990. *The Rational Enterprise: Logos in Plato's Theaetetus*. Albany, New York: State University of New York Press.

Dewey, John. 1927. *The Public and Its Problems*. Denver, Colo.: Alan Swallow.

Gadamer, Hans-Georg. 1990. *Truth and Method*. Second revised edition. Translated by J. Weinsheimer and D. G. Marshall. New York: Crossroad, 1990.

Galston, William. 1998. "Political Economy and the Politics of Virtue: U.S. Public Philosophy at Century's End." *The Good Society* 8 (Winter): 1–12 and 22.

Garver, Eugene. 1994. *Aristotle's Rhetoric: An Art of Character*. Chicago: University of Chicago Press.

Gaus, Gerald F. 1997. "Reason, Justification, and Consensus: Why Democracy Can't Have It All." In *Deliberative Democracy: Essays on Reason and Politics*, ed. Bohman and Rehg, 205–42.

Gutmann, Amy, and Dennis Thompson. 1996. *Democracy and Disagreement.* Cambridge, Mass.: Harvard University Press.

Habermas, Jürgen. [1968] 1971a. *Knowledge and Human Interests.* Translated by Jeremy J. Shapiro. Boston: Beacon Press.

———. [1969] 1971b. "The University in a Democracy." In *Toward a Rational Society,* trans. Jeremy J. Shapiro, 1–12. Boston: Beacon Press.

———. 1981. "Modernity versus Postmodernity." Translated by Seyla Benhabib. *New German Critique* 22 (Winter): 3–14.

———. 1987. *The Philosophical Discourse of Modernity: Twelve Lectures.* Translated by Frederick Lawrence. Cambridge, Mass.: MIT Press.

———. 1995. "Reconciliation through the Public Use of Reason: Remarks on John Rawls's *Political Liberalism." Journal of Philosophy* 92 (March): 109–80.

———. 1996a. "Three Normative Models of Democracy." In *Democracy and Difference: Contesting the Boundaries of the Political,* ed. S. Benhabib, 21–30. Princeton, N.J.: Princeton University Press.

———. 1996a. *Between Facts and Norms: Contributions to a Discourse Theory of Law and Democracy.* Translated by William Rehg. Cambridge, Mass.: MIT Press.

Havel, Vaclav. 1996. "The Hope for Europe." *New York Review of Books* (June 20): 38–41.

———. 1997. *The Art of the Impossible: Politics as Morality in Practice, Speeches and Writings, 1990–1996.* Translated by Paul Wilson and others. New York: Fromm International.

Hirschman, Albert O. 1977. *The Passions and the Interests: Political Arguments for Capitalism before Its Triumph.* Princeton, N.J.: Princeton University Press.

Irwin, Terence. 1985. *Aristotle: Nicomachean Ethics, Translated, with Introduction, Notes, and Glossary.* Indianapolis: Hackett.

Kant, Immanuel. [1784] 1991. "An Answer to the Question: 'What Is Enlightenment?'" In *Kant: Political Writings,* ed. Hans Reiss, trans H. B. Nisbet, 54–60. Second enlarged edition. Cambridge: Cambridge University Press.

Kellert, Stephen H. 1993. *In the Wake of Chaos: Unpredictable Order in Dynamical Systems.* Chicago: University of Chicago Press.

Koziak, Barbara. 2000. *The Retrieval of Emotion in Political Theory.* State College, Penn.: Penn State University Press.

Longino, Helen E. 1996. "Subjects, Power, and Knowledge: Description and Prescription in Feminist Philosophies of Science." In *Feminism and Science,* ed. Evelyn Fox Keller and Helen E. Longino, 264–79. Oxford: Oxford University Press.

Lord, Carnes. 1984. *Aristotle: The Politics, Translated with an Introduction, Notes, and Glossary.* Chicago: University of Chicago Press.

Mara, Gerald. 1995. "The Near Made Far Away: The Role of Cultural Criticism in Aristotle's Political Theory." *Political Theory* 23 (May): 280–303.

———. 1997. *Socrates' Discursive Democracy: Logos and Ergon in Platonic Political Philosophy.* Albany, N.Y.: State University of New York Press.

Marx, Karl. [1845–46] 1978. *The German Ideology, Part 1.* In *The Marx-Engels Reader,* ed. Robert C. Tucker, 147–200. New York: Norton.

Mill, John Stuart. [1859] 1989. *On Liberty*. In *J. S. Mill: On Liberty and Other Writings*, ed. Stefan Collini, 1–115. Cambridge: Cambridge University Press.

Murdoch, Iris. [1970] 1985. *The Sovereignty of Good*. London: Routledge & Kegan Paul.

Nussbaum, Martha C. 1986. *The Fragility of Goodness: Luck and Ethics in Greek Tragedy and Philosophy*. Cambridge: Cambridge University Press.

———. 1990. "Aristotelian Social Democracy." In *Liberalism and the Good*, ed. R. Bruce Douglass, Gerald Mara, and Henry Richardson, 203–52. New York: Routledge.

———. 1995. *Poetic Justice: The Literary Imagination and Public Life*. Boston: Beacon Press.

Rawls, John. 1971. *A Theory of Justice*. Cambridge, Mass.: Harvard University Press.

———. 1996a. "Reply to Habermas." In Rawls, *Political Liberalism*, paperback edition, 372–434. New York: Columbia University Press.

———. 1996b. *Political Liberalism*, paperback edition. New York: Columbia University Press.

Rorty, Richard. 1996. "Idealizations, Foundations, and Social Practices." In *Democracy and Difference: Contesting the Boundaries of the Political*, ed. S. Benhabib, 333–35. Princeton, N.J.: Princeton University Press.

Salkever, Stephen G. 1999. "Precision versus Accuracy: The Capabilities Framework as a Challenge to Contemporary Social Science." *The Good Society* 9: 36–40.

———. 2000. "Aristotle and the Ethics of Natural Questions." In *Instilling Ethics*, ed. N. Thompson, 3–16. Lanham, Md.: Rowman & Littlefield.

Saxonhouse, Arlene W. 1996. *Athenian Democracy: Modern Mythmakers and Ancient Theorists*. Notre Dame, Ind.: University of Notre Dame Press.

———. 1998. "Democracy, Equality, and *Eidē*: A Radical View From Book 8 of Plato's *Republic*." *American Political Science Review* 92 (June): 273–84.

Sen, Amartya. 1987. *The Standard of Living*. Cambridge: Cambridge University Press.

Shell, Susan Meld. 1996. *The Embodiment of Reason: Kant on Spirit, Generation, and Community*. Chicago: University of Chicago Press.

Sherman, Nancy. 1989. *The Fabric of Character: Aristotle's Theory of Virtue*. Oxford: Oxford University Press.

Smith, Thomas W. 1994. "The Protreptic Character of the *Nicomachean Ethics*." *Polity* 27 (Winter): 307–30.

———. 1999. "Aristotle on the Conditions for and Limits of the Common Good." *American Political Science Review* 93 (September): 625–36.

Solow, Robert M. 1997. "How Did Economics Get That Way and What Way Did It Get?" In *American Academic Culture in Transformation: Fifty Years, Four Disciplines, Daedalus* 126 (Winter): 39–58.

Sorabji, Richard. 1993. *Animal Minds and Human Morals: The Origins of the Western Debate*. Ithaca, N.Y.: Cornell University Press.

Strauss, Leo. [1957] 1991. Letter to Alexandre Kojève, May 28, 1957. In *Leo Strauss on Tyranny, Revised and Expanded Edition*, ed. Victor Gourevitch and Michael S. Roth, 276–80. New York: Free Press.

———. 1959. "What Is Political Philosophy?" In *"What Is Political Philosophy?" and Other Essays*, 9–55. Glencoe, Ill.: Free Press.

Tessitore, Aristide. 1996. *Reading Aristotle's Ethics: Virtue, Rhetoric, and Political Philosophy*. Albany, N.Y.: State University of New York Press.

Thompson, Norma, ed. 2000. *Instilling Ethics*. Lanham, Md.: Rowman & Littlefield.

Tulis, Jeffrey K. 1987. *The Rhetorical Presidency*. Princeton, N.J.: Princeton University Press.

Uhr, John. 1998. *Deliberative Democracy in Australia: The Changing Place of Parliament*. Cambridge: Cambridge University Press.

Warren, Mark. 1996. "Deliberative Democracy and Authority." *American Political Science Review* 90 (March): 46–60.

———. 1996a. "What Should We Expect from More Democracy? Radically Democratic Responses to Politics." *Political Theory* 24 (May): 241–70.

Young, Iris Marion. 1996. "Communication and the Other: Beyond Deliberative Democracy." In *Democracy and Difference: Contesting the Boundaries of the Political*, ed. S. Benhabib, 120–35. Princeton, N.J.: Princeton University Press.

———. 1998. "Inclusive Political Communication: Greeting, Rhetoric, and Storytelling in the Context of Political Argument." Paper presented at APSA, Boston.

CHAPTER TWELVE

Aristotelian Autonomy

FRED D. MILLER, JR.

Autonomy is a cardinal value for many modern political philosophers. This is especially true for liberal theorists, for whom the ideal citizens are autonomous—that is, independent, self-directing, self-determining, self-governing, self-ruling. Autonomous individuals act on their own judgment, and not from coercion, fraud, or manipulation. The philosophical defender of autonomy must provide an analysis and justification of this ideal. This has proven, however, to be a daunting task.

An influential modern advocate of autonomy was Immanuel Kant, who understood it as a capacity for self-legislation which moral agents possess by virtue of their rational faculty. By means of "pure practical reason" moral agents can grasp moral principles or laws which authoritatively limit how they may act. Kantian autonomy is the capacity of reason to master one's inclinations when they rebel against the moral law.[1] For Kant reason is in itself "a higher faculty of desire," which can motivate us to obey our moral duty without relying on any prior desires.[2] Heteronomy consists in being motivated by our inclinations (specifically, those not arising from our rational self), including the desire for pleasure or happiness.[3] An action has "moral worth," on this view, only if it is performed autonomously, that is, done out of respect for a law formed by the agent's own reason. The Kantian theory of autonomy, although influential, relies on controversial philosophical doctrines: that our essential nature as moral beings is rational, that pure practical reason is able to formulate substantive moral principles, and that we have free will consisting in the ability of our reason to control our sensuous inclinations in accordance with these moral principles.

Acknowledging the importance of autonomy but wary of the metaphysical hazards of free-will theory, some recent theorists have tried to give autonomy new foundations, assuming a conative psychology closer to that of David Hume, who held that all human motivation is ultimately grounded in the passions and that reason plays a purely instrumental role. That is, roughly speaking, when an agent has a certain desire and believes that the desire can be fulfilled through a specific course of action, an action of that type ensues, provided the agent has the means to act and nothing stands in the way. Proponents of such a view argue that they can account for autonomy: agents are autonomous only if they exercise rational self-control, in the sense that they are able to examine their desires and to act on those which they endorse on critical reflection. Hence, addicts who squander their resources to indulge unreflective cravings are not autonomous. This account of autonomy is ultimately conative: in order to endorse or reject a given desire, the agent must appeal to other desires, such as a higher-order desire to have (or not to have) the desire for a certain drug. Addicts who are incapable of this are heteronomous. This theoretical approach faces a serious difficulty: an agent is autonomous with respect to desire D_1 only if the agent can endorse D_1 on the basis of a higher desire D_2; but desire D_2 may itself be one over which the agent has no control. Wantons may endorse specific desires on the basis of other desires which are themselves unrestrained and unreflective. Or individuals may carry out impulses which they have acquired through brainwashing, indoctrination, or subtle forms of manipulation. Hence, the agent must also be autonomous with respect to higher desire D_2. This poses a dilemma: if we apply the same analysis of autonomy to desire D_2, then the agent must endorse it on the basis of a still higher desire D_3; but this must also be autonomous, leading to an infinite regress of desires, D_4, and so on. Alternatively, if the regress must stop somewhere with desire D_N, the problem arises of whether the agent has control over *this* desire. In spite of ingenious attempts, this dilemma continues to plague the conative approach.[4]

In view of the doubts bedeviling modern theories of autonomy, it seems advisable to consult ancient thinkers like Aristotle, who seem to recognize a kind of autonomy without espousing "free will" in the modern sense.[5] A precursor of the modern idea of autonomy was implicit in the ancient Greek ideal of *paideia,* which Plato defined as "the education in *aretē* from youth onwards, which makes men passionately desire to become perfect citizens, knowing both how to rule and how to be ruled on a basis of justice."[6] Following Plato, Aristotle assigned to the political expert and lawgiver the duty to ensure that all the citizens are good persons.[7] They must be properly educated if they are to possess political virtue and the capacity for self-governance.[8] Accordingly, Aristotle devoted most of his description of the best constitution in *Politics* VII–VIII to its educational program, rather than to legal institutions and political offices.

His philosophy of education presupposes a psychological theory which is set forth in the *Politics, Nicomachean Ethics,* and *Eudemian Ethics.*[9] On this view, animals are composed of body (*sōma*) and soul (*psuchē*), and are, like all natural systems, subject to the principle of rulership:

> ... whenever a number of things ... are combined into one common thing, a ruling component and a subject component appear, and this applies to living things since it holds of all of nature.... Soul and body are the basic components of an animal: the soul is the natural ruler; the body the natural subject.[10]

Human beings are animals of a special kind because their souls have rational and nonrational parts. Aristotle says that he is here following statements about the soul found "in exoteric discussions" which are imprecise but sufficient for his purposes.[11] The irrational (*alogon*) part of the soul is subdivided into vegetative and appetitive elements: "the vegetative faculty (*phutikon*) in no way shares in reason, but the faculty of appetite (*epithumētikon*) and in general the faculty of desire (*orektikon*) in a way partakes of it, in so far as it listens to and obeys it."[12] The rational part of the soul is also twofold: one component has reason in the strict sense, the other component, that is, desire, is rational in the sense that it obeys reason.[13] As a complex system the human soul is itself subject to the aforementioned principle of rulership: "it is natural and advantageous for the body to be ruled by the soul, and for the affective part to by ruled by thought, i.e. the part having reason (*logos*)."[14] But, all too often, reason fails to maintain control over desire, for example, in the case of moral incontinence or weakness (*akrasia*).[15] In particular, when incontinent persons pursue a pleasant object, their desire overcomes their reason.[16]

A virtuous person in contrast is reasonable (*epieikēs*), that is, governed by reason.[17] For example, in a temperate person "the desiring faculty accords with reason; for the noble is the aim of both of them, and the temperate person desires what he ought to do as he ought to and when; and this is what reason directs."[18] A virtuous person also exhibits authentic self-love, in the sense that he obeys the sovereign part of himself, namely, his reason, rather than his passion.[19] But we cannot make most people, especially the young, good by presenting them with arguments, because they are motivated by appetites and passions. "Argument and teaching do not have effect in all persons, but the soul of the student must have first been cultivated by means of habits for noble joy and noble hatred, like earth which is to nourish the seed."[20] The proper aim of education, then, is to habituate the citizens so that their souls are ruled by reason rather than irrational desires.[21]

The modern term "autonomous" derives from the Greek word *autonomos,* which applied primarily to the city-state but could be used by extension for an individual's free action.[22] Although the term is not applied to the individual in Aristotle's own extant writings, the concept is implicit in his notion of the rule of reason in the individual's soul.[23] This idea has important political ramifications, because citizens ought to possess self-ruling or autonomous souls. Aristotle argues that only naturally free adult males meet this requirement. "For the slave has no deliberative faculty at all; the woman has it, but it lacks authority, and the child has it but it is undeveloped."[24] Despotic rule is justified only over natural slaves, whereas political rule is just in the case of naturally free and equal persons.[25] Although nearly all modern philosophers would concur that Aristotle was grievously mistaken to restrict the capacity for autonomy to a narrow subset of humanity, it is still worth considering whether he sheds some light on this concept. And in view of the recent revival of virtue ethics, the question arises whether such a theory can and should validate autonomy.

This essay explores the prospects for "reconstructing" the concept of autonomy in an Aristotelian framework. The first section addresses the difficulties of accommodating the ideal of individual autonomy (i.e., reason ruling over the individual soul) within Aristotle's psychology. Section two explores the related concept of political autonomy, that is, self-governance by citizens. The concluding section considers autonomy as a political ideal—from an Aristotelian, as opposed to a modern, perspective.

INDIVIDUAL AUTONOMY

In view of the importance of reason ruling over the soul, we would expect Aristotle to provide a firm basis for it in *De Anima,* where he offers a theoretical psychology employing the concepts discussed in his *Physics* and *Metaphysics.* In this context, the notions of rule and authority involve causation. Just as, in a human community, the ruler maintains order by means of coercive force or persuasion, similarly, in a natural system, the ruling element holds it together by exercising causality.[26] For example, within a living organism, what unites its elements or matter is the sovereign or most dominant factor (*kuriōtaton*). But, Aristotle remarks, "it is impossible for anything to be superior to, and ruling (*archon*) over, the soul; and even more impossible, over thought; for it is reasonable that this is by nature primordial and dominant (*kurion*)."[27] Aristotle states that "the soul is the cause (*aitia*) and principle (*archē*) of the living body," and expounds this in terms of the four causes. Whereas the elements are the material cause of the body, the soul is the cause in the other three senses: it is the efficient cause (the source of change, and specifically of locomotion), it is final cause or end, and it is the formal cause or essence.[28] This is also required by Aristotle's theory of nature. Insofar as a plant or animal exists by nature, it has an internal principle or cause of motion or rest.[29] This implies that, if the rational part of the soul is also to rule over the desires, it must operate as a comparable causal principle. That is, in order to be the natural ruler of the soul, thought must be an efficient cause in the sense of a source of change.

But this implication seems to contradict Aristotle's own account of human motivation in *De Anima* III.9–10. The idea that reason is the natural ruler over desire is an important theme in Plato's *Republic,* where it presupposes the theory that the soul is divided into three distinct parts or faculties: rational (*logistikon*), spirited (*thumikon*), and appetitive (*epithumētikon*).[30] Aristotle follows Plato in distinguishing among distinct kinds of desire (*orexis*): namely, appetite (*epithumia*), passion (*thumos*), and wish (*boulēsis*).[31] But he rejects Plato's tripartite psychology, on the grounds that desire as such is a single faculty, and it is unreasonable to divide it into three parts corresponding to three parts of the soul.[32] Aristotle thus confronts the unavoidable question: which faculty of the soul is responsible for self-movement? His discussion is tortuous, but his conclusion seems clear: "That which moves therefore is a single faculty and the faculty of desire (*orektikon*)."[33] This suggests that desire, rather than reason, is the primary cause of human action. Reason seems to be conceded a merely subordinate causal role. He says, "Desire is relative to an end; for that which is the object of desire is the stimulant of practical thought; and that which is last in the process of thinking is the beginning of the action."[34] Thus reason is relegated to a mere facilitator of the ends at which one's desire happens to aim. Reason cannot be ruler over desire if desire is the primary cause or source of action. Aristotle thus seems to agree with Hume that reason is and ought to be the slave of the passions.[35]

This presents a problem: the aim of education (*paideia*) as described in the *Politics* and *Nicomachean Ethics* seems to be in tension with the theory of motivation in *De Anima.* One might respond in different ways to this problem. One might concede that the problem is insoluble: that the ethical and political treatises rely upon an "exoteric" psychology, which is incongruent with his own theoretical psychology. Alternatively, one might suggest that the "rule of reason" invoked in the *Nicomachean Ethics* and *Politics* is only a *façon de parler.* Aristotle does not literally mean that reason has primary causal efficacy. He may merely mean that agents are "ruled by their reason" when they *consistently* pursue certain aims, and that these aims are the result of whatever desires the agent happens to have. On this view Aristotle looks like a sort of "closet" Humean, who could not endorse a strong version of autonomy. Further, in education, the cultivation of rationality would play a basically subsidiary role, and the point of moral habituation would primarily be to inculcate certain desires in the students. Thus the aim of education would be to produce well-habituated, or conditioned, individuals, rather than autonomous, self-governing agents. But there is another way of answering the problem: that a careful reading of *De Anima* reveals that Aristotle is really committed to the rule of reason in his theoretical psychology, so that his philosophy of education is after all supported by his psychology. I shall consider the evidence for the third interpretation. If this approach succeeds, it is unnecessary to suppose either that Aristotle's exoteric psychology conflicts with his theoretical psychology, or that he is speaking misleadingly about the rule of reason in the moral and political treatises.

Before considering the argument of *De Anima* III.9–10, it is important to have in view the overall context of Aristotle's philosophy of soul. He has defined the soul in general terms as the first-level actualization of a natural body which potentially partakes in life.[36] He has added that living things possess different powers or faculties whereby they qualify as natural bodies of the sort presupposed in the general definition of soul. These include the nutritive faculty, perception, thought, and the power of self-movement or locomotion.[37] After investigating the faculties of nutrition, perception, and cognition, he turns to locomotion in *De Anima* III.9–11. He has also remarked that the soul is the cause or principle of the body in three senses: the efficient cause, the final cause, and the formal cause.[38] But when Aristotle offers causal explanations, he does not intend to propose that a "ghost in a machine" or "homunculus" is *really* performing the action in question. He remarks, "To say that the soul is angry is like saying that the soul weaves or builds a house. It is doubtless better to avoid saying that the soul pities or learns or thinks, and rather to say that it is the human being who does this with his soul."[39] The same applies when Aristotle speaks of parts or faculties of the soul. He does not deny that human beings act. He is trying to explain *how* they act. Finally, in order to follow his reasoning in these chapters, it is important to keep in mind his aporetic method. He poses a problem (*aporia*), argues for a provisional solution, then critically assesses that answer, qualifies or modifies it, and then resumes the process of critical assessment. If we compare his statements at different stages of the argument, we should not be surprised to find apparent inconsistencies.

Aristotle begins by asking: Which faculty or capacity of the soul brings about movement in the animal?[40] The candidates are the nutritive faculty, the perceptual faculty, thought, and desire. Aristotle rejects both the nutritive faculty[41] and the perceptual faculty[42] by invoking his teleology. If either of these was the source of locomotion, then since nature does nothing in vain, it would have equipped plants and stationary animals like the sea anemone with bodily organs for moving in place. Moreover, thought or intellect (*nous*) is also dismissed because it does not have control (*kuria*) over the soul.[43] This seems clear in the case of contemplative thought. Our knowledge that if we eat a lot of sweets we are liable to become obese and prone to disease is so far merely knowledge of a fact. But even practical thought, which commands us to pursue or avoid certain objects, can lack control if we are incontinent and succumb to our appetites. All too often we eat the fattening foods from which practical thought bids us to abstain. This seems to leave the field to desire (*orexis*), but this is challenged as well on similar grounds.[44] If we are continent, we will resist the temptation to eat fattening foods, and thus obey thought rather than appetite.

Aristotle accordingly draws the interim conclusion that "these two things at any rate are observed to bring about movement in place: desire or thought."[45] But he adds that this applies to nonhuman animals only if we suppose that imagination (*phantasia*) is "thinking of a sort" (*noēsis tis*).[46] For imagination brings about movement in nonhuman animals, and indeed humans in many instances follow imagination rather than thought. Given this qualification, Aristotle seems to conclude that two different sorts of causal factors cooperate to bring about locomotion: a conative cause and a cognitive cause.

So far Aristotle seems to have allowed that thought is at least a partial cause of action. But he further qualifies this claim: thought which brings about movement is practical thought, which reasons for the sake of something. Desire (*orexis*) is also for the sake of something, namely, the object of desire (*orekton*). This object of desire is the starting point of practical thought, and its terminus is the starting point of action. For example, if I want to be healthy, health is the object of my desire. Through practical reasoning I conclude, "Eat non-fattening foods," and I act accordingly.[47] Aristotle infers that thought (and, by similar reasoning, imagination) can bring about movement only because the object of desire brings about movement.[48]

Although Aristotle has so far recognized two sources of action, he now contends that there must be *one* moving principle. If two things brought about movement, they would bring about movement on account of a common form or kind.[49] What is this single kind of cause? He says, "That which brings about movement therefore is a single thing, that is, the faculty of desire (*orektikon*)."[50] He argues that whenever one acts according to calculation, one also undergoes movement according to wish (*boulēsis*), which is a sort of desire. But appetite (*epithumia*), another sort of desire, can also bring about movement contrary to calculation.[51] The argument *seems* to be that sometimes action results from desire accompanied by reasoning, and sometimes it results from desire accompanied by imagination or appearance (*phantasia*).[52] For example, we may skip dessert because we wish to be healthy, having reasoned that this is good for us. Or if we are incontinent, the pastry appears pleasant to us and we indulge our appetite for sweets. But desire is the one element that is always present, so it has a privileged status as the moving principle. Aristotle thus seems to have enthroned desire as true ruler over the soul, and demoted reason to the Humean role of slave of the passions. Moreover, he seems to have done this by means of a shaky argument, since from the fact that desire is always involved, it does not follow that it is the *only* cause.

It is very questionable, however, whether this is Aristotle's point. For he continues[53] his argument as follows: "Thought then is always correct,[54] but desire and imagination are both correct and not correct. Therefore, the object of desire always brings about movement, but this is either the good or the apparent good; and not every [good] but that good which is an object of action."[55] Hence, Aristotle's inference that the faculty of desire is the source of movement—in the sense of a proximate cause of movement—is but a step on the way toward a further conclusion, namely, that the *object of desire* brings about movement, and it does so in two ways: as the apparent (*phainomenon*) good when desire is merely accompanied by imagination or appearance (*phantasia*), and as the good simpliciter when desire is accompanied by correct reasoning.[56] This suggests that the faculty of desire is a source of movement because the object of desire is also a source, but the way in which the object of desire plays this role depends on the cognitive condition of the agent. Let us see whether this suggestion is borne out by the remainder of Aristotle's discussion.

As we have seen, Aristotle has appealed to the phenomenon of incontinence in arguing that the soul's power (*dunamis*) of desire brings about movement.[57] But he now points out that the desires themselves can be opposed to each other.[58] This opposition occurs in agents who are able to perceive time, that is, to distinguish between the present and the future. For example, I perceive a morsel which is sweet but which I know is fattening and will be harmful to my health. In this case my reason commands me to refrain from the morsel because of the future. But appetite commands me to eat it because of what is now the case, "for what is now pleasant seems pleasant without qualification and good without qualification, because [appetite] does not see the future." This results in opposed desires, namely my appetite for immediate gratification and my wish for health.[59] Aristotle concludes, "that which brings about movement is one in kind, i.e. the faculty of desire in so far as it is a faculty of desire; ... but the things which bring about movement are many in number." In the case of continence and incontinence, then, particular desires come into conflict with each other, like countervailing causal forces.[60]

This concluding statement contains, however, an important parenthetical qualification: "but the object of desire is [that which brings about movement] first of all; this brings about movement without being moved, by being thought or imagined."[61] The object of desire in our example is either health or immediate pleasure. Whether health is in fact an object of desire depends on whether the agent understands that health is the good, and whether pleasure is such an object depends on whether it appears to the agent to be good. This supports our earlier suggestion: that the faculty of desire is a source of movement because the object of desire is also a source, but the way in which the object of desire plays this role depends on the cognitive condition of the agent.

Aristotle distinguishes three factors involved in locomotion:

1. That which brings about movement. This turns out to be twofold:
   a. That which is itself unmoved, that is, the good that is the object of action. Aristotle has established that this is the object of desire.[62]
   b. That which also undergoes movement, that is, the faculty of desire, because an animal is moved insofar as it has an actualized desire.[63]
2. That which is made to move, that is, the animal.[64]
3. That by which the animal is made to move: this is a bodily instrument which is to be discussed in biological works such as the *Motion of Animals*.[65]

To conclude, the conative faculty brings about movement in the sense that it is actualized in the form of a sort of movement, which is the *proximate* cause of action, in that it initiates the process in the agent which leads to action (or, in the case of incontinence, interrupts it). The faculty of desire is a conduit of motion, in that it is a "moved mover." The primary cause is an unmoved mover,[66] namely, the object of desire. This depends, however, on thought or imagination playing its role.[67] This is consistent with the object of desire being unmoved, because the object of awareness is not affected by being apprehended.[68]

The cognitive capacities play a different role from that of desire in bringing about locomotion. The distinctive role of reason and imagination must be understood in terms of Aristotle's teleology: an animal naturally seeks its proper end or good, and avoids what is opposed to it. It will be moved whenever its end is present or appears to be present. Thought and imagination play the role of revealing (or seeming to reveal) this end to the agent. When the agent apprehends its good, or apparent good, as attainable it will act in the appropriate way. Deliberate human action involves the following progression:

1. The agent *A* thinks (or imagines) that object *O* is a good (or apparently good) thing attainable by action.
2. *A* has a desire for *O*; i.e., *O* becomes an object of *A*'s desire.
3. *A* deliberates about how to achieve *O*.

4. *A* concludes that *O* ought to be attained by means *M*.
5. *A* chooses to do *M*.
6. *A* does *M*, i.e., *A* undergoes locomotion.

Human action thus depends on complex interactions between the conative and cognitive faculties.[69]

Whether agents do the right thing ultimately depends upon whether they seek a truly good end, as opposed to a seemingly good end, and this depends upon how they exercise their thought and imagination.[70] Both thought and imagination are under the human agent's control in an important sense. Unlike perception, which depends on external objects, thought is up to the agent, since knowledge involves universals which are in a sense in the soul.[71] Similarly, imagination in the case of human beings is up to themselves to a large extent.[72]

The account in *De Anima* seems to be consistent with what Aristotle has to say about choice (*prohairesis*) in the *Nicomachean Ethics*, for example, "The origin of action is choice—its efficient cause but not its final cause— and the source of choice is desire and reasoning for the sake of something."[73] Choice, viewed here as a proximate efficient cause of action, is thus a desire for the sake of an end, for example, good action.[74] Choice is characterized variously as "deliberative desire" (*bouleutikē orexis*), "cognitive desire" (*orexis dianoētikē*), and "desiderative thought" (*orektikos nous*).[75] Deliberation (*bouleusis*), strictly, is concerned with the means to our ends.[76] For example, by deliberation a person concludes that going for a walk will promote his health, and then chooses to take a walk.[77]

Aristotle also uses a political metaphor to describe the role of choice:

> The same thing is an object of deliberation and an object of choice, except that the object of choice has already been determined. For the object of prior judgment resulting from planning is an object of choice. For each person stops inquiring how he will act when he has brought the starting point into himself, and into the commanding part of himself; for this is what chooses. And this is clear also from the ancient constitutions, which Homer depicted. For the kings announced the things which they had chosen to the people.[78]

Aristotle here calls choice the commanding part (*hēgoumenon*) of the self, anticipating the Stoic notion of a commanding faculty (*hēgemonikon*) of the soul.[79] The Homeric analogy plainly implies that the process of deliberation resulting in a choice is finished when action begins. But the analogy seems to have confused the ancient commentators, who equated it with the rule of reason. According to Heliodorus' paraphrase, Homer "presents the kings announcing after planning their prior judgment to the people as if to the choice, so that it will be enacted."[80] This implies that choice is analogous to the people, a recipient of prior judgment. The implication is that thought (*nous*) is the commanding part. Similarly, other commentators compare human *nous* to the kings, and our desire (*orexis*) to the people.[81] But this contradicts Aristotle's explicit identification of choice with the commanding part in this passage. Here it is choice that has command over the parts of the agent which carry out the action.[82]

Nonetheless, this characterization of choice as a commanding element is consistent with the thesis that reason ultimately initiates action. For deliberation and choice concern the means to our ultimate end, whereas the end is the object of wish (*boulēsis*): "wish is rather of the end, and choice is of the things related to the end, for example, we wish to be healthy, and we choose the things through which we will be healthy, and we wish to be happy and say so, but it is inappropriate to say that we choose to be so. For generally choice seems to concern the things which are up to us."[83] Wish is thus the specific form of desire concerned with our ends, and, as remarked above, Aristotle maintains in *De Anima* that reasoning may lead a person to wish for an object. In this case, wish is a form of rational desire.[84]

The foregoing analysis explains how Aristotle could think of reason as having as its proper role the rule over the soul, even though it is not a proximate cause of action on a par with desire. By revealing to agents their natural end, it enables this end, which is as such unmoved, to become an object of action for the agent, and thereby to bring about desire, the movement or change in the soul which is the proximate cause of action. Although he speaks of desire as the source of movement, Aristotle is not a Humean, because thought enables desire to find its proper end.[85] But, although Aristotle speaks of the rule of reason, he is not a Kantian either. For Kant practical reason discovers the moral law by abstracting entirely from human nature and appealing to the necessities of action among rational wills in general.[86] Aristotle differs from both Hume and Kant in that he explains the roles of reason and desire in terms of his natural teleology.

In the *Nicomachean Ethics* Aristotle recognizes—indeed, he emphasizes—that not all humans are receptive to reason. The many pay no heed to rational argument: "living by passion they pursue their own pleasures and the means to them, and they avoid the opposite pains, and have not even a conception of what is noble and truly pleasant, since they have never tasted it. What argument would reform such persons?" One of the main purposes of education is to prepare the young to be receptive to rational argument: "the soul of the student must first have been cultivated by means of habits for noble joy and noble hatred, like earth which is to nourish the seed. For he who lives as passion directs will not hear argument that dissuades him, nor understand it if he does."[87] Practical wisdom, "the eye of the soul," reaches a developed state only if the agent is virtuous. For practical wisdom involves reasoning about what is to be done, i.e., the end or the best thing is such and such. "But this will not be apparent except to the good man. For wickedness distorts and makes one deceived about the starting-points of action."[88] An educated person can distinguish between true good and immediate pleasure, which is only apparently good; and between true evil, and immediate pain, which is only apparently bad.[89] In this respect, education, like art, follows the distinctions of nature, but supplies what is missing in nature.[90] The uneducated person cannot distinguish between what is objectively good and what is apparently good. But students who have been brought up properly are able to become excellent (*spoudaioi*) citizens, who are fully autonomous in that they are able to rule themselves as individuals and to share in governing the city-state.

This explains how human beings can be autonomous individuals as well as interdependent political animals. Aristotle's thesis that "the city-state exists by nature" is derived from the argument that the city-state arises out of natural human potentials and that when it attains self-sufficiency it provides its citizens with all that they need in order to fulfill their natural ends.[91] This presupposes that "a human being is by nature a political animal," a thesis based on the observation that human beings are by nature endowed with moral capacities necessary for political life and with the impulse to form communities with other human beings.[92] Human beings cannot, however, develop these natural potentials on their own. Individuals are not self-sufficient when they are separated from the city-state, and they are therefore unable to develop and exercise their natural functions. Aristotle thus makes the further claim that "the city-state is prior by nature to the individual."[93] Hence, the city-state is one of the greatest human goods: "just as a human being is the best of animals when perfected, when separated from law and the administration of justice he is the worst of all."[94] A human being must be reared and educated under an appropriate constitution, laws, and educational system in order to acquire ethical virtue and practical wisdom and thereby become a rationally self-governing, autonomous moral agent.[95]

In conclusion, when Aristotle declares in *De Anima* that the faculty of desire is the moving principle in human beings as well as animals, he does not compromise his political ideal of reason's rule in the human soul. Even in *De Anima* thought has a role in action which makes intelligible and plausible "the rule of reason" essential to individual autonomy.

POLITICAL AUTONOMY

Political autonomy may be defined provisionally as self-government by the citizens under law. This is, in effect, equivalent to Aristotle's notion of

political rule (*politikē archē*). At the beginning of the *Politics* he claims that
political rule differs from other modes of rule: namely, kingship, despotism,
and household management.[96] He elsewhere remarks that we have often distinguished the modes of rule "in the exoteric discussions."[97] He finds a form
of political rule within the human soul:

> It is possible then, as we say, to observe in an animal first both despotic
> and political rule. For the soul rules the body with a despotic rule, but
> thought rules desire with a political and kingly rule. And it is evident
> in these things that it is according to nature and advantageous for the
> body to be ruled by the soul, and for the passionate part to be ruled by
> thought and the part having reason, but it is harmful for all of them if
> they are ruled equally or in the reverse way.[98]

This passage seems to suggest that political and kingly rule are identical, but
Aristotle's point is instead that both modes involve the rule of reason over
emotion.[99] Kingship differs from political rule in that a king never relin-
quishes authority, although a king, unlike a tyrant, has free and voluntary
subjects.[100] Political rule in contrast typically involves ruling and being ruled
in turn.[101] This is reasonable, since "political" means "of or pertaining to the
citizen." The citizen on Aristotle's general account shares in ruling and being
ruled, although in different ways in different constitutions; and the citizen
of the best constitution does so with the correct aim, namely, the virtuous
life.[102] Political rule is appropriate for a political multitude "in which there
naturally emerges a military multitude that is able to be ruled and to rule
according to a law that distributes offices on the basis of merit to those who
are prosperous."[103] Hence, a population fit for political rule satisfies three requirements: it is capable of defending the city-state, it possesses sufficient
wealth, and it is capable of sharing in governance. Such a population must
know how to rule as well as be ruled, or else they will only be capable of
despotic rule.[104] The hallmark of such a population is equality: "The city-
state wishes to consist of equal and similar persons as far as possible."[105]

It has been intimated that political rule entails the rule of law.[106] Political
rule requires that the citizens share in governance, taking turns in ruling
and being ruled or holding different offices. Each person must be willing
to rule with a view to the advantage of others and to yield up authority when
it is another person's turn.[107] This requires that individuals abide by legal
procedures governing their term of office, the selection of new officials, and
the rights and duties associated with each office. More generally, Aristotle
declares, "where the laws do not rule, there is no constitution."[108]

Aristotle discusses the rule of law in connection with the constitution
of kingship: is it better to be ruled by the best man or the best laws?[109] This

problem arises out of Aristotle's argument that a constitution should assign political rights on the basis of distributive justice, hence in proportion to the merit of the citizens. Merit (*axia*) is defined in terms of their contribution to the political community: this includes of course military and financial contributions, but education and virtue have the most just claim in the dispute over sovereignty.[110] This might seem to imply that kingship would be the best constitution, if there was a supremely virtuous man. Although Aristotle admits this as a theoretical possibility, he recognizes truth in the arguments for popular government based on the purported wisdom of the multitude:

> The many, although none of them is individually an excellent man, can still, when they have come together, be better than [the excellent men]. They will be better, not as individuals but all together. . . . For each of the many persons has a portion of virtue and practical wisdom, and after they have come together, just as the multitude becomes like one man who has many feet and hands and senses, so also with respect to character and thought.[111]

It is not merely that the many outnumber the few, but that when the many "come together" to deliberate and complement each other, so that different individuals are able to judge different aspects of complex matters and pooling their wisdom arrive at a more comprehensive and informed judgment than even a very wise person. Such popular rule can succeed only if it also involves the rule of law.

Aristotle's discussion of this question is complex, dialogic, and aporetic, shifting from one viewpoint to another. Proponents of kingship remark that, like doctors and other practitioners, rulers must deal with particular circumstances and cannot rely simply on written generalizations.[112] Advocates of the rule of law retort that general rules are necessary, and that governors cannot deal with special cases unless they have been educated by means of laws.[113] Further, the law is inherently rational and thus superior to the passionate element found in every human soul.[114] Law as such is not subject to the influence of appetite or spirit which subverts human decision makers, for example, through spirit or favoritism. Again, individuals have difficulty judging themselves, which is apparent even with practitioners of crafts (e.g., doctors and gymnasts) who ask others to judge their performance. The rule of law is preferable because the law is a mean, i.e., impartial.[115] Throughout this discussion Aristotle draws upon the reputable opinions (*endoxa*) of his predecessors. For example, the claim that "law is thought (*nous*) without desire (*orexis*)" echoes Plato's description of law as "the distribution of thought (*nous*)."[116] Understood in this way, rule of law consists in the city-state ruling over itself according to reason, and thus a form of autonomy on the part of the entire city-state.

AUTONOMY AS A POLITICAL IDEAL

Autonomy emerges as an implicit political value when Aristotle considers the aims of the ideal constitution. He argues first that "the best way of life both separately for each person and in common for city-states" is a virtuous life "equipped to the extent that they can partake of virtuous actions."[117] This helps to define the central task of political theory, which is to fashion the best constitution, that is, "that order under which anyone whatsoever might act in the best way and live blessedly."[118] Whether a constitution qualifies as "best" depends on whether it enables the citizens to realize their highest potentials.[119] Aristotle then takes up the issue: Is the virtuous way of life the political life or the philosophical life? Or, in other words, is it the active life or the contemplative life?[120] Aristotle proceeds in familiar fashion, assessing arguments for and against each candidate. The political life is condemned as despotic and unjust, as well as an impediment to one's personal well-being. The philosophical life is also disparaged as inactive and inimical to happiness.

Aristotle considers the case to be made for each way of life, beginning with the political. This should be distinguished from the tyrannical life, because the political life entails the just treatment of foreigners and fellow citizens alike.[121] Also, it is wrong to deprecate the political life on the grounds that inactivity is better than activity.[122] Happiness is action, and the actions of just and temperate persons have as their end many noble things. It does not follow that politicians should strive for unlimited power, so that they can perform the greatest number of noble acts. Instead, they should respect the constraints of natural justice, and share in ruling with those who are equal and similar to themselves.[123] When others are superior in virtue and the power to do the best things, it is noble and just to obey them. Thus the political life should conform to the same requirements of the individual virtuous life, so that the active life is "the best way of life for every city-state in common and for the individual."[124]

Aristotle then argues that it is also wrong to criticize the philosophical life for being inactive.[125] The underlying error is the assumption that a way of life is active only if one leads it relative to other persons, or that a thought is active only if it is carried out for the sake of consequences of actions. Instead, "contemplations and thoughts that are ends in themselves and carried out for their own sakes are much more [active]. For acting well, hence also a sort of action, is the end." The philosopher thus emerges as a fully autonomous agent, with his thought ruling over his soul for the sake of intellectual activity. Similarly, even when actions extend beyond the agent, we say that the master craftsmen by means of their thoughts act in the authoritative sense. Here the master craftsman is again a fully autonomous agent, presiding over a complex project by means of his thought. When a project is carried out, for example, a trireme is constructed, this action is attributable to the master craftsman more than to anyone else, because it is his intelligence which is directing the project.

But Aristotle reaches a rather surprising conclusion, drawing a parallel between the city-state, the individual, and the cosmos:

> Further, city-states that are situated by themselves and have chosen to live this way are not necessarily inactive. For activity can also come about with respect to its parts. For the parts of the city-state have many types of community with each other. This also belongs in a similar way to any human being as an individual. Otherwise god and the entire cosmos could hardly be in a noble condition, since they have no external actions beyond the ones proper to them. It is evident then that the same life must be the best for each individual and for city-states and human beings in common.[126]

The life of action fundamentally involves intelligent self-governance. The cosmos is a system governed by a divine intelligence,[127] just as a human agent is properly governed by reason. Similarly, a city-state will be truly capable of action only if its parts are interrelated according to a similar principle of rational self-governance. Political agency, like individual agency, is fundamentally autonomous. A primary task of the lawgiver must be to prepare the citizens for rational self-rule.

The requirement that citizens possess political virtue is not confined to the "polis of our prayers." The argument that popular government is best, based on the wisdom of the multitude, also assumes that "each of the many persons has a portion of virtue and practical wisdom." Hence, political autonomy (political rule according to law) requires some measure, at least, of individual autonomy (self-governance of the soul): that is, a city-state is (politically) autonomous only if the citizens are (individually) autonomous to some degree. And even in a deviant constitution, it is not enough for the citizens merely to have good laws: "There is no benefit in the most beneficial laws, even when they have been approved by everyone involved in governing, unless they will be habituated and educated in the constitution—if the laws are popular, educated in a popular way; if they are oligarchic, educated in an oligarchic way."[128] This is necessary if the constitution is to be their "way of life."[129]

The need for education in the laws is most evident in the case of the best constitution. This is clear from Aristotle's identification of lawfulness with justice in the universal or broad sense. (He distinguishes universal justice from particular justice, i.e., distributive or corrective justice.) He defends this analysis as follows:

> The laws address all things, aiming at the common advantage of all persons or at that of the best persons or of the authorities according to virtue or according to some other sort of manner. So we say that those acts that tend to produce and protect happiness and its parts for the political community are just in one way. And the law commands that one do the acts of a just person (e.g., not to leave one's post or flee or throw away one's arms), and that of a temperate person (e.g., not to commit adultery or act insolently), and that of a gentle person (e.g., not to strike or malign another), and similarly regarding the other virtues and vices, commanding some and forbidding others. The correctly established law does this correctly, but the law which is made offhand does worse.[130]

He goes on to call this kind of justice "complete virtue, not without qualification but in relation to another person. . . . It is complete because he who has it is able to exercise his virtue in relation to another person also, not only with respect to himself; for many persons can exercise their virtue in their own affairs but cannot do so in relation to another person."[131]

Complete virtue does not, however, consist in unquestioning conformity to the laws, but education under law fosters the development of both ethical virtue and practical wisdom (*phronēsis*). Practical wisdom is more than mere cleverness, because it has a noble end.[132] Ethical virtue, in the authoritative sense, is also more than a natural disposition. Although human beings possess virtues such as justice, courage, and temperance in a way by nature, we need to have them in another way if they are to be fully virtuous. "For the natural states belong to children and beasts, but without insight (*nous*) they are evidently harmful. . . . Just as a mighty body that moves without sight may have a mighty fall, so also in this case. But if one acquires insight, there is a difference in action. And his state, though similar to what it was then, will be virtue in the authoritative sense."[133] Persons educated under law who acquire full ethical virtue and practical wisdom are autonomous in the sense discussed above. J. A. Stewart provides a vivid account of this process:

> *Nomos* [law] (which is *nous aneu orexeōs* [thought without desire]) perceiving the relation which ought to subsist between the tendencies of

human nature, endeavours to effect it in the young, by encouraging some tendencies, and discouraging others. At first the subjects of this educational process are not aware of what is really being done; but in course of time they begin to see for themselves the relation which has been gradually effected. *Phronēsis* [practical wisdom], or the conscious-ness of the proper relation (*ho orthos logos*), dawns in them, and aids *nomos*, and gradually supersedes it in the function of preserving and perfecting the *summetria* [harmony]. Unless, on the one hand, the way-ward tendencies were first regulated in relation to one another by the constraining force of *nomos*, we should never become *conscious for our-selves* of the proper relation in which they ought to stand to one another, as members of a whole; but, on the other hand, unless this conscious-ness supervened in us, our virtue would remain at the level of the mere good behavior of children, who do right without knowing why, simply because they are told to do it: "One cannot be good in the authorita-tive sense without practical wisdom."[134]

The distinctive function of the practically wise person is to deliberate well in pursuit of good ends,[135] and moral habituation under law is necessary to ensure that the virtuous agent is committed to the correct end and acquires the practical wisdom necessary to attain this end in practical circumstances.[136]

According to Stewart's interpretation, Aristotle's practically wise per-son is governed by his own reason, and thus resembles Kant's autonomous moral agent. Stewart goes so far as to claim that "the difference between Kant and Aristotle is not really one of principle, but of detail."[137] Stewart's main point is that there is "no real antagonism between Aristotle's doctrine of Habituation, and Kant's doctrine of the Autonomy of the Will."[138] Al-though he is correct to deny a conflict between habituation and autonomy, Stewart has exaggerated the parallel between Aristotle and Kant. Aristotle does not regard the virtuous agent as ruled by "pure practical reason" in Kant's sense. The characterization of law as "thought without desire," which Stewart cites, occurs in a passage in which Aristotle is summarizing the opinions of "some persons" who are opposed to absolute monarchy.[139] Aris-totle sifts through the arguments for and against the rule of law before reaching his own conclusion. We should consider the context in which Aris-totle's claim that law is thought (*nous*) occurs:

> He, then, who commands the law to rule seems to command god and *nous* alone to rule, but he who commands a human being to rule adds a beast also. For appetite (*epithumia*) is of this sort, and passion (*thu-mos*) corrupts even the best man. Therefore, law is thought without desire (*orexis*).[140]

It is noteworthy that this argument is unsound, when viewed from the standpoint of Aristotle's own psychology, because it mentions only two species of desire—appetite and passion—but ignores the third, wish (*boulēsis*). Further, wish is present whenever reasoning leads to action.[141] Hence, Aristotle himself could not have accepted this as a decisive argument that law consists of thought to the *exclusion* of desire. Nor would the autonomous agent be motivated by "pure" practical reason.

Here Aristotle differs from Kant, for whom autonomy is the "power to restrain and overcome inclinations by reason."[142] The Aristotelian moral agent is self-directed and governed by reason, but Aristotle does not view the rule of reason as consisting in self-legislation, that is, the making and enacting of universal moral laws on the basis of our pure practical reason alone. For Kant, reason is not, in and of itself, a higher faculty of desire. Rather, human beings have natural ends such as health and happiness, and when the agent apprehends these through reason he has a natural desire for them. Kant might dismiss such motivation as heteronomous. For Aristotle, in contrast, the autonomous agent—understood as directing himself to his natural end—is both ruled by reason and motivated by desire.

CONCLUSION

Many modern political theorists hold that political institutions should respect and protect individual autonomy. It is generally supposed that an agent is autonomous insofar as his motivations "derive from the essential character of his will."[143] If an individual performs an action as a result of being intimidated, deceived, seduced, or brainwashed, this crucial requirement is violated. The desires motivating the agent are alien to his will—so that he exhibits heteronomy. There is, however, no consensus among autonomy theorists as to what it means for motivations to derive from the essential character of one's will. The Kantian tradition identifies this essential character with pure practical reason. This allows for a sharp distinction between autonomy and heteronomy, but carries heavy theoretical freight: in particular the view that reason can by itself construct moral laws and motivate agents to act from moral duty in opposition to natural inclinations. The conative tradition allied with Hume identifies the essential character of one's will with desires that have been endorsed, or could be endorsed, through a process of critical reflection. There is, however, no generally accepted account of desire-based critical reflection. Autonomy theorists have sought in vain a conative "Archimedean point": privileged desires in virtue of which the agent is autonomous. Moreover, the Humean view is closely associated with ethical noncognitivism, the view that ethical principles are subjective and cannot be justified on rational grounds. On the

Aristotelian alternative, as reconstructed in this essay, the autonomous agent is motivated by natural desires which have resulted from a rational awareness of what is objectively good in relation to the agent. This theory differs from Humean and Kantian theories in that it accords both reason and natural inclinations an essential role in the autonomous will. The Aristotelian notion of autonomy also has an important place in his political theory. Popular self-governance cannot embody justice unless the citizens are autonomous—i.e., rationally self-governing—individuals. The principle of rule of law which underlies political rule is indispensable not only for protecting the freedom of individuals but for promoting their autonomy. Aristotle's political ideal differs from much of modern liberalism, especially in assuming that there is an objective good for all human beings, and that humans are by nature political animals. Still he has much to offer to modern political theory, to the extent that he succeeds in liberating autonomy from a commitment to ethical noncognitivism, and that he establishes that a moral agent can be both governed by reason and motivated by desire.[144]

NOTES

1. Kant, *The Metaphysics of Morals*, Part II, *The Doctrine of Virtue*, in *Practical Philosophy*, trans. and ed. Mary J. Gregor (Cambridge: Cambridge University Press, 1996), 515.

2. See Roger J. Sullivan, *Immanuel Kant's Moral Theory* (Cambridge: Cambridge University Press, 1989), 45.

3. See Kant, *Groundwork of the Metaphysics of Morals*, in *Practical Philosophy*, 81–89.

4. James S. Taylor gives an illuminating account of the difficulties for the conative approach to autonomy in his doctoral dissertation, "Personal Autonomy: Its Theoretical Foundations and Role in Applied Ethics," Bowling Green State University, 2000.

5. The free-will controversy took definitive shape only after Aristotle, and scholars disagree over whether his various remarks on voluntariness and on responsibility generally imply some version of determinism or indeterminism. The issue is complicated by the fact that the concept of the will (from the Latin *voluntas*) developed later on. See Albrecht Dihle, *The Theory of Will in Classical Antiquity* (Berkeley: University of California Press, 1982) and Charles H. Kahn, "Discovering the Will: From Aristotle to Augustine," in *The Questions of "Eclecticism": Studies in Later Greek Philosophy*, ed. J. M. Dillon and A. A. Long (Berkeley: University of California Press, 1988), 234–59. Aristotle's commentator, Alexander of Aphrodisias criticized Stoic determinism by explicitly appealing to Aristotelian principles in *De fato*, written about 200 A.D. See R. W. Sharples, *Alexander of Aphrodisias On Fate* (London: Duckworth, 1983).

6. Plato, *Laws* 643e, cited in Jaeger, *Paideia: The Ideals of Greek Culture*, trans. Gilbert Highet (Oxford: Oxford University Press, 1945), vol. 1, p. 55.

7. *Pol.* VII.14.1333a11–16; cf. 13.1332a28–38 and *EN* I.13.1102a7–10, II.1.1103b3–6.

8. *Pol.* VII.14.1332b41–1333a11; cf. Plato *Laws* I.643c3–6.

9. See *EN* I.13, VI.1; *EE* II.1; *Pol.* I.2, 5, 13, VII.15.

10. *Pol.* I.5.1254a28–31, 34–6.

11. *EN* I.13.1102a26–8.

12. Ibid., 1102b28–31. Cf. *Pol.* VII.14.1333a16–18. The claim appears to be qualified at *EN* VII.6.1149b1–3 which states that anger follows reason in a sense but (sensuous) appetite does not; cf. III.5.1113b26–30. As James B. Murphy comments, "You might talk someone out of his fear but not out of his hunger."

13. *EN* I.13.1103a1–3. Cf. V.11.1138b5–13.

14. *Pol.* I.5.1254b6–9. Cf. 13.1260a5–6: "The soul by nature contains a part that rules and a part that is ruled."

15. See *EN* I.13.1102b21.

16. Ibid., VII.6.1149b3.

17. *EN* IX.8.1169a17–18: "The reasonable person (*epieikēs*) obeys thought (*nous*)." X.9.1180a10–11: "A reasonable person, since he lives with a view to the noble, will obey reason (*logos*)." The latter passage cites an opinion with which Aristotle evidently agrees. Because the term *epieikēs* is often applied to the excellent or virtuous person (see *EN* III.5.1113b16 and IV.9.1128b28, and *Rhet.* II.1.1378a13, 16), it is often translated as "good person," "decent person," etc. But the passages quoted in this note suggest that reasonableness is a distinguishing trait of the *epieikēs*.

18. Ibid., III.12.1119b15–17.

19. Ibid., IX.8.1168b28–1169a6.

20. Ibid., X.9.1179b23–6. W. D. Ross translation in Jonathan Barnes, *The Complete Works of Aristotle: The Revised Oxford Translation* (Princeton, N.J.: Princeton University Press, 1984). Cited henceforth as "Revised Oxford Translation."

21. Here Aristotle is in basic agreement with Plato: see 1180a5–24 and cf. *Laws* IV.722a and IX.854e.

22. See Sophocles, *Antigone* 821. Some scholars interpret the unusual application of *autonomos* to the heroine by the chorus as disapprobatory. As B. M. W. Knox argues, "the chorus shows no sympathy and places the full responsibility for her imminent death on her own head," because she "lives by her own law" (*The Heroic Temper* [Berkeley: University of California Press, 1964], p. 66 nn. 8 and 9). Martin Ostwald adds that Antigone "has put herself outside the pale of the *nomoi* of the city and has defied them" by invoking the unwritten statutes of the gods (*Autonomia: Its Genesis and Early History* [Scholar's Press, 1982], p. 11).

23. This idea is also suggested by Plato, who says that expressions such as "self-control" (*kreittō hautou*) should be analyzed in terms of the naturally better part of the soul controlling the naturally worse part. That is, it is the rule of reason over the appetites (*Republic* IV.430e6–431a7, 442c5–d1, 444d8–11). The closest Aristotle comes to calling an individual "autonomous" is with his characterization of the virtuous individual as "a law unto himself" (*nomos heautoi*, *EN* IV.8.1128a32; cf. *Pol.* III.13.1284a13).

24. *Pol.* I.12.1260a12–14.

25. *Pol.* I.7.1255b20; cf. *EN* V.6.1134a26–8.

26. This applies to the entire cosmos. See *Metaph.* 12.10.1075a11–25 which compares the unmoved mover to the general of an army.

27. *DA* I.5.410b11–15. Aristotle is criticizing pre-Socratic philosophers who hold that the elements are the most basic entities. His claim is reminiscent of Plato, *Laws* X.896b10–c3.

28. Ibid., II.4.415b8–27.

29. *Phys.* II.1.192b20–3.

30. *Rep.* IV.444d8–12. Aristotle refers to the three parts of the soul at *DA* III.9.432a25–6.

31. See *DA* II.3.414b2; *MA* 6.700b22, 7.701a36–b1; *MM* I.12.1187b37; *EE* II.7.1223a26–7.

32. I discuss Plato's doctrine and Aristotle's critique in "Plato on the Parts of the Soul," in *Plato and Platonism,* ed. Johannes M. Van Ophuijsen (Washington, D.C.: Catholic University Press, 1999).

33. *DA* III.10.433a21. Revised Oxford Translation of J. A. Smith based on W. D. Ross's Oxford Classical Text of 1956. Cf. 433a31–b1 and 433b10–11.

34. Ibid., 433a13–17. Also from the Revised Oxford Translation.

35. See Lynn Holt, "Aristotle on the *archē* of Practical Reasoning," *Journal of Philosophical Research* 24 (1999): 365–69.

36. *DA* II.1.412a16–28.

37. Ibid., 2.413a20–5.

38. Ibid., 4.415b8–12.

39. Ibid., I.4.408b11–15.

40. The Greek verb *kinein* and related noun *kinēsis* present problems of translation. First, these terms have a generic sense of "change," including quantitative change (e.g., growth or diminution) and qualitative change (e.g., change of color) as well as the narrow sense of change of place (locomotion). When the latter sense is intended, *kata topon,* "in respect to place," is sometimes added for clarification, but often the kind of change meant must be understood from the context. Second, *kinein* is used in three different voices—active, middle, and passive—which do not correspond to distinct English verbs. The active (transitive) voice is usually translated as "bring about movement (or change)," the middle as "undergo movement (or change)" or simply as "move (or change)," and the passive as "be moved (or changed)." To complicate matters the middle and passive have identical forms except in the aorist and future tense. There is occasional uncertainty over whether Aristotle is using the passive or middle in other tenses.

41. Ibid., III.9.432b13–19.

42. Ibid., 432b19–26.

43. Ibid., 432b26–433a6.

44. Ibid., 433a6–8.

45. Ibid., 10.433a9–10. He uses *phainetai* with the participle, which generally signifies what is observed to be the case. This is stronger than the verb with the infinitive, which typically means "seems" or "appears."

46. Aristotle's term *phantasia* can be translated as "imagination" or "appearance," depending on the context. Here by *tis noēsis,* he means that *phantasia* is a

mode of awareness comparable to thinking. Here *tis*, "a sort of," indicates indefiniteness of nature. On this usage see H. W. Smyth, *Greek Grammar* (Cambridge, Mass.: Harvard University Press, 1974), §1267.

47. Cf. *MA* 7.701a7–25.

48. *DA* III.10.433a18–21.

49. Ibid., 433a21–2.

50. *DA* III.10.433a21. This passage is very difficult, because two main families of manuscripts disagree over whether *orektikon* (faculty of desire) or *orekton* (object of desire) occurs here and previously at lines 19 and 20. The C family of manuscripts have *orektikon*, the E family of manuscripts *orekton*. The term *orekton* is clearly preferable at lines 19 and 20, and I. Bekker's text accepted it at all three places. However, A. Torstrik argued for *orektikon* at line 21, which was subsequently accepted in the texts of G. Rodier, W. D. Ross, R. D. Hicks, and P. Siwek. H. Richardson has challenged this reading, contending that *orekton* makes better sense at line 21 ("Desire and the Good in *De Anima*," in *Essays on Aristotle's De Anima*, ed. Martha Nussbaum and Amélie Oksenberg Rorty [Oxford: Clarendon Press, 1992], 390–92). Although Richardson is persuasive in emphasizing the primacy of the object of desire (*orekton*), he has not decisively answered Torstrik's main point, that lines 22–26 argue that desire, *rather than* thought, is the common causal form. Hence, *orektikon* is preferable at line 21.

51. *DA* III.10.433a22–5. Aristotle here distinguishes two forms of desire: wish (*boulēsis*) and appetite (*epithumia*). At 433b4 he alludes to a third type: passion (*thumos*). These three forms are listed together elsewhere: see n. 31.

52. Cf. *DA* III.11.433b31–434a5.

53. Ibid., 10.433a26–30. That these lines are a continuation is indicated by the particle *oun*, "then," at line 26 and the conjunction *dio*, "therefore," at line 27.

54. This seems to mean that thought is never in error, which is mistaken and elsewhere denied by Aristotle (cf. *DA* III.6.430a26–b6). A more charitable interpretation, which fits the context, is that the faculty of thought (*nous*) is able to attain a state of knowledge which is certain and inerrant, namely, when it apprehends first principles. In this case, Aristotle uses *nous* in a narrower sense for the comprehension of first principles: cf. *Posterior Analytics* II.19.100b5–7. In the context of *DA* II.10.433a26, Aristotle presumably means that practical thought can attain certainty about human natural ends such as health.

55. Ibid., 10.433a26–9.

56. Aristotle has just said, "whenever one is moved according to calculation, one is also moved according to wish" (ibid., 433a24–5). In the *Nicomachean Ethics* Aristotle also states that wish is directed to an end rather than to a means to an end: for example, we wish for health as an end, but choose particular actions as means to achieving this end (III.2.1111b26–8). Assuming that he understands wish in this way in *De Anima* also, it follows that when one is moved according to reason, one has a desire for a certain end, namely, the good.

57. *DA* III.10.433a31–b1. He adds that this power is "what is called desire (*orexis*)." The reason for this qualification is evidently that *orexis* is also used for the actualization of this power, which is a sort of movement (cf. 433b17–18, reading *energeiai*).

58. Ibid., 433b5–16.

59. Ibid., 433b8–10. This argument assumes something like the hypothesis of opposites which Plato deploys in *Rep.* IV.436b8–c1 to argue that the soul has parts. Namely, it is impossible for the same thing to be moved at the same time with opposing movements with respect to the same object. Aristotle evidently assumes a similar principle at *DA* III.2.425b19–29.

60. Ibid., 433b10–11, 12–13. Cf. *DA* III.11.434a11–14.

61. Ibid., 10.433b11–12. Aristotle uses the instrumental dative—*tōi noēthēnai ē phantasthēnai*—to indicate that the object of desire brings about movement by means of the awareness of the agent. That is, the agent desires the object as an end because the agent is aware of it in the appropriate way.

62. Ibid., 433b15–16; cf. 433a27–9 and 433b11–12.

63. Ibid., 433b16–18. When Aristotle describes the faculty of desire as "the moved mover" (*to kinoun kai kinoumenon*) he is probably using these terms in the generic sense of "cause of change which undergoes change" (cf. n. 40). Insofar as the agent *desires* an object, the agent undergoes a change, which may not involve locomotion.

64. Ibid., 433b18.

65. Ibid., 433b19–27; cf. *MA* 10.703a4–28.

66. Again in describing the object of desire as an "unmoved mover" (*akinēton kinoun*), Aristotle is probably using these terms in the generic sense of "cause of change which itself undergoes no change." The term *akinēton* can also have the stronger sense "immoveable," which it probably has as applied to god in *Metaphysics* XII. In the present context it seems sufficient if the object of desire is unmoved with respect to the desire in question.

67. In a postscript Aristotle remarks that an animal is incapable of desire unless it has imagination, and that all imagination involves reason or perception (*DA* III.10.433b28–30). This is a broader notion of imagination or appearance, which looks forward to III.12.434a5–10, where Aristotle distinguishes perceptual imagination, which is all that other animals possess, from deliberative imagination, which belongs only to rational animals. Thus, when incontinent human beings act according to imagination, this involves conceptualization and reasoning. Humans do not merely succumb to temptation; they also figure out how to satisfy their aberrant urges.

68. Cf. *Meta.* XII.7.1072a26–30: "The object of desire (*orekton*) and the object of thought (*noēton*) bring about movement without undergoing movement. Their primary objects are the same. For the apparently noble is the object of appetite (*epithumēton*), and the really noble is the object of wish (*boulēton*). But we have desire because we have opinion, rather than having opinion because of having desire. And thinking (*noēsis*) is the starting-point (*archē*). But thought (*nous*) is moved by the object of thought (*noēton*)." Norman O. Dahl argues persuasively that this and similar passages are not susceptible to a Humean interpretation, *Practical Reason, Aristotle, and Weakness of Will* (Minneapolis: University of Minnesota Press, 1984), 40–41.

69. The foregoing schema does not apply to all voluntary acts, but only to those which are deliberate and chosen. Voluntary actions are a wider class than the cho-

sen: "Children and other animals share in the voluntary but not in choice, and we call sudden actions voluntary but not chosen" (*EN* III.2.1111b8–10). Aristotle's general analysis of the voluntary agrees with established opinion, including all actions which have their source in an agent who knows the particular circumstances in which action occurs (1.1111a20–2). This includes actions which are caused by passion or appetite (1111a25) even when these are opposed to reason, because "the irrational emotions are believed to be not less human, so that the actions resulting from passion (*thumos*) or appetite (*epithumia*) also belong to a human being" (1111b1–2). The incontinent person, also, acts from appetite but not from choice (1111b13–18). The analysis of incontinence is, however, a paradigm case of being ruled by appetite rather than reason (VI.6.1149b3). The analysis set forth in the text describes deliberate action of the kind exhibited by the autonomous agent.

70. See Stephen D. Hudson, "Reason and Motivation in Aristotle," *Canadian Journal of Philosophy* 11 (1981): 111–35 and Holt, "Aristotle on the *archē* of Practical Reasoning," 382–84 for a similar interpretation.

71. *DA* II.6.417b22–6.

72. Ibid., III.11.427b16–20. In the *Nicomachean Ethics* Aristotle considers the objection that how things appear to agents depends on their character, and he replies that "if each person is somehow responsible (*aitios*) for his state of character, he will also be responsible for appearance." He goes on to suggest that "we are ourselves joint-causes (*sunaitioi*) of our states of character, and by being persons of a certain sort we assume that the end is of a certain sort." (*EN* III.5.1114b1–3, 22–4). Aristotle evidently thinks we are responsible to some extent for our moral characters, but scholars disagree over the extent to which this commits him to any doctrine of "free will."

73. *EN* VI.2.1139a31–3. The parallel with *DA* III.10 is noted by Aquinas, *Commentary on Aristotle's Nicomachean Ethics*, trans. C. I. Litzinger (Notre Dame, Ind.: Dumb Ox Books, 1993 [1964]), 361. My understanding of this passage was enhanced by a posting of Paul Bullen on his Aristotle email list (December 20, 1999, aristotle@lists.enteract.com).

74. Ibid., 1139b3–4.

75. Ibid., III.3.1113a11, VI.2.1139a23; 1139b5; 1139a4.

76. Ibid., III.3.1112b11–12.

77. Ibid., 1113a9–12.

78. III.3.1113a2–9, reading *prokrithen* at 4 with Susemihl and manuscripts except K[b].

79. The Stoics characterized the *hēgemonikon* as "the most authoritative part of the soul" (Diogenes Laertius VII.159; cf. Aëtius *Placita* IV.4.4 = *SVF* II, p. 228, 1–2). Zeno of Citium (335–263 B.C.) and Chrysippus (*ca.* 280–207 B.C.) called it thought (*dianoia*) (see Plutarch *De virt. mor.* 3.441c, Diogenes Laertius VII.110, Stobaeus *Eclogae* II.65, 1 = *SVF* III, p. 75, 9). According to Chrysippus "the whole of the *hēgemonikon* of human beings is rational (*logistikon*)" (Galen *De Hipp. et Plat. decr.* IV.3 = *SVF* III, p. 115, 24–5; cf. Alexander *De Anima* 97.8 Bruns; Diogenes Laertius, VII.110). Note *SVF* refers to Hans von Arnim (ed.), *Stoicorum Veterum Fragmenta* (Stuttgart: Teubner, 1978 [orig. 1905–1924]).

80. *Commentaria in Aristotelem Graeca* XIX.2, p. 49.2–4, ed. G. Heylbut.

81. See the anonymous commentator (*Commentaria in Aristotelem Graeca* XX p. 152.29–153.3) and Aspasius (XIX.1 p. 75.1–3).

82. Similarly, in *Metaphysics* IX.5.1047b35–1048a15, Aristotle speaks of choice as *to kurion*, i.e., as "authoritative" or dominant in a causal sense. The context is a distinction between nonrational and rational potentialities. In the case of a nonrational potentiality, when an appropriate agent (e.g., solvent) meets an appropriate patient (e.g., dissolvent) in the appropriate circumstances, the former must act and the latter be acted on appropriately. But in the case of rational potentiality, found in a rational animal, the agent can act in either of two contrary ways: e.g., a physician can make a patient healthy or sick. Aristotle says that something besides the potentiality—i.e., desire or choice—is "authoritative," because the agent will perform the alternative for which it has a dominant desire (*oregētai kuriōs*) in the appropriate circumstances. "Thus everything with a rational potentiality, when it has a desire for that of which it has potentiality and in the manner in which it has it, must do this." The point is that choice or a comparable desire is the necessitating efficient cause of the action.

83. Ibid., 1.1111b26–30, cf. 4.1113a23.

84. It is not, however, strictly accurate to translate *boulēsis* as "rational desire." Aristotle also observes that *boulēsis*, along with passion and appetite, are present in children from birth, but reasoning and thought naturally come to be in them as they develop (*Pol.* VII.15.1334b22–5). One can also wish for the impossible, for example, for immortality or for the practically unattainable, for example, victory in an Olympic contest (*EN* III.4.1111b22–4, *MM* I.17.1189a5–7). Granted, Aristotle speaks of *boulēsis* as "rational desire" (*logistikē orexis*) for the good (*Rhet.* I.10.1369a1–4), and he says that all *boulēsis* is in the rational faculty (*logistikon*) (*Top.* IV.5.126a13, a passage echoing Plato's tripartite psychology). But it would be more precise to say that *boulēsis* is desire for an ultimate end, and that it is the only kind of desire that can be activated directly by reasoning.

85. See Holt, "Aristotle on the *archē* of Practical Reasoning"; Dahl, *Practical Reason, Aristotle, and Weakness of Will;* and Thomas Olshewsky, "Deliberation and Desire in Aristotle and Hume" (unpublished), for different critiques of the Humean interpretation of Aristotle.

86. See James B. Murphy, "Practical Reason and Moral Psychology in Aristotle and Kant," *Social Philosophy & Policy* 18, no. 2 (2001): 257–99.

87. *EN* X.9.1179b13–16, 24–8; Ross's translation in the revised Oxford translation.

88. Ibid., VI.12.1144a28–34.

89. See Holt, "Aristotle on the *archē* of Practical Reasoning," 378–81.

90. *Pol.* VII.17.1337a1–3.

91. Ibid., I.2.1252b30.

92. Ibid., 1253a1–3.

93. Ibid., 1253a25–6.

94. Ibid., 1253a31–3.

95. This paragraph assumes the interpretation I defend in *Nature, Justice, and Rights in Aristotle's Politics* (Oxford: Clarendon Press, 1995), ch. 2.

96. Ibid., I.1.1252a7–9, cf. 3.1253b19–20.

97. Ibid., III.6.1278b31–2. This calls to mind his aforementioned comment about discussions of parts of the soul. Cf. n. 11 above.

98. Ibid., I.5.1254b2–9.

99. Ross, following Richards, tries to avoid this problem by reading ē ("or") at 1254b6, i.e., "thought rules desire with a political *or* kingly rule." But the manuscripts all have *kai* ("and"), and the substitution is not necessary if one accepts the interpretation defended in the main text.

100. *Pol.* III.14.1285a27, IV.10.1295a15–16, V.10.1313a5–8.

101. Ibid., I.1.1252a13–16.

102. Ibid., III.13.1283b42–1284a3. Aristotle defines the citizen as one who has the right or liberty (*exousia*) to share in deliberative or judicial office (III.-1.1275b18–20).

103. Ibid., III.17.1288a12–15.

104. See ibid., IV.11.1295b19–21.

105. Ibid., 1295b25–6; cf. I.7.1255b19–20; III.6.1279a8–16 and 17.1287b37–1288a5. An exception to this characterization of political rule occurs at I.12.1259a37–b17, which says that the householder ought to rule his wife in a political way, and his children in a kingly way (I.12.1259b1). He recognizes this is unusual: "In most political offices the ruling and ruled elements change, for their nature tends to be equal and not to differ at all." He adds that the male is naturally a superior ruler, and always has a superior status in relation to the female. Aristotle's reason for this nonstandard use is presumably that women have the deliberative faculty, but it lacks authority (13.1260a12–14). This suggests that women are equal in a sense with men, and can share to some limited extent in the governance of the household.

106. Cf. ibid., III.16.1287a17–18; cf. 17.1288a12–15.

107. Cf. ibid., III.6.1279a8–13.

108. Ibid., IV.4.1292a32.

109. Ibid., III.15.1286a7–9.

110. Ibid., III.13.1283a25–6; cf. 9.1281a4–8.

111. Ibid., 1281a41–b7.

112. Ibid., III.15.1286a9–16.

113. Ibid., 15.1286a16–17; 16.1287a23–8.

114. Ibid., 15.1286a16–20; 16.1287a28–32.

115. Ibid., 1287a41–b5.

116. Ibid., 1287a32. See Plato, *Laws* IV.714a1–2, which also associates law with reason (*logismos*) at I.644d1–3 and 645a1–2.

117. *Pol.* VII.1.1324b40–1325a2. Aristotle elsewhere describes the aim as happiness and noble action (1323b30–1; cf. III.9.1281a2), living blessedly (2.1324a24–5), the good life (1325a9), and "the actualization and perfect employment of virtue" (8.1328a38, 13.1332a7–10).

118. Ibid., 2.1324a23–5. Cf. IV.1.1288b21–4 where this is the first task assigned to political science.

119. Ibid., 14.1333a29–30.

120. Ibid., 2.1324a25–9.

121. Ibid., 2.1324a35–3.1325a31.

122. Ibid., 3.1325a31–b16.

123. Ibid., 1325b7–10: among similar and equal persons, the noble and just involve ruling "in turn" (<*en*>*merei*), but unequal rule is "against nature" (*para phusin*) and hence ignoble.

124. Ibid., 1325b15–16.

125. Ibid., 1325b16–23.

126. Ibid., 1325b23–32.

127. See *Meta.* XII.10.1075a11–15 which speaks of a "leader" of all nature.

128. *Pol.* V.9.1310a14–18.

129. Ibid., IV.11.1295a40–b1.

130. *EN* V.1.1129b14–25. The first sentence of this passage presents some textual difficulties disregarded by the Revised Oxford Translation. The Oxford Classical Text follows manuscript K^b in bracketing "according to virtue" (*kat' aretēn*). The passage is also ambiguous as to whether the law aims at the common advantage only in the case of "the common advantage of all" or in the other instances (e.g., the common advantage of the authorities). I have translated so as to preserve this ambiguity. But the passage clearly implies that universal justice is lawfulness in the case of the correct constitution, regardless of what it says about inferior constitutions.

131. Ibid., 1129b15–17, 31–1130a1; the Revised Oxford Translation is mistaken.

132. Ibid., VI.12.1144a8.

133. Ibid., VI.13.1144b4–14. Aristotle here uses *nous* in the sense of a specific intellectual virtue, rather than for the faculty of thought generally.

134. J. A. Stewart, *Notes on the Nicomachean Ethics of Aristotle* (Oxford, 1892), vol. I, p. 201. The passage cited is *EN* VI.13.1144b31.

135. *EN* VI.5.1140a25–8, b20–1; 7.1141b9–10; 12.1144a26–8.

136. Ibid., VI.12.1144a20–2, 13.1145a4–6.

137. Stewart, *Notes on the Nicomachean Ethics of Aristotle,* 206. For a similar, more recent interpretation of 1287a32 see Jennifer Whiting, "Self-love and Authoritative Virtue: Prolegomenon to a Kantian Reading of *Eudemian Ethics* vii 3," in *Aristotle, Kant, and the Stoics: Rethinking Happiness and Duty,* ed. Stephen Engstrom and Jennifer Whiting (Cambridge: Cambridge University Press, 1996), 181–82.

138. Ibid., 207.

139. *Pol.* III.16.1287a10: *dokei de tisin.*

140. Ibid., 1287a29–32.

141. See *DA* III.10.433a23–5, cited in n. 51 above.

142. Kant, *The Metaphysics of Morals,* Part II, *The Doctrine of Virtue* (Philadelphia: University of Pennsylvania Press, 1964), 481.

143. Harry G. Frankfurt, "Autonomy, Necessity, and Love," in *Necessity, Volition, and Love* (Cambridge: Cambridge University Press, 1999), 132.

144. Earlier drafts of the first section benefited from audience comments at the University of Binghamton (October 1999), the 11th International Symposium of the Olympic Center for Philosophy and Culture in Pyrgos, Greece (August 2000), and the University of Oklahoma (April 2001). James B. Murphy offered insightful criticisms, which were especially useful due to his skepticism about the applicability of "autonomy" to Aristotle. My graduate students (Mahesh Ananth, Carrie-Ann Khan, Khalil S. Khan, Pamela Phillips, and James S. Taylor) and my colleague Christopher Morris contributed helpful criticisms and constructive remarks. The editor made many valuable suggestions.

Contributors

SUSAN D. COLLINS is Assistant Professor of Political Science at the University of Houston. She is translator and author of an interpretive essay (with D. Stauffer) published as *Empire and the Ends of Politics: Plato's "Menexenus" and Pericles' Funeral Oration* (Focus Philosophical Library) and editor (with R. Bartlett) of *Action and Contemplation: Studies in the Moral and Political Thought of Aristotle* (SUNY). She is currently completing a book on Aristotle's *Nicomachean Ethics*.

DOUGLAS J. DEN UYL is Professor of Philosophy and Director of the Master of Arts in Liberal Studies Program at Bellarmine College and Vice President of Education at Liberty Fund Inc. His most recent books include *The Virtue of Prudence* (Peter Lang Press) and *Liberalism Defended* (Elgar Press). He has published numerous book chapters and articles that have appeared in such journals as *Review of Metaphysics*, *Social Philosophy and Policy*, *Journal of the History of Philosophy*, *Public Affairs Quarterly*, *International Journal for Philosophy of Religion*, *American Philosophical Quarterly*, and *Studia Spinozana*.

JILL FRANK is Assistant Professor in the Department of Government and International Studies at the University of South Carolina, Columbia. She has published in *Political Theory* and *Revue de la recherche juridique: Droit prospectif*. She is completing a book project about lessons contemporary political theory and practice might draw from Aristotle's ethical and political philosophy.

MIRIAM GALSTON is Professor at the George Washington University Law School. She is author of *Politics and Excellence: The Political Philosophy of Alfarabi* (Princeton University Press). She has published numerous articles

403

that have appeared in a variety of journals including *Tulane Law Review, Columbia Law Review, California Law Review, Texas Law Review, Virginia Tax Review, Ethics, Dialogue, Review of Politics, Israel Oriental Studies, Jewish Quarterly Review,* and *Journal of the History of Philosophy.*

GERALD M. MARA is Executive Associate Dean of the Graduate School and Professorial Lecturer in Government at Georgetown University. He is author of *Socrates' Discursive Democracy* (SUNY Press) and joint editor of *Liberalism and the Good* (Routledge, Chapman and Hall). He is the author of numerous articles that have appeared in *Political Theory, Polity, Journal of Politics, Western Political Quarterly,* and *Journal of the History of Philosophy.*

FRED D. MILLER, JR., is Professor of Philosophy and Executive Director of the Social Philosophy and Policy Center at Bowling Green State University. He has authored four books, co-edited thirty volumes for Cambridge and Blackwell University Presses, and published over forty articles. His most recent book, *Nature, Justice, and Rights in Aristotle's Politics* (Oxford University Clarendon Press), was the subject of a conference in Palo Alto and two special symposia of the American Philosophical Association. Selected papers from these conferences as well as responses by Miller have been published in *Ancient Philosophy* and a special edition of *The Review of Metaphysics.* He is currently writing *A History of Philosophy of Law from the Ancient Greeks to the Later Scholastics* that will be published as the sixth volume of *A Treatise of Legal Philosophy and General Jurisprudence* (Kluwer Academic Publisher).

MARTHA CRAVEN NUSSBAUM is the Ernst Freund Distinguished Service Professor of Law and Ethics (appointed in the Law School, Philosophy Department, and Divinity School, Associate in Classics) at the University of Chicago. She is author and editor of over twenty books (many of which exist in translation) and well over a hundred journal articles. Among her most recent publications are *Cultivating Humanity: A Classical Defense of Reform in Liberal Education* (Harvard University Press) (winner of the Ness Book Award of the Association of American Colleges and Universities), *Sex and Social Justice* (Oxford University Press), *Multiculturalism and Women* (with Joshua Cohen) (Princeton University Press), and *Love's Knowledge: Essays on Philosophy and Literature* (Oxford University Press) (winner of Spielvogel-Diamondstein Prize for best collection of essays).

DAVID K. O'CONNOR is Associate Professor of Philosophy at Notre Dame. He is editor (with Carnes Lord) of *Essays on the Foundations of Aristotelian*

Political Science (University of California Press) and author of several book chapters and encyclopedia articles. He has written for *History of Philosophy Quarterly, Greek, Roman, and Byzantine Studies, Midwest Studies in Philosophy, Ancient Philosophy,* and *Ethics.* He is currently working on a book entitled *Socrates and the Envy of the Gods: A Study of Philosophy's Ambitions.*

CHARLES R. PINCHES is Professor of Theology, Director of Graduate Studies, and Chair of the Department of Theology/Religious Studies at the University of Scranton. His books include *Theology and Action* (Eerdmans) and, with Stanley Hauerwas, *Christians among the Virtues: Conversations with Ancient and Modern Ethics* (University of Notre Dame Press). He has published numerous book chapters and several encyclopedia articles. His articles have appeared in *The Christian Century, Pro Ecclesia, Christian Bioethics, The Journal of Religious Ethics, Modern Theology, International Journal of Applied Philosophy, Southern Journal of Philosophy,* and *Sophia.*

DOUGLAS B. RASMUSSEN is Professor of Philosophy at St. John's University. He has co-authored and co-edited five books, the most recent of which is *Liberalism Defended: The Challenge of Post-Modernity* (Elgar Press). He has published over sixty articles and reviews dealing with issues in epistemology, philosophy of language, ethics, and political philosophy that have appeared in such journals as *Social Philosophy and Policy, International Philosophical Quarterly, The Thomist, Public Affairs Quarterly, Reason,* and *American Philosophical Quarterly.* He was guest editor of the January 1992 issue of *The Monist* on "Teleology and the Foundation of Value."

STEPHEN S. SALKEVER is the Mary Katharine Woodworth Professor of Political Science at Bryn Mawr College. He is author of *Finding the Mean: Theory and Practice in Aristotelian Political Philosophy* (Princeton University Press) and over twenty articles and book chapters. His articles have appeared in *Ethics, American Political Science Review, Political Theory, Polity,* and *PS: Political Science and Politics.* Among numerous papers and invited lectures, he gave the Frank Covey Loyola Lectures in Political Analysis (Loyola University Chicago, 1997).

ARISTIDE TESSITORE is Associate Professor of Political Science at Furman University. He is author of *Reading Aristotle's* Ethics: *Virtue, Rhetoric, and Political Philosophy* (SUNY Press). He has published several articles that have appeared in *American Political Science Review, Political Theory, Review of Politics, Journal of Politics, Polity, Interpretation,* and *The Southern Journal of Philosophy.*

BERNARD YACK is Professor of Political Science at the University of Wisconsin, Madison. He is author of *The Longing for Total Revolution: Philosophic Sources of Social Discontent from Rousseau to Marx and Nietzsche* (Princeton University Press), *The Problems of a Political Animal: Community, Conflict, and Justice in Aristotelian Political Thought* (University of California Press), and *The Fetishism of Modernities: Epochal Self-Consciousness in Contemporary Social and Political Thought* (University of Notre Dame Press), as well as editor of *Liberalism without Illusions: Essays on Liberal Theory and the Political Vision of Judith N. Shklar* (University of Chicago Press). He is currently completing a book entitled *Nation and Individual: Contingency, Choice and Community in Modern Political Life*.

Index